YOU, THE CHOREOGRAPHER, Creating and Crafting Dance offers a synthesis of histories, theories, philosophies, and creative practices across diverse genres of concert dance choreography. The book is designed for readers at every stage of creative development who seek to refine their artistic sensibility.

Through a review of major milestones in the field, including contributions to choreography from the humanities, arts, and modern sciences, readers will gain new perspectives on the historical development of choreography. Concise analyses of traditional fundamentals and innovative practices of dance construction, artistic research methods, and approaches to artistic collaboration offer readers new tools to build creative habits and expand their choreographic proficiencies.

For learners and educators, this is a textbook. For emerging professionals, it is a professional-development tool. For established professionals, it is a companion handbook that reinvigorates inspiration. To all readers it offers a cumulative, systematic understanding of the art of dance making, with a wealth of cross-disciplinary references to create a dynamic map of creative practices in choreography.

Vladimir Angelov is a choreographer, author, and the Executive Director of the International Consortium for Advancement in Choreography, **Dance ICONS, Inc.** — the **I**nternational **C**horeographers' **O**rganization and **N**etworking **S**ervices, a global association for choreographers, based in Washington, D.C., USA.

To Rebecca Ritzel,

I greatly admire your dance writings and I hope you will enjoy mine :)

With all professional respect and gratitude,

Vlad & Angela

June 9, 2024
Washington, D.C.

VLADIMIR ANGELOV

YOU, THE CHOREOGRAPHER
Creating and Crafting Dance

A Guidebook of Artistic Practices

Featuring ICON SMART[SM]

Cover image: Photography © Lois Greenfield, pictured Donna Scro Samori, courtesy of Freespace Dance, 2006

First published 2024
by Routledge
4 Park Square, Milton Park, Abingdon, Oxon OX14 4RN

and by Routledge
605 Third Avenue, New York, NY 10158

Routledge is an imprint of the Taylor & Francis Group, an informa business

British Library Cataloguing-in-Publication Data
A catalogue record for this book is available from the British Library.

Library of Congress Cataloging-in-Publication Data
Name: Angelov, Vladimir, author.
Title: You, the choreographer: creating and crafting dance: a guidebook of artistic practices / Vladimir Angelov.
Description: Abingdon, Oxon; New York, NY : Routledge, 2023.
Includes bibliographical references and index.
Identifiers: LCCN 2022021923 (print) | LCCN 2022021924 (ebook) | ISBN 9780367444457 (hardback) | ISBN 9780367444464 (paperback) | ISBN 9781003009764 (ebook)
Subjects: LCSH: Choreography—Study and teaching. | Dance—Study and teaching. | Choreography—History. | Choreography—Philosophy.
Classification: LCC GV1782.5 .A55 2023 (print) | LCC GV1782.5 (ebook) | DDC 792.6/2071—dc23/eng/20220225
LC record available at https://lccn.loc.gov/2022021923
LC ebook record available at https://lccn.loc.gov/2022021924

ISBN: 978-0-367-44445-7 (hbk)
ISBN: 978-0-367-44446-4 (pbk)
ISBN: 978-1-003-00976-4 (ebk)

DOI: 10.4324/9781003009764

ADDITIONAL COVER IMAGES AND CREDITS:

BOOK I cover image: Photography © Lois Greenfield, pictured David Parsons, courtesy of Parsons Dance Company, 1990

BOOK II cover image: Photography © Lois Greenfield, pictured Fang-Yi Sheu, Ballet Tech, 2008

BOOK III cover image: Photography © Lois Greenfield, pictured Cornelius Brown, courtesy of Dodge Dance Company, 2005

BOOK IV cover image: Photography © Lois Greenfield, pictured Sara Joel and Anna Venizelos, 2008

BOOK V cover image: Photography © Lois Greenfield, pictured Raymond Ejiofor, Naila Ansari, LaKendra Dennard, Michael Bange Jr., Annalee Traylor, courtesy of August Wilson Dance Ensemble, 2012

BOOK VI cover image: Photography © Lois Greenfield, pictured Andrew Pacho,1999

BOOK VII cover image: Photography © Lois Greenfield, pictured Melanie Hamrick, 2010

Supplemental photography and decorative clip art courtesy of 123RF, ShutterStock, Adobe Stock, Pixabay, and iStock/Getty Images

Book design, clip art design of rubrics, and typeset design by Koranjali Alfonseca

Further design and typesetting by Elizabeth Gray, Liz Gray Design, LLC

Rubrics *dance DIALOGUES*, *Let's Imagine*, and *Helpful Tips & Suggestions*, authored by Vladimir Angelov

Recto pages standalone epigraphs and proverbs courtesy of www.goodreads.com

Choreographers are driven by creative impulses and urgencies, which they share and manifest through the making of dance. Choreographers explore and investigate dynamic principles of movement, motion, and embodied meaning—they discover and invent diverse approaches to channeling their creative powers into action.

But who, exactly, are YOU, THE CHOREOGRAPHER, and what kinds of provocative truth-seeking is at the heart of your work? Are you functioning intellectually or intuitively? Are you the one who strives to invigorate your audience with profound ideas, or do you simply stumble upon something and turn it into art? And how do you create and craft dance?

This book explores these questions to help you find your answers.

CONTENTS

ACKNOWLEDGMENTS

Similar to putting together a major dance production, it takes a village to research, fund, write, edit, and assemble a book for publishing. Many individuals and institutions generously contributed their time and resources to this process, and I would like to acknowledge all of them. Foremost, a book would not materialize without a publisher: I am deeply indebted to the team at Routledge/Taylor & Francis Group, and especially to Ben Piggott, for foreseeing the need for this book in the field of choreography and for accepting my proposal to publish it. I also would like to thank Steph Hines for all of her kindness, support, and accommodations.

My very special thanks go to Camilla Acquista, Content Editor and Programming Associate at Dance ICONS, Inc. I asked Camilla to be the "first eyes" to read this manuscript, and she became the First Editor of the book. She spent countless hours, days, and months reading and rereading every single word; rewriting phrases and sentences; ensuring correct grammar, spelling, and punctuation; verifying names and details; and double-checking sentence structure and word flow. Camilla also ensured the accurate wording of every single idea. Her work, dedication, and contribution in the development of this project were monumental.

I am deeply grateful to Charles Scheland, Research Associate at Dance ICONS, Inc. Charles' dedication and research efforts over many months produced numerous critical resources, including stunning photographic materials and art works. I am thankful for Charles' indispensable persistence in negotiating and processing the essential permissions and licensing by contacting many organizations around the globe, as well as for his thoughtful feedback on the manuscript from his perspective as a practicing dance professional.

Instrumental to this project was my dear friend of many years, Michael Lillys, President of the Executive Board of Dance ICONS, Inc. Michael's multilayered contribution encompasses a vast spectrum of activities, including providing major funding for this project, technical and logistical help, and insightful feedback on the manuscript. Michael's encouragement and continuing support during every step of the process were indispensable.

I would like to acknowledge and express my heartfelt gratitude to contributing individuals and organizations for their support and resourcefulness in the following areas:

Major funding provided by Michael Lillys, President of the Executive Board, Dance ICONS, Inc. Additional funding provided by Vladimir, Akiko, and Julia Angelov; Michael Lillys, President of the Executive Board, Dance ICONS, Inc.; National Cathedral School and the Katharine Lee International Programs Grant; Washington DC Deputy Mayor for Planning and Economic Development Grant; Washington DC Commission on the Arts and Humanities and The National Endowment for the Arts—CARES ACT Grant; DC Commission on the Arts and Humanities Fellowship Grant; Stacey and Daniel Kohl Charitable Fund.

Featured art photography created and provided by Lois Greenfield.

Book design, original clip art, and typeset design created by Koranjali Alfonseca.

Typesetting and additional design created by Elizabeth Gray, Liz Gray Design, LLC.

Index created by Pilar Wyman, Wyman Indexing.

Legal counsel provided by James E. Armstrong IV and Glenn Pudelka, Locke Lord, LLP.

Consulting Editors Committee and content peer reading feedback generously provided by Jo Butterworth, PhD; Assis Carreiro, MBE FRSA; Donna Davenport, EdD; Elizabeth Edenberg, PhD; Judith Lynne Hanna, PhD; Ivo Kaltchev, DMA; Robin Kish, MFA, MS; Larry Lavender, PhD; Sandra Cerny Minton, PhD; Julie Mulvihill, PhD; Freya Vass-Rhee, PhD; and Liesbeth Wildschut, PhD.

Field Experts Committee and peer reading feedback generously provided by Mark Bishop, Jeanette Christensen, Helen Hayes, Desi Jordanoff, Anne Liberman, Ben Levine, Carmel Morgan, Elizabeth Naro, Leah Rothschild, Brandon Straub, and Cynthia Word.

Resources and visual materials generously provided by Alvin Ailey American Dance Theater, Atlanta Ballet, BANDALOOP, Bill T. Jones/Arnie Zane Company, Ballet Zürich, Dutch National Ballet, English National Ballet, Hong Kong Ballet, Joffrey Ballet, Kidd Pivot, Mariinsky Ballet and especially Nina Nachkebia, Mark Morris Dance Group, New York City Ballet and especially Wendy Whelan, Norwegian National Ballet, Paris Opera Ballet, Paul Taylor Dance Company, Riverdance, The Royal Ballet, Royal New Zealand Ballet, Scottish Ballet, Sokolow Theatre/Dance Ensemble, Sydney Dance Company, The Washington Ballet, and especially Theo Kossenas.

Additional support with resources generously provided by Levy BAM Archives, George Balanchine Trust, Trisha Brown Archives, Jacob's Pillow Dance Festival and Archives and especially Norton Owen, Jerome Robbins Foundation, New York Public Library and especially Erik Stolarski, Smithsonian Institution, National Museum of African American History and Culture, University of California Los Angeles, and especially Libby Smigel at the Library of Congress in Washington, DC.

My great appreciation goes to my colleague choreographers who kindly contributed to this book with their time, communications, discussions, interviews and in various other ways. They are Kyle Abraham, Jennifer Archibald, Rafael Bonachela, Ted Brandsen, Marc Brew, Sidi Larbi Cherkaoui, Lucinda Childs, David Dawson, Michelle Dorrance, Alexander Ekman, Paul Gordon Emerson, Neil Ieremia, Akram Khan, Liz Lerman, Pontus Lidberg, Nanine Linning, Hans van Manen, Cathy Marston, Dada Masilo, JoAnna Mendl Shaw, Jennifer Monson, Annabelle Lopez Ochoa, Eiko Otake, Steve Paxton, Helen Pickett, Crystal Pite, Yvonne Rainer, Amelia Rudolph, Claudia Schreier, Yuanyuan Wang, Septime Webre, Christopher Wheeldon, and Yin Yue.

And last but not least, I'd like to thank and express my gratitude to my family, Akiko and Julia Angelov, for their immense support and patience while I worked on this book.

THANK YOU ALL!

FOREWORD

The concepts in this book were developed from decades of working as a professional choreographer, and of teaching and writing about choreography. The book also features a new philosophical framework and an innovative approach of systematizing and practicing the choreographic craft embodied in the acronym:

ICON SMART^{SM}

Instruments of Choreography, Objectives and Norms — Systematic Methods of Artistic Research and Training

This functional philosophy and creative algorithm integrate the rich history of choreography with modern research and training and are expressed so that the concepts and techniques can be well understood by budding, emerging, and professional choreographers. My initial goal was to provide the choreographic community with an up-to-date approach and all the necessary tools—intellectual and practical—for development of choreographic skills. These efforts resulted in the emergence of ICON SMART^{SM}.

Furthermore, it was my intention to develop an environment where the choreographic community can gather—digitally and live—and exchange ideas, knowledge, and information. To that end, in 2015 I founded the International Consortium for Advancement in Choreography, Dance ICONS, Inc.—the International Choreographers' Organization and Networking Services, a global association for choreographers, based in Washington, DC, USA.

This book was made possible by the generous intellectual contributions of my many colleague-choreographers, as well as the resources and support of the International Consortium for Advancement in Choreography—Dance ICONS, Inc. Our intent was to produce a book that will serve as a helpful tool for choreographers closely or peripherally affiliated with our organization, as well as the dance community at large: students, educators, dance artists, and anyone interested in the art of choreography. I'm also grateful to the staff, associates, and volunteers of Dance ICONS, Inc. for all of their dedication, time, and hard work to help make this book possible.

To my readers: I would like to hear from you and your organization about your experience with this book. Please contact me directly at www.danceicons.org.

Enjoy using this book and best of luck with your creative work in the years ahead!

Vladimir Angelov, Author & CEO of Dance ICONS, Inc.

You have to learn the rules of the game.
And then you have to play better than anyone else.

Albert Einstein (1879–1955)

INTRODUCTION
– I CHOREOGRAPH, THEREFORE I AM –

This book, a decade in the making, provides a synthesis of histories, theories, philosophies, and creative practices across diverse genres of concert dance choreography. For learners and educators, it is a textbook. For emerging artists, it is a professional development tool. For established artists, it is a companion handbook that may reinvigorate inspiration. To all readers, it offers a cumulative, systematic understanding of the art of creating dance while incorporating abundant cross-disciplinary references. The book aims to establish a dynamic cognitive map of creative practices in choreography in relation to other arts and cultures.

Through a review of major milestones in the field, including contributions to choreography from the arts, humanities, and modern sciences, readers and artists will gain new perspectives on historical developments in choreography. Concise analysis of traditional fundamentals of dance construction, artistic research methods, and approaches to artistic collaboration offer readers and artists new tools to build creative habits and expand their choreographic proficiencies. Emerging choreographers, this book is especially for you!

Let's further introduce this book with a playful word replacement. *Cogito Ergo Sum* is a statement in Latin first made by French philosopher René Descartes in his "Discourse on the Method of Rightly Conducting One's Reason and of Seeking Truth in the Sciences" (1637). The phrase translates as *I think, therefore I am*, meaning that one's own existence serves—at a minimum—as proof of the reality of one's own mind.

For those who are already deeply involved in creating dance and choreography, let's modify this phrase and transform it into *I choreograph, therefore I am*. The phrase now states that as choreographing occurs in one's mind, it leads to self-awareness. Therefore, if you are choreographing, then it is *you, the choreographer*, who now exists through creating!

DO YOU CHOREOGRAPH, AND THEREFORE YOU ARE?

Please check the boxes next to any of the statements below that apply to you:

□ I know the differences between the craft of a performer, a teacher, and a choreographer.

□ I experience creative impulses and urges to make my own dances.

□ I like to experiment with movement ideas, phrasing, and dynamics.

□ I'm already making my own dances and wish to improve my choreographic craft.

□ I can spend many hours in the dance studio creating, rehearsing, and editing choreography.

□ I love research and also understand that choreographing is both creative *and* intellectual engagement.

□ I'm a compassionate and open-minded person who enjoys collaborating with other artists.

The creative mind often behaves like a bird flying freely and randomly from place to place. A spontaneous and subconscious stream of movement ideas is an organic part of the choreographer's creative process. At some point, however, as a choreographer, you might wish to shape and formulate those artistic impulses-in-motion. This is natural. When aiming for an outcome, you are also *engineering* dance and movement, with intentions to *build* and *share* an artful expression in an organized manner. Bringing some structure to a waterfall of ideas often requires a thoughtful approach, grounded in a sense of purpose.

With that in mind, this book offers a helpful feature — **ICON SMART**SM — an acronym that refers to a pioneering system and a new approach with practical strategies for developing creative skills and choreographic craftsmanship. This approach includes and addresses:

➢ **Experiential, research, and exploratory-based creative practices.** The book fosters the exploration of existing and new intellectual and movement knowledge. The goal is to link your movement experiences and discoveries with your intentions and goals as a choreographer. This approach will help you to create while learning and to learn while creating.

➢ **Intellectual references and practical creative tools.** The book includes established and new choreographic devices, ongoing rubrics of artistic research assignments, fun facts, and helpful tips, as well as in-studio creative training exercises that aim to build a bridge between theory and practice. You will have the opportunity to reflect on choreographic work and ideas that resonate with your evolving process.

➢ **Systematized approaches and creative methods.** A daily dance class often begins with simple codified movement, which becomes more complex and technically advanced as dancers gain strength, flexibility, and understanding of the form. Well-established pedagogical principles and methods guide the progression of training for dancers. Similarly, the craft of choreography requires daily practice and growth. Principles and elements outlined in this text could be used selectively, and they could also be modified, edited, adapted, deconstructed, re-structured, reassembled, and reinterpreted. The following pages address:

◆ **What is ICON SMART**SM**?** The acronym is explained, describing the elements of this multidimensional creative algorithm for developing creative skills for choreographers. A detailed account of ICON SMARTSM is offered in Chapter 10, BOOK II.

◆ **How does ICON SMART**SM **relate to the contents of the book?** A diagram offers a visual reference for how the sub-books and chapters are divided, structured, and related. All of these building parts, put together, allow this creative algorithm to function as a comprehensive whole.

◆ **What are the diverse ways of using ICON SMART**SM**?** In a *Straightforward Curriculum*, each week is dedicated to a chapter in two weekly sessions—one as a theory session and one for assignments and in-studio creative exercises—*SmarTraining/ArtInAction*, based on that week's chapter theme. The *Non-linear and Integrative Approaches* offers the choreographers a customized way to use this book as per their creative needs. Readers, educators, and artists may determine to focus only on selected chapters and content of their preference.

WHAT IS ICON SMART℠?

Instruments of Choreography, Objectives and Norms — Systematic Methods of Artistic Research and Training

Instruments of Choreography are the artistic tools, organizing principles and structuring devices applied to movement, as well as sound, costuming, and visual design with which choreographers work. Instruments of choreography may be newly created for a given project or borrowed from diverse histories and traditions of dance and other forms of art.

Objectives and Norms. While objectives are project-specific ideas, parameters, and purposes shared among the participants in a choreographic project, norms could be politically, socially, and culturally predetermined. The choreographers' objectives may challenge these norms. As the work finds its distinct identity, these objectives and norms may be shaped and reshaped, framed and reframed multiple times and in many ways.

Systematic Methods are the activities undertaken and the procedures carried out by participants in a choreographic project to bring the work from imagination to material presence in the world. The journey may be linear—i.e., progressing steadily to a predetermined end, or it may include accidental or intended direction shifts, exploration of emergent possibilities, and revisions to the presumed character and identity of the work.

Artistic Research is the practice of gathering and exploring diverse resources to bring a choreographic idea into sufficient focus for creation to commence, and to support the exploratory and decision-making processes that will bring the project to completion. The following three forms of *artistic research* for choreography may usefully be distinguished:

➢ ***Scholastic Research*** is the examination of such materials as books, articles, art works, case studies, statistical data, archival repositories, and audio and video collections. This kind of research produces connections between one's own and others' artistic intuitions, ideas, and methods for setting and achieving goals.

➢ ***Creative Research*** is the undertaking of such activities as visiting museums, galleries, and various built and natural environments; trying unfamiliar forms of dance and other body/performance practices; and interviewing artists or practitioners in other domains. This research refines one's artistic sensibilities and expands one's repertoire of ideas about how choreography may situate itself.

➢ ***Movement Research*** is kinetic experimentation and improvisation to awaken new body experiences and new ideas about movement. Such research might launch from spontaneous somatic brainstorming, or embodied engagements with selected imagery, themes, scores, actions, tasks, or a particular movement philosophy.

Training is the means by which one gains and strengthens skills and gathers insights about their use in diverse contexts of practice. A high level of artistic proficiency will be achieved through regular exposure to and immersion in familiar and preferred body, mind, and research practices, as well as by deliberately seeking ideas and experiences that challenge one's current creative and conceptual boundaries.

HOW DOES ICON SMART℠ RELATE TO THE CONTENTS OF THIS BOOK?

The diagram that follows visually represents how the approach is structurally linked with the contents of the book, as well as the sub-books. Bullet points list the main topics of the chapters:

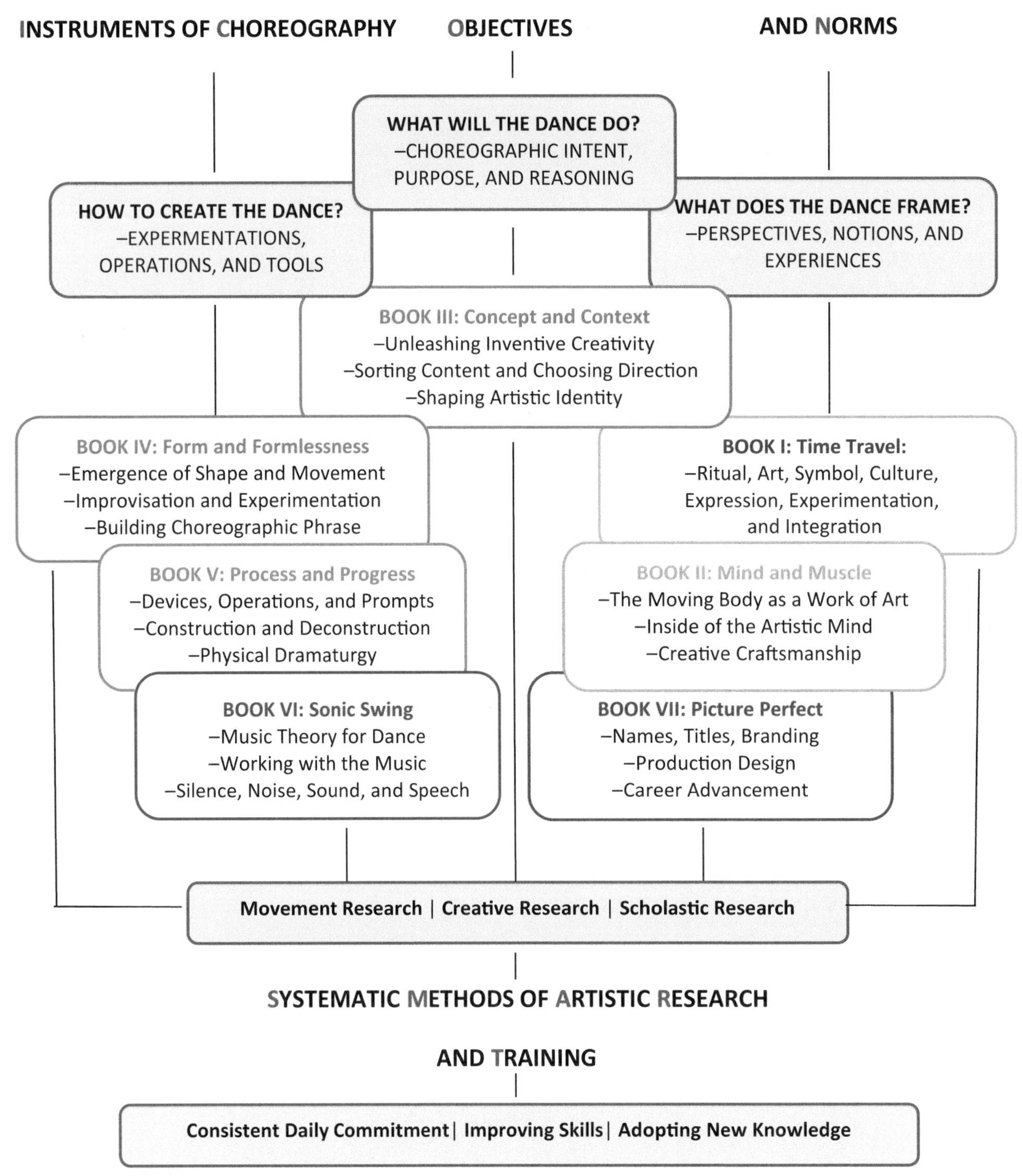

Figure 1

DIVERSE WAYS OF USING ICON SMART℠

Linear Approach—Straightforward Curriculum: As a companion handbook, this book offers independent, self-educating choreographers a panoramic view of choreographic crafts and creative practices. The approach that follows is useful in the format and rhythm of two regular academic semesters of self-didactics.

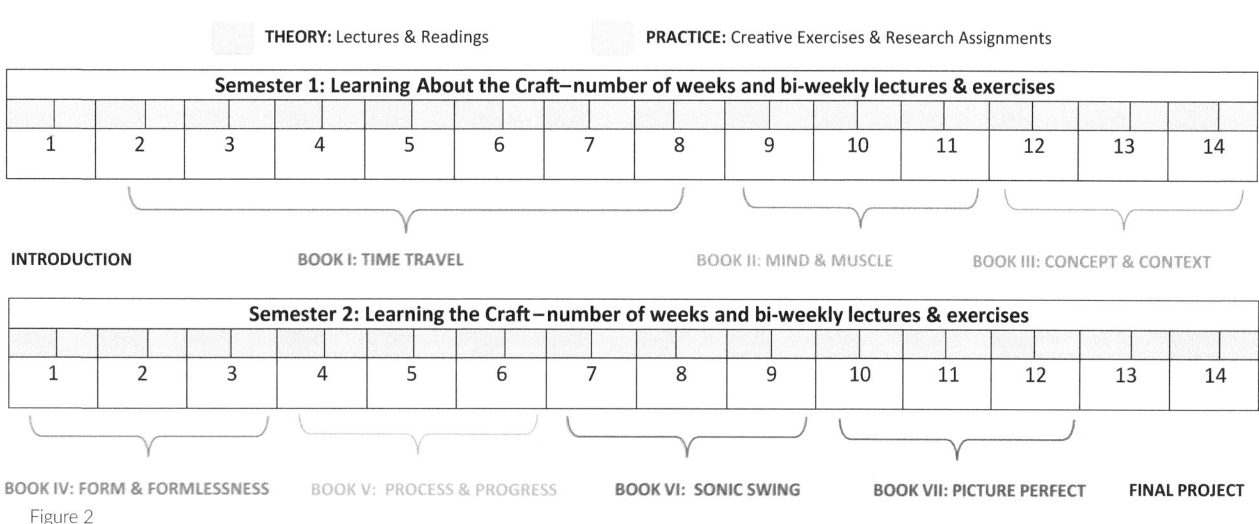

Figure 2

Non-Linear Approach—Modular Implementation: As an academic book, this approach offers a flexible selection of chapters and topics covering choreographic practices. Educators and learners can determine the order and progression based on their needs and connect these with other content and events. For example:

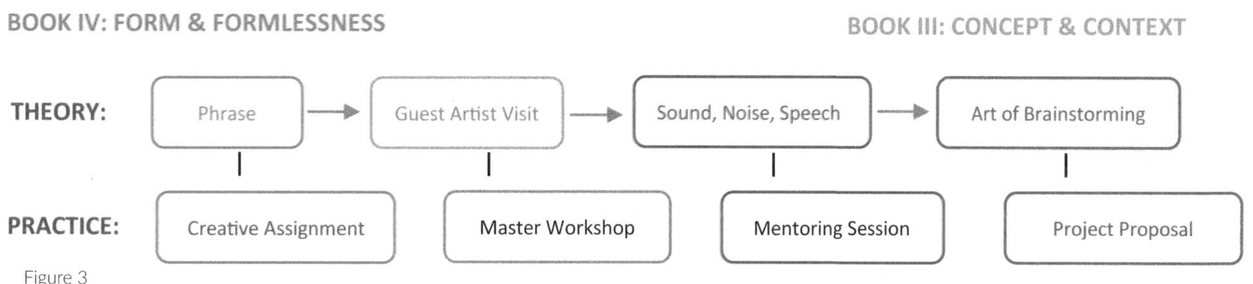

Figure 3

Integrative Approach—Recurring Reference: The book invites experienced and professional choreographers to choose particular sections that are the most suitable for their individual artistic work and to integrate them into their creative environment. In this context, the book may be used as an ongoing reference and resource. Users can actively incorporate their own content. For example:

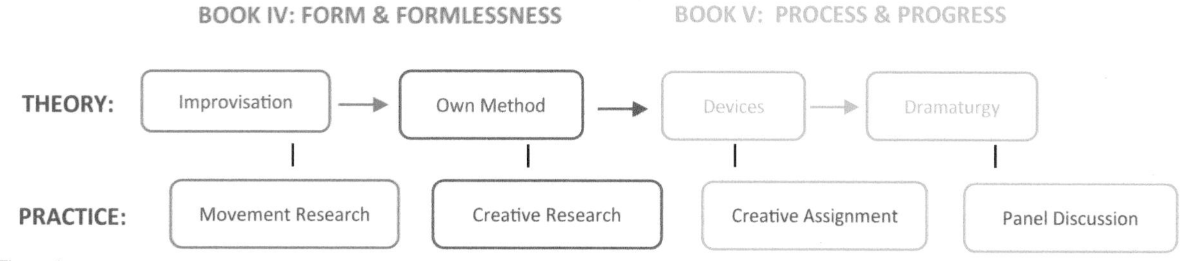

Figure 4

PRESCRIPTION FOR LEARNING TO ACHIEVE

– A HEALTHY [CHOREOGRAPHIC] WELL-BEING –

How much time should an artist commit to learning and developing sustainable working habits and maintaining choreographic well-being? Like any employment, artistic work often involves diverse and even contradictory experiences, as creative energy may vary widely. One day you might be productive and inspired, while the next day your work feels challenging and tedious. Or perhaps you feel frightened one morning, but by the afternoon, success has boosted your confidence. These cycles of ups and downs are normal, especially during an artist's early years of choreographing. Keep in mind that learning how to work is more important than a single piece of work. Learning how to learn is completing half of the learning.

Just for fun, imagine visiting the "choreography doctor" to request a prescription for learning effectively and creating productively every day, while also fighting the emerging choreographer's worst syndrome—*anxiety*! This book already includes the basic knowledge, as well as the exercise and training regimen, to help guide you through the creative process! Here is a humorous physician's prescription for success:

FROM THE DESK OF:

Dr. Awesome Moves
Dance Laboratory, Department of Artistry in Motion
5678 Jump Start Street, Studio B-there
Massive Success, UR #00001

Rx for the emerging choreographer

Diagnosis: Creative impulses and excitement mixed with anxiety

Medication: Use this book regularly, at least for the duration of a year.

Directions, Usage, and Dosage:

Read and learn about dance and choreography
for about 1-3 hours daily at least twice a week.

Practice the exercises and do the assignments
for about 1-3 hours daily at least twice a week.

Experiment with movement and create new choreography
for about 1-3 hours daily at least 3-5 times a week.

Additional Notes:

Drink plenty of water, maintain a healthy diet, and get enough sleep.
Replace stress with anticipation, anxiety with enjoyment.
Share dance with others, be kind, and have fun!

Figure 5

SEVEN MANTRAS

– BRIEF WISDOMS FROM LENGTHY LEARNING IN THE FIELD –

As we step together in this exciting world of creating dance, advancing choreographic skills, and honing artistic expression—let these mantras orbit our thinking, remind us to keep our minds open, and drive us forward when we need it, and we always need it!

Choreographers shall look not only in the dance studio mirror, but also out of the window.

* * *

Choreographers excel by studying other choreographers, not by copying them.

* * *

Choreography can be made from any dance ingredients by putting them together skillfully.

* * *

Research to look for the new; experiment to test the new; innovate to create the new.

* * *

The choreographic realization of an idea is more important than the idea itself:

A great dance with a simple concept may outshine a simple dance with a great concept.

* * *

Consistent hard work propels you faster and farther than intermittent inspiration:

Your passage in choreographing is a marathon, not a sprint.

* * *

There are three paths to creating art—interpretation, experimentation, and innovation.

Unite them to build your artistic highway!

Vladimir Angelov,
Choreographer and Author

PROLOGUE
– YOU, THE CHOREOGRAPHER –

◆ **Who are you, the choreographer, and what do you do?** Choreographers are driven by creative impulses and urgencies which they share and manifest through the making of dance. Choreographers explore and investigate dynamic principles of movement, motion, and embodied meaning—they discover and invent diverse approaches to channeling their creative powers into action.

But who, exactly, are ***YOU, THE CHOREOGRAPHER***, and what kinds of provocative truth-seeking is at the heart of your work? Are *you* functioning intellectually or intuitively? Are *you* the one who strives to invigorate your audience with profound ideas, or do you simply stumble upon something and turn it into art? And how do *you* create and craft dance? This book offers the explorations and inquiries to these questions to help you find *your* answers.

◆ **Why become a choreographe**r? "Becoming a choreographer was not really a conscious choice, but an evolution—a natural progression through my life. Choreography was a way to dovetail my creative impulse with my love of dancing"—says choreographer Crystal Pite.[1] Your answer may be similar or different than the one given here. The fact is that every dance artist has a personal reason. For some, the process of becoming a choreographer is a gradual evolution; for others, it happens by chance. The reason may also change as you explore the creative act of choreography and grow as an artist.

Whatever your starting point may be, you may take pride in the fact that between the moment you first feel the urge to create a dance, and the moment your first new dance is presented to the world, you have crossed the threshold between your old life and the new life as a creator of dance!

◆ **What is choreography?** The word choreography literally means "dance-writing" and derives from the Greek words "χορεία"—circular dance, and "γραφή"—handwriting. Historically, the term choreography often referred to written notation of dance movements. In the United States, the term "choreographer" was first used in 1936 as a credit for George Balanchine in the Broadway show *On Your Toes*.[2] Interestingly, *choreography* first appeared in the American English dictionary in the 1950s, and it has been in popular use ever since. The prior terminology was "ensembles staged by" or "dances staged by."[3]

Nowadays, the term *choreography* has evolved to encompass more than the literal translation of "dance-writing"—today it refers to all forms of "dance-creating." This means you may draw courage from the fact that your approach to dance creating is as valid a form of choreography as anyone else's.

◆ **Why does choreography matter?** In addition to being identified as the art of creating dance, choreography is also part of everyday life. Any sequencing of thoughts and ideas occurring in a mental process is a form of choreography. Take notice of how your thoughts move from one point to another. Sometimes your thoughts reverse course, veer off, circle back, rush ahead, and pair with other thoughts to twist, bend, and spin around. Sometimes, your thought flow might slow down and temporarily halt for a short meditation. A pause?...No. Suddenly your thoughts awaken and jump into action again. The point here is: Thoughts are in constant motion. The brain is a vast dance studio. Ideas waltz around. Thinking is remarkably similar to dancing. The human mind is a choreographer!

◆ **What does it take to become a professional choreographer?** There is no prescribed recipe. Choreographers develop creatively and professionally on their own terms. Yet choreographers strive to train and prepare on multiple levels—physical, intellectual, and emotional; to endure and survive setbacks; to keep finding the creative power and the strength to move forward. Dance creates the choreographer, and the choreographer creates dance—they are connected and in constant motion together: sometimes complementing each other, other times contrasting with each other, just like tango or other partner dancing.

◆ **What is at stake?** Historically, most of the groundbreaking choreographers have dedicated their entire lives to the art form. But great commitment and hard work alone still do not guarantee great accomplishments. The field is crowded, the profession is demanding, and the public taste is unpredictable. You might invest more than you gain. You might be disliked before you are admired. You might first be misunderstood before you are accepted and celebrated, if at all. Here is the good news: Although choreographing well is tough, it *is* possible. Many choreographers in the past have proven it. Will *you, the choreographer*, be *ONE* of them? You won't know until you do it. This book will help you get started and help you keep going. Making it to the top is challenging but also very exciting. You can accomplish a lot, as long as you are strong, courageous, and devoted!

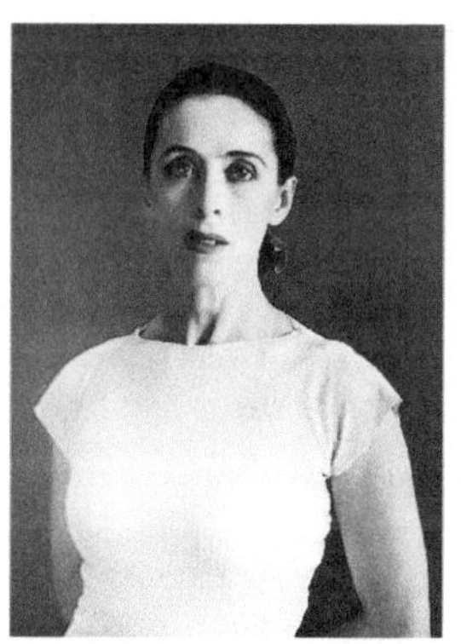

Marius Petipa **Isadora Duncan** **George Balanchine** **Martha Graham**

Figure 6 THEY ARE LOOKING AT YOU! Groundbreaking choreographers who for the last two centuries have shaped the landscape of dance, from left to right: Marius Petipa, photography © Charles Bergamasco, c1855; Isadora Duncan, by anonymous, c1906–12, source and courtesy of Dover Street Studios, London, UK, distributed in the U.S. by Charles L. Ritzmann; George Balanchine, photography © Martha Swope.1968, courtesy New York Public Library; Martha Graham, photography © Barbara Morgan, 1937, courtesy of the Barbara and Willard Morgan photographs and papers, collection of University of California in Los Angeles.

◆ **Is the sacrifice worth it?** Dance is impermanent and ephemeral, like the wind—it emerges instantly and may quickly vanish without a trace. Dance exists with, in, and through the body in motion. A dance may leave behind only a lasting impression and a fond memory. And just like the wind—we can't physically hold it, keep it, and treat it as a material artifact.[4]

Nevertheless, choreographers frequently create dances that capture precious human experience, dances that viewers remember long afterward, and that are preserved and performed again and again. Dance, like life, is fleeting, yet both are worth experiencing to the fullest. Dance and life offer opportunities for us to generously create something that inspires others. But time is passing...The clock is ticking: Are you creating a new dance?

ADMIT [THE] ONE

A new dance cannot emerge without someone creating it—this is where *you, the choreographer*, are needed! A choreographer is also part of a huge workforce contributing to the field of dance, which includes those...

➢ *On Stage, Back Stage, and In-studio:* dancers and performers, technical crew members and production designers, physical therapists and kinesiologists, teachers and educators, rehearsal directors and coaches, restaging consultants and choreographers.

➢ *In Media and Print:* public relations promoters, publicists and writers, scholars and researchers, historians and biographers, notation specialists and archivists, journalists and critics.

➢ *In Management and Leadership:* administrative coordinators and assistants, dance school and studio managers, business leaders and financial clerks, community organizers and board members, curators and programmers, agents and presenters, impresarios and producers, executive and artistic directors.

All of these dance-related positions are equally important. Often, their efforts are coordinated toward one exciting goal—to ensure the realization of a new dance that is about to premiere.

And *you, the choreographer*, are the *ONE* who will create the new dance; the *one* acting as the designated captain and the pilot flying the art form; the *one* who will determine the route, explore new directions, and find new destinations. And everyone will follow you!

Admitting yourself to this special position empowers you to lead and create, to discover and encounter new frontiers. So take a chance and grab your ticket for this special reserved seat. Enjoy the experience, the responsibility, and the privilege!

YOUR DANCE MANIFESTO?
— GENERAL DEFINITIONS IN DIALOGUE WITH UNIQUE VISIONS, EXISTING TRADITIONS IN DIALOGUE WITH INDIVIDUAL ARTISTS —

◆ **What is dance and what is the point of choreography?** It depends on who we ask and where we look for an answer. On one hand, there are numerous definitions in dictionaries and encyclopedias offering general descriptions of what dance is. These summaries often outline collective knowledge rooted in existing tradition and accumulated experience. On the other hand, choreographers have their own unique visions, artistic practices, aesthetic philosophies, and ideologies, often unconventional—and even radical—in the summarized form of manifestos. These manifestos may depict their individual perspective of what dance is. Therefore, it is important to clarify the difference between a general definition and a personal manifesto, where the latter formulates a unique artistic vision.

A *definition* serves to determine or identify the essential qualities of something within a broad explanation and a *general statement* of meaning. Earlier, we identified the etymology and general definition of choreography and choreographer. For dance, Merriam-Webster's Dictionary offers a traditional definition, describing it as:

"an act or instance of moving one's body rhythmically usually to music,"
and "a series of rhythmic and patterned bodily movements usually performed to music."[5]

A *manifesto*, on the other hand, is a declaration of principles, intentions, and ambitions, which might be aesthetic or political in character, in the form of a *personal statement* about the meaning of an artist's work. Perhaps the most famous manifestos in the 20th century are the *Futurist Manifesto*, written by Filippo Marinetti, and the *Surrealist Manifesto*, by André Breton.[6]

In 1760, French choreographer Jean-Georges Noverre described his perspective on what dance is in his book *Letters on Dancing and Ballets*:

Dancing, according to the accepted definition of the word,
is the art of composing steps with grace, precision and facility to the time and bars given in the music,
just as music itself is simply the art of combining sounds and modulations
so that they afford pleasure to the ear.[7]

Although Jean-Georges Noverre began with the disclaimer "according to the accepted definition," one can compare and notice that the dictionary definition of dance is relatively broad: *the instance of moving one's body rhythmically.* Should an athletic team's rhythmic movements to music at a sporting competition also be called dancing? In that particular instance, the movements may actually be referred to as "rhythmic gymnastics."

Noverre's manifesto, in contrast, pairs down dancing as "the art of composing steps with grace" with emphasis on aesthetic provisions and purposes of inventing steps. Therefore, dance is more than an athletic activity in the presence of music—dance is an art form able to capture, synthesize, and communicate precious human experiences.

◆ **Who decides what *good* dance is, could be, or should be?** The fact is, no one truly decides what a *good* dance is or should be. Dance traditions, having established aesthetic principles and movement cultures, tend to be perceived as indisputable and obligatory. But the dance of tomorrow, including *your* dance, may well depart from the constraints of dance traditions.

While established dance forms, such as folkloric dance, courtroom, ballroom, ballet, and many others, offer variable frameworks of what a *good* dance is—only *you, the choreographer*, will decide what *your* dance is. Obviously, the dictionary definition of dance, as provided in the example, may not be sufficient to truly capture the complexity, diversity, and variety of dance as both a fun activity and as an art form.

Proven recipes suggest how to make a *good* dance by complying with pre-determined boundaries in multiple contexts—aesthetic, social, and political. Such a construct raises a question: Is a dance a *good* dance *only* if it complies with certain norms, and should choreographers be concerned with making only dances that others consider good?

You may begin a career in dance by encountering, learning, and embracing certain historic dance traditions and their existing interpretations. You may decide to conform to the established norms indefinitely. You may also choose to not hold on to traditions of the past, but rather use them as "stepping stones" to explore what *your* dance of today is. Furthermore, you might want to explore what a *good* dance of tomorrow could be.

Choreographer Martha Graham famously said: "No artist is ahead of his time. He is his time; it is just that others are behind the times."[8] Brave choreographers may summon the courage to formulate individual interpretations of traditions, to transform dance on their own terms by relating it to their own unique artistic vision—see the following diagram.

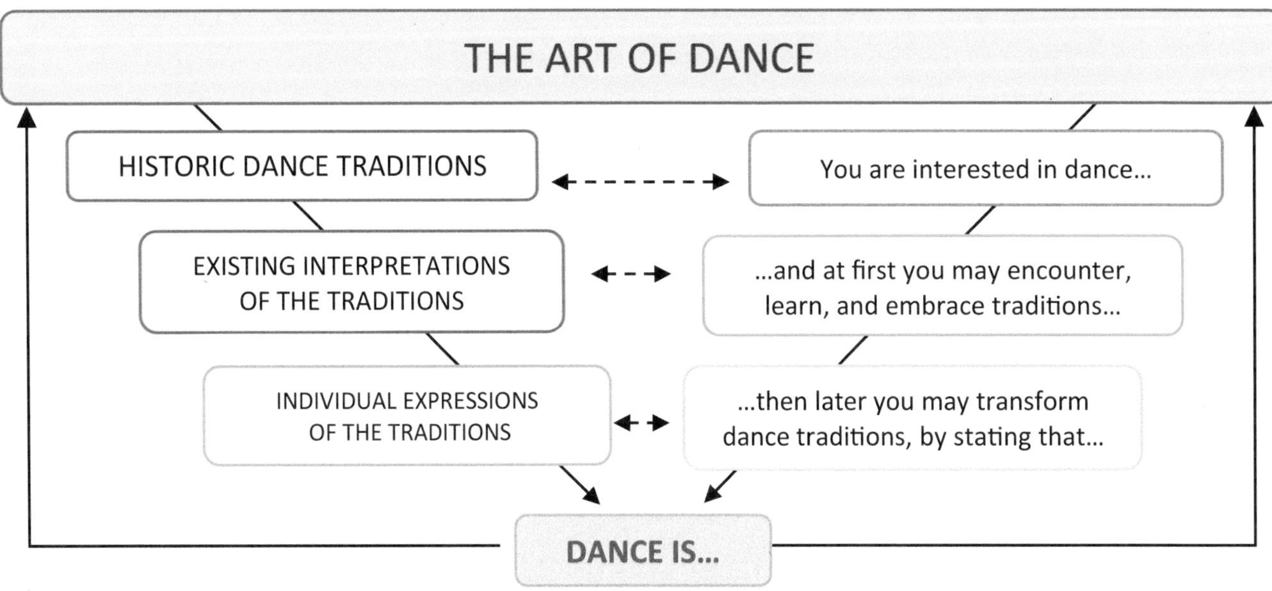

Figure 7

◆ **Explore, discover, and create dance as you *see* it!** Allow yourself to make mistakes and learn from them! Formulate brave and bold normative assertions about what dance is, could be, and should be! Convince everyone that *your* dance contributes transformatively to a living art form that continuously expands in many directions through choreography.

There is no requirement to create your own dance manifesto. Simply having a purpose to create dance is enough. In the past, however, many choreographers have crafted distinct manifestos and found value in describing their performance aesthetics, artistic philosophies, and ideologies—thus formulating notions of what dance is from their own perspectives. Let's provide the following examples in the form of a brief and fun quiz:

?

Can you guess the choreographers who authored or could have authored the following manifestos?

With basic knowledge of dance history and choreography, one may recognize these sample manifestos, as they belong to well-known choreographers. The answers * are disclosed at the bottom of the following page. Here we go:

Dance is freedom. *The spirit of liberation possesses the human body and soul, and therefore relates organically to dance and to the state of the creative mind. One can find freedom in the beauty of nature. The purpose of making dance is to bring out freedom and truth without which the human spirit would exist in agony. Dance is the way to feel free, to be free, and to embrace freedom.*

~

Dance is breathing. *It is essential for dance and it is essential for life. Dance begins with breath! It is the contraction and release of the entire breathing body—particularly in the torso and the pelvis—which creates the pulsation of life and the substance of dance. We are born with breath, we live because of it, and we will keep breathing until we die.*

~

Dance is chance play. *Movement by itself is fascinating, and chance is the only way to experience it directly. Instead of narrative leading the dance, choreography is a random selection method for the choice of steps and step-sequences. Music and dance work together at the same time and place, but as their own entities, without relying on one another.*

~

Making dances is an act of progress. *It is an act of growth, an act of music, an act of teaching, an act of celebration, an act of joy. Dance is for everybody. I believe that the dance came from the people and that it should always be delivered back to the people.*

~

Dance gives form to the unknown. *The body is a location, a place where being is held and shaped. In the dancing body, the unknown appears as something both familiar and extraordinary: we might possibly catch a glimpse of something eternal. But both the dancers and the dance are temporary: their beauty resonates with meaning because of their impermanence.*

These manifestos are distinctly different from one another, and yet they are truthful and persuasive statements. They also demonstrate how a single paragraph can synthesize and encapsulate an artistic vision of a lifelong artistic journey. Are there as many manifestos as choreographers, and how can one keep track of them to avoid disputes?

Choreographers are free to state and pursue whatever they wish. There is plenty of open space in the universe of dance, which offers endless new frontiers to be discovered and inhabited. If a territory is desired, everyone may build and claim a special place within the vast available space. In this text, we will approach choreography and dance making as transcendental and fluid, and not as territorial or static. A manifesto functions autonomously as a unique system of individual expression and, most importantly, it encapsulates the totality of your evolving.

Luckily, no choreographer is the same as another, unless replication is intended. Everyone is unique by nature. Yet the path to formulate one's uniqueness and to claim artistic ownership is not given by nature—it is cultivated through devoted creative work and time. Emerging choreographers may at first incorporate and modify well-known traditions, or "borrow" and alter the artistic practices of other artists. Let's never forget that dance history is brimming with examples of good dances that, in their time, broke or ignored prescribed boundaries.

Over time, you will build your own choreographic instruments to capture and express the ways *you see dance*. These devices could be creative and analytical, artistic and scientific, or a combination of other means of your choice. The core of your manifesto is the persuasiveness of these deliberate artistic decisions, and how they genuinely capture your choreographic agenda and unique creative individuality. So get busy, choreographer: Begin your first manifesto, or add on to an existing one, with these three simple questions:

- ➢ What is dance for you?
- ➢ Why do you create dance?
- ➢ How do you make dance?

A determined, creative mind like yours will not rest until answers are found. Not once-and-for-all answers that end the search, but answers that start a new chapter or the next phase of creative work. And new exciting answers will come when the questioning continues.

A rich and rewarding period of soul-searching, truth-seeking, and self-discovery will begin as soon as you begin it. And the more that *you, the choreographer*, engage creatively with the ideas in this book, the more unique and clearer your manifesto will be. Most likely it will not emerge at first through descriptions and words. So get into the studio and move your ideas! The words will follow.

* Sample manifestos on previous page are authored by or capture in summary the work of from top to bottom in sequence: Isadora Duncan, Martha Graham, Merce Cunningham, Alvin Ailey, and Crystal Pite[9]

BIBLIOGRAPHY AND REFERENCES

[1] Pite, Crystal. TV interview during the 2016 Edinburgh International Festival, 2016, and Direct Quotation via Online Personal Conversations with Vladimir Angelov, December 2020.

[2] Taper, Bernard. *George Balanchine: A Biography*, University of California Press, 1996, pp. 180.

[3] Editors. *Definition of Choreography*, wikipedia.com online dictionary an encyclopedia, accessed September 2012.

[4] Charlotte Van Camp, Julie. *Philosophical Problems of Dance Criticism; Chapter II: The definition of Dance*. Charlotte Van Camp, Julie, Dissertation, Copyright, 1981, Web, September 2012.

[5] Editors. *Definition of Dance*, Merriam-Webster Dictionary, online accessed January 2021, www.merriam-webster.com/dictionary/dance, accessed May 2020.

[6] Editors. *Filippo Tommaso Marinetti, André Breton*, Encyclopedia Britannica, online accessed January 2021, www.britannica.com/, accessed May 2020.

[7] Noverre, Jean Georges. *Letters on Dancing and Ballets*, 1760, translated by Cyril W. Beaumont, Dance Horizons, 1966, pp. 29–30.

[8] Graham, Martha. *Blood Memory: An Autobiography*, Bantam Doubleday Dell Publishing Group, Inc., 1991.

[9] Sample manifestos from the top to bottom in sequence: 1) Duncan, Isadora. *The Art of the Dance*, edited by Sheldon Cheney, Theatre Arts Books, 1969, paraphrased summaries on pp. 50, 63, 77; and *Isadora Speaks: Writings & Speeches of Isadora Duncan*, edited by Franklin Rosemont, Charles H. Kerr Publisher, 1994, paraphrased summary, pp. 33, 36–37, 48–49; 2) Graham, Martha. *Blood Memory: An Autobiography*, Bantam Doubleday Dell Publishing Group, Inc., 1991, pp. 46, paraphrased summary; 3) Cunningham, Merce. "The Impermanent Art," article, 7 Arts, No. 3, Falcon's Wing Press, 1955, pp. 69–77, paraphrased summary; 4) Ailey, Alvin. *Top 24 Quotes of ALVIN AILEY*, source, www.inspiringquotes.us, accessed January 2021: 5) Pite, Crystal. A Direct Quotation via Online Personal Conversations with the author Vladimir Angelov, December 2020.

VISUAL REFERENCES

Figures 1 to 5: Diagrams © Vladimir Angelov

Figure 6: Portraits from left to right: Marius Petipa, photography © Charles Bergamasco, c. 1855; Isadora Duncan, by anonymous, c. 1906–12, source and courtesy of Dover Street Studios, London, UK, distributed in the US by Charles L. Ritzmann; George Balanchine, photography © Martha Swope, 1968, courtesy of New York Public Library; Martha Graham, photography © Barbara Morgan, 1937, courtesy of the Barbara and Willard Morgan photographs and papers, collection of University of California in Los Angeles.

Figure 7: Diagram © Vladimir Angelov

TIME TRAVEL

CHOREOGRAPHING THROUGH THE AGES

Emperor's palace gate. Late fall. Ceremony preparations.

The naked time traveler just finished putting his clothes on and addresses the nearby official.

CHOREOGRAPHER: Please hurry…I need to get everything and everybody ready…

OFFICIAL: Yes, I will escort you in. *(while walking)* You look familiar…

CHOREOGRAPHER: Yes, I have worked for His Majesty before.

OFFICIAL: Offering your services as…?

CHOREOGRAPHER: Choreographer.

OFFICIAL: I see. And exactly what have you been summoned to do now?

CHOREOGRAPHER: Everything!

Excerpt from

dance DIALOGUES

An Anonymous Unpublished Manuscript, 376 BC–AD 2091

WELCOME TO THE TIME TRAVEL GATE

This BOOK I is a portal to a fictitious journey through time which could be linear and chronological, or it could "jump" into different historic periods. This time travel is limited to visiting the past, and not the future. By learning about the past, participating time-traveling choreographers may creatively project what dance of the future could be.

◆ **Why travel through time?** This travel adventure could be an artist's escapist journey to the "good old times." Enjoy sightseeing! Or, this travel could be an artist's exploratory expedition providing an immersive experience and a chance for a choreographer to:

➢ **Consider dance chronologically and contextually:** Dance emerges and forms in relation to various historic circumstances, events, and experiences. What has preceded and followed the creation of a dance provides the framework to understand its function and meaning. By identifying the "time-stamp" of a dance, one can learn how, when, where, and most importantly, why a dance has occurred. Yet does dance always belong to its original environment? What would happen if the environment where a dance first took root is changed or removed?

➢ **Consider dance retrospectively and referentially:** Artists usually welcome great ideas for dance no matter where they come from. Content and concepts in dance that address fundamental human existence such as life and death, love and revulsion, survival and progress, are obstinate and metaphysical; such concepts in dance constantly "travel" from the past to the present and recur in new forms and interpretations. Many contemporary ideas of today have their roots in the past. For example, a particular narrative in dance may be traced throughout history, from early rituals, ancient dances, folkloric traditions, and romantic and classical ballets, all the way to 21st-century contemporary dance. Concepts from the past may fuse, change, and lead to new content that crosses histories and cultures to capture and reflect the human condition.

➢ **Consider dance transcendently and perceptively in relevance to time:** Because live dance is impermanent, it could rightfully be perceived as transitory and temporary; dance also remains relevant and eternal. Live dance exists at/for/in the moment, with an inevitable "nowness" at its core. The appearance of dance coming to be and ceasing to be, as passing or flowing, makes it seem like an occasional phenomenon, and therefore, it appears as unsustainable. Dance by nature is *transcendental*—passing and thriving throughout time. Dance is *beyond* framed time and a consistent purpose. Dance at any point in time is not "more" or "less" relevant than at any other point in time. Although temporal in nature, dance is persistent with possibilities of growing and expanding in many directions, just like a supernova bursting in the cosmos. Therefore, one might argue, but also discover and conclude, that dance from the past, present, and future has equal importance and a perpetual relevance.

DANCING THROUGH THE AGES
– SLICING TIME, MAPPING HISTORY, AND OUTLINING DESTINATIONS –

Time travel might be overwhelming, so having an itinerary, a map, and directions in advance may be helpful. Instead of dividing time conventionally into historic periods, this book offers a structural division applicable to choreography. Slicing time, history, and chronology differently will help us pair together the anthropological stages of humankind with the corresponding constructs of dance. The diagram in Figure 1 serves as a map of seven different ages of human history in relation to dance. Each of the ages will be addressed as separate time travel destinations in the consecutive seven chapters of BOOK I.

Comparably to the distinct *dance manifestos* (see *Your Dance Manifesto*? in the *PROLOGUE* of this book, where individual choreographers define artistic ideologies of what dance is), the classification that follows systematizes *functional constructs* of dance in the context of human history during particular periods. In a choreographic context, each historic age has its own defining dance manifesto! There are no clear borders between the ages; the importance here is the transforming dominant function of dance between ages: Although during each historical age and time frame dance had certain dominant characteristics; dance also did serve many purposes simultaneously.

BOOK I: Chapter	HISTORIC AGE	TIME FRAME	CONSTRUCTS OF DANCE
1	Stone Age	40,000 BC-1,000 BC	Dance as Ritual
2	Ancient Age	9th century BC-5th century AD	Dance as Art
3	Medieval Age	6th century-14th century	Dance as Symbol
4	Renaissance	15th century-17th century	Dance as Culture
5	Industrial Age	18th century-19th century	Dance as Expression
6	Information Age	1900-1999	Dance as Experiment
7	Integral Age	2000-present	Dance as Integration

Figure 1

The generalization above may be arguable at first, but it aims to operate as an easy-to-understand guide addressing the evolving functional constructs of dance within the context of historic periods with corresponding creative forces and patterns. Today's dance is a cumulative progression of all constructs from the historic past to the present, and resulting in convergence and expansion of possibilities:

DANCE COULD BE RITUAL + ART + SYMBOL + CULTURE + EXPRESSION + EXPERIMENT + INTEGRATION

THE CRAFT OF THE CHOREOGRAPHER THROUGH THE AGES

"You, the choreographer—let's create a dance!" Whether this be said by a tribal leader, the gods, the king, the villagers of a newly established settlement, the wealthy industrial family, the government art commissioner, or a choreographer driven by passion to experiment with movement, a new dance emerges in response to and within a framework. The occasion could be an assignment or simply an impulse for self-expression. The choreographer could be employed to craft a dance or motivated to create one.

But how did the choreographer's craft evolve through the ages? On one hand, the "job description" of a choreographer has dramatically changed during the past few centuries—from custom-crafting dance for the king, to radicalizing postmodern dance by inventing new devices. Ironically, the opposite is also true—not a lot has changed during the past few centuries. Principles of early ritual dance continue to appear in contemporary 21st-century dance. Is that a conscious reenactment of past dance histories, or a manifestation of archetypes and the collective unconscious? It could be both, and even more...

The choreographer's creative work through the history of dance could be summarized with short definitions of Choreographer's Craft and daily "job requirements," alongside the choreographer's Operating Mindset and creative force at play. Throughout history, all of these creative purposes and operations do not vanish, but rather accumulate.

HISTORIC AGE	THE CHOREOGRAPHER'S CRAFT	OPERATING MINDSET
Stone Age	Initiate rituals, ceremonies, and celebrations for the survival and spirit of the community.	I worship...
Ancient Age	Define and manifest aesthetic principles and artistic norms of beauty and harmony.	I strive...
Medieval Age	Form and synthesize sacred and secular symbols and metaphors of nature and God.	I embody...
Renaissance	Transpire and exhibit cultural attainments; please and entertain patrons and dignitaries.	I present...
Industrial Age	Invent, define, and display unique individual style and new means of self-expression.	I imagine...
Information Age	Deconstruct, restructure, and redefine ideas, idioms, constructs, and interactions.	I challenge...
Integral Age	Confront, refer to, and integrate complexities of idiosyncratic, cultural, and social change.	I integrate...

Figure 2

A choreographer may be driven by a range of artistic objectives simultaneously. In particular circumstances, a choreographer's creative intentions and operating mindset may act in a single way, or in multiple ways cumulatively:

I CHOREOGRAPH, THEREFORE I WORSHIP + STRIVE + EMBODY + PRESENT + IMAGINE + CHALLENGE + INTEGRATE

GETTING READY FOR A JOURNEY THROUGH THE CHRONICLES OF CHOREOGRAPHIC ART

The approach offered in BOOK I emphasizes the development of choreographic practices in dance throughout history. For that reason, the "history" of choreography presented here differs from a conventional history of dance that would address the chronological development of the art form in a broad spectrum. Nevertheless, choreography is integrated in dance history and linked to human history. The development of consciousness is linked to the expansion of the creative mind, which is the engine of all choreographic practices and their evolutionary development.

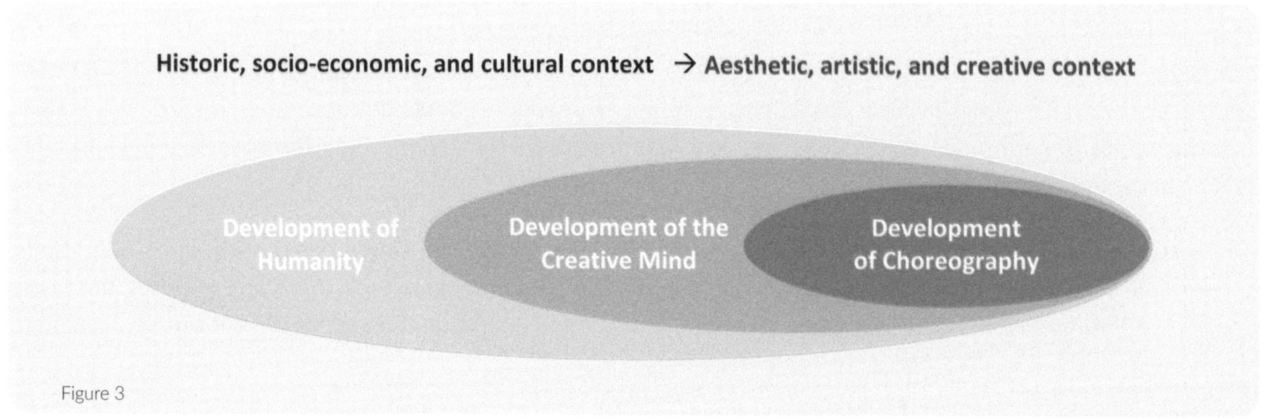

Figure 3

Therefore, the structural flow of each chapter begins with a brief description of the historic, socio-economic, and cultural circumstances of each era, followed by the evolution of consciousness and development of the creative mind. The text addresses various creative constructs and aesthetic frameworks in dance leading to key aspects of the development of choreography. Additional recurring rubrics in the chapters throughout BOOK I are:

◆ ***RETROSPECTIVE AND PERSPECTIVE*** are diagrams with chronology of major choreographic forms serving as historic "maps." These aim to help orient readers to the consecutive flow of the dance ages and enjoy the time travel by hopping backward and forward.

◆ ***THE CRAFT OF THE CHOREOGRAPHER*** are diagrams drawing analogies and systematizing the choreographer's creative work during a particular historic period to help readers envision the purposes and the functions of the choreographer's craft. Each diagram is a pictorial "job description" of what it means to be a choreographer within that particular historical context.

◆ ***LET'S IMAGINE*** are literary sketches in the form of a short essay, story, or dialogue that creatively captures a fictitious event to help readers immerse themselves in a particular historic period and envision what it would be like to live and create in certain historic environment.

◆ ***TRANSCENDING THE AGES and OPERATING CONCEPTS*** are sections and diagrams positioned toward the end of each chapter to help readers envision various functions and constructs of a choreographer's creative work in a broad context across time, and how these constructs transcend history and chronology.

WITH ALL OF THAT COVERED, LET'S GET READY, SET, AND GO!...

⟶

CHAPTER 1

STONE AGE:

THE DAWN OF DANCE – CHOREOGRAPHING RITUAL –

Dance played an integral part in the primal stages of human evolution. The earliest physical evidence of dancing figures was discovered first in Europe and linked to the Aurignacian culture of the Upper Paleolithic era, dating back 40,000 years.[1] Early dance had practical and spiritual functions and was organically connected with ceremonial and celebratory activities. Let's begin with the anthropological context in which early humans lived and the circumstances leading to the emergence of early ritual dance.

In the prehistoric age, early humans inhabited caves, rock shelters, and village-like settlements next to water—on riverbanks and at beaches. They formed small tribal communities that hunted, fished, and gathered wild plants for survival. The priorities of early human communities were to:

- avoid death by carnivorous animals or other early humans
- ensure survival by obtaining shelter and a sufficient amount of food
- procreate to maintain and expand the tribe

In addition to addressing these existential basics, early humans also endeavored to satisfy their deep spiritual urges and needs through rituals, which served practical, rather than aesthetic, purposes. Dance rituals helped early humans feel and think of themselves as:

- united and strong as a community
- connected with the forces of nature and the gods
- enabled to express joy or sorrow in conjunction with life's events

Bonding deeply with nature and striving to survive by all means were existential priorities for early humans—figurative sample photo left. However, daily life was not easy. Besides working hard for their food, they also encountered unpredictable weather, natural disasters, and life-threatening diseases.

The domestication of plants and animals in the late period of the Stone Age brought a better understanding of calendar sequencing and the coordination of agricultural activities. Farmland and hunting grounds were often disputed territories among prehistoric tribes. Early human formations faced conflicts and engaged in battles for control over the land and resources.

Figure 4 Photography © Lois Greenfield, pictured Sam Mosher, 1993

The dwellings of early humans were much simpler than today's homes: the kitchen, the bedroom, the living room, the painting canvas, the music room, and the dance studio were all located within the same space. Figure 5 depicts a speculative view of the San people, a community of hunter-gatherers who lived 4,000 years ago. San people's paintings were found in stone shelters and caves in the Drakensberg Mountains in South Africa.

Figure 5 Vintage engraving of a family of the San people gathered in front of a cave, courtesy of Ferdinand Hirts Geographische Bildertafeln, 1886

The way of dancing is naturally linked to the way of thinking. Prehistoric people were likely practical thinkers with rudimentary needs. Their reasoning and interpretation of themselves and nature were reflected in how they crafted ritual dances. Presumably, mindsets shifted priorities through the centuries. A pivotal transformation of the mindset from the Stone to the Ancient Age was the transition from concrete thinking to abstract thinking, and from practical solutions to imaginative solutions. Compared to prehistoric ancestors, people of the Ancient Age prioritized a thinking mode and cognitive abilities such as writing and mathematics, which may not have been considered of existential importance by early humans. Resolving a simple equation of counting and distributing food supplies, such as 1+2=3, is illustrated in Figure 6 using the two modes of thinking that differentiated these two ages.

PERIOD	RATIONALE	APPROACH	STRATEGY	ENACTMENT	EXAMPLE
STONE AGE	CONCRETE THINKING	Simple assessment	Practical solution	Hands-on tools	+ =
ANCIENT AGE	ABSTRACT THINKING	Complex assessment	Imaginative solution	Mental tools	$\frac{\sqrt{4}}{2} + (1^5)\left(\frac{64}{32}\right) = 27\left(\frac{2}{18}\right)$

Figure 6

Ritual dance during the prehistoric era, according to general resources, likely emerged as a physical expression and kinesthetic arrangement of stylized movement sequences and actions reflecting practical needs and attributed spiritual values. Shamanism and witchcraft were also embedded in the ritual ceremonies and dance festivities, which worshiped and honored the cults of nature by expressing respect, sacrament, and commitment.[2]

In prehistoric ritual dance making and performance, often there were no specific assignments to the roles of the choreographer, the dancers, the musicians, and the audience. All of the participants were involved in various functions. In most early rituals, the act of choreography was not the work of a single person, but likely a group activity and creative communal experience. *Individual identity* was expressed as *collective identity.*

Ritual dances likely took place at different sites: inside the cave, outside at the gathering area around the totem, beside the river, and in the agricultural fields. Dancing activity was accompanied by singing, chanting, drumming, and praying to the forces of nature—all occurring simultaneously. Ceremonial body painting and piercing were often an organic part of ritual dance pageantry. Dance wasn't just a portion of ritual—ritual itself was dance!

> ◆ **Worship rituals and honoring ceremonies** of early humans were likely continuous efforts to understand and connect with nature and improve chances for survival. Humans were looking at the sky and the stars, searching for clues, examining repetition, and studying nature's patterns. The circular shape of the sun and moon, the repetitive cycle of day and night, the consistent changing of the seasons and their impact on humans, were all represented by the people standing and moving in round formations. Archaic circular patterns replicated the patterns of nature and the forces of the Universe. For early humans, observing and understanding the world was often mixed with a great dose of mysticism and a belief in supernatural powers. Religious trance and impersonations of nature through movement were likely the mental and physical frameworks to offer comfort in response to inexplicable natural phenomena. Worship dance rituals and honoring ceremonies were the outlets available to early humans to embody their concerns, beliefs, and hopes.

Circular dance patterns and choreographing in round shapes combined functionality with attributed meaning. The round form of early pottery was likely perceived as a sacred shape given to humans by the gods, and it served vastly functional purposes: to keep food in one place, to contain water, to store items and make them transportable. Early people also positioned themselves in a ring around the bonfire to equally share the warmth and light. The circle formations reflected choreographically the equality among tribal members and the strength of their solidarity.[3] Circle dance rituals were an expression of *togetherness,* closeness, comfort, confidence, and therefore, an assurance of survival.

> ➢ **Combat and warfare rituals** likely had practical aspects: to enact battle and prepare men to fight, improve their military skills, and build physical endurance. Warfare drills in the form of synchronized dance to the rhythm of drumming accompaniment and chanting empowered and energized tribal armies, training them physically and mentally to fight against their enemies in territorial disputes.

> ➢ **Hunting rituals and training in developing coping skills**, guided by a shaman or an experienced hunter, offered essential means for survival and healing, skills for self-help, and most importantly, hunting. Hunting provided food; the animal skin was utilized for multiple purposes, and feathers from hunted birds decorated the sites of worship and the partakers.

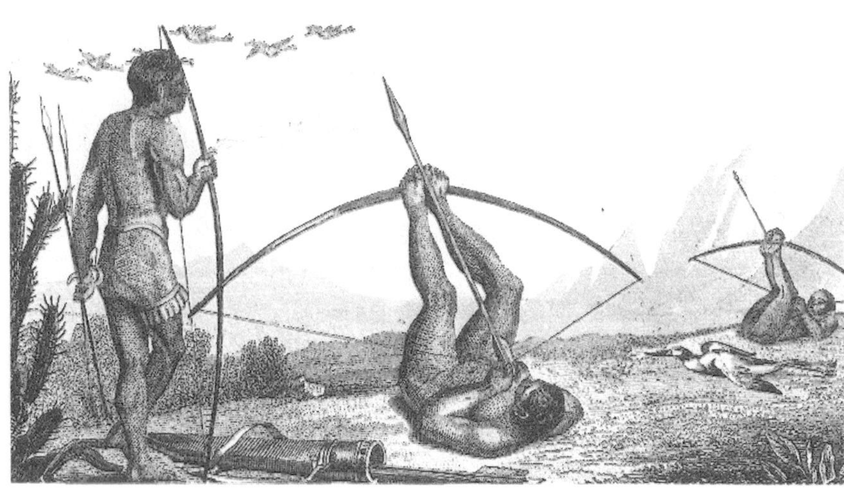

Figure 7 Imaginative scene of hunters, a fragment of engraving illustration, first published in 1851, courtesy of iStock/Getty Images

Shooting arrows, throwing spears, and other coordinated movement sequences, performed by a single individual or a group, served as practical training to improve hunting skills and strategies. In early forms of hunting dance rituals, a selected religious leader—a shaman—wore a carved wooden mask representing an animal. It was believed that the mask had powers that enabled the shaman to connect and communicate with the mystic powers before the actual hunting began. Dance was also prescribed and implemented as a type of healing, medicine, and wellness for the body and spirit. During a ritual, shamans often led the participants into a spiritual trance, which was believed to be the way of divine bonding with the Universe.[4]

➢ **Celebration rituals and communal processions** were likely associated with tribal social events and were designated outlets for the community to express joy or sadness. These activities included acknowledging and commemorating births and deaths, marriages and burials, fertility and procreation, coming of age and rites of passage, seasonal farming and harvests, animal sacrifices, and hunting triumphs. Dance rituals also portrayed public punishments and executions, surrenders and concessions, pilgrimages and migrations, as well as oaths of allegiance and dedication, tribal inaugurations, and combat victories over newly attained territories.[5]

In summary, ritual dance in the early ages likely had both practical and spiritual functions and served the vital necessities of early humans. The acts of choreography and dance were intuitive responses and creative group activities that accommodated tribal needs and reflected communal experiences.

?

What are the advantages and challenges of choreographing in a communal round formation, where all participants are equally spaced and facing each other?

THE CRAFT OF THE EARLY DANCE RITUAL CHOREOGRAPHER

The early ritual dance choreographer's craft is depicted in the diagram below, which maps and draws an analogy to a prehistoric communal circle, by listing key aspects of early ritual dance. Conceptually, the purpose of a ritual dance may be summarized in three major categories: ceremonial worship, communal celebration, and practical training. Kinesthetically, the setting and participants, sound and music, movement imagery and dance vocabulary, and structure and sequencing reflect the content in relation to tribal survival needs. All of these aspects function as a multilayered and dynamic construct to systematize the choreographic processes of early dance rituals.

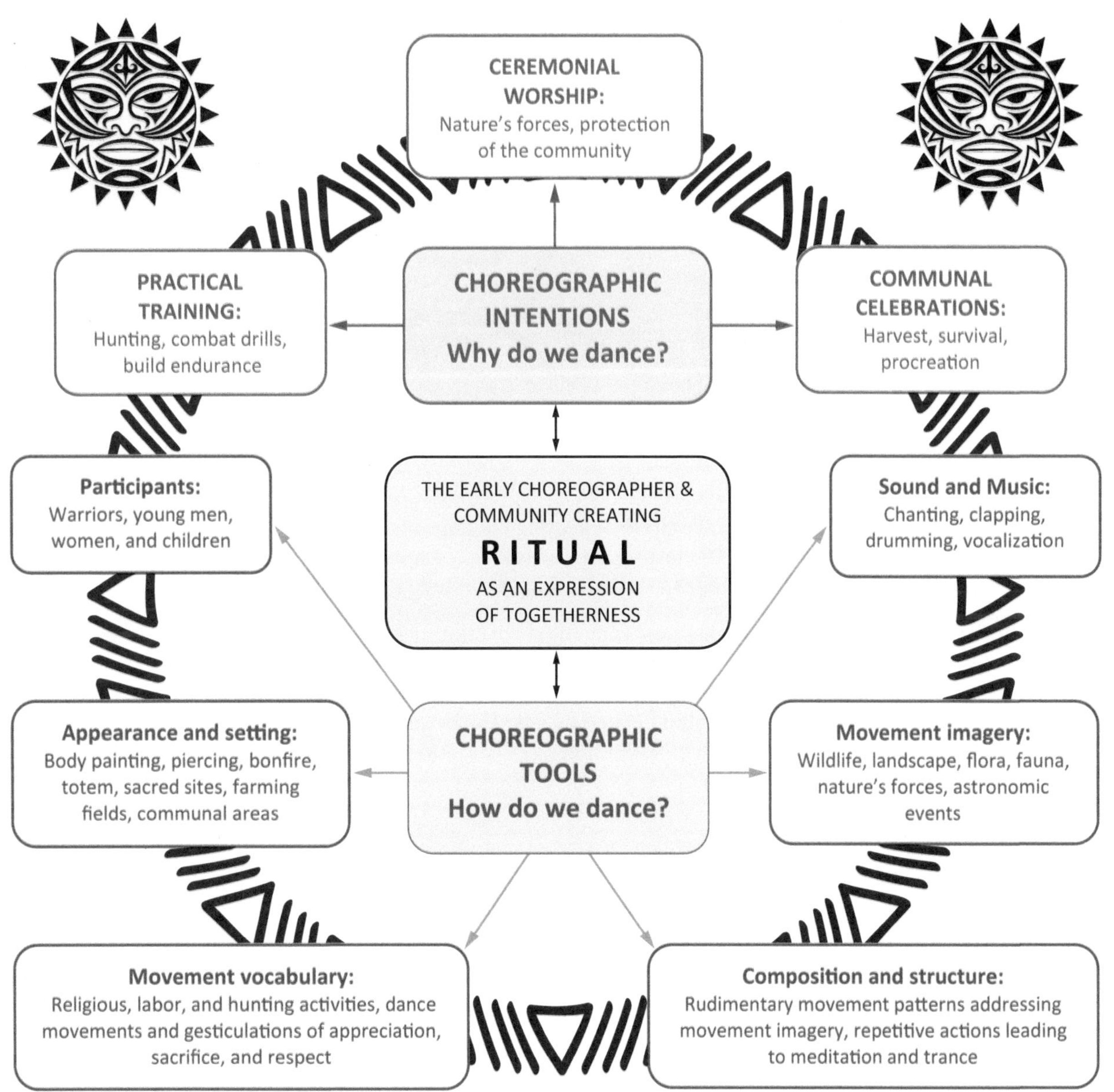

Figure 8

THE HUNTING WARRIORS

HYPOTHETIC LIBRETTO OF FICTITIOUS PREHISTORIC RITUAL DANCE

The choreographic scene set-up: It is early evening at sunset on the beach in front of the cave. Women bring small branches and help set up a bonfire. Men begin drumming, while women light the fire and chant. The rest of the community gathers around the bonfire in a circle, moving rhythmically as a group and performing simple repetitive steps.

The choreographic happening: A warrior uses his spear to draw silhouettes of elands in the sand around the fire. With calculated, rhythmic steps, the warrior slowly begins to circle the sand-drawn elands and the bonfire, whispering and chanting to the beat of the drums. His meditative dance steadily intensifies and takes him into a trance. His heartbeat synchronizes with the rhythm of the drums; his stomping feet, with the pulse of the Earth; his breath, with the wind of the desert...Nature and dancer are united!

Other warriors gradually join him in the dance circle, repeating his steps and moves. During a rhythmic climax, the lead warrior suddenly jumps over the bonfire. While airborne, he tosses his spear at the sand-drawn elands and hits one of them. He lands safely on his feet and continues his dance, uninterrupted.

One by one, the other warriors join the leader, repeating the risky hunting drill. Many spears are now stuck in the sand, as the warriors complete their dance. The warriors then gradually pick up their weapons. They slowly kneel around the fire, leaning back on their spears and facing up toward the night sky. Warriors gaze at the star formation Taurus, and they seemingly whisper a prayer for the hunted horned beasts. The drumming gradually fades out. Only the chanting of the women echoes, glorifying the strength of the hunters.

The choreographic accomplishments: Hunting warriors improve their skills in jumping high above the fire and throwing their spears with precision. The tribe is supportive by singing, chanting, drumming, and moving rhythmically. Dance reflects hunting as a ritual of survival, and it is a unifying experience for the entire community. Dancing warriors express their respect, affection, and appreciation of the forces of nature and for the chance to put in a fair fight for their food.

TRANSCENDING THE AGES
– CHOREOGRAPHING RITUAL IN A BROAD CONTEXT –

Although originating in historic contexts, rituals synthesize and embody hope, values, and truth-seeking rather than facts. Therefore, rituals connect wisdom and experiences of the past with those of the present and future. Transcending and traveling through time, rituals today thrive in many forms and constructs: formal and informal, ceremonial and casual, institutional and vernacular, symbolic and task-based. Rituals bring consensus among people and unite them under the mutual goal of accomplishing a mission. Among many, three categories of transcending rituals appear with distinct characteristics:

- ***TRADITIONAL DANCE RITUALS WITH CONTEMPORARY INTERPRETATIONS:*** A vast number of traditional early human rituals are preserved and still performed by indigenous communities around the globe. Contemporary choreographers also engage with early rituals by choosing various approaches and creative techniques: in some cases, these are authentic reconstructions of early ritual dances based on research, references, and examination of oral and written histories. In other instances, contemporary choreographers approach early dance rituals as a source of inspiration: they interpret, modify, and transform ancestral traditions to serve their creative visions and purposes. The example that follows below illustrates creative work inspired by early dance ritual.

Born in New Zealand and of Samoan heritage, choreographer Neil Ieremia has developed a powerful movement aesthetic and a sensitive, yet fearless, approach to integrating early dance traditions and rituals with contemporary dance. In 1995, he founded the dance company Black Grace, and his work encompasses his native traditions infused with his unique artistic perspective. Contemplating the direction of his work, Ieremia shares:

I believe traditions of Samoa, including its rituals and practices, are still relevant and important, particularly to those who still live in the islands. My work is a direct expression of who I am—made up of viewpoints, opinions, understandings, and experiences—a key component of which is my Samoan heritage and New Zealand upbringing. The resulting tension between the two provides a lens through which I create and organize movement, regardless of its perceived or actual origin.[6]

Figure 9 Photographer © Simon Wilson, *Siva* (2015), choreography by Neil Ieremia, pictured dancers from left to right Otis Herring, Andy Faiaoga, Callum Sefo, Ruby Ala, Black Grace, 2015

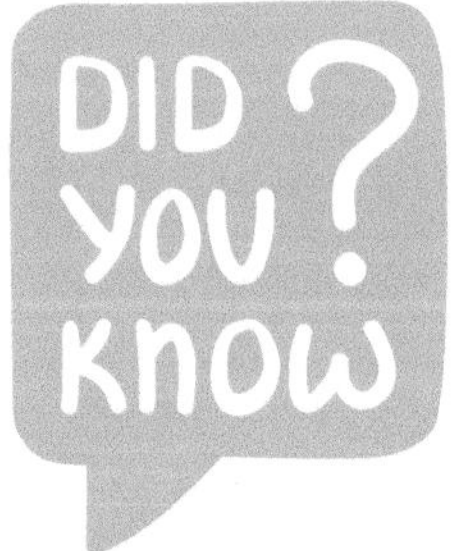

Neil Ieremia proudly shares that the creative practices in Black Grace occur in the form of a communal ritual, where everyone pitches in and works collectively. Humility, respect, and a commitment to togetherness throughout the process are nurtured values. As he describes, besides dancing, the company members sit down together, eat together, and sing together. They also laugh a lot together, and from time to time, they cry together. [7]

Kinesthetically, contemporary interpretations of early rituals may focus on both somatic experiences and spiritual embodiment. Whether or not the movement appears aesthetically pleasing is rarely of concern; instead, the emphasis is on how body, soul, and nature connect. Conceptually, the focus is to reveal human values of the past by relating and integrating them with human values of contemporary times. The work incorporates an unapologetic appeal for social change. The differentiation in interpreting early rituals is not problematic, but rather a healthy distinction that emphasizes the connectivity between dance histories without erasing the importance of differences between choreographic cultures.

◆ ***URBAN DANCE RITUALS, MOVEMENT CULTURES AND TRIBALISM:*** Social dance in big cities and metropolitan areas continually evolves, bringing to life new forms of rituals and movement cultures related to urban society. Origins and belonging are associated with social groups and territories: the "street," the "hood," the "club," the "crew," etc., rather than specific physical locations. New values emerge in response to social stigma and in refuting the banalities of ordinary life. These acts of nonconformity and resistance also encompass commentary on social status, politics, and sensuality. The following groupings describe these forms:

➢ *Disco, House, and Club Dancing* collect large groups of people at indoor or outdoor dance floors to spontaneously dance to loud and bass-heavy electronic music.[8] The disc jockey, also known as the DJ, acts as the "shaman" who controls the music selection, guiding the crowd's repetitive and monotonous, modern contemporary, yet visceral movements to a *group trance*. As in early ritual, the participants enjoy dance as *togetherness*.

Figure 10 Photography © Victor Gladkov, Dancing people in a disco club, courtesy of iStock/Getty Images

The improvised movement vocabulary may include hand-waving, rhythmic steps, stomping, and energetic footwork, combined with ecstatic and sensual rippling movements of the torso—an all-encompassing worship of joy. Various moves and sub-styles of house dance are in use such as bump, hustle, shuffle, jacking, lofting, freestyling, and waacking, among many others. The dancers instantaneously invent their moves and never stop moving when the music is on.

➢ *Voguing*, on the other hand, is a highly stylized movement and dance culture that evolved from the ballroom scene in Harlem, New York City. By the 1980s, voguing had established itself as a distinct dance and movement space for self-expression for urban Black and Latinx LGBTQ+ communities. While the style emerged from an underground social dance culture, it suddenly became mainstream through pop star Madonna's iconic music dance video entitled "Vogue."

Egyptian hieroglyphs are considered the inspiration for the old-way-voguing. Voguing moves mimic the fashion models' postures in *Vogue* magazine: to the beat of the music, dancers strike a series of poses as if they are modeling for a photo shoot. Similar to early ritual, voguing is an idiosyncratic homage honoring beauty and glamour, but also capturing melancholy feelings about inaccessible stardom. Various versions of voguing incorporate exaggerated feminine movements called catwalk, duckwalk, runway, floorwork, spins, and dips, as well as the extensive use of hands and mimicking facial expressions to tell a story. Drag dance and movement competitions eventually shifted from elaborate fashion pageantry to vogue dance battles.[9] Prominent ball culture establishments in the field include House of Aviance, House of LaBeija, House of Ebony, and House of Abundance, to name a few.

➢ *Street dance forms and dance battles* emerge in various formats in which street dancers battle on their own, in duos, or as part of a crew on the street, in a nightclub, or in a competition. As in early warfare and combat rituals, during a dance battle, each dancer or crew stands opposite each other, and they take turns trying to outdo one another's moves. The winner is decided by the crowd or by a panel of judges. Urban street dance forms may include elements from other urban dance styles, such as break dance, popping, locking, shuffle, electro, robot, clowning and krumping, funk, and hip-hop, among others.

➢ *Hip-hop music and dance,* for example, are an earth-based wisdom vernacular with links to shamanic dialects of multiple cultures. The ecstatic rhythms of hip-hop are a rebirth of ancestral power, where thoughts and emotions affect the body and soul, then ripple out and energize all of those engaged. When funk and hip-hop music lyrics talk about "getting down" and are instantly implemented into movement equivalent, they literally mean down in the ritualistic Africanized context of the ground, to Mother Earth, our Goddess.[10]

Hip-hop connects contemporary urban culture to ancient rituals with a giant leap through time, bypassing centuries of heavily Christianized, colonialized psyches. Similar to early ritual, themes and connotations about sensuality and ferocity are not direct incitements, but rather serve as metaphors in poetic, psycho-chanting music and to shock, like lightning on the consciousness. When addressing moral values, hip-hop music and dance deliver existential, rebellious statements with biting wit and political commentary on the status quo of marginalized communities facing the humiliating prejudices of society.[11]

Some of the most noted hip-hop dance makers working for concert dance stage are American choreographers Rennie Harris, Sonya Tayeh, Doug Elkins, Israeli-born American choreographer Ephrat Asherie, French choreographer Mourad Merzouki, and French-Spanish-Korean choreographic duo Sébastien Ramírez and Honji Wang, to name a few.

In the entertainment industry, alongside the legendary choreographer Paula Abdul, the noted pop, rap, and hip-hop music and movement TV celebrities engaged in dance include Jennifer Lopez, Beyoncé, Shakira, Drake, and Kanye West. They regularly use distinguished choreographers such as Paris Goebel, JaQuel Knight, Tina Landon, Chris Grant, Tanisha Scott, Liz Dany Campo Díaz, Sean Bankhead, and the choreographic duo William "WilldaBeast" Adams & Janelle Ginestra-Adams, among many others.

◆ ***EVERYDAY RITUALS, FORMAL AND INFORMAL TASK-BASED PROTOCOLS, AND ACTION SEQUENCING:*** A choreographed ritual may emerge in the form of artful dance work, a distinct social event, or simply an activity that occurs in daily life. A ritual could also take place in the form of individual or group task-based activity such as meditation or action sequencing, such as an exercise routine. These formal and informal rituals provide day-to-day frameworks for how people operate kinesthetically as individuals, and how community interactions coordinate and function together within a beneficial consensus. Ritual activity unites people under one agenda to implement that agenda in efficient and meaningful ways. Such rituals may range from participating in a wedding, to taking a Yoga class, to routine teeth brushing. In this broad context, initiating and implementing any purposeful endeavor involving a task-based activity and action sequencing is an act of choreography. Such pre-created or newly created organized movement structures are *task-based protocols*—a wider and broader understanding and implementing of transcendental ritual activities. Well-known protocol formats are graduation ceremonies and court proceedings, administrative and medical procedures, guidelines and directions in user manuals, and recipes, and routines and habits such as dining and exercising.

?

Have you recently encountered any of the task-based rituals from the list, and how could you re-envision and re-choreograph some of them?

Creating and crafting a ritual of any kind is a fundamentally useful skill for all choreographers. Choreographers may observe, study, and analyze existing rituals and use them as inspiration and a starting point to formulate their own rituals. Choreographing a ritual entails the following basic algorithm:

➢ Determining the purpose, intention, and format of the ritual and/or task-based protocol;
➢ Generating a series of efficient kinesthetic actions and meaningful activities that encompass the objectives and the values of the ritual;
➢ Creating and crafting a movement sequence by involving and organizing the partaking members, and by incorporating the necessary supportive production elements—environment, setting, and practicalities—to facilitate a multi-layered ritual experience.

HELPFUL TIPS & SUGGESTIONS

~ Transform a prayer into a movement ritual by dancing it
~ Approach dance celebrations as a reenactment of what has inspired us
~ Worship and love through dance and embody transpersonal energy
~ Consider rituals as togetherness of body and soul, individual and community
~ Think of ceremonies as bridges between heart and fate, existence and significance
~ Set the stage for dance ritual by setting the stage for enlightenment
~ Honor past movement traditions by building future dance aspirations

CHOREOGRAPHING RITUAL AS AN OPERATING CONCEPT BEYOND HISTORICAL CONTEXT

Beyond the fine art of dance, creating a sequence of physical actions is a subject and an act of choreography. Choreographers are empowered and privileged to be able to create new rituals and use them as part of their creative work and dances. Activities arranged as a ritual could serve a wide range of purposes, from deeply meaningful to simply practical, or purely comforting. A well-crafted choreographic ritual sequence contains and reveals the plan, methods, and mechanisms needed for meeting an objective.

Choreographing a ritual as an operating concept encompasses action-sequenced and task-based protocols—some of them could be strictly predetermined; others could be altered or originally created to fit an occasion. A ritual could involve a single individual, a selected group of partakers, or masses of people brought together to accomplish a goal or share an experience. Rituals could be formal—ceremonial and mandating, officially approved and institutionalized, or they could be casual—pragmatic and informal, flexible and improvised.

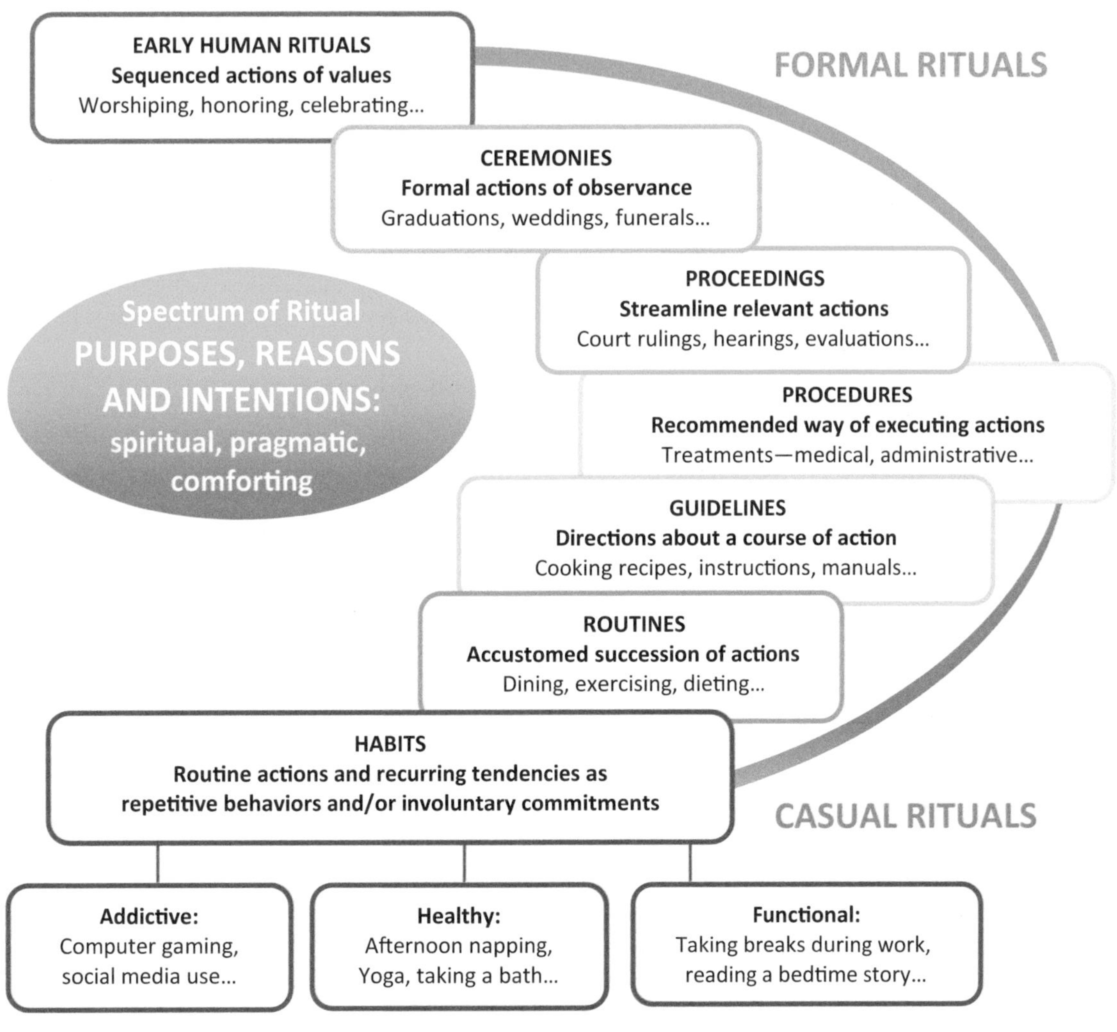

Figure 11

assignments & exercises

RESEARCH ASSIGNMENT: Use online, library, and video resources to research and study a sample of an early dance ritual. The ritual could still be in practice around the world today by indigenous cultures of Africa, Tibet, New Zealand, and others. Describe the purpose of the ritual, the theme, and the actions used in the ritual you researched. Analyze and explain what movement vocabulary and kinesthetic imagery capture the intentions and meaning of the ritual. What elements were the most powerful, and why?

★ **CREATIVE EXERCISE:** Let's practice the creation of a prehistoric and a modern-day ritual:

➥ Imagine being placed in the prehistoric age, where you are in charge of choreographing a ritual. What needs and actions from prehistoric life can you recreate? Choose an idea that will be the content of your early dance ritual. For example, select an animal, plant, or a force of nature that inspires movement generation. How does that subject move? How do you interpret that movement with different body parts or locations in space? Consider using supportive elements such as rhythmic and percussive sounds created by your moving body, as well as improvised props, masks, body painting, etc.

➥ Continue working on developing your movement ritual by expanding it into a longer format of worship, ceremony, or celebration. Refer to and use the circular diagram *The Craft of the Early Dance Ritual Choreographer*. For example, create a circle in your practice space. As you travel around the circle, physicalize your subject matter as part of an activity, which could be hunting, fire making, planting, harvesting, a wedding, or a funeral—what movement and rhythmic patterns emerge as you repeat your ideas over and over?

➥ Shift gears and create your personal ritual based on your current daily life. Refer to the diagram *Choreographing Ritual as an Operating Concept Beyond Historical Context*. Your subject matter might include various activities, such as a morning wake-up routine, getting ready for work, doing laundry, etc. Or you could tackle another popular ceremony of all ages, such as a wedding. However, place the ceremony in an unusual environment, then modernize it and make it humorous. For example, you might consider an underwater wedding with scuba diving gear, which could also be choreographed and presented without being underwater, with improvised swimming accessories and beach props.

COMPARATIVE ASSIGNMENT: Compare and analyze your contemporary rituals with the authentic prehistoric one you have researched and created. What are the differences and the similarities in terms of content, movement material, and performance environment? What are the challenging and exciting aspects when creating the rituals, and why?

BIBLIOGRAPHY AND REFERENCES

[1] Garfinkel, Yosef. "The Evolution of Human Dance: Courtship, Rites of Passage, Trance, Calendrical Ceremonies and the Professional Dancer," Article, Cambridge *Archaeological Journal*, vol. 28, no. 2, May 2018, pp. 283–298.

[2] Garfinkel 2018. "The Evolution of Human Dance..."

[3] Garfinkel 2018. "The Evolution of Human Dance..."

[4] Garfinkel 2018. "The Evolution of Human Dance..."

[5] Hanna, Judith Lynne. "Dance and Religion (Overview)," in The *Encyclopedia of Religion*, 2nd edition, edited by Lindsay Jones, Macmillan Co., 2004, pp. 2134–2143.

[6] Angelov, Vladimir. Conversions with Neil Ieremia and Rehearsal Visits at Black Grace, Quotation provided in coordination and permission by Neil Ieremia, Spring, 2019.

[7] Teague, Jessica. Interviewer, *Neil Ieremia: The Grace of Resilience*, online interview, Dance ICONS, Inc., 2019, accessed February 2021.

[8] Pareles, Jon. "Dance and Music Clubs Thriving in Era of Change," article, New York Times, November 12, 1982, accessed January 2021.

[9] Tsione Wolde, Michael. "A Brief History of Voguing," The National Museum of African American History & Culture, Smithsonian Institution, accessed 13 December 2019.

[10] Cercone, Katie. "*10* Divinations on Hip Hop as Sacred Medicine, Blood Time, Sex, Rituals & Ancestral Communion of the Mother Tongue," September 2014, online article: https://brooklynrail.org, accessed January 2021.

[11] Cercone 2014. *10* Divinations on Hip Hop...

VISUAL REFERENCES

Figures 1, 2 and 3: Diagrams © Vladimir Angelov

Figure 4: Photography © Lois Greenfield, pictured performer Sam Mosher, 1993

Figure 5: Vintage engraving of a family of the San people, gathered in front of a cave. The San people (or Saan), also known as Bushmen or Basarwa, are members of various indigenous hunter-gatherer people of Southern Africa, whose territories span Botswana, Namibia, Angola, Zambia, Zimbabwe, and South Africa. Ferdinand Hirts Geographische Bildertafeln, 1886

Figure 6: Diagram © Vladimir Angelov, including hand banner vector icon, Credit: f9b65183_118, courtesy of iStock/Getty Images

Figure 7: *Scenes from Greenland, Brazil and Patagonia*, a fragment of engraving antique illustration, credit: bauhaus1000courtesy, first published in 1851, courtesy of iStock/Getty Images

Figure 8: Diagram © Vladimir Angelov, including Ethnic symbol-mask of the Maori people—Tiki. Thunder-like Tiki is symbol of God, a sacral tribal sign in the Polenesian credit: KatikaM, and *Set of gold hand drawn ethnic arrows frame*, credit: krolja, courtesy of Adobe Stock

Figure 9: Photographer © Simon Wilson, *Siva*, (2015), choreography by Neil Ieremia, pictured dancers from left to right: Otis Herring, Andy Faiaoga, Callum Sefo, Ruby Ala, courtesy of Black Grace, 2015

Figure 10: Photography © Victor Gladkov, *Dancing people in a disco club*, courtesy of iStock/Getty Images

Figure 11: Diagram © Vladimir Angelov

O divine Muse, join me in this festival dance!

Peace, a comedy by Aristophanes,
Athens, 421 BC

CHAPTER 2

ANCIENT AGE:

GODS AND MUSES IN MOTION — CHOREOGRAPHING ART —

Our time travel through choreographic creativity now takes us to the ancient civilizations of Egypt, India, and Greece to look into societal development, economy, culture, and dance. Over time, prehistoric people and tribal communities started abandoning caves and improvised shelters, and they began to establish larger permanent settlements and villages. There was a growing need for a centralized place for trade within a concentrated population, as well as more extensive civic and military defense infrastructures. Over time, denser populations organized themselves into cities, which faced a new challenge: to set parameters for how urban society should function. Rules of governance and structures of political leadership were established.[1]

For instance, ancient Greece, the birthplace of the modern era *democratic society*, placed a strong emphasis on laws and the participation of elected individuals as representatives in government. The society was divided into *demes* or local areas within the city-state. The *demes* were grouped into political sections to choose council members for the city's government.[2] Athens was testing *democracy*, and the experiment was working!

Money and currency were invented, so the Stone Age practice of trading livestock and goods was no longer the sole means of exchanging resources. Coins were minted and introduced as an abstract equivalent in value. Women were no longer limited to child-rearing and home-keeping, and men were not limited to the roles of "hunters and warriors," effectively changing the structure of the workforce. Ancient citizens began to *specialize* in certain sets of manual and intellectual skills, which they called "crafts" and "professions." Doctors and politicians, philosophers and playwrights, architects and engineers began to identify themselves as *professionals*.

Dance artists also adopted the concept of paid performers and professionals. Employment in dance became a legitimate source of income and an accepted profession that provided services to the community. Performance venues ranged widely: rituals and funerals, religious ceremonies and military celebrations, dramatic plays and seasonal festivals, acrobatic demonstrations and burlesque entertainment. The dance field became populated with sub-specialties of performers, dancers, educators, movement coaches, and choreographers. Artistic expression transformed as well: from a communal group activity into the democratic act of individual creativity—themed art photography sample left.

Figure 1 Photography © Lois Greenfield, pictured Leslie Simpson, courtesy of KDNY Dance Company, 2005

A transition from *concrete thinking to abstract and symbolic thinking* was crucial in transforming the ways ancient people operated. Abstract ideas such as "money," "democracy," and "art" emerged as people in antiquity became less confined to material objects and more concerned with the universal essence of things.[3]

Abstract thinking, in general, involves three processes: a) analytical assessment and thought synthesis to extract the essence of a complex idea by organizing and summarizing the idea into a straightforward, easy-to-understand concept; b) investigation of the relationships between physical objects or topics and how they interact by seeking common properties and forming analogies; c) new concept formation by innovative exploration of how one thing/idea could be multifunctional and be integrated in a range of contexts. Throughout human history, both types of thinking—concrete and abstract—have effectively used the mind's powers. What is the difference between them?

Concrete thinking is engaging the mind to make *functional and practical* decisions and taking action to address an immediate need to gain control over certain conditions or phenomena. For example, one could climb a tree when being chased by a wild animal because it would save one's life. *Abstract thinking*, by contrast, is engaging the mind with ideas that might be intangible at first and that might not provide an immediate outcome, and yet they could lead to a *functional outcome*. For instance, one can think of the same tree from the previous example and use that tree in various ways such as for wood to fuel a fire (branches and logs); a high point for surveillance (observation tower); food supply (apples, maple syrup, and honey); material for building hunting and military weaponry (spears, bows, arrows); a source to craft furniture and musical instruments (desirable objects); or construction material for various large projects (canoes, shelters, fencing, homes), etc.

Abstract thinking rarely leads to a predictable outcome or the achievement of a specific goal. Instead, it is about the act of thinking itself. The strategic questions that drive abstract thinking are what one is curious about and what one can learn when engaging intuitively, intellectually, and creatively with phenomena. In summary, abstract thinking is an open-ended and risk-tolerant activity that invigorates the imagination and fosters innovation—see also Chapter 11.

As abstract thinking permeated ancient life, religion expressed itself in *abstract poetic symbols* and mythical personifications of gods. On the other hand, ancient science and philosophy preferred the language of *non-poetic abstraction* for discussing substance, *cause*, and *matter*. The transition from myths to science required a new rational and sequential approach to understanding nature that discarded mythical explanations for natural phenomena.[4] In the arts, including dance, however, the gods' alleged supernatural intervention in art-making and their recurring representation in artwork continued to prevail throughout the Ancient Age.

?

Does abstract thinking help you to identify the "underlying pattern" and its attributed meaning in a given dance sequence? How?

DANCING GODS AND MUSES

People of the Ancient Age believed that dance was a gift from the gods to the earthly population as a salve for life's struggles and sorrow. While Stone Age dance activities to worship, honor, and celebrate did remain in place, the purpose of ancient dance expanded: dance now served to enlighten, entertain, and even seduce. Prehistoric people engaged deeply in sacred dance rituals centered on nature, animals, and mystic forces, as did ancient people. Ancient people, however, also created dance for dance's sake, while taking guidance from the ancient gods, who were personified as humans.

Human-looking gods of all sorts were present across the ancient world to serve distinct purposes. In Egypt, Amun-Ra was the god of the sun and creation. The Hindu god Vishnu was a protector, while in Greece, Aphrodite was the goddess of love, beauty, and desire. The diagram that follows provides a partial hierarchical list of the ancient gods in three ancient world locations. The existence of ancient *dance gods and muses* assigned explicitly for dance was an endorsement for the art of dance across cultures as a god-like pursuit that provided humans with a path to reach the wisdom and power of the gods.

EGYPT	INDIA	GREECE
Amun-Ra God of Sun and Creation	**Brahma** God of Nature and Universe	**Zeus** God of Sky, Justice, and Fate
Isis Goddess of Life and Motherhood	**Vishnu** God of Protection and Maintenance	**Poseidon** God of Sea and Earthquakes
Hathor Goddess of Dance and Music	**Indra** God of Rain and Thunder	**Aphrodite** Goddess of Love and Beauty
Osiris God of Death and Underworld	**Ganesha** God of Venture and Trade	**Apollo** God of the Arts and Truth
Seth God of Storms and Desert	**Shiva** God of Dance, Destruction, and Creation	**Calliope** Muse of Epic Poetry
Geb God of Earth and Farming	**Varuna** God of Water and Ocean	**Melpomene** Muse of Tragedy
Nut Goddess of Sky and Air	**Hanuman** God of Energy and Power	**Terpsichore** Muse of Dance and Music
Thoth God of Knowledge and Wisdom	**Parvati** Goddess of Female Creative Energy	**Clio** Muse of History
Sekhmet Goddess of War and Destruction	**Saraswati** Goddess of Wisdom and Knowledge	**Urania** Muse of Astronomy

Figure 2

Ancient *religious polytheism,* with its long roster of *anthropomorphic gods,* alongside societal developments and democratic experiments as political reality, provided the circumstances to reframe *dance as an autonomous fine art form,* independent from the other arts. In early ritual dance, a choreographer was likely tasked with multiple creative functions: to craft the dance, the accompanying song, and the accessories and costuming. In ancient dance, a choreographer likely collaborated with other artists specializing in music, drama, and visual art. The emergence of dance gods also helped transform dance from a functional, decorative, and applied art into a fine art form.

Figure 3 Left: *Goddess Hathor*. XVIII Dynasty, 1405–1367. BC, Karnak, Cachette. Diorite. Stone statue, courtesy of Luxor Museum of Ancient Egyptian Art; center: *Shiva as the Lord of Dance*, Nadu, Tamil. India, c. 950–1000, bronze statue courtesy of Los Angeles County Museum of Art; right: *Terpsichore Lyran*, Canova, Antonio. 1816, marble statue, courtesy of The Cleveland Museum of Art

➢ **Egyptian dance goddess Hathor**, also known as "the mistress of life," was seen as the embodiment of joy, love, romance, perfume, dance, music, and alcohol. Hathor was the incarnation of dance and sexuality and was given the epithet "Hand of God," referring to the act of masturbation. A myth tells the story of the god Amun-Ra, who had become so depressed that he refused to talk to anyone. Hathor, who never suffered from a bad mood, danced in front of him, delicately revealing her private parts, which caused Amun-Ra to laugh out loud and return to good spirits.[5]

➢ **Hindu lord of dance Shiva** was often depicted as a dancing figure within a circle of fire. Shiva used his divine powers to destroy in order to create, to tear down in order to rebuild. Therefore, his cosmic dance was either violent and harsh to eliminate old and weary lifestyles, or pleasant and gentle, aiming to depict a new and better world.[6]

➢ **Greek dance muse Terpsichore** was one of the nine muses in charge of arts, sciences, and literature. Terpsichore's name means "delighting in dance," from the Greek words *terpsis* "to delight" and *khoros* "dance."[7] Often depicted with a lyre, she was the muse of choral song and lyrical poetry, but most of all, dancing.[8]

THE TRANSFORMATION OF DANCE INTO AN AUTONOMOUS FINE ART FORM

Ancient religion, with its polytheistic and anthropomorphic aspects, inspired ancient people to strive to be god-like. But how could they attain the gods' beauty, wisdom, and power?

Ancient people soon realized that it's hard to be human because the world does not organize itself to accommodate humans. In general, life is unpredictable and tough. Therefore, structure, norms, and tools were needed and invented to handle life's events and challenges. If such guidelines and tools were created and put in place, humans could better manage themselves, gain a sense of control over the surrounding world, and broaden their perspectives and creativity. Such developments marked a pivotal point in dance: the fundamental purpose of prehistoric ritual dance had been to predominantly capture spiritual experiences and serve communal needs. Ancient dance evolved and became a *fine art form* serving predominantly as an aesthetic experience. Dance-makers engaged in abstract thinking in an attempt to *capture, form*, and *formulate* phenomena:

- **CAPTURING:** *Mimesis*—the means of artful representation in a unique manner. In his book *Poetics,* the ancient Greek philosopher Aristotle introduces mimesis as "art as imitation of the ideal." Translated from Greek, *mimesis* can be interpreted as "imitation," but it does not simply mean "imitation" in a literal and narrative sense. *Mimesis* captures and "represents many things as physical philosophy in measured forms," such as objects, subjects, events, and characters. As Aristotle wrote, the artist can capture and "represent them in a unique manner, not as the things that have happened, but as the things that might occur as probable or necessary."[9]

- **FORMING:** The concept of abstracting within the creative act—matter forming the mind and the mind forming matter. The assumption that creating is forming something out of nothing poses the question: Does a dance idea that is formed conceptually in the mind need to *materialize* in order to exist? In various works, Aristotle discusses that there is no *form* without *content* (or matter) and no matter without form. Aristotle determined that material things constitute the unity of *forming matter* or formed matter. He also wrote about *unformed matter* or nonmaterial form that exists independently and originates in the "form of forms." The idea of God, for example, is a cognitively formed concept without a direct material equivalent.[10] Therefore, the conclusion is that one can conceptualize, create, and choreograph an idea *prior* to its materialization as a physical dance.

- **FORMULATING:** The construct of artistic frameworks—defining creative principles, aesthetic norms, and imperatives. Beauty exists as an environmental phenomenon in the natural world. Ancient thinkers such as Pythagoras, Plato, and Aristotle concluded that beauty as a concept could also be in the possession of humans, who can create in a spontaneous and organized fashion. Humans are capable of summarizing, systematizing, and synthesizing phenomena to create the idea of beauty. Consequently, any experiences may be formulated and expressed through various aesthetic forms and means—art and artistry!

Frameworks for producing and consuming art gradually developed. They included the forming of criteria and aesthetic norms, which ruled the inclusion of compelling content and themes, such as joy and wisdom, beauty and harmony, love and unity, morals and justice. The framing of artistic craft and creative practices introduced guiding art-form principles such as coherence, contrast, symmetry, balance, proportionality, and compositional tools. New types of dance vocabulary emerged in ancient dance, which were organized in *movement systems* with corresponding dance terminology. Dance pedagogy emerged as a framework for cultivating creative and performance skills and transferring existing and new knowledge.

Prehistoric dance ritual was a group activity of spiritual, ceremonial, and festive actions—a functional and applied arts engagement. As people evolved, ancient dance engaged in art making by tapping into the individual's artistry, and by establishing criteria, norms, and principles of creating fine art—a comparison of these features is in the diagram that follows:

Characteristics:	Early Dance as Ritual	Ancient Dance as Art
Creative Intentions	Dance serves communal and spiritual purposes.	Dance serves aesthetic and entertainment purposes.
Places of Dance Performance	The cave, the village square, the totem, and the sacred grounds.	Temples, theater stages, inside wealthy homes, city and festival grounds.
Dance Music and Sound	Drums, wooden flutes, chanting, singing, and vocalizing.	Harps, lyres, flutes, horns, drums, cymbals, vocal and choral music, sung poems.
Creative Process	Dance creation is a collaborative communal process.	Dance creation is an individual artistic process that has collaborative features.
Dance Participants and Performers	The audience, dancers, musicians, and choreographers operate on all tasks at the same time. Dance performance training is not required.	The audience, dancers, musicians, and choreographers operate separately. Dance education is cultivated and required, while the professionalization of dance is ranked.
Choreographic Expression	Choreography emerges from impersonating the movements of cult animals, forces of nature, communal events, labor, and combat activities.	Choreography emerges from "artistic imitation"—*mimesis*. There is a high degree of abstraction and relationship to the qualities of the gods and the complexity of humans.
Choreographic Purpose	Choreography aims to celebrate, train, and empower. Designated communal and collective experiences are transformed into visceral movement.	Choreography aims to capture ideas of joy, beauty, and morality. Concepts are cultivated as *physical philosophy* and represented through movement and refined performance.

Figure 4

CHOREOGRAPHING IN ANCIENT EGYPT

In chronicles dating back to the Old Kingdom of Egypt, circa 2100 BC, dance and choreography were documented as ancient arts occupations in the oldest civilization on the banks of the Nile River.[11] Similar to early ritual dance, dance and choreography in the Ancient Age emerged as creative practices having three main purposes:

- *Dance as a religious experience,* ceremonial worship, and a gateway to the supernatural powers of the gods;
- *Dance as an aesthetic experience,* dramatic and theatrical reenactments, and a reflection of the gods' perfection and definition of beauty;
- *Dance as a social activity,* entertainment, and reflection of human interactions that depicted joy and pleasure, sensuality, and seduction.

Religious dance in Egypt was performed primarily by men. When dancing as part of religious ceremonies, male dancers often wore crowns of reeds. Funeral dances involved leaping or skipping, accompanied by a sung or spoken prayer to the sounds of percussion. Musical instruments for the dance were double flutes and eight- and twelve-string harps in various shapes and sizes.[12] *Secular dance at public and private celebrations* involved dancers of both sexes performing complex choreography that included mimetic and acrobatic sequences in solo or unison group formation.[13]

Harem dancers, on the other hand, were selected from the women servants living in the harem to entertain at social occasions and private parties in the houses of noblemen.[14] The Harem was established by the Egyptians as an institution. Translated from Arabic, harem means "forbidden place." This "women's quarter" in the palace of the dignitaries served multiple purposes: catering to royal women and their children, hosting the tiers of multiple wives, and institutionalizing the employment of female servants, entertainers, and dancers. Wall paintings in Egyptian pyramids depicted harem dancers in elegant poses, sensual postures, and virtuosic body convulsions with strong erotic undertones—a photograph of a contemporary reenactment of a belly dance, left. The harem dancers attracted special attention and held certain powers over their patrons. Harem women were often involved in political intrigues and conspiracies, influencing the outcome of strategic governance decisions.[15]

Figure 5 Contemporary interpretation of belly dancing. Credit: D-Keine, Courtesy of iStock/Getty Images.

CHOREOGRAPHING IN ANCIENT INDIA

Based on archaeological evidence, ancient dance in India began to form sometime around 2500 BC.[15] According to legends, in about 200 BC, the God Brahma inspired a theatrologist and musicologist named Bharata Muni, and possibly other participating scholars, to write a 36-chapter Sanskrit treatise on the performing arts entitled *Natya Shastra*. This principal work of dramatic theory ultimately served as a manual for dance, music, and drama in ancient India.[16]

Like Aristotle's *Poetics*, Bharata Muni's *Natya Shastra* philosophically described artistic practices in the arts, including drama, music and dance, movement gestures, and emotions. In *Natya Shastra*, Bharata refers to *bhavas* (emotional representations)—the imitations of emotions that the actors perform—and rasas (emotional responses)—the emotions elicited in the audience. The eight basic *bhavas* representing emotions are love, humor, energy, anger, fear, grief, disgust, and astonishment. In observing and imagining these emotions, the audience experiences eight principal responses, or rasas: love, pity, anger, disgust, heroism, awe, terror, and joy.[17] In addition, systematized choreographic devices for crafting dance were included: *Stana*, or the body postures and attitude; *Mudra* and *Hastra-prana*, or the system and "language of hand gestures," which gave specific images and meaningful "life" to the mime. Facial expression and the movements of the head and the eyes conveyed different types of emotions—*Rasas*.[18] Dance was performed in temples before and during worship, on festive occasions, and during the seasonal harvest. Dance was also present in the houses of royalty and often was created exclusively for special occasions.

Dance traditions, which were deeply rooted in the ancient Sanskrit text of *Natya Shastra*, developed throughout India's geographical regions and branched into a variety of dance styles. These dances served as the religious performance arts of Hinduism, depicting epic narratives from Hindu mythology. Many of these styles are still in practice today:

- *Bharatanatyam* was a traditional dance form of the Tamil Nadu region in southern India. Originally a temple dance for women, Bharatanatyam often was used to express Hindu religious stories and devotion. The dance movements were characterized by bent legs, while feet kept the rhythm. Hands gestures and mudras were used to tell a story.[19]

- *Kathak* was a regional dance form established in India's northern parts and is recognized as one of the oldest dance traditions in India. Kathak in translation from Hindi means "story" or "storytelling." The pure dance exhibition of this style was characterized by the presence of numerous fast spins and turns, ending in still body positions. In addition, there was intriguing, speedy footwork and stomping of the toes and heels, which was often performed in contrast to the percussive rhythm. Kathak was the ancient predecessor of flamenco dance of southern Spain. The form developed and changed through the centuries, formulating into different schools and sub-styles called *gharanas*.[20]

➢ *Odissi* originated as a dance style in the region of Odisha, formerly Orissa, in eastern India. Besides the specific stampings in the footwork, what distinguished *Odissi* from other dance forms was the significance of stylistic torso placement. A particular dance position called *Tribunga* consists of three bends in the body. The "three-part break" of the dance posture consisted of actual independently tilted movements: at the neck, waist, and knees. Since the torso was oppositely curved at pelvis and head, the body would take on an overall gentle "S" shape. The gods Shiva and Krishna were often portrayed in this sensual *Odissi*-style posture.[21] Traditional dance styles of India were and are *Kuchipudi, Kathakali, and Sattriya, Mohiniyattam, Chhau, Yakshagana, and Bhagavata Mela,* as well as many others.

In addition to depicting regional traditions and rituals, ancient dance in India often illustrated mythological scenes from the gods' lives. Dance and choreography in many instances impersonated, reenacted, and portrayed through movement a particular god or goddess. In Sanskrit, the terms for the heavenly supreme beings translate gender-specificity, Deva for a masculine god and Devi for a goddess.

A contemporary interpretation of Indian traditional dance at left captures a dance posture depicting the powerful Devi Parvati, the goddess of love, beauty, purity, fertility, and devotion. Parvati is also the wife of Shiva, the Lord of Dance and the creator and destroyer of life in the universe. The goddess represented the material universe and she was an embodiment of the Divine Feminine and bestower of human souls. The dancer's facial expressions, synchronized with the defined placement of the hands and position of the legs, combine to create a specific visual iconography—understood by both the performer and the audience. Purposeful symmetry, asymmetry, and balance were pivotal, as well as using movements and postures to capture abstract symbolic values. The upward positioning of the right hand signifies her blessings and protection from evil, whereas the left hand is held down, indicating the granting of benefits.[22]

Figure 6 Photography © Vishal Kanwar, pictured Maya Zhalova-Kanwar in a Devi dance as Goddess Parvati, 2011

Music for dance incorporated various instruments such as the sitar, tabla, pakhavaj, swarmandal, flute, and cymbals. The dancers wore anklets adorned with tinkling bells that made calculated percussive sounds with each movement. Codified techniques were also implemented in which a piece of poetry set to music in a particular metric cycle would merge with the dance movements by synchronizing numerous reference points in the contents of the text, music, and dance.[23] *Dance costuming* varied based on the occasion and region. The most common garment for a female dancer was a sari with bold and vibrant colors, gold borders, intricate embellishments, and multiple drapes. *Accessories* included heavy jewelry: multiple gold necklaces, earrings, and rings, as well as henna tattoos on the hands and feet and flowers adorning the hair.[24]

CHOREOGRAPHING IN ANCIENT GREECE

For the ancient Greeks, dance was one of the most vibrant art forms in religious, cultural, and social life. Choreographers collaborated with artists from other art forms such as drama, music, visuals arts, and rhetoric. Dance was part of physical education and the emotional development of the population and even a subject of philosophical discussion. Dances were integrated into dramatic theatrical productions, celebratory amusement festivals, rituals to obtain good seasonal crops, military triumphs, and also in creating abstract beauty for its own sake. In summary, dance played an essential part in all aspects of Greek life.[25]

◆ ***Sacred ritual*** dance and choreography, for example, portrayed various characters and stories from Greek mythology. *Geranos* was a dance about the legend of the Minotaur, a creature having the head of a bull and the body of a man, who dwelt in the center of a Cretan labyrinth. During *Geranos*, the dancers held each other's hands and moved with synchronized steps in a curved line, following a leader at the beginning of the line. Contrived in a certain rhythm, the dancing line made complex turns and shapes representing the labyrinth's winding twists.[26] Today, a similar dance known as *horo* prevails in the Southeastern Europe.

◆ ***Greek drama*** dance and choreography played an essential role in the genres of tragedy, comedy, and satire. Both Sophocles and Euripides often used dance and pantomime to substitute for verbal interactions and enhance the dramatic plot. In his play *Peace*, Aristophanes wrote a famous line: "*O divine Muse, join me in this festival dance*!" which was followed by a staged dance.[27] With the popularity of tragedy and comedy, choreographers experimented with numerous techniques to organically incorporate the dancers. The chorus's remarkable moving group formations and the occasional virtuoso dance solos with songs turned the dramatic plays into semi-operatic spectacles. In *Poetics*, Aristotle gave directorial suggestions for how ancient Greek drama, theater, and dance should be developed and staged, stating that theatrical performances should be produced with three crucial elements in mind:

➢ Base story—how the plot, simple or complex, develops and unfolds.

➢ Qualitative features—the type of language, movements, etc., used to create the intended environment.

➢ Characters—the main and supporting roles in the dramatic conflict and how all these elements become an integral part of the whole: the unity of action.[28]

According to Aristotle, Ancient Greek drama and dance should draw in the audience and stir their emotions. Aristotle also wrote about using rhythm, language, and harmony as artistic devices, either together or separately. Aristotle wrote: "Rhythm alone, without harmony, is the means in the dancer's imitations; for even he, by the rhythms of his attitudes, may represent men's characters, as well as what they do and suffer." [29]

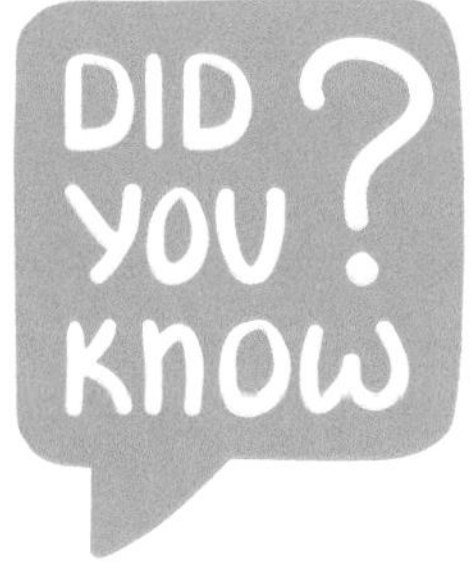

Under the beautiful Mediterranean sky, the ancient Greeks built unique open-air theaters where the public could watch performances of Greek comedy, tragedy, and satire. Europe's first and oldest theater, the Dionysus Eleuthereus, was constructed in the 6th century BC and is located on the south slope of the Acropolis of Athens. Soon after, theaters became a typical feature in all Greek cities. Built initially from wood and later from stone, theaters were constructed on natural hillsides in a large semi-circular shape, which allowed more spectators to have a better view. One of the largest theaters is in Argos and has a seating capacity of 20,000 spectators.[30]

Figure 7 The Odeon of Herodes Atticus is a stone theater located on the southwest slope of the Acropolis of Athens. It was built in 161 AD by the Athenian magnate Herodes Atticus in memory of his wife, Aspasia Annia Regilla. Photograph courtesy of iStock/Getty Images

◆ ***Dionysius festival*** dance and choreography were a participatory dance celebration and mass party for everyone during rural and urban Dionysia, which took place at different times during the year. The festivities lasted for days without interruption. During the day, the performers were involved in song and dance contests called *dithyrambs*—spontaneous poetic and dance expressions, sometimes in the form of dialogue.[31] During the night, male dancers dressed as satyrs and wore horned masks, and semi-naked female dancers ecstatically performed erotically charged dances in celebration of Dionysius—the God of Wine, Theater, and Ecstasy.

Crafting and constructing dance with various creative tools and formal artistic constructs further professionalized dance and the choreographic craft in ancient Greece. There was a method called *cheironomia*, a movement system and set of symbolic arm and hand gestures with predetermined meaning. For instance, the hands stretching heavenward signified worship, and the arms bent over the head expressed grief and suffering. *Cheironomia* was also used by philosophers and politicians in theatrical performances, as well as oratory and rhetoric presentations.[32] *Choreographic devices* and *creative designs* were divided into three constituent elements: *phora*, *schemata*, and *deixis*.

➢ *Phora* was a motion of the body or the mind meant to "carry" a posture as a dancer moved from one place to another. Simple movements such as walking, running, leaping, twisting, or bending could also be performed in a specific manner.

➢ *Schemata* represented "poses in which movement ends" and could be interpreted as taking a form, shape, or figure. Dancers might form geometrical figures, group formations, or brief distinctive floor patterns. They would be visually pleasing during the course of the dance piece, some of them lasting for a few seconds and some longer. The stillness of the dancers was valued as equal to them moving.

➢ *Deixis* meant to "display" and to "portray." Deixis was also the manner of a dancer directly pointing and referring to something nearby—like the sky, earth, or other people. In this context, the dancer might point and act through movements to personify an object such as an animal, a flower, or a flame.[33]

Dance Music was offered by musicians who played instruments such as the flute, lyre, hand drums, and cymbals. The musicians and dancers often performed together or in close proximity of each other. Dancers also frequently carried small musical instruments like cymbals and were part of the main accompaniment. Performers danced not only to musical accompaniment but also to spoken poetry by miming, illustrating, and interpreting a poetic verse through small rhythmic gestures and with full body motion—"danced poetry."[34]

Dance costuming and accessories changed and ranged according to the occasion: from processional robes worn during funerals and grieving *schemata*, to sheer scarves covering completely nude bodies for dances during the Dionysius festivals. Light dressy tunics were used during Greek tragedy and comedy plays and as costumes for dance-for-dance's-sake performances.[35]

Ancient Greek dance inspired and influenced many great choreographers throughout the centuries, most notably, Isadora Duncan during the early 20th century. On the other hand, Duncan's unique artistic interpretations of ancient Greek dancing women inspired ballet choreographer Frederick Ashton to create a masterpiece entitled *Five Brahms Waltzes in the Manner of Isadora Duncan*—see Figure 8.

Figure 8 Photography © David Scheinmann, Five Brahms Waltzes in the Manner of Isadora Duncan, (1975–6), choreography by Sir Frederick Ashton, pictured performer Bregoña Cao, Viviana Durante Company, 2020

THE CRAFT OF THE ANCIENT CHOREOGRAPHER

The ancient choreographer's craft is depicted in the diagram below, which draws an analogy to a Greek temple, capturing the artistic drive and determination to reach the ancient gods' beauty, power, and perfection. Dance creation was a god-like activity, and the choreographer had to be skilled and engaged to develop abilities in four distinct but equally important *pillars*: the abstracting of ideas through the process of summarizing, synthesizing, and systematizing; the defining of aesthetic principles of artistry and craftsmanship; the establishment of tools for the advancement of performance techniques; and the cultivation of dance education as a means of transferring existing and new knowledge.

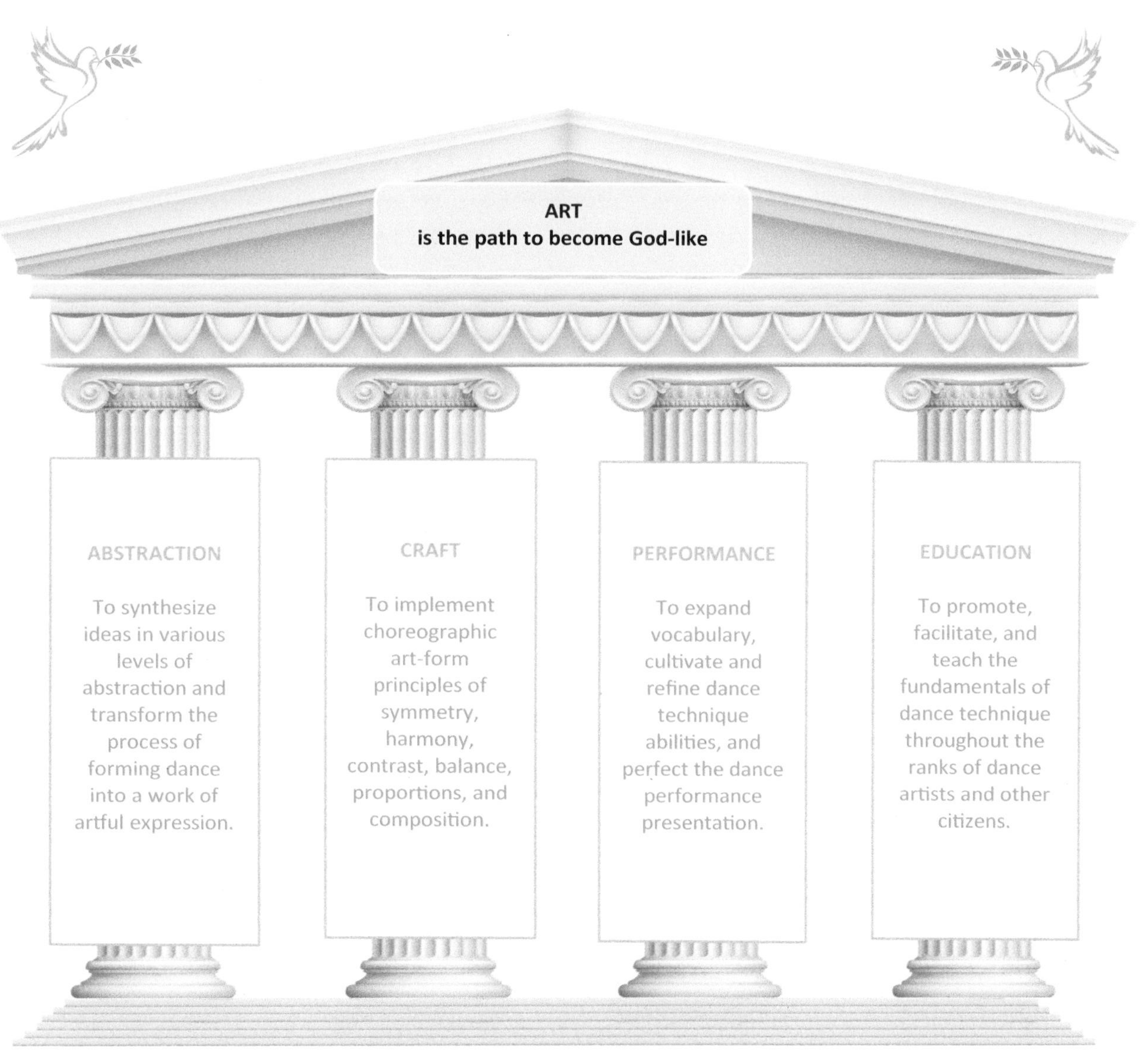

Figure 9

EXCERPTS FROM MY DANCE JOURNAL —ATHENS, YEAR 399 BC*

*Although the author of this historical fiction is fictitious, the events and the individuals described are historically accurate.

February 7: Today, I was very late for my dance appointment with Socrates because my water clock broke. We were scheduled to practice cheironomia—Socrates needs to improve his hand positions, gestures, and body posture during his public rhetoric. In just a few days, Socrates will appear at his court trial to address a jury of 500 Athenians. It will be the speech of his lifetime—to save his life...

***Personal Note:** By the way, what in the name of Aphrodite are those people of the jury thinking?!...I still do not understand why, in a society enjoying more freedom and democracy than in any other place on Earth, a seventy-year-old philosopher would be sentenced to death because of his teachings?! Is he really a threat to our democracy? We live in crazy times...I hate politics!*

February 9: My second dance appointment with Socrates went better. He improved! Meanwhile, he invited me to join him and his family for supper and wine after the rehearsal. I met his three sons. At the dinner table, I mentioned that I know a geranos choreography that could fit the entire family. I said I would love to teach it to them. Socrates' wife, Xanthippe, said that now—during the trial—is not a good time for a geranos dance lesson. She is always a bit mean...

***Personal Note:** On my way out, I bumped into Plato, one of Socrates' students, who was coming to see him. Plato complimented my dances and also expressed his love of dance. He said he has been working on a couple of philosophical works entitled "Laws" and "Republic." He wrote that a man who cannot dance is uneducated and unrefined, while an accomplished dancer is the epitome of a cultivated person. "That is right!" I whispered, full of joy...*

February 10: This afternoon, I met with Aristophanes, a playwright who staged his work "Clouds" more than 20 years ago. In the play, he portrays Socrates as a harmless character who is definitely not a real threat to Athenian democracy. Aristophanes said he would like to restage the comedy and asked me if I wished to choreograph the chorus. "Yeees!" I answered, head over heels...

***Personal Note:** When working on this play, my focus shall be to treat the chorus not as a chaotic mass of individual performers but as a single, unified body. I will use everything I know: phora, schemata, and deixis. And even if the chorus has to wear the ugly 20-year-old tunics and the heavy head masks, I will choreograph beautifully exaggerated movement patterns so that their dancing will look grand in that vast theater...*

February 12: City Dionysia is coming soon. I have to plan and get ready. The dances for those festivals drive me insane! Last year we had too much wine, and I don't even remember what we did in rehearsal...Should I avoid the free wine this time around? Hmmm—tough choice...

***Personal Note:** Honestly, choreographing dithyrambs is not my forte. Not a big fan of dance competitions! Working for the Drama at the theater and staging dances for the chorus is much more fun and rewarding. The stories are so emotional and touching...So sad and beautiful...I often cry backstage. By the way, I just heard that Socrates has been sentenced to death and scheduled for execution on February 15. I can't believe it!...Now I am beginning to cry again...*

TRANSCENDING THE AGES
– CHOREOGRAPHING FINE ART IN A BROAD CONTEXT –

The ideals, creativity, and arts of antiquity were profound, transformative, and transcendent. Their influence continues to *travel forward in time*, leaving its mark throughout the ages. Ancient dance forms, epic stories, and mythological characters were, are, and will remain an inspiration to many generations of choreographers.

In more recent times, Ancient Egyptian themes appeared in the choreography of groundbreaking dance works such as Marius Petipa's *The Pharaoh's Daughter*, Mikhail Fokine's *Cléopâtre*, and Maurice Béjart's *Pyramide*. Ballet interpretations of dance in ancient India and Persia were imaginatively created in Jules Perrot's *Lalla Rookh ou la Rose de Lahore*, Lucien Petipa's *Shakuntala*, Marius Petipa's *Talisman*, and the iconic *La Bayadère*, as well as Mikhail Fokine's *Scheherazade*. Hindu mythology and dance were fascinatingly captured in the work of the early modern dance choreographer Ruth St. Denis' *Radha*. The powerful influence of ancient Greek mythology, culture, and dance can be seen in Isadora Duncan's *Dance of the Furies*, Vaslav Nijinsky's *L'Après-midi d'un Faune*, Martha Graham's Greek cycle—*Bacchanale, Errand into the Maze, Night Journey, Clytemnestra*, and *Phaedra*, among others, and George Balanchine's Greek trilogy—*Apollo, Orpheus*, and *Agon*.

Ancient dance as fine art and its principles, constituted by the ancients, are transcendent—they surpass initial historical circumstances, context, and purpose. Ironically, humans created the ancient gods, who, in turn, helped free human thinking from the material world's constraints, broaden people's perceptions, and embolden them to explore courageously beyond the obvious.

Although ancient artists and thinkers provided a blueprint for what constitutes fine art as such, these initial parameters have been changing in each stage of human evolution. While dance as ritual is an embodiment of celebration, sacrament, and worship with spiritual and aesthetic values driven by functional purpose, dance as fine art is an artistic creation driven predominantly by aesthetic purposes and values. But what transforms functional and applied arts into a fine art with purely aesthetic purposes and values? At any given time, creative expressions and artistic experimentations may or may not result in an artwork.

The parameters of what *constitutes a work of fine art* in dance and movement are always fluid, and yet there are three substantive constants:

- To be human-made, although art could be inspired by and related to nature.
- To contain purely aesthetic purposes and an artistic engagement that captures and communicates essential concepts in creative, imaginative, or interpretive ways.
- To address, summarize, and synthesize human experiences, ideas, ideals, emotions, sensations, impressions, imagery, and truths which are embodied and represented through the individual artist's unique perspective.

CHOREOGRAPHING FINE ART AS AN OPERATING CONCEPT BEYOND HISTORICAL FRAMEWORK

When employing the ancient thinkers' blueprint of art in a broad context, choreography as fine art emerges as the harmonized unity of *content*, *form*, and *process*, which interact dynamically and are inseparable. Various aspects of these three elements could interact proportionally or asymmetrically.

◆ *Content* relates to the choreographer's intentions and goals, the subject matter choice, the conceptual parameters, the artistic direction, and the purpose of the work. *Content* could be *broad* or *condensed*, *free* or *framed*, *narrative* or *abstract*, or in combinations and nuances somewhere in between.

◆ *Form* relates to the choreographer's movement material, kinesthetic language, idea embodiment, and use of other aesthetic means and art forms through which the work emerges. Form could also be *narrative* or *abstract*, *natural*, or *artificial* (a word with art in it), organic or impromptu, synthesized, or systematized.

◆ *Process* relates to the choreographer's creative activities of building the work, the direction, and the methods of experimenting and generating movement material, constructing the dance, and working with dancers and collaborators. The process could shift dynamically from being *intuitive* to *rational*, *neutral* to *pro-active*, as the work grows and develops as an *ordinary* or *extraordinary* performance activity—see Figure 10.

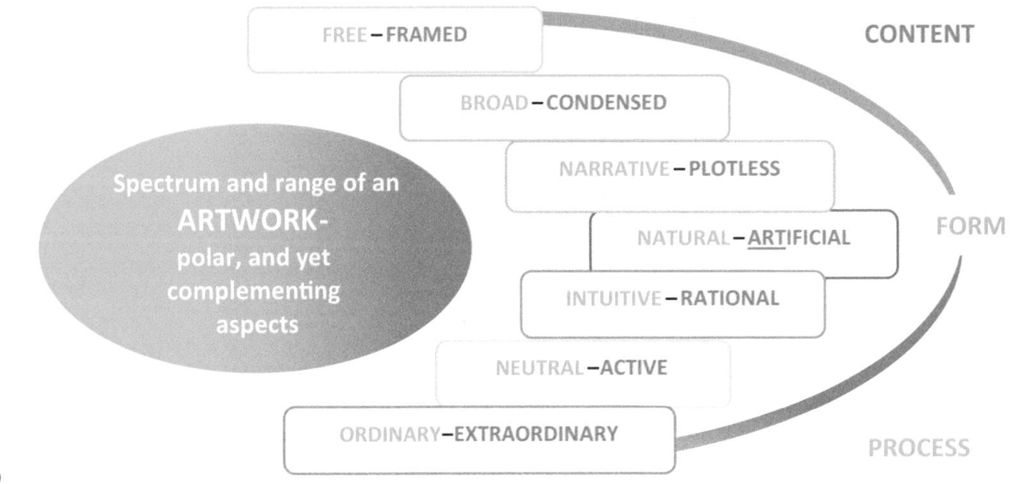

Figure 10

HELPFUL TIPS & SUGGESTIONS

~ Consider abstraction not as a style but as an approach
~ Employ abstraction by letting the mind be in a state of play with itself
~ Engage abstract thinking in dance as thought becoming visible—physical thinking
~ Remember that abstraction is reimagining reality, not replicating reality
~ Approach any imposed norms of art not instructionally but artistically
~ Think of conceiving art as creativity inviting and befriending new ideas
~ Let art speak to you before you speak

assignments & exercises

RESEARCH ASSIGNMENT: Explore various movement systems: Use online, library, and video resources to research an ancient dance form. Choose a region with historical reference to dance between approximately the 5th century BC and 5th century AD. Narrow your research to one aspect of one of the three ancient cultures—Egypt, Greece, and India. For example, you could select *mudras* from classical Indian dance, poses of figures from photos of an ancient Greek vase, or a wall painting from an Egyptian pyramid. For example, if you select India, learn what specific types of movement genres or style divisions existed in the numerous regions of that same culture. Create a worksheet or use notecards to create a list of particular moment postures. Based on your research, create a short movement phrase as a fictitious reenactment of an ancient dance or an impersonation of an ancient god. Demonstrate the phrase to peers and discuss the challenges of your process.

★ **CREATIVE EXERCISE:** Create and formulate your own "homemade" movement system:

➥ Select a scene from an ancient Greek play, a contemporary theater play, or a recent movie you have seen. Extract gestures and movements that represent movement expressions of joy and sadness and basic actions such as working or thinking. Sort the movements and gestures into charts or make handy notecards. Feel free to incorporate western mime or another existing movement system, such as American Sign Language. Alternatively, create your movement system or combine any of these strategies.

➥ Based on the scene you have selected, create a short dance narrative phrase using your movement system. Your initial effort might look like the game "Charades." Add a short music selection that fits your new movement composition.

➥ Demonstrate your work to peers and ask if your presentation was understandable. What was communicated via the movement system? What did and did not work? Use your own movement system again, this time with a different scene, play, or movie.

COMPARATIVE ASSIGNMENT: Analyze the challenges you encountered during your research and creative process. What was distinctly different in the creative modes: dance as ritual—a set of movement actions with attributed meaning to accomplish a goal—versus dance as art—dancing within a codified movement system?

BIBLIOGRAPHY AND REFERENCES

[1] Kassing, Gayle. "Ancient Greece," in *History of Dance*, 2nd edition, Kindle Edition, Web version, 2017.

[2] Kassing 2017. "Ancient Greece," Kindle Edition.

[3] Gilead, Michael, et al. "From Mind to Matter: Neural Correlates of Abstract and Concrete Mindsets," Social *Cognitive and Affective Neuroscience*, vol. 9, no. 5, 2014, pp. 638–645.

[4] Katz, Arnold M. and Phyllis, B. "Emergence of Scientific Explanations of Nature in Ancient Greece: The Only Scientific Discovery?," *American Heart Association Journal Circulation*, vol. 92, no. 3, pp. 637–645, Originally published 1 Aug 1995, accessed March 2021.

[5] Hill, Jenny Hathor. *Ancient Egypt Online*. Published on 2008, online article: https://ancientegyptonline.co.uk/hathor/, accessed February 2021.

[6] Cartwright, Mark. "Shiva Nataraja—Lord of the Dance," *Ancient History Encyclopedia*. 09.08.2015, accessed Web. February 19, 2021.

[7] Theoi Project. *Greek Mythology, Muses*, www.theoi.com/Ouranios/, accessed April 29, 2014.

[8] Britannica, The Editors of Encyclopedia. "Terpsichore," in *Encyclopedia Britannica*, 09.16.2019, www.britannica.com/topic/Terpsichore. Accessed February 24, 2021.

[9] Aristotle. "Poetics," in *The Basic Works of Aristotle*, Random House Inc., Oxford University Press, 1941, pp. 1455–1458.

[10] Aristotle. "De Anima, Physics, *and* Metaphysics," various publishers, and article summary: Ainsworth, Thomas. Form vs. Matter, article, *Stanford Encyclopedia of Philosophy*, published February 2016; substantive revision March 2020, online access August 2019.

[11] Spencer, Patricia. "Dance in Ancient Egypt." *Near Eastern Archaeology*, vol. 66, no. 3, 2003, pp. 111–121. JSTOR, www.jstor.org/stable/3210914, accessed 23 February 2021.

[12] Mark, Joshua J. "Music and Dancing Ancient Egypt," *Ancient History Encyclopedia*. Published on 2017, online article: www.ancient.eu/article/1075/music-dance-in-ancient-egypt/, accessed February 2021.

[13] Hill, Jenny. "Hathor," *Ancient Egypt Online*. Published on 2008, online article: https://ancientegyptonline.co.uk/hathor/, accessed February 2021.

[14] Kassing, Gayle. *History of Dance: An Interactive Arts Approach*, 1st edition, Human Kinetics, 2007, pp. 41–48.

[15] Singh, Upinder. *A History of Ancient and Early Medieval India: From the Stone Age to the 12th Century*. Pearson Education, 2008, pp. 153–163.

[16] Beck, Guy L. *Sonic Liturgy: Ritual and Music in Hindu Tradition*. University of South Carolina Press, 2012, pp. 138–139.

[17] New World Encyclopedia. The Editors of Encyclopedia. "Natya Shastra," *New World Encyclopedia*, online article, accessed February 2021.

[18] Devi, Ragini. *Dance Dialects of India*, Motilal Banarsidass Publishers, 1990, p. 43.

[19] Devi 1990. *Dance Dialects of India*, pp. 50–59.

[20] Devi 1990. *Dance Dialects of India*, pp. 166–174.

[21] Devi 1990. *Dance Dialects of India*, pp. 138–157.

[22] Zhalova-Kanwar, Maya. *Dancing India: A Journey Eastward*, Self-published, 2012.

[23] Vatsyayan, Kapila. "Notes on the Relationship of Music and Dance in India," *Ethnomusicology*, vol. 7, no. 1, 1963, pp. 33–38. JSTOR, www.jstor.org/stable/924145, accessed March 11, 2021.

[24] Zhalova-Kanwar 2012. *Dancing India*.

[25] Lawler, Lillian B. "The Dance in Ancient Greece," *The Classical Journal*, vol. 42, no. 6, March 1947, online article, 2014, pp. 343–349, accessed 2021.

[26] Ragazzi, Gaudenzio. "The Crane, Ariadne's *Thread*, Labyrinth and Dance," *Le Origini della Danza*, online publications, 2019, accessed 2021.

[27] Lawler 2021. "The Dance in Ancient Greece," pp. 343–349.

[28] Aristotle. "Poetics." in *The Basic Works of Aristotle*, Random House Inc., Oxford University Press, 1941, pp. 1460–1475.

[29] Aristotle 1941. "Poetics," pp. 1455.

[30] Cartwright, Mark. "Greek Theatre Architecture," *Ancient History Encyclopedia*, 0422.2016, accessed Web. February 19, 2021.

[31] Kassing 2017. "Ancient Greece," Kindle Edition.

[32] Kassing 2017. "Ancient Greece," Kindle Edition.

[33] Kassing 2017. "Ancient Greece," Kindle Edition.

[34] Lawler 2021. "The Dance in Ancient Greece," pp. 343–349.

[35] Lawler 2021. "The Dance in Ancient Greece," pp. 334–44.

VISUAL REFERENCES

Figure 1: Photography © Lois Greenfield, pictured Leslie Simpson, courtesy of KDNY Dance Company, 2005

Figure 2: Diagram © Vladimir Angelov

Figure 3: Image left: *Goddess Hathor*. XVIII Dynasty, 1405–1367. BC, Karnak, Cachette. Diorite. Stone statue, courtesy of Luxor Museum of Ancient Egyptian Art; Image center: *Shiva as the Lord of Dance*, Nadu, Tamil. India, c. 950–1000, bronze statue courtesy of Los Angeles County Museum of Art; Image right: *Terpsichore Lyran*, Canova, Antonio. 1816, marble statue, courtesy of The Cleveland Museum of Art

Figure 4: Diagram © Vladimir Angelov

Figure 5: *Young girl dancing belly dance*, credit: D-Keine, Courtesy of iStock/Getty Images

Figure 6: Photography © Vishal Kanwar, pictured Maya Zhalova-Kanwar in a Devi dance as Goddess Parvati, 2011

Figure 7: The Odeon of Herodes Atticus is a stone theater structure located on the southwest slope of the Acropolis of Athens. It was built in 161 AD by the Athenian magnate Herodes Atticus in memory of his wife, Aspasia Annia Regilla. credit: Lefteris, Courtesy of iStock/Getty Images

Figure 8: Photography © David Scheinmann, *Five Brahms Waltzes in the Manner of Isadora Duncan*, (1975–6), choreography by Sir Frederick Ashton, pictured performer Bregoña Cao, Viviana Durante Company, 2020

Figures 9 and 10: diagram © Vladimir Angelov

CHAPTER 3

MEDIEVAL AGE:
LEAPING INTO GROUP IDENTITY – CHOREOGRAPHING SYMBOL –

Our time travel through choreographic creativity now takes us to old Europe and the Americas between approximately 500 AD and 1500 AD to look at societal, economic, cultural, and dance development. One of the most important characteristics of this time period was the reconfiguration of empires and the formation of new nation-states. Although some of these geo-political changes were described as "invasions," they were not always instigated by military activity. Large groups of people migrated from one place to another. The medieval *nation-forming processes* emerged when native tribes, kingdoms, and monarchies were declaring, forcefully or peacefully, control and ownership over a section of land. Governing bodies were constituted to unify people based on their origins, cultural similarities, or political interests, and to represent their distinctive group identity.[1]

For instance, in the 6th century, the Lombards settled in Northern Italy, replacing the Ostrogothic Kingdom with a grouping of duchies that selected a king as their ruler. Spain, on the other hand, had a large population of new settlers, some having migrated from as far away as India. Slavonic people settled in Central and Eastern Europe and into the Balkan Peninsula. Greeks occupied the same territories but had to share their northern borders with the new Slav population. Further north, the newly established kingdoms of Poland, Hungary, and Bohemia grew powerful.[2] The Iberian Peninsula gained more land from the Ottoman Empire. The Western Roman Empire was gradually dispersed by branching into different countries with languages based on Latin. The development of new languages like French, Portuguese, and Romanian took several centuries and went through a number of stages.[3] The new settlements were accompanied by changes in culture and language as part of building native pride and national identity.

Dance in the newly forming medieval nations reflected the legends, tales, imagery, and heroes specific to each region. For instance, the illustration at left depicts a scene from *The Pied Piper of Hamelin*. The piper plays his pipe on a beautiful spring day as children dance in the fields near the town of Hamelin in Lower Saxony, Germany. The legend tells of a piper dressed in colorful clothing who removed a plague of rats from the town in 1284, luring them away by playing his pipe. However, when the townsfolk refused to pay him, he enticed away most of their children in the same manner. The earliest mention of the story seemed to occur on a stained-glass window at the Church of Hamelin.[4] The story later reappeared in the writings of Johann Wolfgang von Goethe, the Brothers Grimm, and Robert Browning, among other authors.

Figure 1 Illustration © Kate Greenaway, *The Pied Piper of Hamelin* by Robert Browning, George Routledge & Sons, 1888

The economy and socio-political life in medieval society were structured in two ways: *manorialism*—peasants were organized into villages, and they owed rent and labor services to the nobles, and *feudalism*—the political structure whereby *knights* and lower-status nobles owed military service to their overlords in return for the right to rent from landlords and manors.[5] The economic interest in land expansion and the hunger to search for new territories overseas in the late medieval period led to Christopher Columbus's first voyage to the Americas in 1492.

Intellectual life throughout Europe in the Medieval Age was marked by philosophy and theology fusing into *scholasticism*. Monks were the authors of new works covering history, theology, rhetoric, logic, and other subjects. In addition to the building of castles, monasteries, and Romanesque and Gothic cathedrals, universities were founded. In these early stages of institutionalized education, the focus remained on the training of future clergy. Gradually, medieval scholars recognized that reason operates independently of faith, as they carefully began allowing the separation of science from theology and philosophy.[6]

In religion, the rise of Christian *monotheism* replaced and eliminated the Ancient Age's *polytheism*. The new belief system asserted that Jesus was the son of God, divine, and yet human, and that he would be the single savior of humanity. Jesus's ministry, sacrificial death, and subsequent resurrection are described in the *Gospels* and became the building blocks of the new faith. The belief in one god and the rise of Christianity served as a unifying spiritual catalyst for many new nations in Europe. Yet there were numerous differences between Eastern and Western Europe—theological, political, cultural, linguistic, and the specifics of religious practices. The Eastern Byzantine Church ultimately became the Orthodox Church and the Western Church to the Roman Catholic Church.[7]

In the Middle Ages, religious discipline glorified spiritual struggle, moral sacrifice, and physical suffering. Compared to their ancient predecessors, medieval saints were depicted in a contrasting physical appearance, often with facial expressions suggesting anguish or struggle—image left. The joy of dancing or anything involving the human body became unpopular and was often interpreted as immoral.

Dance as a spiritual expression was strictly canonized, and dancing was often censured. Dance as spontaneous and a less-redacted expression flourished only in the medieval countryside and folklore.[8]

Figure 2 *Christ Pantocrator*, by anonymous, mosaic, cupola of choir, Hosios Loukas Monastery, Greece, early 11th century AD

Medieval arts in Europe went through various periods, from the days of early Christianity through the Romanesque and Gothic periods. Generally, the ways to portray the world were not *realistic* but, rather, decorative by methods of interlacing *decorative* and *symbolic* imagery. Medieval visual artists gave birth to *symbolism*.[9] The images portrayed represented something other than themselves, and they conveyed ideas and beliefs to observers who knew how to interpret them. Choral church music frequently included *polyphony*, a musical texture where independent melodies are played simultaneously. The countryside dance festivities were accompanied by songs and instrumentalists playing bagpipes, harps, guitars, lutes, flutes, percussions, and bells.[10]

THE RISE OF SYMBOLIC THINKING

The mindset of medieval people in Europe distinctly diverged from their ancient predecessors. Generally, Christians in the Medieval Age believed that greatness and joy did not happen during earthly life, but after death for those chosen to go to Heaven. Life on Earth was merely a testing ground to evaluate whether a person was "morally" qualified for a happy afterlife. This ideology was exploited by church and state. The fear of punishment and being sent to eternal suffering in Hell was deeply rooted in the psyche of medieval people. Average daily activities, religious practices, and artistic initiatives were constantly subject to judgement and censorship.

The medieval frame of mind was persistently stretched in a torturing duality between body and spirit, good and evil, heaven and hell, faith and punishment. Speaking the truth could carry severe consequences if that truth conflicted with the church's interests. The restrictions on free expression and the fear of punishment led medieval choreographers to reframe their *creative mindset*, resulting in the domination of *symbolic thinking*.

Symbolic thinking and abstract thinking have common features: they both summarize and reconfigure the characteristics of a phenomenon—see Chapter 2. There are also differences: Abstract thinking develops, explores, and *synthesizes ideas* that may or may not have physical equivalents by engaging the receiver's mind to discover beyond reality. *Symbolic thinking*, on the other hand, codifies ideas of existing phenomena by engaging the receiver's mind to guess, decode, recognize, or interpret a phenomenon, by often using analogies and metaphors. While most symbolic forms are abstract, not all abstraction is symbolic. Symbolic thinking enabled medieval artists to create aesthetic content having a satisfying façade that complied with church doctrine, and yet it also had mysterious hidden messaging.

COURT AND SOCIAL DANCES IN MEDIEVAL EUROPE — A WHEEL OR A WALL —

Medieval court and social dances in Europe were performed indoors and outdoors, as couple and group dances. The dances were characterized by two main choreographic formations and symbolic patterns: circle dances, such as *carole* and *bransle*, which resembled images of a wheel, and line dances, such as *thread the needle* and *estampie*, which resembled images of a wall or walls.

➢ *Carole dance* (from Old French *caroler* which means "to dance in a ring") was a group circle dance in which many couples held hands. Since both men and women participated in the dance, and there was some physical contact and touching in public, moralists at that time regarded it as evil. The legend of the *carole* dance was a tale of a supposed miracle in Saxony in early 11th century AD. The story told of a group of men and women who, despite the protests of the priest, persisted in dancing around a churchyard during mass on Christmas Eve. As a result, they were condemned to dance continuously day and night for a whole year.[11]

➢ *Maypole dance*, another type of circle dance, took place in front of churches during feasts and celebrations. A close ring of men and women danced around a central pole, the maypole, which was festooned in streamers held by the dancers.[12] The maypole with its stripes resembled the Devil caught up in chains and imprisoned by the dancing ring.

➢ *Thread the needle dance* was a line dance where all participants stood with hands joined. The leader and second in line formed a one-handed arch through which the rest of the line passed. When all dancers were through the arch, a new arch was formed at the beginning of the line by the next two dancers.[13] The movement figure aimed to convey a coded message of wisdom by teaching a life lesson: do not talk too much but summarize the content of a relevant statement.

➢ *Sword dances* and *Morris dances* were performed during fairs and social gatherings. Performers danced with wooden sticks resembling swords and weapons carried into battle during the Crusades. The word *Morris* is believed to derive from *Moorish*.[14]

➢ *Pavane* was a sedate dance mostly performed by couples who participated and danced in ceremonial balls, weddings, and garden parties. Small forward and backward steps were combined with simple body rotations aiming to discreetly display the elaborate, fashionable clothing of the participants.[15]

Many of these dance forms, expressing trivial sentiments to accommodate certain occasions, were well suited to church and state. However, many of these dances might have functioned as movement amusement rather than genuine artistic expression. Medieval countryside dances and ***folklore dances***, on the other hand, provided more freedom from the religious canon by capturing meaningful native values, earthly truths, and candid joy.

◆ ***Dance folklore*** did not denounce God and the Church; rather, it used the idea of God as a *spiritual force for unity*, while bypassing the clerical rules and restrictions. The Church as an institution and religion as a subject matter were often omitted from folkloric dances that provided an informal creative space for the average people to express themselves. The *artistic anonymity* of folklore dance artists, creating on behalf of the community rather than individually, served as a *protective shield* from possible punishment imposed by the Church.

Native dance metaphors and symbolic imagery emerged through synthesizing, stylizing, and codifying the native values of the newly forming regions and nations. Through dance symbols, folklore dance sought to capture unique *movement identity* of communities sharing the same set of rituals, myths, beliefs, customs, and attitudes. Dance folklore was the artistic bond allowing ordinary people to creatively express their cultural uniqueness in abundant symbolic movement imagery and native dance metaphors.

UNITY	+	IDENTITY	=	NATIVE VALUE	+	FOLKLORE
One God		One Nation		Symbolic Imagery		Native Dance Metaphor

The following pages reveal how native values and pride, as well as group identity, might have been exhibited through various types of folkloric dance imagery.

SPANISH FOLKLORE DANCE IMAGERY
– HUMAN VS. BULL –

Romani tribes arrived on the Iberian Peninsula, modern Spain and Portugal, around the 11th century, entering from two different directions. One group arrived from India carrying the traditional style of Indian classical dance known as Kathak, and another came from Persia (present-day Iran) and imported its local dance influences.[16] Over time, both dance forms merged into a new genre that retained signature stylistic influences from India and Persia, as well as elements inherited from the former Roman Empire.

One practice, bullfighting, was linked to the gladiator combat of ancient Rome. Besides respecting the ancient spectacle, medieval people also needed the bull's meat to consume or sell. However, Rome's moral principles stipulated that every living creature had the right to live. Humans and animals were given equal chance to fight, survive, or die based on their strength, skills, and courage. Through the medieval centuries, bullfighting became a central cultural practice of the Iberian region: an energizing spectacle of death and victory and a source of national pride that a man "on foot" could kill a bull "face to face."[17] In the medieval context, the bullfighter might have represented a priest, and the slaughter of the bull, a sacrifice symbolic of Christ's death.

In this context, one may hypothesize that Spanish folkloric dance references bullfighting through movement imagery. Some dances resemble movement conversations between a woman (bull) and a man (fighter), where roles could instantly reverse. The choreographic interaction between the two dancers captures the passion and the intensity of a symbolic fight on the border between love and hate, life and death (Figure 3). Traditionally, young men aspired to step into the bullring of hope, fame, and fortune. The matadors were expected to carry out countless fights, and perhaps those surviving to retirement continued to nostalgically portray their fights in the form of dance.

Figure 3 Contemporary interpretation of Spanish folklore-inspired dance. Photography © Lois Greenfield, pictured Marat Bakh, Kristina Staykova, 2009, on the left. Bull skull and bullfighter in a ring, courtesy of iStock/Getty Images—on the right.

Although possibly linked to bullfighting, these folkloric dance forms might not have been intended to express of an act of killing or murder. To the contrary, perhaps they depicted a desire to fight and live with dignity and pride. An actual bullfighter puts his or her life at risk while exercising the highest level of self-control and the artistry of the craft to fight and win. Similarly, the choreography of the dancers in various Spanish folklore forms could have been an effort to skillfully portray a moment on the edge of life by displaying emotional intensity alongside the wisdom and skills to survive. The syncopated footwork present in the Flamenco folkloric form, for instance, might have expressed multilayered choreographic imagery—the resounding command of the matador conquering, the charging hooves of a raging bull, and the propulsive heartbeat of a man in the face of death.

Male dancers moved swiftly with a distinct emotional intensity. They usually lifted up their hips, keeping both legs together and feet on the ground, upper body held in a proud and upright stance. The positioning of a lifted ribcage recalled a matador and a warrior in a soldier's posture. The female dancer's upper body was held in a tense back twist. She would rhythmically move her hips, while her whole body was held tightly, arms engaged in elegant, persistently curved motion. The moves and shapes of her arms often resembled the shape of bull horns. While dancing, she frequently grasped the folds of her long, full dress, using them as an imaginative accessory, such as a fan or a cape.

The music accompaniment of an early version of a guitar, a soundbox with strings, was enhanced by the syncopated patterns of a cajón, a wooden box drum played by a percussionist. Frequently, all of the performers would participate by clapping their hands, singing, and loudly vocalizing their stream of thoughts and feelings.[18]

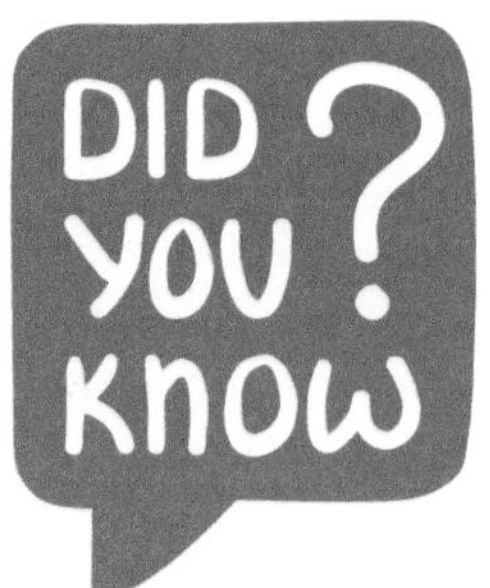

The imagery of a bull was an inspiration to artists across disciplines. The drawing series by 20th-century artist Pablo Picasso is a perfect example of image evolution from realistic to abstract (Figure 4). Picasso's stylization is applicable to choreography and the abstraction and stylizing of movement imagery. The observer might ask: What is it? How do I see it? What am I supposed to see? Is it a bull as reality, a bull as an impression, or a bull as a hint? Is it important for the bull to be of mass or to be of essence?

Figure 4 - Photography © Vahe Martirosyan, Picasso P. *The Bull*, Norton Simon Museum, Pasadena, California, 1946

IRISH FOLKLORE DANCE IMAGERY
– RUNAWAY HORSES –

The Irish were heavily influenced by the culture and language of the Celts. The arrival of Christianity and Saint Patrick in Ireland in 432 AD converted the pagan Celts to Christians, thus combining pagan values with Catholic beliefs. The pagan influence remained as dance began to evolve into sophisticated expression. The Viking invasion in 795 AD and the combined cultures of the Celts and Vikings produced the *Feiseanna*, or *Feis Festival* of trade, politics, and culture, which became a routine display of the arts, music, dance, and sporting events. The Norman invasion in 1169 AD brought the *round dance* to Ireland. By the 15th century, the Normans brought and incorporated the circle dance into Irish dance culture.[19]

Various stylistic changes occurred through time. Old-style Irish step dancers initially carried their arms freely and loosely at their sides. Rules gradually emerged for proper posture and carriage of the upper body and arms, as well as for foot placement.[20] Consequently, the upper body was kept contained, so as to not distract attention from the complex footwork. Different theories emerged to explain the purpose of this dance posture. One theory suggests that the girls dancing at the crossroads needed to hold their skirts down due to the windy Irish weather. Other theories emphasized the Catholic Church's doctrine demanding an "internally controlled body" and moral discipline.[21] The syncopated footwork in the old style recalled the consistent and energizing rhythm of galloping horses.

In this context, one may theorize about the striking similarities between the Irish old-style step dancing and the Irish association and fascination with horses as a native symbol of freedom and an allegory of free thought. The dynamic footwork of the lower body may be an expression of change and exuberance, as the upper body is more restricted, with arms held close to the torso. The speedy footwork and stepping sounds recall a herd of horses racing against the wind. Perhaps the choreographic intention was to translate the fast, syncopated rhythm of four horse legs to two human feet.

Figure 5 At left, contemporary interpretation of Irish-inspired step dance. Photography © Jark Hartin, *Riverdance, Riverdance 25th Anniversary Show*, 2020. At right, herd of horses in motion, courtesy of iStock/Getty Images

Horses in the land of medieval Ireland played an important role in everyday life: farm work, transportation, military crusades, and at sports occasions. The Irish were the first in Europe to establish horse racing as a formal competitive event.[22] Dance was often treated by the Irish as competition in the form of an artistic challenge, while for most of Europe, medieval social dances served as an expression of pleasurable public interaction during communal events. Ireland's equine art and dance art went hand in hand.

In medieval Irish narratives, for instance, the sun was described as "horseman" of the heavens. Another character of Irish mythology was a hero called Morrigan or Masha. She was described as a great runner, and her most celebrated achievement was winning a race against horses.[23] Her personality parallels the continental Celtic goddess of horses known as Epona.[24]

Ancient mythology and medieval mystic imagery glorified horses for their strength, speed, and beauty, and inspired many poets and artists. The image of a *white horse with wings*, rooted the ancient Greek myth of *Pegasus*, symbolized wisdom and inspiration. A unicorn in the European medieval tradition was a horse with a pointed, spiraling horn projecting from its forehead and resembling a cross between a goat and a horse. The wild creature was a symbol of purity and grace, and according to legend, only a virgin could capture it.[25] Images of unicorns appeared frequently on military heraldry, coats of arms, and native emblems—as illustrated in a contemporary rendering in the image left.

Figure 6 Emblem with prancing unicorn, courtesy of iStock/Getty Images

A dance adopted by the Irish was the *quadrille*, initially performed in ancient and medieval military horse parades, in which four horsemen and their mounts performed in square formations. This display became popular and led people throughout Europe to perform quadrilles without horses. The lively dance consisted of four couples arranged in the shape of a square, with each couple facing the center of the square. The dancers might hold hands to connect and move through floor formations or "figures."

Popular Irish group dances were *jigs, reels, hornpipes, sets, half sets*, and *ceili*. A core feature of the Irish dance tradition was the technique of stepping called *sean-nós*, which was the predecessor to Irish step dancing as we know it today. The tempo of the accompanying music was the low-to-the-ground footwork beaten out by the dancer. Sean-nós dance was traditionally a solo improvisational dance occurring in a limited performance space.[26] Various authors suggest that the form was developed on the tabletops of medieval taverns, on the flat surfaces of wooden barrels, and on the surfaces of wooden doors placed on the ground. Groups performing synchronized sean-nós dance were less common. Instead, the dancers might take turns, playing off the energy of the others, or most often, competing against each other.[27] Dances aimed to display virtuosity and endurance and were performed to the music of tambourines, harps, pipes, and bagpipes.

AMERICAN INDIAN FOLKLORE DANCE IMAGERY
– BECOMING AN EAGLE –

The end of the medieval period in Europe was marked by numerous ambitious voyages by explorers Christopher Columbus and Amerigo Vespucci, among others who were striving to discover and colonize new territories. They reached the shores of the American continents and encountered the rich traditions and folklore of indigenous peoples. The land was populated by numerous distinct Native American tribal nations spread out across South and Central America. The North American continent was also well inhabited, from the Great Plains and the Great Basin to the Colorado Plateau, California, and the Southwest. The indigenous North Americans lived in hunter-gatherer societies and used the land for farming and hunting.

For the North American indigenous population, the first natural dancers were not people, but animals. Eagles spread their wings, spinning circles in the sky, deer danced with leaping strides, and fish twirled in the sunlight reflecting off of the river. Not all humans were great movers, but all animals were natural-born dancers. Dance could be found everywhere: in the desert, in the mountains, in the sky, in the water, and in fire. Therefore, a vast majority of ritual and folklore dance imagery was nature- and animal-oriented.[28]

For many Native North Americans, the eagle was associated with supernatural forces, particularly the power to control thunder and rain. For the Iroquois people, the *Eagle Dance* portrayed species of eagles orbiting in flight, high in the heavens amidst the clouds; the Iroquois people called them "cloud dwellers." A Comanche dancer also imitated the eagle. According to legend, the young son of a chieftain was turned into an eagle when he died. Eagle feathers were believed to exert special powers. Members of the Iowa tribe carried an eagle feather fan in their left hand, while the Sioux people wore feathers in their war bonnets to represent victory. The Pawnee, Yuchi, Delaware, and Iroquois people use the feathers in ceremonial fans, brushes, and garment ornaments.[29]

Figure 7 Modern day presentation of an indigenous North American dance. Photography © Mark Miller, *Native American Dance*, Old Town Sacramento, 2015—on the left; flying eagles, courtesy of iStock/Getty Images—on the right

In the Jemez and Tesuque nation communities of today's state of New Mexico in the United States of America, the *Eagle Dance or Condor Dance* took place in the early spring and was often danced by two men. The dancers portrayed different movement aspects of eagle behavior: first, stepping and hopping on the ground, and later spreading their wings, soaring, alighting, and mating. The appearance and the costuming exhibited equal fidelity to nature. Outfits consisted of short skirts around the hip and exposed eagle-like painted legs. Great feather wings were attached and fastened to the arms. The wings were long and extended from the fingers of one hand across the back to the fingers of the other hand.[30]

In the context of native allegory and national symbolism of modern times, the Great Seal of the United States of America features a bald eagle as the symbol of a unified nation. The eagle grasps an olive branch in its left talons and a bundle of arrows in its right—symbols of the power of peace and war. The shield is a warrior's primary piece of defensive equipment, and here, it is supported solely by the American eagle to symbolize that people rely on their own virtue. The colors of the pales are those of the flag of the United States of America; white signifies purity and innocence; red, hardiness and valor; and blue, the color of the chief, signifies vigilance, perseverance, and justice.

Figure 8 The Great Seal of the United States of America

The members of various tribes also used dance in healing ceremonies conducted by their spiritual or religious leaders, as well as to celebrate a successful hunt and to thank the spirits for a bountiful harvest. The American Indians called such a congregation a *powwow*. These gatherings varied in size and duration, lasting anywhere from an afternoon to a week. In addition to serving as large social gatherings or festivals for the entire tribe, powwows celebrated a family member's accomplishments. For longer festivals and parade celebrations, multiple tribes would set up a camp. The music was primarily based on the use of percussion instruments accompanied by vocalization that included singing and chanting in solo, unison, choral, responsorial, and multipart formats.[31]

Other types of American Indian dances included *Sun Dance* by the members of the Plains Nations. This dance took place primarily around a pool and symbolized a connection to the divine as embodied by the sun. *Ghost Dance*, on the other hand, was a ceremony for the regeneration of the Earth and subsequently, the restoration of the Earth's caretakers to their former life of bliss. *War and Peace Dance* of the Cherokee Nation was a group ritual where male dancers holding spears and tomahawks executed a series of movements reflecting the acts and mechanics of battle.[32] These maneuvers included pushing, hitting, stomping, fighting, and eventually celebrating victory in battle. Most *War Dance* rituals concluded with a tobacco rite and smoking the calumet—a peace pipe. Ceremonial pipe smoking was traditionally used to seal a covenant or treaty or as a ritual to offer prayer in religious ceremonies. It was believed that the pipe was a link between the Earth and the sky. Smoking the pipe was a prayer in physical form as tobacco smoke was connecting the worlds—earth through the plant's roots and heaven with the spirits high above.[33]

BULGARIAN FOLKLORE DANCE IMAGERY
– AN ERRAND INTO THE MAZE –

Bulgaria traces its ancient roots back to the powerful Odrysian (Thracian) Kingdom, which was divided among three Odrysian kings and eventually conquered in 340 BC by the rising Kingdom of Macedon under Philip II.[34] King Philip established the city of Philippopolis in the middle of the Thracian Valley, the city of Plovdiv today.[35] Philip invited the Athenian philosopher Aristotle to tutor his son, Alexander the Great.[36] The region was influenced by ancient Greek culture under King Philip, who was a Macedonian, Greek, and Thracian king simultaneously. The same territories became part of the Roman Empire from 46–681 AD. In the second half of the 7th century AD, Bulgar Khan Asparuh expanded his presence in the Balkans. A peace treaty with Byzantium in 681 AD marked the beginning of the First Bulgarian Empire.[37] During the Middle Ages, Bulgaria developed a distinct national identity, while retaining the influence of the Greco-Roman cultures.

There is much speculation about the origin of the folkloric dances of Bulgaria, with roots back to the *geranos* dance of ancient Greece. The *geranos* was a dance often linked to the legend of the Minotaur from Greek mythology. The Minotaur was a creature with the head of a bull and the body of a man that dwelt in the center of a Cretan labyrinth. During geranos, the dancers held hands and moved with synchronized steps in a curved line, following a leader at the beginning of the line. Contrived in a complex rhythm, the line dance unfolded into elaborate turns and shapes representing the labyrinth's winding twists.[38] Syncopated steps included hops, leaps, and crossing of the feet while moving forward and backward. These features resemble the folkloric dance known today as *horo*.

Presumably, the ancient *geranos* dance migrated from the Cretan region, north into the Thracian Valley. From there, it most likely spread throughout the numerous ethnic regions of the country and was adopted by the locals, who creatively modified it into various patterns, formations, and rhythms. Different *horos* today contain unique circular patterns formed by the tracks of the footsteps on the ground. These dancing-into-the-maze pathways or "puzzles," when placed in a circular formation, resemble images present in different types of *horos*, such as a water wheel, a flower, or a star.

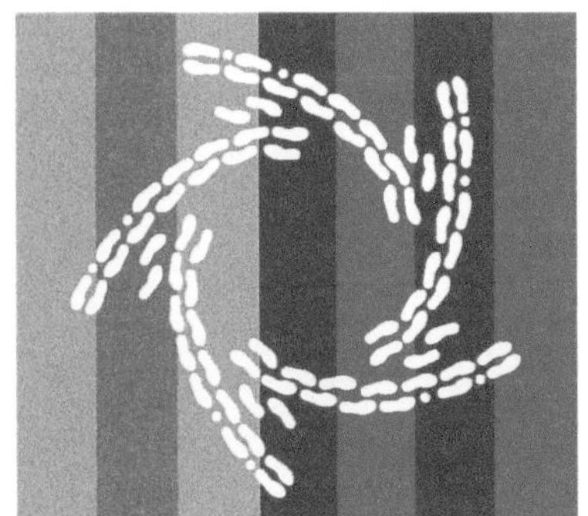

3/4 Douna Pacing horo

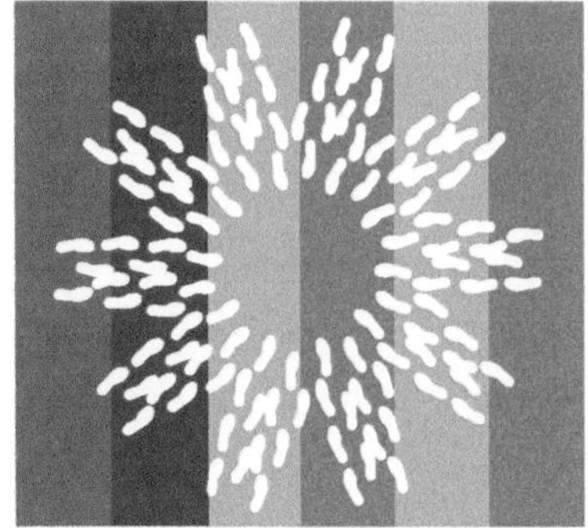

2/4 Pravo Thracian horo

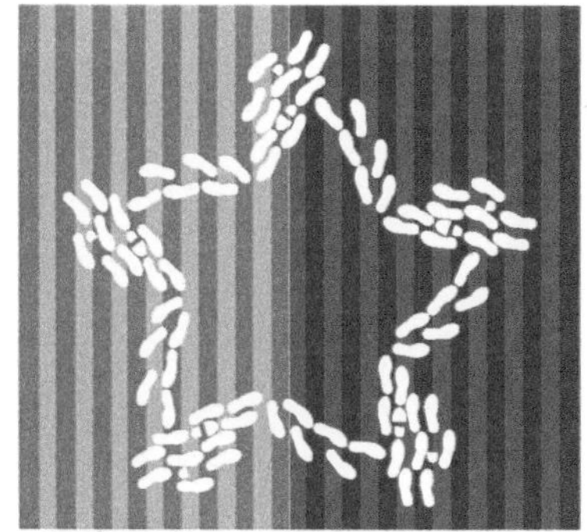

15/16 Bouchimish horo

Figure 9 Images design © Petra Marino, courtesy of Foundation Taratanci, Bulgaria. Three types of horos named are in the colors of the regional traditional clothing. The colored digits are the time signatures of each horo, followed by its title. The numbers of vertical colored lines relate to the rhythmic patterns—the number of beats in a measure of each horo

Perhaps the *allegory* of the dance maze in this folkloric dance form aimed to prove the point that life unfolds in unpredictable pathways. The *metaphor* of the horo's complex rhythmic steps used to enter the maze may be an *analogy* of the various ways one can maneuver through life's complex twists and turns. The *symbol* of dancing into the maze may represent the struggle and striving for orientation that is manageable only through a community effort to resolve a challenge.

In summary, perhaps *medieval dance symbolism* operated with key cognitive devices similar to figures of speech that have transcended time and are widely used today. For instance, in literature, a *metaphor* is a figurative comparison in which an object, activity, or idea is used as a symbol of something else, as in "the calm before the storm." An *analogy* uses a descriptive association to build an argument, such as "Time is a thief because it steals moments of our lives." *Allegory*, on the other hand, is a longer narrative that uses a seemingly unrelated story to teach a lesson or prove a point. *Interpretation* adds another layer of creative perspective. Similar to the stories in the Bible, which were written by multiple authors, folkloric imagery anonymously chosen by a native group might have been uniquely interpreted and modified through the performers' prism. Interpretation may have been used as a strategic gateway to avoid censorship by the religious doctrine and to bring a balance between common people's spiritual and artistic needs and the imposed norms and conventions set by the establishment.

Finding embodied equivalents of certain phenomena or creating movement and dance symbols "from scratch" may encompass a wide scope of strategies including: *concretization*, by producing movement as the outward aspect of specific action and representing it literally; *stylization*, by extracting and summarizing the key features and characteristics of motion; *metaphorical abstraction*, by encoding movement as expression of one thought, experience, or phenomenon in place of another that it resembles.[39] For diagrams outlining the algorithm, see Figures 10 and 11.

?

If you were the leader of your own fictitious nation, what would you name your nation? What animal or phenomenon would you use as the symbolic imagery of your native pride? How would you express it choreographically through your nation's folkloric dance?

HELPFUL TIPS & SUGGESTIONS

~ Think of a metaphor as the carrier of an idea from one form to another

~ Use metaphor as a vessel of meaning and symbol as a vessel of imagery

~ Handle metaphor as sharpening the knife and allegory as doing the cutting

~ Design symbols that embody the hidden and the obvious at the same time

~ Create metaphors that awaken the sense of wonder and the search for truth

~ Treat symbols as caterers of coded knowledge—shapes, rhythms, and patterns

~ Consider that thinking hardly exists without language and imagery; language and imagery hardly exist without metaphors and symbols

THE CRAFT
OF THE MEDIEVAL CHOREOGRAPHER

The medieval choreographer's craft is depicted in the diagram below, which maps and draws an analogy to a cross—the medieval Christian symbol of punishment, salvation, and resurrection. The anonymous choreographers of the Middle Ages who created court and social dance, religious ceremonies, and rituals, as well as those engaged in transforming native rituals and symbols into folkloric forms, may have shared common principles for crafting dance. Various prompts summarize the creative practices of the medieval choreographer.

Figure 10

Dancing in Front of God?

Historical fiction involving the medieval philosopher and teaching priest Thomas Aquinas and two of his monk pupils.*

*Although this account is fictitious, the events, quotations, and individuals described are historically accurate.

"Padre, wake up! Padre! Are you okay...?" the two shaken young monks whispered.

The priest, still convulsing in his bed, finally opened his eyes. Bewildered, he looked at the monks, gasping, "I am...fine, I am fine now!"

One of the monks brought the candle closer to the priest's face:

"We heard you singing and screaming, Padre, and we came to check on you. You behaved as though...as though you were...possessed in your sleep!"

Wiping his sweating forehead, the priest replied, "I am not...possessed. I just had...a nightmare." Annoyed, he gestured towards them in denial.

"You may go now. Giovanni, Antonio, go! Thank you."

The two young men did not move.

"Leave!" the priest raised a commanding voice, and his gaze escorted the runaway monks into the dim, empty corridors of the Santa Sabrina convent.

It was an early morning in the month of May in the year 1265. The sunrise was turning the sky from dark blue to light blue and pink. The priest crawled from the bed to his worktable. He stared for a moment at the rising sun, which was compressed by the narrow window of his cell.

A dozen dispersed writings were on the tabletop. The priest quickly put them in order by carefully lifting the cover page with *Summa Theologiae* written on it and placed it on top of the stack of paper. Then, he slowly closed his eyes and brought his hands together, as if in prayer, for deep contemplation:

"Did I really dance in front of the Lord, or was that just a dream?" Is it even appropriate for Christians to dance? Hmmm...As I recall from the *Book of Psalms*, we are allowed to praise God with spontaneous worship in the form of dance: *Let them praise His name with dancing, making melody to Him with tambourine and lyre*, says *Psalm 149:3*. Dancing on appropriate occasions is not sinful: *A time to weep, and a time to laugh; a time to mourn, and a time to dance*, says *Ecclesiastes 3:4*."—Thomas opened his eyes and defensively sighed with relief.

"On the other hand, our bodies belong to God. Everything we do must honor Him. And if dancing draws attention to our bodies or ourselves, then it is sinful. *Or do you not know that your body is a temple of the Holy Spirit within you, which you have from God? You are not your own, for you were brought with a price. So, glorify God in your body*, says *First Corinthians 6:19, 20.* We must dance in a way that does not tempt others, does not tempt ourselves, and brings glory to God." Thomas stared at the sky though the window, then brought his hands together, lowered his head, and closed his eyes for another meditation and prayer:

"Forgive me, Lord, if I have offended you. I, Thomas Aquinas, promise not to write about dancing in my book, which I dedicate to your name and your heavenly glory. Amen!"

TRANSCENDING THE AGES
– CHOREOGRAPHING SYMBOL IN A BROAD CONTEXT –

The influence of symbols derived from medieval church and state doctrines and from folkloric imagery of native values and pride continued to *time travel* throughout the ages. Medieval metaphors and allegories inspired many generations of choreographers. Dance symbols as an operating concept frequently appear in new works.

A popular medieval-inspired work for dance today is *Carmina Burana*, translated from Latin as *Songs from Buria*, meaning Bauern or Bavaria in today's Germany. The initial medieval manuscript collection of poetry and dramatic texts was written by multiple authors between the 11th and 13th centuries and addressed religious commitment, faith, morality, love, seduction, and death. *Carmina Burana*, widely used for dance today, was written by German composer Carl Orff, who based his work on 24 medieval poems.[40]

Dance folklore has been pivotal in forming movement imagery and in capturing native values, pride, and distinct group identities. Each native group and nation danced about subject matter meaningful to them. For instance, horses existed in both Spain and North America, yet Spanish folklore dance imagery resembled the intensity of bullfighting, while Native American folklore dance displayed the power and magnificence of the eagle.

Through time choreographers have explored these distinct images and symbols of ritual and folklore. For example, imagery of bullfighting can be found in *Carmen*, a ballet choreographed by Roland Petit in 1949 to an orchestrated score of the opera with the same name by Georges Bizet, and to the libretto based on the 1845 novella by Prosper Mérimée. The work used ballet-adapted Spanish folkloric movement, including representations of the bullring and bullfight. In addition, iconography of horses is present in the 1980s ballet *Equus*, which is set to music by Wilfred Josephs and based on the play with the same name by Peter Schaffer. The narrative juxtaposed commercial culture and the worship of nature and spirituality, the sense of belonging, and the loss of one's identity.[41]

Ted Shawn, an early pioneer of American modern dance, wrote about Native American dance: "The art of dance is the fundamental art of the human race, and it is of greater importance that we preserve and record the authentic dances of the Indians now alive than that we preserve all their other arts." Shawn found inspiration in American Indian dance rituals and created numerous dances, including *The Feather of the Dawn* (1923), *Zuni Ghost Dance* (1931), and *Hopi Indian Eagle Dance* (1935).[42]

Another American modern dance choreographer, Martha Graham, drew inspiration for her iconic dance piece *Primitive Mysteries* (1931) from the rituals of Christianized American Indians in the American Southwest.[43] Dancer and choreographer Erick Hawkins was fascinated by dance ceremonies of the American Indians and traveled through New Mexico and Arizona. Hawkins himself cited the reason for the trip as one to settle his own doubts about pursuing a dance career that the world viewed as questionable for men. His mind changed, however, when he witnessed the American Indian men dancing both as a form of worship and as a way of celebrating their own existence.[44]

CHOREOGRAPHING SYMBOL AS AN OPERATING CONCEPT BEYOND HISTORIC FRAMEWORK

When capturing and representing a phenomenon, symbolism and abstraction in art condense elaborate descriptions and details by summarizing the content and form to its very essence. Through the centuries, choreographic creativity has demonstrated that a concrete object, event, idea, or sensation may be abstracted, stylized, codified, and transformed into dance movement imagery—a symbol in motion.

For instance, early modern dance choreographer Loïe Fuller was drawn to depicting the visual and movement characteristics of natural forms by incorporating into her dance the motion of a large piece of silk fabric. One could guess that the intention of these experiments was to artfully capture a specific image—perhaps a butterfly (see Figure 11)?

Often movement imagery emerges spontaneously and unintentionally. Afterward, choreographers may seek to identify imagery's resemblances or corresponding analogies so that they can incorporate them into the fabric of their work. Or in the reverse: A movement symbol could be crafted and produced intentionally and methodically, with a suggested algorithm, as in Figure 11.

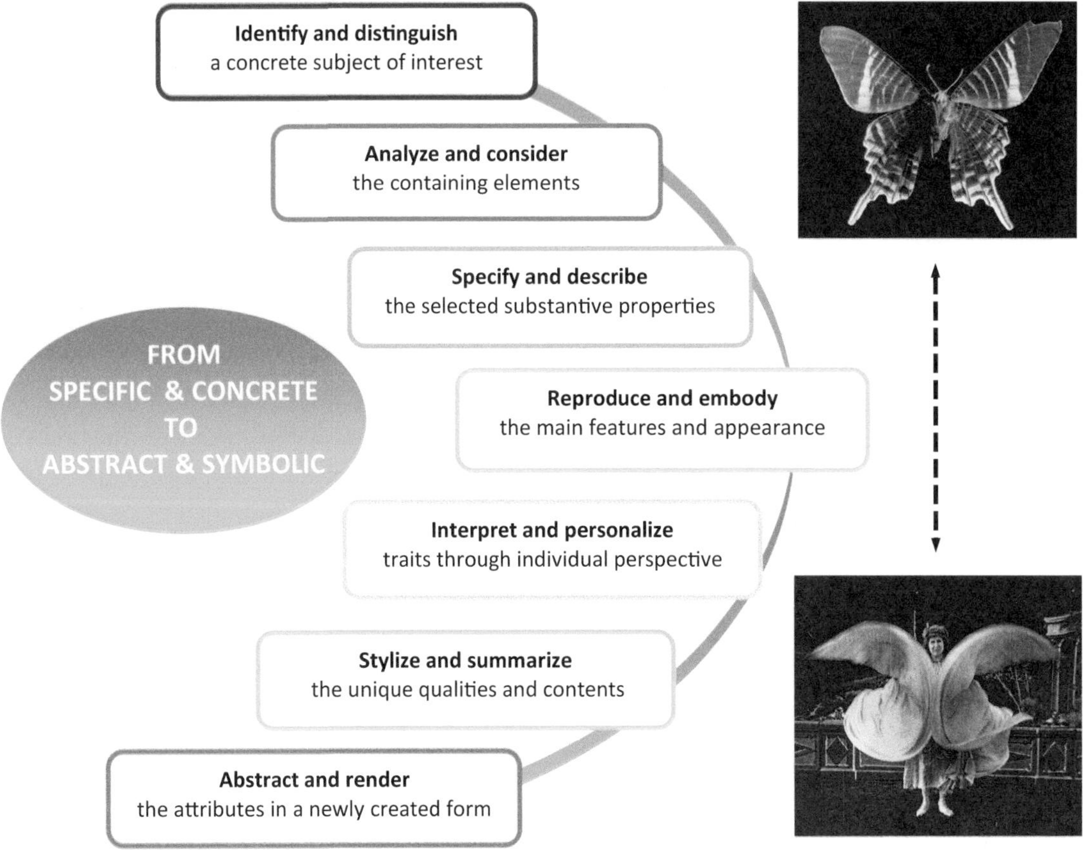

Figure 11 Image © BFI National Archive, pictured Loïe Fuller, FRA 1905, photography by anonymous, hand colored nitrate print by Olivia Kristina Stutz—bottom photo; butterfly, courtesy of iStock/Getty Images—upper photo

assignments & exercises

RESEARCH ASSIGNMENT: Use online, library, and video resources to research a folkloric dance form. You could select a general region having references to medieval dance between the 5th and 15th centuries AD, when nation building took place and the world map of today slowly began to form. Or you could direct your research to locations such as Hawaii, Alaska, Mexico, or other world regions. Questions: a) How did people in these areas celebrate, mourn, and worship through dance, and what were the native values, features, and symbols in dance? b) How did religious practices inform dance iconography, and how were social customs revealed in the folkloric dances of that region? c) What additional elements, such as costumes, masks, props, location, and surrounding environment, were/are frequently used?

★ **CREATIVE EXERCISE:** Think of founding your own *fictitious new nation* and describe its emergence and features. Give your nation a name. Your new nation could be located on the surface of Earth, underground, in outer space, or in an imaginative universe.

➡ Draw a symbol and create a seal capturing your new nation's identity. Then create and draw your national flag. Justify the name of your nation and the design of your seal.

➡ Select an animal of native respect (for example: lizard, tiger, whale) or a distinct natural event (earthquake, volcanic eruption, breaking iceberg, beach breeze), or think of a fictitious unearthly phenomenon, and then establish a movement symbol of native pride based on your selection.

➡ Using the movement symbol, create and stylize movement vocabulary and motion patterns that lead to building a short folkloric dance presentation of your new nation. You can tailor your dance to fit a social occasion that occurs in your nation, for instance a wedding, funeral, birth, or naming ceremony. Use musical instruments, everyday noise-making devices, or electronic sounds to create music and/or soundscape for your new fictitious folkloric dance. In addition, create improvised but unique costuming using fabric, props, masks, or any supportive physical objects to enhance your presentation.

COMPARATIVE ASSIGNMENT: Analyze whether an existing or a fictitious "religion" was present and if it has influenced the creative imagery of your folkloric dance. Questions: a) To what extent was spirituality involved? b) How and where were native symbols and identity reflected in the folkloric dance? c) Compare the expression of your national identity with the expression of your own identity in your folkloric dance. Give examples.

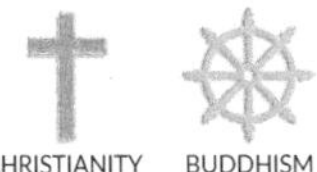

CHRISTIANITY BUDDHISM ISLAM SHINTO TAOISM HINDUISM JUDAISM SIKHISM

BIBLIOGRAPHY AND REFERENCES

[1] Britannica, The Editors of Encyclopedia. "Middle Ages," in *Encyclopedia Britannica*, 09.10.2020, www.britannica.com/event/Middle-Ages, accessed March 2021.

[2] Britannica, The Editors of Encyclopedia. "Premodern Monarchies," in *Encyclopedia Britannica*, 09.10.2020, www.britannica.com/topic/monarchy/Monarchy-in-the-modern-era, accessed March 2021.

[3] Mantello, F. A. C. and Rigg, A. G. *Medieval Latin: An Introduction and Bibliographical Guide*, The Catholic University of America Press, 1996, p. 85.

[4] Reader's Digest. *Reader's Digest the Truth about History: How New Evidence Is Transforming the Story of the Past*. Reader's Digest Association, 2003, p. 294.

[5] Hodgett, Gerald A. *A Social and Economic History of Medieval Europe*, 1st edition, Routledge, 2006, pp. 13–88.

[6] Colish, Marcia L. *Medieval Foundations of the Western Intellectual Tradition*, Revised edition, Yale University Press, 1999, pp. 3–66, 265–270, 302–318.

[7] Stefon, Matt, Lindberg, Carter H., Hogg, William Richey, Wainwright, Geoffrey, Marty, Martin E., Chadwick, Henry, Fredericksen, Linwood, Pelikan, Jaroslav Jan, McGinn, Bernard J., Crow, Paul A., Hick, John, Spencer, Sidney, Benz, Wilhelm, Ernst and Sullivan, Lawrence E. "Christianity," in *Encyclopedia Britannica*, 11.26.2020, accessed March 23, 2021.

[8] Fyfe, Agnes. *Dances of Germany*. Max Parrish, 1951, pp. 8–9.

[9] "Symbolism in Medieval Art," *ukessays.com*. 11.2018, 03.2021, www.ukessays.com/essays/arts/eve-in-medieval-art.php?vref=1, accessed March 2021.

10 Wolfman, Ursula Rehn. Music and the Arts in the Middle Ages, 2011, online article: https://interlude.hk/music-and-the-arts-in-the-middle-ages/, accessed March 2021.

[11] Mullally, Robert. *The Carol: A Study of Medieval Dance*, Ashgate Publishing Company, 2011, pp. 7–19, 31–40.

[12] Britannica, The Editors of Encyclopedia. "Maypole Dance," in *Encyclopedia Britannica*, 02.28.2007, www.britannica.com/art/Maypole-dance, accessed March 2021.

[13] Snodgrass, Mary Ellen. *The Encyclopedia of World Folk Dance*, Rowman & Littlefield Publishers, 2016, p. 14.

[14] Forrest, John. *The History of Morris Dancing*, 1458–1750. James Clarke & Co Ltd, 1999.

[15] Brown, Alan. "Pavan," in *The New Grove Dictionary of Music and Musicians*, 2nd edition, edited by Stanley Sadie and John Tyrrell, Macmillan Publishers, 2001.

[16] Phillips, Miriam. "Becoming the Floor/Breaking the Floor: Experiencing the Kathak-Flamenco Connection." *Ethnomusicology*, vol. 57, no. 3, 2013, pp. 396–427. JSTOR, www.jstor.org/stable/10.5406/ethnomusicology.57.3.0396, accessed April 2021.

[17] Conrad, Barnaby. "Matador," in *Encyclopedia Britannica*, 12.09.2009, www.britannica.com/sports/matador-bullfighter, accessed April 2021.

[18] Edwards, Gwynne and Haas, Ken. *!Flamenco!*, Thames and Hudson, 2000, pp. 160–170.

[19] Flechner, Roy and Meeder, Svén. Editors. *The Irish in Early Medieval Europe: Identity, Culture and Religion*, Palgrave Macmillan, 2016, pp. 231–241.

[20] Brennan, Helen. *Story of Irish Dance*, Brandon and Imprint of Mount Eagle Publications, Ltd, Dinge. Co., 1999, pp. 46–62.

[21] Brennan 1999. *Story of Irish Dance*, pp. 121–131.

[22] McCormick, Finbar. "The Horse in Early Ireland," *Antropozoologica*, vol. 42, no. 1, 85–104, article, 2007, accessed April 2021.

[23] Cartwright, Mark. "The Mórrigan." *World History Encyclopedia*. 02.09.2021, accessed April 2021.

[24] Editors. "Epona." *World History Encyclopedia*. 01.18.2012, accessed April 2021.

[25] Smith, Hillary. "The Unicorn Myth in Ancient and Medieval Folklore," *Ancient History Encyclopedia*, 10.23.2020, under a Creative Commons: Attribution-Non Commercial-Share Alike 3.0 Unported license. Published on December 6, 2020, online article: https://brewminate.com/the-unicorn-myth-in-ancient-and-medieval-folklore/, accessed March 2021. And Casolani, Charles Edward. "Horsemanship," in *Encyclopedia Britannica*, 01.05.2018, www.britannica.com/topic/horsemanship, accessed April 2021.

[26] Brennan 1999. *Story of Irish Dance*, pp. 63–72.

[27] Hall, Frank. *Competitive Irish Dance: Art, Sport, Duty*, Macater Press, 2008.

[28] Evans, Bessie and Evans, May G. *Native American Dance Steps*, illustrations by Poyege, A.S. Barnes and Company Inc., 1931.

[29] Fenton, William. *The Iroquois Eagle Dance An Offshoot of Calumet Dance*, Smithsonian Institution, Bureau of American Ethnology, 1951.

[30] Heth, Charlotte. *Native American Dance: Ceremonies and Social Traditions*, Smithsonian Institution, Starwood Publishing, 1992.

[31] Crum, Robert and Crum, Betty. *Eagle Drum: On the Powwow Trail with a Young Grass Dancer*, Four Winds Press, Macmillan Publishing Group, 1994.

[32] Heth 1992. *Native American Dance: Ceremonies and Social Traditions*.

[33] Editors of Encyclopedia. "Sacred Pipe," in *Encyclopedia Britannica*, 06.05.2013, www.britannica.com/topic/Sacred-Pipe, accessed April 2, 2021.

[34] Archibald, Zosia. "Macedonia and Thrace," in *A Companion to Ancient Macedonia*, edited by Joseph Roisman and Ian Worthington, Wiley-Blackwell, 2010, pp. 326–341.

[35] Delev, Peter. "Thrace from the Assassination of Kotys I to Koroupedion (360–281 BC)," in *A Companion to Ancient Thrace*, edited by Julia Valeva, Emil Nankov and Danver Graninger, Wiley-Blackwell, 2015, pp. 48–58.

[36] Mark, Joshua J. "Aristotle." *World History Encyclopedia*, 05.22.2019, accessed April 2021.

[37] Crampton, R. J. *A Concise History of Bulgaria*, 2nd edition, Cambridge University Press, 2006, pp. 3–12.

[38] Ragazzi, Gaudenzio. "The Crane, Ariadne's Thread, Labyrinth and Dance," *in Le Origini della Danza*, online publications, 2019, accessed March 2021.

[39] Hanna, Judith Lynne. "Movement," in *The SAGE Encyclopedia of Music and Culture*, Vol. 3, edited by Janet Sturman and J. Geoffrey Golson, SAGE Publications, 2019, pp. 1489–1492.

[40] Schaller, Dieter. "Carmina Burana," *in Lexikon des Mittelalters* (in German), 2. Artemis, 1983.

[41] Reference, www.wisemusicclassical.com/work/9722/Equus-ballet-Wilfred-Josephs/, accessed April 2021.

[42] Sherman, Jane. "The American Indian Imagery of Ted Shawn," *Dance Chronicle*, vol. 12, no. 3, 1989, pp. 366–382. JSTOR, www.jstor.org/stable/1567683, accessed April 2021.

[43] Jowitt, Deborah. *Time and the Dancing Image*, University of California Press, 1989, p. 182.

[44] Kriegsman, Alan M. "Erick Hawkins' Dance to a Different Drummer," *The Washington Post*, article, 10.25.1987, accessed April 2021.

VISUAL REFERENCES

Figure 1: Illustration © Kate Greenaway, *The Pied Piper of Hamelin* by Robert Browning, published by George Routledge & Sons, London, Glasgow, Manchester, New York, 1888, Public domain, image courtesy of iStock/Getty Images

Figure 2: Anonymous, *Christ Pantocrator*, mosaic, cupola of choir, Hosios Loukas Monastery, Boeotia, Greece, early 11th century, US public domain

Figure 3: Contemporary interpretation of Spanish folklore inspired dance. Photography © Lois Greenfield, pictured Marat Bakh, Kristina Staykova, 2009 (on the left), *Head skull of bull in smoke isolated on black background*, credit: SandraMatic, courtesy of iStock/Getty *Images*, *Bullfighter* in a bullring, credit: Syldavia, courtesy of iStock/Getty Images (on the right)

Figure 4: Photography © Vahe Martirosyan, Picasso P. *The Bull*, Norton Simon Museum, Pasadena, CA, 1946, CC BY-SA 2.0. public domain

Figure 5: Photography © Jark Hartin, Riverdance, *Riverdance 25th Anniversary Show*, 2020; *Horses herd portrait in motion with dark blue sky behind*, Credit: Nemyrivskyi Viacheslav, courtesy of iStock/Getty Images; *Horse herd run fast in desert dust against dramatic sunset sky*, Credit: Callipso, courtesy of iStock/Getty Images

Figure 6: *Ancient symbol of prancing unicorn in vector graphic style*, credit: Adelevin, courtesy of iStock/Getty Images

Figure 7: Modern days reenactment of American Indian Dance. Photography © Mark Miller, Native American Dance, Old Town Sacramento, 2015, CC BY-SA 3.0. (on the left); *Eagle flies at high altitude with wings spread out on a sunny* day *in the mountains*. Credit: Andreas Nesslinger, courtesy of iStock/Getty Images (on the right)

Figure 8: The Great Seal of the United States of America, public domain

Figure 9: Images design © Petra Marino, courtesy of Foundation Taratanci, Bulgaria. Taratanci is a cultural collective with a mission to promote Bulgarian folk dances through modern artistic representation. Visit our website and enjoy the dance patterns at https://taratanci.com

Figure 10: Diagram © Vladimir Angelov, *An ornate cross design with separate scroll designs which are all ungrouped, these are sharp clean vectored images*, Credit: ANGELGILD, courtesy of iStock, Getty Images

Figure 11: Diagram © Vladimir Angelov Image © BFI National Archive, Loïe Fuller, FRA 1905, photography by anonymous. Photograph of the hand colored nitrate print by Olivia Kristina Stutz, ERC Advanced Grant *FilmColors* (bottom photo); butterfly, Butterfly Farfalle, credit: iacu, courtesy of iStock/Getty Images (upper photo)

Midway upon the journey of our life, I found myself within a forest dark, for the straightforward pathway had been lost.

The Divine Comedy, a narrative poem by Dante Alighieri,
Florence, 1308–1321 AD

CHAPTER 4

RENAISSANCE AND BAROQUE AGE: WALTZING KINGDOMS – CHOREOGRAPHING CULTURE –

The Renaissance was a cultural and intellectual movement that profoundly affected Europe and spanned the period from approximately the second half of the 14th century up to the first half of 18th century. The word *renaissance* derives from Old French, and the Italian word *rinascimento*, which comes from the verb *rinascere*, meaning "to be reborn."[1]

There are various theories about why the Renaissance emerged. One of them attributes its origins to the devastation caused by the Black Death, also known as the Bubonic Plague. The disease, considered one of the deadliest in human history, hit Europe between 1348 and 1350 and killed approximately 75 to 200 million people.[2] The encounter with mass death caused thinkers, leaders, and ordinary people to dwell more on their earthly lives, rather than on the religious promise of an afterlife. The changes brought by the Renaissance, however, were not uniformly experienced across Europe, and yet the Renaissance was a turning point in political and social consciousness.

There is historic consensus that the Renaissance started in Florence, Italy. Renaissance origins and characteristics focused on a variety of factors, including the social and civic conditions and the political structure of Florence at the time. The dominant Medici family of Florence was best known for sponsoring artists such as Leonardo da Vinci and Michelangelo, who inspired the term "Renaissance man"—a person with many skills.[3]

The Renaissance followed by the Age of Reason introduced innovations in many intellectual pursuits: in politics—the development of conventions in diplomacy; in science—an increased reliance on methodology, reasoning, and empirical evidence. In education, a new program was gradually forming called *Studia Humanitatis*, which embraced five subjects in the humanities: grammar, poetry, history, moral philosophy, and rhetoric.[4]

In the dance arts, choreographers still embraced Medieval allegory and symbolism. Geometrical dance patterns were assigned certain meanings. For instance, a triangle symbolized justice, three circles conjoined meant truth known, a square within a square indicated virtuous design.[5]

Choreographers focused on geometrical floor patterns and directed the dancers to move through various figures such as squares, diamonds, ovals, diagonals, and triangles, as shown in image left.

Figure 1 *The Royal Ballet of the Dowager of Bilbao's Grand Ball*, artwork by Daniel Rabel, 1626, collection of Louvre Museum

THE RISE OF ENCYCLOPEDIC THINKING AND THE EXUBERANT DISPLAY OF CULTURAL ACHIEVEMENT

In contrast to the medieval period, which advanced strict social and religious dogmas, the new society of the "re-birth" revived ancient classical ideas by placing *the individual* at center stage. Renaissance doctrine empowered a person to create and speak on behalf of society. While the "ancient man" might have focused on nurturing skills in specific areas of knowledge, arts, and crafts, the "Renaissance man," as a philosopher, sculptor, or architect, nurtured multiple skills and knowledge simultaneously.[6] The spirit of the Renaissance cultivated *encyclopedic thinking* and individuals with inventive, multidisciplinary, and multifaceted mindsets who would creatively contribute to the new society. The artistic and intellectual influences of polymaths such as da Vinci, Michelangelo, and Galileo echoed in the versatile choreographer-authors Pierre Rameau and Jean-Georges Noverre, as well as in multifaceted musicians-actors-authors, such as Molière and Jean-Baptiste Lully. In summary: intellectual drive = encyclopedic knowledge = educated individual = cultured person.

The sweeping societal changes would ultimately provide a new context for the meaning of *culture*. The term culture (from the Latin word *cultura*, meaning "cultivation") was used first by the ancient Roman orator Cicero, who stated that philosophy was *cultura animi*, the "cultivation of the soul."[7] Culture as a social phenomenon in its contemporary meaning first took root during the Renaissance and was cultivated with care during that time period.

In Renaissance Europe, education, arts, science, politics, wealth, and governing power taken together represented *culture*, and its intellectual and artistic achievements were celebrated in the most glamorous and sensational ways. In comparison to the arts during the preceding medieval era, the arts during the Renaissance evolved swiftly and in multiple directions. After 1600 and until the early 18th century, the Renaissance period fused historically into the Baroque period. Baroque art principles included exaggerated motion and easily interpreted detail to produce dramatic tension and exuberant grandeur in all areas of life.[8] The aristocracy used the dramatic style of Baroque art as a means of expressing glamour, triumph, and power.

Baroque royal palaces encompassed grand entrances and opulent, spacious halls. The Palace of Versailles, completed in 1682, served as principal royal residence of French King Louis XIV. Ironically, the late Baroque flamboyance sharply contrasted with the early Renaissance ideals of clear and sober rationality. By the early 1720s in France, Baroque slowly began its cultural decline and was gradually replaced by the Rococo style, especially in the areas of interior design, paintings, and decorative arts.

Figure 2 *Galerie des Glaces—Hall of Mirrors in the Palace of Versailles*, France. Courtesy of Wikimedia Commons

MASQUERADE BALL
– DANCE GAMES AND GLAMOROUS ENTERTAINMENT –

Dance in the Renaissance and Baroque periods flourished in the courts and was linked to court culture, where the priority was to exhibit the wealth and power of elite society. As part of displaying culture, dance gradually became part of court policy and a means to manifest social status, refinement, and good manners.

By the year 1550, the courts in Europe required that each person belonging to royal society be skilled in reading and writing, riding horses, hunting, and court dancing. Possessing such skills and cultured manners was key to advancing within the court ranks and gaining employment opportunities.

Everyone was learning how to dance! Dance was becoming not only a fashionable trend, but also an obsession within the royal courts. In addition to teaching court dance, dance educators and choreographers were expected to set standards of *etiquette* and *deportment*, as well as advise participants on how to manage various social interactions that might arise during the course of a dance ball.[9]

Masquerade balls were one of the major dance events and entertainments of the 15th century. Masquerade (from the Italian word *maschera*, meaning mask) was a form of dance party where the guests wore masks and costumes making them unidentifiable.[10] These gatherings involved pageantry and triumphal processions celebrating dynastic marriages and other entertaining social events. In addition to the dancing, masquerade balls offered games to determine if the guests could reveal each other's identities, or whether they could remain incognito behind their masks. These games gave masqueraders license to spy, gossip extensively, or be verbally vulgar.[11]

During the 16th century, masquerades were extended into costumed public festivities in Renaissance Italy. These celebrations continued to include elaborate dances held for members of the upper classes and were particularly popular in Venice, where the tradition continues today as the Carnevale festival occurring annually before Lent.

Pearls, lavishness, and opulence! There were many reasons for the popularity of wearing masks. People had membership of various orders and belonged to wealthy families, social castes, and groups that often demanded confidentiality and privacy: And yet they would not hesitate to display and demonstrate status and glamour.

"I hate deceit," wrote the infamous Italian adventurer, gambler, poet, violinist, spy, con man, freethinker, and notorious seducer, Giacomo Casanova, in his "*History of My Life*," but the truth was that he consistently hid, deceived, and pursued anonymity.[12]

Figure 3 Couple in masks and costumes at Carnival in Venice nowadays, courtesy of iStock/Getty Images

Dances at festivities and parties were not always formally choreographed. During balls and masquerades, the queen was expected to dance with the king, and perhaps with her brother, but no one else. Everyone in the courts understood those unspoken rituals and protocols. Yet choreographers felt the urge to display more formal dancing during court celebrations. So immediately after the king and queen's anticipated dance introduction, the choreographers would insert dance scenes in which more experienced dancers would take on the choreography of the ball. This strategy served two great purposes: it removed the pressure on the royal dignitaries so that they could enjoy the spectacle, and it helped choreographers introduce new dance ideas for the upcoming dance lessons.[13]

Renaissance dances during royal balls and various types of other social gatherings flourished with popular dance forms such as *pavane, sarabande, courante, branle,* and *le moresques.* Besides processional and sedate dances, there were also the cheerful partnering dances such as *volta,* in which the gentlemen helped the ladies to leap and turn in midair. The choreographed formations for ball and court dances gradually developed into more complex geometrical arrangements. Dancing couples were positioned and moved into well-organized and pre-planned patterns like figures in a chess game. They were also directed to realign themselves into symbolic movement formations by using simple dance steps and anticipated group bodily moves similar to a "wave" performed by spectators at stadiums during modern day sport events.[14]

THE RENAISSANCE SPECTACLE
– SUMPTUOUS PERFORMANCE CELEBRATIONS –

The second half of the 16th century marked an important transformation in the concept of the masquerade ball. The format of "dancing games" and movement playfulness gradually transformed into choreographed movement spectacles and danced exhibitions (*défilé*), which led to the emergence of a new performance format—*the Renaissance spectacle*—as the predecessor of *ballet de cour*. The pivotal force behind this new type of presentation was an Italian royal celebrity: Catherine de' Medici, who was the consort of Henry II of France. She was from the renowned Medici family of Florence, which had long cultural traditions and sponsored such great artists as Leonardo da Vinci and Michelangelo.

At age fourteen, little Catherine was sent from Florence to Paris to marry French King Henry II. As any foreign dignitary in the French court, from the beginning she was treated with discretionary suspicion. The latter motivated her to prove herself and find ways to flatter the French court and nobility. Catherine had an artistic soul and sophisticated taste. No one in the French aristocracy would suspect that her marriage to Henry II would help build a formal alliance between the Italian and the French court cultures.[15] On October 15, 1581, audiences of nobles gathered at the Salle Bourbon near the Louvre Palace to witness splendid entertainment arranged by Catherine de' Medici and choreographed by the musician and dance master **Balthasar de Beaujoyeulx.** The performance was titled *Ballet Comique de la Reine*, but it vaguely resembled the ballet as we know it today.[16] Although the word *comique* was in the title, the performance was not a *comedy*. The word comique sprang from *comédie,* which in French can refer to drama in general.

There was no stage for the performance. The dancing took place on the floor of the hall, while the audience sat above the performers in the galleries. The occasion for producing the spectacle was the marriage of Queen Louise, who also participated in the performance. The Queen made a grand entrance. She was accompanied by court ladies on moving floats adorned with sirens and tritons, which spouted water like a fountain. The spectacle was the most lavish of the dance performances and theatrical entertainment ever seen, and it was quickly noticed across the European continent.[17]

Ballet des Polonaise in 1573 and *Ballet Comique de la Reine* in 1581, image left, were the first "ballet spectacles" recorded in dance history that moved beyond the masquerade ball, establishing the groundwork for the French *ballet de cour*. The purpose of these kinds of festivities was usually to celebrate royal weddings and to entertain *the royal* court.

Ballet Comique de la Reine was nearly six hours long and had a comprehensive libretto.[18] The opening scene shown on this authentic drawing by Jacques Patin depicts a royal courtier, seen in the center of the space, addressing an audience of aristocrats. From the side balconies and the galleries, the observers watched the progress of the performed story, which was an allegory about the release of a man enslaved by the royals in power.

Figure 4 *Ballet Comique de la Reine, Grande Salle du Petit-Bourbon*, illustration by Jacques Patin, 1587, derived from Gallica, 2010

Since there were no theaters during those early days of court ballets, the audience members sat in large chambers around and above the performance area. This improvised space configuration actually allowed the spectators to focus on and enjoy from above the choreographic formations and geometric patterns of the performance, which was led by the king and queen. Since dancing was considered part of socializing, most of the court ballets finished with a "grand finale" followed by a celebration ball in the form of an "after-party" in which the members of the audience joined the participants of the performance. By the end of the Renaissance, the invention of the *proscenium stage* established separation of the audience from the performance. The introduction of a theater-like space allowed the viewer's focus to shift entirely to what was occurring during the dance presentation.[19]

Following the building of the Globe Theater in London in 1599, other European monarchies gradually began to adapt existing halls and buildings into theaters and to construct architectural structures intended for concert dance performances. The proscenium stage prompted choreographers to develop more intricate group movement figures and floor patterns. Dancers soon realized that it was significantly easier to arrive at various choreographic formations and to execute the choreography more gracefully on a designated stage space. The proscenium stage also allowed for the use of elaborate *stage effects* generated by ingenious, custom-made stage machinery, which in turn led to the development of *scenic design* and the employment of backstage personnel—*stage crew*.

HISTORIC ERA	RENAISSANCE 15th century	16th century	BAROQUE 17th Century	18th Century
PERFORMANCES	**Dance festivities** Social dances, Folk dances	**Masquerade balls** & Renaissance spectacles	**Ballet de cour** Court dances, Royal balls	**Ballet d'action** Theatrical ballet performances
LOCATIONS	Gardens, taverns, festival grounds	Multipurpose halls, large rooms	Royal courts, City halls	Theaters with proscenium stage

Figure 5

BALLET DE COUR
– DANCE AS AN EXQUISITE ROYAL AFFAIR–

French court ballet reached its peak under King Louis XIV, who reigned from 1643 until 1715. A medal given at his birth proclaimed him *Orbis Solis Gallici—Risen Sun of Gaul*, and later the famous epithet "The Sun King" was bestowed upon him. Dance was always part of the King's life. Louis began dancing as a young boy and was often accused of spending more time at dance lessons than learning grammar.

Louis first danced in public at age thirteen, and by the time he was a young man, he would appear in court ballets several times a week. He took ballet very seriously, and at one point in his youth Louis became the living embodiment of the dance form, transforming his private and public life into a theatrical spectacle, and placing himself in full view of his subjects. Waking up, dining, or going to bed was for him an occasion with structured formality—measured and performed as dance.[20]

King Louis XIV chose some of the finest talent to collaborate with and further develop the preceding *Renaissance spectacles*, expanding them into new types of lavish productions—*ballet de cour*. The poet Isaac de Benserade contributed intricate librettos while Jean Bérain designed sumptuous costumes and built spectacular scenery. Bérain also introduced stage machines creating the illusion of storms, flying gods, and collapsing palaces.[21]

Many musical scores for court ballets were composed by Jean-Baptiste Lully, who entered in the service of Louis XIV in 1653. Lully came to France as a child from his native Florence, Italy, where he performed as a young comic dancer and musician. He had background in *commedia dell'arte*, an improvisational theatrical form containing comic dialogues and actions that unfolded within a few basic plots, tackling love intrigues and matters of the day. Lully wrote elegant and sophisticated music and collaborated on lighthearted *comédie-ballet* with the great comic playwright Molière (1622–1673). Eventually, Lully also introduced an entirely new genre known as *tragédie en musique*.[22]

King Louis XIV, image right, was personally involved in developing and producing ballet performances. He required for himself an overall appearance of grandeur, while assessing his own capability to dance those ballets. Louis also cast himself in diverse roles, indicating his deep understanding of ballet, his interest in the art form, and his passion to progress as a performer.

Throughout his dancing career, Louis played an Egyptian in *Le Mariage forcé* in 1664, a Moorish gentleman in *Le Sicilien* in 1667, and both Neptune and Apollo in *Les Amants magnifiques* in 1670.[23]

Following a dance performance lesson, Louis XIV often had to rush back to his ultimate role of king to make important decisions regarding national and foreign affairs, economy, and warfare.

Figure 6 *Portrait of Louis XIV of France*, art work by Hyacinthe Rigaud, 1700–1, The Louvre Museum collection

Pierre Beauchamp, the foremost dance master of that time, was the King's personal dance teacher. Beauchamp gave daily dance lessons to King Louis XIV for over 22 years, and he was one of the King's highest paid servants. In addition, Beauchamp codified some of the fundamental ballet positions and terminology still known and used today.[24]

Dance educators and choreographers discovered that the legs and feet turnout used in fencing helped dancers to increase flexibility, speed, and balance while permitting the body to open outward towards the court audience. Turnout of the legs and feet was also introduced into ballet as a theatrical adaptation of fencing postures, which were very fashionable at that time. The outward rotation of the feet became one of ballet's cardinal principles of movement execution, facilitating clarity and visibility of movement. In the 17th century, however, when dancers still wore heeled shoes, heavy wigs, and bulky costumes, turnout and flexibility were required to a lesser degree than today; therefore, the moves were not as dramatic as those performed by today's professional ballet dancers.[25]

Before retiring from performing dance on stage, in 1661 Louis XIV founded *Académie Royale de Danse* in one of the rooms in the Louvre. It was the first formal and professional dance institution established in the Western Europe. Pierre Beauchamp became the newly appointed director. The academy was an association of thirteen dance experts whose purpose according to the preamble of the King's letters was "to restore the art of dancing to its original perfection and to improve it as much as possible" referring to a reuse of Ancient Greek and Roman ideals, and a distance from early dance rituals and folkloric forms.[26]

The group was intended to codify court and character dances and to certify dance teachers by examination. Writing some years after the actual events, Pierre Rameau credits Pierre Beauchamp with the codification of *the five positions of the feet* in ballet, as well as the rules for using and positioning of the arms. Unlike the positions of the feet, however, the use of arms in Baroque dance differs significantly from their use in ballet today.[27]

For mysterious reasons, no comprehensive archives of *Académie Royale de Danse* have been found, making it difficult to historically evaluate its activities and accomplishments. Eventually the dance academy disbanded. In 1669, King Louis founded the *Académie Royale de Musique*, originally known as *Académie d'Opéra*, which had closely linked opera and ballet companies. Ultimately the ballet company would mature and transform into the Paris Opera Ballet, making it the first and the oldest ballet company in the world.[28]

King Louis XIV stopped dancing on stage in 1670 at age 32, after performing 80 roles in 40 different ballet productions. Until his very last days of ruling, the King kept his patronage and financial custody over the French ballet and opera, influencing artistic decisions and retaining respective control over the productions.[29]

Dance and the performing arts during that period reached their peak in terms of government attention and enormous funding. During the reign of Louis XIV, even French public life and culture outside the royal court began to resemble a ballet performance and a theatrical spectacle on a massive scale. People felt the need to see one another and be seen. City ordinance, planners, and architects rebuilt the city of Paris to incorporate wide tree-lined boulevards, thoughtfully designed city squares, parks with wooden benches, and charming alleys with colorful flowers. The city became more friendly and offered urban areas for people to socialize and present themselves to one another.[30]

Following the death of Louis XIV in 1715 and during the post-Renaissance and Baroque periods, court ballet continued to evolve. The newly established ballet genre spread across European kingdoms, gaining popularity in Britain, Sweden, Denmark, Spain, Italy, and Russia. The French *ballet de cour* would continue transforming aesthetically with each generation. As ballet gradually left the royal court facilities and moved into the theater, the kings were no longer the star performers and the center of the spectacle.

Newly trained professional dancers, educators, and choreographers emerged, gaining popularity and rising to fame. One of them was Marie Sallé (1707–1759), a charismatic performer, talented choreographer, and dance innovator. Sallé was known for possessing rigorous discipline and for practicing her performance routines daily. She gained great popularity in both Paris and London, becoming one of the first women to achieve stardom in ballet, which was remarkable at a time when the dance world was predominately masculine.[31]

BALLET D'ACTION
– CHOREOGRAPHING STORIES WITHOUT SPOKEN WORDS –

Meanwhile, French aristocracy and the opera patronage were gradually opening up to choreographers who were not directly related to the royal court and Paris Opera. One of them was the young dance partner, friend, and pupil of Marie Sallé, **Jean-Georges Noverre** (1727–1810), who would eventually become one of the most popular choreographers in Europe.[32] With the ambition to *reform the art of ballet*, in 1760 Noverre published his prolific *Lettres sur la danse, et sur les ballets*—a book still in print today. Ballet was still under the patronage and dominance of the royal court. The audiences in the theaters, however, were gradually expanding in social diversity, which led to the demand for ballet to artistically explore a broader spectrum of themes and common interests.

Noverre aimed to address those new needs and fundamentally reform the art of ballet by taking it beyond fashionable royal entertainment. The elitist, self-indulgent dance skits and pleasure-seeking aristocratic spectacles had to be abolished. The masquerade masks, exaggerated wigs, and over-decorated heavy clothing had to be replaced as well. Noverre felt compelled to substitute this excessive style with new types of ballets that explored classical tragedy and tales of moral dilemmas from everyday life. Instead of choreographing another dance parade for royal dignitaries, Noverre drew ordinary people into dramatic psychological worlds to explore human behavior and strength of spirit.[33]

Noverre focused on the narratives of the ballets as the core of the performance experience. He experimented with improving the flow of the story by paying special attention to pantomime as an organic part of dance sequencing. Noverre became an ambitious advocate of *ballet d'action—storytelling theatrical ballets***.** This new kind of theatrical dance employed psychological realism and dramaturgical unity.

Ballet d'action aimed to convey its dramatic content entirely through movement and *without using spoken words and songs*. This fundamental change enabled choreographers and dancers to gain more creative power and collaborate more closely with the composers and librettists.[34] In a short period of time, many ballet companies across Europe embraced this new ballet aesthetic.

Marie Camargo (right), painted by Nicolas Lancret in 1730, was a contemporary of the choreographer Marie Sallé and famous for her stunning technique and energy.

Camargo was also responsible for many innovations in ballet. She was the first ballerina to introduce and execute *the entrechat quatre*—a step involving "beating" of the legs, in which the dancer jumps into the air and rapidly crosses the legs to the front and back of each other.

Sallé was also the first dancer to wear *ballet slippers* instead of heeled shoes, a *shorter skirt*, and hosiery known today as standard *ballet tights*.[35]

Figure 7 *Mademoiselle de Camargo dancing (fragment)*, artwork by Nicholas Lancret, 1730, The Wallace Collection

RETROSPECTIVE AND PROSPECTIVE:
– ENJOY TIME TRAVEL BY HOPPING BACKWARD AND FORWARD –

The general chronology that follows traces the development and transformation of choreographic forms throughout early human history. During the Renaissance and Baroque Age, *ballet de cour* became the first "hybrid" choreographic phenomenon, by grouping together and incorporating multiple types of dances into one coherent theatrical spectacle. Some of the dance genres with folkloric dance forms maintained a certain independence from the interests of the royal courts and continued to develop on their own. Throughout the subsequent Industrial Age, however, folkloric movement imagery and dance vocabulary were incorporated into Romantic ballets, which will be discussed in the next chapter.

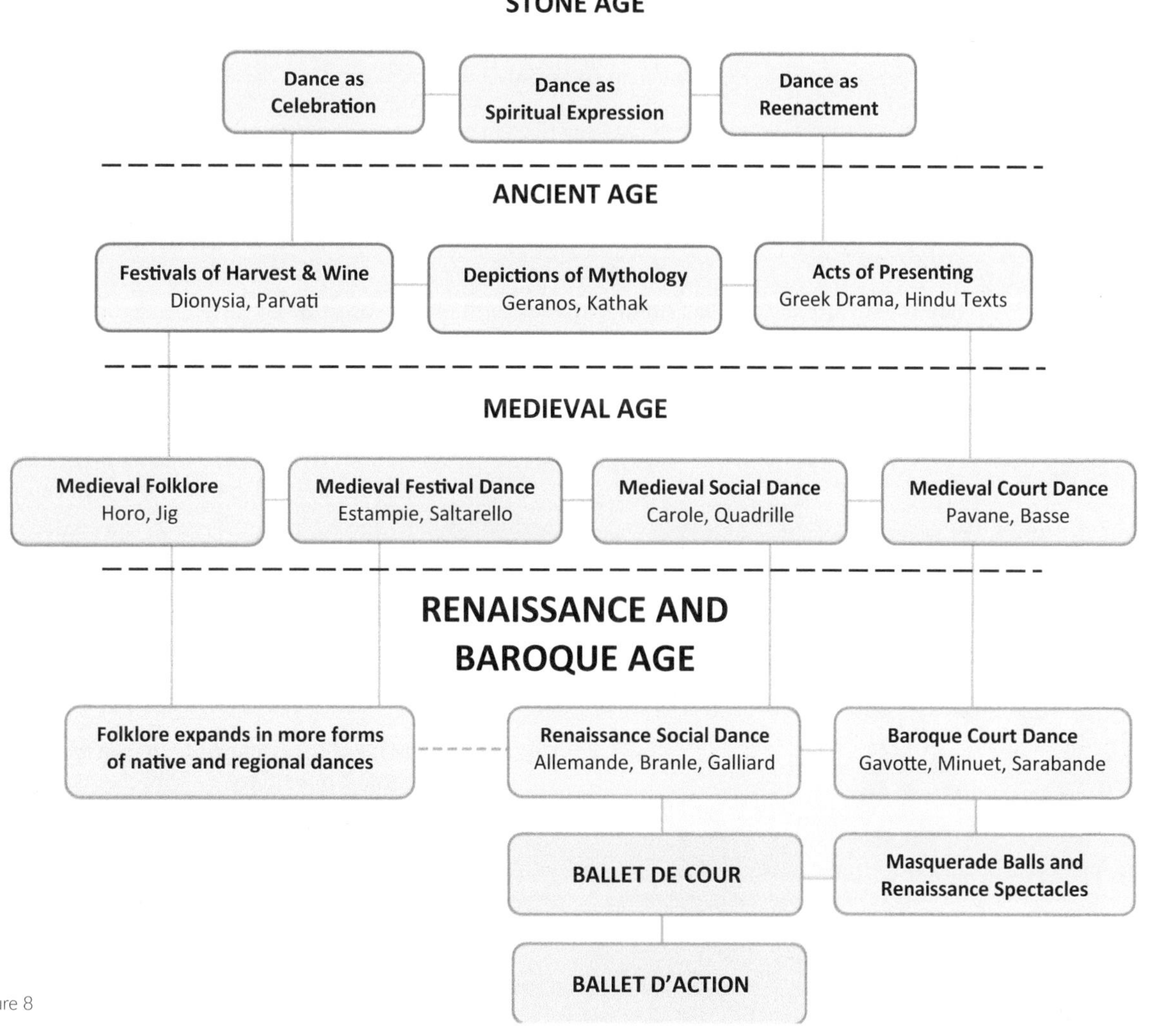

Figure 8

BALLET LESSON WITH THE KING

A FICTITIOUS DIALOGUE BETWEEN KING LOUIS XIV AND HIS FORMER BALLET MASTER, PIERRE BEAUCHAMP, WITHIN AN HISTORICALLY ACCURATE SETTING

The King's royal dance chambers
Palace of Versailles, near Paris, France
May 3, 1682, late morning

King Louis XIV: Oh…I am getting old, but it felt good…Another fabulous lesson, Pierre.

Monsieur Beauchamp: Always at your service, Your Majesty! You are a ballet danseur magnifique and an artiste extraordinaire of all time! (Spoken with a bow)

King Louis XIV: Hmm…Très bon. We have finished and you may dismiss the musicians. Also, order the servants to clean my sweat from the barre* and use more perfume. Speaking of which, Pierre, I am beginning to like that ballet barre you installed in my chambers. It helps me with my balance for these turned-out positions, especially in the morning when I am still sleepy…

Monsieur Beauchamp: At your service, Your Majesty! (Spoken with a bow)

King Louis XIV: Come here, Pierre. Join me for a quick snack. I love croissants, fruit bites, and citron pressé after a workout. Keep me company. Tell me what is new with your dance research.

Monsieur Beauchamp: Merci beaucoup, Your Majesty! With great pleasure! While you were ill, I took a break from working with Lully. I left Paris and traveled south to the sea coast of Provence. One evening during a festivity at the harbor, I saw this dance…It was actually a dance step that intrigued me—three quick syncopated steps with two fast changes of the feet. I think they called it…"Bourrée." Well, we can name it "pas de bourrée." So, I was thinking…perhaps we could try it in our lessons?

King Louis XIV: C'est miserable! Pierre, are you intending to teach me dance steps you have stolen from some drunken sailors and peasants?!

Monsieur Beauchamp: Oh, no…Please excuse my misspoken words, Your Majesty! What I meant…and what I promise is to entirely transform the manner of performing those steps to a highly sophisticated glide before introducing them to you for your kind consideration and fine dance performance. **

King Louis XIV: Hmm…Très bien. Then, I might try it. You may leave now. I was asked to rendezvous with the visiting Spanish ambassador. By the way, he presented himself as a terrible danseur at the welcoming ball last night, n'est-ce pas? Let's hope he will do better as a diplomat this morning and prevent a potential war over Spain.***
See you around, Pierre. Au revoir!

Monsieur Beauchamp: At your service, Your Majesty! (Bowing as he walks away backwards)

* The ballet barre was introduced in that approximate time period to assist the body with feet turn-out during dance warm-up.
** Dance artists might have taken the liberty to modify and implement folkloric dance steps into courtroom dances.
*** After retiring from dance, King Louis XIV was involved in the War of Spanish Succession (1701–1714).

THE CRAFT OF THE BAROQUE CHOREOGRAPHER

The Baroque choreographer's craft is depicted in the diagram below, which maps and draws an analogy to royal banners, by listing the major requirements when choreographing for the king. Creative skills and directorial proficiency, as well as communication and diplomatic thoughtfulness, were crucial for the Baroque choreographer to function successfully in the royal courts. A misstep, a wrong decision or word, could cause dismissal from the courts, which in turn would mean a downturn of economic fortune for an individual. Furthermore, choreographers were not the sole creators of the spectacles nor empowered with excessive creative freedom. Instead, complex factors were at play and various collaborators were involved to produce the massive spectacle. Most importantly, the choreographer's creativity aimed to accommodate the king's needs. In summary, the professional choreographers of that era were also professional servants.

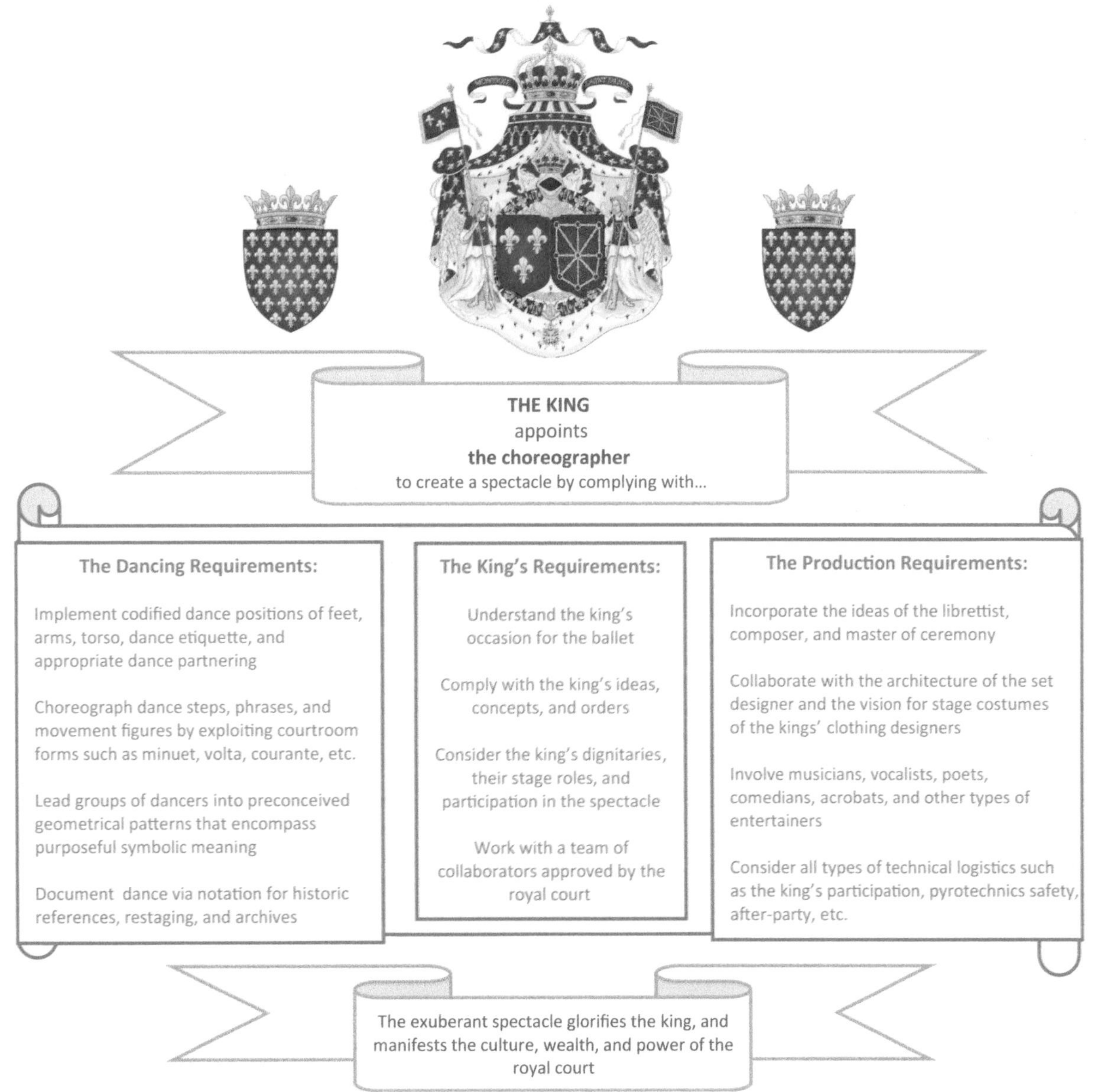

Figure 9 *Grand coat of arms of Louis XIV, King of France and Navarre*, authored by Sodacan, courtesy of Wikimedia Commons

TRANSCENDING THE AGES
– CHOREOGRAPHING CULTURE IN A BROAD CONTEXT –

The reframed parameters of culture derived from the Renaissance and Baroque periods in Europe continued to travel forward in time. The influences and artistic achievements of those eras served as milestones throughout the following centuries. During the European Renaissance, thinkers, artists, and choreographers had an encyclopedic frame of mind and acquired expanded knowledge about the society they lived in. Thus, combined with their multifaceted skills in various disciplines, they were empowered to formulate, cultivate, and represent the values that composed the European Renaissance and Baroque culture. Dance as an art form maintained and further expanded its existing purposes of functioning as ritual, aesthetic engagement, and artful entertainment. In addition, dance and choreography during these eras began to function as a public display and a manifestation of social status, education, good behavior, and proper deportment.

Catherine de' Medici was the initial inventor and first producer of *ballet de cour*—a distinctly new advancement in court entertainment used to celebrate special occasions. She encouraged Italian dance educators and choreographers to accept posts in France and had her own four sons take dance lessons. Many poets, artists, musicians, and choreographers contributed to these elaborate productions, and it was Catherine de' Medici who insisted that the ladies of her court receive basic dance training to perform these ballets.[36]

Considered the first choreographer of the Paris Opéra, Pierre Beauchamp arranged various court ballets and staged the dance sequences in several of Molière's plays, as well as Lully's operas. Beauchamp was largely responsible for the professionalization of ballet by raising the standards of ballet technique required for concert dance performances. Specialized training became necessary, and amateur dancers from the royal court were no longer the sole performers of ballet. Beauchamp also devised a system of *dance notation* that, although never published, was used by his pupils, one of whom—Raoul Feuillet—became the author of one of the earliest published systems of dance notation.[37]

The first reformer-choreographer-author Jean-Georges Noverre was one of the most influential choreographers of the Baroque period, the creator of *ballet d'action*—a precursor of 19th-century narrative ballets. Noverre was an author of great importance both then and now. His birthday is now observed each year on April 29 as International Dance Day.

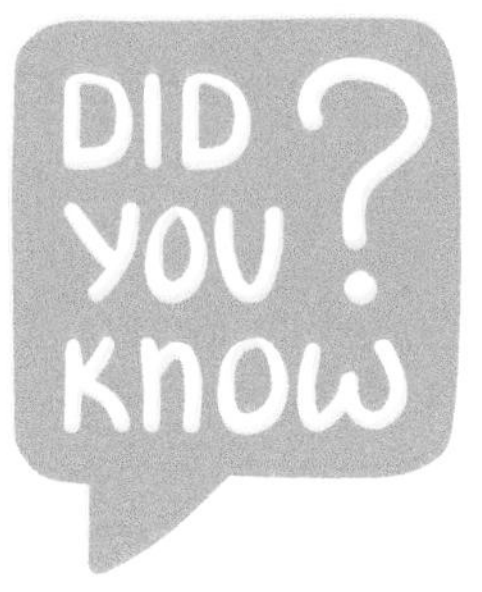

In the early eras of humanity, dance knowledge was commonly transferred through oral tradition from generation to generation, and from body to body. In Europe especially, there were limited manuscripts with in-depth analysis of artistic practices and instructional writings on how to create dance. Pierre Rameau's treatise *Le Maître á danser* (1725) is an eminent source of 18th-century dance technique focusing on the appropriate manner of walking, feet positions, types of bows, and vocabulary of steps. In choreography, Noverre's 1760 book *Lettres sur la danse et sur les ballets (Letters on Dancing and Ballets)* is considered the first European textbook on creative practices in ballet choreography.

The professionalization of dance and its reframing as the embodiment of *cultural status* in France during the Baroque period was caused by exceptional circumstances and set a unique historic precedent: the head of state—King Louis XIV—was an avid dancer devoted to ballet! Therefore, in a short period of time, an enormous amount of resources and funding were poured into the development of the art form. Dance was implemented in many aspects of life and, in a sense, functioned as a state-run enterprise.

French court and aristocracy created a unique cultural phenomenon and dance genre called "ballet." Ballet was a new type of Baroque dance spectacle that reflected and captured the rules of court life and etiquette and the importance of chivalry in society at that time. It also served as a means of exposure to society for the nobility. The new dance genre articulated high ideals and formal principles. Ballet was the living embodiment of anatomic intelligence, physical communication, and visual satisfaction. With the fast-changing political interests and ideals during the Renaissance and late Baroque period, ballet became the most appropriate dance aesthetic to frame a *dance experience* as an elite *cultural experience*. Through time, ballet as a genre would also prove flexible enough to serve different social classes and unify them under its newly invented code of beauty.

Historically, dance and choreography have always functioned within particular socio-economics, which at that time were developing unevenly in different regions of the world. In the later medieval and early Renaissance period, continental geographic distances and lingering human migration prevented the interaction and integration of cultures. However, *exploration of new lands and their colonization* caused redistribution of territorial ownership and domination of native and immigrant populations.

Therefore, the parameters of what would constitute a cultural construct, belonging, and identity were uniformly experienced across the world. Only in the 19th century and the first half of the 20th century did philosophers and anthropologists finally address the uniqueness in the distinctions of cultures in an effort to avoid global *Westernization* and *ethnocentrism*: Human creativity in various national and native cultures was to be understood not only within a universal framework and general definitions, but also in the context of particular cultural conditions. Cultural values were finally contemplated in the environment of the particular human group. Today, the term culture is used within three distinct contexts:

➢ Culture is a cluster of characteristics and features that identify a certain human group based on their common customs, shared beliefs, traditions, norms, and values, for instance: "This is the culture of our community."

➢ Culture is a cluster of accomplishments and the manifestation of the collective achievements in the arts, sciences, education, politics, and humanities of a particular group and society, for instance—"Let's experience culture by visiting our national gallery."

➢ Culture is a cluster of unique and newly cultivated activities (ways of functioning), abilities (ways of proficiency), and actions (ways of accomplishing a goal) emerging as a response to societal conditions, demands, behaviors, and attitudes, for instance—"The current ecological crisis requires a new environmental culture."

Culture and dance, especially in the context of the choreographic practices, are discussed throughout this book: for culture and tradition—see the *Prologue* of this book; for culture and transcultural society, see Chapter 7; for culture and the artistic mindset, see Chapter 9; for culture and aesthetic norms, see Chapter 10; for cultural appropriation and multiculturalism, see Chapter 12; for culture and creative identity, see Chapter 13; for culture and movement systems, see Chapter 14; for culture in communication and branding, see Chapter 23.

?

In what context do you use the term "culture" and what is your understanding of it?

When addressing "choreographing culture" in a broad context, multiple factors should be taken in consideration, including *cultural constructs, uniqueness, and belonging*. These factors could be set or fluid, shaped or reshaped dynamically, via mutual influences and interactions between the individual and collective—the "I" and the "We." These factors are addressed separately below:

◆ ***Cultural construct*** refers to inherited or newly emerged belief systems, common interests, mutual customs, and norms that are usually consolidated and manifested as a cluster of values, characteristics, and features.

◆ ***Cultural uniqueness*** refers to the particularities and specificities that shape the values, characteristics, and features of a culture, as original and distinct.

◆ ***Cultural belonging*** is twofold integration that is similar to the two sides of one coin. First, there is the cultural identity of the "I"—meaning the individual cultivates *selfness* and *otherness*. This factor relates to one's accepting and adopting affiliation and commitment to a certain culture, while considering and consolidating similarities and differences between one's personal views and the culture.

Secondly, there is the cultural identity of the "We"—meaning to collectively cultivate *oneness* and *manyness*. These factors relate to contemplating or contriving influences and transformations initiated collectively or by an individual, leading to retaining or reframing patterns, customs, and traits—see the diagram on the following page.

HELPFUL TIPS & SUGGESTIONS

~ Treat culture as capturing the collective "WE" rather than the individual "ME"

~ Bear in mind that a cultural experience cannot be forced, but only encountered

~ Consider that a unique culture is shaped by unique heritage and experiences

~ Approach culture as a religion but without the cult of one god or person

~ Embrace culture that shapes values, and values that determine the future

~ Grow culture by offering groundbreaking ideas; change culture by editing them

~ Think of symbols as systems of abstract and stylized concepts; think of cultures as systems of existence

CHOREOGRAPHING CULTURE AS AN OPERATING CONCEPT BEYOND HISTORIC FRAMEWORK

Cultural construct, uniqueness, belonging and identity "interact choreographically" with the factors of selfness and otherness, oneness and manyness. The "I" is the individual's unique cultural self-expression—*selfness*—that also contains adopted multiplicity of viewpoints and perspectives—*otherness*. The "We" is the collective cultural expression of unique values, characteristics, and features—*oneness*—that also contains influences and contributions of many individuals to formulate and adopt existing and new traditions—*manyness.*

Figuratively speaking, *the artist* as an individual can be compared to a foot soldier or a military commander who serves in a large army unit—*the culture*. The artist functions as an independent entity within the group and at the same time, as a part of a bigger independent group entity. These two entities consensually *belong* to each other. They also depend on each other through their shared interests, which could be set or fluid, shaped or reshaped dynamically by mutual influences (Figure 10).

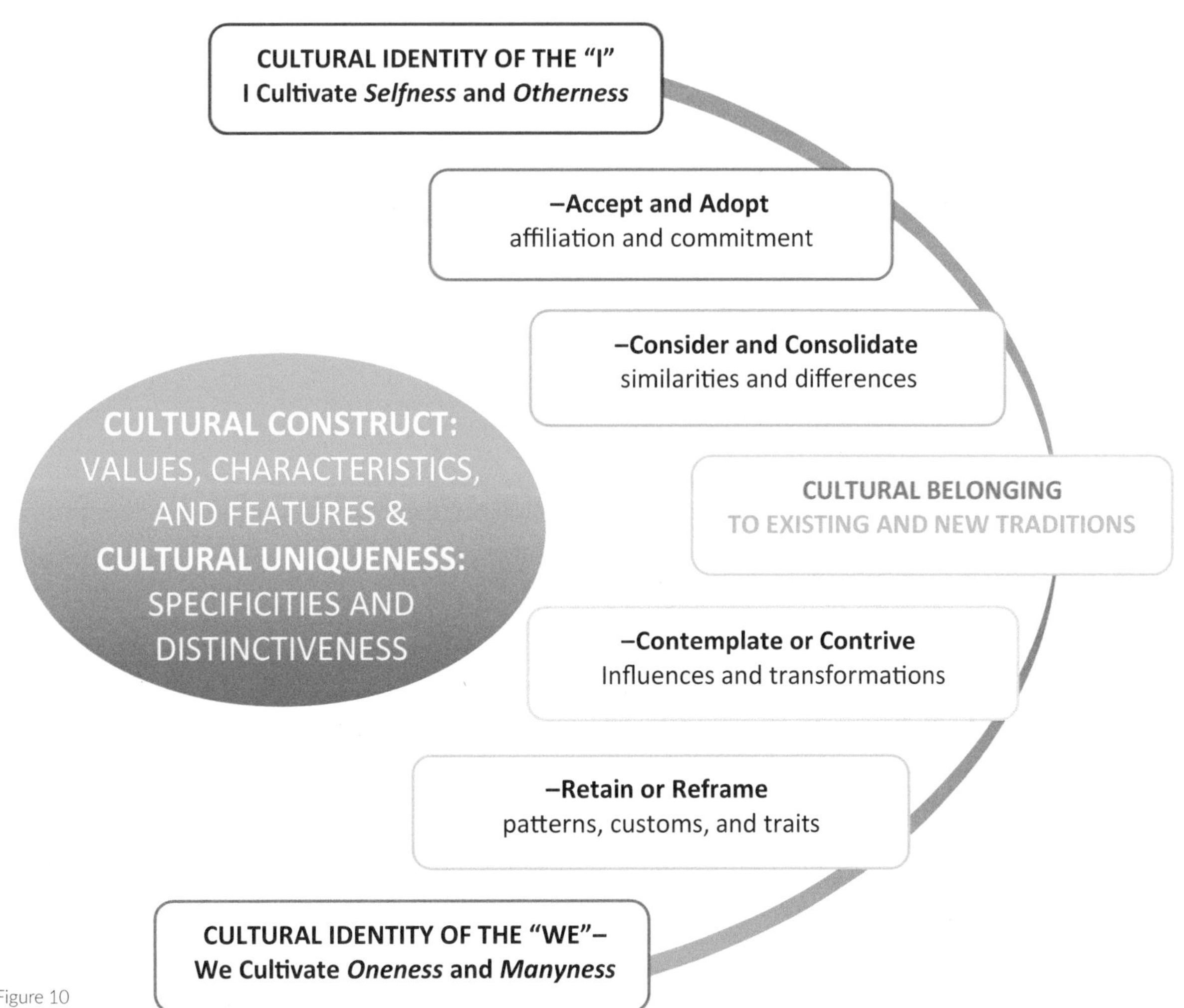

Figure 10

assignments & exercises

RESEARCH ASSIGNMENT: Use library, online, and video resources to research Renaissance and Baroque dance forms in practice today. There are clubs, societies, schools, and dance groups that specialize in reconstruction and practice of historic dance of Europe. Locate one in your area. a) Using the available resources, choose and learn a short Baroque court dance sequence. b) Create a worksheet and use notecards to outline the flow of distinct movement vocabulary used by the arms and legs. Explore how the dance sequence was created by using and repeating only a few steps and gestures. c) Analyze and mark in your journal how and why Baroque dance movements give the impression of "royalty" during the performance of this kind of dance. What makes the dance postures project formality, nobility, and respect?

★ **CREATIVE EXERCISE:** Create your own court dance inspired by and to serve as a royal dance for your nation that you created for the assignment in Chapter 3:

➡ Draw on the dance studio floor a "geo-choreo-map" similar to a hopscotch alley drawing or a Baroque dance notation sheet. Use colored sheets of paper to write simple, specific movement instructions like: *glide*, *pivot*, *hop*, *turn*, and *bow*. Then spread the sheets out across the floor and connect them with colored masking tape.

➡ Choreograph a sequence that can be performed by two dancers as they follow each other by starting at the different points on your "dance map."

➡ Involve a secondary choreography of another "dance map" with a different layer on top of your preliminary map, which functions independently and yet in harmony with the first one. Different dancers should use different layers of paper. Engage a dance partner(s) to learn and perform it. Focus on mobility, posture, and etiquette.

COMPARATIVE ASSIGNMENT: Research two or more distinct historic court, royal, or aristocratic dance systems belonging to countries other than France and genres other than ballet. For example, you could choose the Japanese movement theater "Noh" and "Kabuki," the Indian movement theater "Kathakali," and/or the Indonesian court dances of Java, Bali, and Malaysia that reflect both Islamic and Hindu religions. Analyze and describe in your journal the distinction between the subjects, movement expression, music, costumes, and scenery of your choices. Identify in your journal the similarities and the differences in court and folkloric dance performance modules by referring to the previous chapter.

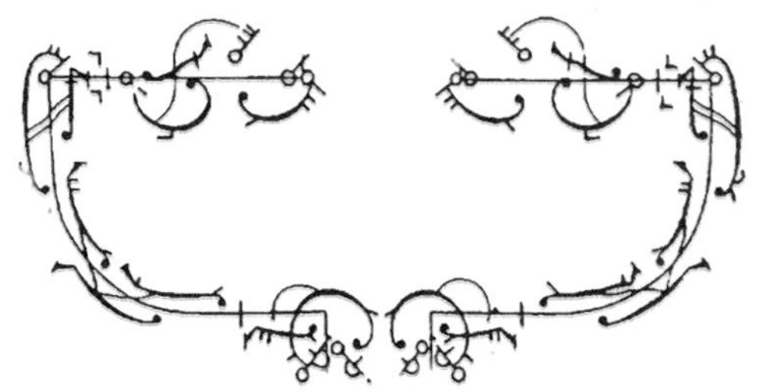

BIBLIOGRAPHY AND REFERENCES

[1] Editors. "Renaissance," *Etymology Online Dictionary*, www.etymonline.com/word/renaissance, accessed May 2021.
[2] Gould, George Milbry and Pyle, Walter Lytle. "Historic Epidemics," in *Anomalies and Curiosities of Medicine*, Blacksleet River, 1896, ISBN 978-1-4499-7722-1. Archived from the original on September 12, 2008, accessed May 2020.
[3] Burke, Peter. *The Italian Renaissance: Culture and Society in Italy*, Princeton University Press, 1999.
[4] Wiesner-Hanks, Merry E. *Early Modern Europe, 1450–1789*, Cambridge University Press, 2006, p. 32, p. 122.
[5] Anderson, Jack. *Ballet and Modern Dance: A Concise History*, Princeton Book Publishing, 1992, p. 35.
[6] Editors of Encyclopedia. "Renaissance Man," in *Encyclopedia Britannica*, 09.13.2020, www.britannica.com/topic/Renaissance-man, accessed May 2021.
[7] Cicéron, Marcus Tullius Cicero and Bouhier, Jean. *Tusculanes*, J. Gaude, 1812, p. 273.
[8] Editors of Encyclopedia. "Baroque Art and Architecture," in *Encyclopedia Britannica*, 01.31.2021, www.britannica.com/art/Baroque-art-and-architecture, accessed May 2021.
[9] Anderson 1992. *Ballet and Modern Dance: A Concise History*, pp. 34–36.
[10] Pierce, Sophie. "The History of Masquerade Balls," *Avas Flowers*, accessed November 9, 2017.
[11] Johnson, James H. *Venice Incognito: Masks in the Serene Republic*, University of California Press, 2011, p. 54, pp. 79–85.
[12] Johnson 2011, *Venice Incognito: Masks in the Serene Republic*, pp. 3–12.
[13] Sim, Catherine. *Renaissance Court Dance in Italy and France*, 2012, online article: https://dancetimepublications.com, accessed May 2021.
[14] Editors. "Renaissance Dance," collection: *An American Ballroom Companion: Dance Instruction Manuals*, ca. 1490 to 1920, Library of Congress, 2021, including reconstruction and video clips reenactment demonstration of Thoinot Arbeau's *Orchesographie* from 1588, accessed May 2021.
[15] Homans, Jennifer. *Apollos' Angels: A History of Ballet*, Random House, 2010, pp. 3–5.
[16] Anderson 1992. *Ballet and Modern Dance: A Concise History*, p. 31.
[17] Anderson 1992. *Ballet and Modern Dance: A Concise History*, pp. 31–33.
[18] Anderson 1992. *Ballet and Modern Dance: A Concise History*, p. 33.
[19] Anderson 1992. *Ballet and Modern Dance: A Concise History*, p. 38.
[20] Anderson 1992. *Ballet and Modern Dance: A Concise History*, p. 39.
[21] Anderson 1992. Ballet and Modern Dance: *A Concise History*, p. 40.
[22] Anderson 1992. *Ballet and Modern Dance: A Concise History*, pp. 41–42.
[23] Prest, Julia. "Dancing King: Louis XIV's Roles in Molière's Comedies-Ballets, from Court to Town," *Seventeenth Century*, vol. 16, no. 2, 2001, pp. 283–298.
[24] Anderson 1992. *Ballet and Modern Dance: A Concise History*, p. 42.
[25] Anderson 1992. *Ballet and Modern Dance: A Concise History*, p. 43.
[26] Homans 2010. *Apollos' Angels: A History of Ballet*, pp. 15–16.
[27] Homans 2010. *Apollos' Angels: A History of Ballet*, pp. 22–24.
[28] Anderson 1992. *Ballet and Modern Dance: A Concise History*, p. 44.
[29] Prest 2001. "Dancing King," pp. 283–298.
[30] Anderson 1992. *Ballet and Modern Dance: A Concise History*, p. 40.
[31] Anderson 1992. *Ballet and Modern Dance: A Concise History*, pp. 55–59.
[32] Anderson 1992. *Ballet and Modern Dance: A Concise History*, pp. 60–61.
[33] Homans 2010. *Apollos' Angels: A History of Ballet*, pp. 74–79.
[34] Homans 2010. *Apollos' Angels: A History of Ballet*, pp. 73–74.
[35] Anderson 1992. *Ballet and Modern Dance: A Concise History*, pp. 55–56.
[36] Yates, Frances. *The Valois Tapestries*. 1959. London: Routledge & Kegan Paul, 1999, pp. 102, 121–122.
[37] Editors of Encyclopedia. "Pierre Beauchamp," in *Encyclopedia Britannica*, 01.01.2021, www.britannica.com/biography/Pierre-Beauchamp, accessed May 2021.

VISUAL REFERENCES

Figure 1: *The Royal Ballet of the Dowager of Bilbao's Grand Ball*, artwork by Daniel Rabel, 1626, The Louvre museum collection, public domain

Figure 2: *Galerie des Glaces* — Hall of Mirrors in the Palace of Versailles, Versailles, France. Photo credit: Myrabella, Wikimedia Commons/ CC BY-SA 3.0

Figure 3: A couple in masks with beautiful costumes at carnival in Venice, credit RelaxFoto.de, courtesy of iStock/Getty Images

Figure 4: *Ballet Comique de la Reine, Grande Salle du Petit-Bourbon*, illustration by Jacques Patin, 1587, image derived from Gallica, 2010, public domain

Figure 5: Diagram © Vladimir Angelov

Figure 6: *Portrait of Louis XIV of France*, art work by Hyacinthe Rigaud, 1700–1701, Louvre Museum collection, public domain

Figure 7: *Mademoiselle de Camargo Dancing* (fragment), art work by Nicholas Lancret, 1730, The Wallace Collection, public domain

Figure 8: Diagram © Vladimir Angelov

Figure 9: Diagram © Vladimir Angelov, including *Grand Coat of Arms of France and Navarre*: from 1589 to 1790. From the ascension of Henry III of Navarre as Henry IV of France (first King of the House of Bourbon) to the changing of Louis XVI's title as King of France and Navarre to King of the French (heraldry and coat of arms having been abolished in France 1790); and *Coat of Arms of France and Navarre*; author: Sodacan, October 15, 2009, Wikimedia Commons

Figure 10: Diagram © Vladimir Angelov

Those are my limbs dancing; I am waking up.

The Devil's Elixirs, a novel by E.T.A. Hoffmann,

Berlin, 1815

CHAPTER 5

INDUSTRIAL AGE:

DANCING THE SELF – CHOREOGRAPHING EXPRESSION –

The Industrial Age in Europe and the Americas, also known as the Industrial Revolution, spanned approximately from the second half of the 18th century through the 19th century and into the beginning of the 20th century. The rising demand for goods stimulated the establishment of the *commercial economy*, as the population migrated into urban areas. Factories and assembly lines enabled mass production. Rapidly growing cities and the broad financial expansion created a new societal structure—the *middle class*. Owning a home and raising large families provided certain social independence. Ordinary citizens gradually demanded better education as means of social mobility.[1]

Following the French Revolution and the Napoleonic era, the reorganization of the economy and society also fostered and provided a broader spectrum of political structures. Introduced were new *political trends* such as liberalism, nationalism, and anarchism, as well as new *political systems* such as constitutional monarchies, dictatorships, fascism, and socialism, which had not existed before. Industrial science and technology led to the use of materials like rubber, aluminum, petroleum, and oil. The invention of the light bulb and the distribution of electricity changed the nightlife in the cities. With advancements in engineering, the oceans became populated with transatlantic ships; the countryside with fast-moving trains; the cities with automobiles and streetcars; and the sky with airplanes. Architecture flourished with the building of railroads, massive bridges, and the first all-steel-framed skyscrapers. The invention of the telegraph, the telephone, and the radio transformed society, enabling an instantaneous exchange of information and mass communication across great distances.[2]

Inventions in dance, especially in the late 19th and early 20th centuries, included stage presentations, which nowadays might be considered "dance installations" or "performance art" rather than "pure dance." One of those artists/inventors of stage effects was Loïe Fuller, who was also referred to as a "creature of light."

Isadora Duncan, who was briefly a member of Loïe Fuller's dance company, testified that Loie was radically inventive and incomparable when it came to achieving subtlety and visual impact with her stage effects. Fuller never intended to tell a story through dance. Instead, her choreography aimed to create lyrical moods and imitate physical phenomena, such as atmospheric illuminations, flowers, and insects. Fuller became a regular performer at Paris's Folies-Bergère—poster of Fuller at left—where she also created an extensive amount of work. Her creative vision inspired numerous French writers, painters, and intellectuals.[3]

Figure 1 *Folies Bergère Loïe Fuller*, poster artwork by Jean de Paleologu, 1893

Discoveries in astronomy and physics, such as Albert Einstein's *theory of relativity*, provided a new frame of reference to explain the physical world. The early stages of new art forms, such as photography and cinematography, emerged in the 19th century, subsequently leading to the 20th-century film industry, television, and computerization.[4]

European poetry and literature of the 19th century offered new aesthetic platforms such as *naturalism*, *sentimentalism*, and *realism* reflecting details of social life. *Romanticism*, on the other hand, was a movement for spontaneity, mystery, and optimism. Early 20th-century literature introduced new trends such as *symbolism*, *modernism*, and *structuralism*. Writers challenged the existing norms by infusing into their work never-before-used subjects such as political conflict, social injustice, sex, and the human subconscious.[5]

Visual artists searched for alternative ways to see and paint the world and people, giving birth to *impressionism*, *expressionism*, *surrealism*, and *abstractionism*. Composers experimented with atonal compositions and the *twelve-tone technique*, searching for unique sonic qualities. The introduction of Sigmund Freud's *psychoanalysis* unlocked the doors to the subconscious, the irrational, and the instinctual. The study of human behavior became a new frontier.[6]

THE RISE OF INDIVIDUALISM, CRITICAL THINKING, AND FREEDOM OF EXPRESSION

One of the Industrial Age's most vital contributions to society and the arts in Europe and the Americas was the emergence of *civil liberties* and an individual's *freedom of expression*. The actual legal terms and the Universal Declaration of Human Rights were not adopted as international law until 1948.[7] However, a century earlier, humanitarians, philosophers, and artists began demanding the right to live, create, and speak without fear.

Philosophy encouraged the separation of state from religion and emphasized reason, skepticism, and scientific thought. Ethical judgment of what was good and evil, right and wrong, was finally removed from the church's control and secured by the federal states and the law. Morality was becoming less religious and more societal. "God is dead!" proclaimed philosopher Friedrich Nietzsche in his 1880s writings, marking an intellectual shift in morality—from external sources like God to internal human consciousness. The newly emerging frame of mind linked the *rise of individualism* with freedom of expression.

TIME TRAVEL	Reality was driven by	Progress was driven by	Art was driven by
MEDIEVAL AGE	God	God	Symbol
RENAISSANCE AGE	Individual	The King	Culture
INDUSTRIAL AGE	Individual	Individual	Expression

Figure 2

During the Renaissance, choreographers were predominantly oriented toward encyclopedic and analytical thinking. Yet their work was expected to comply with the wishes of the patrons funding the arts and culture. In contrast, during the Industrial Age, choreographers were empowered with broader institutional and societal freedom—artistic and personal—than their predecessors. This new state of the self and freedom of expression led to the rise of critical thinking.

Compared to *analytical thinking*, which is grounded in observations, evidence gathering, examinations, and conclusions based on facts, *critical thinking* is primarily concerned with evaluating, judging the truth of statements, and seeking errors. Critical thinking also involves imagination and enables the emergence of alternative ideas that could arise from personal perspectives, interpretations, and opinions. This new construct empowered choreographers to gain full artistic control over their creative work, create the dances they wanted to create, and express the world as they saw it—even if those visions were *ethereal*, *surreal*, and *unreal*.

French Romanticism in art and literature during the 19th century infused ballet with the fascination of the non-rational, the magical, and the supernatural. Ghosts, spirits, elves, and dreamlike creatures began to populate the dance stage, entering the lives of ordinary people to reveal relationships between daily human life and the mysterious, spiritual world. At the same time, the new availability of long-distance travel sparked the audience's curiosity to journey to exotic places and encounter lesser-known cultures, stories, and dances—if not in person, then on stage. The storylines of French and consequent Russian ballets were often purposely set in other countries, such as Spain, Italy, Egypt, and India.[8]

Advancements in dance techniques also contributed to the expressive range of dance. By the early 1800s, a typical daily dance class was very similar to the structure of a ballet class today. The movement sequences included repetition to the right and left, and the dance was organized under a strategic physical goal called a *dance syllabus*.[9]

The French Impressionist painter Edgar Degas (1834–1917) depicted dancers of his time as one of his favorite subjects. The paintings sold well and provided him with needed income. His *La classe de danse (The dance class)*, image left, captured dancers and their teacher during daily training.[10]

Dance lessons would typically continue from one and a half to three hours, followed by numerous repetitions to perfect dance technique. The day then continued with rehearsals of the current ballet repertory. The purpose of this rigorous training and the heavy workload was to improve the dancers' skills and challenge the limits of the human body by exposing the dancers to excessive physical difficulties. The goal was to make dancing on stage look impeccable and effortless.[11]

Figure 3 *La classe de danse*, art work by Edgar Degas, 1875, courtesy of Musée d'Orsay

ROMANTIC BALLETS
– CHOREOGRAPHING MYSTERIES AND GHOSTS –

A pivotal point in ballet during the French Romanticism era was the production of *La Sylphide*, which premiered on March 12, 1832, at the Salle Le Peletier of the Paris Opéra. The music was composed by Jean-Madeleine Schneitzhoeffer, and the ballet's libretto was written by Adolphe Nourrit. The plot of this two-act ballet tells the story of an impossible love between a human and a spirit. On the morning of his wedding day, a Scottish farmer named James falls in love with the captivating vision and spirit of a magical sylph. In an effort to keep the sylph for his own and win her love, James causes her wings to fall off, which to his dismay and surprise leads to her death.[12]

The Italian choreographer **Filippo Taglioni** created this ballet to showcase his daughter, Marie. While experimenting artistically with her, Taglioni did not anticipate that he would be giving his daughter the most celebrated role of her career. For the role of the sylph, Marie Taglioni wore the typical "romantic" bell-shaped white dress, cut just below the knees, with a wasp waist and sleeves puffed at the shoulders. A flower headpiece adorned her hair. Her most important accessory, however, was her pair of shoes, which would lead to the introduction of a new expressive dance technique that would change the future of ballet: *pointe technique*.[13]

Marie Taglioni delivered an astonishing en pointe performance in *La Sylphide*! As she portrayed the magical, ghostly creature, she appeared to glide weightlessly through the air. Filippo Taglioni's idea to use *en pointe* led to an ultimate balance between dance technique and artistic expression and the total choreographic embodiment of the stage character's movement characteristics. The pointe shoe technique became the first significant artistic device in ballet choreography to express the vitality of a dancing sylph, fairy or spirit, in such a profoundly romantic manner. Taglioni's light and effortless *en pointe* dancing rapidly popularized the new technique across Europe.[14]

Taglioni's pointe shoes were made by Janssen in Paris and were not the same as those we know today. The shoes had no box to protect the toe, but rather were adapted satin slippers heavily darned on the toe tip, and with leather on the sides to keep the shoe intact. There was no direct support other than the strength of the feet and ankles. Taglioni was able to go *en pointe* only during *relevé* on two feet, *arabesques*, *attitudes*, and *bourrées*, purposely avoiding extended dance sequences to protect her feet.

Latter modification of the pointe shoes in Italy and Russia led to the inclusion of a box with layers of fabric to contain the toes and a stiffer, stronger sole.[15] Although pointe emerged in the Romantic Era, ballet choreographers and dancers nowadays extensively use the *en pointe* technique in their neoclassical and contemporary ballets. *En pointe* has become the symbol and the embodiment of ballet.

Figure 4 *La Sylphide/Souvenir d'Adieu/de/Marie Taglioni*, art drawing by Edward Morton, 1845, The British Museum, a rendition courtesy of Wikipedia Commons

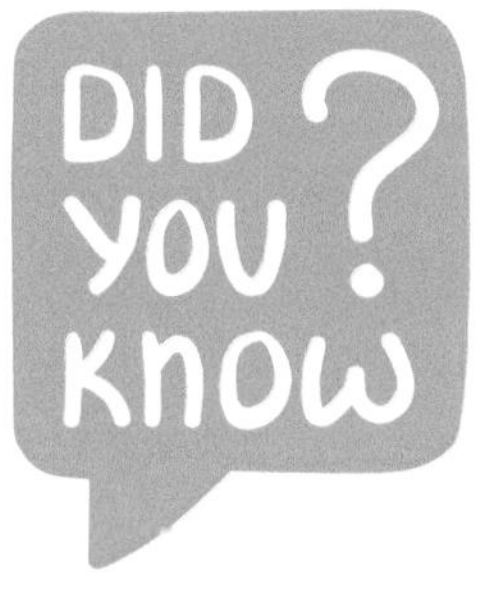

There is no specific person credited as the "inventor" of the pointe shoe. Before Taglioni, many ballerinas in the early 1800s experimented with elevating their bodies and maintaining their balance on the tips of their toes to accommodate more turns and body spins. Ballet training at that time was divided into two opposite camps: the technical–to improve jumps, turns, and suspension; and the expressive–to represent advanced acting and authentic stage characters driving the ballet plot forward.[16] The introduction of dancing *en pointe* helped bridge that divide over time, resulting in a change in how ballet was perceived, and proving that ballet as a form could be both expressive and technical at the same time.

The success of *La Sylphide* quickly spread across Europe and drew the attention of ballet companies and choreographers from other countries. One of them was **August Bournonville**. He was fascinated by the story of *La Sylphide* and the themes of bourgeois domesticity because of the intellectual influence of a key family friend who was not a highly skilled dancer but rather a great writer: Hans Christian Andersen.[17] Bournonville trained in Paris in his early years, and from 1820 to 1828, he danced with Marie Taglioni at the Paris Opéra Ballet. He then returned home and took over the Danish Royal Ballet, which he directed from 1830 to 1877.[18] Bournonville decided to stage his own version of *La Sylphide* in Denmark. Still, when he asked for permission to use the music, the Paris Opéra demanded too high a price. Bournonville then collaborated with the Norwegian composer Herman Severin Løvenskiold on a new score. That 1836 version of Bournonville's *La Sylphide* is the well-known production still widely performed today.[19]

Besides *La Sylphide*, Bournonville choreographed numerous ballets, most notably *Napoli* (1842), *Le Conservatoire* (1849), and *A Folk Tale* (1854). But what was unique about Bournonville's expressive choreographic style? His ballets were about ordinary people dancing their daily lives. Gestures were sincere, and the dance flowed like a smooth conversation. The scale was modest yet intimate and touching. A small leap would portray excitement of the heart; a graceful twist of the shoulders—an *épaulement*—would indicate flirtation among youngsters; and a bolder jump would send a charming signal for attention and affection. The phrasing of Bournonville's choreography was key: the steps were virtuosic, yet never overdone. When a jump was executed, it wouldn't be to show off but to move from one point to another with genuine emotion. Women were treated equally to men by the choreographer—they danced the same movement phrasing as men, but with an affectionate innocence and child-like vitality. The arms were held low and close to the torso to help launch the body into the air, while the feet executed fast and intricate beats during jumps—*entrechat quatre* and *royale*. The energetic lightness and exuberance of such dancing became the signature of Bournonville's choreographic style.[20]

The era of Romantic ballet reached its peak with *Giselle*, which premiered on June 28, 1841, at the Ballet du Théâtre de l'Académie Royale de Musique in Paris. Set to music by Adolphe Adam, Giselle was choreographed for Carlotta Grisi by **Jules Perrot**, Grisi's former dance partner and lover, and **Jean Coralli**, who also danced one of the roles. The libretto was written by Jules-Henri Vernoy de Saint-Georges and Théophile Gautier, who was one of the most prominent writers of that time.[21]

The first act is set in a village. Giselle, a joyful peasant girl with a passion for dancing, finds out that Albrecht, her lover, is engaged to someone else. Giselle dies dramatically of a broken heart. The second act takes place in the moonlit forest, where Giselle's spirit dances along with the ghostly Wilis—young women who have died of unrequited love. Even in death, Giselle protects Albrecht, who finally realizes his passionate feelings towards Giselle and the pain caused by losing her.[22]

The choreographic structure of *Giselle* was ingeniously varied, juxtaposing dance scenes and intense dramatic twists. Hearty peasant dances in the first act were intentionally contrasted with the ghostly movements of the Wilis in the second act, also known as the "white act," because the dancers wore white dresses. Under Jules Perrot's supervision, *Giselle* was restaged by Marius Petipa for the Imperial Russian Ballet and revived multiple times in the 1880s.[23] Petipa's version of *Giselle* is the one we know today. Most accomplished dancers have performed the role of Giselle, including Anna Pavlova, Margot Fonteyn, and Gelsey Kirkland. Famous dancers of Albrecht's role include Marius Petipa's brother and the first dancer of the role—Lucien Petipa, Vaslav Nijinsky, Rudolf Nureyev, and Mikhail Baryshnikov, among many others.

The last great production of the Romantic Era, *Coppélia*, was choreographed by **Arthur Saint-Léon** to music by Léo Delibes and libretto by Charles Nuitter. The ballet premiered on May 25, 1870. The story of *Coppélia* unfolds around a mysterious inventor, Doctor Coppelius, who makes a life-size dancing doll. Like the preceding Romantic ballet productions, the dramatic content of *Coppélia* was driven by many vivid characters. The music, choreography, and mime kept the stage action and the audience on their toes.[24]

A new choreographic structural feature was introduced that became standard in the narrative and construct of most Romantic and Classical ballets: the *grand pas de deux*, from the French words *grand*, which translates as *large and magnificent*; *pas*, meaning *step*; *de*, meaning *for*, and *deux*, *two*. A *grand pas de deux* referred to a distinct, long dance for two people—see Figure 5.

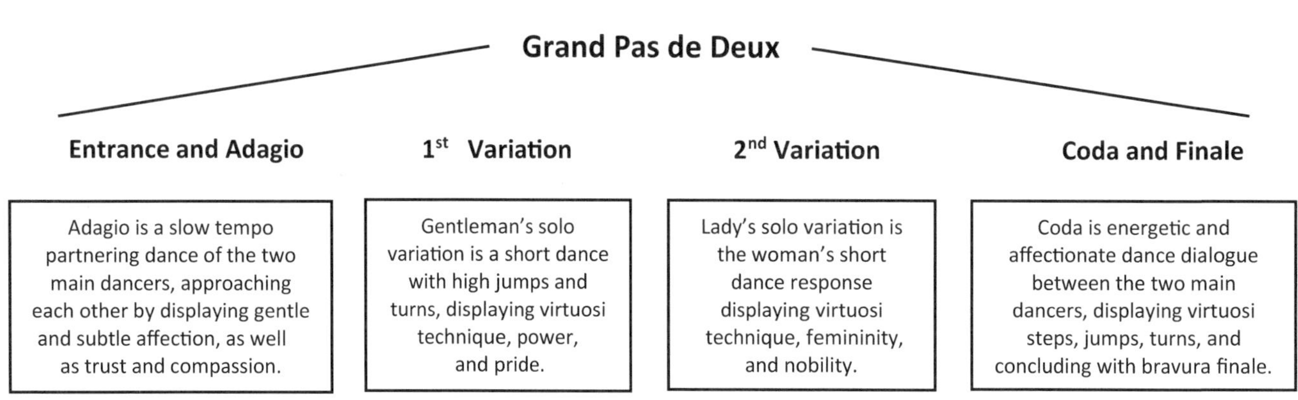

Figure 5

There was certain liberty in the placement and the timing of the *grand pas de deux* within each ballet, which was performed by the lead characters as the climax of the ballet. The choreographers tailored the steps, movements, and partnering to the abilities of the *premier danseurs*, taking into consideration the characteristics of their roles according to the ballet libretto.[25]

CLASSICAL BALLETS
– CHOREOGRAPHING MORAL DILEMMAS –

Imperial Russia gradually became the center of a new period in ballet known as Classicism. The choreographer who fully embodied the ideas and aesthetic of classical ballet was **Marius Petipa**. Born in Marseilles, France, in 1818 to a family of dancers, Petipa arrived at the St. Petersburg Imperial Theatres in 1847 as *premier danseur*, but on a modest salary. He worked in the shadow of Jules Perrot, the ballet director in St. Petersburg from 1849 to 1858 and the choreographer of *Giselle* and *Le Corsaire*. Petipa also served as ballet master under the subsequent director, Arthur Saint-Léon, the choreographer of *Coppélia*, who came to St. Petersburg in 1860 and departed in 1869.[26] A couple of years later, at age fifty-three, Petipa finally became entirely in charge of the world's largest ballet troupe at the time, which today still has a roster of more than two hundred dancers.

Petipa further developed and expanded the choreographic structure of the full-length story ballet by stretching the narrative over three or four acts, even if the story could have been told more concisely. In the narrative of ballet structure, Petipa inserted the so-called *divertissement*, which was a lively dance suite that often accommodated two opposite purposes: to advance the dance story by giving more information about a relationship and to expand the plot because a dance might represent part of a wedding, castle celebration, or brief entertainment for the royal visitors. These dance suites were often performed by the *demi-characters*, or the *corps de ballet*, while the climax of all of Petipa's full-length ballets—the *grand pas de deux*—continued to be performed by the *premier danseurs*.[27]

Petipa's most significant impact as a choreographer was replacing the intimacy, delicacy, and softness of the Romantic ballets when tackling stories with moral dilemmas. His productions mesmerized with their panoramic scale and dynamic sharpness. His ballets were full of mime, character dances, and contrasting lyrical and dramatic scenes. Petipa took artistic liberty and strived for the best possible choreographic effects, even if they were historically inaccurate. For example, in his ballet *The Daughter of the Pharaoh,* set to music of Pugni, Petipa placed an Egyptian princess in a tutu. This grand-style opera-ballet lasted more than four hours and incorporated waterfalls, camels, monkeys, and a lion. Petipa's take on *Don Quixote*, set to music by Minkus, turned into a light comedy ballet loosely based on the Cervantes novel.[28] Although the ballet carried the same name as the novel, the legendary knight was, in fact, featured as a minor character, while the attention was placed on the romantic relationship between two spirited youngers—Kitri and Basilio. Petipa also created a story ballet set in Royal India—*La Bayadère*—also to music by Minkus.

A signature scene called "The Kingdom of Shades" that featured the dancing ghosts of deceased maidens became wildly popular. The scene was inspired by an illustration from Dante's *Divine Comedy*. The vision of the dance took place in the mind of the warrior Solor, who loved a beautiful temple dancer—a *bayadère*. The ballerinas portraying the shades entered the stage, one by one, dressed identically and executing the same steps over and over again. The hypnotic repetition of the steps gradually built to a massive crescendo, with the entire stage full of dancers—all in perfect formation.[29]

Petipa tended to choose ballet librettos with vivid characters entangled in complex relationships and moral dilemmas that ultimately resulted in enlightenment prompted by love and duty. One of Petipa's most acclaimed ballets, which he staged at the age of almost seventy, was *Sleeping Beauty*, which was set to music by Tchaikovsky. The ballet included exquisitely danced court ceremonies portraying the growth of Princess Aurora: her royal birth, coming of age, wedding, and celebration. The magnificent production quickly became popular since it was a metaphorical summation of the Russian court of King Peter the Great. Petipa's next successful ballet was *The Nutcracker*, again to music by Tchaikovsky. The ballet was about a little girl's Christmas dream of a journey into the realm of the Sugar Plum Fairy. Soon after beginning the staging of *The Nutcracker*, Petipa became ill, so the ballet was completed by Petipa's closest collaborator and assistant, the Russian choreographer **Lev Ivanov**.[30]

Petipa's last great classical ballet was his version of *Swan Lake*, created in 1895 to music by Tchaikovsky and with revisions by his chief conductor, Drigo. The 1st and 3rd acts of the ballet were choreographed by Petipa himself, and the 2nd and 4th by Lev Ivanov. *Swan Lake* tells the story of Prince Siegfried, who encounters Odette during a hunting trip. Odette, the queen of white swans, has fallen under an evil spell. Later, Siegfried meets Odile at a ball, who is dressed as a black swan and pretends to be Odette. Deceived by her performance, Siegfried agrees to marry Odile. The story takes various dramatic turns, ultimately ending with the moral triumph of love over deception. In most versions, Odette commits suicide by drowning herself. Prince Siegfried chooses to die as well rather than live without her.[31]

Figure 6 Upper image: photography © Valentin Baranovsky, *Swan Lake*, choreography by Marius Petipa, pictured dancers Anastasia Kolegova and Maxim Zyuzin, 2010. Lower image: photography © Natasha Razina, *Swan Lake*, choreography by Marius Petipa, pictured dancers Anastasia Matvienko and Denis Matvienko, 2011; both images courtesy of State Mariinsky Theatre, St. Petersburg, Russia

The choreographic uniqueness of *Swan Lake* is revealed in the narrative complexity of the movement language: The opposite characters of Odette/Odile simultaneously portray human *and* animal qualities through the use of white *and* black swans. Petipa skillfully created a choreographic depiction of two swan princesses performing bird-like movements while also exhibiting contrasting earthly moral behaviors: Odette represents goodness, and Odile, the incarnation of evil. The lead role of Odette/Odile is still enormously demanding because it is often danced by the same ballerina. In the original casting, the Italian ballerina Pierina Legnani incorporated during the *grand pas de deux* consecutive axis spins, known as *fouettés*, that have become a landmark in ballet virtuosity.[32]

EARLY MODERN BALLET THEATER
– REINVENTING BALLET CHOREOGRAPHICALLY –

Following Petipa's classicism, ballet transformed and reemerged as a new, distinct form—*modern ballet theater*. The primary catalyst for this reinvention was Ballets Russes, the most innovative dance company of the early 20th century. Ballets Russes propelled the performing arts to new heights through groundbreaking collaborations between choreographers, dancers, composers, authors, visual artists, and fashion designers. Founded in Paris in 1909 by Russian impresario Serge Diaghilev (1872–1929), the company combined dance traditions of various cultures with a rich dose of modernism and a powerful fusion of innovative choreography, music sets, and costumes.

"*Astonish me, Jean*!" Diaghilev ordered Jean Cocteau, a young collaborating artist and writer working with Ballets Russes. Diaghilev was energized by bold artistic experiments—his impolitic and intellectual arrogance often intimidated his associates.[33] In addition to his unorthodox taste in art, charming sense of humor, and workaholic temperament, Diaghilev had an exceptional intuition and a remarkable ability to identify and bring together the most innovative artists of his day. Recognizing the vitality of contemporary art, he called upon Léon Bakst, Natalia Goncharova, Pablo Picasso, Joan Miró, Henri Matisse, and Coco Chanel, among others, to create unique set designs and exquisitely decorated costumes. These artists, in turn, brought to the ballet stage the most radical artistic ideas and trends of the early 20th century, including futurism, cubism, and surrealism.

Diaghilev commissioned ballet music and original scores by highly innovative composers such as Igor Stravinsky, Sergei Prokofiev, Erik Satie, Claude Debussy, Manuel de Falla, and Maurice Ravel. Featured choreographers and dancers noted for their technical brio and astounding creativity made the company a breeding ground for musical and choreographic discoveries. Diaghilev engaged five groundbreaking choreographers: Michel Fokine, Vaslav Nijinsky, Léonide Massine, Bronislava Nijinska, and George Balanchine, all of whom invented new movement vocabulary and expanded the range of dance expression. In the 20-year period of the company's existence, Diaghilev and his Ballets Russes transformed romantic and classical ballet into modern art!

One of the signature works in the company's repertory was *The Rite of Spring* (1913) by Ballets Russes' most controversial choreographer—**Vaslav Nijinsky**. The ballet tells the story of a prehistoric tribe experiencing the arrival of spring and reaches its climax when a chosen maiden must dance herself to death to please the gods. The initial idea of staging was to historically explore the ritual within the setting of ancient pagan Russia. The costumes and set design by Nicholas Roerich suited the libretto accordingly. However, Nijinsky's interpretation and choreography soon expanded beyond the historic ritual narrative and suggested that primordial psychic forces might be buried within anyone at any time. *The Rite of Spring* was about the death of an individual and its celebration by the collective spirit. The quintessence of the ballet narrative was the question: *Are we prepared to sacrifice ourselves for the good of others*?

The choreography of *Rite of Spring* resembled an early dance ritual. Unlike a linear narrative, the dance was driven by a cumulative sequence of short choreographic episodes. These included: awaiting and greeting the sunrise, a stomping tribal dance, a ceremonial abduction of the "Chosen One," a solemn procession by the high priest, and finally, the chosen maiden's tormented solo dancing to her death. The movements were non-balletic and erratic. Inspired by *the freed movement* of the early Isadora Duncan, Nijinsky choreographed angular shapes and jerky movements. The dancers would spin furiously in round formations, then were spontaneously thrust out of the ring and thrown into a frantic jumping sequence.

The choreography was often uncomfortable, and even intentionally chaotic, as the arms would follow one trajectory and the legs another. Nijinsky kept an overall solid and comprehensive structure to his ballet despite the unconventional movement vocabulary, with a narrative that was easy to follow. This brave artistic experiment expanded ballet as a genre and reaffirmed that ballet had the capacity to stretch further, modify, and transform under a compassionate choreographic vision.[34]

Afternoon of a Faun (1912) was another signature work of Ballets Russes. Based on Stéphane Mallarmé's poem, it was choreographed and danced by Vaslav Nijinsky to music by Claude Debussy. The costumes were created by Léon Bakst—drawing from the original program cover at left. The dance was only about eleven minutes long and reflected self-absorbed physical instincts. The story unfolded during an afternoon, when a nymph escaped from an amorous fawn, dropping a scarf in her haste. The fawn then slowly lay down upon the scarf, with gestures hinting at fetishism and sexual enactment.

The ballet was performed only eight times and then cancelled because of its alleged obscenity. Nijinsky worked on this ballet patiently and deliberately for two years to invent the unique two-dimensional angular postures and "frozen" positions—some movement vocabulary was drawn from ancient Greek art. Although lacking an immediate bravura effect of classical ballet virtuosity, the physical language still required a lot of muscular discipline to accomplish a cinematically captivating pictorial stream.[35]

Figure 7 Vaslav Fomich Nijinsky in the ballet *The Afternoon of a Faun*, drawing by Léon Bakst, 1912

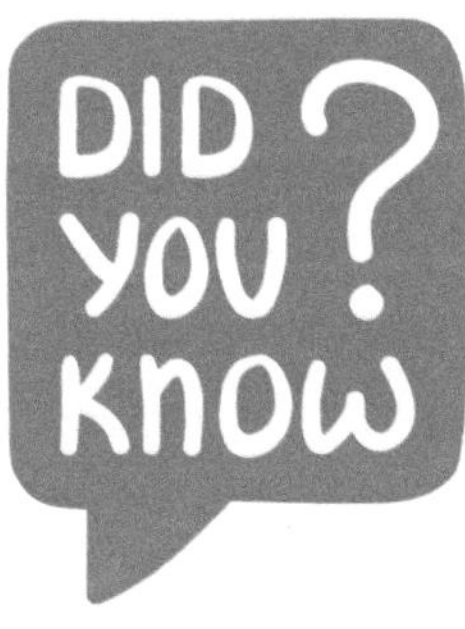

DID YOU KNOW THESE FACTS? BALLETS RUSSES...

- **became the first independent ballet company able to operate without the permanent financial patronage of a royal court.**
- **introduced the one-act ballet format that had a compact, dynamic, and modern feel. These ballets were less expensive to produce in comparison to the imperial ballet productions.**
- **invigorated choreographers to create original movement vocabulary for every dance production, associated with the specific libretto and music.**
- **attracted the most groundbreaking artists of the early 20th century in Europe and provided fertile ground for their collaborations.**
- **cultivated five groundbreaking choreographers in a time period of 20 years, compared to St. Petersburg Imperial Theaters, where Marius Petipa was the single chief choreographer for more than 30 years.**

EARLY MODERN DANCE
– CHOREOGRAPHIC INDIVIDUALISM VERSUS INSTITUTIONALISM –

During the late Industrial Age, countries of substantial political influence and wealth, such as the United States and Germany, did not have ballet companies of major significance. American democratic and cultural values contrasted with those of the European monarchies and royal traditions. For many dance artists in Germany and America, creating and producing dance was a profoundly personal and individual process rather than part of an institutional model. The choreographic approach was also different at its core. For ballet choreographers, creating dance was about serving the art form by contributing new ideas and perspectives. For early modern dance choreographers, creating dance was about finding themselves in the art form and embodying artistic identities. Also, they did not conform to established institutions but instead created new institutions on their own.

In Germany, modern dance was emerging as *Ausdruckstanz* (expressive dance), and it was pioneered by choreographer **Mary Wigman** (1886–1973). Wigman was a student and later an assistant of Rudolph von Laban, who was known for analyzing and formulating scientific principles of dance. After working with von Laban, Wigman went on to study and work with Émile Jaques-Dalcroze, who invented a system of rhythmic exercises designed to increase movement awareness. Wigman's choreography was muscularly physical and noted as quite intense even when her dance themes and music choices were lyrical. She believed that authentic dance occurs beyond causal experiences. She often wore masks as a tool to connect with primordial forces, which she believed possessed her body—similar to ritual trance—and drove her dance creation. Other prominent German choreographers of that time were Harald Kreutzberg, Gret Palucca, Valeska Gert, and Hanya Holm.[36]

In the United States, modern dance was also called "barefoot," "interpretive," and "expressive," and dance pioneers identified their creative processes as "intuitive," "divine," and "revolutionary." One of the most significant artists of early American dance modernism was *Loïe Fuller* (1862–1928). She often experimented with simple, pedestrian movement sequences, delirium-induced movement improvisation, and the integration of a moving dancer with a large, lightweight piece of fabric. She used the motion of the scarf-like fabric to create airy sculptural designs, visually enhanced by intricate lighting effects. In *Serpentine*, Fuller manipulated a long silk dress that she slowly unfolded on stage.[37] Then, her calculated movements caused the excessive amount of cloth to form unexpected shapes and motion with rippling effects, recalling a butterfly, a flower, and flames—see Chapter 14.

Considered by many as the founder of modern dance in America, however, was **Isadora Duncan** (1877–1927). Born in San Francisco, California, Duncan grew up by the sea, where her first dances were inspired by nature. Her mother had a great love of music, and the young Isadora developed an impeccable taste for classical concert music. It was not a coincidence that her major choreographic opuses flourished in conjunction with the music of Gluck, Beethoven, Wagner, Chopin, and Scriabin.[38]

Duncan did not embrace ballet, considering it too restrictive for the body and the mind. She also did not subscribe to dance when presented solely as entertainment. Duncan's philosophy of choreography was that dance is an art form of individual expression that unlocks the imagination and reflects the beauty of nature and the experiences of humanity. "I hate dancing. I am an *expressioniste* of beauty. I use my body as a medium, just as a writer uses his words. Do not call me a dancer." Duncan asserted.[39]

To create her system of movement expression, Duncan took inspiration from ancient Greek arts and costuming, combining it with the American love of freedom. She was opposed to codified postures and calculated steps. Instead, she was attracted to sculptures and images painted on ancient vases, where movement was driven by emotion and purpose. Duncan's choreography had a natural feel and included simple steps, skips, turns, waltzes, and jumps. Her dance vocabulary carried fluidity and endlessness, similar to the motion of sea waves. She believed that all movements originate from a single source—the *solar plexus*, located in the center of the upper abdomen, just below the chest and above the diaphragm.[40]

The legacy of another early modern dance pioneer, **Ruth St. Denis** (1879–1968), started on a small farm in New Jersey. Her mother trained St. Denis in a physical exercise method developed by François Delsarte, a French musician and teacher. The method included physical expression that engaged voice, acting, gymnastics, and the movement dynamics of the human body. The study of emotional connection with physical gestures was central to Ruth St. Denis' early years. In 1894, she debuted as a skit dancer. Later, she performed for the company of the director and producer David Belasco, where she stayed until 1905. St. Denis decided on a career as a solo performer/choreographer and immersed herself in religion and mystical themes influenced by Eastern philosophy and dance.[41]

Ruth St. Denis possessed a mesmerizing stage presence and an extraordinary fluidity in her arm movements as a performer. Her dance technique and mime skills were so strong that she could make a simple choreography look fashionably compelling by extracting and manipulating every bit of dance material. Her choreographic input in terms of expanding on conventional dance vocabulary, however, was very minimal.

For example, Ruth St. Denis' *Cobras* (1906) to music by Léo Delibes, from *Lakmé*, was a solo dance on a platform where St. Denis portrayed with hand gestures the slithering and undulating movement of snakes. In *Incense* (1906), St. Denis depicted the curling lines of smoke, while in *The Yogi* (1908), she revealed a mysterious ritual by using minimalistic moves. These works, combined with others, became one of Denis' East India cycles of dance, which she performed extensively from 1906 to 1910, and they quickly brought her to fame.[42]

The change in the public's taste, however, led to the demand for more dance couples rather than solo female artists, and St. Denis soon began looking for ways to sustain her career and revenue stream. In 1914, she met Ted Shawn, who was taking dance as physical therapy to recover from a recent illness. They became dance partners and soon married. The following year, the new dance couple instituted a private dance school and company in Los Angeles called Denishawn, which attracted numerous talented young dancers, among them Martha Graham, Doris Humphrey, and Charles Weidman.[43]

Denishawn's philosophy of choreography and pedagogy asserted that dance should not be encompassed by a single system of movement expression. On the contrary, dance should include all styles, systems, and schools of dance! Dance as art should be defined as every way that people of any race or nationality—during any period of human history—express themselves rhythmically with dance motion.

Denishawn dance company's concerts were well programmed and offered something for everyone. The shows included solo works, group dances, and longer pieces with simple plots, original stage sets, and intricate costuming. Often the dance works had thematic characters with origins from the Middle East, Asia, and the Americas, or were simply music visualizations. Denishawn School and Company were very successful. The establishment enjoyed wide popularity and toured internationally. However, the dance company never exceeded the artistry and fame of Ruth St. Denis' early solo dance career.

The company disbanded as an institution in 1931, and many of the dancers and key artists went on to pursue their own artistic careers. Ruth St. Denis focused on specializing in religious dances for the rest of her days. Ted Shawn formed his own all-male dance company, which toured successfully during the 1930s. His private property in Massachusetts is now the location of the flourishing Jacob's Pillow Dance Festival, which Shawn founded, and which continues to congregate annually.[44]

Figure 8 Photography © Franklin Price Knott, Ted Shawn and Ruth St. Denis, 1916, courtesy of Jacob's Pillow Dance Festival

With this wide, open-ended aesthetic framework, the curriculum of the Denishawn School included eclectic selection of dance techniques ranging from ballet, ballroom, and Yoga to interpretations of Spanish, Middle Eastern, and American Indian dances. Denishawn Dance Company seized the opportunity to perform on any type of stage or location where they were invited, or even not invited—colleges, theaters, concerts halls, and improvised outdoor locations.[45] Denishawn was the first to experiment with and introduce a format that became known as "site-specific" work.

?

Do you have your own philosophy of choreography and dance?
How would you describe it?

HELPFUL TIPS & SUGGESTIONS

~ Remember that being yourself and being accepted do not always go together

~ Let free expression be the reason and occasion for speaking the truth

~ Consider that in art, there is no right or wrong, but only honesty and ingenuity

~ Know that your free expression will inspire others to seek freedom

~ Think of self-expression as being comfortable with justifying yourself

~ Acknowledge that it is easier to be yourself than to be anyone else

~ Be kind and fair to yourself

FICTIONAL LETTER to Isadora Duncan from Vaslav Nijinsky

Based on selected historical information and quotes from the books and the diaries of both artists.[46]

Ballet Russes
Paris, 1916

Dear Isadora,

My trip back home was safe, and I wanted to write and tell you how happy I was to see you again in New York last month during our tour. It was great to have lunch and not to forget our nostalgic dance improvisation at the studio afterward. I cannot believe ten years have passed by since you first came to Russia to dance. Your inspiring performance back then had the energy of instantaneous creation and the effect of a fresh mountain breeze…When we met again in Paris in 1909, you were already a celebrity.

Remember our endless debates about whether ballet would ever converge with modern dance and if ballet choreography has a chance at originality? I know you do not like classical ballet, but I do like and embrace modern dance. On the other hand, you like using classical composers for your dances, while I prefer to choreograph to newly created music. It seems we are both so different in approach and yet so similar in our aspirations. However, you should know that I have removed all classical ballet vocabulary from my dances and have done my best to create my own movement. Know that your work and perspective had a great influence on me, and I will never forget the words you often repeat, and that everyone knows: "You were once wild here. Don't let them tame you."

I have danced frightening things throughout my career. Now my choreography shocks the audiences. Creativity tends to be a lonely and unpredictable enterprise–no success is guaranteed, yet a personal struggle is inevitable. I often feel I am leaping into madness, like falling into the abyss or dancing endlessly on the brink of insanity. And yet, while the audience treats me like a superstar, I am wrestling with myself and can barely take a breath to stay alive. Some evil demons are entering my head…My wife mentioned that she consulted a fine physician about my episodes–Dr. Sigmund Freud. Perhaps I should make an appointment to see him. I am not sure if I'm going crazy. People call me an eccentric–some even say that I am…a mad clown. Such is the persona of Creativity!

So, my dear, I say goodbye for now. You have plenty of your own struggles, and I am sending you much hope and all my wishes for happiness. Thank you for reading all I wanted to share–please know that I am not crying but have tears in my heart.

Yours,

Vaslav Nijinsky

?

If you are about to write a fictional letter to a choreographer you admire, to which choreographer would you write and what would you say?

THE CRAFT OF THE INDUSTRIAL AGE CHOREOGRAPHER

The Industrial Age choreographer's craft is depicted in the diagram below, which maps and draws an analogy to a steam locomotive—one of the symbols of the Industrial Revolution. Choreographers during that time were powerfully independent and artistically distinct—they were finally able to attain total creative leadership and the rank of a sole creator. As artists, they earned the right to be truthful to themselves and express anything freely to create the dances they wished to create and to capture the world through movement as they saw it.

Choreographers of the Industrial Age still respected preferred traditions of the past. They still referred to and strived to improve conventional dance-making skills, traits, and abilities and to obtain knowledge about various techniques, forms, and the production aspects of the performances. In addition, however, what truly expanded the scope of creative practices was cultivating new and unique visions about movement and the courageous offering of distinct individual perspectives on dance. Artistic originality and innovative breakthroughs in choreographic expression became the new norm.

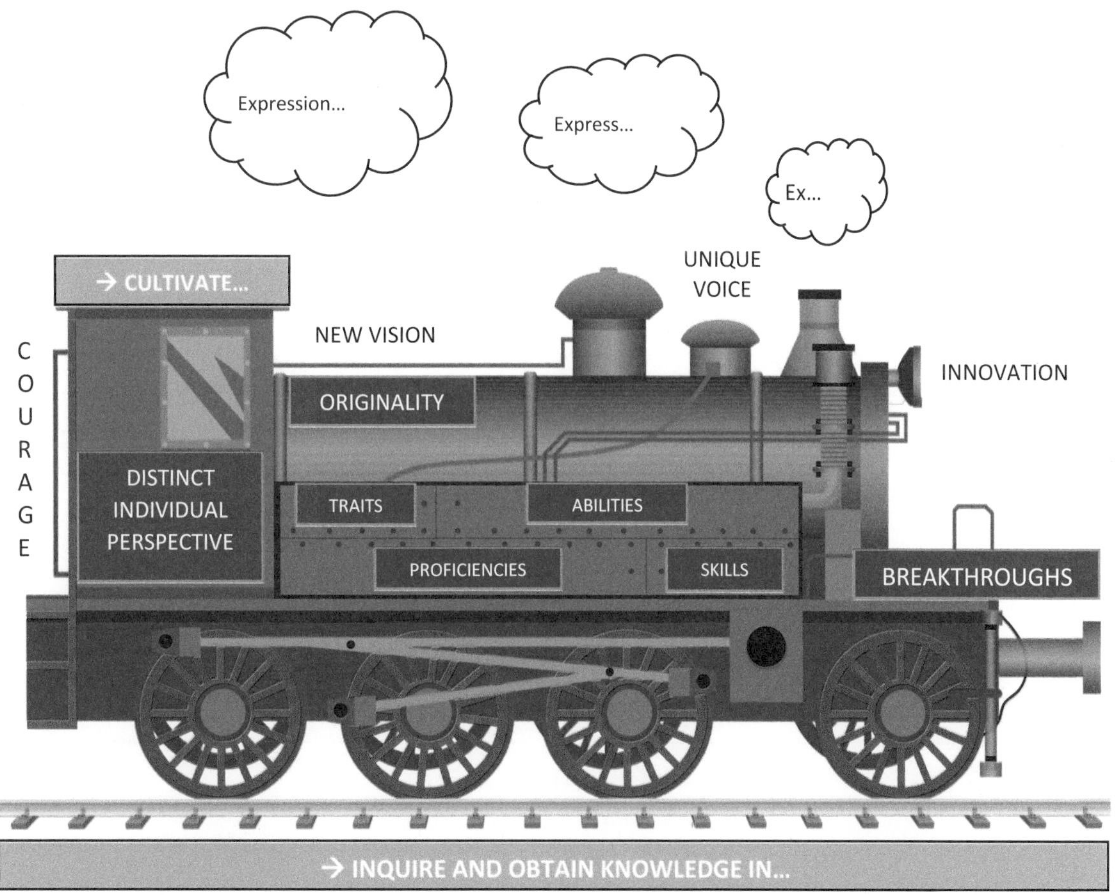

... | VARIOUS DANCE TECHNIQUES | HISTORICAL AND FOLKLORIC DANCE FORMS | MUSICAL FORMS | DESIGN AND PRODUCTION | ...

Figure 9

RETROSPECTIVE AND PROSPECTIVE
– ENJOY TIME TRAVEL BY HOPPING BACKWARD AND FORWARD –

The general chronology that follows traces the development, mutual influences, and transformation of choreographic forms and genres during the Industrial Age. The diagram visually represents the foundation leading to 20th-century *concert dance*. Ballet originated in the Renaissance, Baroque, and Enlightenment court cultures; by contrast, modern dance was rooted far back in history and drew inspiration from the movement identities and expressions of early ritual dance, ancient dance, and medieval folklore. A few key choreographers are indicated as the major creative contributors representing these genres during the Industrial Age.

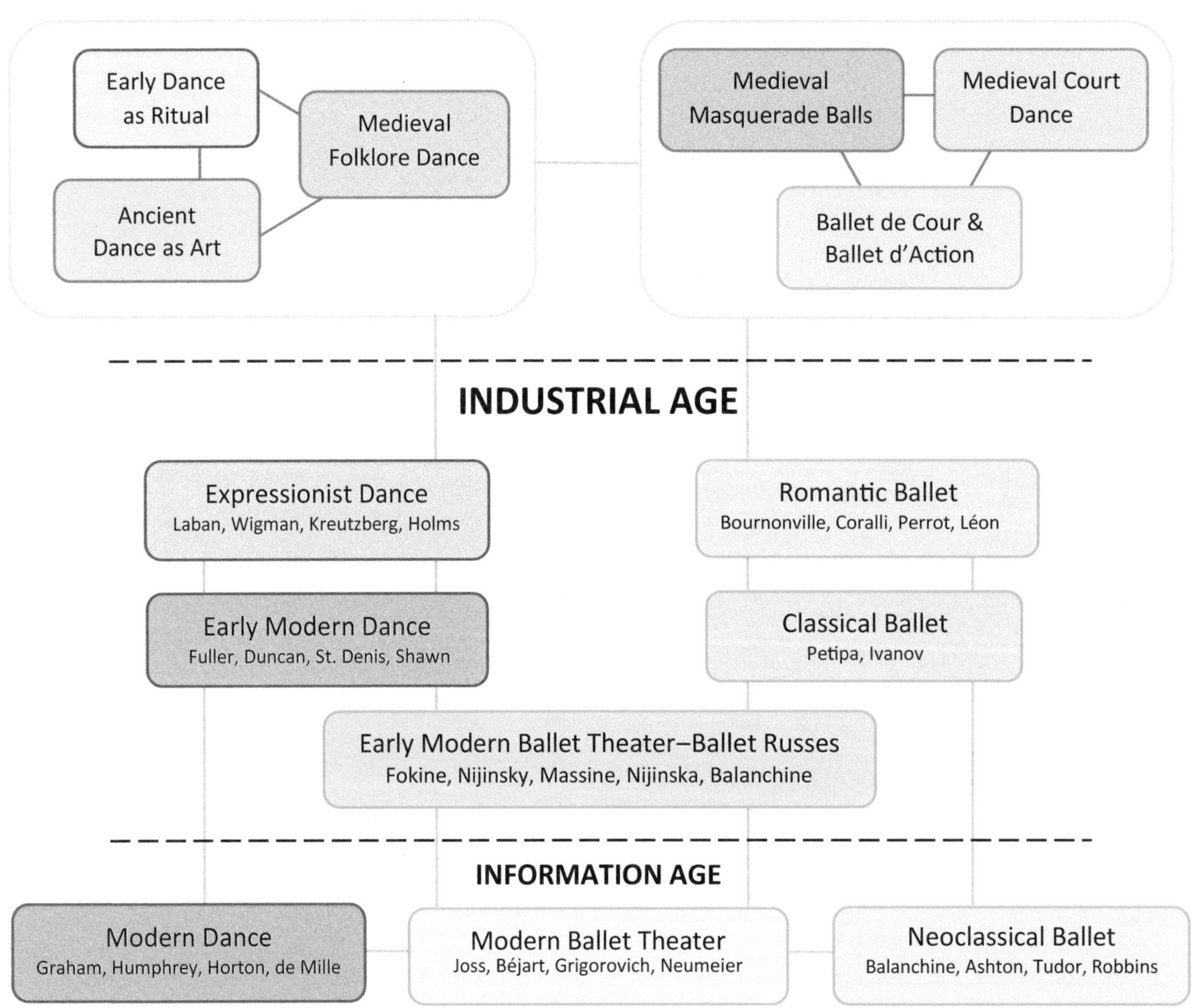

Figure 10

TRANSCENDING THE AGES

– CHOREOGRAPHING EXPRESSION IN A BROAD CONTEXT –

Finding and creating new means of choreographic expression was at the core of the Industrial Age's choreographic practices. Major milestone works of that period continue to exist and travel forward in time. The romantic and classical ballets created by generations of choreographers, from Perrot to Petipa, left a rich heritage of works still performed today by many ballet companies around the globe. Ballets Russes's reinvention of classical ballet and the aesthetic of modern ballet theater can be further seen in various subsequent aesthetics—from Maurice Béjart to John Neumeier and Christopher Wheeldon, among many others. The inherited repertory of Isadora Duncan is continually reconstructed and restaged, and it is an inspiration to many current choreographers.

The choreographic works and the creators mentioned in this chapter began to gradually receive public recognition, attribution, and archival preservation. In most cases, the original dance pieces were appropriately credited with the choreographers' names as sole creators. A handful of these dance productions was preserved either by passing the works from one generation of dance artists to the next or via archival records. Dance historians and other types of scholars provided more accurate accounts of the choreographers' creative processes, the roots of their unique expression, and the sources of innovation.

Choreographers during the Industrial Age finally gained the privilege to uniquely express themselves and be openly innovative. The invention of Taglioni's pointe shoes, Bournonville's fusion of ballet and folklore, and Petipa's white/black swan movement allegory, all speak to the evolution of ballet de cour. Loïe Fuller's inventive visual work with fabric and lighting effects and Nijinsky's animalistic yet authentic movement findings brought forth new means of expression. By the end of the Industrial Age, a choreographer could sincerely form a distinct *artistic individuality and choreographic identity*—see Chapter 13.

At first, unique ways of expression and artistic inventions might have been received as confusing, awkward, and even unpleasant. Yet they were pure and honest statements of personal artistic findings and views. Also, choreographic inventions considered radical during the Industrial Age are part of today's conventions.

Choreographic expression as an operating concept beyond historical origins encompasses capturing and forming unique movement ideas. An expression transforms a mental picture of thoughts and feelings into a physical form that also bridges the gap between emotions and logic, the conscious and subconscious mind. In the search for an authentic inner "I," an artist's self-expression forms an individual perspective: "I see…I feel…and I share my view of the world as I perceive it." However, before even formulating any means and tools of expression, at its core, a choreographic or artistic expression, in general, emerges from the "I." The artist's perceptions and perspectives of reality as the individual's *functioning subjectivity*—the "I"—takes on the world, which is *functioning objectivity*—the "IT." But how do the "I" and the "IT" interact?

CHOREOGRAPHING EXPRESSION AS AN OPERATING CONCEPT BEYOND HISTORICAL FRAMEWORK

Choreographic expression is the artistic manifestation, representation, and implementation of ideas in a particular movement, manner, and form. Content-wise, an expression could capture certain sensations, impressions, imagery, or concepts on any specific subject. Form-wise, an expression could be somatic, idiomatic, or semiotic, and its character could be assertive, measured, or subtle. Process-wise, an expression emerges from the interaction between inner and outer worlds: the "**I**"—the manifestation of a personal perspective—and the "**IT**"—the functioning objectivity of reality, such as nature and culture.

Figuratively speaking, any individual artistic expression is a way of *seeing* the world, the "IT," by using either a regular glass, a colored glass, or a magnifying glass that is chosen by the "I." The "I" and the "IT" are two-fold integrations similar to the two sides of one coin: The ***Internal* I** encompasses how the subjective consciousness accesses, processes, and organizes information about reality with the input of perceptions. The ***External* I** encompasses how inner thought processes and objectives are manifested outwardly through various means. The ***Internal* IT** encompasses an inner subjective model and perspectives of reality formed by the input of the senses and perceptions of the "I." The ***External* IT** encompasses reality as functioning objectively to be encountered by the "I." An individual artistic expression results as the manifestation and artful representation of the ***Internal* IT** by the ***External* I**—see Figure 11.

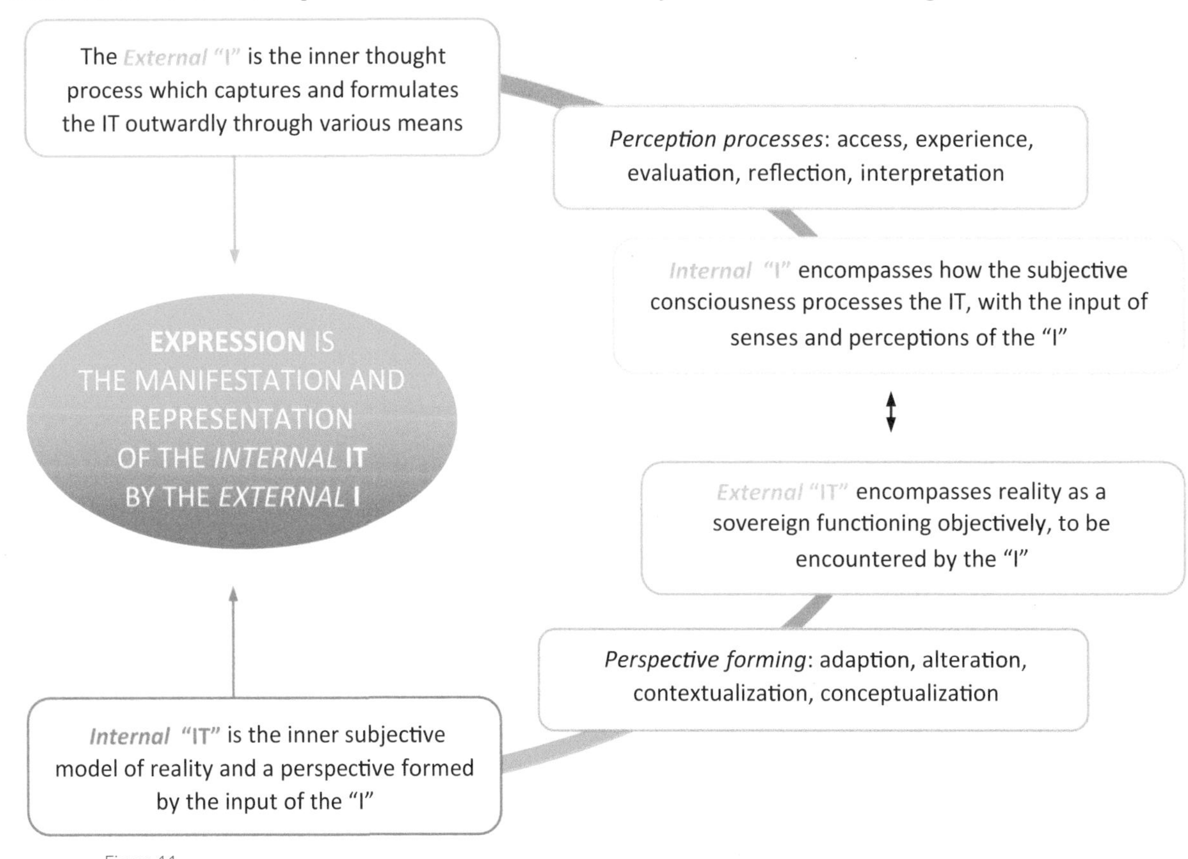

Figure 11

assignments & exercises

RESEARCH ASSIGNMENT: Use library and online resources to research one of the most influential dance and music works of early 20th-century modern ballet—the original production of *The Rite of Spring (Le Sacre du printemps)* choreographed by Vaslav Nijinsky: a) Create an outline in your journal of the content and flow of choreographic episodes in parallel to the music score of Igor Stravinsky; b) Use library, online, and video resources for choreographic research to look at the works of two different contemporary choreographers from the late 20th and early 21st centuries who have choreographed their versions of *The Rite of Spring* by using Stravinsky's original music score; and c) Analyze and describe in your journal how the two different choreographers treat the music score and the choreographic episodes. What do you find most intriguing in their interpretations, concepts, and movement material? Is there anything in common?

★ **CREATIVE EXERCISE:** The founder of American modern dance—Isadora Duncan—said in her book *The Art of the Dance*, "Look at Nature, study Nature, understand Nature—and then try to express Nature."

➡ Think of rudimentary natural forces and elements in a variety of conditions, such as FIRE (candlelight or forest fire); WATER (light rain or a raging river); WIND (a gentle breeze or a devastating storm), as well as trees, clouds, and reflected sunlight. Select one of these natural elements and explore how your chosen element "moves."

➡ Explore your chosen natural element's movement qualities and generate various bodily movements that capture its movement essence. Feel free to create either literal or non-literal movement vocabulary that visually represents the natural element.

➡ Combine the generated dance movements into a short phrase that you can dance either solo or with a partner. Then, select appropriate music to fit it to and present it to your peers or mentors for feedback.

COMPARATIVE ASSIGNMENT: Identify and analyze in your journal the similarities and the differences between: a) the aesthetics of Romantic and classical ballets; b) the aesthetics of modern dance pioneers Isadora Duncan and Ruth St. Denis; c) the aesthetic platforms of the Ballets Russes and the early modern dance pioneers.

BIBLIOGRAPHY AND REFERENCES

[1] Editors of Encyclopedia. "Industrial Revolution," in *Encyclopedia Britannica*, 05.21.2021, www.britannica.com/event/Industrial-Revolution, accessed May 2021.
[2] Editors of Encyclopedia. "Industrial Revolution," in *Encyclopedia Britannica*, 2021, accessed May 2021.
[3] Editors of Encyclopedia. "Loie Fuller," in *Encyclopedia Britannica*, 01.11.2021, www.britannica.com/biography/Loie-Fuller, accessed May 2021.
[4] Editors of Encyclopedia. "Industrial Revolution," in *Encyclopedia Britannica*, 01.11.2021, accessed May 30, 2021.
[5] Read, Herbert. *Grass Roots of Art; Lectures on the Social Aspects of Art in an Industrial Age 1893–1968*, Faber and Faber Limited, 1955.
[6] Editors of Encyclopedia. "Psychoanalysis," in *Encyclopedia Britannica*, 05.28.2020, www.britannica.com/science/psychoanalysis, accessed May 31, 2021.
[7] Andreopoulos, George J. "Universal Declaration of Human Rights." in *Encyclopedia Britannica*, 01.02.2020, www.britannica.com/topic/Universal-Declaration-of-Human-Rights, accessed May 31, 2021.
[8] Kant, Marian. *The Cambridge Companion to Ballet*, Cambridge University Press, 2007, pp. 175–176.
[9] Homans, Jennifer. *Apollos' Angels: A History of Ballet*, Random House, 2010, pp. 127–132.
[10] Trachtman, Paul. "Degas and His Dancers," *Smithsonian Magazine*, April 2003.
[11] Homans 2010. *Apollos' Angels: A History of Ballet*, pp. 127–132.
[12] Anderson, Jack. *Ballet and Modern Dance: A Concise History*, Princeton Book Publishing, 1992, pp. 78–79.
[13] Homans 2010. *Apollos' Angels: A History of Ballet*, pp. 139–141.
[14] Homans 2010. *Apollos' Angels: A History of Ballet*, pp. 154–156.
[15] Homans 2010. *Apollos' Angels: A History of Ballet*, pp. 140–141.
[16] Homans 2010. *Apollos' Angels: A History of Ballet*, p. 138.
[17] Homans 2010. *Apollos' Angels: A History of Ballet*, pp. 185–186.
[18] Homans 2010. *Apollos' Angels: A History of Ballet*, pp. 177–182.
[19] Homans 2010. *Apollos' Angels: A History of Ballet*, pp. 186–188.
[20] Homans 2010. *Apollos' Angels: A History of Ballet*, pp. 189–192.
[21] Anderson, Jack. *Ballet and Modern Dance: A Concise History*, Princeton Book Publishing, 1992, p. 87.
[22] Anderson 1992. *Ballet and Modern Dance: A Concise History*, p. 88.
[23] Homans 2010. *Apollos' Angels: A History of Ballet*, p. 288.
[24] Anderson 1992. *Ballet and Modern Dance: A Concise History*, pp. 90–91.
[25] Anderson 1992. *Ballet and Modern Dance: A Concise History*, pp. 104–105.
[26] Anderson 1992. *Ballet and Modern Dance: A Concise History*, pp. 102–103.
[27] Anderson 1992. *Ballet and Modern Dance: A Concise History*, pp. 104–105.
[28] Anderson 1992. *Ballet and Modern Dance: A Concise History*, pp. 104–106.
[29] Anderson 1992. *Ballet and Modern Dance: A Concise History*, p. 106.
[30] Anderson 1992. *Ballet and Modern Dance: A Concise History*, pp. 107–109.
[31] Anderson 1992. *Ballet and Modern Dance: A Concise History*, pp. 109–110.
[32] Anderson 1992. *Ballet and Modern Dance: A Concise History*, p. 110.
[33] Anderson 1992. *Ballet and Modern Dance: A Concise History*, p. 121.
[34] Anderson 1992. *Ballet and Modern Dance: A Concise History*, p. 126.
[35] Homans 2010. *Apollos' Angels: A History of Ballet*, pp. 308–309.
[36] Anderson 1992. *Ballet and Modern Dance: A Concise History*, pp. 172–174.
[37] Anderson 1992. *Ballet and Modern Dance: A Concise History*, pp. 165–166.
[38] Anderson 1992. *Ballet and Modern Dance: A Concise History*, pp. 166–167.
[39] Duncan, Isadora. *Isadora Speaks*, Illustrated edition, edited by Franklin Rosemont, Charles H Kerr Publisher, 1994, p. 53.
[40] Anderson 1992. *Ballet and Modern Dance: A Concise History*, p. 168.
[41] Anderson 1992. *Ballet and Modern Dance: A Concise History*, p. 169.
[42] Anderson 1992. *Ballet and Modern Dance: A Concise History*, p. 170.
[43] Anderson 1992. *Ballet and Modern Dance: A Concise History*, pp. 170–171.
[44] Anderson 1992. *Ballet and Modern Dance: A Concise History*, pp. 169–170.
[45] Sherman, Jane. *Denishawn: The Enduring Influence*, Twayne Publishers, 1983.
[46] Nijinsky, Vaslav, *Diary of Vaslav Nijinsky*, translated from the Russian by Kyril FitzLyon; edited by Joan Acocella, Farrar, Straus and Giroux, 1999 and *"You were once wild here, don't let them tame you"*—a phrase shouted by Isadora Duncan, as she waved her red scarf at the end of a concert in Boston. Her costume had "malfunctioned," exposing a breast. The proper Boston audience was booing her and walking out. Incident reported by the Chicago Tribune, 10/23/1922, Described in *Isadora: A Sensational Life*, by Peter Kurth, Back Bay Books; Reprint edition, 2002, p. 461.

VISUAL REFERENCES

Figure 1: *Folies Bergère Loïe Fuller*, poster artwork by Jean de Paleologu, 1893, public domain

Figure 2: Diagram © Vladimir Angelov

Figure 3: *La classe de danse*, art work by Edgar Degas, 1875, courtesy of Musée d'Orsay, public domain

Figure 4: *La Sylphide/Souvenir d'Adieu/de/Marie Taglioni*, art drawing by Edward Morton, 1845, courtesy of the British Museum, CC BY-NC-SA 4.0., "Rendition courtesy of Wiki Commons, authored and originally uploaded by Mrlopez2681 at en.wikipedia.org CC BY-SA 3.0

Figure 5: Diagram © Vladimir Angelov

Figure 6: Photography © Valentin Baranovsky, Swan Lake, choreography by Marius Petipa, pictured dancers Anastasia Kolegova and Maxim Zyuzin, 2010, State Mariinsky Theatre, St. Petersburg, Russia; and Photography © Natasha Razina, Swan Lake, choreography by Marius Petipa, pictured dancers Anastasia Matvienko and Denis Matvienko, 2011, State Mariinsky Theatre, St. Petersburg, Russia.

Figure 7: Vaslav Fomich Nijinsky in the ballet *Afternoon of a Faun*, a drawing by Leon Bakst, 1912, public domain

Figure 8: Photography © Franklin Price Knott, Ted Shawn, and Ruth St. Denis, 1916, courtesy of Jacob's Pillow Dance Festival Archives

Figure 9: Diagram © Vladimir Angelov, and *Head of steam locomotive antique model with black tones and red steel* wheels. *On isolated white background and shadow*. Credit: Jpreat, and Railway track, Credit: eestingnef, courtesy of iStock/Getty Images

Figure 10: Diagram © Vladimir Angelov

Figure 11: Diagram © Vladimir Angelov

And let each day be a loss to us on which we did not dance once!

Thus Spoke Zarathustra, by Friedrich Nietzsche (1844–1900)

CHAPTER 6

INFORMATION AGE:

TURNING AGAINST THE NORM – CHOREOGRAPHING EXPERIMENTATION –

The respect for freedom of speech and individuals' human rights that emerged in the Industrial Age became a political and social experiment during the 20th century. As new tools of modern media began to easily transmit facts as well as radical and often contradictory ideas to the entire world, the 20th-century society emerged as a *global society of sharp contrasts.*

World War I and II reminded the world that the cruelest enemy of humans is other humans. For the first time in the history of civilization, the use of atomic energy as a weapon led to the stance for globalism in warfare and sent a warning about the possibility of complete human annihilation. The Cold War (1946–1989) and the struggle for political control over the world between the two superpowers—the Soviet Union and the United States—polarized views between many nations, their cultures, and the arts. During the middle and second half of the 20th century, social protests challenged governments to address issues of political control, religious expression, social justice, racism, civil rights, women's liberation, and individual freedom. Fundamental discoveries in science, technology, physics, and astronomy worked in collaboration with education, business, and government. The first human-crewed missions to outer space were launched. Advancements in medicine and genetic engineering opened controversial possibilities to create new forms of life.[1]

Cultural movements of existentialism and critical thinking influenced new trends in literature and drama. The "Theater of the Absurd" challenged the popular play writing and its conventional characters, and instead examined the sense of meaning and absurdity of existence. There were striking contrasts between the orchestral dissonant compositions and the new music genres such as rock and roll and jazz. In the visual arts, alongside abstract expressionism, the newly introduced pop art captured common objects conveying provocative messages about the rise of a consumer-run society.

In dance, radical ideas introduced new principles of choreographic construction. American choreographer Merce Cunningham experimented with his innovative technique involving circumstance and chance play. He assigned arbitrary numbers to certain movements and then made lottery-defined decisions on how and where movement would occur in space. *Summerspace* (1958) to sonic climate by Morton Feldman-Ixion, and decor and costume by Robert Rauschenberg, contained rapid and often unexpected changing choreographic patterns. New technology in audio, film, video recording, and image projection bridged and connected dance with media.

Figure 1 Photography © Mko Malkhasyan, *Summerspace*, choreography by Merce Cunningham, performers Melissa Toogood and Ashley Chen, a still from "CUNNINGHAM," a 3D film by Alla Kovgan, 2015

Radical improvements of the telephone and radio, as well as the introduction of the television, computer, and the internet, defined the 20th century as the Information Age.[2] The new type of media apparatus instantly provided the public with direct connectivity and an infinite amount of commercial content—news and entertainment. Like the Stone Age, when a tribe gathered around the fire to hear the wise man's words, modern people gathered via electronic devices to follow up on the latest events affecting their lives.

As choreographic knowledge accumulated through history, the tools of collecting and sharing information and knowledge about dance also expanded. The amount of data about dance has become so enormous that it would not be possible to process its total quantity within a single lifetime. Ironically, the Stone Age's principle of creating a dance has remained consistent, despite the modern high-tech gadgets. A choreographer's rehearsal nowadays usually begins with oral communication or/and body-to-body connectivity.

GATHERING AND SHARING INFORMATION AND KNOWLEDGE OF DANCE THROUGHOUT THE AGES					
Stone Age	**Ancient Age**	**Medieval Age**	**Baroque Age**	**Industrial Age**	**Information Age**
Oral tradition, body to body	Oral tradition, body to body	Oral tradition, body to body	Oral tradition, body to body	Oral tradition, body to body	Oral tradition, body to body
	Vase paintings, frescoes	Vase paintings, frescoes	Vase paintings, frescoes	Vase paintings, frescoes	Vase paintings, frescoes
		Manuscripts, drawings	Manuscripts, drawings	Manuscripts, drawings	Manuscripts, drawings
			Early books, artists' archives	Early books, artists' archives	Early books, artists' archives
				Press, newspaper, journals, posters, brochures, photos, early filming, radio, library archives	Press, newspaper, journals, posters, brochures, photos, early filming, radio, library archives
					Mainstream media: radio & TV broadcast, film, video recording, phone, internet with global reach

Figure 2

RISE OF PLURALISM AND ANTAGONISTIC THINKING

The 20th-century contrasting political systems and polarized social factions with opposing world views led to political pluralism and antagonistic thinking. On one hand, there was the recognition and affirmation of diverse convictions and interests and the commitment for their peaceful coexistence. On the other hand, there was the permission to actively resist and even reject prevailing political, social, and artistic constructs. The artists' creative processes were gradually transforming; radical artistic experimentations often replaced traditional craftsmanship. Along these lines, artworks were also transforming into opportunities for political engagement and protest.[3]

Arguably, the rising cultural pluralism and antagonistic views led to the gradual disbandment of common taste and common sense. Lacking also was a universal agreement on what reality, art, and the truth are, or if they even exist. Instead, there was a growing sense that the boundaries of art must be challenged, the definition of dance—redefined, and the concept of *normality* with origins in the past—abandoned. The new norm was either no norm or a self-made norm!

The freshly formed conviction was that any norm-structured activities might lead artists to habitually use conventional creative techniques. A norm-governing mode of creative work may also compete with *artistic originality*. Then what might the creative act be about? The influential French philosopher Gilles Deleuze stated in the 1980s that the creative act is an act of resistance—an artful defiance of the profane and the sacred.[4] Yet the defiance, and even demolition of any existing norms, would ultimately open up the space for new rules and norms to emerge. Then artists may determine their aesthetic norms by choosing which rules to suppress and which to elevate—see Chapter 10.

Alternative and radical viewpoints began to emerge as artists experimented with how to *see and do things differently* than usually expected. The status quo was usually portrayed as problematic. An emphasis was given to the friction between individual and society, the subjective and the objective. Such decentralization and polarization of aesthetic views often resulted in provocative and contradictory concepts without any consensus.[5] A visualization and humorous [optimistic or pessimistic] interpretation of a "glass of water" that triggers a pluralistic range of views is illustrated in the figure below.

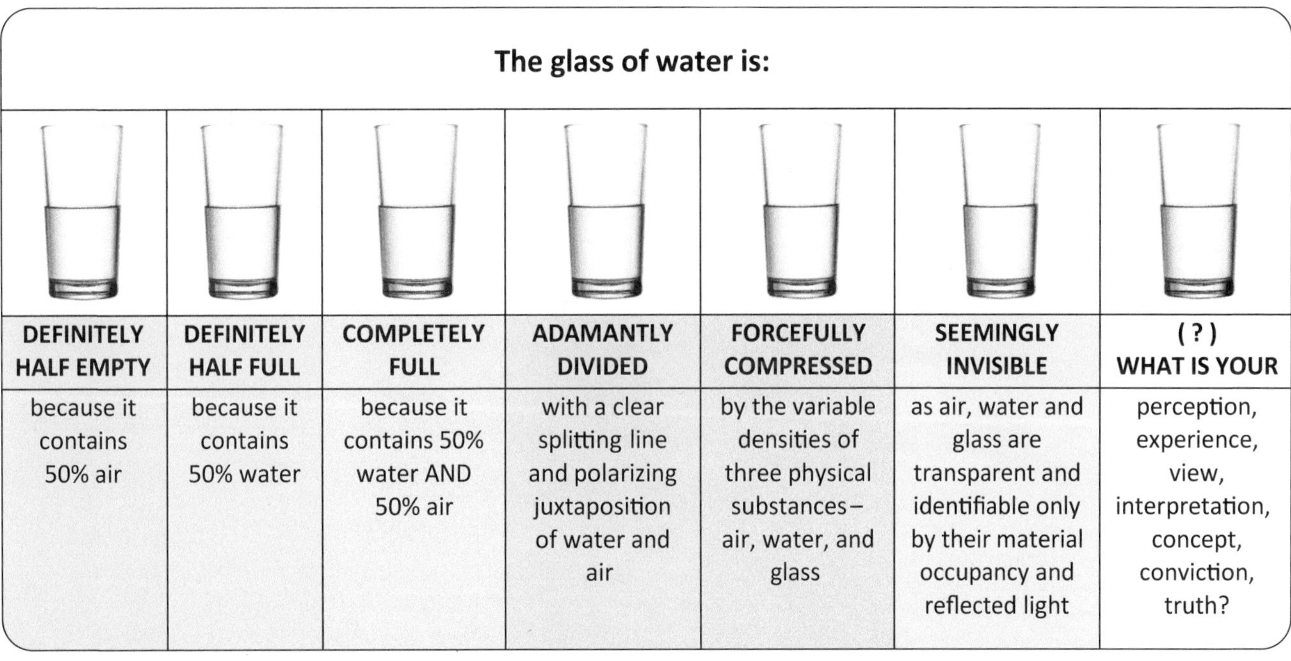

The glass of water is:						
DEFINITELY HALF EMPTY	**DEFINITELY HALF FULL**	**COMPLETELY FULL**	**ADAMANTLY DIVIDED**	**FORCEFULLY COMPRESSED**	**SEEMINGLY INVISIBLE**	**(?) WHAT IS YOUR**
because it contains 50% air	because it contains 50% water	because it contains 50% water AND 50% air	with a clear splitting line and polarizing juxtaposition of water and air	by the variable densities of three physical substances– air, water, and glass	as air, water and glass are transparent and identifiable only by their material occupancy and reflected light	perception, experience, view, interpretation, concept, conviction, truth?

Figure 3

The object in question here is the *same* glass of water! However, the answers do not ordinarily perceive it only as a glass of water. With a particular context and attributed meaning, the answers could transform the glass of water into a social argument, political statement, and artistic conviction. The 20th-century artists were fully empowered to conceive the world through their independent and personal lens. **Any radical views were welcome!**

20TH-CENTURY MODERN DANCE
– THE EMERGENCE OF NEW MOVEMENT PRINCIPLES AND TECHNIQUES –

Early Modern Dance entered the 20th century without a strict definition and commitment to a specific movement technique. Fuller, Duncan, and St. Denis were channeling their creative explorations into forming unique choreographic styles and were seeking a new type of movement imagery. At those initial stages, the focus of defining choreographic styles and codifying specific movement techniques was often diverted by the wide range and the plurality of artistic interests.

Ted Shawn, Ruth St. Denis' dance partner, collaborator, and husband, was a striking example of artistic pluralism in dance. He also became the first American choreographer to address gender disproportionality in dance. Following a separation from St. Denis, he assembled a group of male dancers, and in 1933 he formed Ted Shawn and His Men Dancers. After purchasing a farm property near Lee, Massachusetts, he founded Jacob's Pillow Dance Festival as a summer residence and theater for his new dance company.[6]

Shawn's eclectic choreographic style was a compilation of various European, American, North African, and Pacific Islander dance traditions, mixed with other movement techniques such as gymnastics and acrobatics. His work occasionally included ballet without shoes, as motion focused less on rigidity and more on the freeing of the body. As modern dance evolved, there was an increasing interest in a deeper exploration of the formation of *choreographic style*, as well as the development, codification, and integration of corresponding *movement technique.*

When Ted Shawn selected his original Men Dancers from the athletes he taught at Springfield College in 1933, his stated purpose was to forge a new performance opportunity for men, and to prove that dancing could be an honorable profession for American men. With his company Shawn produced some of his most innovative and controversial choreography at that time, such as *Sinhalese Devil Dance*, *Maori War Haka*, *Hopi Indian Eagle Dance*, and *Kinetic Molpai*. Through these creative works Shawn showcased athletic and masculine movement that soon gained popularity.[7]

Figure 4 Photography © Shapiro Studio, Ted Shawn and His Men Dancers in Shawn's *Kinetic Molpai*, ca. 1935, ourtesy of Jacob's Pillow Dance Festival Archives

While the choreographic style was a particular type and manner of expression, dance technique was the method and principle to develop the particular skills of its execution. Succeeding Fuller, Duncan, and St. Denis, and building upon their pioneering innovations, the next generation of modern dance choreographers attempted to formalize movement principles and modern dance techniques.

One of them, **Martha Graham**, a passionate and driven performer, educator, and choreographer, embodied the most influential principles of American Modern Dance during the first half of the 20th century. Graham developed a unique dance technique and choreographic style built around the primary instinct of life—breathing. Bodily changes and impulsive human motion would occur during inhalations and exhalations, causing contraction and release of the entire torso. Graham defined *Contraction and Release* as the fundamental movement principle of her method. Graham also had a unique approach of distributing energy kinesthetically: While Classical Ballet technique concealed the physical effort of the dancers, making them appear light and at ease on stage, Graham's technique exposed the dancers' physicality and harsh effort to move and breathe, as an inevitable part of being alive. Graham's visceral choreography had an angular look with percussive drive and dramatic convulsions, which sharply contrasted with the preceding lyrical choreographic expressions of Isadora Duncan and Ruth St. Denis.[8]

After establishing her own company in 1926, Graham created *Heretic* (1929) as a sample of her distinct choreographic style and later her acclaimed masterpiece *Primitive Mysteries* (1931). Her repertory included all American-themed works such as *Frontier* (1935), *Letter to the World* (1940), and *Appalachian Spring* (1944). Her interest in Ancient Greece inspired her to create signature dance-dramas such as *Night Journey* (1947), *Errand into the Maze* (1947), and *Clytemnestra* (1958), among others. On multiple occasions, she worked with renowned designer Isamu Noguchi and musical collaborator Louis Horst.

Martha Graham's signature solo *Lamentation* (1930) was about the embodiment of sorrow. In program notes, *Lamentation* was subtitled *Dance of Sorrow*, "not the sorrow of specific person, time or place but the personification of grief itself."[9]

Graham premiered and danced the work herself by sitting alone on a bench, wearing a tube-like shroud of stretchy fabric with only her face, hands, and bare feet showing.

On an emotional level, the work was an expressive narrative of a grieving woman. On a physical level, the solo captured an obsessed body pushing within and against its own skin with unexpected twists, convulsions, and reaches. On a visual level, the solo was a modern architectural homage to a reeling skyscraper standing out on the modern New York skyline.

Figure 5 Photography © Herta Moselsio, *Lamentation*, (1930), choreography and performance by Martha Graham, Martha Graham Dance Company, Library of Congress, Music Division, Washington, DC, date of photo unknown

Doris Humphrey was another pioneering artist who contributed to building the fundamentals of American Modern Dance during the first half of the 20th century, while working alongside her close collaborator Charles Weidman. In contrast to Graham's "contraction and release" technique, Humphrey's technique, method, and choreographic philosophy were based on the concept of *Fall and Recovery*. A simple walk was seen as a partial fall—one foot stepped forward to save the body from falling down and the hands swung in opposition to each other as compensatory movements to help balance the body. In her writing, she formulated her principle in her own words as "falling away from and returning to equilibrium."[10]

When falling, the body extends further to complete contact with the floor, only for the hands to reach out for safety and recovery. Multiple movement occurrences were explored during the process of the body traveling up and down. Gravity and weight played favorably, in contrast to classical ballet, which required the body to jump high, stay uplifted, and "float" above the dance floor. In Humphrey's gravity, the body voluntarily gave itself to the floor by embracing the ground, only to rise when it needed to recover. The principle of *Fall and Recovery* was also applicable to the emotional aspect of dance: the individual's inner emotions and experiences of danger, peace, struggle, and progress.[11]

Doris Humphrey and Charles Weidman worked closely together to co-create *New Dance*, (1935–36) which demonstrated not only Humphrey's groundbreaking choreography but also her principles of movement and dance technique. The work had three sections entitled *Theatre Piece*, *With My Red Fires*, and *New Dance*. Though the three sections were never performed together, they were danced to the score by Wallingford Rigger.

The dance trilogy was an ambitious study of conflict and centered on an individual whose growth was transferred to the group. The theme of how a person's actions would be interpreted by the group—in both movement and emotional contexts—deeply interested Humphrey throughout her career.[12]

Figure 6 Photography © Hans Knopf, Doris Humphrey and Charles Weidman at Bennington College, 1941, courtesy of Jacob's Pillow Dance Festival Archives

Humphrey became the first American choreographer to write a theory and methodology of dance composition and choreography. Her book *The Art of Making Dance* (1959) outlined fundamental principles of modern dance making, improvisation, body language, movement lines, partnering, group dynamics, spatial design, and the use of rhythm and music.

Lester Horton's dance technique included asymmetrical arrangements of the arms and the legs extending from a secure center. Elements of Native American, Balinese, Javanese, and Japanese dances were included as isolations for the upper body, as well as Afro-Caribbean moves like hip circles. Horton's training technique used the principles of *Tension and Extension* and emphasized an anatomical approach toward dance by addressing body flexibility, strength, coordination, and spatial awareness. Horton's signature work, which he described as "choreodrama," was *Salome, The Face of Violence* (1950), set to his music featuring percussion, human voice, and wind instruments.[13]

Katherine Dunham and **Pearl Primus** were among the first prominent Black choreographers in American Modern Dance and were both university-trained anthropologists. Dunham's concentration was Afro-Caribbean dance heritage, which she transformed with fun and clever choreography. Her most popular work *Choros* (1943) was based on the 19th-century Brazilian quadrille. Initially, Primus was interested in authentic African rituals; however, as her career progressed, she produced her masterpiece *Strange Fruit* (1943), a dramatic study of lynching in the Southern States.[14]

RADICAL DANCING AT THE JUDSON CHURCH
– EMERGENCE OF POSTMODERN DANCE AND THE AVANT-GARDE MOVEMENT –

The mid-20th century was historically marked by the Civil Rights Movement and concern for world peace and ecology. A new wave in dance exploration and creation, gaining the name *postmodernism,* surged as a counterculture of the early 20th-century modern dance. Postmodernism became a playground for avant-garde ideas and radical experiments.

In 1963, the Judson Memorial Church in Greenwich Village in New York City served as a center for social action and artistic endeavors. It also became a space for innovative dance for years to follow in which a group of young choreographers and their Judson Dance Theater challenged the norm of the conventional dance genres. Musician Robert Dunn led a dance composition workshop that examined Cunningham's experimental approaches. Participating artists were interested in more than learning about structured expression. Postmodernists objected to the stiff codification of both ballet and the various modern dance techniques and questioned dance performance's fundamentals and nature.[15]

In 1966, choreographer **Yvonne Rainer** created and presented at the Judson Church the work *The Mind is a Muscle,* which contained a prolific segment called *Trio A* that became an exemplary work of postmodern dance. A solo version of *Trio A* performed by Rainier herself is available in a 1978 film version online. That version of the solo was performed in silence. In terms of choreography, *Trio A* looked like a long-running phrase. In terms of execution, the phrasing of all movement vocabulary was performed as equally important. There was neither a movement climax nor intended virtuosity. The movement simplicity and motion flow unfolded as a neutral performance on a human scale.[16]

Figure 7 *Trio A* (1966), choreography and performance by Yvonne Rainer, image © Judson Dance Theater Archives, 1978

In her other works, Rainer generated material and "found" movement through tasks and games, where motion would occur casually and unpredictably. She manipulated her choreography by either *radically juxtaposing movement imagery* or by *deconstructing a conventional dance phrase imaginatively* while verbally slipping in political and social statements. She was letting the dancers be seen as themselves rather than as performers. Props often included ordinary furniture such as a radiator, chairs, and mattresses.

Rainer's 1964 infamous *NO manifesto* and her aesthetic of denial scandalized many dance critics when published in 1965. According to Rainer, however, the manifesto was not supposed to be taken as a prescription for all choreography but rather occurred as a provocation in the context of a particular piece of work.[17] Throughout the years, the *NO Manifesto* evolved with additional commentary and clarity. The following is an excerpt from the original version from 1965 and more recent commentary, which was first published and exhibited in 2008, in "The Manifesto Marathon" at the Serpentine Gallery in London, UK.[18]

1965	2008
No to spectacle	Avoid it if at all possible
No to virtuosity	Acceptable in limited quantity
No to transformation and magic and make-believe	Magic is out; the other two are sometimes tolerable
No to the glamour and transcendence of the star image	Acceptable only as quotation

Rainer and another Judson colleague, **Steve Paxton**, co-created *Words Words* (1963), which featured both performing practically nude as a provocative statement about the effects of gender.[19] Later, Paxton became interested in working with large groups of untrained dancers by directing them as "mutually moving mass." He discovered that any physical activity with intention could be perceived as a dance performance. Paxton's "unrehearsed" dance technique treated choreography as a spontaneous creation and a physical contact capturing togetherness within a community. In this approach, every dancer was also a choreographer interacting with one or more dancers, by improvising and instantly contributing material in an unpredictable and non-repetitive movement flow.[20]

In 1972, Paxton introduced his *Contact Improvisation* as a new and unique approach within the field of improvisation. Surprising spatial configurations occurred while dancers touched, tumbled, rolled, fell, lifted, or were being lifted. Partnering interactions took place primarily in gyms and at first resembled martial arts in slow-motion. The participating dancers-choreographers used Paxton's approach to develop a new type of mental and physical sensitivity—a fast-reacting intuitive "reading" of a partner's intentions.[21]

Another type of artistic experimentation in dance during the 1970s, which gained the umbrella term *minimalism*, explored simple patterns in music and dance that were developed in a complex manner. **Lucinda Childs** often used limited numbers of steps and varied them endlessly in different configurations. Her dances looked like an intricate formalistic design of a newspaper crossword puzzle, where everything was structured, yet it remained unknown and unexpected until completed.[22] On the other hand, **Laura Dean** favored geometric patterns and the repetitions of meditative spinning to reflect the monotonous circular movement of the planets, the universe, and the human condition. Her later work became increasingly more complex and grandiose.[23]

For **Trisha Brown**, dance was ordinary movement with extraordinary execution. Often, her choreography included simple gestural sequences executed in different directions to provide the audience with additional viewpoints. Furthermore, Brown explored multiple new compositional techniques, most notably the *movement progression.* For instance, one additional movement added to a movement sequence after cycles of repetition expanded her four-and-half-minute solo *Accumulation* (1971) into a 55-minute-long dance. She was often told that her compositional tactics went to extremes at the expense of her dancing, as well as emotional and physical presence.[24]

Man Walking Down the Side of a Building, SoHo, (1970) pictured left, was one of Trisha Brown's "equipment pieces" where she used mechanical systems of support such as ropes, cables, and pulleys. *In Man Walking on the Wall* (1971), the dancers were suspended in harnesses allowing them to "walk" on the wall of the New York Whitney Museum, which gave spectators the illusion of looking down from a great height.[25]

In *Planes* (1969) Brown asked the dancers to crawl across a wall constructed with holes for hands and toeholds. The wall was washed in aerial film footage creating an illusion that the performers were falling. Like other Judson alumni, Brown was presenting her works in parks, urban plazas, floating rafts and on rooftops.[26]

Figure 8 Photography © Carol Goodden, *Man Walking Down the Side of a Building*, Trisha Brown Dance Company, 1971

A key principle of postmodern choreographers was to avoid using previously established dance techniques or movement material belonging to traditional dance genres. Instead, they were interested in ordinary movements by ordinary people as a testament to human dignity. Their avant-garde creative practices had either extreme rules, or there were barely any. Such antagonism among collegial creative forces prompted a critical philosophical question about the very nature of dance, which still lingers today:

◆ **If every dance is movement, is every movement dance?** While *dance* is artistically expressed movement, *movement* could be *any* physical activity. Dance as an art form might require training and refinement—therefore dance might be exclusive. Movement as action simply requires acceleration and direction—therefore movement is always inclusive.

Postmodern dance invited all types of movement into the performance activities! The doors opened for exploring an exciting new field where movement could resolve into dance, and dance could dissolve into ordinary movement. A performance could be dance-based or movement-based. Or both. In addition, dance and movement could take place at any location and at any time. Most importantly, *choreography* was no longer equal to *creating and setting a sequence.* Instead, choreography could simply emerge from an activity, or a task, or a prompt. This new frontier became a catalyst for endless experiments!

A PARTIAL LISTING AND APPROXIMATE CHOREOGRAPHIC LINEAGE TREE OF 20TH-CENTURY AMERICAN MODERN DANCE

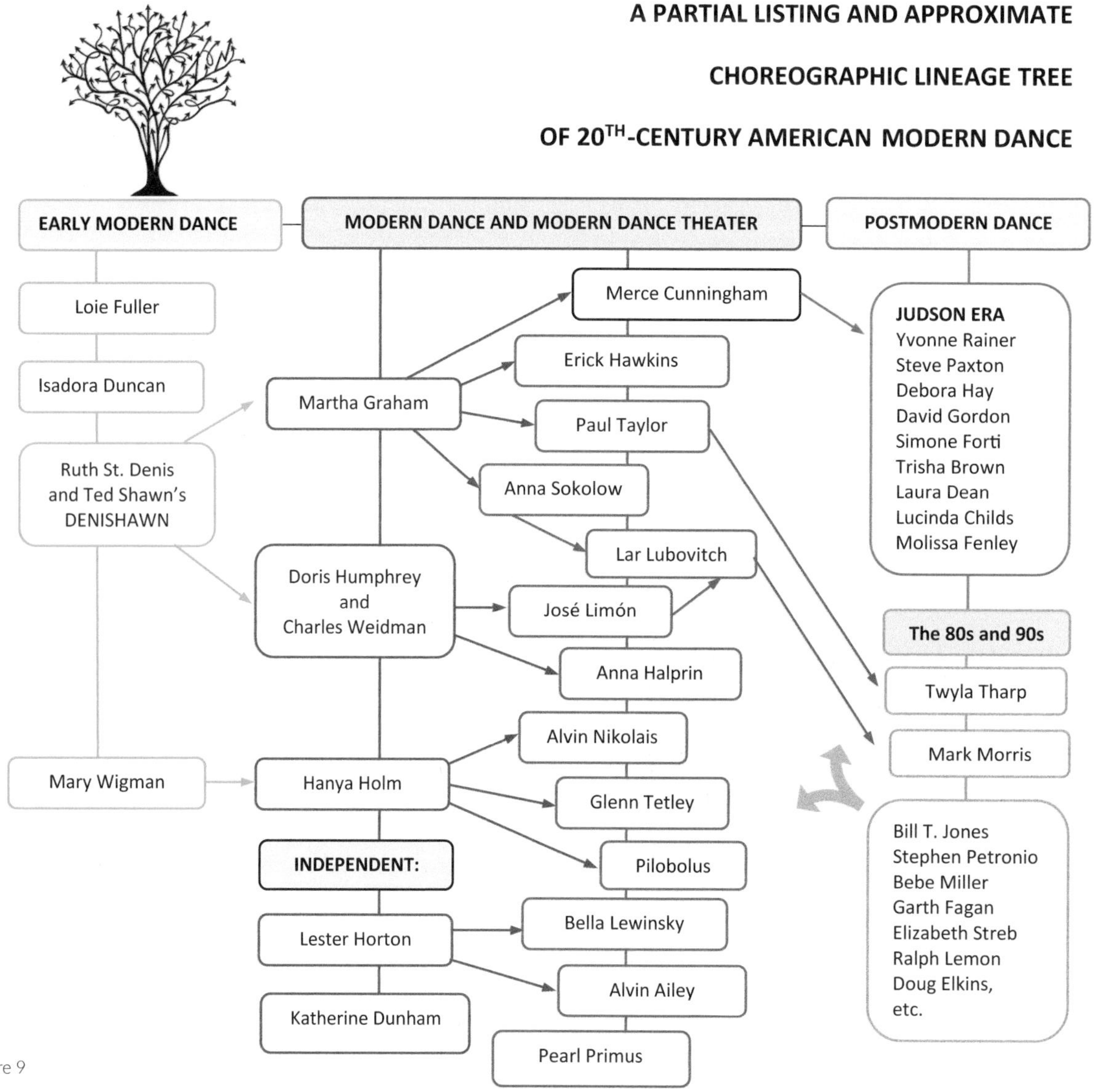

EARLY MODERN DANCE
Loie Fuller
Isadora Duncan
Ruth St. Denis and Ted Shawn's DENISHAWN
Mary Wigman

MODERN DANCE AND MODERN DANCE THEATER
Merce Cunningham
Erick Hawkins
Martha Graham
Paul Taylor
Anna Sokolow
Lar Lubovitch
Doris Humphrey and Charles Weidman
José Limón
Anna Halprin
Alvin Nikolais
Hanya Holm
Glenn Tetley
Pilobolus
INDEPENDENT:
Bella Lewinsky
Lester Horton
Alvin Ailey
Katherine Dunham
Pearl Primus

POSTMODERN DANCE
JUDSON ERA
Yvonne Rainer
Steve Paxton
Debora Hay
David Gordon
Simone Forti
Trisha Brown
Laura Dean
Lucinda Childs
Molissa Fenley
The 80s and 90s
Twyla Tharp
Mark Morris
Bill T. Jones
Stephen Petronio
Bebe Miller
Garth Fagan
Elizabeth Streb
Ralph Lemon
Doug Elkins,
etc.

Figure 9

This multidirectional lineage tree illustrates partial or substantial connections between generations of American choreographers. Relational involvement ranged from repertory participation to choreographic mentorship and significant artistic influences. Antagonism was also present. For example, Graham's and Cunningham's concepts about choreography parted ways in starkly opposing manners. Graham's interest was in translating narratives and imagery into movements for the body, while Cunningham was interested only in movement of the body. In contrast, Doris Humphrey's creative principles became the cornerstone of José Limón's choreography. Limón's approach developed further but was still based on Humphrey's technique. Humphrey did remain Limón's lifetime mentor and artistic adviser.[27]

?

Describe the relationships between you and your past or current mentors and how those artistic interactions have influenced you.

THE MULTIFACETED 20TH-CENTURY MODERN DANCE THEATER

– CROSSOVERS, HYBRIDS, AND ASSIMILATIONS –

The artistic interests of many modern dance choreographers in the first half of the 20th century were to cultivate their systems of movement expression and principles of dance construction. The newly occurring choreographies operated mostly with a select arsenal of movement vocabularies set to chosen music.

During the 1960s and 1970s, the Judson Dance Theater choreographers turned that approach upside down. They used spontaneous improvisation and *chance play* techniques to create their works. Pedestrian movement was substantially employed, including everyday gestures and casual postures. In some cases, choreographers cast non-trained dancers. The works did not follow a determined story plot and sometimes included spoken word. Movement was no longer bound to accompanying music but to actual time.

A rising antagonism among modern dance choreographers led them to question the purposes and the norms of the genre. Should modern dance be confined within traditional choreographic techniques or evolve within open-ended avant-garde creative operations? Furthermore, modern dance was beginning to be treated as a *theatrical experience* by employing narrative content of all kinds linked to the traditions within dance history. The key characteristics of *Modern Dance Theater* as an emerging umbrella term were: a) Genre crossovers between ballet, modern dance, folkloric, and vernacular forms, b) Movement hybrids between the choreographer's unique vision and other performance activities, c) Assimilations of content addressing cultural values and political and social views. A few prominent choreographers made remarkable contributions to the expansion of the form.

Anna Sokolow quickly established a distinct choreographic voice by assimilating a *political dance theater* aesthetic, which also was in tune with the artistic views of the 20th century's "new dance." Her *Anti-War Trilogy* (1933) to music by her partner, Alex North, tackled in full dramatic scale the experiences of Jews in Germany.[28]

In her powerfully choreographed solo *Kaddish* (1945), set to music by Maurice Ravel, the dancer immersed herself in prayer with a leather strap wrapped around her arm to symbolize tefillin—a set of small black leather boxes containing scrolls of parchment inscribed with verses from the Torah. In *Rooms* (1955), Sokolow used chairs as props, each one symbolizing a room in an apartment complex, and tackling the issues of urban alienation, physical isolation, and escape. *Moods* (1975) pictured left, was an intense poetic journey through inner states, serene to violent, exuberant to crushed, struggle to acceptance.[29]

Figure 10 Photography © Steven Pisano, *Moods* (1975) choreography by Anna Sokolow, Sokolow Theatre Dance Ensemble, dancers left to right: Boonyarith Pankamdech, Elisa Schreiber, Brock Switzer, I-Nam Jiemvitayanukoon, 2018

By the 1950s, a second generation of Modern Dance choreographers began creating new works that were a hybrid of traditional and experimental approaches. **Alwin Nikolais** treated the dancers as part of the visual stage environment. Nikolais loved working with the lights, slides, electronic music, and stage props to create a fictional and highly abstract world on stage, which had no narrative. Rather than exploring stories of emotional distress, Nikolais's choreography visually fused shape, color, motion, and sound.[30]

In the 1960s and 1970s, the choreographic crossovers of **Paul Taylor** stood out with a witty and authentic blend of balletic athleticism, originality, and humor. Taylor's choreographic lyricism and music visualizations engaged dance vocabulary with free-swinging arms, runs, leaps, crawls, and walks—all performed with exuberant affection, speed, and joy.

One of the most distinguished choreographic voices in Black Modern Dance Theater was **Alvin Ailey** and his dance company Alvin Ailey American Dance Theater. Ailey's choreographic vocabulary sprang from his years of training with Lester Horton. Ailey's choreographic works gradually evolved to reflect the African-American movement experience, while crossing over and combining the grace and elegance of ballet. Ailey's dance theater encompassed great spiritual depth and embodied emotionality. His most known and beloved work *Revelations* (1960), set to spirituals and blues music, reflected on African-American faith and tenacity from enslavement to freedom.[31]

Figure 11 Photography © Christopher Duggan, *Revelations* (1960), choreography by Alvin Ailey, pictured company members of the Alvin Ailey American Dance Theater, 2012

The dance group **Pilobolus** was founded in 1971, and it was named after an intelligent barnyard fungus flourishing in spores with extraordinary speed and accuracy. None of the Pilobolus choreography was created by a single mind. Instead, group improvisation was used to develop unconventional movement idioms in a collaborative environment. The Pilobolus aesthetic was a well-conceived hybrid of gymnastics, acrobatics, and modern dance. Dancers' athletic physicality formed sculptural configurations blended with contemporary movement lexica and visual stage technology. [32]

Merce Cunningham, one of the most influential choreographers of the second half of the 20th century, introduced an unorthodox choreographic process containing: a) *Chance and circumstance* that involved assigning arbitrary numbers to certain movements and then determining where in space they would occur. This newly assimilated technique of lottery-defined decisions guided how the movements of the legs and the torso would be combined with those of the arms and the head. Cunningham believed that the human mind tended to contemplate stereotypically and would occasionally fall into old "creative" habits. b) *Equal treatment of the space* made all spots of the stage equal. While in classical ballet, the *premiere danseurs* were placed mostly at the decisive center stage and surrounded by the *corps de ballet* in framed formations, in Cunningham's work, the choreographic activities occurred in diverse places on stage and were equally important. c) *Independence of production elements* concept stipulated that music, costume, and décor were created without preplanned relation to each other. The dancers executed steps on the music without any preplanned phrasing, while costumes, lighting design, and décor did not illustrate the choreography. Dance, costume, lighting design, and décor simply occupied the same space at the same time.[33]

By the 80s and 90s, a third generation of Modern Dance visionary choreographers presented new types of cultural, artistic, and choreographic hybrids. **Bill T. Jones** was one of the choreographers infusing postmodern dance with raw passion and social advocacy, political irony and provocative intimacy, solemn grief, and celebration of life.[34]

In 1982 Bill T. Jones formed Bill T. Jones/Arnie Zane Dance Company and deliberately hired dancers of all sizes, shapes, and ethnicities. Jones himself often chose to appear on stage to dance and speak. He mesmerized the audience with his incredible abilities as both performer and philosopher.

Jones chose harsh issues for his dances and often addressed social justice, racism, homosexuality, and terminal illnesses. Jones's well-organized physical theater and elaborate choreography involved complex movement scores, spoken word, projected still images, films, video installations, and other large-scale multimedia elements.

Figure 12 Photography © Lois Greenfield, pictured LaMichael Leonard Jr., Erick Montes Chavero, Shayla-Vie Jenkins, Jennifer Nugent, Talli Jackson, I-Ling Liu, Joe Poulson, Antonio Brown, courtesy of Bill T. Jones/Arnie Zane Company, 2012

The choreography of **Twyla Tharp** revealed itself as an organic hybrid of modern dance, ballet, and jazz-infused pedestrian and athletic movements such as running, walking, and skipping. In her work, dancers seemed casually "relaxed" as the movement phrases of conventional dance steps were intensely "stuffed" with added wiggles, shrugged shoulders, little hops, and jumps. The versatile idioms and movement qualities were often quirky and witty. Tharp's work found an outlet in productions for television, on Broadway, and in Hollywood. On the other hand, the dances of **Mark Morris** were noted for his signature musicality and clever humor. His dancers carried the spirit of community and equality, where men and women behaved as regular earthly people. Morris' work often crossed over and merged fine art and popular culture, ballet, and folklore, formal and casual dancing.

Figure 13 Photography © Sasha Gouliaev, *Nelken* (1982), choreography by Pina Bausch, pictured center performer Julie-Anne Stanzak, Tanztheater Wuppertal Pina Bausch, image taken during performance in Amsterdam, The Netherlands, 2014

In Europe, the German *Tanztheater* was reinvigorated by **Pina Bausch**, who blended modern dance and modern dramatic art. Her choreography merged dance and pedestrian gestures by excessively using repetition. She also incorporated vocabulary from children's games, altered social dancing, and trivial daily rituals. These were effectively mixed with projected images and film, collaged songs, and rearranged instrumental music, text, and stand-up comedy. Bausch's gravitating themes were loneliness, humiliation, and cruelty. Yet she was not a stranger to hope, tenderness, and humor.[35] Bausch treated the theatrical stage as a three-dimensional art space, where the audience observed the dancers, the dancers observed each other, and finally, the dancers observed the audience.

Swedish choreographer **Mats Ek** crossed modern dance with ballet, which resulted in new interpretations of classics like *Giselle* (1982), *Swan Lake* (1987), and *Carmen* (1992), where psychological dilemmas of modern people were combined with subtle humor. Working mainly in the Netherlands, the Czech-born choreographer **Jiří Kylián** believed that the strict vocabulary of classical ballet was no longer sufficient for his creations. On the other hand, modern dance vocabulary also did not have the full potential to grasp all sorts of complex ideas.[36] Kylián synthesized a new hybrid of what he found helpful in both genres. His choreography encompassed fluidity of motion where movements might not have a beginning and end. Within that unique distilled expression, sweeps of movements and continuous motion of the entire body were more important than separate dance steps.

Kylián's diverse body of work included highly regarded early pieces such as *Return to the Strange Land* (1975) set to music by Czech composer Leoš Janáček and choreographed as tribute and dedication to the life and death of Stuttgart Ballet's director John Cranko, and *Simfonietta* (1978) set to Haydn.

His signature ballets such as *Petite Mort* (1991) set to Mozart and *Bella Figura* (1996), pictured left, set to a music collage, made him one of the most significant European choreographers of the late 20th century.

Figure 14 Photography © Gregory Batardon, *Bella Figura* (1996), choreography by Jiří Kylián, Ballett Zürich, pictured dancers Yen Han and Katja Wünsche, Opernhaus Zürich, 2019

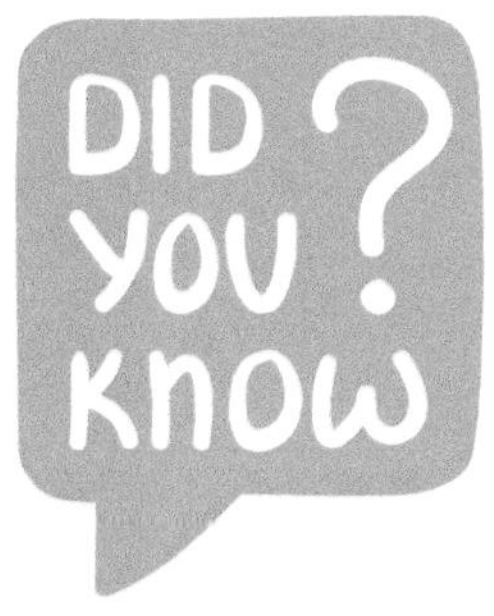

For the first two thirds of the 20th century, ballet and modern dance choreographers were positioned to work on the opposite sides of the dance spectrum. Martha Graham was not into ballet as a technique, George Balanchine was not into modern dance as a genre. The rivalry between "Ballet" and "Modern Dance" was mostly attributed to the discrepancies in historic origins and aesthetic principles. The obvious differences seemed more compelling than the search for common interests and collaboration.

Finally, during the last decades of the 20th century, ballet companies cautiously welcomed the aesthetic diversity and innovativeness of modern dance. Modern dance choreographers, on the other hand, did not resist invitations to work with large groups of ballet-trained dancers and generous budgets. Many modern dance companies also needed dancers who were ballet trained. By end of the 20th century and the beginning of the 21st century, the aesthetics and artists of both genres finally integrated each other in various ways—see Chapter 7.

CATEGORIES	CLASSICAL BALLET	MODERN DANCE
Birth and Early History	Mid and Late 16th Century	Late 19th, Early 20th Century
Pivotal Historical Events	*Académie Royale de Danse* in Paris, by King Louis XIV in 1661	*The Dance of the Future* manifesto, written by Isadora Duncan in 1903
Origin and Purpose	Royal Cultural Entertainment	Individual Self-Expression
Terminology, Language	French	English and any other
Terminology, Vocabulary, and Scope	Uses instructive terms to describe specific dance movements	Uses evocative physics terms to describe motion in general
Samples of Terminology and Prompts	*Plié, Tendue, Développé, Arabesque, Relevé, Chassé, Sauté, Jeté, Glissade, Emboîté*	*Contract, Release, Fall, Recover, Roll, Push, Hold, Reach, Sustain, Shift, Rise, Extend, Stretch, Relax*
Gender Treatment	Men/Women's bodies are different	Men/Women's bodies are the same
Dance Training and Gender	Training for men and women differ, except fundamentals	Training for men and women is the same, including fundamentals
Understanding and Purpose of Dance Technique	Ballet technique is conventionally used for training and it might accommodate different choreographers and their styles	Modern dance technique and choreographic style complement each other, as these might originate from the same individual artist
Scale of Technique	Universal, plain, general	Individual, selective, focused
Understanding of Style	Style captures the unique interpretation of movement	Style captures the unique representation of movement
Movement Philosophy	Dance movement is always a defined movement	Every movement could be a dance movement
Choreographer's Goals	1) Modify existing dance vocabulary, 2) Define unique movement texture, 3) Formulate distinct movement style	1) Discover unique movement vocabulary, 2) Define kinesthetically embodied imagery, 3) Formulate distinct movement philosophy

Figure 15

?

What elements of these two these genres are appealing to you in the terms of your dance training and creative work, and why?

TRANSFORMING BALLET
– 20TH-CENTURY NEOCLASSICISM AND MODERN BALLET THEATER –

While 20th-century American Modern Dance originated as a genuine American enterprise, Classical Ballet was an import from Europe. Young democratic America was not the most fertile soil for the ballet's imperial and aristocratic roots. European ballet choreographers who arrived to work in the US were compelled to transform ballet into a modern and progressive form of dance.

The most influential choreographer in 20th-century American ballet was **George Balanchine**. After arriving in the US in 1933, Balanchine became the founder of the School of American Ballet and the chief ballet-master and choreographer of the company known today as New York City Ballet (NYCB). Throughout his tenure, Balanchine's choreographic style merged the fine European classicism with the American innovative spirit and energy.

Balanchine's boldest choreographic experiments were his plotless ballets with performers clad in only black and white practice clothes. His *Four Temperaments* (1946), set to a commissioned score by Paul Hindemith, was based on Hippocrates's ancient Greek medical theory suggesting the existence of four fundamental personality types. The sequences included distorted steps, angular lines, deep backbends, off-balance kicks, and speedy, syncopated transitions. The torso and the upper body extremities were used as opposing entities, just as in Modern Dance. His *Agon* (1957) was set to an atonal music score by Ballet Russes' alumnae composer and Balanchine's friend—Igor Stravinsky. *Agon* was the Greek word for contest and suggested Olympian Games for young gods. The choreography involved suspended positions, extreme limb extensions, and acrobatic partnering executed with elegant physicality. The phrasing was composed mostly of transitions where the skips, jumps, turns, and runs fused as one continuous flow. Occasional stop-and-pause accents allowed the audience to enjoy the dynamic movement formations.[37]

Figure 16 Photography © Paul Kolnik, image left *The Four Temperaments* (1946) choreography by George Balanchine, performers from left to right Ashley Hod, Isabella LaFreniere, Russell Janzen, Emily Kikta, Claire Kretzschmar, 2018; image right Agon (1957) choreography by George Balanchine, performers Tyler Angle and Maria Kowroski, 2018 © The George Balanchine Trust

Balanchine's experiments introduced a new aesthetic by posing a philosophical question:

◆ **Can ballet thrive without elaborate plots, stage characters, lavish costumes, and grand scenery?** Yes. A ballet can unfold in a simple environment as a progression of movements, no matter if they are bonded by a story. With simply clad dancers on a bare stage, the focus is strictly on the performers, the music, and the dance. Classical ballet form could still be retained while giving it a radical edge. Should these avant-garde ballets be called *abstract*? For his ballet, Balanchine accepted the term *plotless* but not abstract. For Balanchine, the word "abstract" was too vague, as ballet dancing was always about concrete actions.[38] Abstract concepts mainly exist as ideas but not necessarily in a physical form. Another term became commonly used—*neoclassical ballet*, a progressive style determined to emphasize simplicity, purity, musicality, and movement as the sole substance.

Jerome Robbins, a mentee of George Balanchine, became the first American-born prominent ballet choreographer who took a deep dive into various dance styles and aesthetics. Robbins' versatility and interests ranged from neoclassical ballets and narrative modern ballet pieces for NYCB to choreographing a wide spectrum of dances for Broadway musicals and Hollywood. Robbins' choreography had distinctly American features: On the one hand, dancing was confident and persuasive, and on the other hand, it was informal and fun. His first ballet, *Fancy Free* (1944), was a narrative about sailors on shore-leave in New York City. The dance language was relaxed, casual, and felt like an informal ballet staged to the breezy and jazzy score of Leonard Bernstein. *West Side Story* (1957) was also a Robbins-Bernstein collaboration. The narrative zoomed in on a dramatic relationship between Maria and Tony unfolding on the tense backdrop of the two combating gangs—the Sharks and the Jets.[39] Recalling plot elements of Shakespeare's *Romeo and Juliet*, the musical was an urban tale about an impossible love and how prejudice and violence could destroy individual lives.

Robbins' signature plotless neoclassical one-act ballet for NYCB was *Dances at a Gathering* (1969) to music by Chopin. The choreography incorporated everyday movements such as walking, running, and sitting, which were organically connected with refined ballet vocabulary. Dancers' relationships and feeling were distilled in pure classical forms.[40]

Another signature Robbins ballet set to music by Chopin was *The Concert (or, The Perils of Everybody)* (1956). The work was a narrative comedy and a spoof of a classical music concert. During an all-Chopin recital the attendees allow their decidedly imaginative minds to wander.

As the resulting images are danced, human foibles and recognizable insecurities are revealed, as each fantasy is brought comically and vividly to life. The work, still popularly performed today, illustrates Robbins' remarkable insight into the delightful imperfections of human relationships that bring good cheer and laughter.

Figure 17 Photography © Paul Kolnik, *The Concert (or, The Perils of Everybody)* (1956), choreography by Jerome Robbins, pictured performers Kristen Segin, Cameron Dieck, Sterling Hyltin, 2017

Another key figure in the development of ballet in America was British choreographer **Antony Tudor**, who served as resident choreographer for The Ballet Theater (now American Ballet Theater). Tudor found and assimilated new ways to articulate narration in ballet that were deeply psychological and encompassed Edwardian and even Freudian characteristics. Some of Tudor's signature work included *Dark Elegies* (1937), danced to music by Gustav Mahler, where grief was presented but never fully expressed. *Pillar of Fire* (1942) to music of Schoenberg's *Verklärte Nacht* (or *Transfigured Night*) was a ballet about guilt "transformed" through love into happiness.[41] *Leaves are Fading* (1975) to music by Dvořák was a plotless lyrical study of wistful dreaminess, provoking nostalgic feelings.

Meanwhile, in post-war Europe, emblematic works of abstract neoclassical ballets and narrative modern ballets were emerging and evolving continuously.

In the United Kingdom, Ecuador-born, Peru-raised, but ultimately British choreographer **Frederick Ashton** created a body of narrative and plotless ballets infusing the form with distinctive pure lines and sculptural feel. His replacement as director and choreographer of the Royal Ballet was **Kenneth MacMillan**, who created a broad spectrum of works. These ranged from a rich collection of short pieces such as *Danses Concertantes* (1955), set to music of Stravinsky, and *Elite Syncopations* (1974), set to music of Scott Joplin and others; to full-length narrative ballets such as *Manon* (1974) set to music of Massenet, and *The Prince of the Pagodas* (1989) set to music by Britten, among many others. MacMillan's work is known for its panoramic and yet intimate, dramatic, and poetic features.

In Germany, **Kurt Jooss** and his emblematic work, *The Green Table* (1932), brought to ballet political satire on the futility of war, which is still relevant today. The South Africa-born and Royal Ballet trained **John Cranko** settled as director and house choreographer of Stuttgart Ballet. His signature full-length ballet drama *Onegin* (1965) was an adaptation of the verse novel *Eugene Onegin* by Alexander Pushkin, set to music by Tchaikovsky.

The German modern ballet scene expanded further during the 1980s and 1990s owing to two American-born choreographers. Hamburg Ballet's director and choreographer **John Neumeier** became known for his full-length, narrative ballets based on book adaptations and biblical and mythological subjects. Among them were *Daphnis et Chloe* (1972), *A Midsummer Night's Dream* (1977), *The Lady of the Camellias* (1978), and *Streetcar Named Desire* (1983). His thoughtful approach to the chosen subjects resulted in the works' great emotional depth and immersive theatrical experience.

Frankfurt Ballet's director and choreographer **William Forsythe** created his signature one-act plotless work for Paris Opera Ballet, entitled *In the Middle Somewhat Elevated* (1987), to music of Thom Willems. The fast-paced syncopated steps were fused with twisted balletic partnering with off-balance angular lines. Movement passages and non-linear phrasing had an active continuity, where chronological events were replaced by sporadically occurring episodes of dancers' interactions. In general, Forsythe's choreography is entirely movement driven, with dancers perceived as kinetic art objects. His postmodern and deconstructivist approaches reformulated ballet lexis for the 21st century.[42] Forsythe was no stranger to using various modern dance improvisational techniques, which resulted in his method known as *Improvisation Technologies*—see Chapter 15.

In France, the theatrical predispositions and idealized sensibility of **Roland Petit** often resulted in an extensive use of mime, literal, and explicit dramatic actions. His postwar existentialist one-act ballet, *Le Jeune Homme et la Mort* (1946), choreographed to music of Bach and libretto by Jean Cocteau, was considered radical at that time.

The choreography of **Maurice Béjart** for his company Ballet du XXe siècle (Ballet 20th Century), on the other hand, was a hybrid of ballet and modern dance, sprinkled with shocking sensuality and philosophical messaging. In his erotically charged version of *Rite of Spring* (1959) to music by Stravinsky, a sexual act became the ultimate sacrifice. His *Bolero* (1960) to music by Ravel features a dancer on a tabletop, surrounded by seated men, who slowly participate in the dance, culminating in a climactic union of the dancers atop the table.[43]

In the Netherlands, the ballets of **Rudi van Dantzig** were abstract-expressionistic and symbolic, culminating in his signature plotless work *Four Last Songs* (1977). He was one of the founders of Netherlands Dans Theater (NDT). Van Dantzig shared his life and career with his partner **Toer van Schayk**, also a prominent choreographer, set designer, and costume designer with the Dutch National Ballet. His work *Landscape* (1982) had a strong social focus on warfare and environmental pollution. Van Schayk's choreography was impressionistic with a fluid, ethereal feel and distilled linear movements.[44] The neoclassical choreography of **Hans van Manen** focused on plotless movement with clean lines, abstract shapes, and bold movement imagery. His well-known works include *Grosse Fugue* (1971), *Five Tangos* (1977), and *In and Out* (1983), among many others. After co-directing Nederlands Dans Theater, he became a resident choreographer—first with the Dutch National Ballet (1973–87) and then with NDT (1988–2003). Since 2005, he has held the post of resident choreographer with the Dutch National Ballet.[45]

Figure 18 Photography © Hans Gerritsen, *In and Out* (1983), choreography by Hans van Manen, performed by members of the junior company of the Dutch National Ballet, 2021

In Russia, known then as the Soviet Union, **Yuri Grigorovich**'s choreography to Sergey Prokofiev's *The Stone Flower* (1957) and *The Legend of Love* (1961) brought him fame. While serving as artistic director and choreographer of the Bolshoi Ballet (1964–95), his most notable productions were *Spartacus* (1967) to the music of Aram Khachaturian and *Ivan the Terrible* (1975) to music by Prokofiev. Whether he chose folk tales or epic stories for his ballets, Grigorovich's signature skills, notable instantly when seeing his work live or on film, were using the *corps de ballet* to propel a ballet's narrative, create persuasive stage characters, and build dramatic tension through movement.

WELCOME TO A LATE-NIGHT TV SHOW FEATURING A CHOREOGRAPHER STAND-UP COMEDIAN

ENJOY A COUNTDOWN OF ONE-LINERS THAT HUMOROUSLY ANSWER THE QUESTION:

WHAT COULD BE THE TOP 10 REASONS TO BECOME A CHOREOGRAPHER?

10. When I was a teenager, my aunt took me to the kitchen and asked me to redirect the traffic of ants across the floor.
9. Tango and I have been dating for a while, but our romance heated up during one group dance session when I was no longer stepping on anyone's toes.
8. I can work on a dance while I am still in bed.
7. Spatial orientation helps me find my toothbrush easily...Oh, here it is!
6. My morning breath is reconfiguring the breakfast cereal into predictable patterns on the surface of the milk.
5. The postures of people waiting at the bus stop have much more meaning.
4. It turned out that dancing crazily with an imaginary friend is part of the job.
3. They gave me my own dressing room, which I remodeled for Stone Age rituals.
2. Talking nonsense to the dancers and making them do anything that comes to mind is completely legitimate and totally "part of the process."

...AND THE NUMBER ONE REASON TO BECOME A CHOREOGRAPHER COULD BE...

1. To use dance to shake things up!

?

What were your motivations to become a choreographer, and could you reframe these reasons to make them sound humorous?

THE CRAFT OF THE 20TH-CENTURY CHOREOGRAPHER

Do you need energy to power a choreographic experiment or a new dance? The 20th-century choreographer's craft is depicted in the diagram below, which maps and draws an analogy to a battery. Emerging as a widely popular power source during the Information Age, a battery converts chemical energy into electrical power by using charged ions and electrodes with polarities—*positive* (+) and *negative* (-). In the context of a choreographic creation, one could refer to (+) *complexity* and using elaborate tools, and (-) *simplicity* and using minimal tools. Various elements on the wide spectrum between polarities could be seen as charged ions in a battery. For example, two different artists—Choreographer A and Choreographer B—would make distinct choices of the choreographic instruments and production elements from the sampled ranges. Depending on the choreographer's artistic intentions, a determination of simplicity and complexity will always be in dynamic opposition, bringing in the energy to experiment with the ranges of the variables remaining.

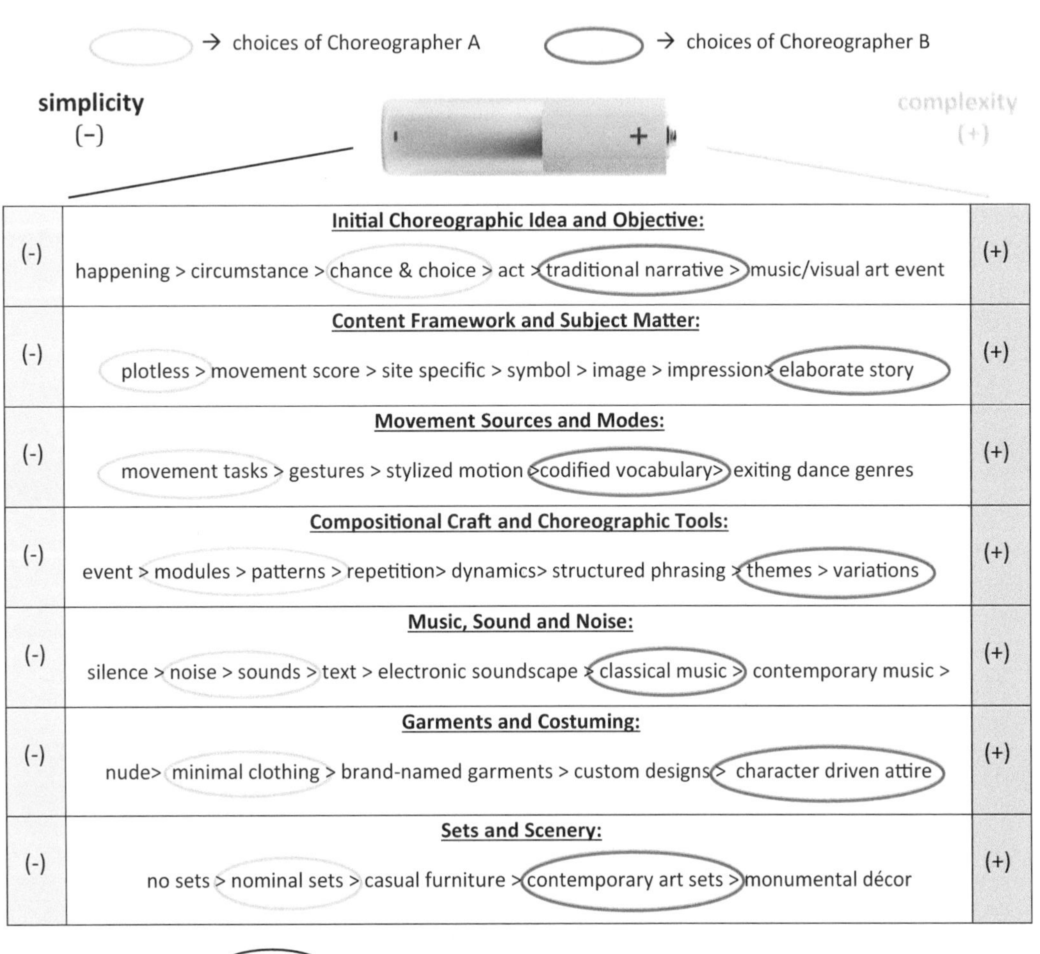

Figure 19

RETROSPECTIVE AND PERSPECTIVE
– ENJOY TIME TRAVEL BY HOPPING BACKWARD AND FORWARD –

The early 21st century, characterized here as the Integral Age, inherited the tendency to break down the boundaries between genres. The experimental, cross-over, and blending approaches in concert dance choreography at the end of the 20th century resulted in the dance theater fusions commonly described today as contemporary dance and contemporary ballet. This latest stage of development of choreographic forms will bring our time travel in choreography to a temporary and active pause, finishing our chronology chart with anticipation and the question— what is next?

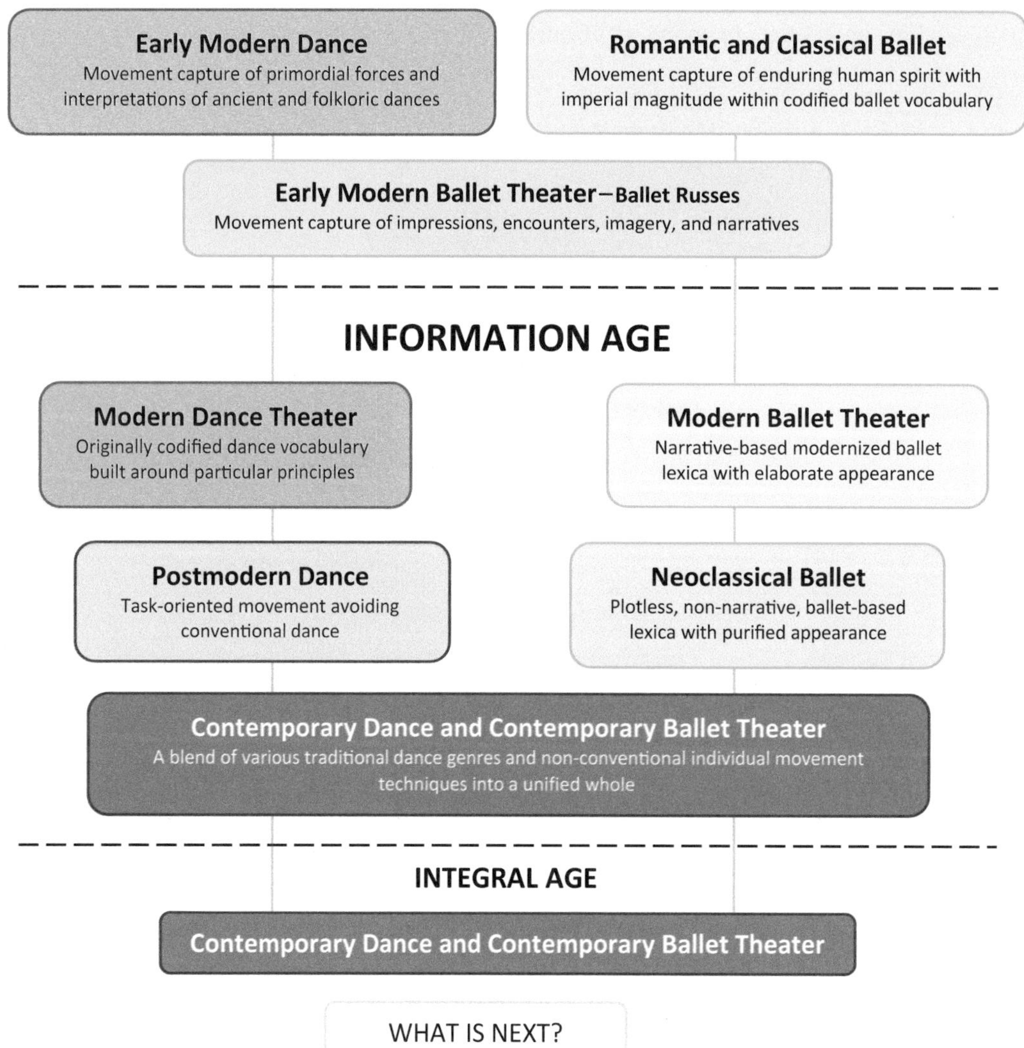

Figure 20

TRANSCENDING THE AGES

– CHOREOGRAPHING EXPERIMENT IN A BROAD CONTEXT –

The cultural experimentations during the mid- and late 20th century arose as society questioned truths and ideologies in politics and the arts. Radical ideas and experimental approaches were introduced and fostered by a wide range of choreographers such as Graham and Humphrey, Holm and Sokolow, Cunningham and Rainer, Paxton and Brown, Nikolais and Pilobolus, Bausch and Kylián, Tharp and Jones, Béjart and Van Manen, Balanchine and Forsythe, among many others.

Modern and postmodern choreographers' references to various historical periods of dance may be seen as more fragmented and module-based. Many experimental plotless works tended to be non-linear, non-climactic, and non-psychological. In ballet, neoclassicism rebelled against the overly dramatized styles of romantic and classical traditions and distanced itself from the notion that "dances [must] tell stories." Detailed narrative and heavy theatrical setting were stripped in favor of minimalism in costumes, scenery, and lighting. Yet key techniques, such as pointe technique, were retained.

Most of the mentioned experimenting revealed that a simplified external presentation allowed for the dancers' movement to become the main artistic medium. As more edgy choreographic ideas floated around, the act of artistic experimenting became the reliable procedure to test any radical proposals. But how does one conduct an experiment?

There is difference between a *scientific* experiment and an *artistic* experiment: The former aims to produce proof of a theory, while the latter explores the potential of a concept. In the arts, statistical evidence is not needed or in question; the goal, rather, is to test various modes of perception and interpretation. A scientific mindset relies predominantly on data and analytical thinking, while an artistic mindset—on imaginative thinking. Yet there is a common denominator, which is the desire to experiment and explore, invent and innovate—see *Inventive Creativity—In Art, Everything is Possible*, Chapter 11. Choreographing experimentations as an operating concept encompasses a few helpful tips, outlined here, and a general outline on the following page.

HELPFUL TIPS & SUGGESTIONS

~ Stay within your comfort zone but make it larger and remodel it

~ Explore a dream concept within the reality of an experiment

~ Build an experiment as a bridge between *wanting* and *having*

~ Consider that an experiment may naturally lead to more experiments

~ Conduct experiments driven by curiosity rather than judgment

~ Recognize that assumption is passive, while experimentation is active

~ Experiment when you do not know what to do

CHOREOGRAPHING EXPERIMENT AS AN OPERATING CONCEPT BEYOND HISTORICAL FRAMEWORK

Let's imagine that somebody gives you a cake that you don't like, so you decide to bake your own cake and experiment with your own recipe. You still need a kitchen with an oven, all of the cake ingredients, as well as the sequence for mixing them. During the baking, nuanced details may need attention and unpredicted variables may arise. Similarly, getting lost in the woods would force you to experiment and look for a way out.

The practical steps for planning and conducting an experiment include: setting the goal of the experiment, choosing the components, and developing a framework. Designing and running the experiment could be very exciting, but also unpredictable. Finally, observing the process and analyzing the outcome might lead to a conclusion or consequent decision.

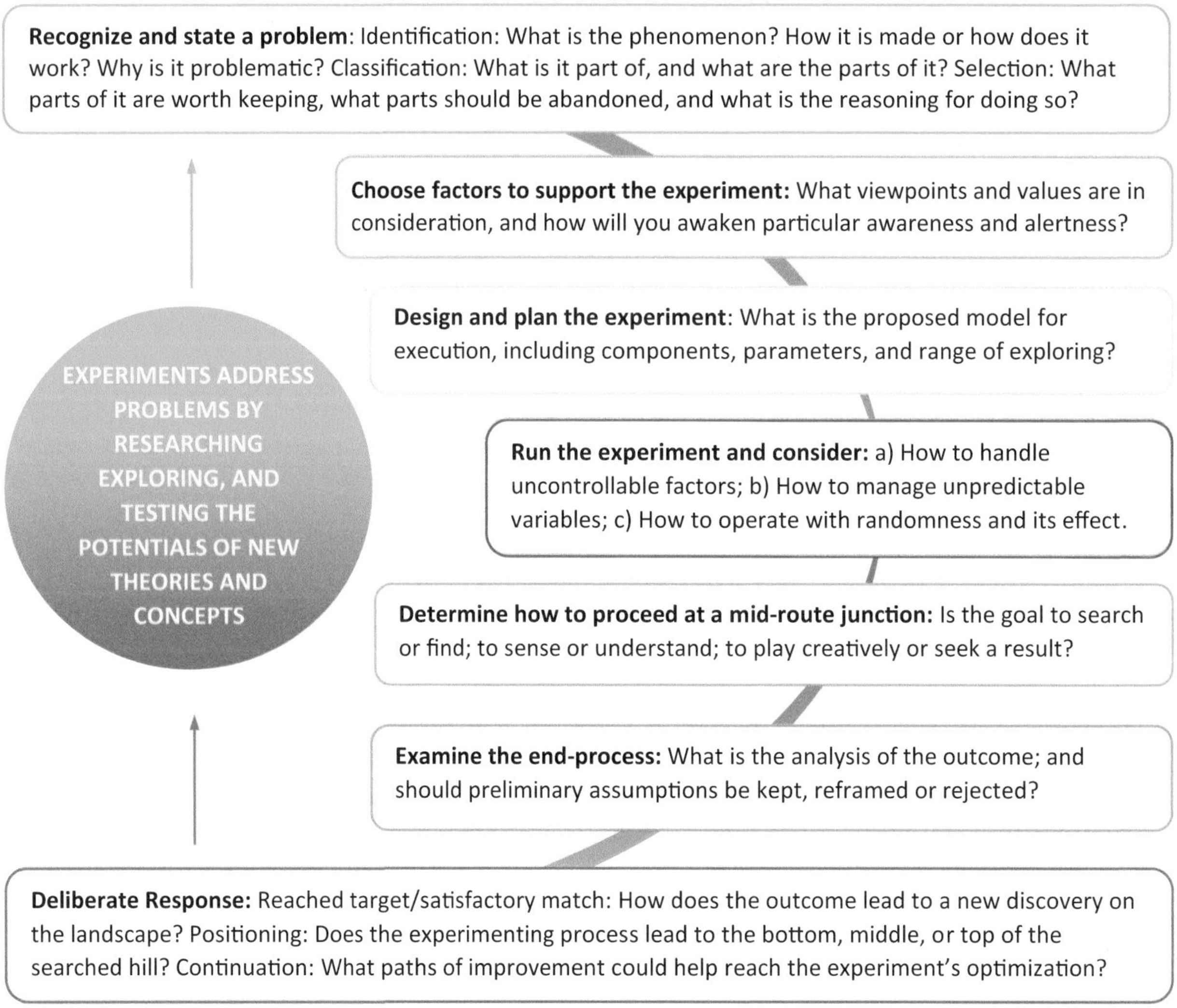

Recognize and state a problem: Identification: What is the phenomenon? How it is made or how does it work? Why is it problematic? Classification: What is it part of, and what are the parts of it? Selection: What parts of it are worth keeping, what parts should be abandoned, and what is the reasoning for doing so?

Choose factors to support the experiment: What viewpoints and values are in consideration, and how will you awaken particular awareness and alertness?

Design and plan the experiment: What is the proposed model for execution, including components, parameters, and range of exploring?

Run the experiment and consider: a) How to handle uncontrollable factors; b) How to manage unpredictable variables; c) How to operate with randomness and its effect.

Determine how to proceed at a mid-route junction: Is the goal to search or find; to sense or understand; to play creatively or seek a result?

Examine the end-process: What is the analysis of the outcome; and should preliminary assumptions be kept, reframed or rejected?

Deliberate Response: Reached target/satisfactory match: How does the outcome lead to a new discovery on the landscape? Positioning: Does the experimenting process lead to the bottom, middle, or top of the searched hill? Continuation: What paths of improvement could help reach the experiment's optimization?

EXPERIMENTS ADDRESS PROBLEMS BY RESEARCHING EXPLORING, AND TESTING THE POTENTIALS OF NEW THEORIES AND CONCEPTS

Figure 21

RESEARCH ASSIGNMENT: Research existing works: a) Use library or online resources to select and view one dance documentary of your choice about an influential choreographer and modern dance company of the second half of the 20th century. For example, you might choose a DVD of *An Evening with Kylián and the Nederlands Dans Theate*r with choreography by Jiří Kylián, or a documentary about Pina Bausch and Wuppertal Tanztheater, or a documentary about Bill T. Jones; b) Outline experimental approaches that the choreographers used to create their work; and c) Analyze what is unique about each approach. How are these methods applicable (or not) in your creative work?

★ **CREATIVE EXERCISE:** Experiment by combining time travel with creative interpretation. Based on your understating of the aesthetic of different stages of Modern Dance, create short dance sequences that identify and recreate the choreographic characteristics of these different aesthetics. For example:

➡ Imagine you are a *modern dance choreographer*. Create a dance sequence of 16 movements dedicated to the choreographic philosophy of known modern dance choreographers. Adapt and modify movements to correspond to a particular movement aesthetic—for instance, free flow, contract and release, tension and extension, and others.

➡ Imagine you are a *postmodern choreographer*. Create a dance sequence of 16 movements that do not involve any conventional dance steps or movement vocabulary from established dance traditions. Explore what type of movement material is left—for instance, pedestrian movements, gestural language, athletic and exercising activities, arbitrary movement behaviors, and task-oriented bodily engagement.

➡ Imagine that you are a *contemporary dance choreographer*. Create a dance sequence of 16 movements by blending these aesthetics and adding new elements—for instance, use randomly selected steps from folkloric or vernacular dance. Focus on crafting smooth transitions, even if the phrase contains a selection of eclectic movement vocabulary.

COMPARATIVE ASSIGNMENT: a) Analyze and compare the differences and the similarities between experimental approaches in ballet and modern dance; b) Analyze and compare the differences and similarities in aesthetics between early modern dance, modern dance, and postmodern dance; and c) Analyze and compare the differences and the similarities in the work of two different 20th-century postmodern dance choreographers—for example, Merce Cunningham and Twyla Tharp.

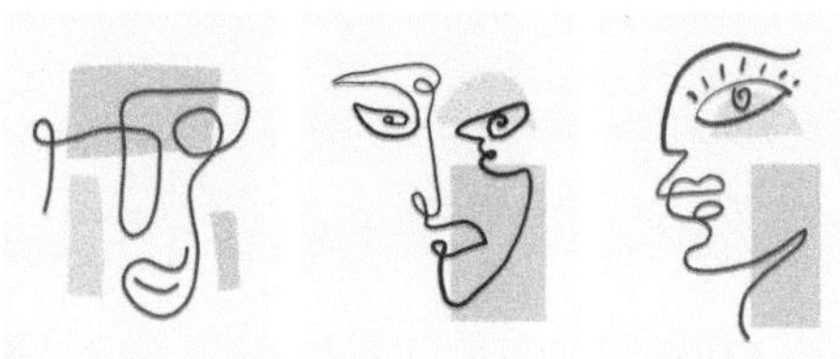

BIBLIOGRAPHY AND REFERENCES

[1] Sherman, Dennis and Salisbury, Joyce. *West in the World: A History of Western Civilization*, McGraw Hill Companies, 2001, pp. 685–773.
[2] Manuel, Castells. *The Information Age: Economy, Society and Culture*. Blackwell, 1996.
[3] Banes, Sally. *Terpsichore in Sneakers: Postmodern Dance*, Wesleyan University Press, 1987, pp. 3–20.
[4] Deleuze, Gilles. *What Is the Creative Act*, 1987, video recording with English subtitles, accessed on YouTube in August 2020, part of Two *Regimes of Madness*. Texts and Interviews 1975–1995 Gilles Deleuze (1925–1995), edited by David Lapoujade, translated by Ames Hodges and Mike Taormina, Semiotext(e), 2006, pp. 312–324.
[5] Stobbart, Kate. "You're So Not Worth It" Article, *Wunderbar Festival, 2010, and Art, Antagonism and Relational Aesthetics*, December 2010, article, original version published in CANNED Magazine, Issue 1.
[6] Benbow-Niemer, Glynis. "Shawn, Ted," in *International Dictionary of Modern Dance*, edited by Benbow-Pfalzgraf, Taryn, St. James Press, 1998.
[7] Foulkes, Julia L. Modern Bodies: *Dance and American Modernism From Martha Graham to Alvin Ailey*, The University of North Carolina Press, 2002, pp. 79–104.
[8] Foulkes 2002. *Modern Bodies*, pp. 51–78.
[9] Kisselgoff, Anna. "Dance: Powerful Emotions Distilled," *The New York Times*, September 13, 2001.
[10] Humphrey, Doris. *New Dance: Writings on Modern Dance*, selected and edited by Charles Humphrey Woodford, Princeton Book Company, 2008, pp. 6–7.
[11] Humphrey 2008. *New Dance: Writings on Modern Dance*, pp. 5–6.
[12] Humphrey 2008. *New Dance: Writings on Modern Dance*, pp. 92–96.
[13] Blumberg, Naomi. "Lester Horton," in *Encyclopedia Britannica*, 01.19.2021, www.britannica.com/biography/Lester-Horton, accessed September 2021.
[14] Allen, Zita. *A Tale of Two Pioneers*, Online article, The WNET Group, www.thirteen.org/freetodance/behind/behind_tale.html, accessed September 2021.
[15] Banes 1987. *Terpsichore in Sneakers: Postmodern Dance*, pp. 3–20.
[16] Banes 1987. *Terpsichore in Sneakers: Postmodern Dance*, pp. 41–58.
[17] Angelov, Vladimir. *Yvonne Rainier: Reimagining Dance with Parts Unknown*, an in-person interview with Yvonne Rainier, online article, Dance ICONS, Inc. October 2021, www.danceicons.org
[18] Rainier, Yvonne. *No Manifesto* (1965 and 2008), reprint of the text as excerpt, with permission by Yvonne Rainer. First published/exhibited in "The Manifesto Marathon" at the Serpentine Gallery, 2008, based on the original version published in Tulane Drama Review, Vol. 10, No. 2, Winter 1965 in an essay: "Some retrospective notes on a dance for 10 people and 12 mattresses called 'Parts of Some Sextets'," performed at the Wadsworth Atheneum, Hartford, Connecticut, and Judson Memorial Church, New York, in March 1965.
[19] Banes, Sally. *Democracy's Body: Judson Dance Theater, 1962–1964*, United Kingdom, Duke University Press, 1993, pp. 85–86.
[20] Banes 1987. *Terpsichore in Sneakers: Postmodern Dance*, pp. 57–76.
[21] Novack, Cynthia Jean. *Sharing the Dance*, University of Wisconsin Press, January 1990, Chapters 2 and 3.
[22] Angelov, Vladimir. *Lucinda Childs: From Chaos to The Day of Dancing Memories*, an in-person interview with Lucinda Childs, online article, Dance ICONS, Inc. December 2019, www.danceicons.org
[23] Craine, Debra and Mackrell, Judith. "Laura Dean," in *The Oxford Dictionary of Dance*, Oxford University Press, 2010.
[24] Banes 1987. *Terpsichore in Sneakers: Postmodern Dance*, pp. 77–91.
[25] Rosenberg, Susan. *Trisha Brown, Choreography as Visual Art*, Wesleyan University Press, 2016, pp. 77–81.
[26] Rosenberg 2016. *Trisha Brown, Choreography as Visual Art*, pp. 65–71.
[27] McDonagh, Don. *The Complete Guide to Modern Dance*, Doubleday & Company, 1976, various chapters.
[28] Warren, Larry. *Anna Sokolow: The Rebellious Spirit*, Routledge, 1998, p. 8.
[29] Kosstrin, Hannah. *Honest Bodies: Revolutionary Modernism in the Dances of Anna Sokolow*, Oxford University Press, 2017, various chapters.
[30] Grauert, Ruth E. "The Theater of Alwin Nikolais," online resource article, *Bearnstow Journal*, 1978, http://bearnstowjournal.org/theaterAN.htm, accessed October 2021.
[31] DeFrantz, Thomas. *Dancing Revelations: Alvin Ailey's Embodiment of African American Culture*, Oxford University Press, 2006, pp. 29–30.
[32] DeFrantz, Thomas. "Pilobolus Dance Theater," article, in *International Dictionary of Modern Dance*, St. James Press, 1998, pp. 631–634.
[33] Kostelanetz, Richard. *Merce Cunningham: Dancing in Space and Time*, Essays 1944–1992, A Cappella Books, 1992, multiple chapters.
[34] Kissellgoff, Anna. "Bill T. Jones In a Quest For Truth," Review, article, *The New York Times*, November 9, 1990.
[35] Felciano, Rita. *Bausch Pina, International Dictionary of Modern Dance*, article, St. James Press, 1998, pp. 42–44.
[36] Barnes, Patricia. "New Faces: Jiří Kylián," Ballet News, December 1979, Jiří Kylián's paraphrased quotation; Sanders, Lorna and Martha Bremser. *Fifty Contemporary Choreographers*, Routledge/Taylor & Francis Group, 2005, pp. 176–179.
[37] Homans, Jennifer. *Apollos' Angels: A History of Ballet*, Random House, 2010, pp. 526–532.
[38] Balanchine, George. "Marginal Notes on Dance," reprinted in Sorel, Walter. *The Dance Has Many Faces*, 3rd edition, A Cappella Books, 1992, p. 39.
[39] Homans 2010. *Apollos' Angels: A History of Ballet*, pp. 488–493.
[40] Homans 2010. *Apollos' Angels: A History of Ballet*, pp. 497–499.
[41] Homans 2010. *Apollos' Angels: A History of Ballet*, pp. 470–484.
[42] Gradinger, Malve. "William Forsyth," in *International Dictionary of Modern Dance*, St. James Press, 1998, pp. 513–515.
[43] Strauss, Marc. *Looking at Contemporary Dance, a Guide for the Internet Age*, Dance Horizons Books, Princeton Book Company, 2012, pp. 56–59.
[44] Lanz, Isabella and van Nieuwpoort, Marcel-Armand. *Toer van Schayk: Drie Dimensions in Dans*, Walburg Pers, 1998.
[45] Editors. *Has van Manen Foundation, Stichtin Hans van Manen*, online resources: www.hansvanmanen.com, accessed September 2021.

VISUAL REFERENCES

Figure 1: Photography © Mko Malkhasyan, *Summerspace*, choreography by Merce Cunningham, performers Melissa Toogood and Ashley Chen, a still from "CUNNINGHAM," a 3D film by Alla Kovgan, 2015

Figure 2: Diagram © Vladimir Angelov

Figure 3: Diagram © Vladimir Angelov, clip art: tall half full glass of water isolated on white clipping path in, Credit: Andrey Kuzmin, courtesy of Adobe Stock

Figure 4: Photography © Shapiro Studio, Ted Shawn and His Men Dancers in Shawn's *Kinetic Molpai*, ca. 1935, courtesy of Jacob's Pillow Dance Festival Archives

Figure 5: Photography © Herta Moselsio, *Lamentation*, (1930), choreography and performance by Martha Graham, Martha Graham Dance Company, Library of Congress, Music Division, Washington DC, photo date unknown

Figure 6: Photography © Hans Knopf, Doris Humphrey, and Charles Weidman at Bennington College, 1941, courtesy of Jacob's Pillow Dance Festival Archives

Figure 7: *Trio A* (1966), choreography and performance by Yvonne Rainer, images © Judson Dance Theater Archives

Figure 8: Photography © Carol Goodden, *Man Walking Down the Side of a Building*, Trisha Brown Dance Company, 1971

Figure 9: Diagram © Vladimir Angelov

Figure 10: Photography © Steven Pisano, Moods, choreography by Anna Sokolow, Sokolow Theatre/Dance Ensemble, dancers left to right: Boonyarith Pankamdech, Elisa Schreiber, Brock Switzer, I-Nam Jiemvitayanukoon, 2018

Figure 11: Photography © Christopher Duggan, Revelations (1960), choreography by Alvin Ailey, pictured company members of the Alvin Ailey American Dance Theater, 2012

Figure 12: Photography © Lois Greenfield, pictured LaMichael Leonard Jr., Erick Montes Chavero, Shayla-Vie Jenkins, Jennifer Nugent, Talli Jackson, I-Ling Liu, Joe Poulson, Antonio Brown, courtesy of Bill T. Jones/Arnie Zane Company, 2012

Figure 13: Photography © Sasha Gouliaev, *Nelken* (1982), choreography by Pina Bausch, pictured center performer Julie-Anne Stanzak, Tanztheater Wuppertal Pina Bausch, image taken during a performance in Amsterdam, The Netherlands, 2014

Figure 14: Photography © Gregory Batardon, *Bella Figura*, (1996), choreograph by Jiří Kylián, Ballett Zürich, pictured dancers Yen Han and Katja Wünsche, Opernhaus Zürich, 2019

Figure 15: Diagram © Vladimir Angelov

Figure 16: Photography © Paul Kolnik, image left: *The Four Temperaments* (1946) choreography by George Balanchine, performers from left to right Ashley Hod, Isabella LaFreniere, Russell Janzen, Emily Kikta, Claire Kretzschmar, 2018; image right: *Agon* (1957) choreography by George Balanchine, performers Tyler Angle and Maria Kowroski, 2018 © The George Balanchine Trust

Figure 17: Photography © Paul Kolnik, *The Concert (or, The Perils of Everybody)* (1956), choreography by Jerome Robbins, pictured performers by Kristen Segin, Cameron Dieck, Sterling Hyltin, 2017

Figure 18: Photography © Hans Gerritsen, *In and Out* (1983), choreography by Hans van Manen, performed by members of the junior company of the Dutch National Ballet, 2021

Figures 19, 20, and 21: Diagrams © Vladimir Angelov

We dance for laughter, we dance for tears,
we dance for madness, we dance for fears,
we dance for hopes, we dance for screams,
we are the dancers, we create the dreams.

A short poem by Albert Einstein (1879–1955)

CHAPTER 7

INTEGRAL AGE:

CONCEIVING PROGRESSIVE COHERENCY – CHOREOGRAPHING INTEGRATION –

The 21st-century society embarked on further development of digital technology inherited from the 20th-century Information Age. The commercial popularization of the World Wide Web in 1993 and the internet turned the Earth into a global village of borderless nations. Mobile phones enabled instant connectivity, and social media platforms became a new playground of societal engagement. Technological advancements in computerization and robotics continued to expand as a substitute for manual labor. New branches of digital technology such Artificial Intelligence (AI), Augmented Reality (AR), and Immersive Art (IA), as well as crypto currency, established new types of interactions and connectivity—an increasing *human-machine togetherness*. People, technology, and phenomena today are all connected and integrated! Still, if society operates divisively and without regard to the natural world, innovations will not be sustainable. Instead, if society integrates advancements with consideration of the world today, it has a better chance of survival. Such hope for a better future may characterize the 21st century as the Integral Age.

In science, great thinkers of the past such as Newton and Einstein developed their ideas mostly by themselves. By the end of the 20th and in the early 21st century, scientific communities introduced new work practices such as team research, group brainstorming, and collaborative problem solving. New trends emerged in the arts, fusing a wide range of aesthetics and merging cultures. In visual art, painters explored pictorial hybrids of abstract expressionism with figurative work. In symphonic music, with polystylism and musical eclecticism, composers were combining elements of diverse musical traditions and compositional techniques into unified and coherent musical works. In contemporary literature, the "new novel" tackled fictional wars, mystic realities, futuristic mythologies, urban melancholy, and social utopias. Using new technologies, electronic games accelerated content into an interactive digital experience.

New directions and integrations were revealed in dance as well. Choreographer David Parsons thrilled his first audience as a teen with a gravity-defying exit from a trampoline at an arts camp show. His most popular piece *Caught* is a solo in which a strobe flashes repeatedly as a dancer leaps, making it appear as if the dancer never touches the ground.

The idea sprang from a years-long collaboration with prominent photographer Lois Greenfield. The choreography uses a principle in photography in which the camera captures a moving body in a split second, making a dancer appear to hover in midair.[1]

Figure 1 Photography © Lois Greenfield, pictured Elena D'Amario and Ian Spring, courtesy of Parsons Dance Company, 2014

Trends of consolidation and integration were also obvious in politics and business. The United States considered itself a world superpower—economically and militarily—while addressing the political, social, and economic challenges of its democratic model. World politics witnessed an economic alliance with the European Union, which by the early 21st century had enlisted 28 member states. Additionally, Brazil, Russia, India, China, and South Africa formed their own corresponding coalition of emerging markets known as BRICS.

In the late 20th century, dominant establishments such as IBM, Coca-Cola, and McDonald's were eclipsed by new 21st-century mega corporations such as Apple and Microsoft, Google and Facebook, Amazon and Starbucks. These new business entities offered greater advancements in technology and an overwhelming variety of products and services to accommodate a new type of a *consumer-driven society*. Big and small businesses continually restructured their marketing and sales tactics to boost profit, using strategies of consolidating and integrating that blend, brand, and bundle or the "3B's" (Figure 2).

The 3 B's are	The Business Meaning	The Intentions Behind	The Consumer Thinking
BLENDING	Mergers and acquisitions of companies and corporations.	Establishing new efficiency, commodity, and excitement.	"I need to buy the latest, which is always the best."
BRANDING	Desired product association targets specific consumers.	Aligning an emotional attachment with a product.	"I feel great owning something new and superb."
BUNDLING	Several products are offered as one combined product.	Anticipating necessity and potential expansion.	"If I have this thing, then I need the other thing too."

Figure 2

Advanced global economies emerged across the geopolitical map: While Europe and North America were the dominant industrial zones during the 19th century and the early 20th century, the new millennium added more competition with Australia, South America, East Asia, and the Middle East. New mega-cities such as Tokyo, Beijing, Hong-Kong, Dubai, Sydney, Buenos Aires, and São Paolo now offer equal economic and cultural opportunities.

The persistent human desire for limitless economic growth and material security, however, is leaving a dramatic mark on the environment on a planetary scale. Polluted air and water, constantly shrinking forests, and the overuse of many natural resources around the world have been identified as causes of global climate change. More organizations and ordinary people are voicing their concerns. Demonstrations with slogans such as "There is No Planet B" aim to alarm political and business leaders to take action toward developing alternative energy solutions and to reevaluate the use of natural resources.

As the new 21st-century multipolar society opens new frontiers, it also brings new challenges. Resolving many pending issues in the world today cannot be achieved by only one person, one government, or one strategy. Instead, multiple perspectives must be considered, leading to the development of new integrative solution models. Consequently, the effectiveness of these models will be tested and further advanced. Selection, synthesis, and integration of the most potent ideas will lead to conceiving an overarching *progressive coherency* that could be adopted as a new functioning solution.

THE RISE OF INTEGRATIVE THINKING

The pluralistic tendencies and antagonistic thinking throughout 20th century postmodernism in the arts and philosophy began to argue that there is NOT only one "correct" approach to thinking and creating. There are many, even opposing, approaches that could be put to work together. This stance further developed and invigorated a new practice of organizing knowledge and operating creatively, which gained dominance in the early 21st century—*integrative thinking*.

The dynamic relationship between *differentiating* and *integrating* as an evolutionary and hierarchical phenomenon of growth is one of the fundamental principles of existence. In biology, for instance, a single cell divides into two, four, eight and more cells. While multiplying and differentiating, the cells also begin to connect, intersect, and integrate, blurring the boundaries in order to form various organisms and new systems of existence.

The model could be illustrated as a progression in an *upward spiral*, a process that also applies to the evolution of consciousness and development of wisdom.[2] While climbing upward in the spiral, each next level of integration reflects the previous level and leads to a new differentiation. The latter subsequently would result in the integration of the formerly differentiated entities. The higher someone progresses up the spiral cone, the wider the capacity of differentiating and integrating, which in turn results in managing greater complexity.

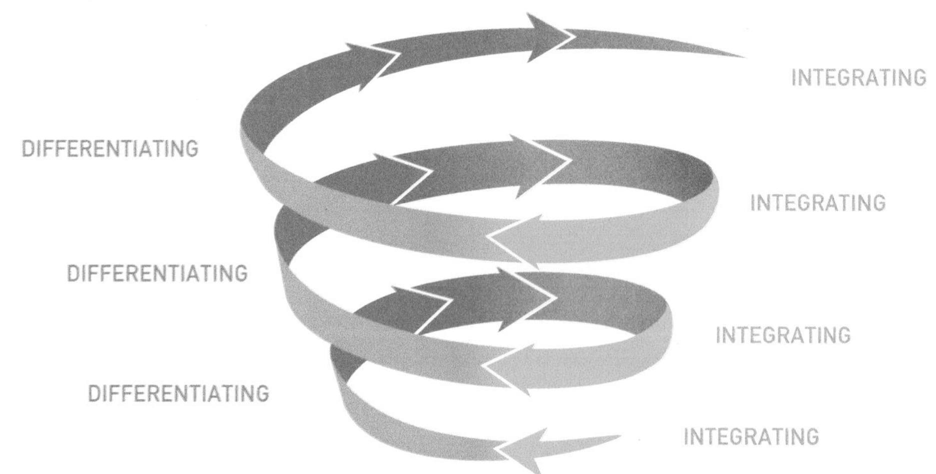

Figure 3

Although the spiral cone seems proportional and steady, climbing it is not. Moving upward could be an uneven experience, especially at the "radical turns" on the peripheries. The *differentiating* on the left side may function as "rest stops" and occur when identifying differences in ideologies. These are easier to manage. The "steep uphill drive" of *integrating* these opposing views on the right side is more challenging to handle. The periods of division tend to be prolonged and contemplative. The periods of unification, on the contrary, require energetic action with calculated timing. In this context, integrative thinking is not a passive, meditative state of mind, but rather a rigorous engagement resulting in a radical twist and revolutionary shift of the creative consciousness.[3]

New ideas, models, and systems arise from the cycling and the interplay between opposites: truth and deception, accuracy and error, progress and regression. Experiencing and understanding the dichotomy of conscious processes and the resulting revelations will foster the ability to handle polarities and unify them in a functional harmony.

Practicing choreographers, for instance, regularly encounter various dynamic states of the creative mind. These include "never-ending" shifts between confidence and doubt, swings from expressing-self to denying-self, and dilemmas about whether to adopt or to resist a certain creative choice. However, the consequent experiences of differentiative and integrative thinking and labeling them as good or bad is not productive. Instead, identifying their advantages and disadvantages may prove more beneficial.

→ DIFFERENTIATIVE THINKING ←	
ADVANTAGES	DISADVANTAGES
- Emergence of new perspectives that are usually opposed to standardized models and the status quo.	- Contention in the investigative and problem-solving processes caused by the collision of either partially contrasting or polarized views.
- Amplification of the uniqueness of an idea and its *standing out*, achieved by separating, sorting, and choosing from a basket full of colorful ideas.	- Proposing either an *anarchic* perspective or an *anti-* and *against* position as a dominating *stance of denial* instead of a solution.[4]
- Attaining a panoramic view of a mosaic of options.	- Problematizing an idea by taking it out of context.

Figure 4

➢ Integrative thinking emerges with the willingness and the ability to constructively face the tension arising from opposing ideas that are seemingly incompatible. Instead of choosing one at the expense of the other, the goal is to explore multiple options for reorganizing the content. A newly formulated idea will emerge as a solution to the tension because it will contain elements of the opposing ideas, but it will be superior to each of them.

➢ Integrative thinking facilitates the coexistence and harmonious functioning of two or more initially contradictory ideas into a new model of *progressive coherence*—a reformist state of "unity-in-diversity." Progressive coherence is the strategic milestone proving that an individual artistic practice has gained the operational capacity to advance inclusiveness.

➢ Integrative thinking and progressive coherency are accessible and achievable, but not bestowed. As the individual act of choreographing tends to be intensely subjective, it may often contradict the framework of integrative thinking. Artists often refuse to step outside of their subjective orbits to explore options other than their own. Only a purposeful engagement and continuing effort will link creative practices with integrative thinking. Such striving by individual choreographers encompasses: *going outward* to acquire relevant knowledge, a broad spectrum of viewpoints, and useful references; and *going inward* to invigorate self-transformative processes and openness to incorporating new learning and discoveries into the creative work.[5] The functioning model is not circular, but an upward spiral of intuitive craftsmanship—see Chapter 10.

THE CONTEMPORANEOUSNESS AND INTEGRATIVENESS OF 21ST-CENTURY DANCE

By definition, the term "contemporary" relates to something belonging to the present and being up-to-date. In dance, the term "contemporary" is used within a wide range of meanings and contexts: as an aesthetic platform, stylistic category, genre marker, and also as a historical periodization related to the current state of dance. Is "contemporary" always about new narrative in dance? Even when a past traditional dance production has been interpreted and recreated in relation to the present day, it could also be called contemporary. Vivid examples are re-envisioned and unconventional productions of the ballet *The Nutcracker*, choreographed by Maurice Béjart, Matthew Bourne, Mark Morris, Christopher Wheeldon, and Christian Spuck, to name a few.

Generally, the term "contemporary work" in dance is used as an indicative characteristic of a piece's *newness* and *nowness.* Contextually, the term "contemporary work" in dance suggests a contrast with the past. Yet the dance piece might also encompass the connectivity, synthesis, and *integration* of developmental stages of various traditional dance forms, with an emphasis on new creative approaches and current artistic views.

A catalyst for the contemporaneousness of dance is the emergence of new types of integrations that are in synchrony with the 21st-century realities. These new integrative constructs will also carry the potential to transmit the choreographers' views on the urgencies of today and the future of the present:

◆ **INTEGRATIVE GLOBAL PERSPECTIVES AND EMERGING STYLISTIC VERSATILITY:** With the development of technology, dance today is no longer confined to theater stages or a specific geographic location. Borderless media coverage and the availability of the internet have turned dance into universal transmedia carrying a message for all of humanity.

Advancements in dance education, training, and nutrition began producing better-conditioned dancers with greater technical abilities and *stylistic versatility.* Dancers in ballet companies train not only to perform classical ballet repertory, but also to handle modern techniques. Dancers in modern dance companies may no longer feel confined to the aesthetic of the choreographer heading the company. Most dancers today are able to execute a wide-ranging repertoire and adjust to different choreographic aesthetics.

Respectfully, choreographers living and working in different parts of the world are becoming less self-centric and more world-centric. Surging interest in global cultures raises the question of how to integrate unique traditions into creative practices. New works are emerging, crossing over stylistic boundaries, genre confinements, and cultural constructs, resulting in *cross-cultural* and *transcultural art.* The latter does not confront pure idiomatic forms or cultural and stylistic integrity; choreographers are becoming increasingly aware of cultural appropriation and various cultural constructs, as they dive into the extensive assortment of available integrative models—see also Chapters 4 and 12.

◆ **INTEGRATIVE COHERENCY INSTEAD OF AESTHETIC REFERENCE AND STYLIZED COLLAGE:** One of the advantages of postmodern dance was that it addressed the distinctions between conventional dance and movement in general—see Chapter 6. While movement could be styleless and generic, ballet during Romanticism and Classicism, on the contrary, exhibited distinct stylistic features. Are stylistic frameworks in dance threatened by the "contemporary ways of thinking and moving," which might appear to be an eclectic patchwork? Not necessarily—it depends on the choreographer's approaches and intentions. For instance, certain folkloric dances continue to retain their authenticity and stylistic coherency, other folkloric dances become stylized, and a third category are synthesized and fused into the fabric of newly integrated hybrid forms of dance. The latter two categories encompass a choreographer's unique aesthetic views. These newly emerged forms consequently stand as unique styles of certain choreographers' aesthetics.

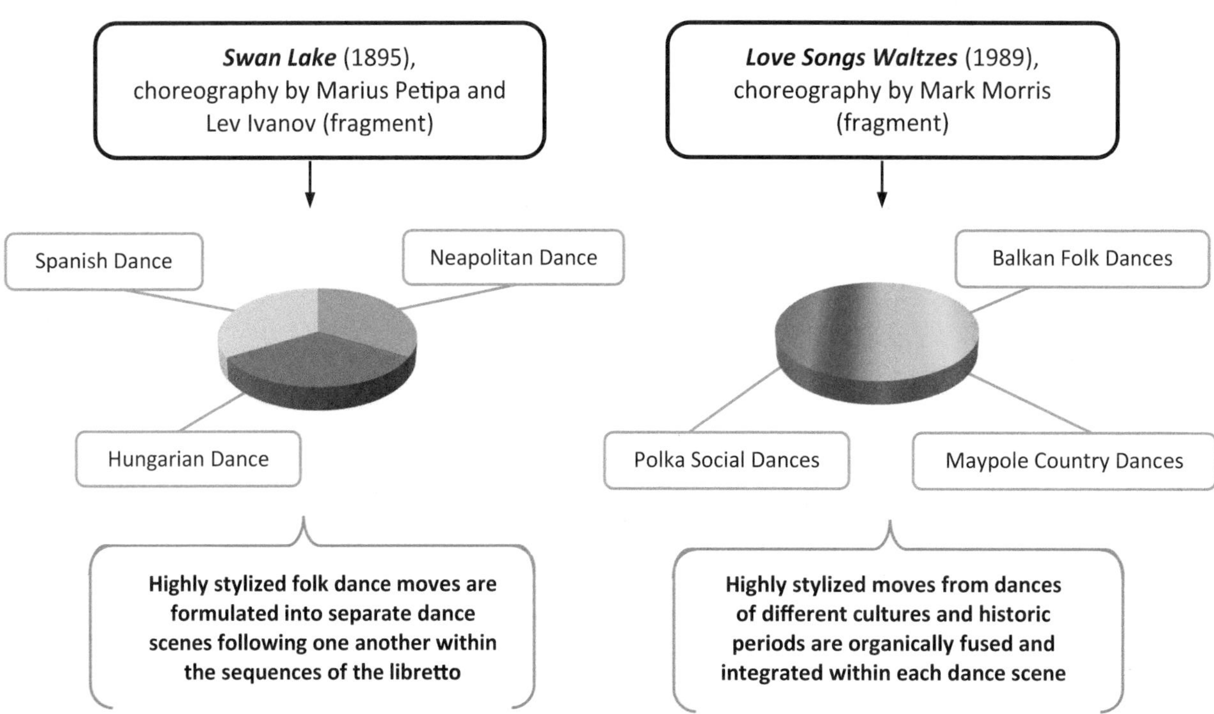

Figure 5

◆ **INTEGRATIVE THINKING AS INVENTIVE THINKING, AND VICE VERSA:** The common perception is that inventive thinking is about "starting from zero" and building hypotheses, models, and systems from the ground up. Integrative thinking, on the other hand, operates with the critical response to a variety of existing models, their compatibility, and the potential to merge them. These two distinct approaches of "generating new ideas" versus "fusing existing ideas," are actually not contradictory but complementary. As critical thinking and creative thinking often go hand-in-hand, so do integrative and inventive thinking. They both start from a place of consideration and with an openness to exploring new possibilities and models. Various techniques are described in this book—see *Inventive Creativity—In Art, Everything is Possible*, Chapter 11.

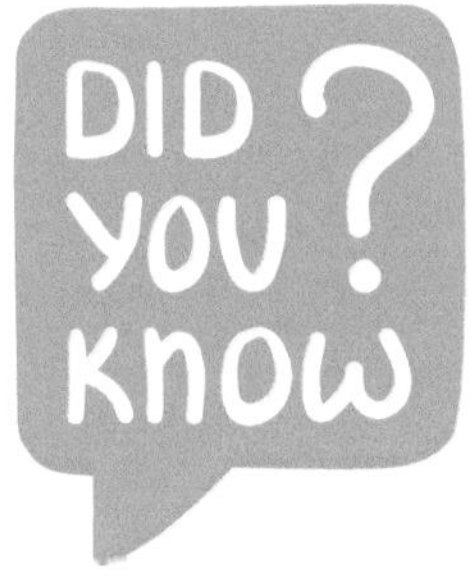

The meaning and use of *ballet* have changed radically during the past 450 years. Terms such as Court, Romantic, Classical, Neoclassical, and Contemporary have been used to place ballet's development in historical context. Over time, the dance form has been abandoning its privileged and hierarchal roots and nowadays is no longer as closely guarded and out of reach for ordinary people.

Ballet is contemporizing its codified movement vocabulary framework and the use of pointe technique; it simultaneously embraces and resists tradition by transforming itself from within. Intersections with other dance genres, arts, technology, and science disciplines are aligning ballet with the latest pioneering strategies in training and performance. The contribution of unique choreographic perspectives, the enduring integration of new content, and the infusion of innovative artistic approaches have been pivotal in the continuing renewal of ballet and its universality.[6]

Integrative thinking and approaches, as features comprising innovative and inventive strategies, play a leading role in the artistic development of a choreographer. They are also a part of the three substantial ingredients which ultimately form one's unique choreographic practice. Addressed elaborately in BOOK III, these integrative factors are:

➢ The past and current *artistic influences* and their role as a conduit in shaping one's unique choreographic perspective, identity, and individuality—see Chapter 13

➢ The forming of *new contents*, as well as the mutation, modification, and modernization of existing content found in traditions and well-known practices—see Chapter 12

➢ The implementation of *integrative approaches*, inventive and innovative artistic techniques, and interdisciplinary connections—see Chapter 11

The accumulation and integration of many other factors will also contribute to advancing one's choreographic craft, including the use of various operating systems and concepts featured in Books I and II. Additional instruments of choreography, including creative tools—both traditional and new—are covered in BOOKS IV–VII.

Serving as quick markers of integrative approaches, the following are selected samples from productions of various choreographers working in the field today. Highlighted are different points of entry and creative constructs showcasing what it means to be "contemporary."

At the dawn of the 21st century, ballet choreographer **Christopher Wheeldon** timely crafted a mission statement in the form of three innovative one-act ballets: *Polyphonia* (2001) and *Morphoses* (2002) for New York City Ballet, as well as *Continuum* (2002) for San Francisco Ballet—all staged to music by the Hungarian-born composer Gyorgy Ligeti. A driving force in contemporary music, Ligeti is well-known for his film scores, including Stanley Kubrick's *2001: A Space Odyssey* and *Eyes Wide Shut*. Ligeti's haunting and dissonant tunes range widely, often within the same piece. His innovative works are deemed polyphonic because of his layering of melodies, an unusual sonic mixture recalling the likes of Debussy and Schoenberg. Ligeti's music is well-suited for choreography, with its sculpturally shaped sound and mysterious tonal textures.

Morphosis according to Merriam-Webster dictionary is "a mode of formation or development of organisms or any of their parts."[7] Watching the ballet *Morphoses*, a spectator might wonder how a choreographer could possibly tackle and integrate the idea of complex models in biology. How does science inspire dance? The ballet begins with four dancers rising from the floor as a single moving organism that contracts and expands before breaking off into two couples, each unfolding into a complex pas de deux. The dancers then return to their opening formation as a united, breathing organism.[8] Wheeldon's nonnarrative choreography grows stunningly physical, sculptural, and sensual. His loyalty to the classical ballet lexica is infused with modern sensibility and receptive musicality.

Figure 6 Photography © Lois Greenfield, *Morphoses* (2002), choreography by Christopher Wheeldon, pictured performers Craig Hall and Wendy Whelan, courtesy of The Wheeldon Company, 2007

Another ballet choreographer implementing a range of contemporary integrative approaches is the highly productive **Justin Peck**, who, in the first part of the 21st century, choreographed more than 30 ballets in less than ten years.[9] In most of his work, Peck invents patterns recalling Petipa and Balanchine; however, the formations are modernized by contemporary geometries and infused with the dynamic feel of the present times. In Peck's *The Times Are Racing* (2017), set to music from Dan Deacon's 2012 album *America*, one could notice influences of Jerome Robbins and the integration of a hybrid of styles such as ballet and theatrical jazz dancing, in addition to tap and street dancing. Peck has successfully developed a unique fusion of dance genres. His stylistic versatility brings a non-classical approach to the classical ballet lexica.

There are passages recalling youthful competition in *The Times Are Racing*, (2017). The dancers are clad in streetwear and sneakers. The traction with the floor provided by the sneakers enhances the dancers' distinct physical rhythm that also astounds with its athleticism. The movements and steps are vigorous, demanding stamina, power, and speed. At the same time, the dance gives the impression of release and freedom, as opposed to the control of classical ballet. The casting is gender-neutral. No one in the cast has only one partner, and the pairing of who dances with whom constantly changes. There is a sense of equality, the possibilities of variations, and an openness to change. The dancers do not portray any specific characters, but rather play joyfully and immerse themselves in the movement.[10]

Figure 7 Photography © Paul Kolnik, *The Times Are Racing* (2017), choreography by Justin Peck, pictured performers Gretchen Smith, Sean Suozzi, and Brittany Pollack, New York City Ballet, 2017

Integrative stylistic versatility can also be seen in the work of **Kyle Abraham**, who has extensive background and accomplishments in contemporary dance. His dance company, A.I.M. (Abraham In Motion), has created its own space in today's dance scene. He calls his style "postmodern gumbo," an inclusion of everything he knows.[11] A new work commission for the New York City Ballet gave him an opportunity to infuse a new type of energy and diverse movement vocabulary into the ballet lexica.

The Runaway (2018), is set to music by Nico Muhly, James Blake, Jay-Z, and Kanye West, and with imaginative costumes by Giles Deacon. The ballet opens with and returns to a series of extended solos alongside chamber group configurations. Abraham integrates neoclassical technique into a mix of contemporary dance styles and inspirations from street dance, hip hop, break dance, and African dance. There are hints of internal and societal tensions—not through words or a story but more subtly, in Abraham's movement vernacular. Abraham had never choreographed on pointe shoes before but decided to use them for this ballet. He staged the dance in a collaborative manner by inviting the dancers to contribute movement ideas.[12]

Figure 8 Photography © Paul Kolnik, *The Runaway* (2018), choreography by Kyle Abraham, pictured performers Peter Walker and Jonathan Fahoury, New York City Ballet, 2018

The works of ballet choreographer **Claudia Schreier** distinguish themselves with a unique combination of youthfulness and nuanced dance geometries. Her musically responsive choreography is an expressive force that looks agile yet at ease, while constantly shifting into many patterns.

Claudia Schreier's ballet *Pleiades Dances* (2021), set to Takashi Yoshimatsu's wildly knotty and impressionistic piano compositions, is organically connected with the musical score. Integrating dynamic geometrical forms and playing with symmetry and asymmetry, Schreier masterfully moves groups of dancers as in cosmic constellations. Her movement sculptures reveal tasteful eclecticism and playful surprises. During a particular group section, wave after wave of dancers moves diagonally across the stage, lunging forward and back and forward again, creating architecture in motion. Although women wear pointe shoes, Schreier gives them so many fast gallops, runs and skips in such strongly grounded, jazzy variations, that conventional toe work takes a back seat.[13] Her partnering choreography is full of innovative lifts.

Figure 9 Photography © Brian Wallenberg, *Pleiades Dances* (2021), choreography Claudia Schreier, pictured performers Sergio Masero and Emily Carrico, courtesy of Atlanta Ballet, 2021

The work of contemporary choreographer **Nanine Linning** explores kinesthetically the primal tension between life and death as it plays out in human behavior. She often contrasts spirituality and beauty with the backdrop of dramatic and pervasive darkness.

In her piece *BACON* (2006), set to music by Jacob ter Veldhuis, Nanine Linning integrates the graphic imagery and unfiltered energy in the work of the visual artist Francis Bacon. Bacon was an Irish-born British figurative painter known for his raw, unsettling imagery that included crucifixions, portraits, and abstracted figures sometimes positioned in geometrical structures. In Bacon's art, the portrayal of fundamental behavior is accompanied by the mystery of what the painting does not show—the hidden space around and behind the portrait. Linning's "choreographic paintings" use bodily movement, sound, light, scenery, and video projection to draw a kinesthetic depiction of Bacon's emotional cosmos.[14] The choreography's excessive physicality and visceral intensity reveals fundamental patterns of behavior such as the struggle of the individual for affirmation. The line between human desires and animalistic impulses is blurred. As light beams are pointed at the abysses of the human soul, archaic instincts are revealed through the glass prism of modern sensibility.

Figure 10 Photography © Kalle Kuikkaniemi, *BACON* (2006), choreography Nanine Linning, pictured performer Pamela Campos, Stephen Quildan, and Naomi Kamilhigashi, Dance Company Nanine Linning, 2018

Integration of visual art and choreography is also revealed in the sculptural works of **Dimitris Papaioannou**. An innovative blend of Asian and Western sensibilities, on the other hand, is present in the work of **Shen Wei**, who often treats dancers' movements as human calligraphy immersed in three-dimensional multi-media performance installations. The work of **Yin Yue** draws movement material and energy from the substantive elements of nature.

Alongside a wide range of kinesthetic experimentation aiming to fuse various genres and styles, the choreographer Yin Yue forms a "new dialect" in dance by integrating Chinese folk dance traditions with innovative contemporary movement forms. Her technique called *FoCo* (FolkContemporary) incorporates five elements: earth/root, wood/axis, water/surroundings, metal/tension and fire/kinesphere, and three rhythmic stages (pulse, drop, flow) across three training segments for dancers—triggering, rooting, and mapping.[15] The technique trains dancers to execute grounded, circular, fluid, and dynamic performance that is rhythmic and powerful, yet sensual and graceful.[16] Yin's repertory pieces are mostly nonnarrative, as subject matter and main themes are drawn from emotional experiences, visual imagery, and impressions translated into complex physical phrasing with contrasting movement dynamics.

Figure 11 Photography© Anton Martynov, pictured performer Yin Yue, Yin Yue Dance Company, 2014

Exploring powerful narrative content and how it integrates in dance is also of great interest to many 21st-century choreographers. More works of literature, novels, plays, and biopics of famous individuals are revealed in corresponding contemporary ballet theater adaptations. Notable productions are **Septime Webre**'s full-length production of *The Great Gatsby* (2010), based on the novel by F. Scott Fitzgerald, as well as Dutch National Ballet's **Ted Brandsen**'s full-length cinematic production of *Mata Hari* (2016), which offers glimpses into the life of the notorious Dutch dancer and spy of the same name. On the other hand, **Akram Kahn's** full-length production of *Creature* (2021) had a hybrid narrative inspired by Georg Büchner's expressionist classic *Woyzeck*, with shadows of Mary Shelley's *Frankenstein*.

Helen Pickett's full-length productions of *Camino Real* (2015), based on Tennessee Williams' play, and *The Crucible* (2019), based on Arthur Miller's play, skillfully use movement theater and innovative ballet lexica to portray complex relationships between the characters. **Annabelle Lopez Ochoa**'s full-length production of *Frida* (2020) is based on the life of the visual artist Frida Kahlo. It integrates visual inspirations from Kahlo's colorful paintings with imagery rooted in indigenous Mexican culture. Lopez Ochoa continuously expands her collection of biopic ballets by zooming in on powerful and inspiring women in the ranks of Eva "Evita" Perón and Gabrielle "Coco" Chanel, to name a few. **Cathy Marston**'s *The Cellist* (2020) reveals an original narrative and ballet libretto inspired by the extraordinary life-force and musicianship of cellist Jacqueline du Pré.

Innovations in technology lead many 21st-century choreographers to gradually explore and embrace the blending of the digital and physical worlds. Current achievements in Artificial Intelligence, Augmented Reality, and Immersive Art are already in use and available via projection mapping and mesmerizing 3-D illusions. Technology is finally doing for dance what it has been offering to other art forms and countless areas of daily life—expanding current capabilities and elevating the ceiling of creative potential. And while it may seem counterintuitive that digital tools can enhance and even replace the physical properties of dance, new technology can be integrated with dance in ways that continue to celebrate the living, moving human body and free spirit.

?

In your creative practices, do you implement integrative approaches and stylistic fusions, and if yes, how?

HELPFUL TIPS & SUGGESTIONS

~ Handle a new choreographic creation as research in motion

~ Consider that all types of movement might be connected in one way or another

~ Incorporate choices "of" rather than "either/or" and in "between"

~ Seek creative resolutions instead of forfeiting with known substitutions

~ Integrate by keeping an open mind and options open

~ Remember that often the big picture emerges by connecting tiny dots

~ Strive for simplicity without simplifying

FIRST SUB-ORBITAL CREATIVE COMMISSION

FICTITIOUS TEXT EXCHANGE BETWEEN A CHOREOGRAPHER IN OUTER SPACE AND HIS CLOSE FRIEND ON EARTH

John, we saw your successful liftoff into space. How U feel?

Amazing! We are approaching 340K feet above Earth

Wow!... Astonishing ^.^

...and we're still climbing *.*

How does it feel to be the first Dancestronaut who's about to create a zero-gravity ballet?

Excited! Can't wait

Gr8t! Congrats again on the new dance comMission in cosmos!

Tnx, Alicia

All humanity will be watching the live broadcast from the International Space Station

Fingers X-ed. Look 4ward to it too

I mean... That will be a *world* premiere – literally!

Haha... Good one. See you back on Earth

Rooting 4 you, Space nerd, and safe flight!

Figure 12

THE CRAFT OF THE 21ST-CENTURY CHOREOGRAPHER

The 21st-century choreographer's craft is depicted in the diagram below, which maps and draws an analogy to a smartphone. Emerging as a widely popular multifunctional device during the Integral Age, a smartphone exceeds the initial purpose of a phone in a historical context, which was to accommodate a live verbal communication from a physical distance. The latest smartphone version integrates an alarm clock, calendar, calculator, music player, camera, and endless resources via the internet, not to mention email, maps, news, and social media. If you have ANY QUESTIONS, then simply ASK YOUR PHONE! Information and resources on a global scale are available instantly. Even the basic settings are an example of creative integration and multidimensionality in choreography. The choreographer can implement integrative strategies within multiple creative components such as artistic intentions and concepts, approaches and devices, movement vocabulary and sequencing, dramaturgy and structure, and collaborations with artists from other disciplines.

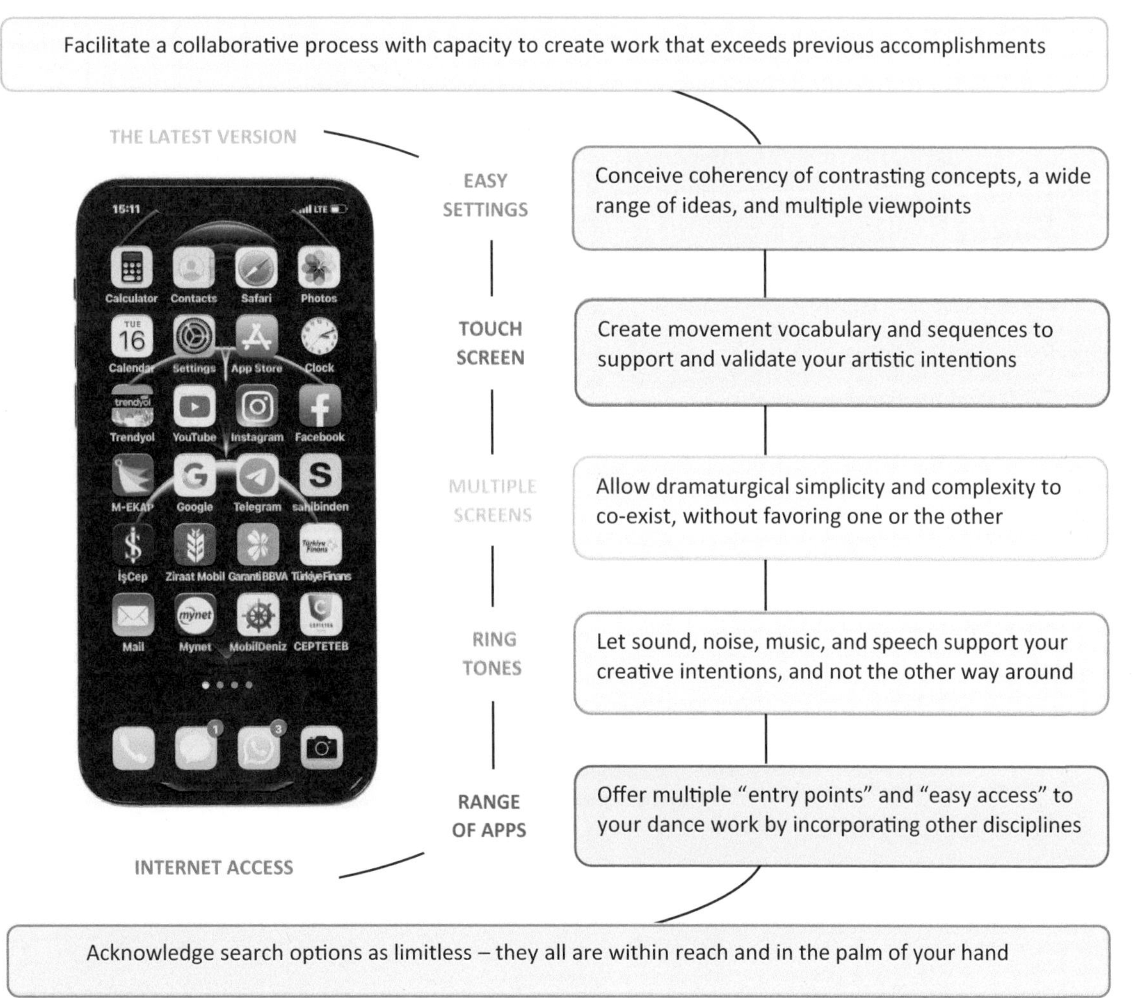

Figure 13

TRANSCENDING THE AGES

– CHOREOGRAPHING INTEGRATION IN A BROAD CONTEXT –

The integration of new perspectives, devices, and content in choreography can be traced throughout the history of dance. Choreographic craft continues to evolve in a cumulative progression as each historic period inherits the accomplishments and the advancements of the previous period.

Prehistoric ritual choreographers integrated dancing, singing, body painting, and various group activities to accommodate the community's needs. Ancient choreographers systematized aesthetic principles in order to abstract complex mythological narratives. Medieval choreographers integrated sacred and secular symbols through movement metaphors. Renaissance and baroque choreography incorporated cultural synthesis of social values, political power, and wealth. Choreographers of the Industrial Age integrated their unique movement expressions and artistic perspectives about art and life. Choreographers of the Information Age infused in their work a broad spectrum of aesthetic acquisitions regarding the affirmation and contradiction of certain political, social, and artistic ideologies.

The choreographer's integrative thinking in the 21st century encompasses the complexities and the multidimensionality of the current times. Diverse cultural constructs are at play. For example, an international team of artists would work *collaboratively* on an interactive dance production involving various arts disciplines. An *intersective* approach would explore the connectivity of the ideas and the artists' consensus to educate one another, collaborate, and formulate how the project will emerge by engaging various modalities of perception through music, dance, visual art, and other disciplines. Most importantly, what will make the project *integrative* and *substantive* is the synthesis and the fusion of various constructs that will transcend a developing framework beyond its initial form.

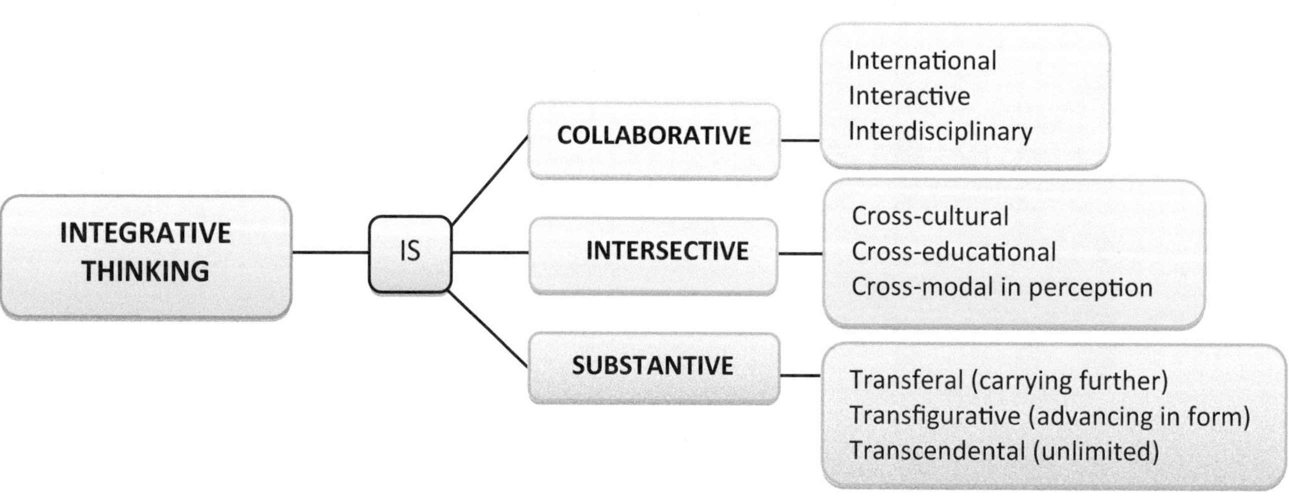

Figure 14

CHOREOGRAPHING INTEGRATION AS AN OPERATING CONCEPT BEYOND HISTORICAL FRAMEWORK

Integrative thinking as an operating concept empowers artists to consider the value of available and competing ideas from more than one perspective. A key strategy is to make sense of the tension between various models and then consider their functioning in mutually beneficial ways. Rather than simplifying a complex model and compromising its advantages, the priority is to understand its multifaceted features and identify what works and what is missing. A reorganization of existing ideas and models might explore various types of connectivity between their elements, leading to the synthesis of new ideas and models.

New ideas and models initially may seem to "never work," but this is a defensive reaction linked with a fear of the unknown. Therefore, conducting experiments with the new prototypes will test their potential and efficacy. Unexpected outcomes may at first feel uncomfortable. Further trials, reframing, and adjustments might be needed to reach and prove the overarching progressive coherency of the new idea and model.

Identify the principles, essence, and complexity of existing and new ideas, models, patterns, processes, and constructs, their incompatibility and the tensions between them. Search for overlapping interests and features and their potential intersectional relations.

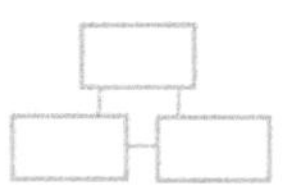

INTEGRATION is the forming of a new idea that contains elements of competing ideas, but it is superior to each

Amplify key characteristics, consider a range of values, look for a possible underlying consensus and connections between the ideas. Then reframe and reorganize their functions to facilitate co-existence and mutuality.

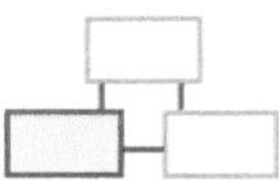

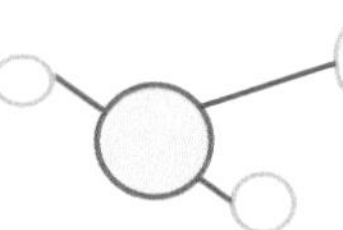

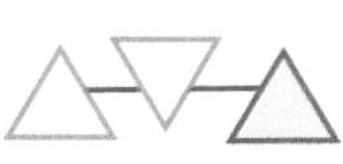

Synthesize, create, and formulate an overarching progressive coherency. Then explore the potential with tests and experiments to reframe and further develop the effectiveness of the newly integrated prototypes of models, patterns, processes, and constructs.

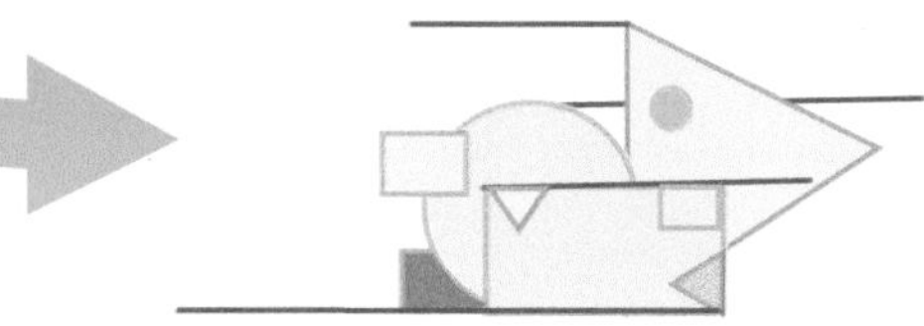

Figure 15

RETROSPECTIVE AND PERSPECTIVE
– ENJOY TIME TRAVEL BY HOPPING BACKWARD AND FORWARD –

Dance functions in many ways and serves many purposes simultaneously. The following generalization may be arguable at first, but it aims to operate as an easy-to-understand guide addressing the evolving functional constructs of dance within the context of historic periods. The different modes of thinking may be present during all historical periods, although some may be more prominent in one era. Creativity and craft could be seen as expanding in a cumulative progression from the historical past to the present and may merge to suit the contemporary time. Therefore, dance today could include one or many of the following constructs:

DANCE COULD BE RITUAL + ART + SYMBOL + CULTURE + EXPRESSION + EXPERIMENT + INTEGRATION

A choreographer may be driven by a range of artistic objectives simultaneously. In particular circumstances, a choreographer's creative intentions and operating mindset may act in a single or in multiple ways:

I CHOREOGRAPH THEREFORE I WORSHIP + STRIVE + EMBODY + PRESENT + IMAGINE + CHALLENGE + INTEGRATE

A choreographer's creative approaches and preferred practices will determine how the choreographer's work will situate in the context of various histories—shared and owned, existing and new, segregated or integrated. Rest assured that *You, the Choreographer*, are part of history, just as history is part of you.

HISTORIC AGE: constructs of dance	MODE OF THINKING	THE CHOREOGRAPHER'S CRAFT THROUGH THE AGES	OPERATING MINDSET
STONE AGE: Dance as Ritual	Practical Thinking	Initiate rituals, ceremonies, and celebrations for the survival and spirit of the community.	I worship...
ANCIENT AGE: Dance as Art	Abstract Thinking	Define and manifest aesthetic principles and artistic norms of beauty and harmony.	I strive...
MEDIEVAL AGE: Dance as Symbol	Symbolic Thinking	Form and synthesize sacred and secular symbols and metaphors of nature and God.	I embody...
RENAISSANCE: Dance as Culture	Encyclopedic Thinking	Capture and exhibit cultural attainments; please and entertain patrons and dignitaries.	I present...
INDUSTRIAL AGE: Dance as Expression	Critical Thinking	Invent, define, and display unique individual styles and new means of self-expression.	I imagine...
INFORMATION AGE: Dance as Experiment	Antagonistic Thinking	Deconstruct, restructure, and redefine ideas, idioms, constructs, and interactions.	I challenge...
INTEGRAL AGE: Dance as Integration	Integrative Thinking	Encounter, refer to and integrate complexities of idiosyncratic, cultural, and social change.	I integrate...

Figure 16

assignments & exercises

RESEARCH ASSIGNMENT: Find out if there is a live presentation of a recently created contemporary dance work in your community: a) Attend the performances and, if offered, a live post-performance discussion with the choreographer. If this option is not available, then recall a contemporary dance work you have seen recently and reviews you have read about it; b) Summarize what you saw: what was unique about the dance production, the concepts, and the movement material? How do the ideas of the work appeal to you, and do you connect with them? c) Would you consider the work integrative, interdisciplinary, or both? If yes, why? If no, why not? Analyze whether the work has multiple conceptual layers. Are you able to distinguish them and what they are?

★ **CREATIVE EXERCISE:** In an effort to create an integrative dance work, let's begin with cross referencing a concept and exploring it creatively by using interdisciplinary research.

➡ Look into anthropology, physics, technology, or other art forms and disciplines. Choose a concept, for example—survival. That same concept might appear in politics, social justice, or the environment. Think of the concept's kinesthetic features and how they can be expressed through movement.

➡ Describe your concept as an image, an impression, or a cultural construct. Then, research how that same concept has been presented by other artists in various art forms and disciplines such as music, literature, visual art, film, theater, photography, and fashion.

➡ Create a short movement sequence presentation that captures your concept. Incorporate elements of the same concept expressed in different mediums by using the various interpretations but without incorporating other mediums into the dance. To clarify: create an *integrative movement presentation*, but not an *interdisciplinary presentation*. Focus on developing your concept, and integrate its appearance in different art forms, disciplines, and mediums by using only human movement as the main medium. For instance, create a short TV advertisement dance about a certain product and its appealing signature features, without physically incorporating the product in the dance.

COMPARATIVE ASSIGNMENT: a) Compare and contrast two modalities of the creative consciousness: the 20th-century antagonistic thinking and the 21st-century integrative thinking; b) Compare and contrast choreographic approaches in the 20th century and those of the 21st century; c) In general terms, what are the similarities and the differences in the works of ballet and modern dance choreographers belonging to two different centuries—for example, George Balanchine and Christopher Wheeldon, or Merce Cunningham and Kyle Abraham?

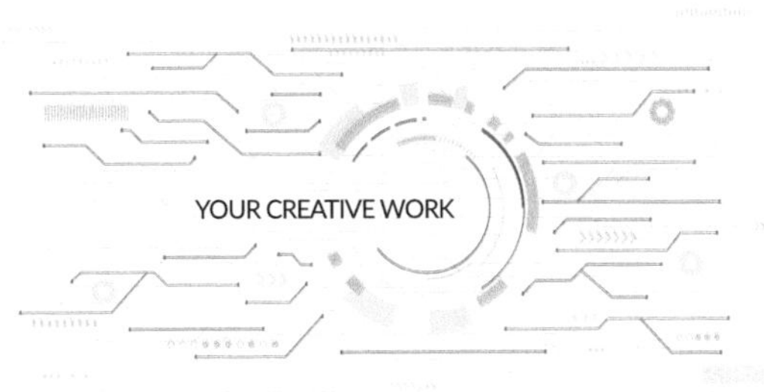

BIBLIOGRAPHY AND REFERENCES

[1] Hoedel, Cindy. "In Conversation with David Parsons," interview and article, *INKASASCITY*, 12.01.2020, www.inkansascity.com, accessed October 2021.
[2] Beck, Don Edward and Cowan, Christopher. *Spiral Dynamics: Mastering Values, Leadership and Change*, Blackwell Textbooks in Linguistics, 1996. Multiple chapters.
[3] Wilber, Ken. *A Theory of Everything, an Integral Vision for Business, Politics, Science and Spirituality*, Shambhala, 2016, pp. 1–16.
[4] Locke, Karen. "Constructing Opportunities for Contribution Structuring Intertextual Coherence and "Problematizing" in Organizational Studies," *Academy of Management Journal*, vol. 40, no. 5, 1997, pp. 1023–1062, online article: www.jstor.com, accessed September 2021.
[5] Macdonald, Copthorne. "Deep Understanding: Wisdom for an Integral Age," *Journal of Conscious Evolution*, no. 2, Article 11, 2018. https://digitalcommons.ciis.edu/cejournal/vol2/iss2/11, accessed October 2021.
[6] Farrugia-Kriel, Kathrina and Jensen, Jill Nunes. Editors. "Contemporaneity in Ballet: Exchanges, Connections, and Directions in Form," Introduction, in *The Oxford Handbook of Contemporary Ballet*, Oxford University Press, 2021, pp. 1–9.
[7] Editors. "Morphosis." Merriam-Webster.com, *Dictionary*, *Merriam-Webster*, www.merriam-webster.com/dictionary/morphosis, accessed November 2021.
[8] Editors. "Morphoses," description, Ballet Repertory *New York City Ballet Website*, www.nycballet.com/discover/ballet-repertory/morphoses/, accessed November 9 , 2021.
[9] Aloff, Mindi. "Justin Peck, Everywhere We Go (2014), A Ballet Epic of Our Time," Chapter 45, in *The Oxford Handbook of Contemporary Ballet*, edited by Kathrina Farrugia-Kriel and Jill Nunes Jensen, Oxford University Press, 2021, pp. 772–788.
[10] Janzen, Russell. "Contemporary Partnerships," Chapter 53,in *The Oxford Handbook of Contemporary Ballet*, edited by Kathrina Farrugia-Kriel and Jill Nunes Jensen, Oxford University Press, 2021, pp. 918–920.
[11] Donnell, Elisabeth. "Kyle Abraham on the Runaway," Stories, *New York City Ballet Website*, www.nycballet.com/discover/stories/kyle-abraham-on-the-runaway/, September 26, 2018, accessed November 2021.
[12] Burke, Siobhan. "The Choreographer Kyle Abraham Mixes Things Up at City Ballet," *New York Times*, September 21, 2018.
[13] Renault, Gillian Anne. "Atlanta Ballet Makes a Strong Return with Schreier's *Pleiades Dances*," review in ArtAtl, May 4, 2021, www.artsatl.org/review-atlanta-ballet-makes-a-strong-return-with-schreiers-pleiades-dances/ accessed November 2021.
[14] Editors. "Repertory Listing and Description of Body of Work," *Nanine Linning Dance Company Website*, www.naninelinning.nl/ and Foyer, Maggie. "Nanine Linning: Dancing on the Edge of Darkness and Light," interview, Dance ICONS, Inc. March 2019, www.danceicons.org, accessed November 2021.
[15] Posth, Veronica. "Movement Language: Yin Yue's FoCo Technique," interview and article, *Fjord Review*—an online dance magazine, https://fjordreview.com/yin-yue/, accessed November 2021.
[16] Editors. YYDC – *Yin Yue Dance Company Website and New Dialect Website*, www.newdialect.org/yin-yue, accessed November 2021.

VISUAL REFERENCES

Figure 1: Photography © Lois Greenfield, pictured Elena D'Amario, Ian Spring, courtesy of Parsons Dance Company, 2014

Figure 2: Diagram © Vladimir Angelov

Figure 3: Diagram © Vladimir Angelov, and clipart illustration © James Steele, *Spring*, 1922, edited by Charles Schelaand, public domain

Figures 4 and 5: Diagrams © Vladimir Angelov

Figure 6: Photography © Lois Greenfield, *Morphoses*, (2002?), choreography by Christopher Wheeldon, pictured performers Craig Hall and Wendy Whelan, courtesy of The Wheeldon Company, 2007

Figure 7: Photography © Paul Kolnik, *The Times Are Racing*, (2017), choreography by Justin Peck, pictured performers Gretchen Smith, Sean Suozzi, and Brittany Pollack, New York City Ballet, 2017

Figure 8: Photography © Paul Kolnik, *The Runaway* (2018), choreography by Kyle Abraham, pictured performers Peter Walker and Jonathan Fahoury, New York City Ballet, 2018

Figure 9: Photography © Brian Wallenberg, *Pleiades Dances*, choreography Claudia Schreier, pictured performers Sergio Masero and Emily Carrico, courtesy of Atlanta Ballet, 2021

Figure 10: Photography © Kalle Kuikkaniemi, *BACON*, (2006), choreography Nanine Linning, pictured performer Pamela Campos, Stephen Quildan, and Naomi Kamilhigashi, Dance Company Nanine Linning, 2018

Figure 11: Photography© Anton Martynov, pictured performer Yin Yue, Yin Yue Dance Company, 2014

Figure 12: Diagram © Vladimir Angelov, photo *Front view of Apple iPhone 12 Pro Max smartphone with 6.1-inch display, isolated on white* background. Credit: guvendemir, courtesy of iStock/Getty Images

Figures 13, 14, 15, and 16: Diagrams © Vladimir Angelov

Hopefully,

YOU, THE CHOREOGRAPHER

enjoyed this exciting time travel,

and it helped you realize

the treasures of the past,

the future of the present,

and the dance of tomorrow.

BOOK II

MIND AND MUSCLE

THE BODY, INTELLECT, AND CREATIVE SPIRIT

Backstage. Green Room. 10 minutes to curtain opening:

CHOREOGRAPHER: You think she will pull it off?

PHYSICAL THERAPIST: I hope so. Luckily...the injury is not that bad, but she is in pain.

CHOREOGRAPHER: She really wants to dance it. Last minute re-casting won't be good for morale.

PHYSICAL THERAPIST: Yes. But she still needs to take care of her body, you know...

CHOREOGRAPHER: Of course.

PHYSICAL THERAPIST: What doesn't seem like a priority today, will become a priority tomorrow.

CHOREOGRAPHER: Understood. We will take care of her. Meanwhile... (loud) Places, everyone!

Excerpt from

dance DIALOGUES

An Anonymous Unpublished Manuscript, 376 BC–AD 2091

CHAPTER 8

THE MOVING BODY AS A WORK OF ART

– *CORPUS COGNITUS* –

The moving human body is the choreographer's main instrument for artistic expression. Dance depends on human movement. As a dance is about to begin, the human body emerges onto the stage, alive and well, conscious and aware—a *Corpus Cognitus*. The dancing body is a work of art, a celebration of life as movement and movement as life.

Many of our cheerful greetings and daily expressions of good wishes address the importance of our physical well-being, such as "All the best," "Take care" (of your being and health), and "Live long." A healthy body is our most precious and important asset. Our bodies are always there for us, and our hearts beat, whether we notice or not.

Throughout the history of civilization, the human body has been approached and treated in many ways: it has been celebrated, idealized, studied, tortured, dissected, healed, loved, and choreographed. During the last few centuries in the Western world, especially with the beginning of the Renaissance in Italy, scientists increasingly gained a better understanding of the body's anatomical functions and movement capacities. Scientific breakthroughs and new knowledge are reflected in the humanities and the arts—including dance.

The emergence of specialized disciplines such as human biology, dance anatomy, kinesiology, biomechanics, and movement awareness has helped choreographers to better understand the anatomical and scientific aspects of the human body in motion. We might creatively use the term *physiology of choreography* to refer to such biological and physiological aspects—see Figure 1.

In the upcoming pages we explore these topics to gain knowledge that we can implement in our artistic practices. Understanding the moving body will lead us to more efficient, healthy, and productive choreographic approaches when we work with it.

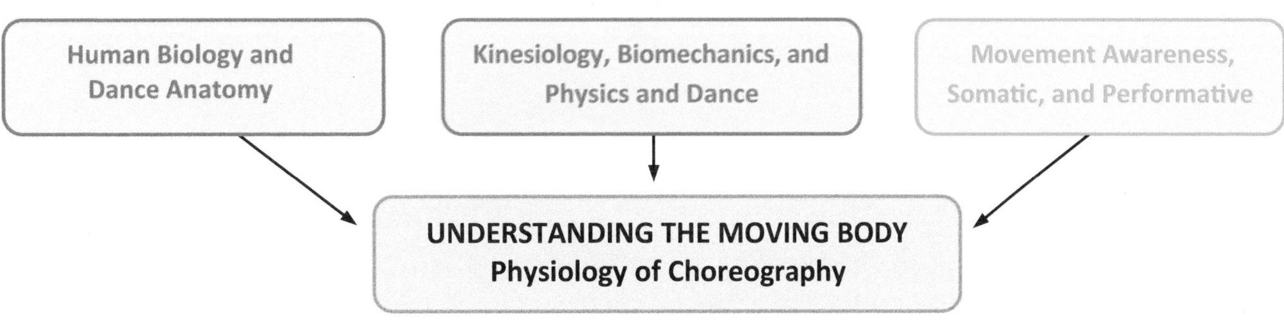

Figure 1

DANCING ANATOMY IN BRIEF

A basic knowledge of human anatomy and biomechanics helps the choreographer gain a better understanding of the anatomical origins of motion. Movement ideas can be expressed more accurately, and the choreographer can monitor how an aesthetic expression becomes a biomechanical event, and vice versa. A better anatomical knowledge helps the choreographer prevent injury to dancers and transform natural body responses and habits into healthier and safer dancing. While there are eleven major organ systems of the body that work together to perform major body functions, of primary interest to choreographers are the cardiovascular, respiratory, muscular, skeletal, digestive, endocrine, and nervous systems—see Figure 2.

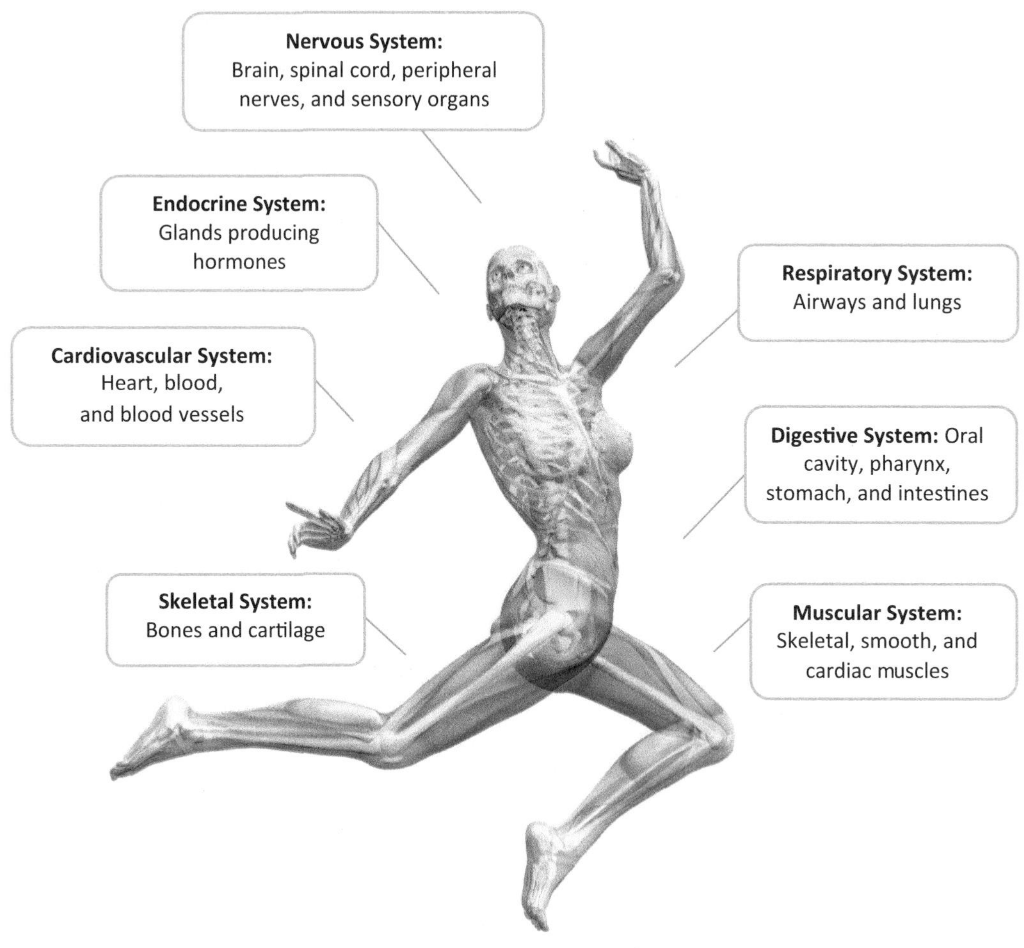

Figure 2

PHYSIOLOGICAL UNDERSTANDING OF THE DANCING BODY

The human body is a sophisticated creation that is organized into efficient systems with specialized functions. A healthy and active human body is mesmerizing and fascinating—it is a well-choreographed natural masterpiece.

A choreographer coming into the studio has expectations, time constraints, and a responsibility to the dancers. During the choreographic process, sometimes it is easy to lose sight of the fact that even with the best trained and physically fit dancers there is a limit to their capacity. Unlike musicians, who can replace a string on a cello if it breaks, a dancer's instrument is the body, and it is irreplaceable. A choreographer does not need to become an expert in dance anatomy and human biology; however, it is beneficial for the choreographer to know the *basic systems* and consider them for a healthy creative process:

- Cardiovascular: The heart, blood, and blood vessels are responsible for transporting blood to the cells of the body in need of nutrients and for the removal of waste. Adequate cardiovascular fitness/endurance is the ability of this system to successfully bring oxygen into the body to fuel the dancer, by matching the aerobic demands of the choreography.[1] Dancers progressively improve their cardiovascular endurance throughout the rehearsal process. The better this system, the longer it will take for a dancer to become fatigued.

- Respiratory: The lungs provide the body with sufficient oxygen needed to execute and maintain physical activity. When oxygen enters the *lungs*, it is taken into the blood. The size and volume of the rib cage changes with breathing. Respiration is the means of revitalizing tissues.[2] Choreography or costumes which impact the ability of the ribs to expand and contract may impact a dancer's ability to fully utilize this vital system. Besides sustaining life, breathing also helps the dancer gain awareness of physical states like muscle tension and relaxation.

- Muscular: The involuntary contractions of cardiac and smooth muscles and voluntary contractions of skeletal muscles create movement, maintain posture, and circulate blood throughout the body. Muscular strength is necessary for a dancer to support the alignment of their bones and joints as well as move gracefully through space.[3] As dancers are innately wired to please, they will work tirelessly to achieve the choreographic vision. In this process, however, they may not have the muscular strength to accomplish this goal safely. Dancers strive to adapt to unfamiliar movements, and yet, there could be a mismatch between the dancers' training and the choreography's demands. Anticipating the time for adaptation in the rehearsal process will help limit the extent of muscle soreness as the body adapts to new movement vocabulary.

- Skeletal: The bones and connective tissue create the internal framework of the body, protecting internal organs and supporting joint movement.[4] A choreographer exploiting the beauty of a hypermobile dancer will be stressing the connective tissue around joints, and with each run of the dance or repetition of a singular movement, a hypermobile joint is at greater risk of being compromised.

➢ **Digestive:** This system breaks down food into small enough components for the nutrients to be absorbed and used by the body for fuel, growth, and cellular healing. Inadequate nutrition and hydration will contribute to fatigue and injuries. Providing short breaks during rehearsal for water or lunch breaks to refuel during longer rehearsals allows the body to refresh its energy stores, clear mental fog, and be prepared for the work ahead.

➢ **Nervous and Endocrine:** The nervous system coordinates voluntary and involuntary actions and transmits signals between different parts of the body. It is divided into the *central nervous system* (the brain and spinal cord) and the *peripheral nervous system* (all the nerves branching out from the brain and spinal cord). The latter is divided into *sensory* and *motor* functions. The *motor nervous system* is functionally divided into *somatic* (voluntary) and *autonomic* (involuntary).[5] Often, choreographers are excited to see their vision come to life, and they may become more demanding, expecting the product to be perfect during the rehearsal process. When the dancers are mentally and physically fatigued, the nervous system will become slower to react, impacting the muscles' ability to work on demand. The *endocrine system* is a collection of glands that produce hormones, which regulate multiple systems in the body including metabolism, tissue function, mood, and growth. This system produces *adrenaline* when the brain senses a challenge or becomes overexcited. The choreographer's positive attitude may mitigate the dancers' level of *anxiety* before a performance.

FIGHTING FATIGUE

– HAULING HARM AWAY –

Fatigue is a significant risk factor for injury for dancers during training, rehearsal, and performance. If a dancer is struggling to learn new work, or the execution of technique is not reaching the expected level, this could mean the dancer's mind-body is in a state of exhaustion.[6] This level of fatigue begins to slow reaction time, greater physical and mental effort is being exerted with less success, poor habits can begin to develop and the risk of injury increases greatly. Choreographing shall do no harm!

While fatigue is a natural part of the training process, there are steps a choreographer can take to support the dancer's ability to reach the choreographic vision. The human body needs time to warm up and to cultivate the ability to stay warm throughout the rehearsal process. A good warm-up may consist of an at least 30-minutes dance/company class or an individualized program focused on warming up the physical body and centering the mind.[7] Once a dancer is *warm*—it's time to choreograph, because now the challenge is *keeping* the dancer *warm*. A 30-minute period of non-motion makes the dancer *cold* again. The cycle repeats.

The nature of the choreographic process involves starting, stopping, waiting, and repeating small sequences of movement. During this time dancers are working the anaerobic system, which excels at short bursts of energy, but fatigues quickly. Once the choreography has built longer movement sequences and rehearsal is focused on running sections for general feedback, the body now moves into using primarily the cardiovascular/aerobic system.

Before starting on a project, a choreographer may consider providing the dancers with advanced information regarding the intensity level of the choreography, which can help them better prepare for the workload. Dancers who incorporate changes in their physical capacities in preparation for a new choreographic work can benefit them greatly. This will help them achieve the demands of the choreography at the intensity required for performance, without experiencing undue levels of fatigue that could increase the likelihood of injury or cause a deterioration of the standard of artistry.[8]

BODY FEATURES, TYPES, AND STEREOTYPES

Beautifully proportioned human bodies are the subject of admiration in many classical paintings and sculptures. Classical masters of visual arts strove to capture the perfection of human figures, using their imagination without limits! However, young dancers might realize that they do not have the stereotypical *ideal body* that enables perfect dance technique. What is an *ideal body* in the first place, and what does it do choreographically?

Each dancer has a certain type of *body features*. The stereotype of what a typical dance body *should* look like often pressures dancers to struggle with maintaining their body weight and to set healthy limits to their physical conditioning. What is too much or too little? Many dancers might feel they have just one choice: to train at their best and to stay fit for the physical demands of the work. At the same time, a dancer's physical characteristics might become a choreographer's creative advantage. An atypical body composition can be perceived as unique in comparison to the stereotypical or "ideal" dancer's body type.

Dancers can be tall, petite, broad, slim, strong, athletic, or anywhere in between. Besides having varying body types, range of motion, flexibility, strength, and endurance, dancers also have differing personalities, temperaments, and stage presence. Therefore, it is essential for the choreographers to identify a dancer's individual characteristics and unique qualities, and to use them effectively during the creative work. That is ideal!

◆ Experienced choreographers are aware that dancers may struggle with their own physical and technical limitations. Dancers often compare themselves to other dancers, and such competitiveness can be harmful, both physically and psychologically. Choreographers may sense that dancers are most happy when they perform movement material that fits their body type and abilities. The choreographer's empathetic and positive attitude in the studio will energize the dancers. When dancers feel supported instead of criticized, they can work around their own physical limitations and set forth realistic goals.

?

How would your movement look on dancers with different shapes and sizes of bodies, and how would that experience enhance your choreographic vision?

KINESIOLOGY, BIOMECHANICS, AND PHYSICS OF DANCE

– THE DYNAMIC FORCES AFFECTING THE DANCING BODY –

Kinesiology is the study of human movement in physiological, mechanical, and psychological contexts. The term comes from the Greek words *kinesis*—movement, and *logía*—study. The discipline studies professional practices centered in physical activities, as well as the science of proper physical exercise.[9] Dance kinesiology grew as a specialization out of the sports medicine field to deal with physiological, biomechanical and psychological elements of dance practice.[10] Thinking of dancers as artistic athletes combines the training of the physical body and mind while addressing the unique nature of an artist. Applying a few kinesiology concepts within the choreographic process can support the dancer and improve the experience for all involved.

- **Specificity** comes into play as a tool to build up the dancer's physical needs for success.[11] Specificity focuses on introducing movements, skills, and conditioning exercises directly related to the movements required in the choreography. By working on the physical demands outside of the rehearsal process and preferably before the rehearsals begin, the dancer will be ready for the challenge and less likely to fatigue or develop an injury.

- **Periodization** is a concept which supports rest, recovery, and peaking in performance. Similar to dance, any organized competitive sport has a pre-season, regular season, post-season, and an off season. In each of these time periods, there are smaller cycles of rest, practice, scrimmages, and then performance.

- **Prioritize the balance of training with rest and recovery** to optimize when the athlete will peak in their performance. As choreographers, if we take this principle and apply it to the dance world, we will discover multiple options to manage rehearsal time. Small adjustments in the schedule to allow breaks, a day off, working with smaller groups at a time, or holding a shorter rehearsal one day—will all make a difference in the ability of the body to recover and make the next rehearsal more effective.[12]

- **Repetition** of choreography reinforces technique and performance but also has a downside. How often are the phrases "One more time," "Practice makes perfect," or "We need additional rehearsals" spoken? While the perfectionist drive in most dancers triggers the urge to do more, the cost can be great. More may not be better! Excessive repetition can lead to overcompensation in the body, resulting in fatigue, boredom, and staleness.

- **Lateral Bias** is the overwork of one side of the body over the other. While the human body is built symmetrically, typically with artistic choices and training dancers become asymmetrical, such as by favoring a right-leg movement and a left-leg stance, turns to the right, and partnering lifts consistently to one side. While it is important to honor the choreographic process, it is helpful to evaluate biases in leg use or side of the body to determine the amount of fatigue on the musculoskeletal system and the risk of repetition leading to injury.[13]

There are a few considerations and efficient approaches for how these dynamic forces could be helpful to the choreographer's daily work with the dancers:

◆ Choreographers may consider beginning each rehearsal with a *review* of the dance sections set previously. Using their bodies and mental memory, the dancer would be *recalling* the sequences and *marking* the movements. This is to serve as a preparatory phase—a *mental and physical warm-up before* the material will be performed in *full-out*. Such a strategy helps refresh the memory and prevent injuries.

◆ Choreographers may engage with the dancer in physically *learning* new movement material that might require *memorizing* through repetition. Dancers' memory is an expanded complex memory that activates *movement memory* and *muscle memory*. This leads us to *neuroplasticity*, which addresses how motor skills and brain activities are related. Many physical activities, including dance performance and choreography, change how the brain functions. With *adaptive plasticity*, specific areas of the brain or the entire brain are affected when acquiring new dance skills with long-term training.[14]

◆ Choreographers may repeatedly rehearse the newly learned material to *improve* and refine the movement sequences. The dancers continuously analyze the choreographer's feedback and adopt new strategies to adjust the level of force and nuances of each movement. The ongoing calculated repetition—without overdoing it to avoid fatigue and injuries—could help to execute the choreography of the dance better and more accurately. As *repeating* becomes a *routine skill*, the practiced skills turn into *advanced skills*.

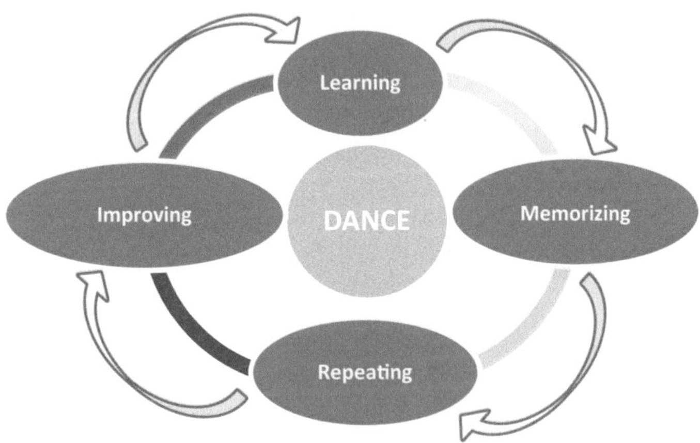

Figure 3

Motor control and redundancy involves the process of how dancers activate and coordinate their muscles and limbs to perform a specific movement task. The human body can generate many configurations of the joints. With creative thinking, the dancers can produce multiple versions to complete the same task, where the nervous system directs the motor system in unlimited ways to achieve the intended movement.[15]

◆ Choreographers are often interested in exploring opposition and counterbalance—for example, by placing body parts against each other in search of complex and unusual moves. At the same time, choreographers are also curious to investigate and find the optimal and efficient ways the body can execute a dance phrase or partnering sequence.

Biomechanics, along with kinesiology, studies and analyzes mechanical principles of living organisms and their movement as they are related to physics and engineering sciences. Newtonian laws of physics, for example, interact and affect all human motion. Proper understanding of biomechanics and its application to the muscular, joint, and skeletal actions of the human body can improve the execution of a given task and improve physical performance.[16]

◆ Choreographers deal directly in the creation of movement and its specific execution; therefore biomechanics can assist with strategies to teach the performers how to execute the choreography with the most efficiency, in relation to the laws of physics. A choreographer might frequently wrestle with three important questions:

➢ Which principles of physics govern human motion?

➢ What is the relationship between laws of motion and the mechanics of specific movements?

➢ How does the human body performing an intended task interact with the internal and external forces of the physical world?

Physics and dance—a field cross-related to kinesiology is a branch of learning about the relationship between these two disciplines. To answer these questions, we examine how Newton's laws of physics apply to a dancer leaping into the air, for example. First, a dancer in stillness encounters the Earth's gravity, the pressure of the dance floor against the human body, and the air's resistance. As the dancer leaps, a physical principle described by Newton as the *Law of Inertia* is enabled.[17] The law states that a body in rest or in motion will stay at rest or in motion until an external force acts on the body.

A dancer who is about to leap must engage effort, energy, and motion in the vertical direction. As the dancer leaps and moves upwards, the velocity and the upward motion remain strong only up to a certain point of elevation, until the external force of gravity acts on the dancer, leading to a landing.[18]

Another physical law present here is the *Law of Action-Reactio*n, which states that for every action, there is an equal or opposite reaction.

◆ Therefore, when the choreographer wants the dancer to land smoothly and then to move forward, backward, sideways, or upward as quickly as possible, the choreographer instructs the dancer how to approach movement most effectively—with and against gravity.[19]

?

Do you find gravity advantageous or disadvantageous to your choreography—would you turn off gravity if you could, and why?

DANCING PHYSICS

Multiple forces and physical laws affect the body while in motion. Biomechanical principles refer to the mechanical principles and the laws of nature applicable to any living being. As physical laws of gravity, momentum, and energy affect dancing bodies as they move through space and time, the same physical laws also affect substantial functions that occur inside the human body.

Choreographers gradually develop skills to identify the most relevant physical principles governing the impressive lifts and dynamic locomotion executed by the moving partners during a dance, as well as the subtleties of balance and the techniques of turns and big leaps.

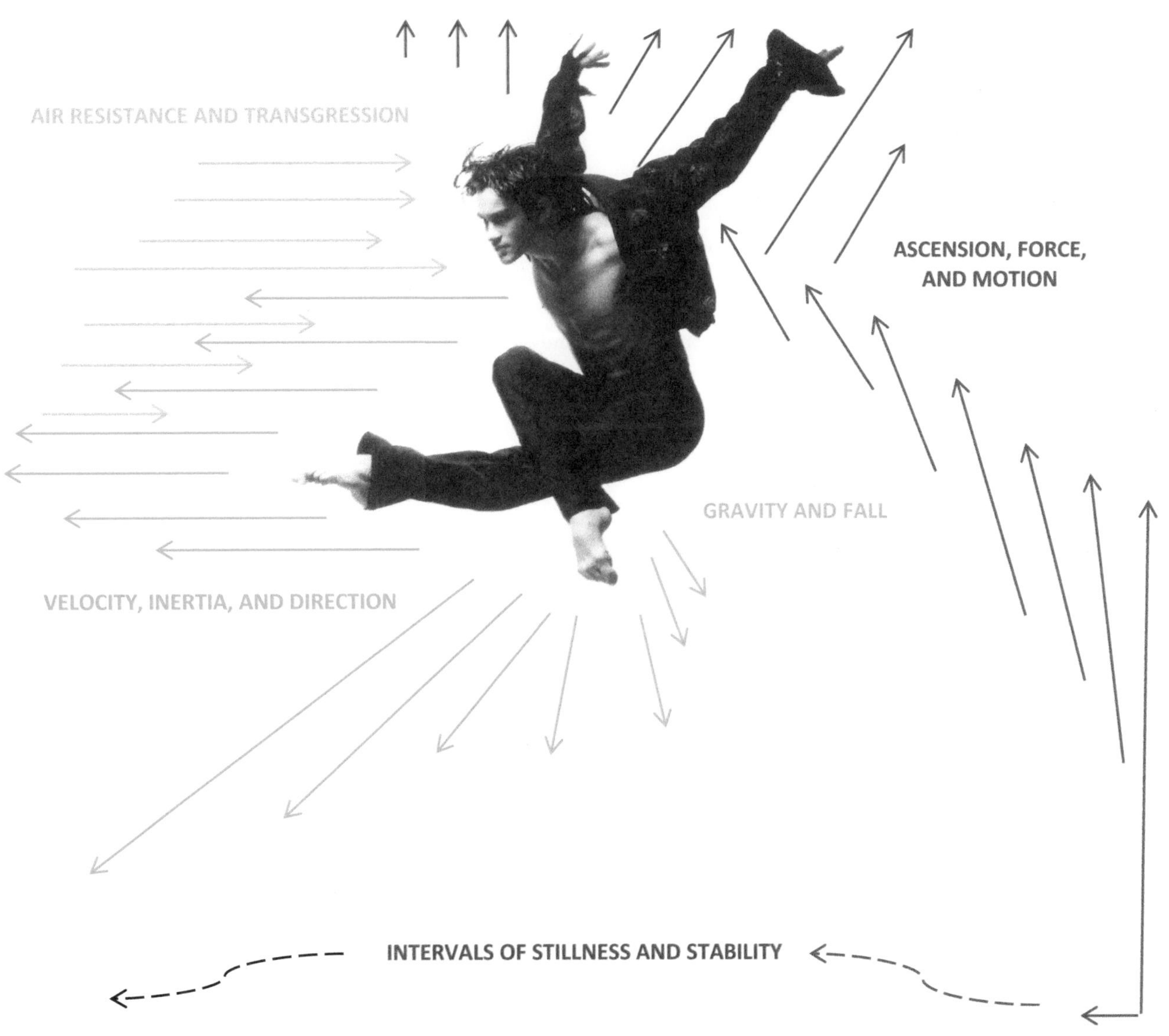

Figure 4 Photography © Chris Dame, *Nostalgia* (1996), choreography by Vladimir Angelov, pictured performer Rasta Thomas, courtesy of Monica and Isabel Dame, 1999

BODY AND MOVEMENT AWARENESS

– THINKING, SENSING, AND MOVING VS. MOVING, SENSING, AND THINKING –

As part of their artistic curiosity and creative experimentations, choreographers are often drawn into a variety of established and developing movement approaches and techniques. These could range from therapeutic methods to various exploratory somatic practices and techniques—all aiming to explore and study multisensory awareness, body responsiveness to motion, and movement sensibility. These aspects combined lead to the development of an umbrella discipline and term—*movement awareness*—that unites the body and the mind in wholeness.

Movement Awareness in this context can be understood as a result of an *inner observing*, and it is differentiated from the notion of *self-consciousness*, which often might include an *evaluation* of what it is being observed. Body and movement awareness practices are organized into what are known as *somatic techniques*. Some of them are:

➢ **Feldenkrais Method** is recognized as a strategy to improve posture, flexibility, and coordination ability, and to help those with restricted movement, muscle pain and tension, as well as neurological, developmental, and psychological concerns. Unlike traditional dance exercises, where movements are objective, repetitive, and mechanical, the Feldenkrais Method suggests processes of learning movement organically, practices of letting go of habitual patterns and allowing for new patterns to emerge.[20]

➢ **Alexander Technique** has similar goals and teaches the use of the appropriate amount of effort for a specific activity, thereby preserving and reserving sufficient energy for the full scope of daily activities. The method addresses freedom of movement, balance, support, and coordination, and a reeducation of the mind and body.[21]

➢ **Laban/Bartenieff Movement System** is the culmination and ongoing development of the philosophies, theories, and practices of Rudolf Laban and Irmgard Bartenieff. Laban's work focused on human movement patterns by mapping the space of human movement. He explored various aspects of human action by developing a theoretical framework and clearly delineated language for describing movement. Laban's protégé Bartenieff utilized Laban's ideas, and worked not only in dance, but also as a physical therapist with a focus on optimizing both functional and expressive aspects of body action. Their system identifies, represents, and interprets macro and micro patterns of human movement. Examined are also universal and group patterns common to all humans, including culturally relevant patterns, as well as patterns that identify an individual's unique characteristics.[22]

While somatic practitioners tend to engage analytically in *movement studies* with a focus on experiential work of movement re-patterning that supports the body-mind integration, choreographers tend to engage creatively in *movement research* with a focus on experimental work on how movement is found and how it operates as an artistic expression. Are dancers, performers, and movers caught in the middle between these two practices?

In somatic practices the dancers focus on *internal sensation and observation-based techniques*, with an emphasis on personal physical experience. In contrast, in the performing arts, the dancers pay close attention to the positions and motion of each part of the body and on developing *performative techniques*. This is because most forms of concert dance, such as ballet or modern dance, emphasize the external observation of movement by an audience. These two approaches initially might seem to be opposites, and yet they are integrated under the concept of movement awareness:

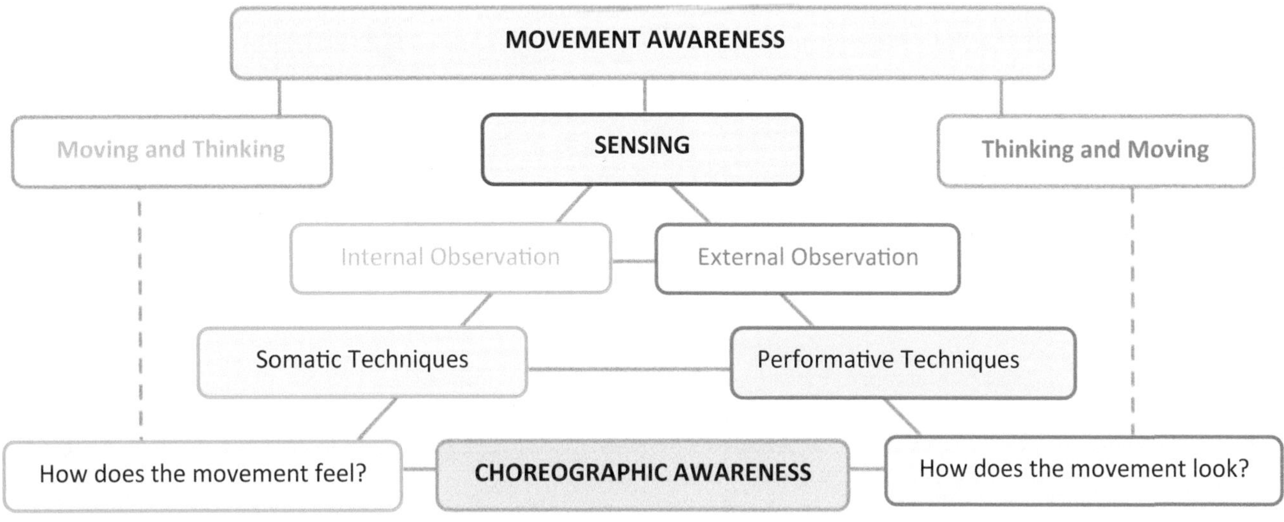

Figure 5

There is an organic kinesthetic unity between inner sensation and outer appearance. As somatic practitioners and performance creators engage with movement experience, could somatic and performance techniques merge? Spontaneity of moving will be lost without *somatic response* and trust in instincts. Inspiration in concert choreography will be lost without *performative explorations* of new movement designs. Mutual growth is about identifying patterns, only to re-pattern them to lead to new directions, discoveries and integrations.

The choreographer is in the position to lead, facilitate, and share the creative process in the dance studio, and propose working algorithms, which could be:

(representational) **THINKING → SENSING →MOVING** (external observation)

and/or

(experiential) **MOVING→ SENSING→ THINKING** (internal observation)

From a choreographer's perspective, a movement as a *kinesthetic experience* emerges and can be observed within three possible inquiries:

- ➢ How is movement replicated by the body, and how does it look when it is performed in various ways when observing and evaluating it externally?
- ➢ How does movement originate in the body, and how does it feel when observing and evaluating it internally?
- ➢ How does movement emerge and define itself while observing and evaluating it internally and externally?

The choreographer approaches the dancer's body by employing the following strategies to activate, sense, think about, and observe movement:

◆ Replicating and Reproducing: The dancer's *body is a vessel replicating* external choreographic imagery. The choreographer demonstrates and teaches pre-created movement material such as shapes, steps, and moves. Feedback is given based on external observation in order to accomplish an anticipated and desirable performance outcome—see figure 6. Many choreographers working in concert dance genres choose this process—see *Movement Ownership: Giving, Taking and Receiving Movement* in Chapter 14. This approach is presentation oriented, where replication leads to representation.

REPLICATION		
THE CHOREOGRAPHER	⟷	THE DANCER
DEMONSTRATES movement **VERBALIZES** actions and intentions **SETS TIMING**, rhythm and counts		**SEES**–Be observant **HEARS**–Be alert **THINKS**–Be attentive
+		+
–Elaborates on movement detail –Explains contentand context –Provides feedbackand corrections based on external observation	⟷	–Memorizes sequencing –Understands objectives –Considers nuances and timing –Retains, displays and executes
REPRESENTATION		

Figure 6

and/or

◆ Sensing and Responding: The dancer's *body is actively sensing and responding* to the ongoing directions from the choreographer, who provides various prompts and triggers. These could be tasks, scores, imagery, and others aiming to initiate and provoke body sensations and to awaken a movement-generating process. The choreographer might solicit movement material based on the dancer's internal observation, bodily feedback, and somatic intelligence—in an experiential, interactive, and collaborative manner. Many improvisational artists choose this process—see *Twelve Leaders in Dance Improvisation and Their Methods of Movement Research and Movement Findings* in Chapter 15. This approach is exploration oriented, where interaction leads to somatic responses and collaboration.

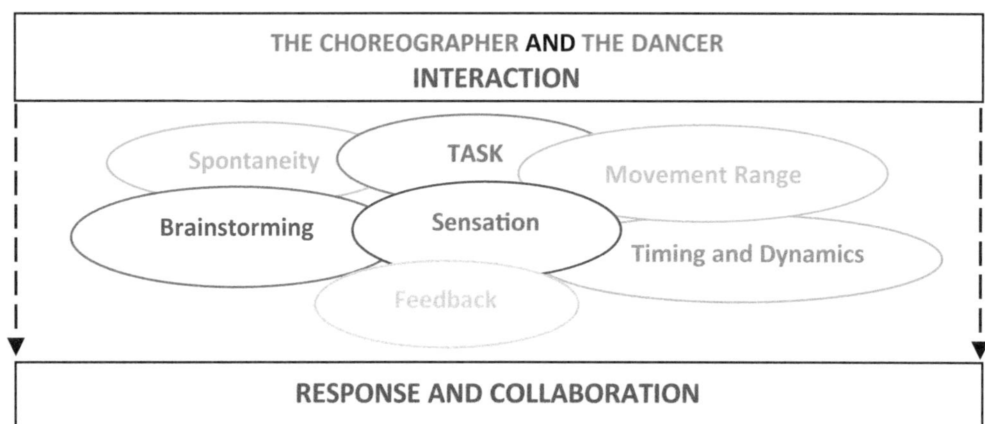

Figure 7

and/or

◆ **Adapting and Embodying:** The dancer's *body is creatively adapting* movement material generated mutually with the choreographer, the choreographer, while simultaneously implementing internal observation and external appearance. Their mutual goal is a movement embodiment and ownership with skillfully controlled execution and performative qualities—this means to embody a type of being, rather than to only represent a type of being. Many choreographers who are interested in pursuing a definitive artistic outcome by involving exploratory movement feedback from the dancers choose this process—see *Movement Initiation and Origination: Generating, Manipulating and Defining Movement* in Chapter 14. This approach is adaptive, where integration is driven by mutual intent and movement embodiment.

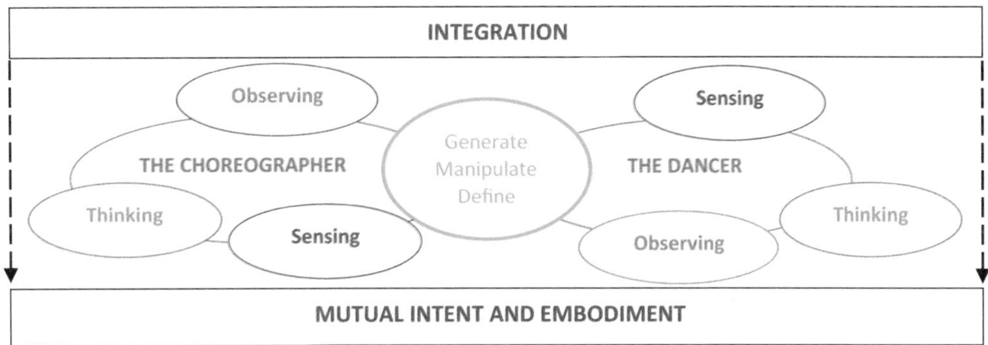

Figure 8

◆ Choreographers tend to react to what they observe dancers do. Dancers, on the other hand, tend to react to what they sense, while form-searching and/or form-fitting the movement on their bodies. Finally, the teachers and rehearsal directors tend to react to and focus on improving the movement's accuracy. This active-reactive occurrence unfolds within three processes: generating movement, teaching it, and performing it. Observational goals could be identifying, describing, and improving, or *fixing* the movement experience and the appearance execution. The somatic goals and performative observations of movement—seeing, sensing, and responding—could have multiple perspectives:

➢ Observational viewpoint: Who is watching: a dancer, a teacher, or a choreographer?

➢ Observational context: What are the focus and the objectives of the surveillance?

➢ Observational feedback: What sensations and/or appearances will be addressed?

For example, the given movement in a dance studio is a simple "arm swing." A dancer most likely will focus on how the arm swings efficiently, expressively, and effortlessly; a dance teacher and a repetiteur most likely will focus on the mechanics, alignment, precision, and movement quality; a choreographer most likely will focus on how the arm swing captures the movement's intent, purpose, reason, and its interpretation/sense-making.

If *somatic* is about communication within the body itself, and *performative* is about the communication of the body to others, what would the body/mind prioritize?

QUESTIONS OF THE THINKING BODY AND THE DANCING MIND

Besides being a movement creator, the choreographer often steps into the role of performer in order to demonstrate movement to the dancers. There is also a teaching aspect to choreography, as the choreographer instructs dancers in movement elements to implement and memorize. Finally, there is the coaching perspective and the repetiteur, who adjusts the movement for accurate execution. Performing, teaching, and choreographing, however, are distinct professions that demand specialized attention. Each has a different point of view on what the body/mind should focus and work on.

During the creative process in the dance studio, varying inner monologues and questions might run through the minds of a performer, a teacher, or a choreographer. These inquiries may involve internal and external observations of movement, pending concerns, and layers of performative issues that need to be addressed. Can they be summarized in short queries about what the "*body is thinking*" while the "*mind is dancing*"? Let's provide a few hypothetical examples:

TASKING	PERFORMER	TEACHER	CHOREOGRAPHER
Dance Pose/Balance	How do I find my center to balance longer?	What is the right alignment of the hip, upper torso, and limbs to accommodate this balance?	How does this balance encompass the overall meaning?
Dance Movement	How do I perform effortlessly and save energy?	What is the most efficient and accurate way to execute this movement?	What is the purpose of this movement and how does it contribute to a phrase?
Dance Phrase	How do I move organically and seamlessly?	Are all movements in correct order and are all transitions properly executed?	How does this movement phrase align with the concept of the entire dance?
Movement Quality	What is the feeling to guide the expression of the movement?	What imagery should I use to help the dancer understand the specific quality?	What are the features that best explain my unique movement style?
Rhythm, Timing, and Musicality	What is the lead: the melodic line, the counts, or sound cues?	How do I help the performer transition from counting to listening to the sound cues?	Is the dance of substance, and are the music and sound supportive to the concept?
Stage Presence and Performance	Am I correctly presenting the choreographer's intentions?	How do I bring out a clear presentation and the best of the performers' skills?	To what extent do I give liberty to the performers to interpret the material?
Costuming and Production	How can I move comfortably in the tightly fitted costume?	Do the costumes fit the dancers properly, and do they look flattering on them?	Does the costuming complement the concept of the choreography?

Figure 9

?

If you are simultaneously choreographing, performing, and rehearsing on your own, how do the different points of view affect you?

Does movement support thinking? Let's look into different concepts, practices, and "embodymental" dynamics: In his work *Republic*, the Greek philosopher Plato outlined how gymnastics and good health were important parts of education. He emphasized that *thinking and intense physical exercising* go hand in hand.[23] Gymnasiums in ancient Greece soon became places for more than physical fitness. Plato assembled his students to give them lectures during workouts in the less structured setting of a gym. Ultimately, Plato founded a school of philosophy at a gymnasium in Athens called the *Academy*, after which the school was named. Plato's school made the gymnasium famous.[24]

An artistic rendition of a philosophers' gathering is masterfully portrayed in a Renaissance fresco at the Vatican called *The School of Athens*, by the Italian artist Raphael—Figure 10. The two center figures walking forward are Plato, on the left in the orange toga, and his pupil, **Aristotle**, to the right in the blue toga. After Aristotle left Plato's Academy, he formed his own school of philosophy known as *Peripatetic*, which generally meant *thinking while walking*. Aristotle and his colleagues gathered at a gymnasium called the Lyceum, which was popular with its covered walkways and colonnades.[25]

Figure 10

In the 20th century, **Albert Einstein** had a different kinesthetic approach toward the thinking process. He used a mediation technique and *thinking while being still and stationary*. Basically, he either sat on a chair or stood still—*sitzenbleiben*. Stillness allowed his body to settle into a uniquely deep state of rest to restore physiological balance and unlock a higher state of consciousness. As Einstein famously noted, it was the way to get answers even before asking the questions.[26]

In conclusion, multiple scientific disciplines such as dance anatomy, kinesiology, biomechanics, and movement awareness are helpful in understanding the essentials of how the body in motion operates. This knowledge can assist choreographers in developing their unique approaches for interaction when working on movement with dancers.

HELPFUL TIPS & SUGGESTIONS

~ Identify the strengths and the limitations of the dancers' natural capabilities

~ Facilitate the growth of the dancers' kinesthetic potential

~ Embrace the fact that everybody is a body, and no body type is a prototype

~ Exercise efficiency and attentiveness when experimenting with movement

~ Befriend physical forces and take advantage of velocity, inertia, and momentum

~ Address internal and external observations, no matter which one comes first

~ Consider elaborating on physical sensations as part of thinking dance—call it *wisdom of the senses*

assignments & exercises

RESEARCH ASSIGNMENT: a) Dance anatomy and kinesiology: Define the difference between major organ systems of the body. How does the understanding of fighting fatigue affect artistic practices? Define how the kinesiology concepts of periodization, rest, repetition, and lateral bias can be used to support the choreographic process; b) Physics and dance: Define how the laws of physics affect the human body in motion. How can the choreographer use the basic principles of physics advantageously? c) Research somatic practices: Define the difference between various somatic practices. How are these somatic techniques useful in performative practices?

★ **CREATIVE EXERCISE:**

➡ BODY STORIES: Choose a part of the body, organ, muscle group, skeleton, joint, nerve, fluid, or entire internal system. Envision that the part of the body or system you have chosen has a dance story to share and it asks you to perform it. Create a movement phrase that portrays your choice and show it to your peers for feedback. To test if your portrayal is accurate, ask them to guess what exactly your bodily selection is.

➡ BODY SENSES: Choose one of the five senses—touch, sight, hearing, smell, and taste—and visualize its function. What actions and motion are involved for this sense and its organ(s) to gather information? Create a movement phrase based on the motion of this sense. Then create a phrase as if a sense is missing. Explore how we compensate with other senses so that we can continue to function without the missing sense.

➡ BODY RESPONSES: Choose an obstacle or a type of barrier to explore how the body mechanisms and intuition respond to challenges in the environment. This could be moving in a very small, confined space, dealing with hurdles, restricting furniture, or with randomly selected objects causing movement discomfort. Build a dance phrase as a creative response to challenges occurring in the performance space or the physical objects placed in it. First, portray the physical obstacles and the ways of interaction. Next, present the struggle and the possible resistance. Finally, propose a movement invention that allows you to overcome those physical obstacles.

COMPARATIVE ASSESSMENT: Work with the dancers on the execution of a simple movement, for example, an arm swing. Interview the dancers about their internal observation and sensations and compare these to the external observation and appearance of the movement. Analyze how the two observations relate (or not). What is the difference between the sensation and the performance of that same movement? Does what the dancers "feel" become obvious in the execution of the movement? Why or why not? Could the "feel" and the "look" of the movement be linked? How?

BIBLIOGRAPHY AND REFERENCES

[1] Fitt, Sally Sevey. *Dance Kinesiology*, Shirmer Books, 1996, pp. 255–265.
[2] Fitt 1996. *Dance Kinesiology*, pp. 262–265.
[3] Fitt 1996. *Dance Kinesiology*, pp. 101–173.
[4] Fitt 1996. *Dance Kinesiology*, pp. 17–20.
[5] Fitt 1996. *Dance Kinesiology*, pp. 266–280.
[6] Quin, Edel, Rafferty, Sonia and Tomlinson, Charolette. *Safe Dance Practice*, Human Kinetics, 2015, pp. 114, 252.
[7] Kish, Robin and Morton, Jennie. *Dancing Longer Dancing Stronger*, Princeton Book Company, 2019, p. 310.
[8] Quin, Rafferty and Tomlinson 2015. *Safe Dance Practice*, p. 76.
[9] Harris, Janet and Hoffman, Shirl. *Introduction to Kinesiology: Studying Physical Activities*, Human Kinetics, 2000.
[10] Quin, Rafferty and Tomlinson 2015. *Safe Dance Practice*, p. 107.
[11] Kish and Morton 2019. *Dancing Longer Dancing Stronger*, pp. 18.
[12] Kish and Morton 2019. *Dancing Longer Dancing Stronger*, pp. 19–20.
[13] Quin, Rafferty and Tomlinson 2015. *Safe Dance Practice*, pp. 129, 253.
[14] Burzynska, Agnieszka Z., Finc, Karolina, Taylor, Brittany K., Knecht, Anya M. and Kramer, Arthur F. "The Dancing Brain: Structural and Functional Signatures of Expert Dance Training," Original Research, Journal Article, *Frontiers in Human Neuroscience Online Magazine*, 2017, www.frontiersin.org/articles/10.3389/fnhum.2017.00566/full
[15] Fenton, Julia A. *Principles of Movement Control That Affect Choreographers' Instruction of Dance*, Honors Thesis Projects, University of Tennessee, 2011. https://trace.tennessee.edu/utk_chanhonoproj/1436
[16] Aruin, S. Alexander. *Biomechanics*, Article, Encyclopedia Britannica online, Encyclopedia Britannica, Inc. March 2019, www.britannica.com/science/biomechanics-science, accessed April 2019.
[17] Lucas, Jim. *Inertia & Newton's First Law of Motion*, Live Science, article, 09.27.2017, www.livescience.com/46559-newton-first-law.html, accessed October 2018.
[18] Collin, George. *Physics and Dance*, Physics Honors Program presentation at the University of Illinois, Power Point, 2001, University of Illinois in Urbana Champaign, accessed 2015.
[19] Laws, Kenneth. *Physics and The Art of Dance*, Oxford University Press, 2002.
[20] Content Editors. *About Feldenkrais Method*. Feldenkrais Institute New York, website content, accessed May 2016, https://feldenkrais.com/about-the-feldenkrais-method/
[21] Content Editors. *About Alexander Technique*. Alexander Technique, website content, www.alexandertechnique.com/at.htm, accessed May 2016.
[22] Studd, Karen A. Content Editors. *Whole Movement, Transforming Lives thought Movement*, December 2018, https://wholemovement.org/what-is-the-laban-bartenieff-movement-system-lbms/, accessed May 2018.
[23] Plato. *Republic*, John Wiley & Sons, 2014.
[24] Multiple authors. *Sport as Training for Virtue in Classical Greek Philosophy*, article 5: *Plato's Gymnasium, Sport, Ethics and Philosophy*, Magazine, vol. 4, no. 2, Taylor & Francis, August 2010.
[25] Liddell, Henry and Scott, Robert. *Greek-English Lexicon, Peripatetic School*, entry, Oxford University Press, 1982.
[26] Pearson, Craig. Ph.D., *Albert Einstein—There Is Neither Evolution nor Destiny; Only Being, Transcendental Meditation*, online article, accessed September 21, 2011.

VISUAL REFERENCES

Figure 1: Diagram © Vladimir Angelov

Figure 2: Diagram © Vladimir Angelov, Image: *Anatomy in Motion—Woman Leaping*, 3D rendering of a woman leaping, side view, showing muscles and bone structure, photo ID:140442260, authored by LindaMarieB, courtesy of iStock/Getty Images

Figure 3: Diagram © Vladimir Angelov

Figure 4: Diagram © Vladimir Angelov, photography © Chris Dame, *Nostalgia*, (1996) choreography by Vladimir Angelov, pictured performer Rasta Thomas, courtesy of Monica and Isabel Dame, 1999

Figures 5, 6, 7, 8, and 9: Diagrams © Vladimir Angelov

Figure 10: *The School of Athens* by Raffaello Sanzio da Urbino, painting and fine art fresco, The Vatican, courtesy of Wiki Commons, 2020, public domain

Knowing yourself is the beginning of all wisdom.

Aristotle (384 BC–322 BC)

CHAPTER 9

DISSECTION OF A GLORIOUS MIND

– INSIDE THE BRAIN OF THE CHOREOGRAPHER –

If we wish to reach our fullest potential, we must first get to know our own mind, mental functions, and thinking mechanisms. A choreographer may wonder and even be concerned about the following: "Am I naturally talented? Will I succeed gloriously?" Each person is born equipped with great abilities and many gifts waiting to be discovered and explored. With time and in the right circumstances, individuals may grow motivated to fully realize their special talents. The secret to being talented in a particular area might be easily demystified. A child generates at an astonishing rate impressive drawings, charming songs, and cute dances while jamming. Creativity in the form of "kids-at-play" seems to be fun and easy. Every child is a natural born artist and every adult has been a child. Is playfulness indicative of natural talent and the potential of a glorious mind?

Children are uninhibited and often unaware of how to control their mental forces—their creativity flows freely. For the average working adult, on the other hand, imaginative thinking and spontaneous artistry are no longer a regular daily activity. Choreographers are perhaps positioned somewhere between a child and an adult, as they strive to develop *goal-oriented* and *purpose-driven creativity* to produce dances in an intentional and controlled manner.

Choreographers are *physical thinkers* who transform abstract ideas and mental images into bodily shapes and moves. When it comes to creatively engaging the body and mind, the question is: Do our minds control our bodies, or do our bodies control our minds? The human brain is a complex mechanism, run by conscious experiences and unconscious psychological functions.[1] How our mind/brain works and manifests itself can be unveiled with the help of psychology, cognitive neuroscience, and behavioral science.

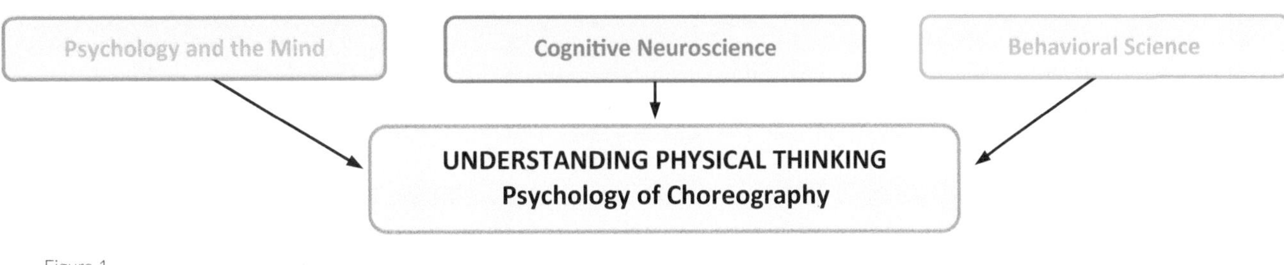

Figure 1

In psychology, the *conscious mind* is responsible for awareness, knowledge, logic, reasoning, intentions, and all planned actions such as locomotor movements and eating. The *unconscious mind* is responsible for involuntary actions such as breathing, subliminal perceptions, and automatic responses. Many of these conditioned *reflexes* are executed without a person having to learn or initiate them.[2]

Contemporary psychology and *cognitive neuroscience* suggest that many activities in the arts and the creative professions also involve conscious and unconscious mental processes.[3] The question remains: How do these processes interact?

Onstage, dancers often perform steps, moves, and jumps at a rapid tempo, while not being consciously aware of each single action performed with different parts of the body. Great baseball athletes have reported that if they try "to think" of the position of the ball in mid-air as it comes at them, they will be less likely to hit it well. The players' quick physical response and judgment based on training and skills enable them to move faster and perform more skillfully. The same type of less conscious response occurs in many sports. In the book *Inner Skiing*, the authors indicated one could ski more skillfully if the mind remained quiet and did not interfere while performing this activity.[4]

These findings lead us to the conclusions that: a) unconscious mental functions proceed at a higher speed than conscious functions; b) there is no immediate synchronization between the conscious and the unconscious; and c) the conscious and unconscious streams might proceed as separate events.

The speed of *processing* and *responding* to input demonstrates the difference between the two modes of mind and of thinking. The conscious mind processes at a slower pace and with a long-term devotion, just like a marathon runner is expected to consciously focus on the end goal. The subconscious mind, on the other hand, seems to process information immediately and reactively—behaving like a sprinter.[5] This is why the phrase "pay attention" is used to bring extra awareness, focus, and control over an automated speedy response, and therefore more mindfulness. This is what dancers do when asked to describe how a movement felt in their body after having performed it.

For example, when reading a textbook, we may constantly force ourselves to remain focused on reading and understand the meaning. On the other hand, parts of our brain want to understand everything with just one quick glance at the page in order to capture the essence of its meaning. Developing the ability to "switch" the modes of the mind and change the speed of thinking is especially important to deliberate control of the creative process and its outcome in choreography.

There are also various forms of thought processes such as visual, auditory, and even "emotional" thinking. For example, it is possible to think in pictures, remember sounds, or make decisions based on emotions. The two basic categories of thinking are most commonly described as: *analytical thinking*, which is information- and fact-oriented, and *intuitive thinking*, which is instinctive and speculative, and therefore imaginative.[6]

Based on varying observations and experiences, we can conclude that the minds of the choreographer, dancer, and dance scholar work in related and yet different modes.

In this book we introduce the classification of and relationship between the **Knowledge Mindset** and **Skills Mindset**, as an interaction between the two minds most efficiently explains the choreographer's combined **Artistic Mindset**—see diagram on next page.

- **Knowledge Mindset** emphasizes intellectual and analytical processes, rationale, logic, and reasoning.

- **Skills Mindset** is interpretative and exploratory with a focus on improvement of abilities by repetitive training, pattern formation, and establishment of habits.

- **Artistic Mindset** is imaginative, creative, and conceptual. It offers space for expansion of ideas, and therefore it is transformational in its core function.

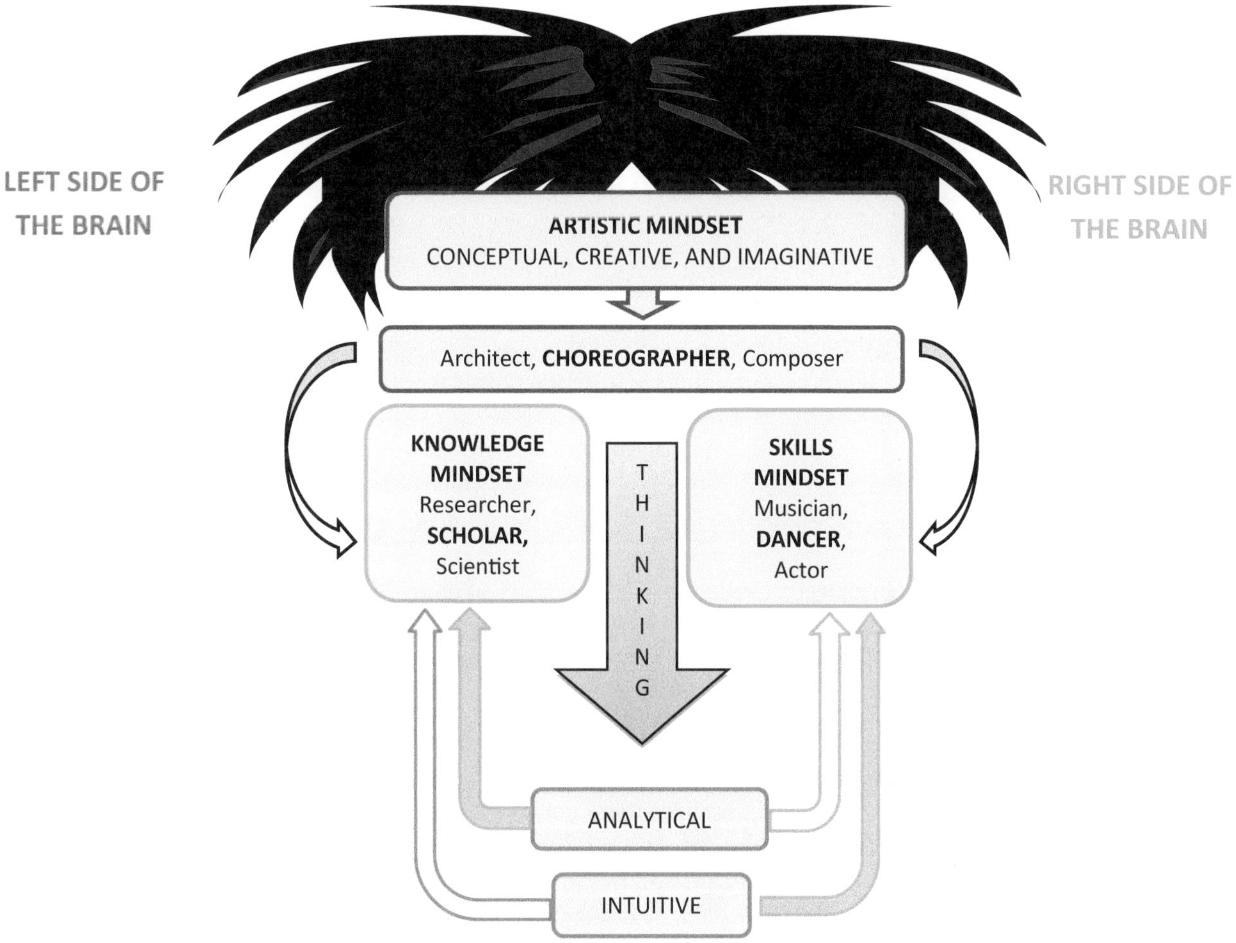

LEFT SIDE OF THE BRAIN

RIGHT SIDE OF THE BRAIN

ARTISTIC MINDSET
CONCEPTUAL, CREATIVE, AND IMAGINATIVE

Architect, **CHOREOGRAPHER**, Composer

KNOWLEDGE MINDSET
Researcher,
SCHOLAR,
Scientist

THINKING

SKILLS MINDSET
Musician,
DANCER,
Actor

ANALYTICAL

INTUITIVE

Figure 2

?

What do choreographers use the most, images or words?

We can answer this question by examining Nobel Prize-winning psychobiologist Roger W. Sperry's research.[7] Sperry found that the brain is divided into two hemispheres: the left side, which relates more closely to logical reasoning, and the right side, which corresponds more directly to imaginative and emotional processes. Although the two sides of the brain are different, neither is dominant. We can think of the *left side* of the brain as our *Knowledge Mindset*, which governs analytical thought like the processes used in science and mathematics. Similarly, the *right side* of the brain is related to our *Skills Mindset*. It allows us to imagine, visualize, feel the music, and understand non-verbal cues. The two sides of the brain are connected by the *corpus callosum*.

◆ Choreographers engage both mindsets when creating a dance. Choreographers physically demonstrate movements by using the right side, while analyzing and counting syncopated music beats for the dancers by using the left hemisphere. Both hemispheres provide choreographers with a harmonious Artistic Mindset. In truth, creative problem solving requires activity between many parts of the brain that are not normally connected.[8]

DANCING NEUROSCIENCE

– ANATOMY OF THE CHOREOGRAPHIC BRAIN –

The brain is a unique organ like any other. Different areas of the brain are assigned specific functions and yet work united in synchrony. The brain does not simply expand during learning or creative problem solving, but rather develops new connections, sequences or patterns between its cells or neurons.[9] The mechanisms of brain activity give rise to conscious thoughts, allowing mental processes to emerge from the physical brain.

A choreographer's mind, personality, and intelligence are often attributed to genetic potential given by birth (nature) and/or by the methods used to rear a person (nurture). In both cases, the day-to-day life of a healthy and productive choreographer moves forward exclusively with the support and the full involvement of the brain's centralized operations.

Just like a choreographer, who is in charge of synchronizing a variety of dancers and their movements, distinct parts of the brain are actively involved in each choreographic function, so that a subjective physical experience eventually is processed as an exemplified mental phenomenon.

➢The ***frontal lobe*** is the brain's center for attention, planning, problem solving, time management, and smell. Speech articulation is located in the left hemisphere, and more specifically in the left temporal lobe. The motor cortex system generates neural impulses that control the execution of movement. This system is in charge of deliberate movement, the sensory guidance of movement, and the spatial orientation of actions. The motor cortex and its components internally generate the planning, the choreographing, and the sequences of movement execution, as well as the coordination and synchronization of the two sides of the body—the left and the right. In other words, the motor cortex is the brain's "choreographer" responsible for all conscious kinesthetic undertaking.

➢The ***right parietal lobe*** integrates sensory information from various parts of the body. Also, the somatosensory system, which is made up of a number of important receptors to receive and process information for pressure, temperature, and pain, is located in this lobe. Touch is a somatic sense reflecting a variety of multisensory mechanisms to establish sensations, such as pressure, skin stretch, vibration, and temperature. The ***left parietal lobe*** functions in visual word recognition and language processing, reading, writing, and mathematics.[10]

➢The ***temporal lobe*** consists of structures that are vital for long-term memory. Declarative (or explicit) memory is conscious memory divided into semantic memory (facts and their meanings) and episodic memory (events). Sections of this lobe called the hippocampi are responsible for forming memories, although only spatial memories are stored in this structure. The temporal lobe also contains the primary auditory cortex, which is involved in the primary auditory perception of hearing. This cortex receives sensory information from the ears, and the data are processed into meaningful units, such as speech and words. Finally, this part of the cortex is in charge of speech comprehension, speech recognition, semantics, verbal memory, and name recollection.

➢The ***occipital lobe***, on the other hand, is the visual processing center of the choreographer's brain. The subregions of the lobe specialize in different visual tasks, such as visuospatial processing, color differentiation, motion perception and the ability to scan depth and distance.[11]

➢The ***cerebellum***, which translates from Latin to "little brain," is in charge of the coordination and the balance of a dancing body. In addition, the cerebellum supports cognitive functions such as language, sharpened attention, precision, and timing. For choreographic work, the cerebellum functions as a large memory bank of motor learning and for micro-adjustments of the parameters of movement.[12]

➢The ***insular lobe*** is folded deep within the fissure separating the temporal lobe from the parietal and frontal lobes. The insular lobe is responsible for interceptive awareness such as timing the heartbeat, controlling blood pressure as well as the sensation of pain. In addition, the insular lobe plays a substantial role in emotional experiences, translating them into conscious feelings. The lobe is also believed to be the "choreographer in charge" of various feelings and emotions, including maternal and romantic love, fear, anger, sadness, happiness, unfairness, uncertainty, disbelief, social exclusion, empathy, trust, sense of justice, and beauty.[13]

➢The ***spinal cord*** is an extension of the brain, connecting it to the peripheral nervous system and the rest of the body. The spinal cord serves as a main pathway for neurological information and transmits upper motor neuronal signals coming from the cerebral cortex. Neural circuits formed in the spinal cord direct motor behavior and locomotive programs with impressive precision, ensuring that the muscles in a particular limb are activated in a strict order.[14]

Besides controlling the complex sensory feedback systems of the five senses—sight, hearing, touch, smell and taste, which are processed in the lobes—the spinal cord hosts circuits permitting the execution of the mysterious "sixth sense," called *proprioception*.

For choreographers, this is an intriguing and important sense which tells the human body how to respond in three-dimensional space. *Proprioception* is the accuracy of motor commands sent by signals from the brain, permitting us to change motor strategies moment by moment and accommodate to obstacles without the involvement of sight or sound. This sense is also thought to detect gradations of effort, tension, and speed; aid balance and rhythmic accuracy; and permit dancers to duplicate movement as demonstrated.[15]

The presence of *proprioception* was first indicated back in 1769 by the French philosopher Diderot: "What really sets a limit to the space you feel you occupy?" With the response: "My sight and touch." Diderot then asked: "Yes, by day, but at night in dark, or even by day when the mind is preoccupied?" The fact is that we can touch our nose with the tip of our finger with closed eyes. This demonstrates that besides involving partial visual memory, we also use an extra sense or *proprioception* in this action.[16]

THE BRAIN'S PARTS AND FUNCTIONS RELATED TO THE CHOREOGRAPHER'S WORK

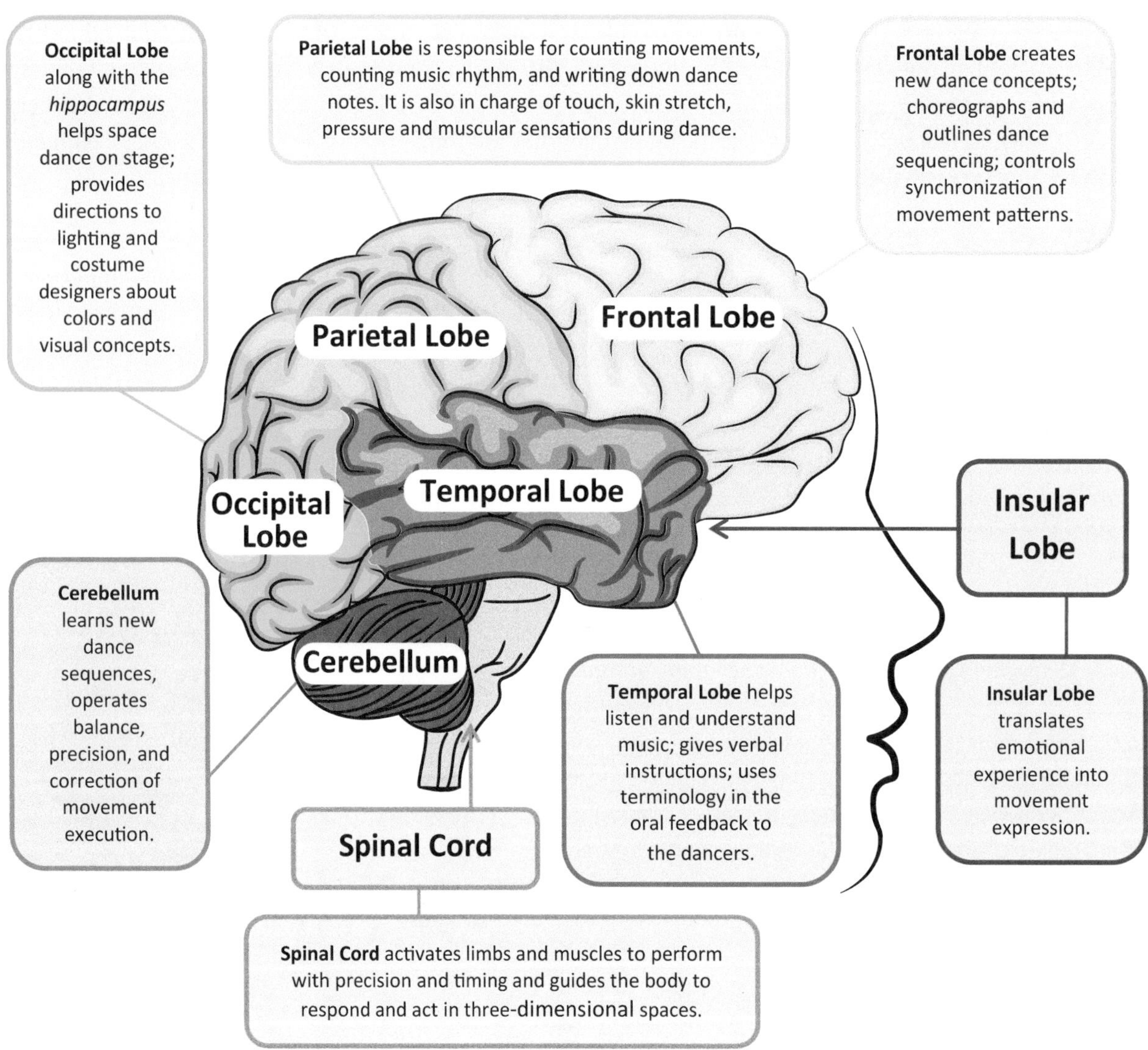

Figure 3

HELPFUL TIPS & SUGGESTIONS

When you suddenly feel "out of ideas" and "stuck" while choreographing, how do you use the knowledge about brain lobes and their functions to recover from creative fatigue? After long and concentrated logic-based work (**Frontal Lobe**), the brain might indicate involuntarily that this lobe needs a rest. At this point, it is helpful to "switch gears/lobes" and think creatively about the same subject from different perspectives—by playing music (**Temporal Lobe**), or by looking at images (**Occipital Lobe**), or by dancing an improvised duet with someone (**Parietal Lobe**).

MAGICAL MEMORIES BY THE MAGIC OF MEMORY

– CHOREOGRAPHER'S MIND COLLECTION OR RECOLLECTION –

Memory is the choreographer's best friend and worst enemy. On one hand, our dance memory retains valuable impressions, learning experiences, and practical information. Recalling important skills makes our creative practices more efficient. On the other hand, memory might confine us to using repetitive movement patterns that are not always exciting and innovative. Certain memory might have a dramatic effect on our artistic inspiration. Wise elderly people often joke that the reason for their life longevity is a good diet and a bad memory.

We can use the best of our dance memories by understanding how they work in the dance studio. Our choreographic memory functions similarly to a computer memory. It stores events in single frame bytes of still images by loading and accumulating kilobytes and megabytes of experiences. Our choreographic memory could be generally classified as:

➢**Photographic memory** is remembering someone's face, movement composition, or choreographic images from dances seen previously, even when they are no longer in front of us. A choreographer can mentally recreate and re-experience the intensity of the dance images and the occasion when they were viewed.

➢**Experiential memory** is the choreographer's internal emotional time traveler. Experiential memory is often referred to as *episodic memory*—the conscious recollection of a personal experience that contains information on what has happened and also where and when it happened. Episodic memory is extremely sensitive to cerebral aging and related to what we wish to remember and what we would like to forget. For instance, imagine visiting the abandoned building of the dance school where you first took lessons many years ago. When you are mentally back in that place it helps you reconnect with the past. You touch the ballet barre, you gaze at the ceiling, and you stare at the huge half-broken wall mirrors. You relive your past experiences and may feel nostalgic. You compare what *it was*, what *is left*, and what *has changed*. You realize how much you have grown, how far you have traveled, and how distant you are from your past. For choreographers, experiential memories are often a source of inspiration and a reason to make a dance.

➢**Movement memories** are mysterious bits of choreography, which seem to be stored in the body rather than in the conscious. By using these memories, a dance that has not been performed for a long time could be restored—shape by shape, movement by movement. One might not remember the whole dance but still have the *bodily feeling* of it. Movement routines rise from the ashes, recreated by the movement memory that contains biomechanical *motor habits*. Movement memory acts as a *kinesthetic instinct*, where repetitive motion experiences are captured. We can swim or drive a bicycle during our lifetime by using our movement memory.

THE INFORMATION AND MEMORY PROCESSING PLANT

Memory is variously classified psychologically. Located in the crucial *frontal and parietal lobes*, the *working memory*, also known and functioning as *short-term memory*, is the dynamic ability of the brain to maintain a temporary representation of information. Working memory is limited in its capacity to take in large amounts of data. The brain's short-term processing system promptly offers strategic sorting, disposal, collection, manipulation, organization, and integration of the data.[17] The processes used to filter information that is vibrant, creative, and subliminal often result in great works of dance art. The short-term memory, however, cannot retain a long complex dance sequence and the process of arranging movements may need to be spread out over time.

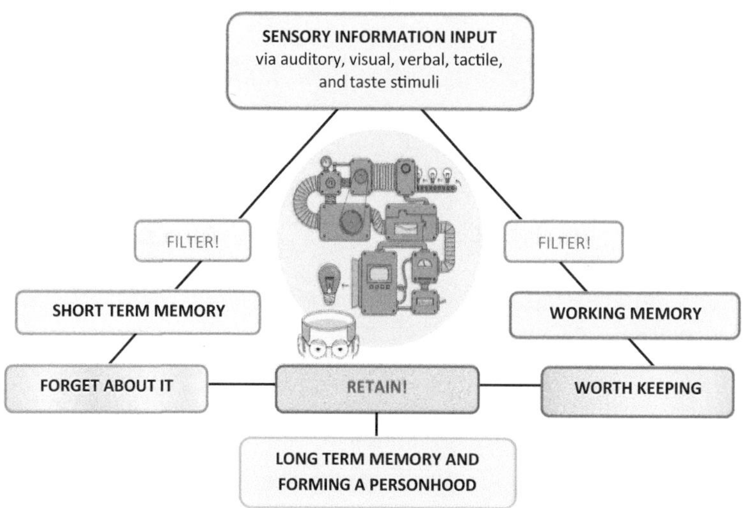

Figure 4

Long-term memory is the ability to remember specific events, perhaps for a lifetime, as well as remembering important facts, dates, names, and relationships. This form of memory is created in the *hippocampus*, but most memories are encoded in other parts of the brain. Memories can be lasting or can change, so remembering a large number of details might decline gradually with time. However, broad, bold concepts, inspiring ideas and generalization are usually remembered very well.[18] Long-term memory can also help establish individual characteristics and behavioral patterns, or what we know as a "personality."

Memory is extremely important in the choreographic process, during which there is interplay between short- and long-term memories. *Short-term memories* are retained for a brief time when movements are held in the brain while being changed, arranged, and rearranged. Once encoded in long-term memory, movements and movement sequences are remembered using a variety of sensory modalities.

◆ Choreographers often develop and remember movements which have somatic meanings and function as their vocabulary, while episodic memories, often associated with emotions, can lead to creating anew. Spatial memory is important when arranging the movements created into dances. A choreographer is expected to remember the location of each dancer with respect to other dancers and to the performance space. Recalling previously created movements is also triggered by remembering body shapes, musical cues, body sensations, or how individual movements are organized in a sequence or pattern.[19]

CULTIVATING A FUNCTIONAL ARTISTIC PERSONHOOD AND SEEKING THE TRUTH ABOUT WHAT MOTIVATES US

In addition to the internal physiological functions of the brain and the lobes as part of the creative work, an individual also processes sensory information and input from the surrounding reality. Many behaviors and actions are influenced by experiences in early childhood and the way information has been processed by the brain. These factors include upbringing circumstances, home environment, powerful memories, present experiences, social surroundings, siblings, friends, educators, cultural exposure, demographics, personal goals, creative drives, and emotional health. This macro universe is the basis of the choreographer's complex individuality and artistic personality.

The Latin word *persona* was originally used to denote the mask worn by an actor and applied to the role assigned on the stage.[20] Nowadays, a personality may be defined by the signature characteristics of an individual and their particular attitude towards life. Our personalities are often manifested via our actions and in what we choose to do.

Why do we do what we do? We believe that we know our own personality very well because we have already lived with ourselves our entire lives. We must admit, however, that often we might purposefully avoid addressing questions about our inner desires and the reasons for our actions. To find out the purpose behind our creative actions and the source of our motivations, we enter and explore the space of *behavioral science*. Author Daniel Pink's book *Drive, The Surprising Truth about What Motivates Us*, offers help and great insights into these areas.[21] Three important questions related to choreographers will help us face the truth about what motivates us to do what we do:

WHAT DO OTHERS EXPECT FROM YOU?

◆ **Expectations and Demands:** A long list of expectations is always placed in front of us. We do not always ask for them and we do not always want them. Personal and work-related expectations and demands are regularly presented to us and we have to deal with them.

Choreographing a new dance project handed to us with predetermined parameters could be frustrating. We feel the pressure to unconditionally accept demands as rules that we didn't establish. We may blindly follow instructions even when we disagree with them. We force ourselves to endure and reach a goal given to us without our mutual consent. Why? Because *if* we do the unpleasant job, *then* there will be a reward. Alternatively, we fear that we will suffer criticism and some punishment if demands are not met as expected.

This dilemma becomes the turning point when the "reward-punishment" behavioral algorithm is turned ON full force. Beyond this point, our creativity stops being creative. Our mind is now trapped in a vicious cycle, bouncing between the fear of punishment and the rewards of doing as expected. It seems as if there is no way out: Creativity will rapidly decline, and the monotonous "work as expected" will turn us into human machines.[22]

WHAT REWARDS AND ACKNOWLEDGMENT DO YOU NEED?

◆ **Reward and Acknowledgment:** We can put aside the "punishment" for now and take a closer look into rewards as mental phenomena. Are they always the ongoing source of inspiration? We all have experienced a time when we do something well once and we have been rewarded for our effort. It feels great! At least for that moment.

Receiving rewards could easily turn into habit, and gratification could become an automatic expectation. We get rewards in different forms: trophies, titles, monetary awards, salaries, feedback, acknowledgment, and compliments. We easily establish a behavior mindset of *when* and *if* we do something well, *then* our effort will be well rewarded and compensated. Once this behavioral system is in place, we keep performing the rewarding activity again and again.

A choreographer's self-esteem and confidence could be crushed by a bad review in the press or negative feedback from a trusted friend. A compliment, on the other hand, can be energizing and inspiring. In the short term, the "*if-then*" behavioral pattern can bring positive outcomes by maintaining steady motivation and predictability of work routines. However, in the long term, anticipated rewards gradually have a detrimental effect on the choreographic mind. They set forth patterns of controlled activities and they focus on expected results. Scheduled rewards turn creativity into *anticipated repetitiveness in work*, and *that work* is not always inspiring.[23]

WHAT DO YOU WANT FROM YOURSELF?

◆ **Inspiration, Purpose and Intrinsic Motivation:** When you, the choreographer, create without any pressure and expectation of external rewards and acknowledgment by peers and society, then you are at your very best! Doing things for your own pleasure and self-satisfaction gives you creative autonomy beyond the need for external gratification.

The most effective reward is a person's own internal reward system. We love to do things simply because we *want to*. External rewards can help, but they cannot substitute for intrinsic motivation. Only a liberated mind can capture the concepts of *how we think* about what we do and *how we do* what we do. The best reward is the satisfaction experienced when one comes to the end of the creative process and dance is realized in its final form.[24] The best-defined purpose, goals, and rewards are those given by choreographers to themselves. This is not to say that external rewards are wrong and undesired. Choreographers need to get paid for their hard work in order to maintain resources and function in society. A choreographer should seek to achieve balance and fairness in the extent of rewards and to realize how reward systems might affect the delicacy of honest and true artistic practices. A focus on finding and adopting new information, learning, and improving skills can turn work into creativity and inspiration.

WHAT MOTIVATES YOU?

REWARDS AND ACKNOWLEDGMENTS	REWARDS AND ACKNOWLEDGMENTS
Money, wealth, awards	Truthfulness, honesty, peace of mind
Compliments, praise, gratification	Accomplishments, recognition, respect
Fame, popularity, celebrity status	Authenticity, love, joy, happiness

WHO IS IN CONTROL?

YOUR SURROUNDINGS ARE IN CONTROL OF YOU	YOU ARE IN CONTROL OF YOURSELF AND YOUR SURROUNDINGS
Expectations and Demands	Purpose and Instinct Motivation
Please others and short term goals	Strive to learn – develop *skills*
Always play by the rules set by others	Be your best on your own – gain *autonomy*
Blindly follow instructions without question	Do what you believe in – define *purpose*

Figure 5

➢We need *skills* to make us better in our artistic craft that we share with others.

➢We need *autonomy* because we want to be directly in charge of our art, our lives and ourselves.

➢We need *purpose* because we believe, think, create, and serve something larger than ourselves. The most noteworthy and significant choreography will be produced when it is developed based on a highly meaningful inner purpose or inspiration rather than an outwardly determined motivation.[24]

PERSONALITY, [IN]TENSIONS, AND BALANCE

– FINDING HAPPINESS THROUGH PASSION, MISSION, SKILLS, AND REWARDS –

Choreographers reach fulfillment and happiness when their works are performed with precision, presented in the best way possible, understood, and appreciated by the audience. A choreographer's source of happiness also emerges and relies on the effort and happiness of collaborators. Healthy creativity begins with a confident and happy mind.

Happiness comes from within us. Our drive and passion, combined with peace of mind, are powerful forces in our internal universe. Often these forces are polarized and at odds with each other. That dynamic tension can be a powerful engine, which, on the other hand, often needs a resolution and a period of rest. We can discover or create a reason for being and a mission to accomplish. Realizing a passion and a mission are important because a choreographer is a person on a mission; however, completing a dance does not always have a predictable path. The way to face such challenges is to meet them with feelings of excitement and a flexible approach.

Well-known choreographer Twyla Tharp once announced she was working on a choreography based on Euripides' *Bacchae*. However, when she began to create this work, Tharp discovered the story included more information than could be communicated effectively in a dance. Instead, she switched gears and decided to focus on the conflict between the two main characters, representing it symbolically as a river.[25]

This selectiveness of prioritizing an interpersonal conflict leads us to *Ikigai*. *Ikigai* is a Japanese concept that means the reason for being. The word roughly translates as things that we live for.[26] What brings meaning to life springs from a harmonious conversion of elements of what you love (passion); what the world needs (mission); what you are good at (vocation); what you can get paid for (profession).[27]

Figure 6

"I am not sure what I want," says an emerging choreographer. Very often, choreographers may find themselves operating in chaos—internal and external, personal, and artistic. It's part of the profession to find purpose and bring some structure to the disorder. Choreographing is also about the urgency and desire to share something important to you with others.

Interpersonal conflicts also emerge when an individual sets forth an unrealistic goal or is driven by fixated desires. On one hand, it is natural for a person to wish for betterment of their lives and art. On the other hand, it is healthier and more productive for that person to sooner realize what is wishful and what is possible.

Self-awareness is the ability to accurately analyze and identify one's own strengths and weaknesses—both personal and artistic. Responsiveness and openness to feedback, advice, and the acceptance of strategies to correct mistakes is a great asset to advance artistic skills. Do we tolerate ourselves and others? How well we do know ourselves? As artists, we can figure out how to be good to ourselves and others by learning more about our inner nature. By taking these steps and "looking in the mirror," choreographers leave room and time for realizing and absorbing new knowledge and experiences—their own and those of others.

?

Do you think you know yourself very well? Let's practice self-awareness. Please answer quickly and without thinking too long the following questions in Figure 7.

QUESTIONS FOR YOU	YOUR BRIEF ONE-PHRASE ANSWERS
WHAT IS MOST IMPORTANT TO YOU, AND WHY?	
WHAT DO YOU DO OFTEN THAT YOU ARE NOT AWARE OF?	
WHEN DO YOU FUNCTION MENTALLY AT YOUR BEST?	
WHEN DO YOU FUNCTION PHYSICALLY AT YOUR BEST?	
WHAT IS YOUR PRESENT GOAL AND WHY IT IS IMPORTANT?	
WHAT DO YOU LIKE/DISLIKE ABOUT YOURSELF, AND WHY?	
WHAT MAKES YOU SMILE?	

Figure 7

THE MANY HATS FOR A SINGLE HEAD
— THE CHOREOGRAPHER AS SOCIALLY INTERACTIVE ARTIST —

Dance is a cooperative art form. Choreographers, in most cases, work with dancers and collaborators, and therefore they constantly engage in social interactions. The Greek philosopher Aristotle said in his book *Politics* that man is by nature a social animal and that "society is something that precedes the individual."[28] In many respects, we are who others think we are. While working, choreographers are both *givers* and *receivers*. On one hand, choreographers give the dancers creative input, choreography, and artistic assignments. On the other hand, choreographers receive feedback from the dancers, collaborators, and the audience.

Choreographers manifest themselves in social interactions on two fronts: as private individuals and as artists. Personal and artistic characteristics and qualities are not set in stone. Life experiences—struggles and successes—can change attitudes and personalities. Therefore, choreographers' public interactions and social behaviors may vary during different periods of their careers. As socially dependent artists, choreographers might feel self-conscious when communicating with performers and collaborators because they realize their interactions may have an impact on others. There is a clear distinction between a choreographer's *personal qualities*, the focus of this chapter, and a dance creator's *choreographic personality*, which ultimately reveals itself onstage as *artistic identity*. For more about the latter, please see *Choreographic Individuality and Artistic Identity—The Search for Who I Am* in Chapter 13.

For example, by looking at a dance without meeting the choreographer in person, one might not be able to tell if the choreographer has an adventurous personality or a more cautious one. Although we cannot identify a choreographer' *personal qualities* from their dances, we can identify their *artistic identity* and even their *choreographic individuality*. It is also possible that we might like the artist, but we might not like the actual person.

HELPFUL TIPS & SUGGESTIONS

~ Enjoy being happy—it is contagious

~ Enjoy being passionate—it is inspiring

~ Enjoy being confident—it is motivating

While striving to create and communicate in the dance studio, choreographers learn to manage multiple facets of their own complex personalities. Wearing many different hats with ease and mastering various types of intelligence are part of the choreographer's work.

Now, here is our "hat collection"—a hat that feels good also looks right. When we engage in multiple types of social interactions, the way we come across has an impact on others.

THE CHOREOGRAPHER IS AN EMOTIONAL CREATURE

Feelings are important and they drive inspiration. Choreographers strive to channel their feelings towards their artistic work. Otherwise, feelings without control could be destructive and problematic. When learning dance technique or movement skills or choreographic craft, choreographers gradually self-train to manage their feelings. Emotions are often complicated and even contradictory. In such cases, a closer look and extra effort are needed to understand their source, reason, and how they can be handled.

Throughout their careers, choreographers develop emotional complexity and maturity. With the input of society and surroundings, choreographers determine which feelings are okay to express, and which feelings are best kept private. Each individual has a unique ***emotional intelligence*** and ways of acting upon it. Some artists may feel comfortable with expressing compassion and love, while others have difficulty dealing with sadness and disappointment. And there are common emotions that we all share and act upon.[29]

How feelings are managed can be a great advantage or a hindrance. Feelings exist and happen, and they should not be ignored or dismissed. A choreographer's feelings are like the dancers' legs and arms—available, alive, and moving when needed. Emotions are an important part of motivation. What we feel is what we get!!

THE CHOREOGRAPHER IS A PERSUASIVE INTELLECTUAL

In addition to being the creator and the expert in their own work, choreographers follow their intellectual curiosity. Through their work they continuously educate themselves and their project participants, audiences, and communities about dance. When it comes to inventing new dances, choreographers are the public representative of the art form!

Attending professional development events about intelligent use of movement essentials and dance making tools helps expand choreographers' intellectual repertoire and the scope of creative practices. These activities also involve learning about various dance cultures and dance history. A choreographer's intellectual spectrum is further broadened by acquiring knowledge of the dance-related arts, including music, visual arts, fashion, architecture, literature, and philosophy.

While being intelligent is often perceived as acting smart and practical, being intellectual is about increasing knowledge and expanding one's range of thinking.[30] A choreographer's horizon expands intellectually by using strategies such as research and investigation, information gathering, learning, and the development of critical thinking.

Intuition and instinct play an important part in creativity in the form of ***intuitive intelligence***. Intuitive intelligence is being able to think of multiple possibilities at the same time. It also means being able to move between the rational to the creative and instinctive.[31] Intuitive intelligence is about considering the unusual and the paradox, sharpening perception, and cultivating a sense of how to "read between the lines." The best decisions are often made when we rationally take into account the most useful bits of information and apply (or adopt) them intuitively to resolve a dilemma.

Finally, the choreographer develops excellence in oral and written communication. Sharing with collaborators concepts and meaningful information related to the work is most productive when those concepts are communicated in a thoughtful manner.

THE CHOREOGRAPHER IS A CHARISMATIC LEADER

On most occasions, in contrast to the writer or the visual artist, choreographers do not communicate in person and directly with the audience. A choreographer's ideas are presented through a dance. The performers, directed by the choreographer, present the dance production to the audience. In addition, the technical crew, production team, producers, and publicity team are led by choreographers, who provide clear instructions and guidelines in an articulated manner about the vision and the execution of the dance.

The choreographer as a person becomes invisible during a dance performance. What we see onstage is the result of the choreographer's artistic identity, choreographic individuality, and last but not least—inspiring leadership. If the choreographer decides to appear and dance onstage with the rest of the cast, then the dance maker becomes a visible performer, but remains invisible as a choreographer.

Choreographers guide people. Therefore, choreographers first need to be in complete control of themselves before instructing others. The process takes great communication, interactive skills, and ***social intelligence*** to turn the choreographer's work into a manageable shared task.[32]

The necessary abilities include respectful interaction, sensible behavior, professional competence, as well as having a powerful personality, charisma, and even a sense of humor. The more intelligently choreographers interact with their dancers and collaborators, the better their ideas will be reenacted and presented.

Choreographers are leaders. As military commanders and their troops train to enter battles and encounter danger, choreographers train to lead the dancers/collaborators into the creative unknown and encounter new challenges. The choreographer's greatest skill is feeling comfortable in a zone of discomfort. There is no victory in avoiding risk during a battle.

THE ADVANTAGES AND DISADVANTAGES OF BEING PERFECT

We all have individual personal values, agendas, and interests. Others look at our qualities through their personal lenses, which change how we appear to them. There is no perfect human characteristic no matter how long and hard we analyze ourselves. The state of perfection is not fixed: finding a balance requires considerable self-awareness. Although we all embody parts of various personality types, one type is usually dominant.

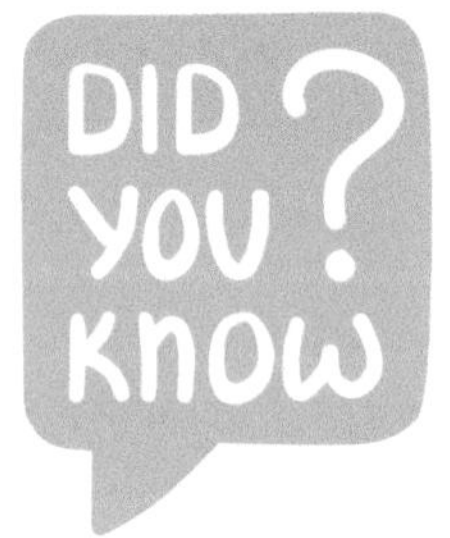

It is natural to feel that you are perfect! However, you might feel perfect only when you are by yourself. As socially interactive creatures, we might never be able to completely please others. Obviously, what we think about ourselves may not be what others think of us. Others might perceive our good qualities as disadvantages.

Here are several major types of creative temperaments and artistic personalities that appear during three distinct phases of choreographic inspiration to creation, and interaction.

?

Please check one dominant trait for each of the phases, and then look into your advantages and disadvantages.

WHEN I AM in the process of	THEN I AM	CHECK ✓	ADVANTAGES	DISADVANTAGES
Searching for Inspiration and Artistic Pursuit	INTUITIVE	☐	Perceptive, spontaneous, sensitive, provocative	Uncertain, unreasonable, irrational, wild, reckless
	INTELLECTUAL	☐	Knowledgeable, cerebral, analytical, logical, wise	Traditional, formal, distant, impersonal, emotionless
	INNOVATIVE	☐	Groundbreaking, creative advanced, original	Unrealistic, bizarre, naïve, extreme, unusual
Working Creatively and Crafting Dance and Movement	GENERALIST	☐	Profound, embracing, abundant, persuasive	Arbitrary, insensible, stiff, excessive, assertive
	SPECIFIST	☐	Insightful, sharp, accurate proportionate, clever	Skeptical, complex, demanding, resistant
	ADVENTURIST	☐	Courageous, engaging, daring, brave, dynamic	Risky, unsafe, random, antagonistic, challenging
Responding, Collaborating and Interacting	STRONG MINDED	☐	Powerful, convincing, disciplined, confident	Stubborn, indisputable, unpersuasive, reserved
	FLEXIBLY MINDED	☐	Generous, tolerant progressive, flexible	Compliant, submissive, conforming, obeying
	OPEN-MINDED	☐	Free-spirited, friendly, accessible, willing	Unclear, elusive, indistinct, dreamy, ambiguous

Figure 8

assignments & exercises

By combining research assignments, creative exercises, and comparative assignments, let's imaginatively play learning games and assume the roles of:

- **THE DANCE PSYCHOLOGIST:** Choose several choreographers from the past in the ranks of Duncan, Nijinsky, Graham, Balanchine, and Robbins. Briefly research their personalities, backgrounds, and private lives. Compare how their individuality in private corresponds with their artistic work displayed in public, and note if there are any connections.

Do you think that these choreographers' temperaments, personalities, and lifestyles are reflected in their aesthetic views, dance subject matter, and movement material? If you create a short dance solo about your temperament, how might you do this?

- **THE INTERNAL (E)MOTION INVESTIGATOR:** As an outside visitor, imagine walking inside the archives of your own life. You just gained rare access to your Department of Memorable Moments. You are about to embark on a very special collection of scenes and highlights capturing the most joyful, dramatic, funny, and romantic moments of your life.

Why are those moments so special to you in the first place? Do you think you can/ might/may/will be able to capture the feelings of those moments in your dances? If you create a short dance solo about one of your experiences, how might you do this?

- **THE CHOREOGRAPHY DETECTIVE:** Ask one of your colleague(s) to show you a couple of short and anonymous dance videos. One work should be a lesser-known work by a well-known contemporary choreographer, and the other one should be created by someone who is a less established contemporary choreographer. Use "reverse-engineering" and analyze how much each dance "tells" you about the choreographers. Finally, predict each choreographer's age, gender, experience, and name based on the style of movement and their point of view found in each dance.

What is the basis of your findings and what is your hypothesis? Check with your colleague(s) to find out if your guesses and estimates are correct. How close were you to the truth in your prediction?

BIBLIOGRAPHY AND REFERENCES

[1] Radwan, Farouk M. *Conscious vs Subconscious Mind*, Article, 2knowmyself Books, Web, January 2015.

[2] Libet, Benjamin. *Mind Time: The Temporal Factor in Consciousness*, Harvard University Press, 2005, pp. 92–99, 109–112.

[3] Finke, Ronald A., Smith, Steven M. and Ward, Thomas B. *The Creative Cognition Approach*, Massachusetts Institute of Technology, A Bradford Book, 1996.

[4] Gallwey, Timothy and Kriegel, Bob. *Inner Skiing*, Random House, 1977, p. 19.

[5] Kahneman, Daniel. *Thinking Fast and Slow*, Farrar, Strauss and Giroux, 2011.

[6] John-Steiner, Vera. *Notebooks of the Mind: Explorations of Thinking*, University of New Mexico Press, 1985.

[7] Pietrangelo, Ann. *Left Brain vs. Right Brain: What Does This Mean for Me?* Medically reviewed by Deborah Weatherspoon, Ph.D., RN, CRNA, COI, 2017. online article: www.healthline.com/health/left-brain-vs-right-brain, accessed January 2015. Smith, Kosslyn. *Cognitive Psychology: Mind and Brain*, Prentice Hall, 2007, pp. 21, 194–199, 349.

[8] Minton, Sandra C. and Faber, Rima. *Thinking with the Dancing Brain: Embodying Neuroscience*, Rowman & Littlefield Education, 2016, p. 139.

[9] Minton and Faber 2016. *Thinking with the Dancing Brain*, p. 124.

[10] Kosslyn 2007. *Mind and Brain*, Prentice Hall, 2007, pp. 21, 194–199, 349.

[11] Caraway, Kimberly. *Designing Instruction to Increase Retention: Strategies for Designing Instructions Informed By Cognitive Neuroscience*, A Power Point Presentation by Kimberly Caraway, PhD, National Cathedral School, 2014, pp. 1–5.

[12] Koziol, Leonard F. et al. *Consensus Paper: The Cerebellum's Role in Movement and Cognition*. Cerebellum, London, England, vol. 13, no. 1, 2014, pp. 151–177.

[13] Craig, A. D. Bud. "How Do You Feel—Now? The Anterior Insula and Human Awareness," *Nature Reviews Neuroscience*, vol. 10, no. 1, 2009, pp. 59–70.

[14] Jessell, Thomas M. PhD. *Making Your Mind: Molecules, Motion, and Memory Lecture 3–Plan of Action: How the Spinal Cord Controls Movement*, Video lecture, Howard Hughes Medical Institute, Online Lectures Series, 2008, Web, accessed January 2015.

[15] Minton, Sandra and Steffen, Jeffrey. "The Development of a Spatial Kinesthetic Awareness Measuring Instrument for Use with Beginning Dance Students," *Dance: Current Selected Research*, vol. 3, 1992, pp. 73–80.

[16] Thomas 2015. *Making Your Mind: Molecules, Motion, and Memory*.

[17] Alloway, Tracy and Alloway, Ross. The Working Memory Advantage: Train Your Brain to Function Stronger, Smarter, Faster, Simon & Schuster, reprint edition 2014.

[18] Haller, Nancy. *I Don't Know How Long My Short Term Memory Is...: Strategies for People with Brains*, Lifetime Connections, 2012.

[19] Minton and Faber 2016. *Thinking with the Dancing Brain*, pp. 77–92.

[20] Bishop, Paul. *Analytical Psychology and German Classical Aesthetics: Goethe, Schiller, and Jung*, Volume 1: *The Development of the Personality*, Taylor & Francis, 2007, pp. 157–158.

[21] Pink, Daniel. Drive, *The Surprising Truth about What Motivate Us*, Riverhead Books/Penguin Group, 2009.

[22] Pink 2009. Drive, *The Surprising Truth about What Motivate Us*, pp. 22, 49–59.

[23] Pink 2009. Drive, *The Surprising Truth about What Motivate Us*, pp. 44–68.

[24] Pink 2009. Drive, *The Surprising Truth about What Motivate Us*, pp. 77–78, 210–220.

[25] Tharp, Twyla. *The Creative Habit: Learn It and Use It for Life*, Simon & Schuster, 2003, p. 142.

[26] Garcia, Hector and Miralles, Francesca. *Ikigai: The Japanese Secret to a Long and Happy Life*, Penguin Books, 2017.

[27] Oppong, Thomas. *Ikigai: The Japanese Secret to a Long and Happy Life Might Just Help You Live a More Fulfilling Life*, https://medium.com/thrive-global/ , online reference, accessed November 2019.

[28] Aristotle. *Politics*, Oxford University Press, Reprint edition, 2013, various pages.

[29] Heen, Sheila, Patton, Bruce and Stone, Douglas. *Difficult Conversations: How to Discuss What Matters Most*, Penguin Books, 1999, 2010.

[30] Dweck, Carol S. *Mindset, the New Psychology of Success*, Ballantine Books, 2008.

[31] Francis, *Definition: What Is Intuitive Intelligence?* Web article, Posted on May 2008, https://thehumancompany.com/definition_what_is_intuitive_intelligence/, accessed June 2019.

[32] Tuhovsky, Ian. *Communication Skills: A Practical Guide to Improving Your Social Intelligence*, Presentation, Persuasion and Public Speaking, CreateSpace Independent Publishing Platform, 2015.

VISUAL REFERENCES

Figure 1: Diagram © Vladimir Angelov

Figure 2: Diagram © Vladimir Angelov, clip art: graphic design hairstyle men illustration vector on anime or comic style, credit: iestudio, Adobe Stock

Figure 3: Diagram © Vladimir Angelov, clipart: Human brain organ parts anatomy diagram illustration by ambassador806

Figure 4: Diagram © Vladimir Angelov, illustration by Mustafahacalaki, clip art courtesy of iStock/Getty Images

Figure 5: Diagram © Vladimir Angelov

Figure 6: Ikigai illustration, credit by StudioBarcelona, clip art courtesy of iStock/Getty Images

Figure 7 and 8: Diagrams © Vladimir Angelov

CHAPTER 10

INTUITIVE CRAFTSMANSHIP

– HANDLING PERFECT IMPERFECTIONS –

By definition, artistry involves cultivating one's talents to create fine works of art: dance, music, theater productions, and visual art. Creativity, on the other hand, is an act of imagination and the emergence of original ideas that may be subjective and may defy rules and norms. Although a creative act is not always an artistic act, an artistic act is always a creative act. Artistry seeks craft and intuition, creativity, and invention. Therefore, looking at the guiding forces and recurring patterns in the acts of learning and discovering might provide insight about links between creativity in general and artistry in choreography.

In an effort to formulate a new approach to systematize the creative act of choreography, this chapter offers a creative algorithm and functional philosophy of choreography—*ICON SMART*.

The chapter also discusses how the creative act of choreography functions; how the choreographer functions as a creator; and what the function of the choreographer's art could be. Key aspects of creativity as intuitive craftsmanship are outlined as:

- Spontaneity and deliberation, creating and crafting
- Acts of learning and discovery, which may be chaotic or organized processes
- Choreographic instruments for artistic practices, formulating intentions as artistic objectives, and the nature and types of norms
- Strategies of artistic research and their implementation in practice
- Artistic training, advancing skills, and developing proficiency
- Fixation with perfection as an inspiration or hindrance to creativity
- Aesthetic directions and channeling the creative act

As choreographers mature artistically and undergo professional and personal transformation, the formulation of their creative acts might change, and their initial aesthetic routes might shift. The following summary simplifies three major dynamic aspects of the creative act as functional philosophy of choreography – see Figure 1.

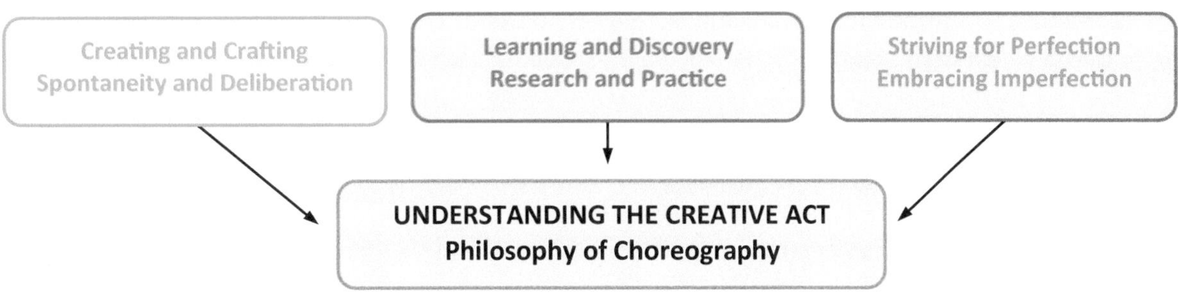

Figure 1

THE CREATIVE PARADOX
– SPONTANEITY AND DELIBERATION –

What is the point of art and creativity? The answer to this philosophical question changes with every epoch and generation—and even with every artist. Conventionally speaking, the point of art is to enlighten humanity and make us better people, to help us bypass the often-narrow landscape of our daily routines, and to enable us to *sense* and *see* beyond the horizon. An individual engaging in creative activities is satisfying an intimate urgency to experience a better self, to encounter a different self, and to communicate and reach beyond the self to a new otherness. Therefore, a creative process may not only be an act of "self-expression" and of making something out of nothing, but also a self-inventive way to l*earn about the world* and *discover the self.*

◆ **If all dance art is self-expression, is all self-expression dance art?** Consider a child who spontaneously and joyfully dances to the bubbling rhythms of random music in the living room, while down the street at the opera house, a choreographer deliberately crafts a monumental new dance that took months to conceive and prepare. In both cases, dance as self-expression emerges honestly and beautifully – in the first case as an impulsive expression, in the second case as a fine work of art resulting from *intuitive craftsmanship.*

"I have commissioned the creation of a new work"—an artistic director announces. There is a general perception that creating already includes crafting, and that creating and crafting are inseparable, which is not always the case. Creating may contradict crafting, which is a creative paradox. A chef can *craft* and prepare dozens of breakfast omelets by following a tried and true recipe. Or that same chef may *create* new recipes and different omelets each morning depending on the mood of the day, the available ingredients, and the customers. As new recipes emerge, some might be more successful than others.

◆ **There is a distinction between *creating* dance and *crafting* dance.** While creating is predominantly impulsive and instinctive, crafting is algorithmic and analytical. Creating is perceptive, progressive, and passionate; crafting is cognitive, calculative, and cultivating. Creating tends to be spontaneous and desultory, while crafting tends to be systematic and deliberate. Creating is imaginative; crafting is illustrative. Creating is senses-based; crafting is skills-based. Creating and crafting may function separately; however, it is magical when they work together simultaneously and in perfect harmony. Senses and skills connect by intuition, and they manifest in various levels of abilities and proficiencies—all united under *intuitive craftsmanship*:

Figure 2

A higher degree of *proficiency* comes with regular immersion in familiar and preferred body-mind artistic research practices and ongoing training. Choreographers also deliberately seek new experiences and practices that challenge the boundaries of their *intuitive craftsmanship.*

ACTS OF LEARNING

Choreographers have their individual ways of accessing and processing new information, retaining knowledge, and advancing their skills. Some choreographers learn best from auditory, visual, and illustrative devices, others from the embodiment of ideas in the dance studio, and still others, from observational and analytical approaches.

There is a long-standing belief that emerging choreographers learn from and are inspired by the work of other choreographers. Where and how can they acquire this knowledge? There are three learning settings where emerging choreographers *experientially* encounter the craft, and these can be cyclical, synchronous, or in various combinations:

➢ *Academic setting*: where emerging choreographers gain knowledge and training in the academic sector through curricular instruction; by directed study and analysis of devices and patterns derived from preferred dance works; and from visiting artists, scholars, and other resources in the dance field.[1]

➢ *Professional setting*: where a fortunate few are part of a professional dance company. In addition to dancing a diverse repertoire and keeping up with busy performance seasons, these emerging choreographers may complete apprenticeships and professional development programs that provide regular and direct access to the wisdom of prominent choreographers.

➢ *Self-learning setting*: where emerging choreographers decide on their own terms the design of their learning experience and the methods to advance their skills. Many choreographers may avoid structured learning and prescribed knowledge that ultimately may also require the theorization of their own dance making processes. And yet practical, theoretical, and virtual learning could be relevant to any choreography that is approached as an art-practice-as-research based activity.[2]

◆ **What advantages and disadvantages may a choreographer encounter when considering conventional tool-based craftsmanship to develop skills?** Some disadvantages are that the choreographic process could be understood as a rule-based activity with identifiable conventional tools. Even when a choreographer deviates from conventions, these conventions may still operate as references. Therefore, such a norm-governing mode of choreographing may compete with *artistic originality*. Concern may arise that following any composition rules, engaging in structured artistic research, and acquiring new knowledge—all may *contaminate* the choreographer's unique vision and approach.

In addition, by engaging and training in craft-building and norm-structured activities, a choreographer may habitually use conventional creative techniques. Following that path, as the creative act becomes more predictable, the imaginative aspects of the work may be negatively affected.[3]

Lastly, a choreographer may be less interested in learning "the craft's general principles and casual laws" and more interested in exploring what cannot be generalized. Such an approach may be better suited for tackling the subjective particularities of unique life situations and deeply individual experiences. Creating original choreography evolves more around the artist as a person and less around the specifications of craftsmanship. Therefore, the choreographer's objective detachment from an artistic concept may be replaced by the choreographer's subjective involvement in the artistic process.[4]

There are also great advantages to tool-based craftsmanship. In most instances, a new and unique dance rarely emerges from a strict plan developed in advance. Yet a dance may be created and crafted according to exact specifications in a well-defined style and aesthetic that contains the criteria for artistic excellence. A choreographer as a craftsperson may choose to create deliberately and consciously with predetermined parameters, and by doing so, may achieve ambitious artistic goals.

Although creative decisions are not always based on a rational view, choreographers' creative solutions may arise from the circumstances of the moment. Realizations and determinations could be based on responses to the environment, the dancers, the needs of the project, and other factors. Cultivating skills and proficiencies is particularly important in choreographers' artistic conduct—not only within their own work, but also with the contributing dancers and collaborators.

In summary, craftsmanship does not limit uniqueness, but along with advancing skills, it fosters learning and cultivates greater sensitivity. Regardless of a choreographer's preferred way to acquire the craft, a *learning experience* during the creative act is always beneficial. Obtaining knowledge involves various types of learning, such as:

Learning how...deals with practical knowledge. *Learning that*...deals with empirical knowledge, established rules, concepts, and reasoning of natural and universal laws, such as principles in action that cause an effect. *Learning about*... deals with knowledge of virtues and the broader knowledge that ultimately cultivates a value system within the social and moral domains.

Learning how to jump and remain suspended in the air, for example, gives us the practical understanding and the knowledge to execute this action skillfully. *Learning that* jumping with suspension in the air deals with physical forces gives us the knowledge that the body will comply with physical laws related to this action. *Learning about* jumping into the air as an integral part of dance and physics gives us broader disciplinary knowledge; such awareness ultimately builds a value system that enables sound decision-making. For example, it would be unreasonable—and even unfair—to demand that a dancer jump into the air and remain suspended for longer than gravity allows.

This concept is not new, but an adaptation for choreographers based on the ancient Greeks' view of knowledge. In the *Nicomachean Ethics*, Aristotle (384–22 BC) described and classified three different types of knowledge: *Techné*—skills and crafts, *Episteme*—scientific knowledge, and *Phronesis*—practical wisdom and virtues.

ACTS OF DISCOVERING

The unknown is usually beyond immediate reach. Discovery is inseparable from the unknown—to discover is to seek, find, and reveal something that was previously unknown. Discoveries are often unpredictable and surprising because they are not anticipated or guaranteed.[6] A few fundamental questions may unveil the variables of available knowledge and the scope of the unknown: How much do we know, how much do we not know, and finally—do we know what we do not know?

The last question is critical because it may indicate *innocent ignorance*. A phrase that begins with: "Oh, sorry...I didn't know," defensively expresses a lack of information, which does not nurture a spirit of discovery. Instead, the phrase acts as a protective barrier to what we are *expected* to know but were *unable* to know for various reasons. Discovering is not about what we *need* to know, but what we *want* to know.

◆ **How to approach discovering?** The first step of willingness to discover is an evaluation and honest disclosure about what we do not know. The next step is to identify and formulate the scope of the unknown as we focus on what to observe and study. The third step is driven by an abundance of curiosity, devotion, and a strategy to gather resources to *learn how.../that.../about*...the subject. Most excitingly, when there is no large quantity of knowledge available on a subject, or the resources are limited and scattered, we proceed to *investigate and explore* the subject on our own terms and, if necessary, to *formulate new knowledge.*

◆ **What types of discoveries are there?** Choreographers who strive for innovation and uniqueness are drawn to the act of discovering. Whether in art, science, or life, choreographers may make different types of discoveries during their creative work and personal experiences. For example, finding and bringing new knowledge to the dance field at large would be a *groundbreaking discovery*, like an astronomer's discovery of new inhabitable worlds in the universe. Choreographers also may make personal journeys to uncover existing facts and truths about themselves and claim these as *personal discoveries*, like children who learn that they have curly hair after looking in the mirror for the first time. There are also the *enlightening discoveries* which assemble facts and evidence to reveal and demystify existing realities and expose truths that may not have been obvious, like when a detective solves a complex criminal case.

◆ **How does discovering work?** Creativity and discovery have been subjects of study by scholars, psychologists, philosophers, and inventors. There are various long-term strategies and short-term tactics, including a few general considerations, about discovering.[7] For creative individuals and choreographers, the most applicable factors are:

➢ Discovering is predominately process-oriented rather than results-driven; for example, a more productive mindset for a rock climber would be to enjoy the climb, not to focus solely on reaching the top of the mountain.

➢ Discovering uses all possible means—it is art and science combined because it deals with the senses, imagination, intuition, style, virtuosity, and judgment, as well as theory, system, and method-building to test and prove a new concept.

➢ Discovering is about acting independently, alone, and outside of the mainstream, and yet with committed project participants such as contributing dancers and collaborators.

➢ Discovering is rebelliousness that is smart, not reckless—it means recognizing an opportunity, capitalizing on it, and moving a concept through multiple phases.

➢ Discovering is about opening up space and welcoming new ideas that lead to unpredictable outcomes—one can encourage dynamic events by tapping into randomness and seeking out chance occurrences in beneficial ways.

➢ Discovering is adopting and adapting various techniques and inventing new tactics for exploration—taking a non-traditional approach.

➢ Discovering is rarely a sudden explosion of new knowledge and learning, but rather a marathon run on a long and uneven landscape: it might begin with great enthusiasm and rising speed in the early phases, then flatten and almost halt for a moment, only to speed up again in a sprint to the finish line.

However, there is a small but important disclaimer: some creative discoveries are based solely on pure luck and happy accident; therefore, they may have nothing to do with formalized reasoning, lasting exploration, or innovative craftsmanship. In such a case, a choreographer may argue whether those reasonings *could be* or *must be* formalized.[8] There are multiple ways to generate, test, and formulate an idea. Yet for a groundbreaking discovery to be legitimized, accepted, and used by others, it should be supported by an articulated algorithm—what is it, and how did we get there?

Creating and discovering bring into being novel ideas and new opportunities. Creating and discovering do not belong to the past; they are meant to function today and tomorrow. Creating and discovering partner with inventive and innovative thinking—see *Inventive Creativity - In Art, Everything is Possible*, Chapter 11 of this book.

While respecting the choreographers-extraordinaire of the past who shaped and developed the art form, choreographers of today should craft dances to not only continue historic legacies and traditions, but also to move dance forward and reflect the current times. Just like the well-known classical artists in their time—today's groundbreaking choreographers aim to create, discover, and innovate the dances of today and tomorrow.

THE CREATIVE ACT
– BOUNDARIES AND FREEDOM –

The creative act is an imagination-driven, dynamic pursuit of content-inventing, truth-seeking, and sense-making. The complexities and transformative functions of the creative act are so entangled and vastly disorganized that it seems impossible to identify the boundaries and the freedom in the field. Yet the creative act is also a decision-making act, where some ideas will be worth keeping and others will be discarded.

Therefore, during the creative act choreographers use their intuitive craftsmanship to choose purposefully or unintentionally which artistic devices they will use and which they will avoid. Choreographers also tend to determine their own aesthetic norms by choosing which concepts to suppress and which they will elevate. Artistic boundaries are often set to frame the creative scope, but soon afterwards, those same boundaries may be challenged and demolished in an effort to restore unlimited freedom.

According to the influential French philosopher Gilles Deleuze, the creative act is an *act of resistance*—an artful defiance of the profane, the sacred, and the ever-present reality of death, which is certain for every human being.[9] On the other hand, the creative act is also the freedom to discover and celebrate beauty, love, and life.

The creative act often seems chaotic and unpredictable. Choreographers strive to orient themselves in a vast cosmos of ideas so they can formulate artistic ideologies that best represent their creative visions. Creative freedom and artistic boundaries may be expected and imposed, or fluid and unknown. How does the choreographer's intuitive craftsmanship function creatively, and is it possible to systematize the creative act?

To answer these questions, offered here is ***ICON***, a non-linear, dimensional, and dynamic concept to formulate the practicalities of the creative act in choreography and organize them in a creative algorithm. The acronym stands for ***I****nstruments of* ***C****horeography,* ***O****bjectives, and* ***N****orms*. These three components function differently and yet synchronously. The detailed definitions are:

◆ ***Instruments of Choreography*** are the movement material, artistic organizing principles, and structuring devices applied to movement, as well as sound, costuming, lighting, and scenery with which choreographers work. Instruments of choreography may be newly created for a given project or borrowed from diverse histories and traditions of dance and other art forms. Multiple conventional devices and formally determined tools, as well as new and uniquely created techniques, are at the choreographer's disposal. These include, but are not limited to, embodied engagement, methods of creating original movement vocabulary through improvisation, techniques of building movement phrases, formats and acts of structuring and restructuring, constructing and deconstruing a dance, principles of physical dramaturgy for dance, use of music and sound, and production aspects, among many others. The choreography-in-practice fundamentals of the creative act as learning and discovery are discussed in BOOKS IV, V, VI, and VII.

◆ ***Objectives*** are the intentions, project-specific goals, ideas, plans, frameworks, and purposes shared among the participants in a choreographic project, and with any others whose input may be solicited. Through experimentation and decision-making as a work finds its distinct identity, these objectives may be shaped and reshaped multiple times and in many ways. The origination and shaping of choreographer's objectives could be nurtured and influenced by various strategies such as brainstorming techniques, tactics of innovative thinking, discovering and problem solving, the determination of various conceptual frameworks and constructs to organize content, and the development of unique choreographic identity, perspective, and vision—all of them discussed in BOOK III.

A choreographer's objectives may converge and formulate the intentions and purposes of a specific piece of dance or encompass the overarching principles of a creative act. Then the choreographer's general creative practices and artistic objectives could be unified, and they can capture the core of specific interests and visions. The resulting parameters shape the choreographer's performance aesthetic and artistic philosophy and culminate in the summary form of an artistic *credo* and *manifesto*—see the *PREFACE* of this book.

◆ ***Norms*** are recognized as preferred habits, standards, rules, or imperatives that may function with a variable degree of influence or enforcement. Norms could be politically, societally, and culturally predetermined. Traditions in art, established aesthetics, and conventional principles of art making often impose sets of norms that are formed and dictated by historical, geo-political, and socioeconomic circumstances—see Chapters 1 to 7, BOOK I.

Norms could be particularized and generalized, conceptualized, and contextualized. A creative act could be outside the norms, or against the norms, or in perfect alignment with the norms. Norms have their own ostensible meaning and independence, which might run counter to or align with the creative act. Often, norms = values, and this is when things might turn personal. The choreographer's objectives may challenge certain or all types of existing and imposed norms. Such an approach recalls Deleuze's concept of the *creative act* as an *act of resistance*. Yet the ultimate defiance, and even demolition of any existing norms, opens up the space for new rules and norms to emerge.

In summary, the creative act is a grand cycle involving all of the processes and elements described earlier. Realizing the immense dimensional complexity of a thoughtful artistic journey might be intimidating at first. Yet this cognitive map of the creative act could provide a cumulative, systematic understanding of the art of creating dance. Over time, choreographers tend to figure out intuitively or intellectually their positioning on the interactive map and sort out routes and desired destinations. The choreographer's *decision-making processes* are guided by and based on the interactions between the chosen choreographic instruments, objectives, and norms.

What has proven to speed up a choreographer's advancement is the ongoing desire for learning and discovery, along with the endeavor to understand and develop craftsmanship. The latter means to proficiently use the instruments of choreography, to formulate artistic objectives, and to define individual aesthetic norms. Only then can choreographers engage confidently in the creative act—when they can skillfully handle the flexibility of artistic boundaries and the responsibility of artistic freedom.

EDUCATING AN IDEA

The creation of a new dance may begin with the bright flash of a simple idea. The idea may spring from anything—a movement, a feeling, or a piece of music. Suddenly, the ripple effect caused by the "big bang" of imagination will awaken and magnetize the moving particles of cosmic dust—a new dance is about to form. But will this newborn dance be a planet or a star? Will it be identifiable in the vast space of the universe in motion, without becoming the center of a formation, system, or galaxy of other ideas? The initial idea might be barely noticed without gravitating and pulling in other ideas to cluster together and join in a new cosmic dance. The nucleus of a space system is similar to a family—the presence of the parents and extended family are needed to raise, support, and educate the newborn.

The development of a dance idea is one of the most laborious and absorbing parts of dance making. Assuming that the choreographer is already proficient with the fundamentals of the craft and equipped with compositional devices, cultivating a set of *research abilities* is essential to the creative process.

Artistic research is a set of guiding practices to *educate an idea* though learning and discovery and to help establish the conceptual and working parameters of a new dance. Artistic research typically consists of: a) identifying and organizing resources; b) gathering and analyzing data; and c) experimenting and testing various movement ideas.

◆ **How does artistic research unfold?** A choreographic initiative develops through gradual phases and undergoes multiple stages of shaping and reshaping of the work. Therefore, artistic research is an ongoing practice for the duration of the choreographic initiative. However, choreographers may allocate and distribute an uneven amount of time and effort to various aspects of research based on the artistic needs of the work. A generalized progression of artistic research may unfold as:

➢ *research-before-creating*, which involves activities to allocate targeted resources, scholarly produced studies, and other public information on the subject matter; to conduct initial movement experimentation and any related activities that would further inform the choreographer's intentions about the work as a whole.

➢ *research-during-creating*, which involves activities to analyze, understand, and reconfigure the gathered knowledge; to mix learned methods and researched approaches; to test studied algorithms; and to explore movement and visual analogies.

➢ *research-while-evaluating*, which involves generating resources to support a mid-point analysis of the creative activities and the characteristics of the work-in-progress, which may include conversation with the performers and the collaborators to propose and produce strategies to improve the effectiveness of the creative process—leading the choreography towards the desired outcome.

A summary of practical implementation and hands-on use of these principles can be found at other places in this book —for example, please see subchapter *Intellectual Investigations During the Creative Process: Brainstorm as You Create, Research as You Stage*, as part of *Growing the Dance Garden—Choreographic Devices and Operations*, Chapter 17.

◆ **How does artistic research commence?** There are multiple entry points for starting the research and learning process.[10] Some of the possibilities are:

➢ *problem-based research*, which suggests a specific subject of interest that must be studied, evaluated, and resolved creatively.

➢ *activity based research*, which encompasses interactions with communities, programs, and collaborators to broaden the choreographer's perspective on how the work could emerge.

➢ *project-based research*, which relates to determining the applicable materials and their organization in ways relevant to creating the work.

◆ **How does a choreographer organize a cosmos full of chaotic ideas and gathered knowledge into the building components of the work?** Each work of dance has unique, complex processes and multiple components. Some of them are the subject matter and conceptual direction of the work, the structuring of the work, and the methods of generating movement material and inventing movement vocabulary. The choreographer as a creative practitioner often addresses the multiple facets of the work simultaneously. The act of designing unique artistic research methods is part of the creative act—it is finding and establishing the most effective ways to sort and organize ideas, synthesize gathered data, and channel the acquired knowledge to build the components of the work.

◆ **What are the building components of a dance work that the choreographer may consider when engaging in artistic research?** The question here is also about how a dance idea *materializes*. In various works, the Greek philosopher Aristotle discusses that there is no *form* without *content* (or matter) and no matter without form. Aristotle determined that material things constitute the unity of forming matter or *formed matter*. He also wrote about *unformed matter,* or nonmaterial form, that exists independently and originates in the "form of forms"—the idea of God, for example, is a cognitively formed concept without a direct materialized equivalent.[11]

Based on these concepts, it is fair to state that philosophically, a choreography emerges in the harmonized unity of three major components: *content, form*, and *process*. These three components interact dynamically, in unity, and are inseparable. Yet it is important to also examine them as acting independently. There is no hierarchy or prescribed order for starting the creative act in terms of these components, nor is there a sequence for artistic research to support a dance idea. Many choreographers begin with the part of the work that they feel most informed and confident about. Brief definitions of the components are:

➢ ***Content*** relates to the choreographer's intentions and goals, the subject matter choice, the conceptual parameters, the artistic direction, and the purpose of the work. Helpful questions to determine the content are: What are the reasons and the urgency to create the dance, and what will the dance do?

➢ ***Form*** relates to the choreographer's movement material, kinesthetic language, idea embodiment, and use of other aesthetic means and art forms through which the work emerges. Helpful questions to determine form are: What shape does the dance take as it emerges, and how will it materialize and appear?

➢ ***Process*** relates to choreographer's creative activities in building the work: the methods of generating movement material, the construction and structuring of the dance, and working with dancers and collaborators. Helpful questions to determine the process are: How do you create and build the dance, and what strategies and approaches are in use?

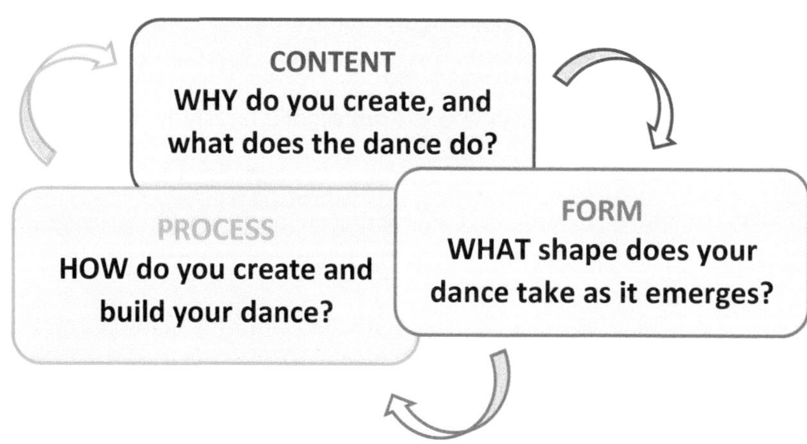

Figure 3

Simple questions are often the most challenging to answer. How do we explain complex matters in simple terms and distill a lot of information to craft a brief response?

Crafting a functional philosophy of choreography begins with exploring complex ideas, and it results in articulating them in simple statements. The crafting of a single dance work is similarly challenging because of the complex interactions among its components. Therefore, it may not be sufficient to approach content, form, and process with just one type of linear research. Instead, the education of a dance idea and project may demand a multilayered and multidimensional approach involving various activities and perspectives, all of which serve as resources and contribute to the complexity of the creative act.

This chapter also features a new *structured approach* to artistic research-as-practice to prepare the choreographer to engage in the creative act.

SMART is an acronym that stands for *Systematic Methods for Artistic Research and Training*, an individually customized framework to adopt either for a specific dance project idea, or to approach the creative act in general. The approach offers ongoing, cyclical, and alternating activities during the multiple stages of the creative act by balancing intellectual processes with intuitive processes. It brings together scholastic, exploratory, and movement engagement in an organized fashion, with the aim to minimize an extended period of trial and error. The following paragraphs describe the components of the *SMART* framework and algorithm:

◆ ***Systematic Methods*** are the activities undertaken and the procedures carried out by participants in a choreographic project to bring the work from imagination to material presence in the world. While formulating a personalized *system* would provide the choreographer with ways to organize knowledge, formulating a personalized *method* will provide the choreographer with ways to practically implement that knowledge. The process of creating a new work may be linear—i.e., progressing steadily to a predetermined ending, or it may include accidental or intended direction shifts, exploration of emergent possibilities, and revisions to the presumed character and identity of the work.

◆ ***Artistic Research*** is the practice of gathering and exploring diverse resources to bring a choreographic idea into sufficient focus for creation to commence and to support the exploratory and decision-making processes that will bring the project to completion. The following three forms of *Artistic Research* for choreography may be usefully distinguished:

➢ *Scholastic Research* is the examination of such materials as books, articles, art works, case studies, statistical data, archival repositories, and audio and video collections. This kind of research produces connections between one's own and others' artistic intuitions, ideas, and methods for setting and achieving goals.

➢ *Creative Research* is the undertaking of such activities as visiting museums, galleries, and diverse built and natural environments; trying unfamiliar forms of dance and other body/performance practices; and interviewing artists or practitioners in other domains. This kind of *experiential research* refines one's artistic sensibilities and expands one's intellectual repertoire about what choreography is and how it may situate itself. While scholastic research may focus on analyzing existing literature, references, and discoveries made by others, creative research is an opportunity for choreographers to invent and design their own methods of research involving direct and personal interaction with their subjects and objects of interest.

➢ *Movement Research* is ongoing kinesthetic experimentation and improvisation to awaken new body experiences and new ideas about movement. Such research might launch from spontaneous somatic brainstorming or embodied engagements with selected imagery, themes, scores, actions, tasks, or a particular movement philosophy.

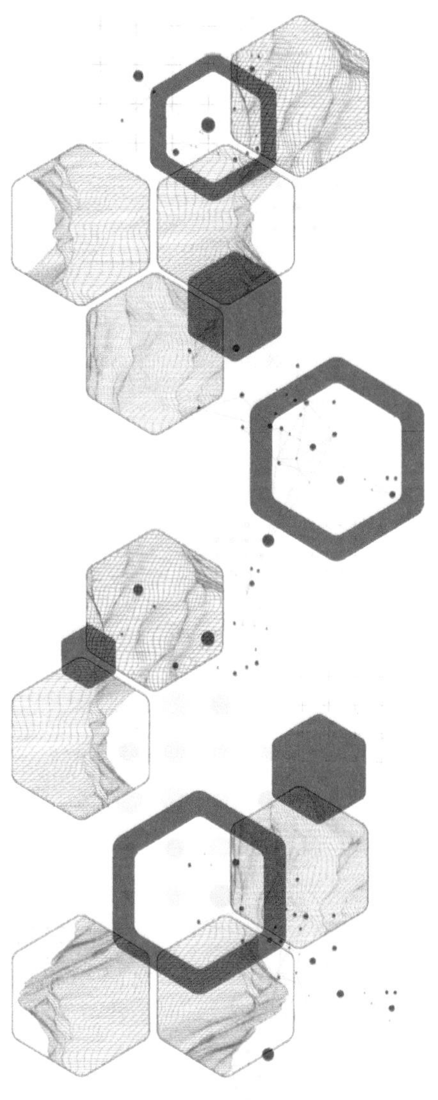

◆ ***Training*** is the means by which one gains and strengthens skills and gathers insights about their use in diverse contexts of practice. A high level of artistic proficiency will be achieved through regular exposure to and immersion in familiar and preferred body, mind, and research practices, as well as deliberately seeking ideas and experiences that challenge one's current creative and conceptual boundaries. A choreographer must work daily in a disciplined manner to expand knowledge, sharpen senses, and develop proficiencies.

The introduction of ***ICON*** in the previous pages and ***SMART*** earlier gives us the unity of **ICON SMART**^{SM}—a newly formulated dynamic *functional philosophy* and *creative algorithm* that systematizes the creative act of dance making. Choreographers, with their intuitive craftsmanship, may already implement these approaches without realizing it—just as cosmic forces and Earth's gravity act upon us without our regular notice. Do you intentionally or unintentionally already use this creative algorithm, and what are the specifics of *your own* ICON SMART^{SM}?

STRIVING FOR PERFECTION AND EMBRACING IMPERFECTION

– THE MASTERPIECE SYNDROME AND THE *CIM*-FACTOR –

People admire great works of art because perfection in art contrasts with the imperfection of life. Iconic works of art are timeless examples that human beings are capable of brilliance and wisdom. Conventionally, perfection is the ultimate goal of any creative and artistic act. Masterpieces of dance, visual art, music, sculpture, theater, architecture, and literature are mesmerizing to watch, listen to, read, or think about over and over again. For many emerging choreographers, they are a source of inspiration and even competitiveness—not with the art itself, but with the artist.

Figure 4 Samples of masterpieces: Left: Leonardo da Vinci's portrait of Mona Lisa (1503–1519) with her enigmatic smile has captured the attention of spectators and scientists for centuries; Center: Photography © Costas, *Apollo* (1928), choreography by George Balanchine, performed by soloist Nilas Martins, Isabelle Guerin, and members of the New York City Ballet, NYC, 1997 © The George Balanchine Trust. The ballet features the Greek god of music and poetry with three muses who are visible, yet they are not. Right: Frank Lloyd Wright's architectural masterpiece *Fallingwater* (1937) has an ingenious treatment of space and integration of natural surroundings

◆ **Is striving for perfection embedded in the nature of craftsmanship?** Yes, and yet there is a catch: a fixation and an unhealthy preoccupation with reaching perfection might drive a choreographer to skip important phases in the creative process. The choreographer might focus solely on reaching a desired result rather proceeding through exploratory practices. Striving for perfection and trying to create a masterpiece actually undermines one's ability to create one—let's call it the *masterpiece syndrome.*

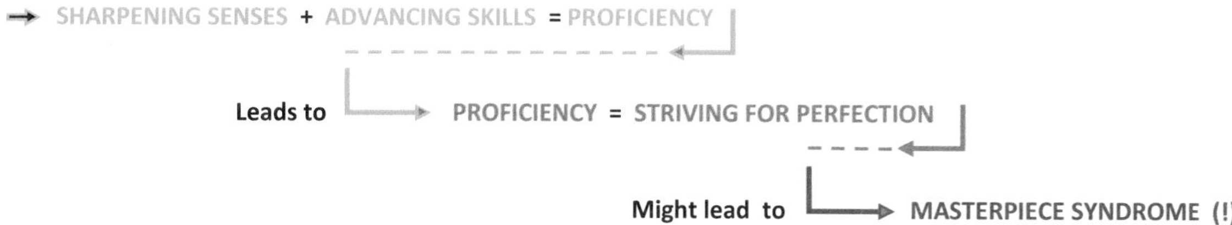

Figure 5

Learning about masterpieces and discovering what makes them so special is part of the creative act. A choreographer can continue to study, admire, and be inspired by masterpieces without becoming fixated on creating one. The masterpiece syndrome is preventable once the focus shifts to curiosity and excitement.

◆ **What makes a masterpiece exceptional and sets it apart from other works of art?** A masterpiece is often perceived as self-explanatory, and yet much remains unexplained about how it was made. Three major factors must be in perfect alignment to produce a masterpiece. Let's call this alignment the ***CIM-Factor***, which can be expressed as the following formula:

CRAFTSMANSHIP + INNOVATION + MYSTERY = CIM-FACTOR

➢ **Craftsmanship** is the knowledge, application, and command of exceptional skills and proficiencies. Craftsmanship and proficiency are achievable through various strategies of learning and discovery, and rigorous artistic training to advance skills—see the previous pages of this chapter, as well as BOOKS IV, V, and VI.

➢ **Innovation** is a novel idea, solution, device, discovery, or process that challenges conventional wisdom and imposed norms. Innovating is achievable through strategies and exploratory processes that often aim to challenge mainstream reasoning and traditional logical thinking—see Chapter 11, Book III.

➢ **Mystery** is a phenomenon or anything that is unexplained or inexplicable. Mysteries are enigmatic and secretive, provocative, and challenging. Mysteries are often identifiable and solvable. As there is no other reference to mystery in this book, let's give it some attention in relation to masterpieces.

Masterpieces tend to be mysterious. These works of art appear as questions rather than statements, as half-solved puzzles rather than straight directives. There are always "clues" or "hints" that convert the spectator into a detective, eager to search for a treasure trove of enlightening knowledge. Uncovering the mystery of a masterpiece is deeply satisfying. Gathering facts and evidence, analyzing them, and hypothesizing might solve the mystery. And yet these activities also might perpetuate the mystery by raising additional puzzling questions. Is this endless cycle intentional? Let's "demystify a mystery" by considering a master-piece-quote from the brilliant physicist and philosopher, Sir Isaac Newton:

"If I have seen further, it is by standing on the shoulders of giants."

The figurative expression is derived from Greek mythology: the blind giant Orion carried his servant, Cedalion, on his shoulders to act as the giant's eyes. This sentence encompasses the perfect balance of a metaphor and profound wisdom—the proverb *is* a masterpiece about discovering truth by building on previous discoveries. The content seems straightforward, yet there are fine nuances.

The mystery is not what is *said*, but what is *not said* in the sentence. The important events are mysteriously omitted, or only suggested. The acts of learning and discovering, and the skill of climbing and walking around (the creative act), are delicately concealed within the context of the sentence. Events are captured as time unfolds in opposite directions, in both retrospective and chronological progression—see Figure 6.

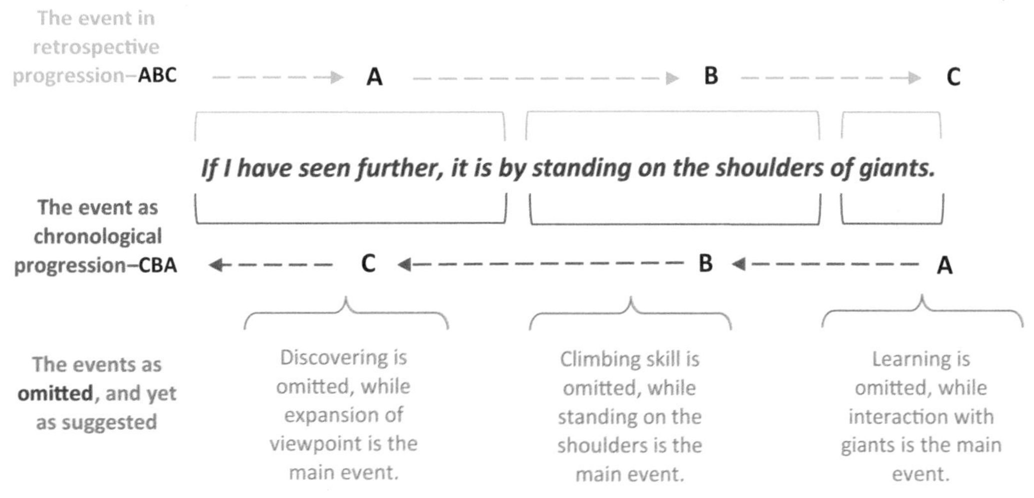

Figure 6

The A-B-C retrospective progression of accomplishing the actions: A) seeing further, B) standing, and now C) discovering harmoniously mirrors the chronological progression: 1–2–3 (as 3–2–1) of reconstructed past events: 1) meet giants, 2) climb on shoulders, 3) see further. This advice for the future captures the past and circles back and forth, creating an endless cycle of wisdom and determination. The suggested mysterious formula is a three-phase action plan that includes: learning/inspiring, skills/opportunities, and discovering/innovating—all said poetically, mysteriously, and practically as the author intended.

The *CIM-factor* described earlier aims to articulate the building factors of a masterpiece; however, it is not necessarily a formula to create a masterpiece. Ironically, one of the crucial factors to reach perfection and to create a masterpiece is to *embrace imperfection*. As in Newton's sample, the proverb with a formula to discover implies his acknowledgment of imperfection with mysterious imperfect omissions, which makes the proverb perfect.

?

Which works of art are your favorite masterpieces, and are there any mysteries about them?

◆ **Why is embracing perfect imperfection the most admirable paradox of a creative act?** A creative act begins as an imperfect act. Our daily lives may be imperfect, though the glamorous images on advertisement billboards present a picture-perfect experience that might be unattainable or unrealistic. Ironically, in a world obsessed with perfection, the imperfect stands out as more humane, vigorous, and fun. The masterpiece syndrome and striving for perfection have many disadvantages, some of which are that they:

- ➢ Cause anxiety and self-censorship, which obstruct the experience of making mistakes, learning from them, and laughing at them.
- ➢ Eliminate the excitement of accidental discoveries, which on most occasions emerge from mistakes, misplacements, or misunderstandings.
- ➢ Tamper with the manifestation of authenticity and uniqueness, which can be special, beautiful, and perfect in its own way.
- ➢ Hinder the spirit of unconventional thinking and the opportunity to draw inspiration from something that is imperfect.
- ➢ Force a directional change in the creative act from process-oriented to outcome-oriented.
- ➢ Suppress the truth that perfection in art is a product of an imperfect human act, and therefore, they conceal the fact that perfection is within reach.
- ➢ Solicit external approval and public praise, rather than personal achievement and satisfaction.

In summary, the masterpiece syndrome and the fixation and striving for perfection may be counterproductive and hinder the creative act as learning and discovery; this reality prompts a clarification of our initial formula and equation:

Proficiency = Striving for Perfection + EMBRACING IMPERFECTION

By resisting and eliminating the masterpiece syndrome, choreographers can fully explore the endless potential of their own artistic identity and the betterment of their work. The creative act becomes humane when we embrace the fact that we all are *perfectly imperfect!*

It takes an average of seven to twelve hours to complete an oil portrait painting. Leonardo DaVinci, however, began painting Mona Lisa in 1503 and continued working on it until his death at age 67 in 1519. Many experts regard the painting as unfinished.[12] But why did DaVinci take sixteen years rather than twelve hours to complete his work?

One theory is that the artist had a hand injury; another is that he was discovering new techniques for future portraits. For example, the soft curves of the woman's hair and clothing are echoed in the undulating valleys and rivers behind her. Adding to the overall harmony achieved in the painting is Mona Lisa's smile, which affirms DaVinci's craft of finding a cosmic link between humanity and nature.

AESTHETIC DIRECTIONS OF A CREATIVE ACT:

MAKING ART = WORKING HARD, PROCEEDING SMART OR TAKING APART?

A creative act in choreography can be channeled in various aesthetic directions based on the choreographer's artistic interests. Guiding questions delve into the fundamentals such as: What is the function of art, and how does this function align with the choreographer's individual aesthetic? The solutions to these two questions define the features of one's choreographic agenda, artistic ideology, and identity—see *Prologue* and *Choreographic Individuality and Artistic Identity—The Search for Who I Am*, Chapter 13.

Existing aesthetic directions may be defined by particular genres spanning across mediums, styles, and time periods. Instead of referring to specific choreographic pieces, samples of visual art may help in choreographing the dance equivalents to visual art. To illustrate the distinctiveness of aesthetic directions, let's generalize three distinct genres: classical art, pop art, and conceptual art.

CLASSICAL ART **POP ART** **CONCEPTUAL ART**

Figure 7 Left: portrait painting by Vermeer, Johannes, *Girl with a Pearl Earring (Het meisje met de parel)*, oil on canvas, circa 1665, public domain; Center: portrait painting © Sherman, Paul, *Marilyn Pop Art*, public domain; Right: photography © Jeff Bergen, *Studio shot of a woman's hand holding a black apple*, public domain, sourced from iStock Photos/Getty Images.

Within Western European traditions, *classical art* is primarily based on ideals of beauty and meaningfulness to serve aesthetic and intellectual purposes. An academic education and training in classical art aesthetics would emphasize the use of creative principles such as subject matter, form, and processes with distinct rules of composition. The choreographic equivalent of classical art would be works rooted in tradition, and yet that provide expandable content and re-envisioning of conventional movement principles.

While classical art tends to explore the complexities of humanity, *pop art* offers an accessible approach to art, with an emphasis on popular culture and imaginative interpretations of commercial products and interests. Pop art operates on the line between art and entertainment, providing easy-to-understand content and likely pleasure. Pop art is usually mass-produced at low cost, and it is often geared toward youth in the short-term. Works are characterized as witty, flashy, gimmicky, and glamorous. A choreographic equivalent of pop art would be dance creations to popular music with movement material that is enjoyable and amusing. The works may be produced to suit commercial venues.

Derived from postmodernism and minimalism, *conceptual art* emphasizes the idea behind the work rather than its aesthetic qualities. The *concept* of the work *is* the actual *work*, while the execution and the function of the concept are less relevant. This radical form pushes the boundaries of art to polar extremes, making art become either overly intellectualized or overly contradictory.[13] Conceptual art is less concerned with the artist's object/subject as such, and instead purposefully breaks apart form from content. The work poses provocative questions that challenge the nature and function of art, such as: What makes art "art"? What is post-art, non-art, and anti-art?

In contrast to classical art, which expresses consciously and subconsciously the subtleties of the universal human condition, postmodern and conceptual art may accommodate very specific creative interests.[14] The trivial may take over the enigmatic. Cleverness may take over genuine creativity and craftsmanship. A choreographic equivalent of conceptual art would appear as a convergence of multi-disciplinary forms, unorthodox techniques, and movement concepts; conventional dance may be featured peripherally or deconstructed unrecognizably.

The practicalities of the creative act may also be taken into consideration when choosing an aesthetic direction. Choreographers are under pressure to continually create and *deliver* new work to satisfy the audience's craving for something new. Often, however, limited time and circumstances prevent a creative act from fully flourishing. In the background, competitiveness in the field and limited employment opportunities fuel tension within the choreographic community. A possible solution is to randomly toss in any unorthodox ideas with the hope of generating interest and excitement. Unfortunately, not everything new and different might be of substance and worth.

Therefore, choreographers may thoughtfully consider the scope of their creative goals and practices in relation to their artistic priorities, and even their living circumstances. Exploring a connection between artistic experiences and real-life experiences may inform a solution. A creative act can be anything a choreographer chooses—a spontaneous activity or a deliberate crafting, a random innovation or a systematic method to develop skills, the striving for perfection or the embrace of imperfection. Regardless of which modality and aesthetic direction choreographers choose, the creative act is always worth pursuing when it is driven by intuitive craftsmanship and the desire to learn and discover.

HELPFUL TIPS & SUGGESTIONS

~ Lose yourself in art to find yourself creating

~ Learn by understanding, improve by embodying, criticize by encouraging

~ Allow accidental innovation by being open-minded while being in control

~ Accept that a work is never finished and never perfect

~ Strive to sharpen your senses and intuition rather than to explain them

~ Strive to become more skilled rather than more clever

~ Strive to be prepared instead of perfect

assignments & exercises

ᔑ **RESEARCH ASSIGNMENT:** Choose a choreographer that you admire and/or whose body of work is familiar to you. By using the outlined principles of content, form, and process, as well as the ***ICON*** approach, research, analyze, and characterize the work of this choreographer within the following parameters:

➥ *Instruments of Choreography:* What type of movement vocabulary, methods of construction, dramaturgical cohesiveness, and art forms are incorporated, predominant, and recurring in the existing repertoire of this choreographer?

➥ *Objectives:* What kind of subject matter, concepts, intentions, and overarching artistic messages can be identified in the overall body of work, and why do you think this choreographer has chosen these topics as recurring themes?

➥ *Norms:* What framework and artistic scope define this choreographer's aesthetic norms and the working parameters used in the created dances? What kind of established norms—political, societal, and cultural—are of artistic interest to this choreographer, and how are these norms revealed in the work? How does the choreographer's individual set of norms complement, oppose, or challenge the existing political, societal, and cultural norms? In what ways does their interaction unfold?

★ **CREATIVE EXERCISE:** Implement elements of ***SMART*** and practice various types of *Artistic Research* that incorporate scholastic, creative, and movement research:

➥ Research and analyze the aesthetic characteristics of works of *classical art* created from the time period of ancient Greece to the end of the Renaissance. What important elements should be in place to formulate a work of classical art, and what would be the choreographic equivalent? Draft a few bullet points of criteria applicable to dance. By using the criteria, improvise and explore various movement ideas and create a short choreographic phrase capturing these characteristics.

➥ Research and analyze the aesthetic characteristics of works of *pop art* of the mid-20th century in the United States and the United Kingdom. What important elements should be in place to formulate works of pop art, and what would be the choreographic equivalent? Draft a few bullet points of criteria applicable to dance. By using the criteria, improvise and explore various movement ideas and create a short choreographic phrase capturing these characteristics.

➥ Research and analyze the aesthetic characteristics of works of *conceptual art* as set apart from contemporary art that formally handles materials, tools, and methods. Look at it from the perspective of a movement that challenges the nature of dance art. What important elements should be in place to formulate a work of conceptual art, and what would be the choreographic equivalent? Draft a few bullet points of criteria applicable to dance. By using the criteria, improvise and explore various movement ideas and create a short choreographic phrase and/or segment to incorporate the human body in a *kinetic installation* and/or *performance art* capturing these characteristics.

COMPARATIVE ASSESSMENT: For this assignment, be prepared to choose a colleague choreographer to work with. Alternatively, you can choose to work with a choreographer "in absentia," meaning that by knowing the work and personality of a specific choreographer colleague, you can make a comparison hypothetically:

➡ Systematic method: How do you organize and structure your work? For example: by personally looking for specific resources to support your initial idea, by trying to make sense of elements that are not yet connected, or by formulating a specific idea and inviting dancers and collaborators to bring in their ideas. Compare your method with your colleague's. What proves effective for each practice? Why?

➡ Ways of learning and discovering: How do you learn best and in what ways do you process information most efficiently? For example: I'm a visual learner; I'm a kinesthetic learner; I learn best when I read. How do you come up with new and innovative ideas? For example: mostly by accident, after working for a long time on certain ideas, by playing with various ideas and exploring what springs out of an improvisation. How do your methods compare with colleagues' works? If there is something in common, what is it?

➡ Training: How do you best advance your skills? For example: by learning from past experiences, by ongoing repetition of what you do best, by seeing works of colleagues and analyzing them, or by consulting an artistic confidant. How does your method prove to be most effective for you? Compare your approach to your colleague's. Analyze why and how common methods prove efficient within each practice.

Comparison of proficiency between works of art: Choose two works of visual art from different eras that are considered masterpieces. For example: a Renaissance masterpiece and a 20th-century masterpiece. Explore each work separately and focus on what characteristics and elements make those pieces masterworks. It is very possible that different sets of components comprise the strengths of each work:

➢ Consider whether there are overlapping components that make these works masterpieces. If so, what are they?

➢ Compare which components are applicable specifically to one work. How do these components make the work distinct from the other?

➢ If you hypothetically exchange and reverse the components that make each piece a distinguished masterpiece, would they still be masterpieces?

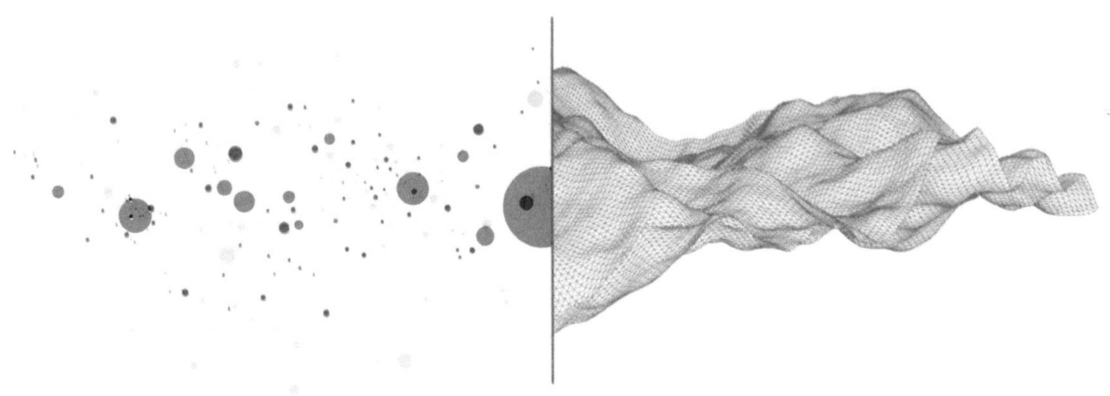

BIBLIOGRAPHY AND REFERENCES

[1] Butterworth, Jo. "Choreographer as Researcher: Issues and Concepts in Postgraduate Study," in as part *Contemporary Choreography: A Critical Reader*, 1st edition, edited by Jo Butterworth and Liesbeth Wildschut, Routledge, 2009, pp. 152–167.
[2] Pakes, Anna. "Knowing through Dance-Making; Choreography, Practical Knowledge and Practice as Research," in as part *Contemporary Choreography: A Critical Reader*, 2nd edition, edited by Jo Butterworth and Liesbeth Wildschut, Routledge, 2018, pp. 10–21.
[3] Pakes 2018. "Knowing through Dance-Making..."
[4] Pakes 2018. "Knowing through Dance-Making..."
[5] Aristotle. *The Nicomachean Ethics*, Book VI, Penguin Classics, 2004.
[6] Oliver, Jack E. *The Incomplete Guide to the Art of Discovery*, Columbia University Press, 1991.
[7] Oliver 1991. *The Incomplete Guide to the Art of Discovery...*
[8] Butterworth 2009. "Choreographer as Researcher..."
[9] Deleuze, Gilles. "What Is the Creative Act," 1987, video recording with English subtitles, accessed on YouTube, August, 2020, part of *Two Regimes of Madness*, Texts and Interviews 1975–1995 Gilles Deleuze (1925–1995), edited by David Lapoujade, translated by Ames Hodges and Mike Taormina, pp. 312–324.
[10] Henry, Jane. "Managing Experiential Learning; the Learner's Perspective," in as part of *Learner Managed Learning*, edited by N. Graves, World Education Fellowship and Higher Education for Capability, 1993.
[11] Aristotle. "De Anima, Physics, and Metaphysics," various publishers, and article summary: Ainsworth, Thomas. "Form vs. Matter," article, *Stanford Encyclopedia of Philosophy*, published February 2016; substantive revision, March 2020, online access August 2020.
[12] Da Vinci, Leonardo. Editor. *Encyclopedia Britannica*, www.britannica.com/, accessed August 2020.
[13] Karg, Alexandra. "Conceptual Art: The Revolutionary Movement Explained," article from *The Collector*, online magazine July 6, 2020, www.thecollector.com/, accessed August 2020.
[14] Kuspit, Donald. *The End of Art*, Cambridge University Press, 2005.

VISUAL REFERENCES

Figure 1, 2, and 3: Diagrams © Vladimir Angelov

Figure 4: Masterpieces triptych: Left image: Painting © Da Vinci, Leonardo, *Mona Lisa*, 1503–19, Creative Commons Zero, CC0; Center image: Photography © Costas, *Apollo*, choreography by George Balanchine, performed by soloist Nilas Martins, Isabelle Guerin, and members of the New York City Ballet, NYC, 1997 © The George Balanchine Trust; Right Image: Photography © Highsmith, Carol M., *Fallingwater*, 2007, public domain

Figure 5 and 6: Diagrams © Vladimir Angelov

Figure 7: Image triptych with samples of classical art, pop art, and conceptual art. Left image: portrait painting by Vermeer, Johannes, *Girl with a Pearl Earring (Het meisje met de parel)*, oil on canvas, circa 1665, public domain, photography © Janson, Jonathan, sourced from *Girl with a Pearl Earring*. essentialvermeer.com—The Complete Interactive Vermeer Catalogue, retrieved in April 2020, Wiki Commons; Center image: portrait painting © Sherman, Paul, *Marilyn Pop Art*, public domain, sourced at WPClipart; Right image: photography © Jeff Bergen, *Studio shot of a woman's hand holding a black apple*, sourced from iStock Photos/Getty Images

BOOK III

CONCEPT AND CONTEXT

INNOVATION, INTENTIONALITY, AND INDIVIDUALITY

Ancient Greece. 331 BC. A conversation while walking from the academy to the theater:

CHOREOGRAPHER: We need some tension…you know…some friction…

PHILOSOPHER: What do you mean?… in the dance?…around the dance?

CHOREOGRAPHER: Yes. A conflict should be taking place—a drama of confinement and freeing.

PHILOSOPHER: Well…there are three types of conflict—which one do you prefer?

CHOREOGRAPHER: What are they?

PHILOSOPHER: *(Lists by raising his fingers, one by one)*

A person versus the surroundings

A person versus another

A person versus him or herself

CHOREOGRAPHER: Well, I'll use…all of them…at the same time!

Excerpt from

dance DIALOGUES

An Anonymous Unpublished Manuscript, 376 BC–AD 2091

CHAPTER 11

INVENTIVE CREATIVITY
– IN ART, EVERYTHING IS POSSIBLE –

One of the most exciting challenges for choreographers is to train themselves to love challenges, both artistic and logistical. Generally, dealing with obstacles is neither easy nor inspiring, and yet they are part of everyday life. Handling problems is the essence of our existence, survival, and progress.

Choreographers may have a substantial advantage when facing challenges because choreography by nature demands creativity in work habits and daily behavior. Traditionally, when facing a challenge, we might think of it as a "problem"—a deviation from what is considered normal and expected.[1] The process of resolving problems is also known as *problem-solving*. But what if a *problem* is not a problem at all? What if a problem turns out to be an *opportunity*? Two exciting strategies then come into play: a problem will involve resolving, while an opportunity will involve exploring.

During daily creative practices, a choreographer's mindset approaches problems and obstacles not as disturbing issues, but rather as exciting challenges and procedural equations needing a solution. Problem solving is not a burden, but a motivating, imaginative activity that attempts to strike a balance between criticism and compliance, a personal agenda and the agendas of others, and artistic objectives and technical barriers. In all problematic scenarios, if we take a chance and time to truly explore what is possible, sooner or later we'll find out that in art, *everything* is possible!

Figure 1 Photography © Dean Alexander & Design Army, Hong Kong Ballet 2018–19 Season campaign, choreography by Septime Webre, pictured Ye Feifei, courtesy of Hong Kong Ballet, 2018

The most well-known strategy for problem solving and exploring opportunities is brainstorming—a spontaneous process of generating and streaming random ideas. By removing inhibitions and suspending judgment, brainstorming—alone or in a group—is a liberating activity to toss out, share, and suggest any sort of unconventional thoughts and imaginative solutions.[2] Brainstorming is not analytical thinking, which may precede a brainstorming session in order to identify the problem needing a solution.

Choreographers may have another substantial advantage—art operates within the realm of fictitious and imaginary reality. Therefore, an unconventional solution to a realistic challenge can be expressed in figurative and dream-like ways. For example, instead of swimming across a large body of water, a dancer can jump over it with an elegant *jeté*, as in this photo.

Inspiration is the driving factor that transforms problem solving and creative thinking into an energizing and fun experience. Choreographers draw their inspiration from multiple sources, such as movement, music, and Nature—arguably, the greatest of all inventors. Choreographers may also draw inspiration from the challenge itself by using various approaches to transform that challenge and make it serve their artistic objectives.

Choreographers are *creative thinkers* by profession, but are they also *innovators* and *inventors*? While the objective of problem solving might be to address a deficiency or "fix" something that is not working, the objective of innovating and inventing is to advance ideas and concepts that may not necessarily appear to be "problematic." We say: "*Be creative!*" meaning *Explore, no matter whether it will be successful!* We say: "*Be innovative!*" meaning *Take an existing concept to a new level.* We say: "*Invent and discover!*" meaning *Search, find, explore, and originate a concept that did not exist previously.*

Figure 2 Photography © Dean Alexander & Design Army, Hong Kong Ballet 2019–20 Season campaign, choreography by Septime Webre, pictured from left: Li Jiabo, Venus Villa, courtesy of Hong Kong Ballet, 2019

A new and original dance is often created "from scratch" by spontaneously generating movement ideas to music, images, or impressions; these ideas are then linked to subject matter and content by inviting collaborators to participate in the creative process. Choreography often emerges from these initial random impulses rather than from prescribed algorithms. For example, the choreographer might simply say—"*Let's get to work, create, and have fun with a few dance steps and exuberant jumps!*"—photo left.

In summary: *brainstorming* is thinking of something new; *innovating* is introducing something as new and improving something that exists.

Inspiration is a starting point for creativity, but it is not always sufficient for creation. *Creativity* is a starting point for innovating, but it is not always sufficient for innovation. *Innovation* is a starting point for invention, but it is not always sufficient for invention and groundbreaking discoveries. The unity of all of these processes is the activity of coming up with new ideas, which we call ***inventive creativity*** in choreography. It is the subject of this chapter.

For choreographers, inventive creativity is not a special one-time event, but a part of daily work. How do brainstorming, innovative thinking, and inventive problem-solving devices relate to choreography and individual artistic practices? Perhaps the answer is hidden in the words of the architect and engineer R. Buchminister Fuller, who said:

> *When I'm working on a problem, I never think about beauty. I think only how to solve the problem.*
> *But when I have finished, if the solution is not beautiful, I know it is wrong.*[3]

THE SCIENCE OF INVENTING: WHAT IS TRIZ?

How do we come up with new ideas? Are these ideas really groundbreaking inventions or only modifications of existing ideas? Is there any science behind inventive and innovative thinking, and if so, how does it work?

Creating does not always mean inventing. In choreography and the arts, invention and innovation are manifested through individual talent, unique perspective, and skillful use of aesthetic means. Evaluating the "inventiveness" and the quality of a dance, however, may be subjective in nature. Technical data in science, on the other hand, is quantitative and statistical, and therefore objective in nature.[4] Luckily, there are overlapping areas where the arts and the sciences can learn from each other. Choreographers may use *inventive creativity* to generate, discover, and develop new concepts for dance.

Since the beginning of humanity, the act of inventing has been linked to survival and progress. And yet it was only within the past century in Russia that a *scientific method* for inventive and innovative thinking emerged. Meet *TRIZ!* The acronym stands for теория решения изобретательских задач. *TRIZ* translates literally from Russian as Theory of the Resolution of Invention-Related Tasks, a translation that is also rendered as the *Theory of Inventive Problem Solving*.[5] *TRIZ* in its original form was developed by the Soviet inventor and science fiction writer Genrich Altshuller (1926–1998) and his associates. While working as a clerk at the patent office of the Soviet Navy's Caspian Sea flotilla, Altshuller realized that *unresolved contradictions* in patent literature caused problems that required inventive solutions. Altshuller studied over 200,000 patents and discovered that less than 25% were genuine inventive solutions, while the rest were variable.[6]

A) Routine design for an existing system–32%
B) Minor improvement to an existing system–45%
C) Fundamental improvement to an existing system–18%
D) Expanding the primary functions of a system–4%
E) **Rare scientific discovery and a pioneering new system–1%**

IMPROVEMENTS (A–C)
INNOVATIONS (B–D)
INVENTIONS (C–E)

Figure 3

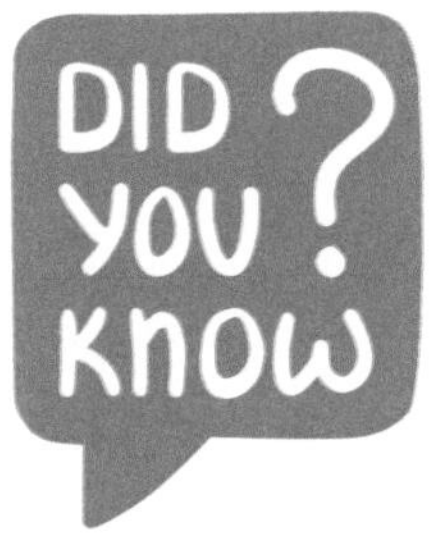

Altshuller observed creative individuals and looked for patterns in their thinking. He analyzed the techniques they used in inventing and subsequently published his book *Creativity as an Exact Science*, Gordon & Breach Science Publisher, 1984. In 1986, Altshuller switched his attention away from the technological approach of *TRIZ* and began to study its application to the development of individual creativity. In 1989, the *TRIZ* Association was formed, with Altshuller as its leader until his death in 1998.

Figure 4 Photography © Gennady Ivanov, Genrich Altshuller, personal archive and courtesy of Alexander Selioutski, 1984

TRIZ-theory is based on the finding that the vast majority of challenges reflect the need to overcome a dilemma or a trade-off between two contradictory elements. Altshuller defined the first series of 40 inventive strategies, some of which can be summarized as follows: [7]

➢ **Segmentation** means to separate into smaller parts that can easily be interchanged and then put back together.

➢ **Extraction** means to take out or separate something or single out the critical parts of a system and replace/substitute them with others.

➢ **Asymmetry** as the opposite of symmetry means that varying asymmetrical shapes give the opportunity for one shape to do one thing and another shape to perform another function.

➢ **Cushion in advance** means to invent and prepare alternatives for events that might fail or go wrong in some way.

➢ **Equipotentiality** means finding ways to avoid heavy physical work and exert less energy to get work done.

➢ **Spheroidicity** means to consider curves, curvature, and changing the radius when designing. Movement tends to be smoother and more efficient when it curves rather than when it is angular.

➢ **Inversion** means doing the opposite of what might seem normal. For example, reverse order, lift instead of lower, or turn things upside down.

Many of these devices can be applied in choreographic practices and might lead to exciting outcomes. Most importantly, implementing Altshuller's statistical classification of the variable degree of innovation and the relatively limited number of groundbreaking discoveries helps us identify and understand the range of inventiveness of a choreographer's practice. The practice may aim to:

◆ ***Improve*** and refine existing concepts in dance and movement

◆ ***Innovate*** and radically modify existing concepts in dance and movement

◆ ***Invent*** and formulate a fundamental new vision and concepts in dance and movement

Inventing and formulating a new vision of what the art of dance would be or could be is a long-term, enduring task. In the context of TRIZ, invention and innovation in the sciences and technology translate into *ingenuity* and *originality* of new choreographic approaches and principles, concepts and styles—as mentioned throughout this book:

√ *Genuine improvisation principles and movement approaches* of somatic experiences and embodied choreographic investigations—see Chapter 8 and Chapter 15.

√ *Genuine conceptual, structural, and dramaturgical approaches* in performative frameworks and interpretational contexts—see Chapter 12 and Chapter 19.

√ *Genuine integrative models incorporating dance with the arts, sciences, global cultures, art as activism for social change, and environmental issues* in interdisciplinary, multidisciplinary, and transdisciplinary forms—see Chapter 7, Chapter 12, and Chapter 19.

TYPES OF CREATIVITY AND MODES OF THINKING

We all have witnessed how children easily generate short poems, impressive drawings, charming songs, and cute dances at an astonishing rate. In many ways, all youngsters are artists by nature. Various forces working in pairs drive children's creativity, among them: Seeing → Sensing, Interaction → Reaction, Necessity → Satisfaction. "Kids-at-play" artistic activities don't aim to problem-solve or reach a desired outcome but rather emerge as *spontaneous creativity* driven by pure enjoyment. Most little children's plays and games tend to be hands-on and physical rather than mental, which activates a mode of *pragmatic thinking*.

Adults, on the other hand, strive to cultivate *goal-oriented* and *purpose-driven creativity*, operating primarily in an intentional and controlled manner.[8] The developed consciousness engages mature cognitive forces working in pairs, among them: Drive → Strive, Cause → Effect, Probability → Possibility. Grownups' creativity could be practical and problem-solving-driven, but not always. It could often be curiosity-driven with a desire to explore and see beyond the obvious. Furthermore, making sense of reality by interpreting physical phenomena as abstract concepts activates a mode of *conceptual thinking*.

Choreographers' *inventive creativity* is positioned somewhere between that of a child and an adult, and yet might combine *pragmatic thinking* and *conceptual thinking*. Both modes provide originality and richness of ideas, which may emerge as imaginative yet applicable, illogical yet smart, direct yet discrete.

WHEN WITNESSING THE SAME RANDOM EVENT – A FALLING APPLE...

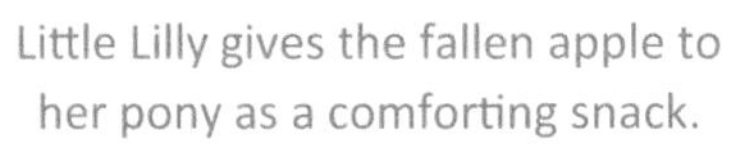

PRAGMATIC THINKING

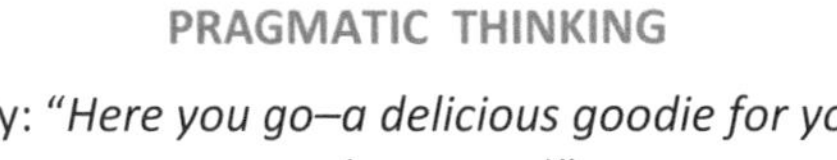

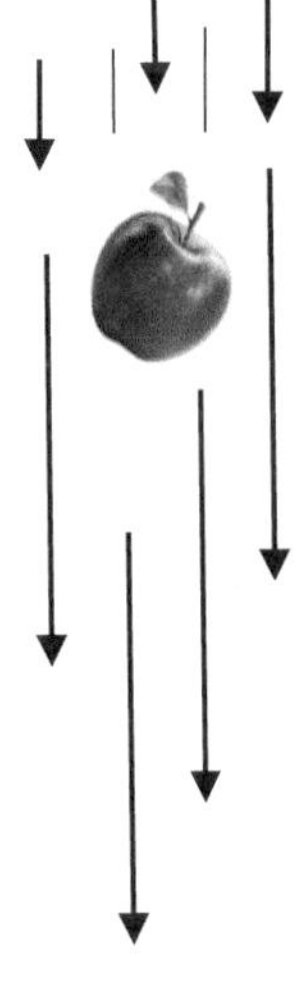

Isaac Newton defines gravity as a groundbreaking principle in physics

CONCEPTUAL THINKING

Newton: *"Gravity is not just a good idea. It is the law:* $F = G\frac{m_1 m_2}{r^2}$ *"*

Figure 5

HEY INSPIRATION, WHERE ARE YOU?

– INVITING INVENTIVE CREATIVITY –

"What inspires you? What made you choreograph this dance?" These are the two most common questions posed to choreographers. The answer usually will involve elaborating on these two topics: *inspiration* as a source of a dance, and *concept* as a summary of the idea and intent of a dance. We think of concept as developed and formulated content often in the form of a synopsis—the *aboutness* of a dance. We think of inspiration as an energizing creativity and motivating enthusiasm.

◆ **Do we find inspiration, or does inspiration find us?** Inspiration that initiates inventing doesn't really emerge out of nowhere. Waiting passively for inspiration to come could be a waste of time. The Austrian neurologist and founder of psychoanalysis, Sigmund Freud, once said: "*When inspiration does not come to me, I go half way to meet it!*"[9] Choreographers are actively involved in originating or inviting inspiration—either intentionally or unintentionally. Inspiration might seem an enigmatic and mysterious phenomenon. However, if we look at the anatomy of inspiration and dissect it, we will discover that inspiration is a cluster of dynamic processes grouped as *initiation*, *actualization*, and *determination*, all of which may ultimately result in the emergence of a new concept for dance.

Curiosity, encounter, and engagement are the three major experiences that separately or together initiate and trigger inspiration. *Curiosity* is driven by the desire to learn more about something. At times, this drive may emerge from an emotional connection; at times, it is the intellectual curiosity about a subject. This initiation may often trigger a temporary feeling of "losing myself," as new knowledge and experiences may contradict preexisting patterns of consistency.[10] An *encounter* is a powerful occurrence that triggers inspiration because it might emerge unexpectedly and casually. A choreographer may simply stumble upon or randomly encounter a phenomenon and decide to turn it into a dance. *Engagement* is linked to encounter and includes the desire to purposefully get involved and act upon something that a choreographer finds important, meaningful, and valuable.

Inventive creativity emerges during the process of *actualization*, which at its core is a cluster of the multilayered activities of *searching, exploring, and developing* various ideas. For these activities, long-term strategies and approaches could be applied, as well as short-term devices, tactics, and techniques, which we will cover in the upcoming pages.

A **concept** finally emerges as a result of a *decision-making* process that unfolds as a dynamic interaction between the choreographer's evolving *objectives* and the shaping of various norms, where final determinations emerge—see the *ICON SMART* creative algorithm as part of *Intuitive Craftsmanship—Perfect Imperfection*, Chapter 10. While the choreographer's objectives tend to cover a broader field of reasoning and goals—the big picture—the choreographer's *intentions* tend to be more specific, streamlined, and directional.

Figuratively summarized, a new concept may emerge and evolve when one wildly imaginative and inspiring idea triggers another idea, which then bounces back and forth, contradicting itself, only for a third idea to emerge. Then, completely accidentally, a fourth idea jumps into the mix. Now, all of the ideas form a *chain reaction* by further multiplying new ideas. The process of inventive creativity and the emergence of a new concept may evolve in exciting and unpredictable ways, with unexpected twists and turns, shuttling back and forth between various options—a *collision of ideas*. Finally, these numerous ideas are streamlined and distilled into the elegant simplicity of a new concept.

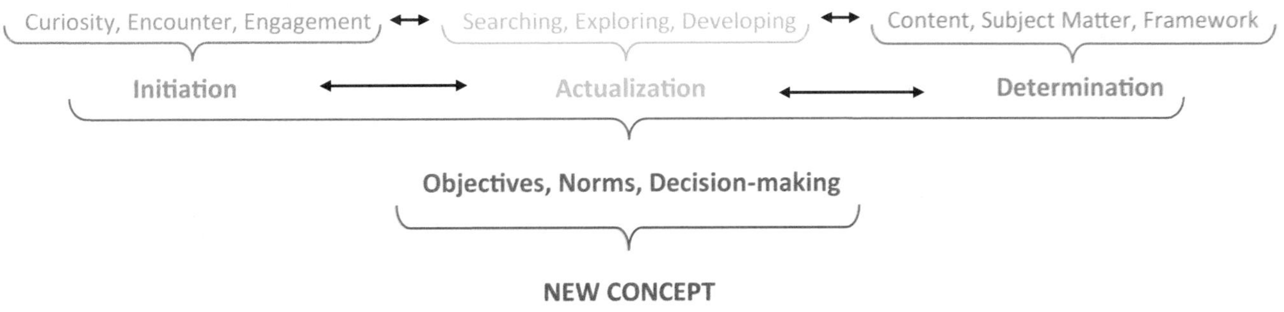

Figure 6

Choreographers are surrounded by moving dancers on a daily basis, where dance and movement mutually inspire movement and dance. A routine choreographic process, however, tends to be a closed-circuit system often within an institutional creative structure. For example, classical ballet operates with an established and historically codified framework. Choreographers working in this genre my feel intimidated to alter and fundamentally modify proven concepts, norms, and traditions. Yet, purposeful innovation, invention, and revolutionary breakthroughs are possible and needed. Inspiration alone is not sufficient for groundbreaking ideas to emerge. Various approaches, strategies, and devices may be used as working tools. For instance, when composing a story plot dramaturgically and developing the narrative for a new dance, a choreographer can choose from three distinct approaches to generate new and intriguing concepts:

CAUSALITY AND CUMULATIVE APPROACH
Searching and discovering why and how events unfold
in life and in dance, and why one occurrence leads to another

CHANCE AND RANDOMNESS APPROACH
Exploring coincidences as random events that happen
in life and in dance—art contains a chance factor

CONNECTIVITY AND RELATIONAL APPROACH
Searching, creating, and discovering possible hidden links
between unrelated events in life and in dance—movement, music, visual art, etc.

Let's explore each approach in detail with the following illustrative examples by using works by choreographer Septime Webre and dancers of the Hong Kong Ballet:

CAUSALITY AND CUMULATIVE APPROACH

Searching and discovering why and how events happen in life and in dance, and why one thing leads to another

Imagine a cargo area full of ideas. These ideas could be selected, elevated, and stacked logically to construct a "concept-tower." There may be multiple ways to assemble this tower. For example, you could find the letters to make a word by successive addition while using the guiding principle that a cause is responsible for an effect, and the effect is dependent on the cause:

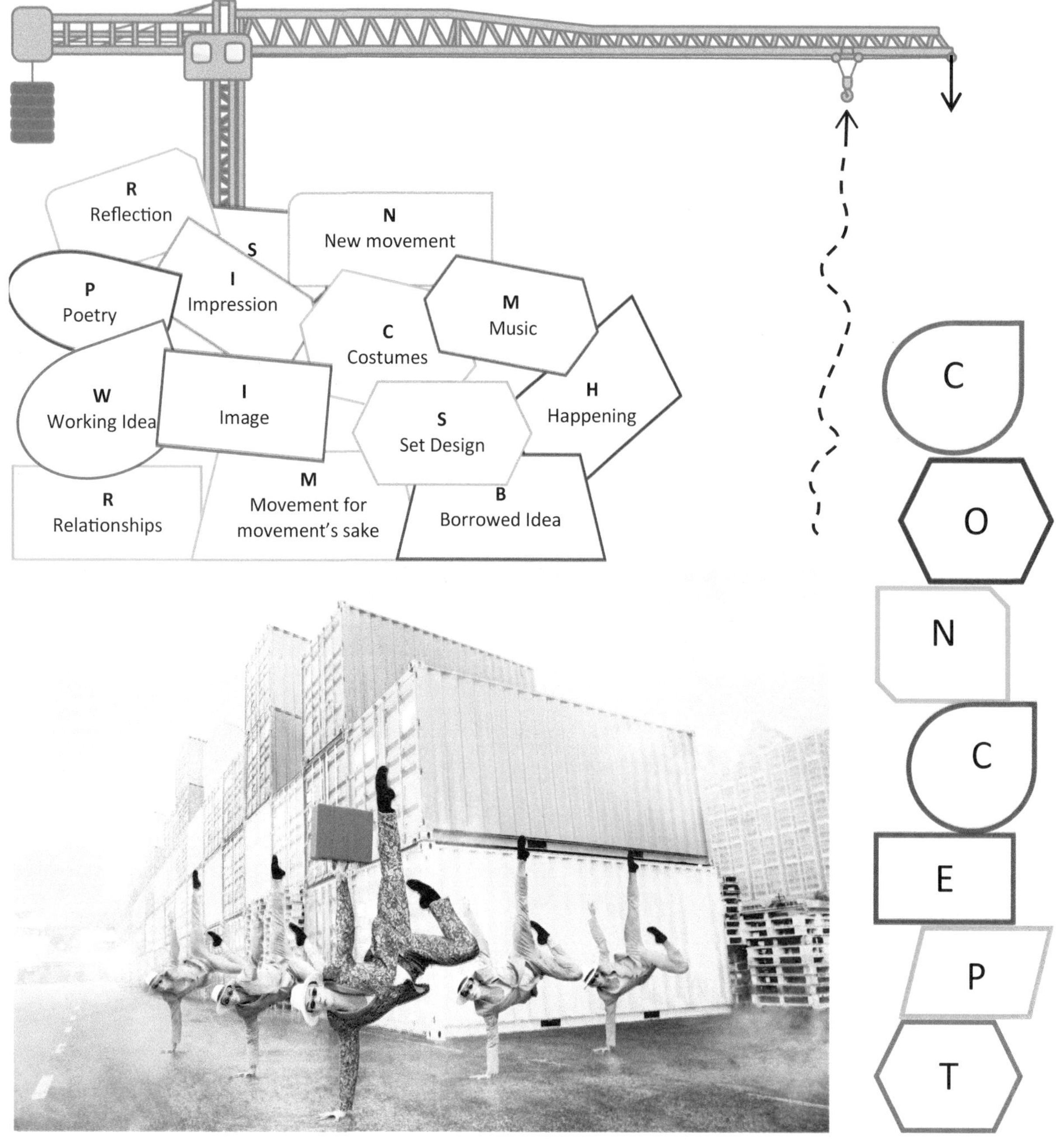

Figure 7 Photography © Dean Alexander, Creative: Design Army, Hong Kong Ballet 2019–20 Season campaign, choreography by Septime Webre, pictured from left: Henry Seldon, Luis Cabrera, Li Jiabo, Li Lin, Lin Chang-Yuan Kyle, courtesy of Hong Kong Ballet, 2019

◆ CHANCE AND RANDOMNESS APPROACH
Explore coincidence as random events that happen in life and in dance—art contains a chance factor

Imagine that after playing a game of dice, a game of cards will follow. Each of the cards is assigned and linked to an intriguing situation or story that you have read as child. As you pull out a random card, that card-story now becomes the idea for a dance—for example, take the whole story or one single idea from *Alice in Wonderland*. What would your version and ideas of Alice's journey look like? To start exploring, select a few devices from the following list and experiment with how the idea will change direction and develop differently:

- Pick a random object nearby and insert it into the idea! – How does the idea change?
- Choose a random song as a playback for the idea! – What parts match accidentally?
- How is the idea related to you? Is it important? – Can you add your life experiences to it?
- Look at the idea with fresh eyes! – What would be a new take on a well-known theme?
- Look at the idea with critical eyes! – What part would you take out, elaborate on, or edit?
- Look at the idea from a different angle! – What did you miss the first time?
- Reverse the sequencing of the idea by swapping elements! – What would you swap?
- Leave the idea alone for a bit. Then come back! – What has changed while you were gone?
- Get up and play with movement based on the idea! – Where does the movement lead you?
- How much can you modify the idea? – Could a conventional concept appear unconventional?
- What if the main idea brings in its "new friends" ideas? – Could you handle bundled ideas?
- How is the idea expanding so far? – Ask what your collaborators can add to it.

Figure 8 Photography © Conrad Dy-Liacco, *ALICE (in wonderland)*, choreography by Septime Webre, pictured Hong Kong Ballet Dancers, courtesy of Hong Kong Ballet, 2018

◆ CONNECTIVITY AND RELATIONAL APPROACH
Search, create, and discover possible hidden links between unrelated events in life and in dance

Imagine, envision, and propose the connections or hidden links between unrelated situations. While looking at the images in Figure 9, think imaginatively to discover, recreate, and restore the possible events developing within and between each of the events:

– What actions took place before and after this situation? How did it begin and end?

– What actions took place in the middle that connected the two situations?

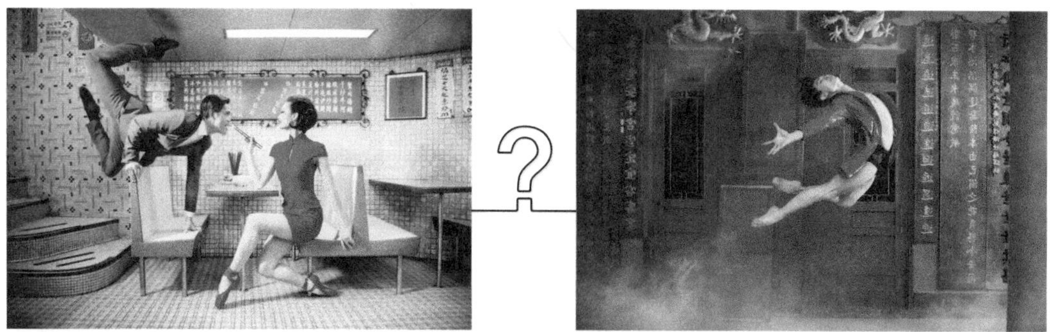

– What actions took place in between these situations that relates them to each other?

Figure 9 First row: Photography © Conrad Dy-Liacco, *ALICE (in wonderland)*, choreography by Septime Webre, dancer Li Jiabo and child dancers, 2018. Second row: Photography © Dean Alexander & Design Army, Hong Kong Ballet 2018–19 Season campaign. Image left pictured Li Jiabo. Image right pictured from left Garry Corpuz, Wang Qingxin, courtesy of Hong Kong Ballet, 2018. Third row: Photography © Conrad Dy-Liacco, *The Great Gatsby*, choreography by Septime Webre. Image left pictured dancers—center Brooklyn Mack, and Hong Kong Ballet dancers. Image in the center pictured dancers from left: Yang Ruiqi, Ye Feifei. Image right pictured Hong Kong Ballet Dancers, courtesy of Hong Kong Ballet, 2019

12 STRATEGIES FOR INVENTIVE CREATIVITY

– EXPLORE EXISTING CONCEPTS AND GENERATE NEW IDEAS –

Coming up with new ideas can be challenging, fun, or both. In the path to formulate creative intentions and distill concepts for dance, a choreographer would probably favor a large pool of ideas to explore, consider, and choose from before developing and implementing them. Great ideas are always needed—the more the merrier.

No matter which comes first—a spontaneous movement idea or an intended concept for a dance—it is helpful for choreographers to be equipped to operate and maneuver their choreographic instruments with as many available options as possible. Various choreographic tools—devices, prompts, and operations—are at the choreographer's disposal to experiment and develop the available movement material—see *Growing a Dance Garden—Choreographic Devices and Operations*, Chapter 17.

When generating and conceptually exploring ideas for abstract or narrative dances, choreographers could adapt inventive strategies used in the sciences and technology to originate new ideas or explore and experiment with existing ideas. In addition to Genrich Altshuller, many contemporary authors such as David Perkins, Edward de Bono, Michael Michalko, Daniel Pink, Michael Gelb and others have proposed various theories and strategies for inventive creativity.

A choreographer might already be using some of these techniques in their creative practices, while others might be new; some of them might lead to anticipated results, others—to less predictable or even surprising outcomes; some could aim to gently alter an idea; others—to substantially revise and re-envision an idea. Here is a short list with strategies for action:

1. **IMPROVISE** by unrestricted brainstorming and generating of ideas. In dance, new ideas can emerge as movement spontaneity or intuitive and somatic responses based on specific directions, scores, frameworks, prompts, and provocations. Various types of dance improvisation can be outlined in three major categories: *spontaneous improvisation*, *structured improvisation*, and *chance improvisation*. Countless improvisational choreographers and movement practitioners have developed and contributed their individual approaches to this field—for more see *Dance Improvisation—Embracing Choreographic Adventures*, Chapter 15.

2. **SEARCH** for ideas that already exist. The thrill of searching for specific ideas is that you might unexpectedly make a great find—a discovery that is better than the initial subject of your search. In that same context, the starting point of a search may be different than the ending point. The focus and priorities of the search might change with the arrival of new information.[11]

3. **GATHER** ideas by collecting as many viewpoints as possible from any available sources. The emphasis is on stockpiling a large quantity of ideas. An important condition here is to eliminate judgment so that any idea can be counted as applicable and may have the potential to be modified and used for various purposes.[12]

4 **FOCUS** on an idea by looking at it from different perspectives, angles, and contexts. Explore the idea's multiple facets and alternative functions.[13]

5 FOLLOW the evolution of an idea and its potential mutations. As in the children's game "Tag," explore the idea by "chasing" its development. Continuation and persistence are key, as some ideas will be more fruitful than others. Let go of ideas that are not compatible and keep only those with greater potential.[14]

6 FIND by making mid-process choices; it is not efficient to endlessly explore ideas and possibilities. Evaluation may be used temporarily to function not so much as the "decision maker," but as a temporary assessor and "crowd-controller."[15]

7 **COMBINE** ideas by putting them together and building a new idea from the different smaller ones. First, practice combining ideas that have supporting elements in common. Next, practice combining unrelated ideas that do not seem to have anything in common. Finally, practice combining extreme or polarized ideas and subject matter.[16]

8 **DISASSEMBLE** an idea by breaking it down into smaller components, which may create new, independent ideas. Explore how these new ideas maintain function in their own "independent" and "minimalistic" way.[17]

9 **MULTIPLY** small attractive ideas and enlarge them in capacity and functionality. Give the ideas a critical mass and power to function autonomously.[18]

10 TRANSFORM an idea by adding existing or new functions to it in order to invent a new version or variation of the idea. This process might also involve building a substitute or an alternative that is able to perform the same and additional functions.[19]

11 **REARRANGE** by randomly mixing ideas, components, and patterns—partially or completely, logically or illogically—by adding "out-of-the-ordinary" elements.[20] For example, imaginary mythical creatures such as a minotaur, dragon, and unicorn do not exist in reality, but only in the arts and literature. Some of their body parts seem realistic and familiar—they are those of horses, lizards, and birds—but assembled differently.

12 **PLAY** by first eliminating formalities, and then engage, explore, and experiment with an entire group of activities and ideas. Play is the opposite of seriousness, and therefore, the outcome of play may be forgiven. Humans play with ideas and language to joke, relax, entertain, and cheer each other up. Humans play games to spiritedly challenge each other about who will win or lose. Humans play roles—social, political, and cultural—and these roles may have an impact—hypothetical or realistic, "underwhelming" or influential.

In his book *Homo Ludens: A Study of the Play-Element in Culture*, the Dutch philosopher Johan Huizinga describes the act of play as a defining characteristic of humanity and as a central activity in flourishing societies. Playing is often an act of freedom and joyfulness. Playing could be an orderly activity, as in *playing by the rules*, or it could unfold as an improvised response—*playing by ear*. Whether *playing alone* or *playing together*, the purpose of play is to bring excitement and festivity. *Homo Ludens*, translated from Latin as *Human at Play*, identifies play and playfulness as fundamental to creativity, discovery, and innovation.[21] What does it mean to play, and what forms of play may be the engine for inventive creativity?

Figure 10 Photography © Dean Alexander & Design Army, Hong Kong Ballet 2019–20 Season campaign, pictured Ye Feifei, wardrobe provided by Victoria Hayes and (Nude), courtesy of Hong Kong Ballet, 2019

Contest is a form of play that is a competitive game against someone or many. The contest could also be within oneself. Playing games is both exciting entertainment and a light-hearted struggle to express superiority. Games have rules, and ironically, within this "strict rules world," creativity flourishes, stimulated by fun, challenge, and competitive spirit.

Pretending is another attribute of play evolving around the concept of *stepping in and out of reality or truth* for a moment. Pretending does not completely eliminate reality and its laws, but rather, it avoids them temporarily. In that "rules-free world," play and fun are pure, voluntary, and unrestricted activities. Pretending can also be mocking, imitating, and playing by exaggerating something or someone.

Humor is an intriguing form of playfulness and one of the most significant functions of the human consciousness—often more important than reasoning and logic. Humor emerges when the mind composes asymmetrical patterns that may not initially make sense and yet are perfectly logical.[22] Humor can be inspired by the realization of an entertaining mistake, which could also be encouraged by a role-reversal or a fun "game of oppositions."

For example, consider two choreographers walking along a small river, one on each side of the river. The first one shouts to the other: "Would you like to come over to the other side?" The other replies: "But I'm already on the other side." This *switch of perception* initially sounds awkward, but it actually makes perfect sense.[23] By using a different focus and looking at the idea from a different perspective, the information has been *rearranged* and *reorganized*, making it sound funny.

?

If you're tasked with creating a dance in the form of a playful movement game rather than delivering a formulated artistic statement, how would your choreographic process change?

LEARNING FROM THE ARTISTRY OF NATURE
– CREATIVE ENVIRONMENTS AS SELF-SUSTAINING SYSTEMS –

A romantic sunset, a gloriously tumbling waterfall, a cheerful spring cherry blossom—observing Earth's creations is exciting and inspiring. Nature is an artist and an outstanding choreographer by nature!

In addition to its majestic artistry, Nature is also an inventor-in-charge! Nature's breakthrough choreography creatively shapes and reshapes the environment by reinventing the richly imaginative, self-sustaining habitat on Earth. Does Nature *think* and *create* through geological, biological, and zoological evolution?[24]

As we strive to protect and preserve the environment by further studying and understanding it, let's explore how Nature's inventive creativity and "choreographic actions" merge techniques such as **disassembling**, **combining**, and multiplying:

Figure 11 Photography by Kanenori from Pixabay

◆ **Volcanic eruptions of breakthroughs:** In a heated environment, a new earth is born with bursts and showers of fire. A volcano is a mountain that opens downward into a pool of melted rock below the surface of the earth. When pressure builds up, eruptions occur with dancing leaps of fire and twisting jumps of lava.

◆ **Earthly crushes of possibilities and dance battles:** The varying seasons and different geographical regions on Earth give Nature a creative practicality in each environment. In the Sahara Desert, life forms are very selective and "minimalistic," with a few plants and fauna such as lizards, snakes, and birds. The dramatic dance battle of the species is to survive the desert. Meanwhile, the Brazilian Amazon Rainforest is a biological extravaganza displaying lavish flora and fauna. The dramatic dance battle of the species is a survival competition among them.

◆ **Carving rivers and curving explorations:** It took about 17 million years for the Colorado River and its tributaries to carve channels through layer after layer of rock to form the Grand Canyon in its present-day configuration. It is a massive geological phenomenon created by the simple motion of water and erosion of rock! Was it the carving movement flow of the river or the river as a curving movement flow? Perhaps life and dance are a metaphor for the curving and carving river—a progressive series of important moments, joined together in one continuous flow of breakthroughs. In addition to geology and biology, let's look at zoology and the creative variety and inventiveness in the animal world.

HUNTING RITUALS as *choreographic sequencing*, for example, could illustrate various ways that predators use and merge strategies such as **searching, finding, focusing, following, improvising,** and **gathering** to obtain food, enhance their chances of survival, and sustain the lineage of their species:

➢ **Aerial strike:** an eagle soars high in the sky, surveilling for prey. The eagle soon spots its quarry and plunges into swift attack, seizing it with razor-sharp talons.

➢ **Gliding elegance:** a pair of crocodile eyes appears just above the water's surface, silently stalking prey; while underwater, the crocodile deliberately positions its body for an instant assault.

➢ **Motion sensing:** a spider meticulously constructs a web to capture insects and detect their presence by the vibrations created by their movement, due to the spider's poor vision that prevents it from seeing its prey.

?

By considering Nature's inventive hunting rituals, can you think of *choreographic analogies* that could be implemented in dance?

Luckily, Nature's creativity is embedded in humans, enabling them to invent, adapt, and survive. Yet the human mind works differently than Nature. While Nature tends to function as a complex, self-organizing, and self-sustaining system, human creativity and actions tend to be multidirectional, often contradictory, and vastly chaotic.

Like Nature, choreographers strive to originate and facilitate ***creative environments*** for ideas to flourish. Although choreographers lead the creative process, in most cases they don't create alone. Many choreographers "lead by following" by soliciting contributions from the project participants. Exploring competitive ideas with a group of contributing artists allows choreographers to establish a functioning creative environment—a diverse, and yet unified, multi-layered, self-sustaining system, where everybody is needed and involved. Just like in Nature! The choreographer's to-do list for a collaboration may include:

◆ **Nurturing circumstances:** a) communicate the goals, formulate the scope, and reveal the working concepts and context of the creative project, as well as the challenges; b) provide all possible resources and share the artistic research available to date; c) disclose the boundaries of the project, as well as the working parameters for taking calculated risks.

◆ **Driving forces:** a) facilitate brainstorming sessions with an equal playing field for all participants; b) share the various approaches and creative techniques and encourage participants to add their own strategies; c) allow messy, confusing, ambiguous, and non-linear idea-generating processes before beginning to streamline and organize ideas.

◆ **Inspiring interactions:** a) offer a safe and non-judgmental space for the exchange of ideas; b) determine lines of communication and encourage honest feedback; c) appreciate and acknowledge all contributed ideas, even if an idea may not seem useful at the moment.

THE DARK SIDE OF A BRIGHT IDEA

...AND WHY IT IS DIFFICULT TO MAKE THINGS EASY?

The human brain is not designed to instantly think creatively. In our daily lives, we generally prefer to follow patterns and conform to repetition. We are creatures of habit, which keeps life practical and predictable. When we, as choreographers, step out of this comfort zone and engage with the volatile nature of inventing, should we also anticipate the great amount of risk taking, and be aware of a mysteriously dark side of creativity?

Inventive creativity emerges when we purposely challenge our automatic thinking. We voluntarily enter an uneasy mental landscape, a psychological state of ambiguity and paradox that may cause stress and frustration. Feelings of self-doubt and disbelief might lead to a negative impact on our creativity, and even our wellbeing.

Struggling is an organic part of the creative process, but suffering is not. Working hard and persistently is usually followed by artistic reward. However, enduring pain while creating or becoming obsessed as a "mad scientist," is definitely not sustainable. Dance and choreography are meant to engage and connect the body and mind in harmonious and healthy ways—very few other activities or professions do the same!

Purposeful self-awareness training is needed for a choreographer to establish a comfortable relationship with contradictory ideas that may end up inspiring and fostering creativity. Let's look for humor when challenged with a puzzling problem. Let's find fascination when researching and resolving mysteries. Let's build endurance for challenges and failures and persistently seek the clues leading to a new discovery.

Inventing and innovating are not easy. They are frequently accompanied by a substantial amount of struggling, risk taking, and disappointment before a choreographer reaches the desired outcome. But is the reward worth the struggles and risks? On one hand, nobody is enforcing progressive thinking, so the *status quo* of choreography could remain unchanged. On the other hand, *inventive creativity* may lead to new concepts and principles that could have a fundamental impact on the art form of dance. So yes, it's worth it!

HELPFUL TIPS & SUGGESTIONS

~ Think of an obstacle as an exciting and playful challenge rather than a burden
~ Train to endure ambiguity—find order in disorder and disorder in order
~ Accept that to move forward, you might first need to take a step back
~ Remember that there is always more than one way to solve a problem
~ Be wildly imaginative and yet practically conservative
~ Seek diversity by building a shared vision
~ Lead by following

RESEARCH AND EXPLORATORY ASSIGNMENT: Ideas that could serve as *concepts for dance* may emerge intentionally or unintentionally from a variety of sources.

For this exploratory research assignment, focus on experiences from your own life, and avoid investigating external resources. Use the following three categories to generate ideas for dance concepts:

➥ **Ideas that emerge from your existing knowledge and skills**—a cluster of ideas that might arise by answering the following question:

In what area(s) have you obtained a significant level of confidence and/or skills?

Your answer could cover ideas that vary in scope of knowledge and parameters of skill. Broader topics might include areas such as philosophy, physics, or scholarship in a specific subject. For example: "I have read, re-read, and studied all books by Ernest Hemingway." More narrow skills related to your passions might involve personal interests like bird watching, Japanese origami, or martial arts, etc.

➥ **Ideas that emerge from your personal experiences and intimate memories**—a cluster of ideas that might arise by answering the following question:

What event(s), situations, relationships, or occasions in your life have had a significant and enduring impact on you?

Your answer could cover ideas related to a significant life changing circumstance or experience. These memorable events may vary in emotional impact. For example, a traumatic experience from childhood or adolescence, moving to a new location and closing a chapter in your life, or the death of someone close to you: "I lost my brother who served in the military and fought for peace." They could also be happy circumstances such as a special reunion, overcoming a major obstacle, or achieving a long-desired goal.

➥ **Ideas that emerge from intriguing encounters and persistent curiosity**—a cluster of ideas that might arise by answering the following questions:

What did you accidentally discover?

What did you always want to explore but felt too intimidated or never had the chance to pursue?

Your answer could cover ideas or wide-ranging subject matter that sparked your interest or activated a long-lasting emotional or intellectual attachment. For example, "Yesterday, I stumbled upon something and I would like to learn more about it," or "I have been listening to this music/reading this novel/looking at this image for long time, but I haven't had a chance to make a dance out of it."

★ **CREATIVE EXERCISE:** After answering the questions from the three categories, choose one of your ideas. Transform the initial idea into a working concept for a dance by formulating and crafting a short verbal/written summary. Explain the experience/idea, why it is important to you, and how it could be relevant to other people in the context of a shared human experience.

➥ Look for and identify tangible visual or auditory illustrations of your idea such as authentic memorabilia, photographs, works of art, poetry, movies, music scores, physical objects/props, etc., to help you conceive of a physical representation of your idea unfolding as a dance.

➥ Use these tangible resources and identify physical actions that come to mind as movement flow and embodiment. Begin moving by engaging in a brief dance improvisation using these supporting resources. While improvising, focus on movement material and select movement vocabulary that closely exemplifies the initial idea. Create a short movement phrase that illustrates the idea. This movement phrase will serve as the first building block for the new dance.

➥ Experiment with the movement phrase by applying the *12 strategies for inventive creativity* to explore and elaborate on the idea by using, for example—*Focus, Follow, Find, Combine, Multiply, Transform, and Rearrange.* Once you have an extended version of the movement phrase, invite colleagues and collaborators to contribute their artistic suggestions and to apply their own strategies to the initial idea.

⤮ **COMPARATIVE ASSESSMENT:** Ideas from a single source or category can be combined with other ideas. Revisit your answers to the three questions and the ideas that you generated in your preliminary research. Explore whether there are overlapping elements among the three ideas. What are they? How do the three ideas relate to each other? Could the ideas be combined into one, and if so, how would they function together?

BIBLIOGRAPHY AND REFERENCES

[1] De Bono, Edward. *Think Before It Is Too Late*, The McQuaig Group, 2009, pp. 26–30.
[2] De Bono, Edward. *Lateral Thinking: Creativity Step by Step*, Harper & Row, Publishers, 1970, pp. 148–165.
[3] Fuller, Richard Buckminster. "Part of Darling," David, J. *The Universal Book of Mathematics*, John Wiley and Sons, 2004, p. 34, public domain source at: https://simple.wikiquote.org/wiki/Richard_Buckminster_Fuller#cite_note-2
[4] Altshuller, Genrich. *Creativity as an Exact Science, The Theory of the Solution of Inventive Problems*, Gordon & Breach Science Publisher, 1984, pp. 6–7.
[5] Lerner, Leonid. *Genrich Altshuller: Father of TRIZ*, Altshuller Institute, online article: www.aitriz.org/, accessed on May 2018.
[6] Zlotin, Boris and Zusman, Alla. *Levels of Inventions and Intellectual Property Strategies*, Ideation International Conference, online paper, Michigan, 2003.
[7] Altshuller 1984. *Creativity as an Exact Science, The Theory of the Solution of Inventive Problems*, pp. 148–172.
[8] Pink, Daniel H. *A Whole New Mind*, Riverhead Books, 2005, pp. 48–49
[9] Sigmund Freud re-question. Tharp, Twyla and Reiter, Mark. *The Creative Habit: Learn It and Use It for Life*, Simon and Schuster, 2003.
[10] Gelb, Michael J. *How to Think Like Leonardo Da Vinci*, Delacorte Press, Bantam Doubleday Dell Publishing Group, 1998, pp. 151–159.
[11] De Bono, Edward. *Lateral Thinking: Creativity Step By Step*, Harper & Row, Publishers, 1970, pp. 176–186.
[12] De Bono 1970. *Lateral Thinking: Creativity Step By Step*, 1970, pp. 57–60.
[13] De Bono 1970. *Lateral Thinking: Creativity Step By Step*, 1970, pp. 239–240.
[14] De Bono 1970. *Lateral Thinking: Creativity Step By Step*, 1970, pp. 148–165.
[15] De Bono 1970. *Lateral Thinking: Creativity Step By Step*, 1970, pp. 207–236.
[16] Michalko, Michael. *Thinkertoys, a Handbook of Creative Thinking Techniques*, Ten Speed Press, an imprint of the Crown Publishing Group, a division of Random House Inc., 1991, 2006, pp. 305–337.
[17] Michalko 1991. *Thinkertoys*, 2006, pp. 53–65.
[18] Michalko 1991. *Thinkertoys*, 2006, pp. 88–91.
[19] Michalko 1991. *Thinkertoys*, 2006, pp. 79–82.
[20] Michalko 1991. *Thinkertoys*, 2006, pp. 78–79.
[21] Huizinga, Johan. *Homo Ludens: A Study of the Play-Element in Culture*, Martino Fine Books, 2014.
[22] De Bono, Edward. *Think Before It Is Too Late*, The McQuaig Group, 2009, pp. 33–40.
[23] De Bono 2009. *Think Before It is Too Late*, pp. 33–40.
[24] Perkins, David. *The Eureka Effect: The Art and Logic of Breakthrough Thinking*, W.W. Norton & Company, 2000, pp. 240–251.

VISUAL REFERENCES

Figure 1: Photography © Dean Alexander & Design Army, Hong Kong Ballet 2018–19 Season campaign, choreography by Septime Webre, pictured Ye Feifei, courtesy of Hong Kong Ballet, 2018

Figure 2: Photography © Dean Alexander & Design Army, Hong Kong Ballet 2019–20 Season campaign, choreography by Septime Webre, pictured from left: Li Jiabo, Venus Villa, courtesy of Hong Kong Ballet, 2019

Figure 3: Diagram © Vladimir Angelov

Figure 4: Photography © Alexander Selioutski, Genrich Altshuller, personal archive and courtesy of Alexander Selioutski

Figure 5: Diagram © Vladimir Angelov. Clip art images: *Red apple stock photo*, illustration by bravo195, iStock/ Getty Images; *Vector illustration with a girl who gives a horse an apple*, illustrations by svaga, iStock/Getty Images; *Cute Isaac Newton is sitting under an apple tree*, illustration by bilhagolan, iStock/Getty Images

Figure 6: Diagram © Vladimir Angelov

Figure 7: Photography © Dean Alexander & Design Army, Hong Kong Ballet 2019–20 Season campaign, choreography by Septime Webre, pictured from left: Henry Seldon, Luis Cabrera, Li Jiabo, Li Lin, Lin Chang-Yuan Kyle, courtesy of Hong Kong Ballet, 2019, *Tower crane crawler crane*, illustrations by Alex Yustus, iStock/Getty Images. + Clip art: *Colorful books stacked*, illustration by soberve, iStock/ Getty Images

Figure 8: Photography © Conrad Dy-Liacco, *ALICE (in wonderland)*, choreography by Septime Webre, pictured Hong Kong Ballet Dancers, Courtesy of Hong Kong Ballet, 2018 , and clip art: *Two red dices vector*, illustration by Sergei Korolko, iStock/ Getty Images

Figure 9: First row: Photography © Conrad Dy-Liacco, *ALICE (in wonderland)*, choreography by Septime Webre, dancer Li Jiabo and children dancers, 2018. Second row: Photography © Dean Alexander & Design Army, Hong Kong Ballet 2018–19 Season campaign. Image left pictured Li Jiabo. Image right pictured from left Garry Corpuz, Wang Qingxin, courtesy of Hong Kong Ballet, 2018, Third row: Photography © Conrad Dy-Liacco, *The Great Gatsby*, choreography by Septime Webre. Image left pictured dancers—center Brooklyn Mack, and Hong Kong Ballet dancers. Image in the center pictured dancers from left: Yang Ruiqi, Ye Feifei. Image right pictured Hong Kong Ballet Dancers, courtesy of Hong Kong Ballet, 2019; Additional clip art: *The question mark is made in line-art*, illustration by Dzyuba, iStock/ Getty Images; Additional clip art: *Flat design style vector illustration concept of blue, red, yellow and green jigsaw puzzle pieces symbol icons connected on white background*, illustration by emrVectors, iStock/ Getty Images

Figure 10: Photography © Dean Alexander & Design Army, Hong Kong Ballet 2019–20 Season campaign, pictured Ye Feifei, wardrobe provided by Victoria Hayes and (Nude), courtesy of Hong Kong Ballet, 2019

Figure 11: Image by Kanenori from Pixabay, pixabay.com/users/kanenori-4749850/?utm_source=link-attribution&utm_medium=referral&utm_campaign=image&utm_content=2305606

Everything you can imagine is real.

Pablo Picasso (1881–1973)

CHAPTER 12

FRAMING CONTENT AND SORTING CONCEPTS
– LOGISTICS OF THE UNLIMITED –

"What is your dance *about*?" is a common question posed to choreographers, who are expected to provide a concept summary of their work. However, when a choreographer first begins to craft a dance, the answer to this question might not be straightforward. A dance, for example, may emerge from a choreographer's random physical encounters, intuitive movement responses, or interest in a particular subject matter. As a dance materializes, however, choreographers may gradually rationalize, crystalize, and define their *intentions* and *objectives* into a *synopsis* that is the summarized *content* and the *aboutness* of their dance.[1] The choreographer may engage with an unlimited number of emerging and evolving ideas to create and craft a performance. Although the creative act may begin ambiguously, an initial idea will ultimately shape, reshape and form as a concept that will emerge as a performance within a *conceptual framework*.

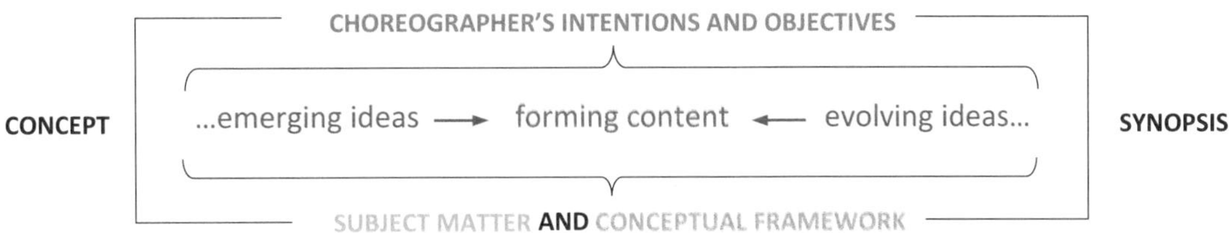

Figure 1

A choreographer's intentions—Figure 2, column one—may give rise to various approaches to the subject matter—column two. These intentions, consequently, may engage a single or multiple conceptual frameworks to serve as preferred performance formats—column three. Any combination of choices is possible as multiple ideas may fuse with one another. A *synopsis* will emerge—a conceptual summary of the content—which will answer the question addressing the *aboutness* of the dance.

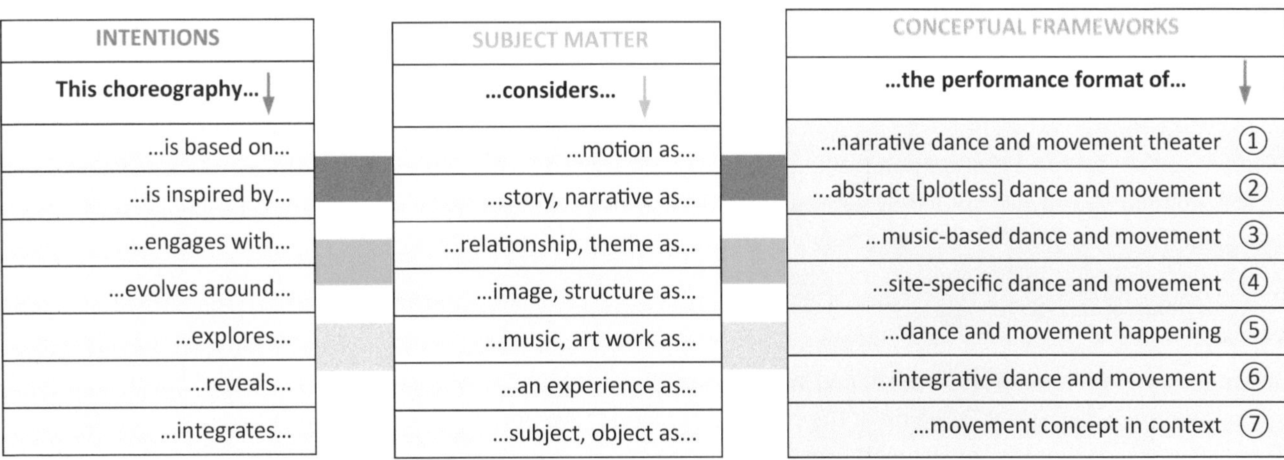

Figure 2

The *intentions*, presented in the first column in the form of passive and active verbs, capture the creative approaches and treatment of the subject matter. For example, "based on" and "inspired by" tend to be reflective and interpretative, while "reveals," "evolves around," and "explore" tend to be descriptive and investigative. Finally, "engage with" and "integrates" may directly interact and literally incorporate the subject matter into the dance. The *subject matter* in the second column offers a few broad categories of core content. Broad or specific meaning can be assigned—for more see Chapter 19. The *conceptual frameworks* in the third column offer various ways to channel intentions, concepts, and subject matter into preferred structural and performance formats.

◆ **Why is framing content needed?** Choreographers' creative processes of building a new work, and the audience's observational process of perceiving the new work, are not in synchrony, but in opposition, like a mirror image. A time-reversal phenomenon also takes place—as the dance performance progresses, the audience perceives it contextually and retrospectively—see Figure 3:

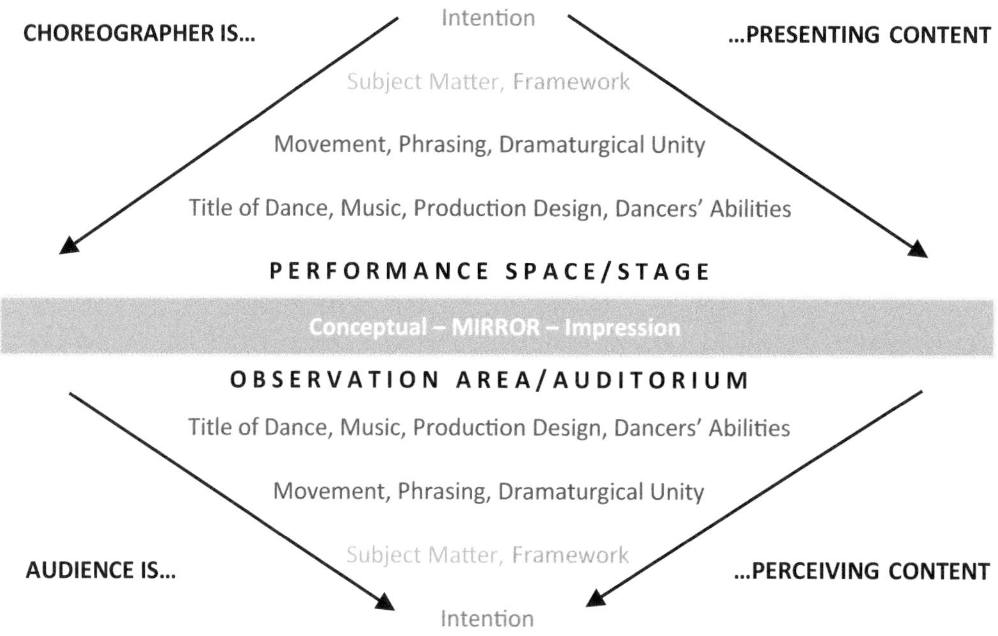

Figure 3

The formed *content* as a *concept* determined by intention, subject matter, framework, and the contributing elements of the production, will also ultimately determine the impression that the audience forms after watching the dance. For example, if a choreographer creates a dance with the intention for the work to be a "playful, plotless dance," by the end of the performance, the audience may be left with the "mirror" impression and the summary that the work was a "playful, plotless dance."

Intent with clear direction and determined subject matter will aid in distilling and consolidating various ideas into an overarching concept, which is the tip of the content "pyramid." Conceptual frameworks help to streamline intentions, frame content, and convey subject matter in an organized and controlled manner. A chosen framework might serve as "main," while other frameworks could be added to serve as "supportive." For example, a mainly narrative dance might also use a site-specific location as a supportive framework. Seven conceptual framework samples are summarized in the upcoming pages.

NARRATIVE DANCE AND MOVEMENT THEATER
– ONCE UPON A TIME... –

There is nothing more exciting than a great story! When searching for current information and news, we turn to radio, TV, and the internet. When searching for inspiration and wisdom, we turn to great stories from literature, Hollywood, and life itself! A story told through dance is a leading conceptual framework that serves as the dance's structural organization.

While a *narrative* may portray people, describe circumstances, and explain events in unrelated order, a *story* has a *plot* revealing the progression of an intriguing series of events. Telling a story by using dancing bodies and physical imagery requires the choreographer to convert a narrative into stage action and find movement equivalents. The *adaptation* of a narrative for dance is executed though skillful *physical dramaturgy*—see Chapter 19.

The foundation of a [dance] story is laid by three major questions: a) *What* happened? The story unfolds as a descriptive account of a specific event or a series of events, and it is built upon circumstances, participating characters, and their agendas; b) *Why* did it happen? The plot reveals why a situation has occurred through connective reasoning between the events and participants in the story; c) *How* did it happen? The story sequence is the arrangement of these episodes, their relationships, and logical-causal bonds. This order could be chronological or structured in various types of sequences: a linear or non-linear way, episodically, retrospectively, or with "jumps" between the past, present, and future. All of these ingredients, when combined, form a story worth telling through words and dance.

THE SEVEN MAIN INGREDIENTS OF A STORY ARE:

CIRCUMSTANCES – the introduction of the conditions relevant to the story, which also involve...

CHARACTERS – the participants, each carrying distinguished qualities, have...

AGENDAS – the known or unknown motives and interests of the characters, initiating...

ACTIONS – the efforts and endeavors of the characters, aiming to reach results of desires, leading to complications, crisis and...

CONFLICTS – the struggles of the characters arising from clashing interests and the eagerness to achieve compatibility of agendas and actions, reaching....

CLIMAX – the decisive moment of intensity and the turning point of the plot in search of a solution and change of course, finally ending with...

RESOLUTION – the answer to the problem, a reconciliation of the situation with lessons learned

Figure 4

These ingredients can create countless stories, each one distinct. Yet all stories have common characteristics and overlapping rationales. Many stories have similar *plots* and can be grouped together under a compatible, overarching narrative. The center of each plot is the *conflict*, where an individual faces one or more challenges. Various types of plots could involve various types of conflicts—see Figure 5:

SEVEN TYPES OF PLOTS	SEVEN TYPES OF CONFLICTS	
A battle to overcome something, which leads to victory.	An individual VS	Nature/Surroundings
A story of renewal and rebirth – a new chapter without ending an old one.		Circumstances/Events
A mission from point A to point B, as a quest for accomplishment.		Machines/Technology
A journey of transformation through venturing out and returning.		Supernatural/Mystery
A rising from the ashes and from rags to riches.		God/Religion
A tragedy where learning from disaster makes us better.		Other individual(s)
A comedy where optimism gives us hope.		Self

Figure 5

?

What stories from dance, literature, and film vividly illustrate these types of plots and conflicts?

The stories' subject matter could be based on facts or fictional events, with origins in mythology, scripture, legend, and Gothic tales. *Classical genres* include comedy, drama, non-fiction, realistic fiction, romance, satire, tragedy, and tragicomedy. *Modern genres*, especially in film, include sub-genres such as fantasy, erotic, mystery, spy, horror, apocalyptic, war, epic, western, superhero, action thriller, and science fiction.[2]

Narrative elements and storytelling in dance can be traced throughout history, from early rituals, ancient dances, folkloric traditions, and romantic and classical ballets, all the way to the 21st-century contemporary dance theater, which uses, fuses, and originates stories, crossing over histories and cultures to capture and reflect the human condition.

Canadian choreographer Crystal Pite and collaborating writer Jonathon Young used as a starting point Nikolai Gogol's 1836 farce *Revisor*. The plot was revised to serve as the basis for a hybrid choreography of contemporary dance and theatre. A blend of body language and stylized movement performed on recorded text captures a new interpretation of the prominent satirical tale of political corruption.

Figure 6 Photography © Michael Slobodian, *Revisor*, (2019), choreography by Crystal Pite, Pictured Ella Rothschild, Cindy Salgado, Jermaine Spivey, Tiffany Tregarthen, Doug Letheren, David Raymond, Rena Narumi, and Matthew Peacock, Kidd Pivot, 2019

ABSTRACT [PLOTLESS] MOVEMENT

– DANCE FOR DANCE'S SAKE –

A movement and dance performance without a storyline or literal references can be wildly imaginative, expressive, and engaging. A performance with such a conceptual framework is usually categorized as a plotless work, or an *abstract dance and movement.*

Abstract doesn't mean pointless or meaningless. Dance for dance's sake and movement for movement's sake express how human motion is *generated, structured, and perceived,* rather than how human motion is *telling something.* Abstract human motion may be fully purposeful, intentional, and functional in terms of conception and perception.[3]

In terms of conception, abstraction engages the choreographer's ability to focus creatively on what is most essential. Concepts are formulated by extracting common properties of movement ideas and building kinesthetic imagery not associated with any specific references. Abstraction may emerge randomly; then, creative ideas may be condensed and purposefully channeled in a controlled manner toward a desired outcome.

In terms of perception, abstraction engages the observer's ability to interpret imagery in order to comprehend it. The human brain is wired to *make sense* of things. In an effort to *decode* abstract ideas, the mind may consciously attribute or imaginatively assign reasoning and meaning. The mind may search for analogies. Or a subjective perception based on individual experiences may be projected onto a personal interpretation—see Figure 7.

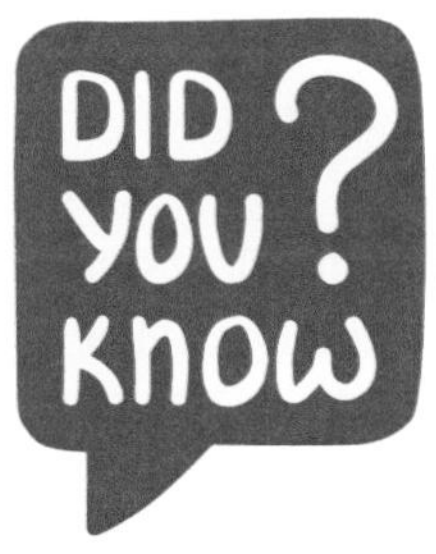

The *inkblot* test was published in 1921 by Swiss psychiatrist Hermann Rorschach—one of his cards is shown here. Until the 1950s, the test was popular among clinical psychologists as a personality test involving the evaluation of a subjective reaction. People were shown different inkblots and then asked to respond to what they saw in the blots. The test served as a perception assessment to determine personality characteristics and emotional functions. Let's do such a test now.

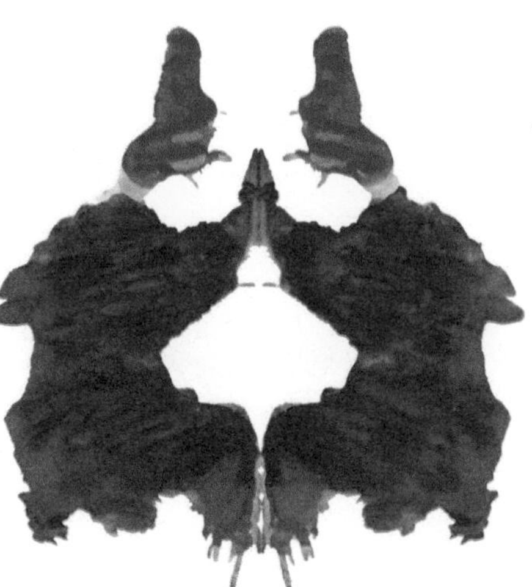

What might this image be?

What specific things do you see?

What does your mind make out of it?

Which part of the image do you focus on?

Which elements form your interpretation?

Which parts are pleasant or disturbing?

Figure 7

Is something abstract really abstract? The mind—artistic and perceptive, choreographic and observational—can separate abstraction from ambiguity and obscurity. Although plotless, an abstract piece of choreography can be organized and meticulously constructed. A non-narrative dance can capture concrete movement shapes, precise partnering, and distinct group formations dancing through well-defined movement patterns and pathways. But will subjective meaning still be assigned by the audience, and if yes, to what extent?

While choreographers might not be in full control of how their abstract creations will be perceived and interpreted by the audience, choreographers still *determine the narrative* and its scope.The choreographer may decide to keep (or not) the narrative elements, while *abstracting movement*—see Chapters 3 and 14. There are different degrees of abstraction:

➢***Semi-narrative:*** essential narrative elements are kept as realistic representation to serve as references and hints. Gestural movements, descriptive encounters, partial mime, and even realistic sentiments may still be incorporated. For example, a semi-narrative dance could still depict various emotional and romantic relationships without an elaborate, detailed storyline.

➢***Semi-abstract:*** narrative elements are stylized, simplified, and pared down to their essence. For example, a semi-abstract dance could still reveal various personalities and relationships by using stylized, minimalistic forms rather than realistic portrayals.

➢***Abstract:*** narrative elements are removed completely and replaced by plotless movement forms, expressed unrestrictedly in non-narrative and stylized configurations. For example, a purely abstract dance would not include any realistic depictions, nor relate to specific instances and literal imagery.

Spanish-born Australian choreographer Rafael Bonachela, also the Artistic Director of Sydney Dance Theater, said in an interview: "My work is never a narrative in a straightforward way. For me, narrative is linked to the themes that inspire me. I don't want to provoke a prescribed response from the audience; I can't control, and nor should I, their subjective interpretation of what they are experiencing. I am not telling them how to think or what to feel, but ultimately am provoking an emotional reaction where they leave the performance space feeling moved and altered by the experience."[4]

Figure 8 Photography © Pedro Greig, *ab [intra]*, choreography by Rafael Bonachela, dancers of Sydney Dance Company, 2018

MUSIC/SOUND-BASED DANCE
– SONIC FORMS AND/FROM THE MOVING BODY –

Silence, noise, speech, sound, and music are *sonic forms* that may be considered as the auditory environment and a leading conceptual framework for a dance work. Historically, music and dance have co-existed such as when drumming and stomping, and chanting and singing were an organic part of early dance forms.

When searching for music for dance, a choreographer may consider various general or specific musical characteristics that draw sound and movement together. Attractive features could be music that is melodic or rhythmic, dramatic or impressionistic, programmatic or abstract. Music could range in the ways it is produced sonically: vocal and instrumental, acoustic and electronic. Formats could also vary—chamber and symphonic, sonatas and concertos, short songs and complete operas. Music could be used in its historical context—such as Baroque and Romantic, or by genres such as folk and jazz.

When choosing and working with precomposed music, a choreographer may consider the mood and the harmonic complexities, the timing and tempo signatures, the structural patterns and framework, the development of a piece in sections, as well as the composition of the climax and variations. Various *choreographic applications* could be at play regarding how sonic forms, music, and dance could complement each other. For example, the dance may initiate, produce and illustrate a sonic score, or a music score may be used as a rhythmic accompaniment or a supportive ambient to a dance.

Along with the use of traditional music, other acoustic forms such as silence and noise, sound, and spoken word may be well-incorporated into a dance. The performers may be choreographed to produce noise, speech, sound, and music, and such *sonic emergence* may range from vocalization, verbalizations, and singing, to tapping, stomping, and clapping. Elaborate exposition of sonic forms and their implementation in movement and dance can be found in BOOK VI, Chapters 20 to 22, and its brief summary—Figure 9.

Figure 9

Music could be composed specifically for a dance or previously composed. Dance music could be created independently from the dance and then used as an accompaniment. The choreographer may take into consideration the composer's intentions behind a music composition. There are also various types of relationships between the choreographer's work and the composer's work, the dance, and the music. These relationships could be dependent, interdependent, or independent, or humorous compared to married, separated, or divorced.[5] Legendary collaborations between choreographers and composers in the past—between Petipa and Tchaikovsky, Balanchine and Stravinsky, Robbins and Bernstein, Cunningham and Cage—led to the creation of numerous masterpieces.

In addition, the human body in motion acts as a musical instrument capable of creating various sounds and rhyming patterns. A rich heritage of choreographic forms produces integrated sound and percussive noise as a signature element of dance, where the choreographer emerges as composer and acoustic performer simultaneously. Popular percussive dance forms are northern Indian Kathak, Māori Haka, Spanish Flamenco, Irish step dancing, American Tap dance and Step dancing, among others, including creative approaches for generating sound in many works of Modern and Contemporary dance.

Whether the complexity of music, sound, and noise leads to the complexity of dance, or vice versa, dance and sonic forms have autonomy and their own principles of organization. As a choreographer's specialty is human movement as the substance of dance, and a composer's specialty is sound as the substance of music, there is always a goal to reach a fine balance of connecting music and dance, sound and movement—two independent art forms that enhance and complement each other.

Music is central and essential to the work of American choreographer Mark Morris. His choreography is guided by musical structure and often interprets the music score in a literal way. Melodic lines are frequently illustrated by the dancers' movement. For example, when a melodic line goes up, a dancer may climb up onto a chair; when it goes down, a dancer may fall to the floor. When the violin plays, the "violin dancers" will dance, and when the clarinet chimes in with the violins, a "clarinet dancer" will join the "violin dancers," and so on.[6]

Figure 10 Photography © Elaine Mayson, *L'Allegro, il Penseroso ed il Moderato* (1988), choreography Mark Morris, dancers of the Mark Morris Dance Group, London Coliseum, 2010

4 BEING [SITE-] SPECIFIC
– A MOVEMENT RESPONSE TO A PHYSICAL ENVIRONMENT –

When we enter any space, enclosed or outdoors, we experience and interact in various ways with the space surrounding us. A choreographer's physical involvement, movement engagement, and artistic response to particular non-proscenium dance spaces are subject to a dance and movement conceptual framework known as a *site-specific performance.*

Moving and dancing in the *interior* of a gallery, a church, or a warehouse, all of which have determined purposes, may lead to vastly different kinesthetic engagement than dancing in a dance studio, a ballroom, or a disco club. A creative choreographic response might also emerge in smaller, confined spaces such as doorways, windows, and staircases. There are also open *exterior* locations to move and dance in, such as streets, plazas, railroads, train stations, and parks—small and large, local and national.

The choreographer's engagement with a site could become a leading conceptual framework. Various improvised or structured approaches might result in *making-sense of the site* through dynamic attraction, interaction, integration, and collaboration among the space, the choreographer, the performers, and the observers—see Figure 11.

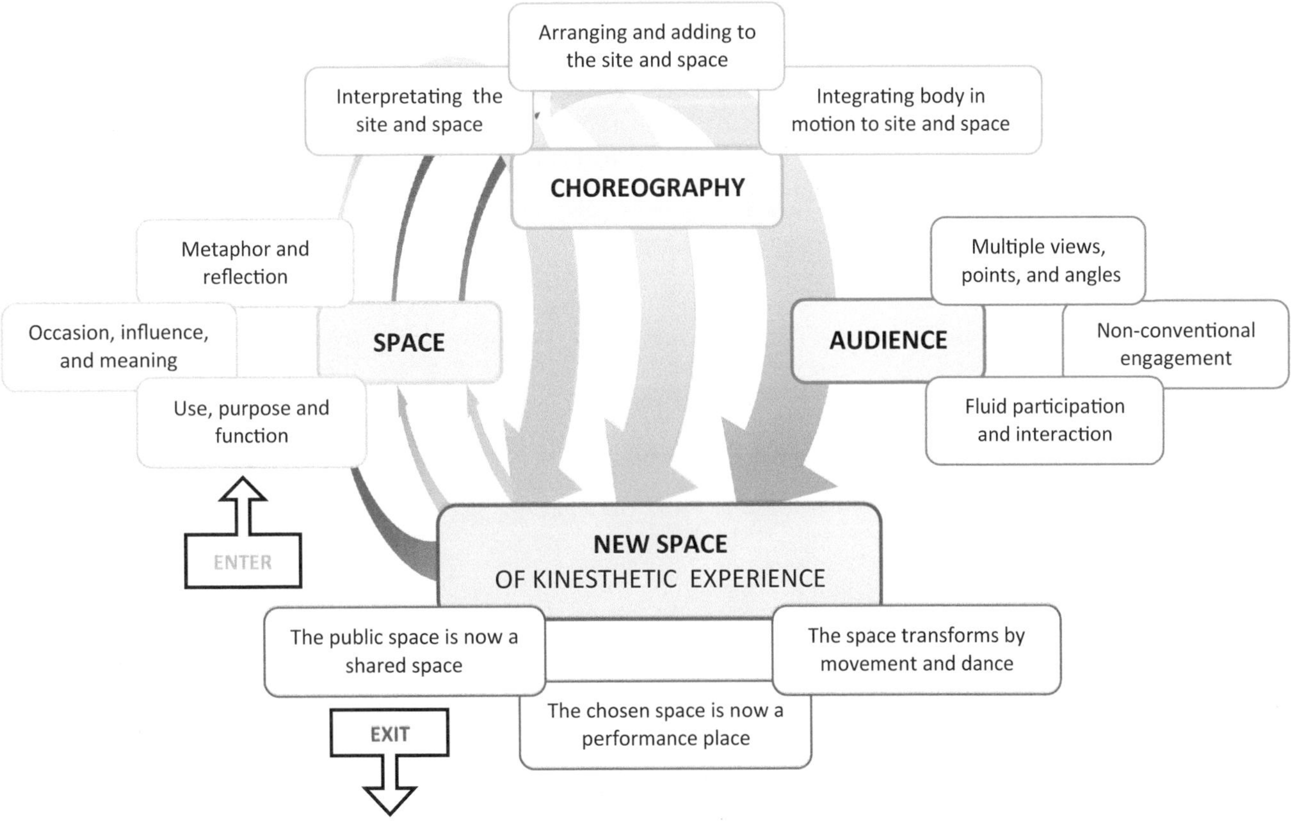

Arranging and adding to the site and space
Interpretating the site and space
Integrating body in motion to site and space
CHOREOGRAPHY
Metaphor and reflection
Occasion, influence, and meaning
SPACE
Use, purpose and function
ENTER
Multiple views, points, and angles
AUDIENCE
Non-conventional engagement
Fluid participation and interaction
NEW SPACE OF KINESTHETIC EXPERIENCE
The public space is now a shared space
The space transforms by movement and dance
The chosen space is now a performance place
EXIT

Figure 11

Site-specific work is an integrative experience—it is both a creative and a perceptive phenomenon that offers great variety and flexibility. The *SPACE*, site, or location could be randomly picked or purposely selected. The *CHOREOGRAPHY* could be a spontaneous movement response, structured improvisation, or pre-choreographed movement, or a combination.[7] The *AUDIENCE* could be seated, or moving along with the performers, or assigned to certain locations and areas to observe the performance from specific angles.

The choreographer *receives* and *reconstructs* the space to make it *feel* unique—a *NEW SPACE OF KINESTHETIC EXPERIENCE*, by shaping a new perception of the space with sight, sound, and motion. The choreographer forms a movement relationship with the physical environment, integrating movement and space into *choreographic architecture.*

The choreographer may *read* the space differently than an architect or a park ranger. The initial function and purpose of the place could be altered and then interpreted differently. The insertion of a moving human body into a structured physical environment not only brings visual changes, but may also trigger social, emotional, and intellectual responses. In summary, the *actual space* will transform into an *imaginative space*, only to convert into a *kinesthetic space* with a new function, content, and context.

The choreographer also makes choices regarding the placement and positioning of the audience and the angles to observe the performance. The audience could be seated or standing, stationary or mobile, and could frequently change their viewing perspective. The audience's role may also transform from *observing visitors* into *integrated bodies* that are part of the dimensional, site-specific choreography, aspiring to transform the perception of those involved, and how movement and dance interact with space.

American rock climber, community leader, dancer, choreographer, and Founding Artistic Director of BANDALOOP, Amelia Rudolph, has created her *vertical choreography* on the walls of skyscrapers, toll bridges, mountains, and in theaters. Her thrilling choreography requires exquisite skills in turning upside-down and sideways, maneuvering the body in space in unexpected relationships to gravity, while the granite mountain rock becomes the most trusted dance partner[8] (Figure 12).

Figure 12 Photography © Braden Mayfield, pictured choreographer and dancer Amelia Rudolph, on location at Dana Plateau, Inyo National Park, CA, 2014

5 DANCE AND MOVEMENT HAPPENINGS – IMPROVISATIONAL AND INSTANTANEOUS CHOREOGRAPHY –

A choreographic process can entail movement that is created, contemplated, and taught by the choreographer to the performers. Dance could also transpire through collaboration between the choreographer, performers, and artistic team. In addition, movement and dance may emerge spontaneously, instantaneously, and unredacted—a leading conceptual framework that we can define as *dance and movement happenings.*

Dancing happens and, at its core, it is a spontaneous movement expression. Any child or adult can dance in some form or another. Whether for fun or for a desire for self-expression, one can simply get up and tango, waltz, club-dance, or improvise without a *set choreography*. The intimate act of creating dance and movement—spontaneously and instantaneously, instinctively and without restrictions—is also an act of choreography.

If dance occurs spontaneously, and creating movement instantly on the spot is choreographing, then what is the focus of the choreographer? Although a dance could emerge randomly and seemingly without a prescribed structure, the creative effort may still seek a purpose. Experimentation, exploration, and improvisation approaches may also necessitate the formulating of objectives and directives.

Dance improvisation is creating, exploring, and performing all at the same time—an instantaneous, less codified movement expression that is capable of producing dramatic and thought-provoking content. During the 1960s, American Postmodern dance redefined improvisation as *freeing* the body from habitual movement patterns. The emphasis was on instinctual, unpredictable, unrestricted movement flow and imagery. Three distinct types of dance improvisation—*spontaneous, structured*, and *chance*—offer unlimited possibilities for movement research and artistic experimentation—see Chapter 15. Various artistic tools and principles are available to choreographers to initiate and channel creative efforts; these tools can function separately or in combination—see Figure 13.

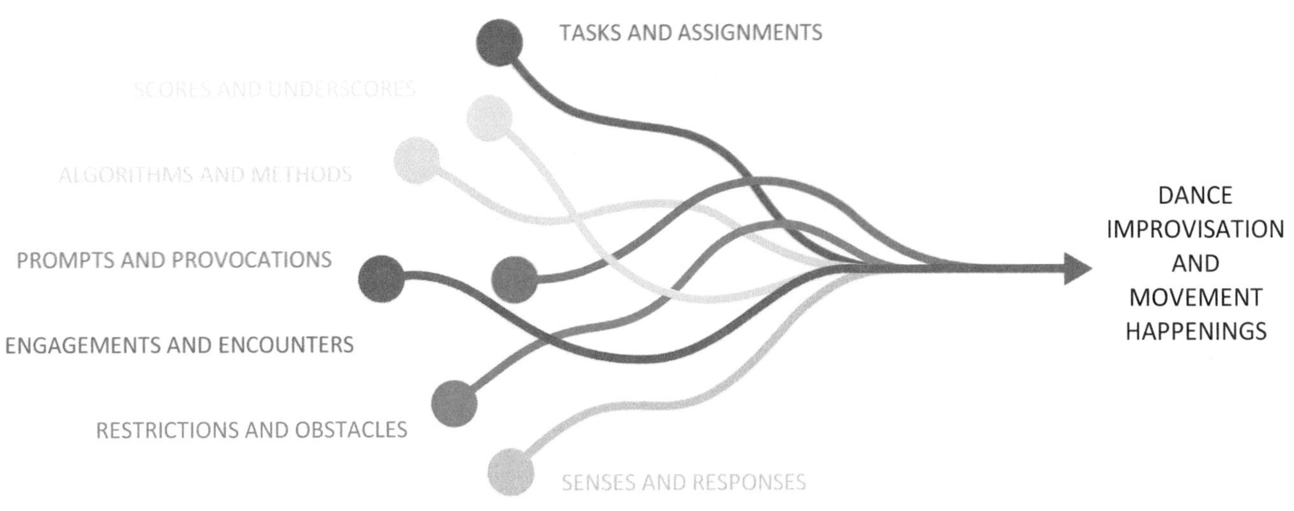

Figure 13

Tasks and Assignments are formulated activities to direct and redirect, channel and allocate, appoint and position exploratory processes. *Scores and Underscores* are the outlined mechanisms, sets of instructions, and maps of improvisational activities in the form of verbal directives, written scripts, drawings, and templates to generate, explore, and develop movement material through exploratory episodes. These means could lead an improvisation towards specific activities, objects, subjects, and sites, by awakening sensations through listening, touching, observation, and imitation.

Algorithms and Methods are guiding principles and patterns of framing improvisation activities by providing sets of rules and operational guidelines for how to maneuver movement material. *Prompts* and *Provocations* are specifically designed requests and creative directives aiming to activate various creative alternatives and to manipulate, transform, and re-envision movement material.[9] *Prompts* and *provocations* can also be used as development devices to contemplate and set choreography—see Chapter 17.

Engagements and Encounters are the kinesthetic initiation and purposeful involvement in movement experimentation, and the physical experiences that occur in dealing with tasks, subjects, objects, and surroundings. *Restrictions and Obstacles*, physical or imaginative, are not to obstruct the movement experience, but to stimulate the development of alternative solutions to movement tasks and to cultivate specific movement qualities. *Senses and Responses* explore how movement may originate somatically and performatively by the awakening of kinesthetic awareness and embodiment. For example, mental imagery may be manifested through specific external bodily shapes, forms, and moves. Such awareness will link sensitivity with sensing, perception with perceiving, and reaction with responding.[10] Improvisation at its core is an exploratory creative practice that may or not may result in a formal dance showcase. Improvisation's time-based nature captures a *movement idea in the moment*, without the pressure to produce and deliver an aesthetically pleasing performance. Improvisers may simply enjoy discovering their kinesthetic selves, the freshness of a spontaneous creation, and the newness of movement.

What if your dance partner is an equine? JoAnna Mendl Shaw, choreographer and founder of The Equus Projects, taps into dancers' movement intelligence and physical listening skills in her interspecies choreography. Such uniquely created kinetic dialogue merges improvisation with horsemanship and transforms equine herd behavior into a shared and co-created movement language.[11]

Figure 14 Photography © Nancy Halsey, *Seven Games* (2006), choreography by JoAnna Mendl Shaw, pictured Gina Paolillo, Bates Dance Festival, 2006

INTERSECTING DISCIPLINES
– CHOREOGRAPHIC MOBILITY BEYOND DANCE –

Choreographers traditionally create and craft movement by operating predominantly with the human body in motion. Dance, however, is an interdisciplinary art by nature. While the marriage between dance and music traces its roots to early human history, choreographers continually seek and implement new, innovative approaches to integrate dance with other disciplines. Newly invented "hybrids" that merge dance with other fields by constantly stretching, flexing, and redrawing the boundaries of dance as an art form, create a conceptual framework that *intersects dance with the other sectors of humanity and science.*

What types of approaches establish relations with other disciplines? *Interdisciplinary* refers to ideas and concepts from different disciplines that are integrated into new structural patterns to organically connect all of the disciplines. *Multidisciplinary* is when a contributing discipline engages with other disciplines in a particular function and purpose, within the boundaries of that discipline, or engages across disciplines, which is also known as *cross-disciplinary,* where one discipline reaches out to the other. *Transdisciplinary* is when different disciplines work jointly to create new conceptual integration that *moves beyond* a discipline-specific field.[12] Many, if not all, of these integrational approaches can merge conceptually and dramaturgically within a single performance—see Chapter 19.

Subject matter can be drawn from various disciplines in science and technology, such as digital innovations and neuroscience; the arts and humanities, such as philosophy, literature, architecture, and global cultures; and topics related to social change and the environment, as illustrated in Figure 15.

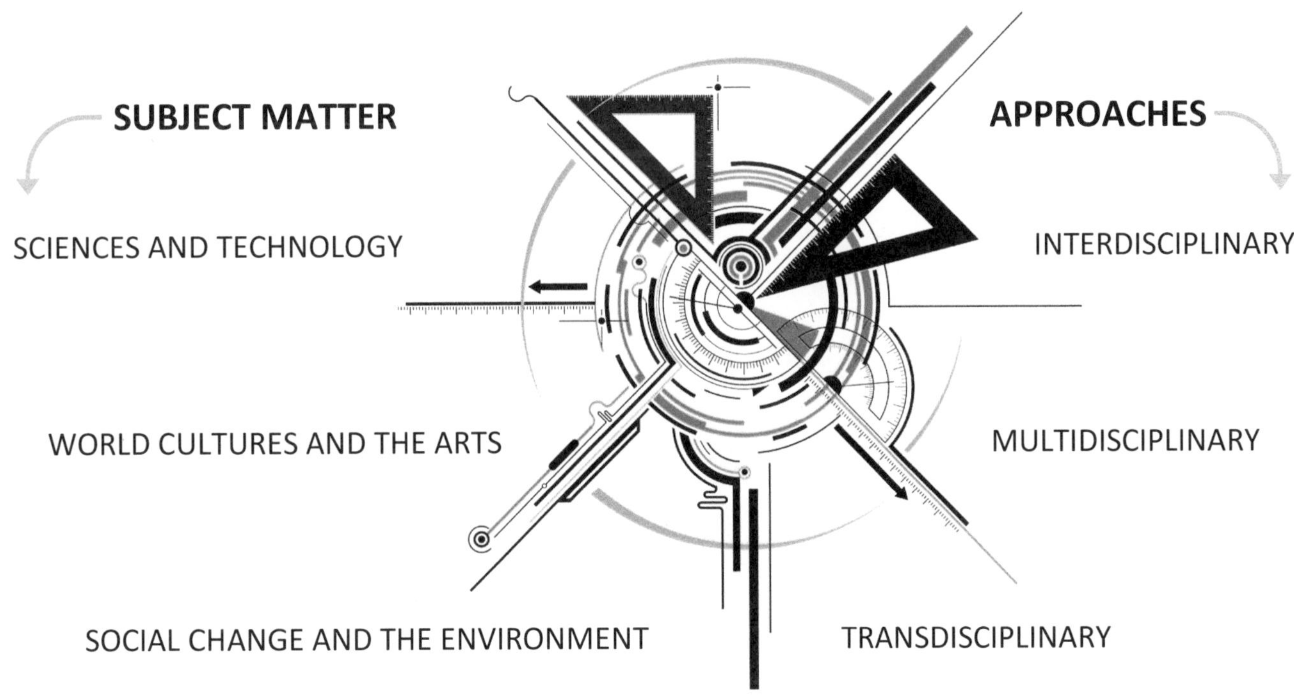

Figure 15

Dance and the sciences integrate the work of choreographers with scholars and researchers to cross-reference and reframe the relationship between the arts and sciences—for example, using cognitive studies to understand deep levels of the human psyche and creativity. *Multicultural and intercultural choreographic discourses* integrate distinct characteristics of indigenous and folkloric dance traditions, in the context of *global society,* as choreographers develop awareness of cultural appropriation and misappropriation. *Dance and social change*, or art as activism, brings awareness to the issues of race, gender, inequality, distribution of wealth, opportunities, and privileges within society. Addressing *the environment* reminds us of the fragility of our lone planetary existence.

Dance and the arts explore new pathways of integration. For example, *Dance on Camera* is a screen-based medium—a hybrid incorporating choreography and film making. *Multimedia dance installations* redefine the architectural and visual use of space by exploring new possibilities to communicate in highly experimental and visceral ways.

Digital technology and design systems serve as new choreographic instruments for film editing, digital animation, and electronic sound. New programs enable choreographers to integrate in their creations motion capture, real-time biofeedback, and interactive digital "mapping." Stimuli-response software and action-reaction models *translate* gesture to sound and gesture to video output.[13] The transition from analog ancestors to digital successors and advancements in Immersive Art (IA), Augmented Reality (AR), and Artificial Intelligence (AI) offer new active-reactive environments, where computers replicate reality, reproduce human behavior via data-response-awareness, and instantaneously generate algorithmic solutions when interacting with humans.

?

Do advancements in digital technology bring us closer to our physical senses or distance us from them?

Centaur, the work of choreographer, filmmaker, and Danish Dance Theater Artistic Director Pontus Lidberg, was inspired by the half-horse, half-human creature from Greek mythology. *Centaur* is also the name of a computer-science concept that examines human qualities by combining Artificial Intelligence with human intelligence, and explores the relationship between Creator and Creation, Man and Machine.

Figure 16 Photography © Raphael Frisenvænge Solholm, *Centaur* (2020), choreography by Pontus Lidberg, courtesy of Danish Dance Theater, 2020

CONCEPT IN CONTEXT

– REVISIT, REIMAGINE, REDEFINE –

Attractive ideas are often authored by someone else and may belong to other people, places, and traditions. When experimenting, choreographers sometimes "borrow" the ideas of others and alter the creator's intentions. While playing with one's own genuine ideas is fine, modifying the ideas of others by taking them out of their original context may bring all sorts of complexities—some celebrated and some unwelcome. This possible scenario leads us to explore a leading conceptual framework that we can define as a *concept in context.*

What is context? The three basic definitions are: a) the circumstances that form something, b) the framework to understand something, c) the parts that precede and follow something to clarify its meaning. Content in the form of an event, statement, or idea emerges in a specific environment. However, does content always belong to its original environment? What would happen if the content is kept but the environment where it has occurred is taken away or changed?

A choreographer, for example, may be inspired to use aesthetic elements of an indigenous culture. In such an instance, the resource should be respectfully acknowledged, credited, and compensated. It is acceptable to borrow, but not to steal. It is appropriate to celebrate, but not to ridicule. Therefore, artistic research should go beyond cherry-picking attractive, decorative elements, and dive deeper into understanding the original cultural context. Taking cultural or aesthetic elements out of context and using them irresponsibly could lead to *cultural misappropriation*. The latter may result in misinterpretation and misperception. For example, something important suddenly may seem less important, right may seem wrong, the serious—trivial, and the large—small.

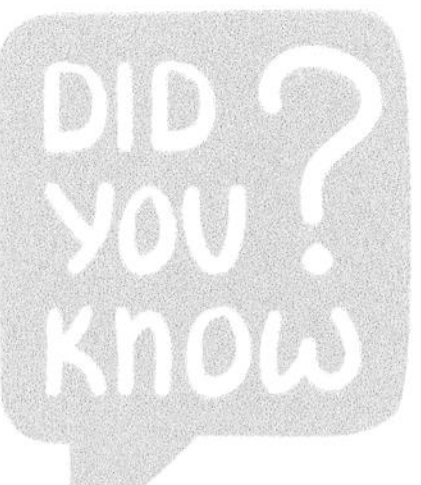

The two golden balls at the center of each ball formation are exactly the same size, yet the golden ball on the right appears larger. This *Ebbinghaus illusion* uses *Titchener circles* to create an illusion based on relative size perception. Shrinking the size of the silver balls and tightening their positioning alters the visual balance and creates the dominant appearance of the golden ball in the image on the right.

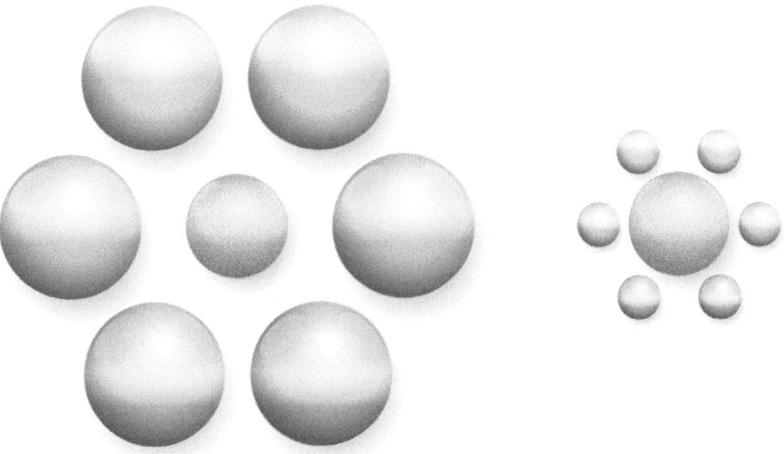

Figure 17

On the other hand, revisiting, reimagining, and redefining traditional ideas by giving them new context and meaning is at the heart of the creative process. Guarding cultures and subcultures in efforts to preserve them becomes increasingly naïve and counterproductive. The exchange of ideas, styles, and traditions is one of the advantages of the global, multicultural 21st-century society. Cultural appropriation is inevitable and potentially great when used properly—in a way that is both creatively open and culturally sensitive.[14]

Many choreographers, for example, are inspired to revisit and re-envision traditional tales, historic works of dance, and masterpieces of dance music—see *Gravitating Towards Well-known Dance Music* in Chapter 21. For example, the ballet *Swan Lake*, composed by Tchaikovsky and based on Russian and German folk tales, such as "The White Duck" and "The Stolen Veil," has been re-staged and re-envisioned many times with various degrees of innovation. Some productions aim to be authentic and historically accurate, while others are updated contemporary adaptations with calculated modernity. There are also renditions where a transformative context has nurtured experimental and radical versions of the classical work, as in the samples below. In summary, context is a powerful creative tool that can redirect and reformulate ideas.

South African choreographer Dada Masilo's *Swan Lake* (image left) integrates African dance movements with technical ballet phrases, while British choreographer David Dawson's rendering of the ballet (image center) is known for its neo-classical minimalism, conceptual boldness, and contemporary feel. Swedish choreographer Alexander Ekman's *A Swan Lake* (image right) takes place in an actual onstage lake of 5,000 liters of water that serves as both backdrop and musical instrument.

Figure 18 From left to right: Photography © John Hogg, Dada Masilo's *Swan Lake* (2010), choreography by Dada Masilo, performed by the dancers of Dada Masilo/The Dance Factory, 2010. Photography © Andy Ross, *Swan Lake* (2016), choreography by David Dawson, pictured Sophie Martin and Christopher Harrison, courtesy of the Scottish Ballet, 2016. Photography © Erik Berg, *A Swan Lake* (2014), choreography by Alexander Ekman, Dancers: Melissa Hough, Camilla Spidsøe, Norwegian National Ballet, 2014

HELPFUL TIPS & SUGGESTIONS

~ Think of dance not only as moves, but also as the framing of movement ideas
~ Envision how a narrative could reveal an imaginative reality, instead of actuality
~ Remember that dance is already abstract—no need to make it more abstract
~ Consider that actions without music might seem boring, like...paying bills
~ Reimagine any space and make it a dance and movement place
~ Use context to reinterpret, redirect, and redefine a concept
~ Integrate life in dance so that dance comes to life

assignments & exercises

RESEARCH AND EXPLORATORY ASSIGNMENT: Conduct online research to find sample video excerpts from the works of the choreographers mentioned in each framework. Watch the videos to analyze how these choreographers used the principles of a framework:

➡ What characteristics and specific elements of each framework did the choreographers use, and to what extent, to help them reveal their ideas?

➡ What supportive frameworks did the choreographers choose to complement the leading framework, and how did the supportive frameworks fuse with each other?

➡ Why might other frameworks not have been appropriate for consideration?

★ **CREATIVE EXERCISE:** Think of a working idea. Use the diagram in Figure 2 of this chapter to define your intention and approach from the first column. Choose your subject matter from the second column and a leading framework from the third column.

➡ By using Figures 1 and 2 as a reference, formulate a synopsis of the content that captures your initial idea and overarching concept. Your synopsis should include a description of your intention, the specific subject matter, and your chosen leading conceptual framework that will serve as a performance format.

➡ Explore imaginatively, or if possible, with in-studio practice and a field reenactment, what would happen if you place your concept in a different framework. For example, if your leading framework is *narrative dance*, how would the same concept function in other conceptual frameworks—for example, as a *site-specific dance*? Or, if your chosen leading framework is a *music-based dance*, how could it be transformed into a *narrative dance*?

➡ Explore how your originally formulated concept will function, change, and transform within all seven conceptual framework samples outlined in the chapter: 1) *Narrative Dance*, 2) *Abstract (Plotless) Dance*, 3) *Music-based Dance*, 4) *Dance Happening*, 5) *Site-specific Dance*, 6) *Integrative Dance*, and 7) *Dance Concept in Context.*

As an example, let's use a classical dramatic play—Shakespeare's *Romeo and Juliet*—to explore how the functions of various frameworks might transform the well-known work:

① *Narrative Dance*: Shakespeare's original play centered around the dramatic relationship between two lovers. How would you reverse the narrative and transform this love drama and tragedy into a comedy of errors?

② *Abstract (Plotless) Dance*: What type of movement and dance would you use to capture the essence of this love drama—without using literal elements, sets, and costumes?

3. *Music-based dance*: The original music of the ballet was written by Prokofiev. If elements of the original score remain intact, how would the insertion of contemporary electronic music and sound effects transform this music-driven dance?

4. *Dance happening*: How might the dance narrative transform if you use the concept for a spontaneous movement and dance improvisation? For example, gather a diverse group of improvisers and ask them to randomly divide themselves into couples, trios, and small groups, and engage movement exploration of various intimate attractions.

5. *Site-specific Dance*: How might various scenes of the ballet *Romeo and Juliet* be transformed when placed in a real physical setting and imaginatively mixing-up the selection of locations? For example, what if the ballet's ball scene takes place in a warehouse with fancy sports cars, the Tybalt and Mercutio fight scene—in a large puddle of water in the street, and the balcony love scene—around a campfire, a tent, and a tree?

6. *Integrative Dance*: How would the narrative of *Romeo and Juliet* be transformed by integrating electronic and digital equipment, such as an installation with live video feeds, digital motion capture, 3D projections, small flying drones, and robots?

7. *Dance Concept in Context*: How would the narrative be transformed if you place it in a contemporary context? For example, imagine that Romeo comes from a wealthy family of oil producers that is trying to obtain permission to drill in a wildlife refuge, while Juliet works for an environmental organization that is trying to prevent oil drilling.

COMPARATIVE ASSESSMENT: Return to your initial synopsis. In order to compare various strategies for handling subject matter, randomly change the approach—for example, from "based on" or "inspired by" to "engage with" or "integrate." Analyze how this strategy might change your creative approach:

- Will it benefit the initial concept, or will it impair it?
- Will the different strategy redirect the concept in exciting or unwanted ways?
- Will this approach bring an unanticipated outcome? If so, how will the new outcome compare with the one you had anticipated?

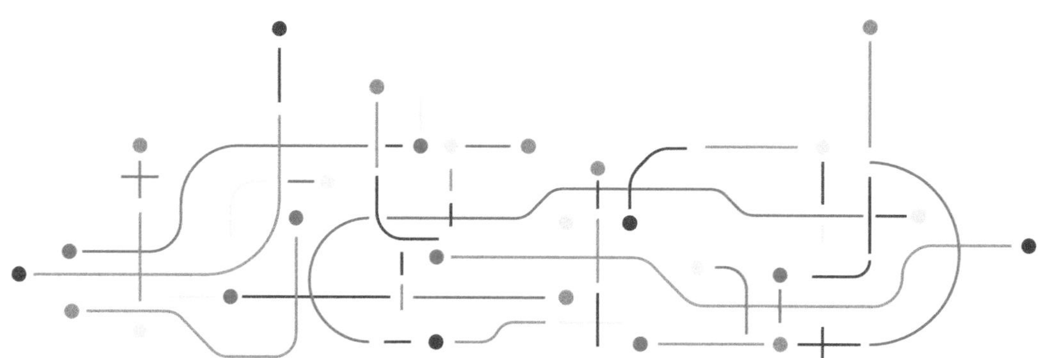

BIBLIOGRAPHY AND REFERENCES

[1] Lavender, Larry. "Facilitating the Choreographic Process," in *Contemporary Choreography: A Critical Reader*, article, 2nd edition, edited by Jo Butterworth and Liesbeth Wildschut, Routledge, 2018, pp. 107–123.

[2] Frensham, Raimund G. *Screenwriting*, Teach Yourself Books, 1996.

[3] Aviv, Vered. "Abstracting Dance: Detaching Ourselves from the Habitual Perception of the Moving Body," *Frontiers in Psychology*, vol. 8, no. 776, May 2017.

[4] Teague, Jessica. *Rafael Bonachela: Dancing Down and Under*, Online interview and article, Dance ICONS, Inc. November 2018, www.danceions.org, accessed November 7, 2020.

[5] Butterworth, Jo, *Dance Studies: The Basics*, Routledge, 2012, pp. 56–57

[6] Acocella, Joan. *Mark Morris*, Farrar, Straus and Giroux, 1993.

[7] Hunter, Victoria. "Experiencing Space: The Implications of Site-Specific Dance Performance," article, 2nd edition, edited by Jo Butterworth and Liesbeth Wildschut, Routledge, 2018, pp. 277–294.

[8] Traiger, Lisa. *Amelia Rudolph: Vertical Choreography*, an interview and online article, published online by Dance ICONS, Inc. March 2017, www. danceicons.org accessed November 10, 2020.

[9] Lavender 2018. "Facilitating the Choreographic Process."

[10] Wait, Nalina. "Embodied Consciousness," in *The Oxford Handbook of Improvisation in Dance*, edited by Vida L. Midgelow, Oxford University Press, 2019, pp. 135–149.

[11] Lindenmuth, Christina. *JoAnna Mendl Shaw: Dancing with Horses*, Online interview, Dance ICONS, Inc. June 2017, www.danceicons.org

[12] Aboelela, SW. Larson, E. Bakken, S. et al. "Defining Interdisciplinary Research: Conclusions from a Critical Review of the Literature," *Health Serv Res*. vol. 42, no. 1 Pt 1, 2007, pp. 329–346.

[13] Birringer, Johannes. "Choreographic Performance Systems," in *Contemporary Choreography: A Critical Reader*, article, 2nd edition, edited by Jo Butterworth and Liesbeth Wildschut, Routledge, 2018, pp. 107–123.

[14] Avins, Jenni. "The Dos and Don'ts of Cultural Appropriation," *The Atlantic*, online article, October 20, 2015, accessed November 15, 2020.

VISUAL REFERENCES

Figure 1, 2 and 3: Diagrams © Vladimir Angelov

Figure 4: Diagram © Vladimir Angelov, image: *A vector illustration of an old feather quill pen writing with black ink*, illustration by grimgram, courtesy of iStock/Getty Images

Figure 5: Diagram © Vladimir Angelov

Figure 6: Photography © Michael Slobodian, *Revisor* (2019), choreography by Crystal Pite, Pictured Ella Rothschild, Cindy Salgado, Jermaine Spivey, Tiffany Tregarthen, Doug Letheren, David Raymond, Rena Narumi, and Matthew Peacock, Kidd Pivot, 2019

Figure 7: Diagram © Vladimir Angelov, image: *Rorschach inkblot*, photographed and retouched in PS, illustration by Zmeel, courtesy of iStock/Getty Images

Figure 8: Photography © Pedro Greig, *ab [intra]*, choreography by Rafael Bonachela, dancers: Chloe Leong, Davide Di Giovanni, Petros Treklis, Nelson Earl, Chloe Young, Todd Sutherland, Emily Seymour, Victor Zarallo, Izzac Carroll, Bernhard Knauer, Jesse Scales, Janessa Dufty, Holly Doyle, Charmene Yap, courtesy of Sydney Dance Company, 2018

Figure 9: Diagram © Vladimir Angelov, image: *Music note vector image*, illustration by Achmad Fandhy Akhbar, courtesy of iStock/Getty

Figure 10: Photography © Elaine Mayson, *L'Allegro, il Penseroso ed il Moderato* (1988), choreography Mark Morris, performed by the Mark Morris Dance Group, London Coliseum, 2010

Figure 11: Diagram © Vladimir Angelov, image: *Colorful arrow symbol*, illustration by Oxign, courtesy of iStock/Getty Images

Figure 12: Photography © Braden Mayfield, pictured choreographer and dancer Amelia Rudolph, on location at Dana Plateau, Inyo National Park, CA., 2014

Figure 13: Diagram © Vladimir Angelov, image: *Arrows coming together*, illustration by Ivcancy, courtesy of iStock/Getty Images

Figure 14: Photography © Nancy Halsey, *Seven Games* (2006) choreography by JoAnna Mendl Shaw, pictured Gina Paolillo, Bates Dance Festival, 2006

Figure 15: Diagram © Vladimir Angelov, image: *Creative geometry tools illustration*. Illustration by Visualgo, courtesy of iStock/Getty Images

Figure 16: Photography © Raphael Frisenvænge Solholm, *Centaur* (2020), choreography by Pontus Lidberg, courtesy of Danish Dance Theater, 2020

Figure 17: Diagram © Vladimir Angelov, image: *Ebbinghaus illusion with golden and silver balls*. Illustration by Peter Hermes Furian, courtesy of iStock/Getty Images

Figure 18 From left to right Photography © John Hogg, Dada Masilo's Swan Lake (2010), choreography by Dada Masilo, performed by the dancers of Dada Masilo/ The Dance Factory, 2010. Photography © Andy Ross, Swan Lake (2016), choreography by David Dawson, pictured Sophie Marti n and Christopher Harrison, courtesy of the Scotti sh Ballet, 2016. Photography © Erik Berg, A Swan Lake (2014), choreography by Alexander Ekman, Dancers: Melissa Hough, Camilla Spidsøe, Norwegian Nati onal Ballet, 2014

Creativity is intelligence having fun.

Albert Einstein (1879–1955)

CHAPTER 13

CHOREOGRAPHIC INDIVIDUALITY AND ARTISTIC IDENTITY
– THE SEARCH FOR WHO I AM –

We never stop being ourselves. And yet, ironically, it can be difficult to describe to others who we actually are artistically and personally, because identity and individuality are multidimensional constructs with complex characteristics.

Identity may be defined as awareness of the unique self, as understood through the assimilation and the integration of otherness.[1] A person's uniqueness forms dimensionally and dynamically through intersecting aspects in the following three categories:

◆ *Physiological and Genetic Uniqueness* are identity parameters that have biological origins: parents and date of birth, for example. Also, at birth, a name is given to each person—please, feel free to fill out the sticker (Figure 1) and think about what your name means. These physiologically-based identity features and biometric data are found on one's birth certificate, ID, passport, face capture, and recorded fingerprints. One's genetic code is also unique and unchangeable. All of these parameters of identity are also known as *identification*.

Figure 1

◆ *Psychological and Cognitive Uniqueness* are fluid constructs that often form in private, as self-consciousness, self-awareness, and self-value are developing. They are influenced by family environment, upbringing, education, and interactions within the surroundings. These factors help to shape and reshape *self-identity*.

◆ *Sociological, Social, and Cultural Uniqueness* are the shared characteristics with response to belonging, as one relates to sameness—*group and collective identities*. A *social identity* conveys a person's perceived identity within a communal environment. Moral and spiritual beliefs form one's *spiritual identity*. A set of cultural, aesthetical, and ethical values determine one's *cultural identity*. And a homeland shapes one's *national identity*, which could also be a migratory *multinationality* or *transnationality*—often related to immigrants.

Individuality, on the other hand, is a person's distinctiveness in behavioral qualities, decision-making, and life perspectives that develop over time. Individuality as a construct is mostly dynamic rather than static, complex rather than basic, asymmetrical rather than symmetrical, intersectional rather than one-directional. A uniquely singular approach towards a circumstance may demonstrate one's individuality and identity.

Generally speaking, one *inherits* identity, and one *forms* individuality that shapes and reshapes one's identity. To simplify the construct and the origins of *being different*, one can compare identity and individuality to a tree. Imagine a forest of oak trees—all of the trees are oaks (identity), and yet every oak is distinct (individuality). Then imagine a forest of many species and identities of plants and trees, where the oak is still identifiable. Just like a tree, the deep roots of ancestry expand in opposite directions from the tall and distinctive tree crown of individuality and personality—all part of the same single body:

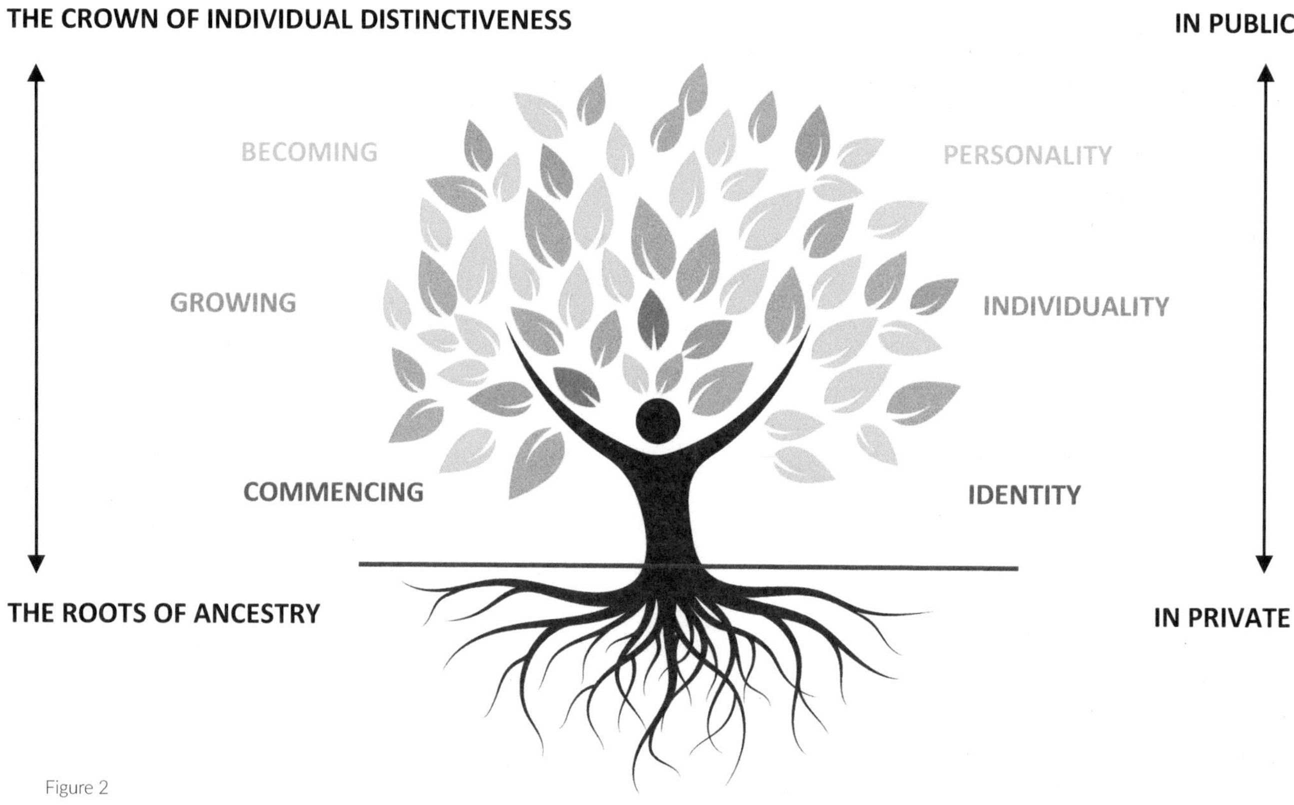

Figure 2

Personality as a "treatment of the self" is not exclusively modeled by cultural environment and social processes.[2] Individuals are the creators of their own social conduct and behavior during any form of social interaction. Personhood and identity develop and mature over time through various processes: from introspection through gaining greater self-awareness to self-realization—see *Dissection of Glorious Mind, Inside the Brain of the Choreographer*, Chapter 9.

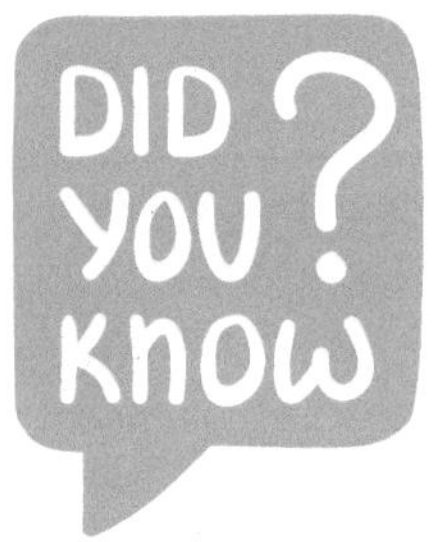

Individuality as associated with personality is often manifested through personal traits and the way we interact with others. Behavioral characteristics can be described by using hundreds of different adjectives, such as patient, persistent, cheerful, sensitive, tolerant, diplomatic, etc.[3] Creating a profile by describing one's own personal characteristics may be a fun experience. The question is whether the image of who we aspire to be in public is an accurate reflection of who we actually are.

CHOREOGRAPHIC INDIVIDUALITY AND ARTISTIC IDENTITY

Choreographers may work differently each day, and yet there is a particular artistic sensitivity during the creative process that remains consistent. We can think of a choreographer's individuality as a cluster of aspects of one's artistic personality, such as privately held thoughts, wishes, and intentions, as well as individual preferences including artistic interests and choices, working approaches, and creative habits.

◆ ***Choreographic individuality*** forms based on the choreographer's own life experiences and history, family upbringing, educational and artistic influences, movement sensibility, creative tendencies, and what type of dance content and specific concepts that the choreographer chooses to suppress or elevate. Choreographic individuality develops as choreographers explore on their own terms how to work and what they will create.

◆ ***Artistic identity***, on the other hand, refers to how choreographers manifest aesthetically their unique concepts, beliefs, and artistic ideologies. Choreographers' individual viewpoints, creative intentions, and artistic discoveries are revealed though a cluster of key concepts and distinct features embedded in a single work or a body of works.

While choreographic individuality may give rise to various means and systems of expression in a controlled manner based on individual choices and decisions, artistic identity is often a social construct of others—dancers, audiences, observers and critics—who experience the choreographer's work. In summary, choreographic individuality *speaks* through the work, while the artistic identity of the work *speaks* for itself to others.

Bridging choreographic individuality to artistic identity are questions such as *"What am I interested in?"*, *"What do I choose to do?"*, and *"Who am I artistically?"* A random movement of bodies can be organized logically and uniquely by experimenting and making different kinds of decisions. The choreographer's intuitive craftsmanship and governing consciousness construct a distinct pattern of purposefully organized artistic choices. The core of one's artistic identity is the persuasiveness of these deliberate decisions, and how truly these decisions reflect one's choreographic individuality.

For example, two different choreographers may use the same movement in very distinct ways. The positioning of that movement and its attributed meaning could be reorganized and reformulated through the unique approaches in each *system of individual expression*.

On a micro-level, certain movement qualities, features, or decorative elements recurring in one's choreography could casually be characterized as an individual *movement style*. On a meta-level, the individually-invented principles of initiating, generating, and formulating kinesthetic imagery, and the uniquely developed systems of distinct movement expression are what form one's *artistic identity*. Identity is far more substantial than style! Furthermore, the idiosyncratic concepts and inventive determination of one's vision of dance could also provide the foundation for building one's *artistic philosophy*, *ideology*, and *performance aesthetic*—see *Your Dance Manifesto?* in the *Preface* of this book.

In summary, choreographic individuality answers the question: *"What shapes you as an artist and informs your work?"* By contrast, artistic identity answers this question: *"What characterizes your work as truly and distinctly yours?"* Artistic philosophy, ideology, and performance aesthetic address the questions: *"What is creating dance according to you? What would be, could be, or should be the art of [your] dance?"*

Artistic identity may often be perceived independently of choreographic individuality and may be *seen as* one thing or another, as similar or different with respect to other artistic identities. Observers or audiences may never learn in great detail about a dance maker's choreographic individuality unless they are engaged in research about how that individual was *shaped* as an artist.

Misconceptions could also occur. For example, the work of indigenous choreographers incorporating characteristics of their own native culture through the lens of their personal experiences may be labeled as *unorthodox* and *weird*, rather than *authentic* and *unique*. Can art be weird? Or does such an unsettling perception actually depend on social perspective, familiarity, and cultural context?

Curiously, artistic identity is often, if not always, a part of a social and cultural construct. The work may be placed accidentally in a false context, as the choreographer is not always in complete control of how the work will be perceived and identified artistically. A certain artistic philosophy and performance aesthetic may also challenge established norms when a choreographer's artistic vision may deliberately confront societal and cultural dogmas and rules—read about *Norms* as part of ICON SMART^{SM} in Chapter 10.

Identity is never really in a *state of stability* despite its core consistency. Instead, artistic identity forms and changes dynamically, as various aspects of one's identity remain fluid. The forces of such changes could be external or internal. For example, external circumstances and changing conditions in the living and creative environment could alter the direction of the choreographer's interests. Newly presented knowledge and situations may lead to a change in one's artistic perspective. The artist may then realize the need to adopt the new information, or the situation may demand that the artist adapt.

Identity also reflects the mind of a choreographer, which often experiences the internal and dynamic complexities of personal and artistic struggles. Many artists may deal with their own *inner angels and demons*—some from the past, others in the present, or some unknowingly repressed to be handled in the future. Emotions and passions could be inspiring but also antagonistic, especially when an artistic expression captures a collision of contradictory feelings, such as experiencing love and anger at the same time.

As artists mature, so do their artistic identities. At the early stages, an emerging choreographer may be driven by inner impulses to create motion in and with the body, guided by personal experiences and artistic influences. Then a choreographer gradually summons the courage to push against the norms and conventions drawn from the past.

An artistic identity truly matures when a choreographer's kinesthetic sensibility leads the artist to discover unique paths of movement; when individual experiences transform into an artistic vision and purpose; and when a dance expresses not what is expected by others, but what the choreographer genuinely intended to express.

FORMING CHOREOGRAPHIC INDIVIDUALITY AND SHAPING ARTISTIC IDENTITY

– PAINTING A SELF-PORTRAIT –

The *PERSON-ARTIST* construct is built by intertwining elements such as personal history and upbringing; the empowering influence of educators and artists who have shaped an attitude and perspective towards art and life; interests in specific concepts; unique approaches to movement embodiment; and distinct principles for creating.

Imagine painting a colorful self-portrait—a visual example of spontaneous brush stokes capturing the dynamic elements and dimensions that shape, reshape, and fuse choreographic individuality with artistic identity.

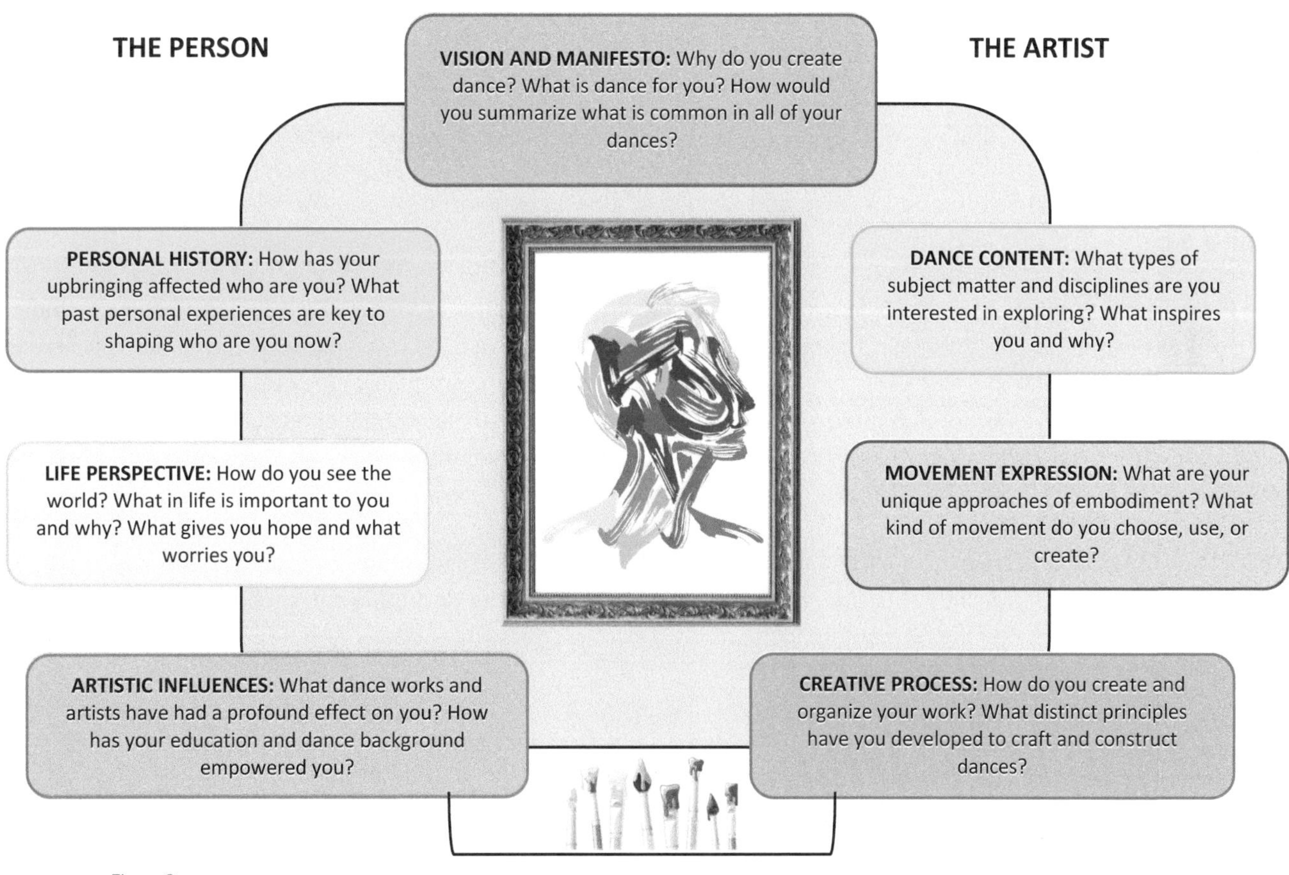

Figure 3

Developing an artistic identity is hardly a dance-skills–based activity; rather, it is a process of forming decision-making skills often tested in situational circumstances and by the questions posed earlier. Choreographers might be subject to environments and experiences that are beyond their control. Thus, to understand a choreographer's individuality and identity is not to ask: *"How good are you at what you do?"* but to ask: *"Who are you, what makes you the way you are, and what defines your artistry?"*

HELP ME SEEK ME!
– FINDING YOUR WHY –

Artistic influences, whether direct or indirect, purposeful or unintentional, fundamental or supplemental, play a role in forming one's choreographic individuality. History speaks loudly about artistic influences and mentorships when choreographers "pass the baton," as in a relay race, while moving the art of dance forward.

In the days of romantic, classical, and modern ballet theater, August Bournonville, through his father, was influenced by the ideas of Jean-Georges Noverre; Marius Petipa, the choreographic "father of classical ballet," was an apprentice of Jules Perrot and Arthur Saint-Léon. While the Ballet Russes' impresario Serge Diaghilev did not directly mentor his choreographers at the dance studio, he personally took them to art galleries, operas, and concerts to educate them, and he introduced them to groundbreaking poets, composers, artists, and designers.[4]

The 20th-century early modern dance pioneers Ruth St. Denis and Ted Shawn had great influence on Doris Humphrey and Martha Graham. Humphrey later became the choreographic mentor to José Limón and Anna Halprin, while Martha Graham inspired choreographers such as Erick Hawkins, Paul Taylor, and Merce Cunningham. Lester Horton mentored Alvin Ailey, while Merce Cunningham become an inspiring force for a generation of postmodern choreographers such as Yvonne Rainer, Steve Paxton, Debora Hay, and Lucinda Childs, among others[5]—see *Choreographic Lineage* tree in Chapter 6.

The New York City Ballet's George Balanchine took under his wing plenty of young choreographic talent including his close associate, Jerome Robbins.[6] Balanchine's neoclassicism was also an inspiring force for Hans van Manen, Jiří Kylián, William Forsythe, and Christopher Wheeldon. Jerome Robbins's replacement of ballet pointe shoes with sneakers could be seen as a choreographic reference in the works of Twyla Tharp and Justin Peck. William Forsythe has been an inspiring figure for an entire generation of 21st-century contemporary choreographers such as Jodie Gates, David Dawson, Emily Molnar, Helen Pickett, Richard Siegal, Wayne McGregor, and Crystal Pite, among many others.

There is wide variance in how the mentor and mentee relate and *feed* off of each other. For example, Doris Humphrey's movement and creative principles became the cornerstone of José Limón's technique and choreography. José Limón's approach developed further but was still fundamentally based on Doris Humphrey's technique. Humphrey remained Limón's lifetime mentor and artistic adviser.

In sharp contrast, Graham and Cunningham's choreography parted ways with starkly opposing ideas regarding what their dances should be about. Both dancemakers developed their own independent techniques, approaches, and choreographic principles. Graham was predominantly interested in translating mythical imagery into movement for narrative dances, while Cunningham was interested only in movement for movement's sake.

Naturally, an emerging choreographer might seek guidance from an experienced choreographer by asking: *"Help me discover who I am artistically and why."* The request might be mistakenly interpreted as *"Help me be like you."* This discrepancy triggers a search for how an emergent choreographer will acquire guidance. A mentor, on the other hand, should discreetly consider the boundaries of the help needed and offered.

Mentors and their potential engagement with mentees (or lack thereof) could be classified as: a) choreographers who are strictly focused on their own work and barely interested in mentoring; b) those who while creating their own work occasionally mentor others out of curiosity or contractual duties; c) those who alongside their own work are full-heartedly willing to mentor others by diligently offering guidance, feedback, and support.

Mentees, on the other hand, have their own strategies for obtaining learning experiences, either by formal arrangements with a mentor or on their own terms:

➢ **Direct influences:** when an emerging choreographer has direct access to choreographers/mentors through live in-studio interactions, while still performing.

➢ **Indirect influences:** when an emerging choreographer remotely studies the creative approaches of preferred choreographers by observing and analyzing their works, with or without their knowledge.

➢ **Inspirational influences:** when an emerging choreographer has limited resources and access to observe and study the works of preferred choreographers—especially if they are deceased and there is limited archival material. Then the core ideas of these notable choreographers become learning tools and inspiration.

There could be overlapping combinations of all of the above. Historically, direct influences and mentorships have proven to be the most impactful. In such instances, a *mentee choreographer* might seek knowledge, guidance, feedback, and affirmation; a *mentor choreographer* would provide resources, suggestions, advice, and encouragement. In these interactions, most important is finding the right balance of how/what/when/why help is needed and offered. Learning, mentoring, studying and teaching of artistry can be pared down to a few essential aspects, as summarized in Figure 4.

↳	MENTEES COULD SEEK TO...		**MENTORS** COULD HELP AND...
KNOWLEDGE	- Gain understanding of the field	↔	- Recommend resources and references
CRAFT	- Identifying own strengths and weaknesses - Formulating own goals and direction of work - Develop own skills and proficiencies	↔ ↔ ↔	- Engage in analysis and evaluation - Offer personalized strategies and advice - Provide feedback and suggestions
IDENTITY	- Formulate own choreographic individuality - Discover own unique artistic self - Nurture intrinsic motivation	↔ ↔ ↔	- Identify distinct virtues and qualities - Reassure truthfulness and confidence - Extend support and encouragement

Figure 4

THE EVOLVING ARTIST AND IDENTITY

A choreographer needs an average of one to two decades of complete immersion in choreographic activities in order to challenge recurring creative and conceptual boundaries, gain and strengthen skills, and confidently develop the proficiencies of the choreographic craft. As in many other professions, investing a substantial amount of time is essential for a choreographer to mature artistically and climb the professional development ladder: from an *emerging choreographer* to a *mid-career*, *established*, and *prominent choreographer*—see *A Career in Choreography* in Chapter 25.

As choreographers mature artistically, their knowledge expands and their creative practices and identity evolve. Various activities and experiences take place simultaneously: the emerging artist conducts research and analyzes information from resources, mentors, and influencers. New information and experiences are synthesized, personalized, adapted, and selectively assimilated in an effort to advance skills.

Courageous acts of inventing and discovery lead to the emergence of new creative theories and artistic practices, which will undergo further experimentation and testing. Decision-making processes increase confidence and clarity when the choreographer chooses, cultivates, and refines the creative direction of the work. With the accumulated experiences, artistic identity begins to take shape and it becomes evident in the work.

There is no strict border separating an *emerging artist* from a *mature artist*, as the process of growth and advancement is ongoing. The characteristics of a mature artist are revealed through the work and the degree of thoughtfulness, proficiency, and identity uniqueness.

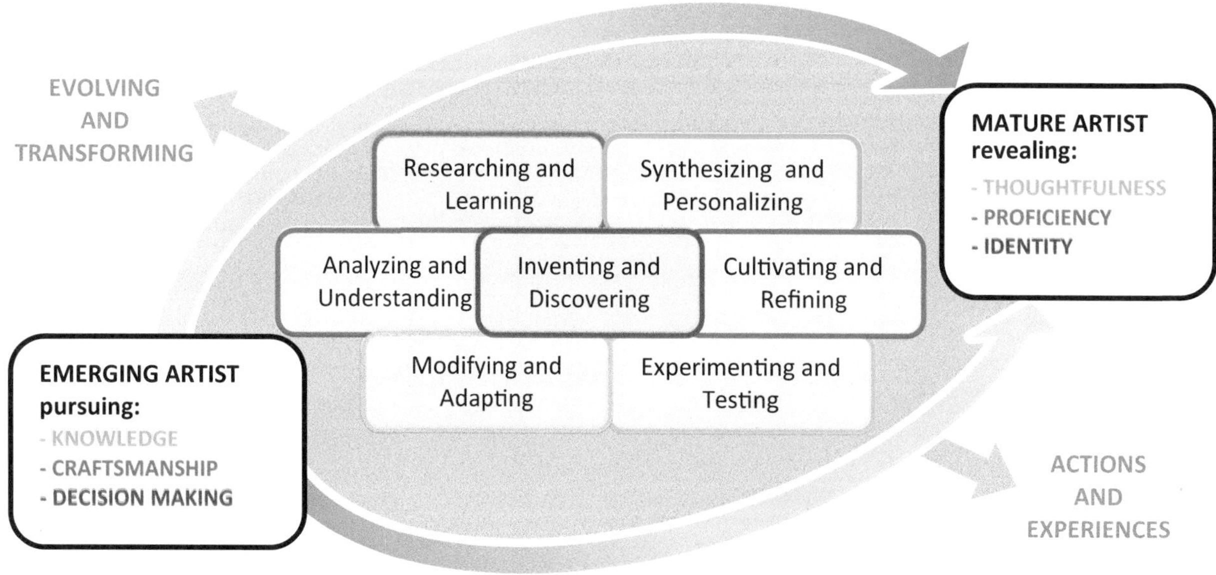

Figure 5

PORTRAITS IN MOTION

Self-portraits by prominent 21st-century choreographers capture their perspective on what informed and shaped their choreographic individuality and artistic identity. These candid revelations include details of family background and upbringing, personal and artistic struggles, the overcoming of challenges, and the shaping of unique artistry.

After dancing with various European dance companies, **Annabelle Lopez Ochoa** turned her focus solely to choreography. She has created new works for the New York City Ballet, San Francisco Ballet, Dutch National Ballet, Finnish National Ballet, and English National Ballet, among others. Raised by her Belgian mother and Colombian father, Lopez Ochoa recalls her early experience as a dancer growing up in Belgium:

> *Growing up as a mixed-race child was very confusing. Until the age of 7, I even thought I was white until my mother put me in front of a mirror and pointed out my tanned skin next to her white skin. I grew up in a white neighborhood and my color was exotic. I overheard the director of the ballet school saying that a classical ballerina was white as she hushed us out of the sun and I saw her startle as our eyes crossed.*
>
> *Now many years later I dare to unveil unabashedly who I am to the world and present it on a stage through the ballets I make. It's been a journey of self-acceptance and healing. And yes, people still can't enunciate my name correctly, I'm still short and brown, and I am still a woman in a predominantly male dominated dance world, but now, in 2020s, I am proud of being different.*[7]

Figure 6 Photography © Laurent Liotardo, *Broken Wings* (2016), choreography by Annabelle Lopez Ochoa, center featured lead principal dancer Tamara Rojo, English National Ballet, 2016

David Dawson is a British choreographer and an associate artist of the Dutch National Ballet in the Netherlands and Semperoper Ballett in Germany. He has created new works for The Royal Ballet, Mariinsky Ballet, Royal Swedish Ballet, Royal New Zealand Ballet, Vienna State Opera, Berlin StaatsBallett, and Norwegian National Ballet, among many others. *Citizen Nowhere* (2017)—one of his works for the Dutch National Ballet—takes on the subject of uncertainty, belonging, and isolationism. He shares:

I failed as a dancer—because of fear. When I started to choreograph, I became free of that fear. I spent so much of my childhood and my dance career being a very insecure person. I was gifted, but I was very much in need of guidance and direction from others. When I was asked to make my first piece in Amsterdam, I felt I had some control of my art for the first time and it became addictive to choreograph because it was in the act of creating that I felt free.

Figure 7 Photography © Hans Gerritsen, *Citizen Nowhere*, choreography by David Dawson, pictured performer Edo Wijnen, Dutch National Ballet, 2017

My ballet Citizen Nowhere *(photo left) started off as a response to my own artistic journey. Through the years I've discovered what I need for my process. I know that I need time. I know that I need clarity.* Citizen Nowhere *came as an antidote to everything I'd experienced in the last three years. I've lived in continental Europe and I built my life here. I was totally heartbroken with the results of the British referendum to leave Europe. I woke up the next day and just kept saying, "I am European. I am. No one can tell me any differently.*

Then, shortly afterwards, the British Prime Minister said, "If you believe yourself to be a global citizen, then you are a citizen of nowhere."

This raised feelings that I had never felt before in my entire life. I had no choice but to take it as a personal insult based on an isolationist mentality that is sweeping the globe. We have come up against a 21st-century problem that affects so many people unjustly.[8]

Crystal Pite is a choreographer and the Artistic Director of Kidd Pivot. Her work is well-known for depth and rigor, sharp exactitude and risk. Pite's distinct choreographic sensibility fuses theatrical elements with the complexity and freedom of structured improvisation, and it is marked by a strong sense of wit and invention. She shares:

> *Becoming a choreographer was not really a conscious choice, but an evolution—a natural progression through my life. Choreography was a way to dovetail my creative impulse with my love of dancing.*
>
> *When I was about 13 years old, my ballet teacher gave me the key to the studio and permission to use the space whenever it was available. It was life-changing to be able to go there by myself and create. I remember experiencing intense, luminous joy in my mind and body as I worked alone on a piece of choreography.*
>
> *Sometimes I still create alone, but often I'm with a dream team of collaborators. We've built trust over time, through many challenges and victories. I'm grateful to share my artistic life with inspiring people that I trust and admire and love. I also choose the subject matter for our creations with a great deal of care, knowing that we will have this content in our lives for years. I seek a subject that demands great courage and rigour from us, and that in return will bring us insight and joy.*
>
> *The things we make, make us too. So it's important to choose deliberately and lovingly what we bring our attention to.*[9]

Figure 8 Photography © Michael Slobodian, *Betroffenheit* (2015), choreography by Crystal Pite, pictured, from left to right Cindy Salgado, Bryan Arias, Jonathon Young, David Raymond, Tiffany Tregarthen, and Jermaine Spivey, a production of Kidd Pivot, 2015

Sidi Larbi Cherkaoui is a choreographer known for his eclectic approach and inventiveness. Influenced by Islamic tradition, he is the son of a Moroccan father and a Flemish mother. His name "Larbi" literally means "Arab," while Cherkaoui means "coming from the East." When he established his own company in 2010, he appropriately called it Eastman.[10] In 2015, he became the artistic director of the Royal Ballet of Flanders in Belgium and currently directs Ballet of the Grand Théâtre de Genève. He shares:

I didn't grow up in a high art-oriented environment: my parents didn't have a lot of money, and the only art that would come into our house was either traditional music from Morocco or TV things. I would learn moves from video and invite my friends from school to my house to teach them and rehearse. I was a jazzy boy, growing up with Prince music, and I mixed a lot of styles, from African dance to voguing.

Then I went to P.A.R.T.S.—Anne Teresa De Keersmaeker's school, which really helped me because we learned composition, how to choreograph. Even if I often do the opposite of what I was taught, I know how you can build a structure. It started with the composition of music, phrases, counter-phrases, repeated elements, refrains...I learned about the way the body could move, from release technique to Forsythe's geometry, Anne Teresa's spatial awareness, Pina Bausch's emotional commitment to a movement.

As a choreographer, I've always been a bit of a chameleon. I'm very good at learning to abide by the rules of others—I grew up having to. What is constant about my work is a certain melancholy, a sense of displacement, the feeling of being at the margins of society. But I also realized, the more I talked with choreographers, that all of them feel like they don't belong. And I'm definitely communicating that in my work.[11]

Figure 9 Photography © Agathe Poupeney, *zero degrees* (2005), choreography by Sidi Larbi Cherkaoui and Akram Khan, pictured Sidi Larbi Cherkaoui, 2015

Jennifer Archibald, a graduate of the Alvin Ailey School, founded her own company The Arch Dance Company in 2006, and is the program director of ArchCore40 dance intensives. Jennifer has created work on major ballet companies around the globe. She is currently on the faculty at the Yale School of Drama and is the resident choreographer of Cincinnati Ballet. Jennifer encapsulates her personal journey and experiences as a choreographer, and shares:

> *As a Black female choreographer in ballet, especially without having a performance career in the ballet field, my artistic journey has been challenging and yet exciting. Although I come from a hip hop background and I have never danced in a ballet company, I knew that I wanted to do thought-provoking work that challenges me artistically, as well as my audience.*
>
> *My teacher always told me to be insightful and take the world in. Being sensitive to humanity is what makes my work humane. My aesthetic falls between borders of social, economic, gendered, and political theories. I demand independent expression in my work and that transcends the color of my skin.*
>
> *My work reflects my background and who I am. There's usually a really powerful hip hop phrase. There's strong drum-based and heavily gestural-driven movement in my work. That pulsing phrase builds and grows; it goes down and then it ends with a very strong exclamation mark. That's where my hip hop aesthetic comes through. A dance section like that appears consistently in my work, to the point that when one sees it, one would say, "That must be Jennifer's work."*[12]

Figure 10 Photography © Peter Mueller, *Never.Nest* (2017), choreography by Jennifer Archibald, pictured from left to right Christina LaForgia Morse, Melissa Gelfin De-Poli, Sirui Liu, Jake Casey, courtesy of Cincinnati Ballet, 2017

Marc Brew is an acclaimed Australian choreographer and former artistic director of AXIS Dance Company in California. Marc's unique choreographic approach pushes the boundaries of physicality and explores new and exciting movement that he has devised on his own body or in collaboration with dancers.

He has created a vast spectrum of work that includes physically integrated dance, while working alongside or in collaboration with fellow groundbreaking artists in the field, such as Mary Verdi-Fletcher, Marisa Hamamoto, and Alice Sheppard. Marc Brew describes how he created opportunity and beauty out of adversity:

> *At age 11, I started classical ballet and I really enjoyed the challenge. I graduated from the Victorian College of the Arts Secondary School and went to the Australian Ballet School. From there I was offered a job in South Africa with PACT Ballet. I moved to Pretoria.*
>
> *After acquiring my disability from a car crash in South Africa, I was paralyzed from the neck down; I knew I wanted to keep dancing. The problem was I had to make up my own dances if I wanted to keep dancing. No one knew how to work with me. I didn't fit into the ballet world anymore...and back then there was no such thing as an integrated company in Australia.*
>
> *I wondered: Could I still even call myself a dancer? I didn't look like a classical ballet dancer now that I used a wheelchair, but I still felt like a dancer. It's just going to be different. I can still move, I can still express myself, through my body and also through my chair, and the use of floor work and partnering. I started exploring with my fellow dancers to discover how we could work together. Through difference there is beauty.*[13]

Figure 11 Photography © David DeSilva, *Radical Impact* (2017), choreography by Marc Brew, pictured performers from left to right: James Bowen, Dwayne Schuneman, Yuko Monden Juma, Lani Dickinson JanpiStar, and Edisnel Rodriguez, courtesy of AXIS Dance Company, 2018

Yuanyuan Wang is one of China's leading choreographers and artistic director of the Beijing Dance Theater, which she founded in 2008. Born and raised in Beijing, she prides herself on being rooted in Chinese traditions, while simultaneously producing innovative, authentic, and thoughtful contemporary dance works for the world stage.

She served as a resident choreographer of the National Ballet of China and was one of the main choreographers for the Beijing Olympic Games. Her pioneering activities in the development of contemporary dance in China have been pivotal. Her works have been presented at major venues around the globe. She shares her experiences:

> *I grew up learning the folkloric dance tradition of Chinese culture. I studied dance and choreography at the Beijing Dance Academy and completed my master's degree at CalArts in the United States. My education in China was curriculum- and methodology-based, while my education in the United States was research- and exploration-based. I'm lucky to have experienced the best of both approaches.*
>
> *As a choreographer, I have committed my work and artistic sense to capturing common human values, rejuvenating traditions, and reflecting on our modern global society—where East meets West, where the ancient meets the contemporary.*
>
> *Therefore, in my work I'm equally interested in exploring and merging stories from Chinese traditions as in exploring the profound wisdom of William Shakespeare and Oscar Wilde, for example. My work seeks what unites us as people.*[14]

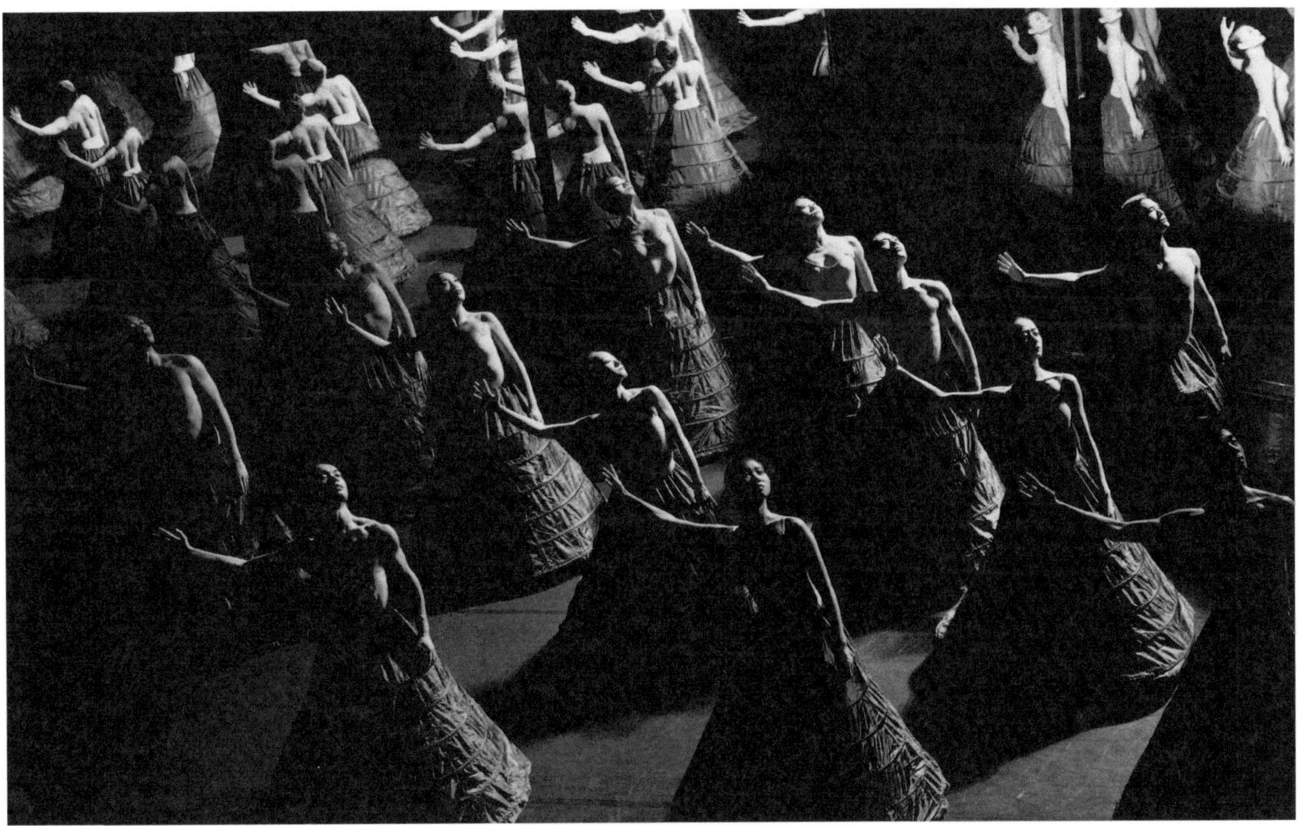

Figure 12 Photography © Han Jiang, Oscar Wilde's *The Nightingale and the Rose* (2015), choreography by Yuanyuan Wang, pictured performers members of Beijing Dance Theater, China, 2015

Capturing the continuity and connectivity between a choreographer's past, present, and future self is a cyclical process of self-realization during a choreographer's career. Emerging choreographers may often replicate the artistic works of others unintentionally. As they seek and form their artistic identities, they will ultimately replace the influence of others with their own discoveries and revelations. Recognizing and reorganizing one's personal experiences and the related artistic inventions are part of the evolution and shaping of one's uniqueness.

?

What would you include in a brief statement about what informs your artistic identity?

In closing, let's address an important question about originality and artistic uniqueness:

◆ **Does every dance embody and transmit choreographic individuality and artistic identity?** The answer depends on whether the choreographer present in the so-called "dance house of embodied movement ideas" acts as the owner or renter, or as the host or guest. Forming one's choreographic individuality is an ever-evolving process. Personal history, inspiring artistic encounters, and newly discovered kinesthetic experiences are recurring influences embodied and manifested in the construct of a dance work. In the early creations of a budding choreographer, the resulting choreographic outcome and embodiment architecture may not appear to be uniquely articulated and one of a sustainable build. With persistence, determination, and confidence, it is possible to construct one's "own dance house" and progress toward creative and artistic autonomy.

The searching and discovering, the shaping and reshaping of one's artistic identity may not transpire quickly and easily. The journey for an emerging choreographer may unfold as a *cacophony* of contradicting concepts and a *polyphony* of movement ideas. An eager choreographer should allow opposing views and concepts to exist in *harmony*. Choices and decisions will "set the tone" for a basic melody to emerge that will, in turn, expand into a *unique symphony of the self.*

When a choreographer is fortified with commitment and endurance to overcome any personal and creative challenges, then the distant horizon is within reach—the discovery of self becomes the most important discovery in one's life.

HELPFUL TIPS & SUGGESTIONS

~ Consider that identity personifies, while individuality diversifies
~ Acknowledge teachers and mentors; through others we become ourselves
~ Always be yourself. If you don't like yourself, then become your better self
~ Ignore others' opinions of you; instead, assert who you actually are
~ Find comfort with yourself and you will find confidence in your work
~ Explore and discover what you want to liberate your potential
~ Don't try to fit in if you want to stand out

assignments & exercises

RESEARCH ASSIGNMENT: Choose an inspiring choreographer who has influenced you and your work. Research extensively the choreographer's biography, body of artistic work, and writings, if any.

➡ Using the sample format from the statements in the sub-chapter *Portraits in Motion*, create a portrait of your chosen choreographer within 160 words.

➡ Applying the format of *Portraits in Motion*, create your own portrait within 160 words about what has informed your choreographic individuality and artistic identity.

➡ Employing the format of *Portraits in Motion*, select a dance photograph from your current or past works that best accompanies your statement and represents your artistic identity. Why did you choose this particular image?

★ **CREATIVE EXERCISE:** Think of subject matter, ideas, and concepts that are most pressing and important at this moment in your life, such as topics that bring hope or worry, or that make you happy or sad, or choose an experience from your childhood that shaped you as a person.

➡ Identify and explain why this particular topic is so important to you and how it relates to your personal view of life and the world. Why did you choose this particular experience, idea, or subject matter?

➡ Which elements of this experience/idea could be translated into movement? Based on the kinesthetic potential of this working idea, generate a series of movements.

➡ What kind of movement material did you choose? Which movements are your own original inventions and which are borrowed from existing movement and dance traditions? As the movement vocabulary emerges, how uniquely personal and how generic is this vocabulary? How are the movements related to you and your idea?

➡ While creating, focus on experimenting and generating your own unique and authentic movement material that specifically captures the ideas related to your individual life experience and your type of personality. Do you tend to move speedily or calmly? Do you prefer fighting gravity or giving in to it? Do your movement gestures tend to be simultaneous or successive?

➡ While creating, observe the approaches you use to organize your creative work, including how you generate the movement material, use dance improvisation, and assemble the movement phrase.

➡ While creating, examine to what extent you stay true to your initial ideas and how you capture the essence of your personal experiences and your chosen idea.

➡ Once a movement phrase is completed, showcase it and share it with peers and colleagues without telling them the source of your inspiration. Ask them to identify the source of the idea for your movement and solicit their feedback.

COMPARATIVE ASSIGNMENT: For this assignment, be prepared to look back at your past experiences and the shaping of your choreographic individuality. Make a list of choreographers that you admire and continue to view as role models; think of educators, mentors, and those who have left a lasting impression during your upbringing and dance education; think of artists and thinkers who have influenced your creative work. Then, for each name, answer the following questions:

- **Probing your role models:** a) What principles and methods of experimenting and testing of creative ideas have you "borrowed" from others, and how have they served as a foundation for developing your own principles? b) Which elements of their artistic and educational work had the greatest influence on you, and why have you decided to incorporate them into your own work? c) Which principles were essential in building your choreographic individuality and shaping your artistic identity?

- **Probing your creative influences:** a) How would you compare and distinguish your own principles from the principles of the mentors who have shaped your choreographic individuality? b) To what extent have you modified, adapted, and assimilated these influences and why are they applicable to your work? c) How has your decision-making process transformed as you have synthesized the knowledge and experiences of your mentors and influential figures?

- **Probing your artistic ancestry and uniqueness:** a) Draw an illustration of your choreographic individuality and artistic identity in the form of a *Choreographic Genealogy Tree.* b) What elements encompassing your uniqueness would you assign to the tree crown branches? c) For the root branches, what life experiences, artistic influences, and mentors have shaped you as an artist, and who would you assign to the root branches?

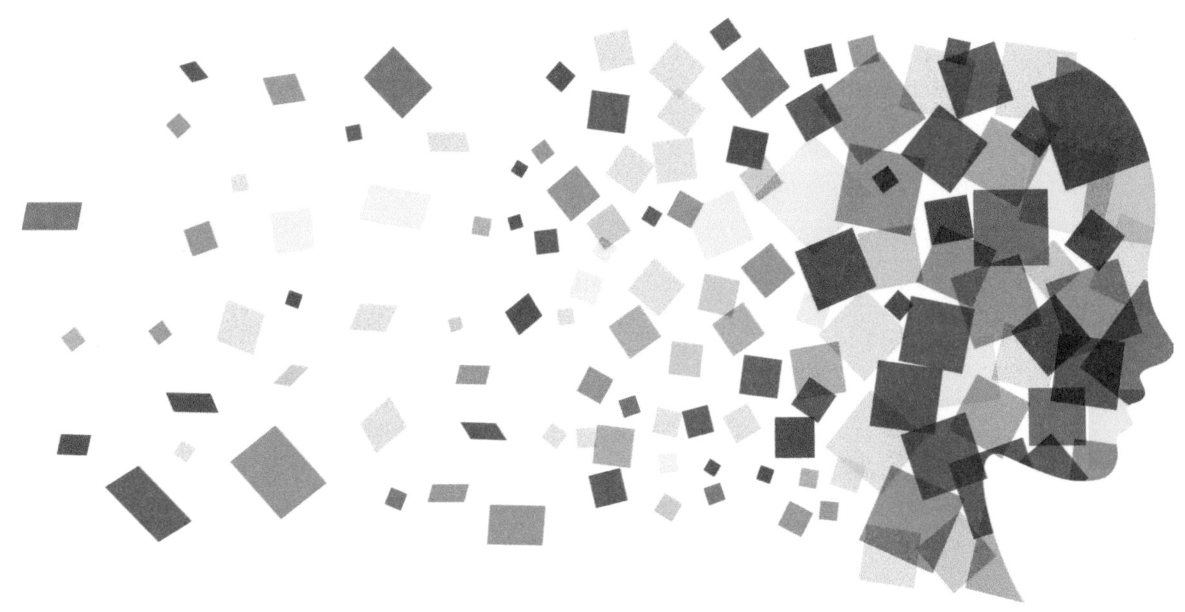

BIBLIOGRAPHY AND REFERENCES

[1] Sibony, Daniel. *L'origine en partage*, Seuil, 1991, pp. 340–341.
[2] Cohen, Anthony P. *Self-Consciousness, An Alternative Anthropology of Identity*, Routledge, 1994.
[3] Leising, Daniel, et al. "What Types of Terms Do People Use When Describing an Individual's Personality?" *Psychological Science*, vol. 25, no. 9, September 2014, pp. 1787–1794.
[4] Anderson, Jack. *Ballet & Modern Dance, a Concise History*, 2nd edition, Dance Horizon Books, 1995, pp. 51–138.
[5] Anderson 1995. *Ballet & Modern Dance*, pp. 165–203.
[6] Anderson 1995. *Ballet & Modern Dance*, pp. 139–164.
[7] Traiger, Lisa. Interviewer, *Annabelle Lopez Ochoa: Navigating Two Cultures & Breaking Into Ballet Choreography as a Woman, A Choreographic Portrait*, Dance ICONS, Inc. monthly global newsletter publication, November 2016.
[8] Teague, Jessica. Interviewer, *David Dawson: Citizen Nowhere, a choreographic portrait*, Dance ICONS, Inc. monthly global newsletter publication, March 2017.
[9] Pite, Crystal. TV interview during the 2016 Edinburgh International Festival, 2016, and online personal conversations with Vladimir Angelov, December 2020.
[10] Cools, Guy. "Sidi Larbi Cherkaoui and Akram Khan: Intertwined Journey In-Between Dance Cultures," in *Contemporary Choreography*, article, 2nd edition, edited by Jo Butterworth and Liesbeth Wildschut, Routledge, 2018, pp. 372–402.
[11] Cappelle, Laura. Interviewer, *Sidi Larbi Cherkaoui: Art as a Creative Paradox, A Choreographic Portrait*, Dance ICONS, Inc. monthly global newsletter publication, May 2019.
[12] Howard, Theresa Ruth. Interviewer, *Jennifer Archibald: The Choreographer as Dance Alchemist, A Portrait of Jennifer Archibald*, Dance ICONS, Inc. monthly global newsletter publication, January 2019.
[13] Traiger, Lisa. Interviewer, *We Will Never Stop Dancing: Physically Integrated Choreographers Speak, Choreographic Portraits Including Marc Brew*, Dance ICONS, Inc. monthly global newsletter publication, April 2019.
[14] Teague, Jessica. Interviewer, *Yuanyuan Wang: Passion in China, A Choreographic Portrait*, Dance ICONS, Inc. monthly global newsletter publication, February 2018.

VISUAL REFERENCES

Figure 1: Red name tag. *Hello my name is – label*, credit: Oleksii Arseniuk, courtesy of iStock/Getty Images

Figure 2: Diagram © Vladimir Angelov, image: *People Tree icon logo template vector design*, credit: sangidan idan, courtesy of iStock/Getty Images

Figure 3: Diagram © Vladimir Angelov, Images: *Man, with colorful image, credit*: artqu, and *Paintbrushes*, credit: alst; *Luxury golden classic painting frame*, credit: WDnet, courtesy of iStock/Getty Images

Figure 4 and 5: Diagrams © Vladimir Angelov

Figure 6: Photography © Laurent Liotardo, *Broken Wings* (2016), choreography by Annabelle Lopez Ochoa, featured lead principal dancers Tamara Rojo, English National Ballet, 2016

Figure 7: Photography © Hans Gerritsen, *Citizen Nowhere* (2017), choreography by David Dawson, pictured performer Edo Wijnen, Dutch National Ballet, 2017

Figure 8: Photography © Michael Slobodian, *Betroffenheit* (2015), choreography by Crystal Pite, pictured from left to right Cindy Salgado, Bryan Arias, Jonathon Young, David Raymond, Tiffany Tregarthen, and Jermaine Spivey, a production of Kidd Pivot, 2015

Figure 9: Photography © Agathe Poupeney, *zero degrees* (2005), choreography by Sidi Larbi Cherkaoui and Akram Khan, pictured Sidi Larbi Cherkaoui, 2015

Figure 10: Photography © Peter Mueller, *Never.Nest* (2017), choreography by Jennifer Archibald, pictured from left to right Christina LaForgia Morse, Melissa Gelfin De-Poli, Sirui Liu, Jake Casey, courtesy of Cincinnati Ballet, 2017

Figure 11: Photography © David DeSilva, *Radical Impact* (2017), choreography by Marc Brew, pictured performers from left to right: James Bowen, Dwayne Schuneman, Yuko Monden Juma, Lani Dickinson, JanpiStar, and Edisnel Rodriguez, courtesy of AXIS Dance Company, 2018

Figure 12: Photography © Han Jiang, Oskar Wilde's *The Nightingale and the Rose* (2015), choreography by Yuanyuan Wang, pictured performers of Beijing Dance Theater, China, 2015

BOOK IV

FORM AND FORMLESSNESS

GENERATING MOVEMENT MATERIAL

4:30 PM, Rehearsal Studio 3:

CHOREOGRAPHER: Is this confusing you?

DANCER: What you are asking me to do…it doesn't make sense…

CHOREOGRAPHER: I know. Let me demonstrate by exaggerating the details.

(showing movements)

DANCER: Oh, I see…But it is quite unusual…and beautifully disorienting…

CHOREOGRAPHER: I know. Did you get it, however?

DANCER: Yes, I think so. But it is still…either crazy or genius…or both…

CHOREOGRAPHER: I know. Let's do it!

Excerpt from

dance DIALOGUES

An Anonymous Unpublished Manuscript, 376 BC–AD 2091

CHAPTER 14

THE EMERGENCE OF MOVEMENT
– FIRST CRAWL AND WALK, THEN RUN –

Choreographers create shapes and movements in their own ways. New ideas may spring from music, visual art, poetry, choreography created by others, or from simply moving freely and seeing where the movement goes. A dance may emerge in a physical manner from moving and dancing, or in a cerebral manner from thoughts and ideas. The chapters ahead address ideas, methods, and tools of formal dance construction for the creation of "set" works of choreography for the concert stage.

◆ **Concert choreography engages with the processes of physicalizing ideas, then organizing them and sharing them in the form of a distilled kinesthetic expression.** The choreographer *thinks* and *speaks* by generating shapes and movements, or with prompts to which dancers may respond with movement. Movement may be organized into dance phrases and sections or remain open to improvisation during each performance. Shapes, poses, movements, and physical actions are among the fundamental instruments needed to craft and present a choreographic expression.

As choreographic ideas gain independence and strength, the cumulative process of *forming* and *building* a dance also accelerates in terms of movement complexity.[1] The emerging work begins to advance kinesthetically. The process is similar to the way a baby first crawls, which is gradually followed by walking, then running.

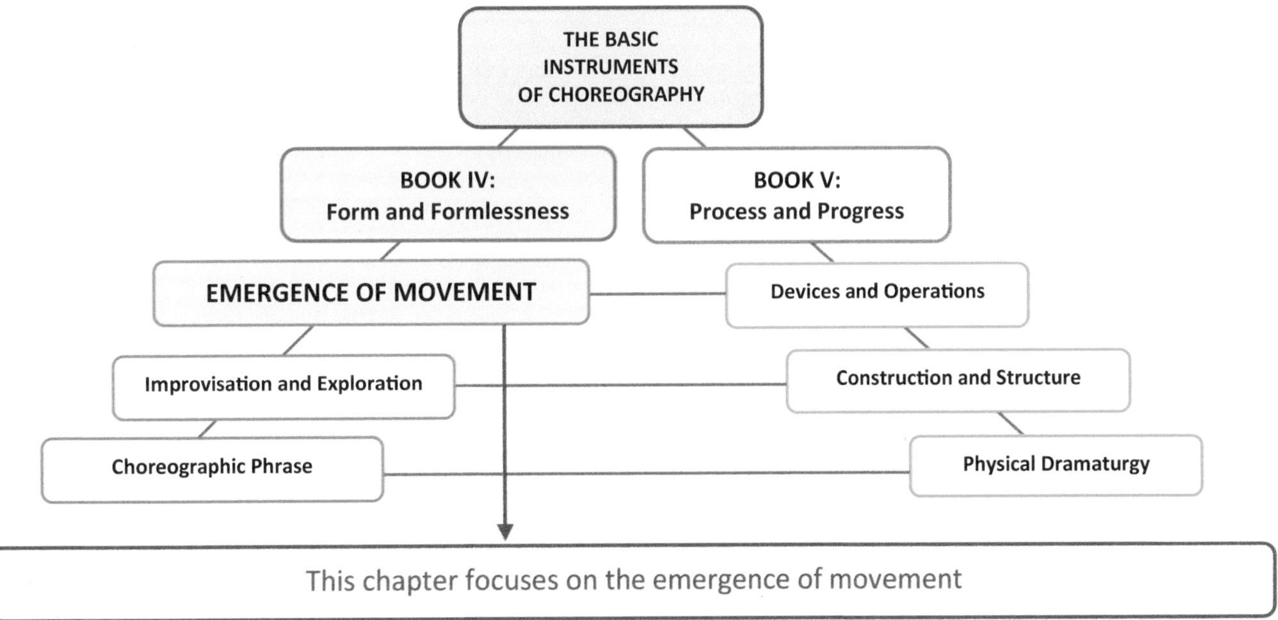

Figure 1

EXPANSION OF DANCE AS AN ANALOGY WITH SPEECH

A piece of dance arises in ways that are similar to the development of language and speech. A baby's first vocalizations are the murmurs of vowels, such as "Ah...Oh...Ah-hum." Then the baby begins to put vowels and consonants together in simple words like "Mom...Yes...Apple." Gradually the toddler puts together simple sentences such as "I am hungry."

Instead of words, choreographers use human motion to form and develop dances. Just like spoken language, movement undergoes a gradual evolution: smaller units are combined into larger chunks of movement. Extended movement statements are built gradually, from elemental units into complex choreographic expression. The more thoughtful the expression is, the more powerful is the artistic impact.[2]

Similar to writers using grammar, choreographers are engaged in all dimensions of this expressive movement system. Often, a choreographer's goal is to compose a short single dance work, or a full-length evening dance performance. Other times, the creative challenge includes generating a new language of movement, upon which current and future works are based.

Just as writers use grammar, syntax, and punctuation in unique ways to develop their "voice," choreographers develop and refine an intuitive and/or intellectual understanding of movement to express their ideas. Measured words can be equated to thoughtful moves. Other times, accidental utterances, or "Freudian slips," also known as *parapraxis*, can be compared to unconscious and spontaneous movement revelations. Figure 2 details similarities between words and movement, as linguistic systems of expression.

DESCRIPTION	SPEECH	DANCE	DESCRIPTION
Vowels, consonants, and sounds used in alphabet	LETTERS	SHAPE	Appearance of motion in stillness
Single meaningful element of speech or writing	WORD	MOVEMENT	Act of changing a physical position and/or location
Set of words completing a statement or decision	SENTENCE	PHRASE	Elements together forming conceptual unit
Short piece of writing dealing with a single theme	PARAGRAPH	SECTION	Distinct part of something that can be divided or made up
Brief narrative of imaginary or real people and events	CHAPTER	PIECE	Conceptual unit assembled from individual parts
Narrative of book length with characters and actions	NOVEL	PERFORMANCE	Large work of staging and presenting dance
System of communication used by a particular community	LANGUAGE	MOVEMENT SYSTEM	Set of principles and procedures in an organized method

Figure 2

BODY IN STILLNESS
– SHAPE, POSE, FIGURE, AND IMAGE –

When a choreographer asks a dancer to adopt a still posture or to arrest their motion, this still shape or pose affects a viewer's perception of time, and it suspends motion. The human shapes in space allow viewers to grasp distinct lines, sense volumes of the bodies in space, and absorb energies at play. A non-moving body is still a dancing body because that dancer has a vital role within the dance. Still dance shapes and poses permit viewers to perceive movement as action unfolding in time. After all, active movement only occurs as the body transitions from *one shape to the next* or shifts from *one step to another*.

A dance consists of multiple poses and shapes in motion, similar to the frames of film in sequence that create motion on the screen. *Serpentine Dance*, created by the pioneering dancer and choreographer Loïe Fuller, performed in an 1897 film by the Lumière Brothers, coincided with the birth of cinema and the ability to present still images in fast progression to create the appearance of motion. In the series of photographs in Figure 3, Fuller is depicted in motion, as a visual metamorphosis of elements from the natural world: a butterfly, a flower, and a tongue of flame.

Figure 3 Images © BFI National Archive, Loïe Fuller, FRA 1905, photography by anonymous. Photograph of the hand colored nitrate print by Olivia Kristina Stutz, ERC Advanced Grant *FilmColors*

Each moment of motion in a dance work might be an image worth isolating through stillness. Choreographers make artistic decisions about when to halt motion and pose the body in a particular shape, how long to hold the stillness, and how often to repeat the still shapes in variations. Shapes and poses can be symmetrical or asymmetrical, balanced or off-balance, curved or straight, angular or rounded, or combinations of these qualities. Angular shapes, for example, tend to produce emotionally sharp, inflexible, hard-edged, and rigid impressions. The characteristics a shape may possess and project such feelings as lyricism or tension, grace and strength, and softness and resilience. No less than movement, still shapes in action communicate experiences and attitudes of the body, as well as distinct choreographic ideas.

In choreography, of course *stillness* does not mean *stasis*. Although the dancing body may be at rest, it maintains a specific design, and its expressive potential remains as potent as that of a body in motion. Still shapes and poses continue to carry artistic momentum, physicality, and emotion.

THE POWER OF STILLNESS

We live and work in a world of constant motion. Lack of movement, especially in a dance, may seem unnatural and even shocking, causing some choreographers to neglect to consider the expressive power of still images. Stillness and motion are choreographic tools, and the lack of motion can be even more riveting than movement. Stillness can arrest attention where movement can dull the senses. Stillness encapsulates time, and motionlessness can elicit a sense of endlessness. Ironically, the lack of movement makes us seek movement. What happens before and after the moment of stillness? Some of the most captivating moments in a dance are when the choreography leads into and out of stillness.

Motionlessness changes the pace of life. Stillness makes us observe clearly. We begin to pay attention. We gain more time to think. Depending on how long and how frequently we look at still shapes, figures, and images, unique modes of perception may awaken in our minds. The artful interplay between motion and stillness in dance sharpens our attention to consider what is being moved or stopped, and how and why. The presence of stasis within the choreography of moving bodies can be explored and found useful in various ways.

FIRST LOOK: **INFORMATION**

Let's take a look at one of the finest examples in the ancient Greek tradition: the sculpture group of the Trojan priest Laocoön and his sons being attacked and fighting off a huge snake monster—Figure 4. This work is considered the archetypal icon of human agony in Western ancient art.[3]

> ◆ **Stillness invites an examination of the subtleties of motion.** The realistic depiction of the sculpted subjects' physical suffering is fascinating insofar as even this painful scene retains beauty and grace. As our observation continues, we grasp more details about the relationships between the bodies and the intensity of their straining muscles. Laocoön's sons look towards their father with fearful, horrified eyes. Laocoön, however, is already embroiled in his own struggle and reaches towards the sky, as if begging to understand the reason for his suffering.

We turn our attention to the tilted head and tormented face of Laocoön. The agonized shape of his eyes and mouth offers a visual depiction of pain and vulnerability. *Laocoön and His Sons* is an epic story of struggle, masterfully condensed into a single sculpted moment within an agonizing narrative. The insight for choreographers to take away from these mythical figures is that the artful moment of stillness can transport the viewer into an elaborate meditation on life and art. The longer we see, the more we see.

Figure 4 Photography © Livio Andronico, *Laocoön and His Sons*, also known as the *Laocoön Group*, a marble copy after a Hellenistic original from ca. 200 BC, found in the Baths of Trajan in 1506, courtesy of Wiki Commons, public domain

SECOND LOOK: **ELABORATION**

Even though the still images of Shen Wei Dance Arts dancers (Figure 5) do not give us many details about the rest of the dance, we receive plenty of information about the choreographer's overall artistic vision, and we can detect movement beneath and beyond the stillness. We can read "between the lines" of text and intuit content that is not explicit. In choreography, by observing stasis one can speculate about the nature of the content and where it may lead.

◆ **Stillness provides elaborate details about the potential of motion.** We may instantly interpret the genre, the mood, and the possible purpose of the dance. Depending on our background in dance, we may identify the name of the style of the movement and recognize the work's historic time period. We may form an opinion about the degree of artistic innovation in the work and determine what level of challenge the work presents to the performers.

Figure 5 Photography © Lois Greenfield, *RE-(III)* (2009), choreography by Shen Wei. Image left: pictured Brooke Broussard, Hunter Carter, Sara Procopio; image center: pictured Joan Wadopian, Hunter Carter, Jessica Harris, Sara Procopio, image right: pictured Sara Procopio; courtesy of Shen Wei Dance Arts, 2009

THIRD LOOK: **TRANSFORMATION**

There is a poignant moment of stillness in the First Act of the ballet *The Nutcracker*, when the young Clara falls asleep. As we take in the image of her resting motionless body, the scene around her begins to change: the room transforms as the furniture grows to immense proportions; creatures begin to populate the stage; and a battle is imminent. Clara's moments of stillness mark a powerful turning point in the story; she falls asleep in one reality and awakens to find herself alive within a different reality—a fantasy world.

◆ **Stillness is a dynamic catalyst for movement and change.** Clara's stillness as she sleeps is part of the plot—it contributes to the transformation of the plot and it alters the movement actions that follow. As Clara wakes up, change has occurred. Her surroundings now portray Clara differently, and she identifies herself differently too. The new reality forces her to adapt. She realizes that her sleeping has led to a transformation around her, for her, and in her. Clara's stillness is multifaceted: a focal point, a contrasting background, and an inviting foreground where movement and change occur. The dynamic shift in the environment causes a figure in stillness to become a figure in motion by transforming Clara into a catalyst figure who drives the narrative forward.

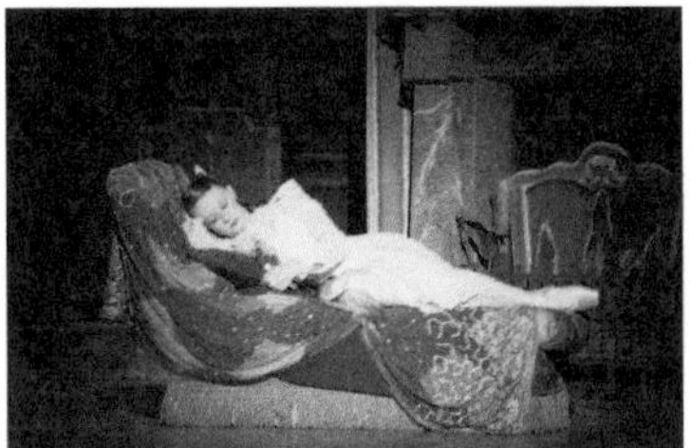

Figure 6 Photography © Theo Kossenas, *The Nutcracker*, choreography by Septime Webre, pictured performer Christianne Campbell in a production of the Washington Ballet, 2010

HOW DOES STILLNESS BECOME MOTION?

We turn now from the way the stillness in *The Nutcracker* ushers in a transformation within the ballet's storyline, and we consider the physical transformation that takes place as stillness becomes motion. From a physics perspective, Newton's first law of motion states that: an object at rest stays at rest, and an object in motion stays in motion with the same speed and in the same direction, unless acted upon by an unbalanced force. Balanced force occurs when two forces are of equal magnitude and moving in opposite directions, as they balance each other.[4]

Of course, Newton's law begins by examining the forces of *motion in objects*. There are complexities when it comes to *motion in living bodies*. For even when they seem to "hold still," the involuntary movements of the muscles continue, causing the heart to beat and the lungs to breathe. From a biomechanical perspective, still dance shapes are defined as the body's resistance to being accelerated and moved out of a present state of motionlessness. Still dance shapes continue to require muscular action and force to resist motion.

Movement occurs when the brain sends signals to the body. The body changes from a static mode to a dynamic mode, and from a stable state of equilibrium to an unstable state of equilibrium. For example, during running, the body is in a *continuous state of falling and recovering*, as the body changes its original location by being periodically displaced. Dancing bodies move along a continuum of equilibrium states, as bodies eventually change their positions and locations, by moving fast or slowly, suddenly or gradually.[5] As will be discussed later in this chapter, dance shapes and still poses may be understood and analyzed through the dimensions and conceptual lenses of ancestry, genre, originality, approach, initiation, range, type of vocabulary, and intention—just as movement can be.

BODY IN MOTION

– PHYSICAL LAWS AND METRICS OF MOVEMENT –

Creating dance involves physicalizing somatic intentions and ideas. We move because we want to or we feel the need to. Making dances enables us to imagine, express, and experience the world in motion through our bodies.

We might move before knowing why. A kinesthetic event of the dancing body might occur spontaneously and precede our mental determination and choreographic intentions. Therefore, a choreographer engages with *movement's physical laws and metrics* in parallel with the effort of creating a choreographic expression. Dance, as a kinesthetic architecture of the human body, unfolds in **SPACE**, **TIME**, AND **ENERGY**.

◆ **SPACE** is where movement occurs dimensionally and where we observe it and perceive it. Three metrics determine and identify the consistency of *static space*: *height*, *depth*, and *width*. All static or kinetic objects with *dimensional access* occupying space relate architecturally to those metrics.

Choreography is kinesthetic art related to space, and dancers are *dynamic space occupants*. At any given time, the dancers' movement can change the volume and consistency of the metrics of a static space. Choreographers and the dancers' bodies generate *dynamic spatial tension and attention* by *interacting with space* in three distinct ways:

➢ ***Positive and negative space:*** Parts of the body may create positive and negative space in relation to each other. *Positive space* is the space occupied by a body part itself. *Negative space* is empty of any detectable physical thing. For example, stand up and put a hand on your hip with the elbow bent out and away from the torso. The triangle between your torso and the inside of your arm is *negative space*; we can see right through it because there is nothing in it. The lack of occupied space is still viewed as use of space.

➢ ***Framed space:*** A proscenium stage is a predetermined and bounded area in which a theatrical performance occurs. The viewers are usually located on one side—"the front"—and they look into the framed area, as if looking through a big window to watch "the performance" on the stage. The positive and negative spaces created by moving bodies on stage become *spaces within* the *framed space* of the stage.

There are areas designated by theatrical conventions of the stage. There are also dynamic spots and intriguing places within this frame that we perceive in relation to it. A body may move upstage (away from the audience), or downstage (closer to the audience), or stage left (to the right of the performer who faces front), or toward stage right (to the performer's left). The body may also locate itself close to the floor, a *low space*; it can orient itself by leaps and jumps, toward the *high space* above the head, and either centrally or peripherally. The relations and combinations of the stage space and body space can generate a variety of perceptions and contrasting choreographic outcomes.

➢ ***Relational complexity in space:*** The *framed space* of a performance may be occupied by multiple bodies, along with stage sets, props, and the effects created by lighting design. The spaces between and among bodies, and the objects with which they may interact, can expand, shrink, open up, or clutter the perceived focus of the performance. For example, bodies may huddle or be pressed together to create such *intimate space* that it is impossible to see where one body ends and another begins. Or, one or more bodies may be placed at a *distance* from other bodies to create a sense of isolation.

Different groupings of bodies may exist and interact to create images of static and dynamic patterns of motion in space. Bodies may lift, carry, climb on, or go beneath such objects as furniture or other props, or create complex shapes and spatial arrangements among them. The transitions between such interactions might also create a new sense of space.

In summary, by placing bodies in various changing formations, choreographers kinetically create a *dynamic space* of *relational complexity* that could contain *positive* or *negative space* or be within and against predetermined areas of a *framed space.*

◈ TIME: Movements in space exist in time. Movements arise, progress, evolve, and conclude in time. Three basic questions orient an analysis and understanding of movement in time metrics, such as *interval*, *duration*, and *speed*:

➢ *When?*—The starting point of a given period determines the beginning of an interval in time. Time—past, present and future—is a continuing astronomical event, experienced in constant intervals, commonly marked by the clock and the calendar.

➢ *How long?*—The duration of a movement may be determined by how long it ordinarily takes to execute it. Or a choreographer may purposely choose to extend or reduce the ordinary duration to generate intrigue with distortion. For example, a walk across a given space that in a "real world" context might take 8 seconds, might be stretched out to take 8 minutes, or sped up to 3 seconds. Other movements carry a consistent duration that is less easy to modify. For example, a jump usually takes a second or less to accomplish because gravity exerts a downward force on the upward trajectory of the jump.

➢ *How fast or slow?*—The speed is the pace of the movement. The speed of movement might create particular perceptions and emotional responses. Most often, a happy dance is a fast dance, while themes of sadness and melancholy might take the choreography to a slow pace. Funny gestures tend to be quick and energetic, while formality traditionally carries more weight, and is therefore lingering.

The speed of movement is measured by the *beat*, a pulse that provides a particular tempo to the movement. A series of beats creates a *rhythm* that might be *regular* if the interval between individual beats or groups of beats is the same each time, or *irregular* if there are different intervals of time between beats. The organization of beats into rhythms can create a sense of speed that remains *steady* or it can create *momentum* by accelerating or slowing down the tempo. For more on beat, rhythm, and tempo, see Chapter 20.

◆ **ENERGY** provides the power needed to initiate, sustain, and stop movement. A dancer holding a still posture is similar to a marble sculpture—an object that does little else than occupy space as time passes. The presence of energy emerging from internal and external forces allows the body to kinetically reconfigure its position and attitude. Gravity, on the other hand, is an ever-present external physical force that we can comply with or resist. The metrics of energy are *power capacity*, *intensity*, and *distribution*. We can interpret these metrics in the following factors that initiate and sustain body movement:

➢ **Gathering the force** and energy to initiate movement to surrender or overcome gravity; dancers need to push against the floor to locomote in space and jump into the air.

➢ **Directing the force** and velocity of movement in particular directions, with the desired degree of intensity.

➢ **Distributing the force** of movement between and among parts of the body to create distinct qualities of movement, such as sharp, floating, herky-jerky, or fluid.

Energy is not just a stationary power source needed to get the work done; neither is it a physical force for a single purpose. Energy is dynamic and interactive. Energy is variable and transformative. Can we be powerful with very little energy?

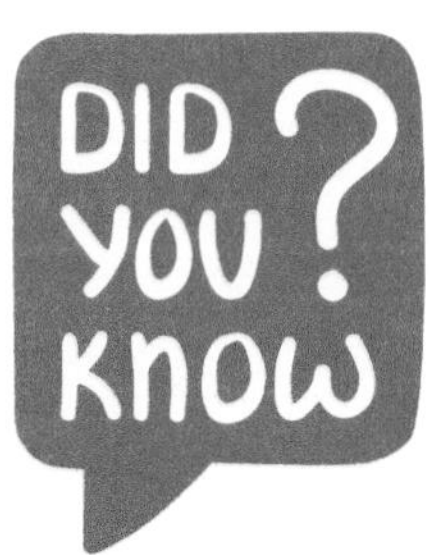

Tai Chi is a type of martial arts and defense technique. Its powerful movement energy has evolved over the years into a slow-motion sequence that is an effective means of alleviating stress and anxiety. The intense energy needed to fight the enemy has been replaced by a gentle inner force, sending the body into serenity and peace through a meditation in motion. The movement vocabulary of the martial art sequence and the meditative practice sequence are technically the same; however, the energy amount, intensity, and distribution are the opposite.

In summary, when employing movement within their individual artistic practices, choreographers continuously operate within the fundamental laws of physics and maneuver the metrics of movement in their own way.

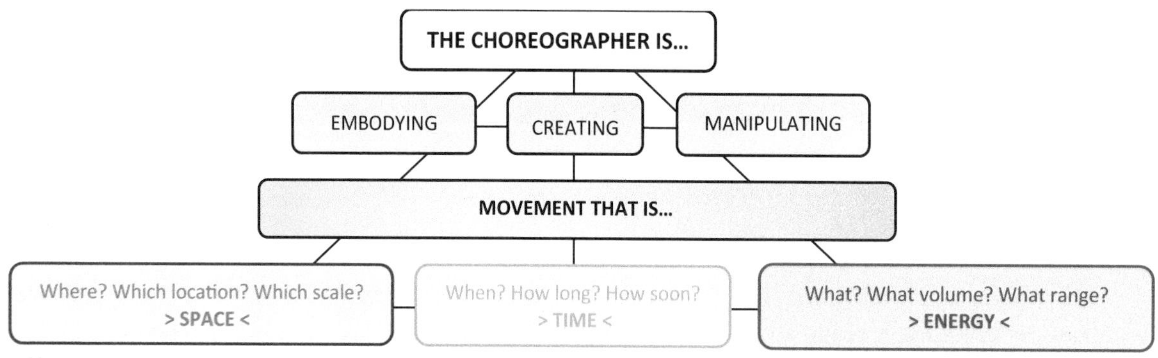

Figure 7

MOVEMENT DYNAMICS

Movement Dynamics is the umbrella term choreographers frequently use to describe a playful interaction between the physics of movement—**space**, time, and **energy**— and the variety of ways dance artists can manipulate and execute movement. *Movement Dynamics* add and change the *quality*, *texture*, and *nuance* of movement to enhance the idea, content, and mood of a dance. *Heavy*, *explosive*, or *forceful* could suggest the energy used. *Smooth*, *jagged*, or *freed* could describe the quality of the movement.

Endless combinations of movement and numerous evocative descriptors can express different dynamics and movement qualities. However, the same words describing movement qualities can be used in different contexts and might cause confusion in a terminology crossover. For example, the word *control* could be used in terms of movement quality—as controlled energy; or in terms of tempo—as controlled speed; or as spacing—as a controlled area. Therefore, when choreographers use descriptive prompts to suggest *movement dynamics* to the dancers, they must consider adding context and metaphors. For example, the prompt "You need to be *gliding* like an ice-skater," or "You need to be an eagle *gliding* in the sky" would bring distinct nuances of groundlessness into the dancers' interpretation of *gliding*.

Movement could be manipulated by a single prompt expressed with *adjectives* or with a combination of variable dynamics that might overlap, interact, or contrast each other.

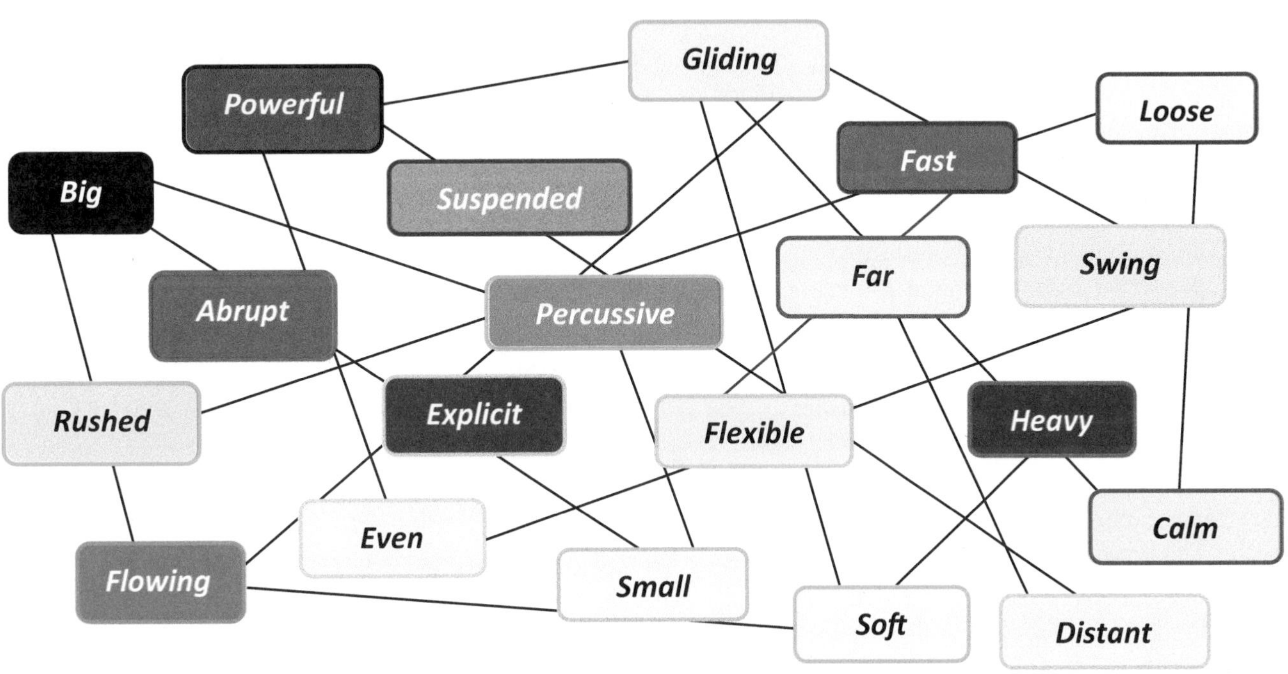

Figure 8

Operating within the physics of movement and manipulating movement dynamics and qualities are the mere *basics of choreographic craft*. We move now to dimensions that are more complex and examine conceptual lenses of the body in motion such as ancestry, genre, originality, approach, ownership, initiation and range, type of vocabulary, intention and meaning.

MOVEMENT ANCESTRY, DANCE HISTORIES, AND GENRES

– WHERE DID DANCE MOVEMENTS COME FROM? –

"I have no idea what the next movement will be...I am stuck," complains a choreographer to the dancers in the studio. The creative flow has suddenly stopped, and ideas no longer come with ease. Artists often experience moments of feeling stuck or puzzled. There is pressure to continue choreographing, and yet nowhere to take the work.

A creative impasse is never caused by a shortage of movement, for it is impossible to *run out of movements*. The human body contains an anatomical variety of over 230 movable and semi-movable joints,[6] the engagements of which can generate virtually endless movement arrangements. Yet many choreographers struggle to create original movements and hesitate to borrow and modify movement from a vast reservoir of sources at their disposal.

In their search for the right movements for dance, choreographers would do well to keep in mind that there is an abundant movement and dance ancestry available to study and use. A vast dance genealogy traces the roots of global historic, vernacular, folkloric, geo-political, socio-economic, and cultural traditions. Many dance traditions emerged during the distant past and continue to evolve today alongside newly emerging styles, forms, approaches, and systems of movement.

In addition, for consideration are established dance genres that emerged in different time periods, including our own. For example, to name only a few, Indian classical dance may be traced back 2500 years.[7] Ballet emerged around 400 years ago, Modern Dance, around 120 years ago,[8] while Hip-Hop dance, tied to the music genre by the same name, is only about 50 years old, even as its origins in Africanist cultural traditions date back far longer.[9] Movement styles, genres, and traditions including Flamenco, Chinese Dance, and Irish Step may be considered individually or merged to create fusions and new movement languages.

Based on its origins, each dance genre has distinct vocabulary that remains stable, even as it may also evolve with each new generation. A genre might also be divided into sub-genres. For example, Postmodern Dance is a sub-genre of Modern Dance, while Neoclassical ballet is sub-genre of Classical ballet, and Afro-Modern is a fusion of modern dance and dances of the African Diaspora. In addition to the social and concert dance forms, which actually represent only a small fraction of the totality of human movement, all physical activities may be used as a movement resource for dance making.

MOVEMENT FORMS → Physical Activities, Sports, Fitness, Yoga, etc.
↳ DANCE FORMS → Historic, Social, Vernacular, Concert Dance, etc.
↳ DANCE GENRES → Ballet, Modern Dance, Jazz, Hip-Hop, etc.
↳ DANCE SUB-GENRES → Neoclassical Ballet, Postmodern Dance, etc.
↳ INDIVIDUAL DANCE AESTHETICS → Contact Improvisation, Gaga Technique, etc.

Figure 9

MOVEMENT ORIGINALITY

– MOVEMENT AS OBJECT AND SUBJECT, CONVENTIONAL AND UNIQUE –

Most choreographers gain stage experience first as performers. Prior to becoming dancers at any level of the profession, we were children dancing freely in our homes, on the street, and at social events. Our naïve urgency to dance was perhaps soon replaced or influenced by formal dance training to prepare us for a performing career. As young dancers, we have listened to a perhaps intimidating dance teacher and obediently reproduced the movements demonstrated as "the correct way" to dance. Later, as choreographers, we approach and create movement material that falls within the following three categories:

- **PRE-EXISTING AND CONVENTIONAL MOVEMENT:** WE LEARN, REPRODUCE, AND BORROW MOVEMENTS CREATED BY OTHERS. When we first enter into dance as a field, we might readily accept movements into our bodies that some teachers and choreographers call the *fundamentals of dance techniques*. Later, in making our own dances, it is likely that we *borrow* this inherited movement vocabulary *fed* to us in our past. In a manner of speaking, we begin our choreographic journey *on credit*. At this early point in our choreographic careers, it would be fair to say that we regard *movement as an object*, in the sense that movement is a "thing" given to us by others, that is now ours to further implant in the bodies of the performers in our dances.

- **INTERPRETED AND MODIFIED MOVEMENT:** WE REVISE AND TRANSFORM EXISTING MOVEMENTS TO FIT OUR INDIVIDUAL CREATIVE NEEDS. In hindsight, we might soon realize that the movements learned during basic dance training may not be suitable to effectively express unique choreographic ideas and artistic identities. Arguably, inherited movement was never intended to express unique ideas and identities; it was meant to enable us to express someone else's unique ideas and identities, or the values of a training system. To truly serve our *subjective creative purposes*, we must modify, or even abandon completely, inherited movements and conditioned values.

Modifying or abandoning inherited movement to serve the purpose of movement invention poses a double challenge. First, we must summon the courage to push against the boundaries of conformity. Second, we must develop an approach to reconfiguring, manipulating, and personalizing conventional movement vocabulary, and/or generating fresh movement ideas that lean as little as possible on conventions drawn from the past.

- **AUTHENTIC AND UNIQUE MOVEMENT:** WE CREATE ORIGINAL MOVEMENT MATERIAL INTUITIVELY AND/OR INTELLECTUALLY. Once we marshal the courage to set aside old habits, tactically forgetting the so-called "rules and tools" of movement passed down by former teachers and choreographers, movement invention guided by intuition, may begin by inviting inner impulses to create motion in and with the body. We move and create by following the interests of the body, transcending movement habits and concerns about expected appearances. Our physical sensibility discovers and investigates paths of movement that are *unique* and *our own*. Movement has become a *subject*.

MOVEMENT OWNERSHIP

– GIVING, TAKING, AND RECEIVING MOVEMENT –

Once movement material—conventional, modified, or original—emerges within/from the body, options arise if the intent is to transfer the movement to the body of someone who did not participate in its creation. The movement, considered complete, is ready to be "set" on the other's body through a traditional *training & setting approach* as the teacher or choreographer "speaks" in movement, and the dancer listens, memorizes, and speaks back through the body as accurately as possible. Movement ownership is restricted.

In this approach, the dancer may be conceived strictly *as a body* whose purpose is to serve *as a vessel* carrying choreographic imagery created by another. The choreographer teaches specific pre-created material, and then trains the dancer to perform it in an automated manner deemed by the choreographer to be correct. The movement is *copied* and *pasted*, so to speak, from the choreographer's body to the dancer's body. Dancers might strive to fit their body into the mold of the choreographer's movements, sometimes to the point of suppressing their natural movement inclinations.

Alternatively, movement may be offered to another body as a starting point for continued exploration, discovery, and modification, based on a *collaborative & intuitive processing approach* used by the choreographer in generating the material in the first place. Distinct conceptualizations of the dance drive the choreographer's approach in creating material that others will ultimately inhabit and perform. Movement ownership is shared.

In this approach, the choreographer might grant the dancer a greater degree of *agency* and *autonomy* than using the body as a vessel. The choreographer may prompt the dancer with improvisational tasks to adjust, re-order, and manipulate the movement material, taking the dancer's intellectual and embodied somatic perspectives into consideration. Here the notion of *dancer as vessel*—mute and waiting to be filled—is replaced by a notion of *dancer as collaborator*, or as an active participant who shares in the creation.

For instance, imagine a female ballet dancer who is given the task to replicate a specific sleeping dance pose while performing as the character of Aurora from a ballet production version of *Sleeping Beauty*. In this case and in terms of ownership, the pose given to the dancer to execute has nothing do with the individual dancer as a person but with the stage character she has been tasked to portray. In comparison, imagine that a female modern dancer is given a prompt by a choreographer to fall asleep on the floor in a movement manner that she would naturally fall sleep. In this case, the modern dancer might appear not only as a body that is sleeping, but also *as that particular person* who is sleeping in a way specific to the unique identity of that individual. The ballet dancer's body will function *as a vessel* holding a *given stylized pose*, while the modern dancer will appear as the *actual person* representing herself. The latter is a collaborative approach resulting in a choreographer/performer co-ownership.

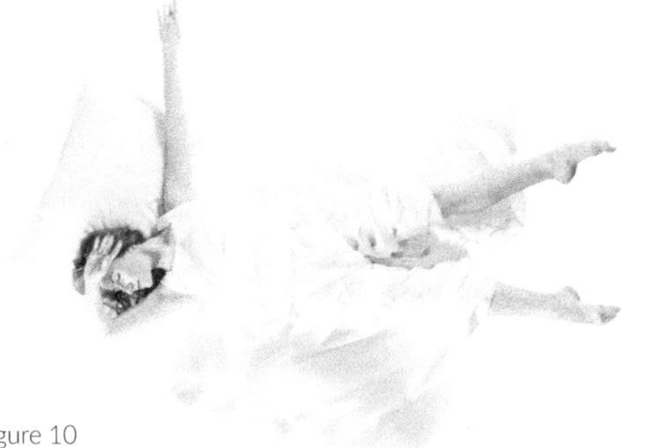

Sleeping Beauty
or
Sleeping Beauty

Figure 10

MOVEMENT INITIATION AND ORIGINATION

– GENERATING, MANIPULATING, AND DEFINING MOVEMENT MATERIAL –

Choreographers use dance improvisation—purposely or unintentionally—as a creative instrument for generating movement and to search for, experiment with, manipulate, and define movement material. Various improvisational techniques by distinguished improvisational choreographers are covered in Chapter 15. Ongoing complexities might occur during improvisation. A list of a few questions, grouped in three modes of operations, offers a starting point for choreographers to engage in non-linear maneuvering throughout these processes. ***Generate*** aims to produce movement, while ***Manipulate*** explores possible renderings and variations. ***Define*** is a choice-making and analytical process that might lead to "set" choreography and stylized movement directed towards a specific aesthetic outcome.

GENERATE

a) What movement could emerge from free and spontaneous movement flow, assigned tasks, or movement scores?

b) What movement could emerge from visual or auditory sources such as observing, enacting, and embodying imagery, as well as listening to music, sound, and speech?

c) What movement could emerge as a response to specific life situations and personal experiences?

MANIPULATE

Spatially: a) What part of the body and what part of the movements are visible? b) How do the movements expand and develop in height, width, and depth? c) Where in space could the movement take place?

Timing: a) What is astronomical time length? b) What is the duration of movement in consideration of the dramatic effect? c) What are appropriate changes in intensity, speed, beat, rhythm, and tempo, and how do those elements contribute to and affect the movement material?

Energy: a) What is the nuance and intensity of the movement? b) How much pressure and force are necessary for the movement to be executed? c) What are the volume, size, and range of the movements in the phrase?

DEFINE

Biomechanically: a) What is the breakdown of the external objective motor activity? b) Which skeletal and muscle groups are engaged, and how? c) How is movement performed accurately and safely?

Kinesthetically: a) What are the instructions for the kinesthetic use of spacing, timing, and intensity? b) What are the ongoing directions to fit accurate body placement? c) How could the dancer's body best adapt creatively to the movement material?

Intentionality: a) How did the movement originate as stimuli and initiation? b) What is the history of the movement as a specific situation, imagery, feeling, or personal experience? c) How is this meaning communicated to the dancers?

Figure 11

MOVEMENT SIZE AND RANGE OF MOTION
– WHAT ARE MICRO-, MEDIUM-, AND META-MOVEMENTS? –

Each movement can be performed with varying degrees of complexity based on the choreographer's intentions and the dancers' abilities. Known in kinesiology as *range of motion*, the *size of movement* in choreographic terms encompasses: a) anatomical engagement of specific or all parts of the body and the muscle groups; b) kinesthetic modes of stability and mobility; and c) biomechanical complexity of the movement execution, also applicable and known as *movement coordination* and *dance technique*. The diagram below, which depicts a ball being thrown, visualizes a range of movement sizes, speed, and qualities.

EXPERIENCE	COMPLEXITY	MOVEMENT RANGE AFFECTING BALL'S DISTANCE AND SPEED
NOVICE	Body remains stationary. Weight is equally distributed between the legs. The torso does not move.	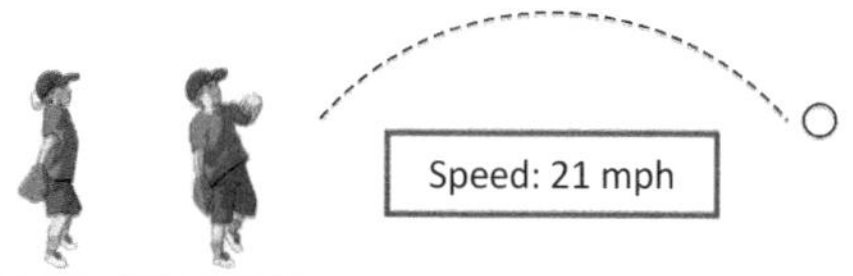 Speed: 21 mph
JUNIOR	Body weight is divided between both feet. Both hands move. The torso shifts to support the acceleration of the hand movements.	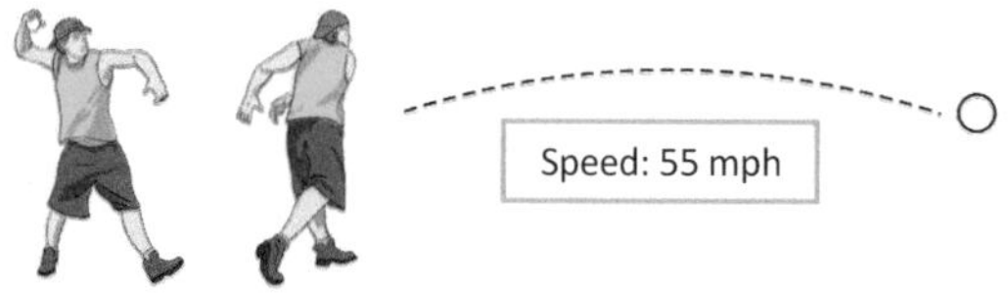 Speed: 55 mph
PRO	Body weight shifts from one leg to the other leg. There is a full rotation of the torso, coordinated with simultaneously moving limbs aiming to gain *momentum* and reach maximum *acceleration*.	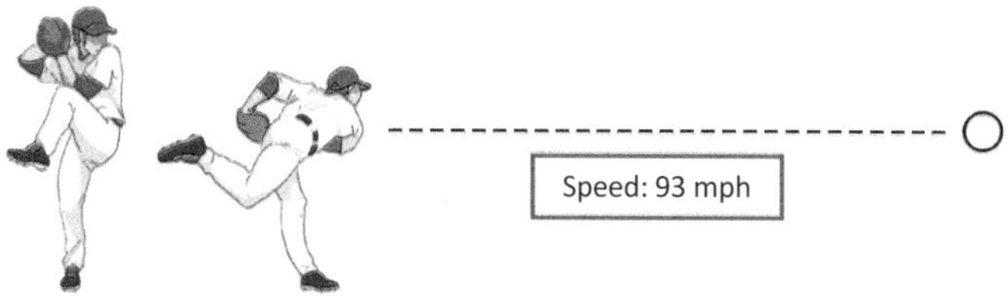 Speed: 93 mph

Figure 12 Illustration © Archer Forsyth

We can creatively classify these ranges and adopt new terminology to name them:

➢ ***Micro-movement*** is a small motion or a series of movements contained within a movement. For example, the single motion of throwing the ball contains a few micro-movements in a short sequence, such as grab, twist, flex, swing, and toss. See our **Novice** in the diagram above.

➢ ***Medium-movement*** is the common way to execute movement. For example, our **Junior** in the diagram above, will automatically execute medium-movements, engaging more muscle groups than necessary to accomplish the goal.

➢ ***Meta-movement***, as per the Greek translation of the word *Meta* meaning "above" and "beyond," is when the movement engages the full and often extreme capacity of the body. The **Professional** in the diagram above, uses extreme mobility, advanced movement techniques, and motion complexity that contains over one hundred micro-movements. Like athletes, dancers enjoy physical challenges. Bringing attention to the vast continuum of movement increases choreographers' movement awareness and makes them both efficient and effective as artists.

MOVEMENT VOCABULARY
– ORGANIZING THE CHOREOGRAPHER'S DRAWER –

There must be millions of movements available for choreographers to use! Is there a system to organize the vastness of dance material? In music, there is a *scale* of only seven basic notes (Do, Re, Mi, Fa, Sol, La, Ti), which can create an endless number of melodies. When it comes to dance—how can we conceptualize a *scale for movement vocabulary*?

Similar to musical notes that can be played together, different movement and dance vocabularies can be used in parallel or combined and layered. For example, a *jump* can also incorporate a *turn* in the air. *Limb movements* can also be accompanied by a few *steps*. Stomping could be *travel/locomotive* and occur with *gestures* of the hands. Rolling can be a *floor movement* with *turning* and *traveling*. And some choreographers might be inclined to use only limited vocabulary, for example, gestures.

Millions of movements could easily be sorted out by introducing a *scale* of only *seven movement categories* across all dance genres. Another helpful analogy: These movement categories are similar to a clothing drawer used to sort and store garments—underwear, pants, and shirts that correspond to *types of movement vocabulary*. Choreographers might use vocabulary just like fashion designers to costume themselves or the dancers.

STEPS–walking, tapping, stomping, any feet motion with full feet, top of the foot, toes or heels, and any transferring of body weight via the feet, etc.

LIMBS & TORSO MOVEMENTS–using hands, legs, torso, chest, back, neck, and head to reach a position, stretching, swinging, extending, touching, grabbing, lifting, catching, rotating, twisting, etc.

TURNS–rotating and changing positioning from facing front by pivoting, spinning, twisting, rotating, revolving, whirling, pirouettes, fouettés, etc.

JUMPS–leaping from the ground into the air by traveling from one foot to another, from two feet to two feet, from two feet into one foot, from one foot to other, or the same foot, etc.

FLOOR MOVEMENTS–using gravity and limbs-torso-floor contact to execute falling, rising, gliding, floating, rolling, pushing, pressing, rocking, slipping, tossing, relaxing, inversions, etc.

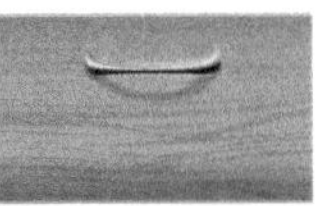

TRAVELING & LOCOMOTIVE MOVEMENTS–using walking, skipping, jogging, running, sprinting, hopping, bouncing, jumping, gliding, skating, etc.

GESTURES & MIME–pedestrian and literal, casual and formal body gesticulations, pantomime, sign language, body emotion, body language, nodding, body signaling, waving, etc.

Figure 13

DOES MOVEMENT AND DANCE HAVE [TO HAVE] MEANING?

"What were you thinking!?"—We might ask this question when we are distressed by a loved one's actions and when we do not understand the reasons for their behavior.

Here is an example that we can call "The Way of Walking Away." At a train station, a woman says goodbye to a man right before she departs. As she walks away to board the train, she turns and looks at the man. Perhaps to him, her last look means that she has affection for him and she does not want to leave. Yet perhaps she has decided long before she walks away that that she will never return, and therefore, she takes a last glance at him before leaving forever. These are two legitimate, yet opposite, views of the same situation. Which story is accurate? What were they thinking!?

It is human nature to seek an explanation and assign meaning to what we see and experience. We tend to justify the behaviors of others and might voluntarily create a fictitious narrative to understand or speculate about someone's intentions. We might even convince ourselves to accept and live with that narrative, despite the fact that *our narrative* might not hold the *true meaning.*

Why? Because we tend to believe that if a *thing* or a *happening* engages and affects us, then it could not be *unintended* or *accidental.* We relentlessly seek answers to *What?* and *Why?* and strive to decode intentions, uncover motives, and understand reasoning. Our questions to "The Way of Walking Away" example would be "What is happening between them? What is the relational narrative? What does the walking away mean?"

Does movement have (to have) a meaning? It might, or it might not. As a starter, it depends on whether the movement actions are intentional or unintentional. Perhaps the most important considerations and challenges for concert dance choreographers are: Must movement have intention and purpose, and to what extent does movement capture, express, and communicate meaning, if any?

In many movement practices—yoga, body-mind awareness, and dance improvisation—movement has purpose and intention: it is done for a reason. Yet, the reason is not to convey a specific message that others will understand beyond, or in addition to, their understanding of the *movement itself*, i.e., bend, twist, and reach. In such instances, movement practitioners do not have the pressure to deliver any artistic statements. Movers arch backwards to reap the bodily benefits of bending, not necessarily to show or convey something for others to interpret. In such instances, there is an intention and purpose for each movement, but no meaning.

In dance, some choreographers want their movements to *convey* to audiences something other than the movements themselves; they imagine a linguistic analog for the movements in their dances. Choreographers might even intentionally seek a one-to-one correspondence between *movement* and *meaning*, which can be interpreted and described in words. For example, a raised fist *means* anger, holding one's head in one's hands *means* sadness, and so forth. Some choreographers and viewers refer to this approach as *literal* meaning.

Choreographers working in this way believe that their dances will, or should, mean whatever they envision, regardless of the creative and intellectual *sense-making* activities of diverse viewers in the audience. The latter may not care what the *choreographer means* because their own meanings are satisfying. The viewers might generate their own meaning just as much, if not more, than the choreographer might. Meaning might not be at all fixed such that it is assigned to specific actions, nor is meaning limited to what the choreographers think, wish, or convey it to be. In such instances, there is an imposed meaning that might not mean much.

Interestingly enough, movement *communicates* intentions and purpose, no matter if there are identifiable reasons and a meaning to interpret. We understand kinesthetically what is behind a stretch in Yoga, yet we might need to engage more deeply if we attempt to interpret a plotless contemporary dance. Coding and decoding of meaning in movement might trigger multiple interpretations, all of which are subjective. In fact, meaning not only *can* be viewed subjectively, it can *only* be viewed subjectively: there are no meanings that exist independently of a subject/person. Meanings are social constructs, not natural artifacts.

In daily life, certain events may provoke specific feelings that trigger and initiate a reason, leading to subsequent actions. In dance, however, the process might be the opposite. Often choreographers create movements with determination and purpose, but initially these movements might not carry a meaning or a reason. Then choreographers decide if meaning should be added or intended, and if so, whether it will be explicit and to what extent it will be communicated.

To help navigate these complexities, three involved entities, which create, communicate, and encounter a dance work, need to be recognized. These are the choreographer, the performers, and the viewers. Also, let's distinguish three separate modes of functioning: **intent/purpose**, **reason/meaning**, and **interpretation/sense making**, and the interaction between them. Will the intentions and the artistic message of the choreographer be truthful, then communicated to the performers, and *correctly* interpreted and understood by the viewers? Is there ever *one correct way* to interpret a dance? Could a message-miscommunication lead to an interpretation-misunderstanding?

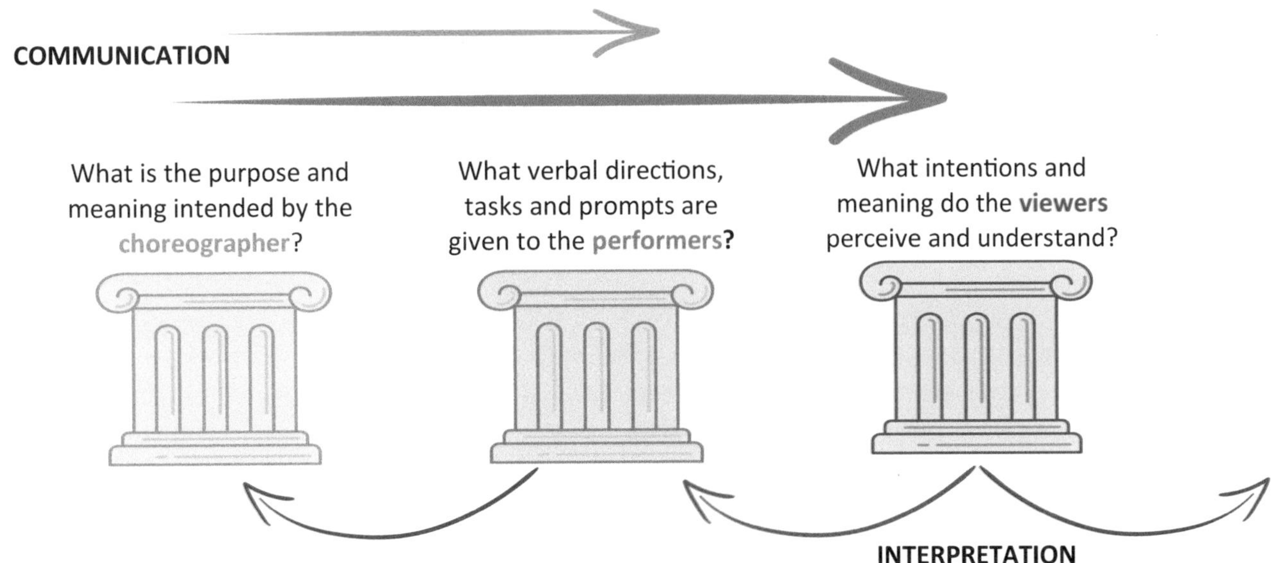

Figure 14

In conclusion, creating unique movement and engaging in the processes of choreographing an original dance share common intentions—the urge to explore, authentically capture, and thoughtfully communicate imperative ideas through the moving human body.

Whether searching for a *true* movement or a *pure* movement, choreographers ultimately strive to find their *own* movement. Whether a movement has been captured in action or in stillness, a movement has the potential to transmit powerful ideas which at first might not be intellectually comprehensible; however, they could be intuitively felt. For instance, the photographs in Figure 15 capture dance imagery that unites movement and meaning, momentum and motion, while depicting dancing bodies in stillness.

Figure 15 Left: photography © Arnold Genthe, pictured choreographer and performer Isadora Duncan, image taken in the early 20th century, public domain; center: photography © Adolf de Meyer, *The Afternoon of a Faun* (1912), pictured choreographer and performer Vaslav Nijinsky, 1912, public domain; right: photography © Jack Mitchell, *Cry* (1971) choreography by Alvin Ailey, pictured performer Judith Jamison, courtesy of Alvin Ailey Dance Foundation, Inc. and Smithsonian Institution, 1971

The ultimate act of choreography goes beyond the basic skill of coming up with conventional steps and moves and putting them together into a sequence; it is about creating, crafting, and expressing movement ideas. *Movement ideas* are comprised of movement with purpose, intention, and meaningful objectives that capture the choreographer's unique perspective, creative individuality, and artistic identity. Only then will movement ideas "speak loudly" without using a single word.

HELPFUL TIPS & SUGGESTIONS

~ Approach movement in the present moment—there is no past or future as you dance
~ Think of movements as people, each with a different personality
~ Seek movement that is yours rather than any movement
~ Share movement—what belongs to you, belongs to all
~ Strive to create movement that moves others
~ Look for meaning beyond words
~ Dance life and let life dance you

"SPECTRAL ANALYSIS" OF A MOVEMENT
– HERE COMES THE SUN –

In summary, we conclude that a single movement has multiple dimensions, conceptual lenses, and classifications. The process of distinguishing and defining movement characteristics helps a choreographer better understand, invent and work with movement.

?

Do you identify a movement as a simple or a complex entity?

In admiration for The Beatles' exceptional song *Here Comes the Sun*, let's make a comparison: movement is similar to the simplicity and the complexity of sunlight passing through a prism and separating into a spectrum of colors. Imagine sunlight and colors being physical experiences. Once we understand and become comfortable with the movement's visible light, we might wonder what movement's invisible light and the nature of its infrared and ultraviolet spectrum would be. Read more about it in the next chapters...

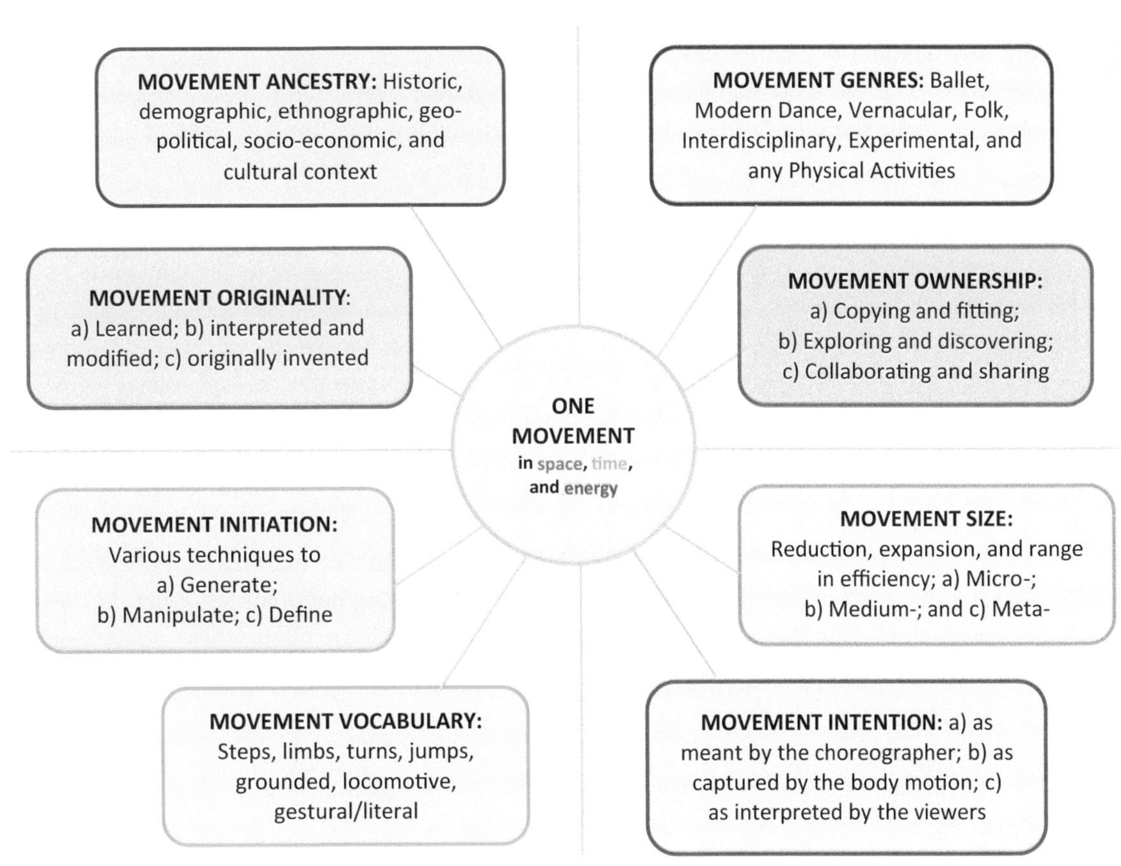

Figure 16

assignments & exercises

Modern dance choreographer Martha Graham once said: ***"Movement never lies."*** Her statement reveals that our mind and self are genuinely expressed through our subconscious body language and physical reactions. And yet no one would suggest that all dances are transparent in their purpose or that their interpretations are not highly variable. With a few exercises, we explore different facets of movement expression and how we send cues to others with our bodies' movements:

➡ **Body Language:** Become a movement detective and describe what you assume to be the purpose and meaning of different positions of human bodies in space, alone or in relation to each other. Reflect on ways in which cultural assumptions may play a role in your formation of meanings: 1) During stillness: sleeping posture, sitting posture, standing posture; 2) During movement: stepping while avoiding obstacles, wandering with confusion, 3) During circumstances: when admired, confronted, afraid, or in pain.

➡ **Movement and SPACE:** The practice of being, embracing, and transforming space: 1) Create a physical motion, abstract gesture, or movement phrase that demonstrates how different parts of your body relate to each other spatially; 2) Generate a movement that conveys how your body interacts with another body: 3) Generate a movement that communicates how your body reacts to and/or engages with an art installation, theatrical props, or static surroundings. What are the differences among these body responses to space?

➡ **Movement and TIME:** The practice of interval, duration, and speed of time: 1) Create a short movement sequence by dancing different sections of the phrase in very slow to very quick speed; 2) Explore the same movement sequence with sporadic "stop-and-go" intervals; 3) Explore the same movement sequence with a variety of rhythmic patterns such as an even pulse, uneven beats, or syncopation. How does this variation of time change the perception of the movement?

➡ **Movement and ENERGY:** The use of power, velocity, and dynamics of energy, or the deliberate absence of energy: Create a short movement phrase for a few dancers and then manipulate its movement quality by asking them to perform it: 1) as though their limbs are very heavy and suddenly become weightless; 2) very angular and then very round; 3) tiny and minimal and then huge, extending across the performance space. Consider how the choreographer and the dancer might decide on each moment of qualitative precision.

➡ **Movement Ancestry:** 1) Investigate and select movements that are similar in motion but originate in different historic time periods and put these movements together into a movement phrase. 2) Trace the development of movements as a historic progression based on cultures and national identity. 3) Locate and describe movement distinctions and similarities in different cultures and nationalities. What do the nuances say about the values of each of the cultures and the lives of people who embody these distinct movement vocabularies?

➥ **Movement Vocabulary:** 1) Select one movement (turn, kick, tilt, jump, slide, fall, etc.) from one genre of dance and explore the same motion within another genre. For example, compare a turn in ballet with a turn in modern dance. 2) Create a dance action or movement phrase that combines at least two or three types of movement. For example, a movement could be a jump and a turn at the same time. Explore movements from different movement categories by sampling choices from conventional dance vocabulary and more originally invented movement. Which movements are the most satisfying or memorable to you?

➥ **Movement Image and Movement [Literal] Meaning:** The goal of this exercise is to create original movement vocabulary stimulated by images, words, situations, and memories. The choreographer generates movement by expressing a personal feeling in movement. For example, "emptiness" might be expressed when one dancer uses the body of another dancer to "knock on the door without a response." As a choreographic choice, consider the differences among movement invention, conventional gesturing and pantomime, and the use of traditional steps or codified technical vocabularies.

A movement image could be symbolic rather than literal and descriptive. Yet it could also be self-explanatory and clear, carrying emotional depth. Select an image from Nature, for example, water. Create three versions of your own signature movement image in three distinguished modes – literal, semi-narrative, and highly abstract.

➥ **Movement Size and micro-movements within a medium movement:** Explore the limits of prompts, instructions, and commands with the following exercise in the form of a game between a performer and a choreographer: The performer is sitting in a chair. The choreographer's goal is to get the performer to stand up from the chair by giving only three simple commands, except the command to "stand up." Each command should include only one verb and name of the body parts engaged in the action. For example: "Bend your upper body forward" and "Press your feet against the floor." The choreographer shall use no more than three commands by addressing an action by a single body part. The performers should follow the commands precisely without adding any additional movements and with the intention to remain sitting on the chair.

The exercise demonstrates the limitations and challenges of the choreographer's verbal prompts. One movement might contain multiple micro-movements, without which it might not be possible to execute the movement. In summary, it is challenging for the performer to stand up straight from the chair with only three choreographic commands, because simply standing up straight (one movement) includes more than three micro-movements.

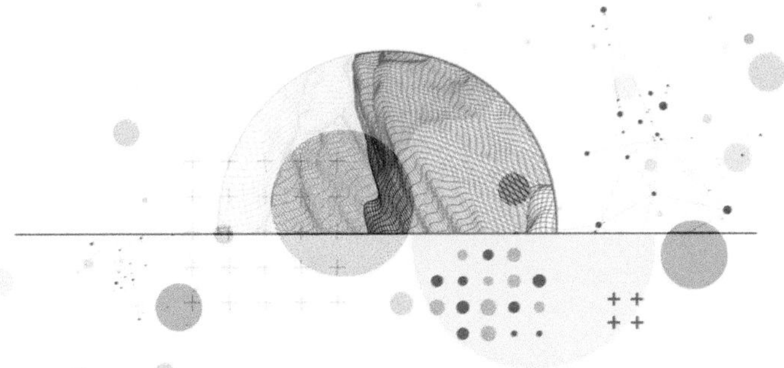

BIBLIOGRAPHY AND REFERENCES

[1] Blom, Lynne Anne and Chaplin, L. Tarin. *The Intimate Act of Choreography*, University of Pittsburg Press, 1982, pp. 31–82, 83, 90.
[2] Bannerman, Henrietta. "Is Dance a Language? Movement, Meaning and Communication," *Dance Research: The Journal of the Society for Dance Research*, vol. 32, no. 1 (SUMMER 2014), pp. 65–80.
[3] Lessing, Gotthold Ephraim. *Laocoön: An Essay on the Limits of Painting and Poetry*, The Johns Hopkins University Press, 1984.
[4] Physics Classroom, Newton's Fist Law of Motion, 1996–2019, online article and resource: www.physicsclassroom.com/, accessed November 2019.
[5] Kibele, Armin, Granacher, Urs, Muehlbauer; Thomas, Behm. David G. "Stable, Unstable and Metastable States of Equilibrium: Definitions and Applications to Human Movement," *Journal of Sport, Science, and Medicine*, December 2015, vol. 14, no. 4: 885–887. Published on November 24, 2015, accessed November 2019.
[6] Winston Medical Center. *Human Bones, Joints, and Muscles Facts*, online resource: www.winstonmedical.org/human-bones-joints-and-muscles-facts/, accessed November 2019.
[7] Venkataraman, Leela. *Indian Classical Dance: Tradition in Transition*, 1st edition, Roli Books, 2004.
[8] Anderson, Jack. *Ballet and Modern Dance: A Concise History*, Princeton Book Company, 1993.
[9] Rajakumar, Mohanalakshmi. *Hip Hop Dance*, Series: The American Dance Floor, Greenwood, 2012.

VISUAL REFERENCES

Figures 1 and 2: Diagrams © Vladimir Angelov

Figure 3: Images © BFI National Archive, Loïe Fuller, FRA 1905, photography by anonymous. Photograph of the hand colored nitrate print by Olivia Kristina Stutz, ERC Advanced Grant *FilmColors. Timeline of Historical Film Colors*: https://filmcolors.org/

Figure 4: Photography © Livio Andronico, *Laocoön and His Sons*, also known as the Laocoön Group, a marble copy after a Hellenistic original from ca. 200 BC, found in the Baths of Trajan in 1506, 2014, courtesy fo Wiki Commons, public domain

Figure 5: Photography © Lois Greenfield, *RE-(III)* (2009), choreography by Shen Wei. Image left: pictured Brooke Broussard, Hunter Carter, Sara Procopio; image center: pictured Joan Wadopian, Hunter Carter, Jessica Harris, Sara Procopio, image right: pictured Sara Procopio; courtesy of Shen Wei Dance Arts, 2009

Figure 6: Photography © Theo Kossenas, *The Nutcracker*, choreography by Septime Webre, pictured performer Christianne Campbell in a production of the Washington Ballet, 2010

Figures 7, 8, and 9: Diagrams © Vladimir Angelov

Figure 10: Left: Adobe Stock File # 94602973, *Ballet dancer rehearsing in her sleep dressed in white with white sheets, on white background. Expressive woman in action, dreaming concept. Dreaming of becoming professional dancer.* by alexandrum01. Right: Adobe Stock File: 135270210, *Model is sleeping on the floor and snuggling*, by demphoto

Figure 11: Diagrams © Vladimir Angelov

Figure 12: Illustration © Archer Forsyth, *Baseball players in various developmental phases*, 2020

Figure 13: Diagram © Vladimir Angelov, clipart: *Drawer front set*, credit: SM Web courtesy of Adobe Stock

Figure 14: Diagram © Vladimir Angelov, clipart: *Antique column vector line icon isolated on white background*, credit: Visual Generation

Figure 15: Left: photography © Arnold Genthe, pictured performer Isadora Duncan, image take in early 20th century, public domain; Center: photography © Adolf de Meyer, *The Afternoon of a Faun* (1912), choreography and pictured performer by Vaslav Nijinsky, 1912, public domain; Right: photography © Jack Mitchell, *Cry* (1971) choreography by Alvin Ailey, pictured performer Judith Jamison, courtesy of Alvin Ailey Dance Foundation, Inc. and Smithsonian Institution, 1971

Figure 16: Diagrams © Vladimir Angelov

CHAPTER 15

DANCE IMPROVISATION
– EMBRACING CHOREOGRAPHIC ADVENTURES –

Dance improvisation is a free, seemingly unstructured, less technically codified, instantaneous movement expression capable of evoking dramatic and thought-provoking content. Historically, improvisation is deeply rooted in rituals, ancient dance, and forms that accompanied them. Improvisation is both dance experimentation and movement research. It can be dance-based or connected to any or all movement forms. Improvisation, movement research, and exploration are the basic and fundamental instruments of choreography.

During the 1960s, Postmodern Dance in America redefined improvisation as *freeing* the body from habitual movement patterns. The emphasis was on instinctual, unpredictable, unrestricted movement flow and imagery. By avoiding conventional movement vocabulary, the post-modern dance improvisation and movement artists were interested in exploring deeper kinesthetic awareness and authentic ways of moving.[1]

◆ **Contemporary dance improvisation focuses on how movement is found rather than on what movement means or says.** Most improvisational artists are not concerned with conventional production elements, such as costumes, sets, props, and lighting design, although accompanying sound is often live and chosen with care. The human body is the sole instrument of dance improvisation, where creativity meets simplicity of production and complexity of expression. The goals are to search for new approaches to movement and to investigate instantaneous sequencing and patterns through space, time, and energy.

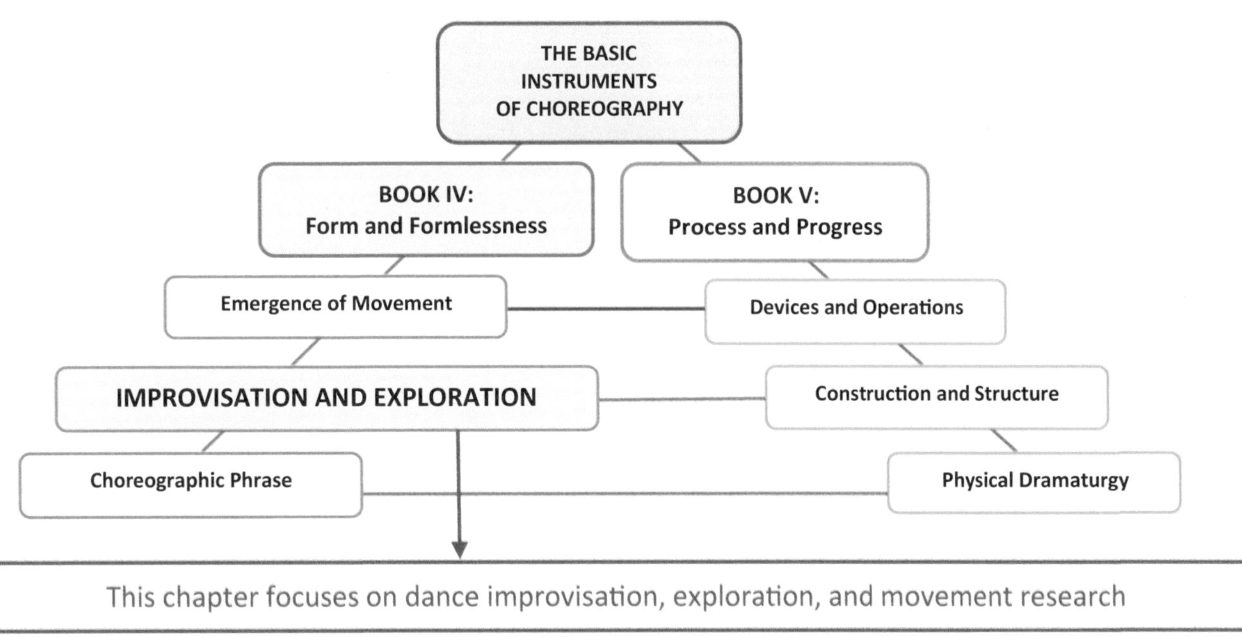

Figure 1

EMPHASIS ON PROCESS RATHER THAN OUTCOME

In March of 2016, The International Consortium for Advancement in Choreography—Dance ICONS, Inc. conducted a survey: *Is Improvisation Choreography?* One group of dance makers responded "Yes," because it involves the intentional creation of movement. Another group responded "No," because they interpreted choreography as a set arrangement of steps, movement, and patterns. A third group responded that improvisation is a tool to generate and experiment with movement in preparation for set choreography.[2] The survey proved that the questions about improvisation were also questions that relate to dance creation. Is choreography a process or an outcome? How much control and navigation of the outcome do we desire in favor of the unruly creative process? Are improvisation and set choreography friends or rivals?

Creating a dance by engaging in movement research might commence at different entry points and develop through a variety of stages, which may lead to set choreography—see the Figure 2. *Initiation/Task* is the first impulse that results in a feeling, idea, and approach to movement. Second, the creation of a dance progresses into an instinctive flow of playful *Experimentation* and then to Improvisation, where one movement leads to others. The improvisation *SCORE*, or thematic outline, helps frame the movement research into an *Exploration* within specific parameters based on a selected *Structure*. Finally, *Construction* solidifies the dance to become *Set Choreography*, which can be memorized, taught, preserved, and recreated. Improvisation can be an organic tool in the process of developing set choreography, leading to structured dance—*outcome driven*. Or improvisation as a creative practice-as-research could be an ongoing exploration of movement ideas—*process driven*.

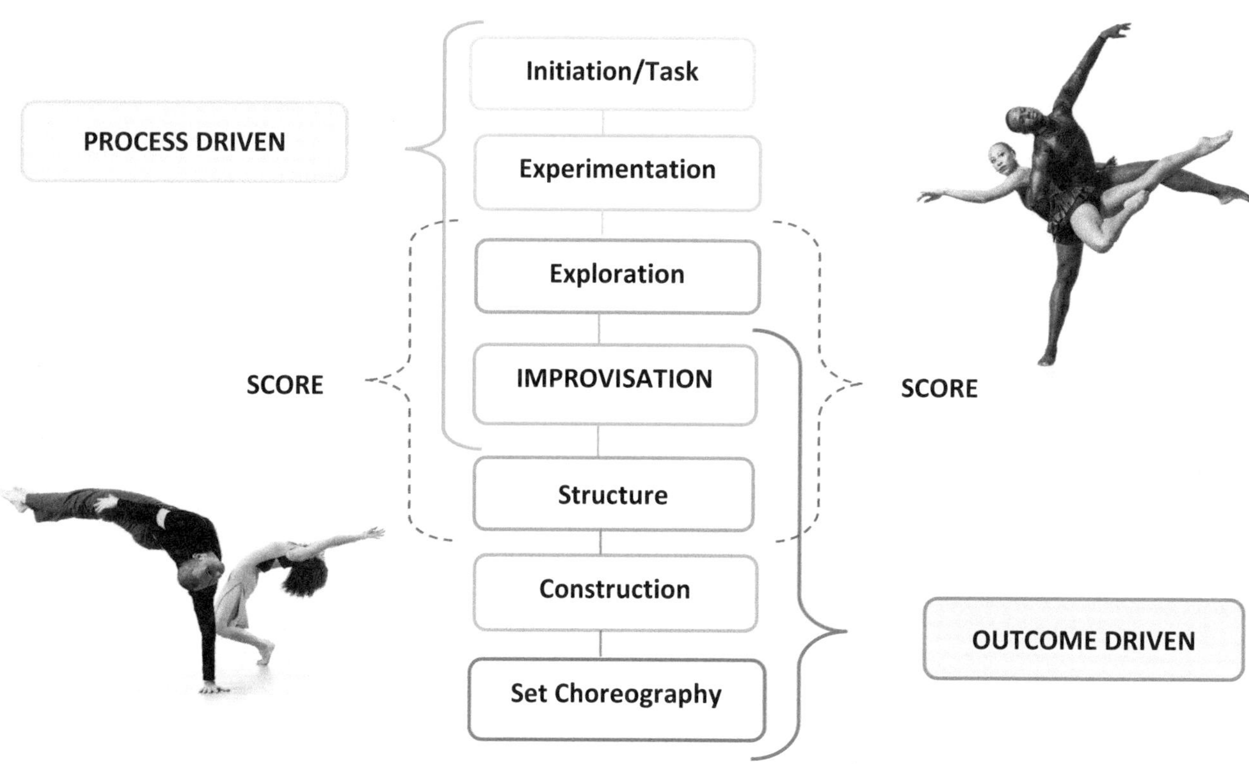

Figure 2 Photography © Lois Greenfield, image left pictured Karen De Luna, Victor Manuel Ruiz, courtesy of Aspen Santa Fe Ballet, 2004, image right: pictured Courtney Robinson, Tommie-Waheed Evans, courtesy of Philadanco, 2014

THE COMFORT OF FEELING UNSETTLED

Most of the time, people like to be in control of their surroundings and themselves, or at least able to anticipate what will happen. How comfortable do we feel, however, when we get lost along the route during the creative process, or in life in general? The reasons for feeling unsettled could be: a) we sense a blank mind and *nothingness*, and as a result we might feel the urge to initiate an orienting framework of clues and directions; b) the clues and directions may be challenging to follow, which leads to introducing a new set of *limitations*, and as a result, we might edit the directions to stretch the limitations; or c) we perceive an overwhelming number of options leading to uncontrollable *chaos*, and we might seek the *chance* to create order.

◆ **Dance improvisation is response-based.** We react to what we encounter in our environment and within our inner selves. Our sense of displacement and our *unsettled feeling* could be demystified by classifying three possible modes of improvisation:

EMERGING FROM NOTHINGNESS → **SPONTANEOUS IMPROVISATION**
Led by a blank mindset or an empty space

- There is no dance yet. What movements do we create for a dance to emerge?

EMERGING FROM LIMITATIONS → **GUIDED IMPROVISATION**
Led by specific structure, framework, and principle to aid movement search

- There are directions about movement making. How can we widen these directions?

EMERGING FROM DISORDER & RANDOMNESS → **CHANCE IMPROVISATION**
Led by offering unlimited capacity to organize movement findings

- There is an abundance of movements. How do we shape these movements into a dance and make sense of them?

Figure 3

By encountering these modes in a linear or non-linear progression, we might engage in processes such as: a) freely experimenting without the pressure to accomplish a specific look or purposeful outcome; b) proposing a framework and guiding principles for movement research and findings; and c) fostering a collaborative environment and open-mindedness. In summary, when we improvise, we explore ways to handle...

...**FREE FLOW** that we might decide to channel by introducing movement...

...**PRINCIPLES** serving as a stepping-stone to set forth a framework for ...

...**COLLABORATIONS** by integrating multiple viewpoints/artists leading to...

...**OPENNESS** as a non-restrictive decision-making process of movement research.

SPONTANEOUS IMPROVISATION AND THE BEAUTY OF NOTHINGNESS

– CHOOSING NOT TO CHOOSE –

Choreographers' lives are often stressful. Today's dynamic and complex world overwhelms our senses with new information and experiences. Our minds are set on default to sort out facts and solve problems within brief time increments.

An addiction to logical thinking and the use of recurring movement material contained in our memory often hinder our ability to escape and relax the over-worked mind. Often, we desire to concentrate and kinesthetically explore the world around us in spontaneous and intuitive ways.[3]

Developing improvisational skills is also about developing a certain mindset, where training might begin with *clearing the mind*, allowing a *blank mindset* to take over. It is challenging, however, to force our mind not to *think of anything!* How do we get to nothingness? A sense of nothingness has to do with relaxing, meditating, and letting go of unnecessary thoughts. We invite new ideas to occur via *inner awareness* and ***meditative improvisation***. There are various techniques suitable to dance practices that can help us clear our minds. The art of Zen and its principles can help clear the mind.

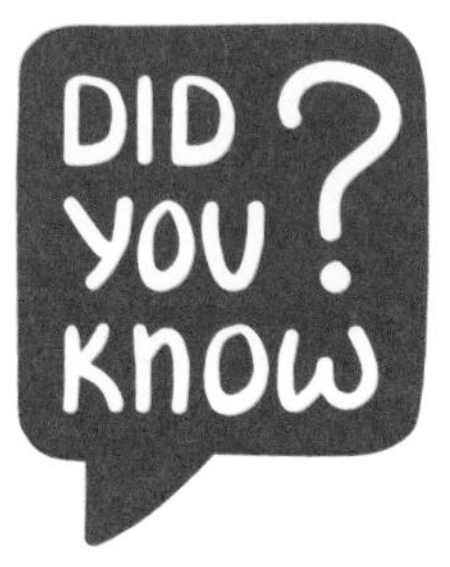

Zen is a school of Buddhism focusing on attaining enlightenment by clearing the mind of all thoughts and concepts, in favor of meditation, which leads to a sudden breakthrough of insight and awareness of ultimate reality.[4] A Zen garden, photo right, is a traditional Japanese meditative garden with minimalistic landscape composed of a thoughtful arrangement of rocks, water features, and gravel or sand that is raked to represent ripples in water.

Figure 4

As a starter, we turn off all noise, face an empty space, and eliminate any outside sources of stimulation. We focus on the self, body, and mind. Several suggestions follow for achieving this mental state.

We can escape from automated mental processing and conventional decisive thinking when we avoid thinking about persuasive arguments. We substitute the latter with a flow of metaphoric and visual imagery that aims to trigger physical sensations. In summary, we replace internal *mental dispute* with *motion imagining*.

We can use a technique which is to *slice*, *divide*, and *eliminate* chunks of mental images and recurring movement material that congest the mind. Similar to a big bucket, our mind contains a load of information and pending tasks waiting to be processed. We can take it apart and begin deleting it until the mind bucket is empty.

We can concentrate and pause our thinking by controlling our *speed of thinking*. We act as an outsider observing our own mental and choreographic processes—particularly how they accelerate and slow down. We can also observe how our mental processes become more or less intense. We can even gradually *slow down* the speed of our thinking processes until we ultimately hold our thoughts in perceived *stillness*.

Small Dance, for example, is a self-awareness exercise developed by Steve Paxton in which the individual focuses on the minimal activities of the body that are noticeable during mental stillness. Here is a narrative excerpt from his Body Cartography Project that describes this approach—a great example of using *motion imaging* for relaxation and centering.

Figure 5 Photography © Rahav Segev, pictured Steve Paxton in the Jennifer Miller production *Cumulus Frenzy*, part of *Brooklyn Bred* during BAM Next Wave Festival, 2012

"Relax deep into the cone of the eye socket. Imagine a line that runs between the ears. That's where the skull rests. Make the motion, very small, for "Yes." This rocks the skull on the top vertebrae, the atlas. You have to intuit the bones. Like the hole of a donut. The sensation around it defines it. Do the motion for "No." Between these two motions you can determine the length of the vertebrae."

"Ballooning of the lungs. Breathe from the bottom of the lung up to the clavicle. Can you expand the ribs out and up and back easily?"

"You've been swimming in gravity since the day you were born. Every cell knows where down is. Easily forgotten. Your mass and the earth's mass calling to forgotten. Your mass and the earth's mass calling to each other."[5]

A great effort is required to think productively. Ironically, even greater effort of a different kind is necessary to avoid needless thoughts and to empty the mind of mental debris. By freeing our choreographic mind, we also free our body, allowing the exploration of a wider range of movement possibilities. We approach our *body as a canvas*, where we can *attend and receive, feel and capture* new kinesthetic sensations. "Freeing the mind" occurs when we choose not to choose, and simply open space for things to happen.

Meditative improvisation might naturally lead to ***spontaneous improvisation***, an unredacted, somatic spontaneity allowing various random stimuli to influence the body's movement experience. This unfettered dance represents *random physicalizing* of free thought and impulsive ideas.

Improvisational discoveries in movement might organically lead to a search for organizing principles. Freshly discovered somatic and movement findings could serve as new improvisational play tools. These tools might be organized into a movement structure or form a new set of parameters for movement invention. The possibilities are both stimulating and creatively challenging for the artists.

GUIDED IMPROVISATION AND BEING FREE WITHIN LIMITATIONS

– THINKING OUTSIDE THE BOX WHILE INSIDE THE BOX –

Assignments, rules, structures, sets of principles, and limitations often require compliance and might hinder the free flow of thinking. Yet setting a *framework of limitations in dance improvisation* can also open up opportunities to help us discover new pathways to solutions. This is an experience similar to entering a labyrinth or a maze. Welcome inside!

Improvisational artist Richard Bull introduced improvised choreography, or *structured improvisation*. He created and codified sets of assignments and structures intended to manipulate, navigate, and direct the flow of an improvisation.[6]

The point of bringing specific assignments, directions, and limits into the improvisational work is to clarify movement tasks before letting improvisers dive into creating. The clear directions and set parameters of structured improvisation are like keeping *SCORE*, which helps participants focus. For example, when exploring pathways and spatial figures such as the maze in Figure 6, the goal is to manipulate specific movement material in a particular way to encourage one to improvise within certain parameters.

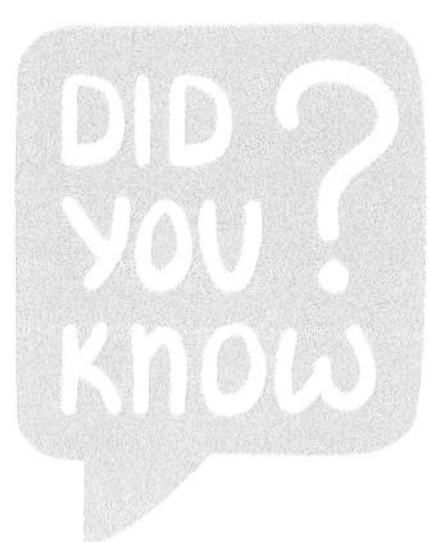

A labyrinth is an elaborate structure, designed by the legendary artist and builder Daedalus for King Minos of Crete at Knossos. Its function was to hold the beast Minotaur—half man, half bull. Daedalus had constructed the labyrinth so well that he could barely escape it after he built it.[7] While a labyrinth might be intimidating, a maze is fun—it is a collection of simpler, non-branching pathways or more convoluted paths, which typically extend from an entrance to an end. The solver must find a route in and out of the maze—and that would be aMazing!

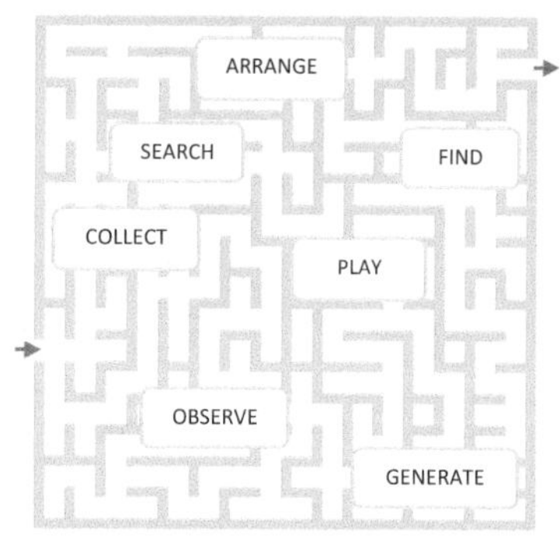

Figure 6

We can refer to *guided improvisation* as a *structured improvisation*, or a *rules-based improvisation*, or a *score-based improvisation*. Using a set of verbs as guiding principles for limiting play with movement has proven to be inspiring. When we improvise, we *generate* new movement material spontaneously. Structured improvisation, however, might require us to *search for*, *find*, and *collect* movements and to *arrange* them instantly.

Improvisers can *play* with the use of space, timing, energy, and repetition while they are in the process of movement searching and finding. They can also *observe* the created material and continue adding levels of complexity, and ultimately *arrange and re-arrange* most or all of the initially collected improvised material.

The similarity between a maze and a guided improvisation is that there is an absence of evaluation during both processes. The difference, however, is the lack of pressure to *solve* the problem of being trapped in a maze, and the sense of joy within the improvisational process. Guided improvisation aims to strengthen the link between the body, mind, feelings, imagination, and actions, and focuses on creativity with greater discipline than spontaneous improvisation.

In contrast with the ancient labyrinth structure, from which Daedalus could barely escape, structured improvisation develops in a playful and interactive way, eliminating a sense of urgency and the need for achievement.

While improvising, dancers might decide to work in groups. They may step onto the floor, step away to observe other dancers, or decide instantly to be part (or not) of the movement experience. In such a group setting, improvisers may prefer to explore movement in a solo format, or engage in collaborative kinesthetic relationships, where two or more improvisers mutually investigate movement material by supporting each other.

This brings us to *collaboration!* Collaboration in improvisation is an enriching engagement of additional artists, multiple viewpoints, and a variety of movement forms. Collaboration brings new solutions to the process and might expand the initial score of the improvisation. Collaboration changes the mindset of the improvisers—the walls of the maze begin to form new patterns and present more movement possibilities.

CHANCE IMPROVISATION AND THE URGENCY OF MAKING SENSE – MERGING THE CONCEPT OF CHAOS WITH THE CONCEPT OF CHANCE –

Dance improvisation is an ever-changing, dynamic, and often chaotic practice. Unpredictable dance movements and patterns emerge. Unpredictability also recalls the randomness of pedestrians walking in urban areas or the changes in weather. Random and chaotic systems are complex systems, which also evolve over time. Under the right conditions, chaos could reduce itself to a specific pattern or a fixed point. For example, a random mix of red, white, and yellow produces a new unique color labeled as "brick."

Dance improvisation invites the concept of ***chaos***, while presenting a few challenging questions: How much uncertainty are we willing to tolerate as part of the creative process? How far forward in the process are we able to accurately forecast and respond to random circumstances that arise? How do we implement a meaningful framework for any chaos created?

This brings us to ***chance improvisation***. In contrast to spontaneous and structured improvisation, *chance improvisation* deals with movement material that is already available in abundance to the choreographers. The avant-garde choreographer Merce Cunningham originated a semi-improvisational technique called *chance dance*, also known as *choreography by chance*, that here we call *chance improvisation*. He was intrigued by the potential of random phenomena as determinants of structure. The basic principle is *providing potential* for movements to emerge by *random chance* and to make sense of them in a sequence, even if at first they do not appear to belong together. Cunningham's intentions were to challenge the traditional methods of constructing a dance by breaking down the stigma of the more traditional beginning, middle, and end narrative format. Some of his chance techniques were to create dances by randomly picking up cards with descriptions of motions on them, rolling dice, or flipping a coin to determine which movement to use in a dance and in what order—see also Chapter 6.

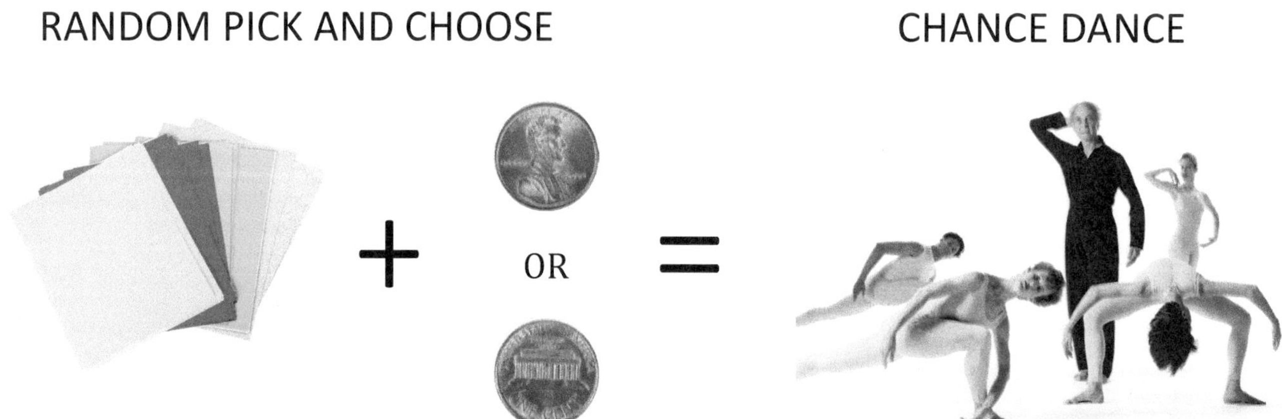

Figure 7 Photography © Lois Greenfield, *Enter*, choreography by Merce Cunningham, pictured Michael Cole, Emma Diamond, Merce Cunningham, Patricia Lent and Carol Teitelbaum, courtesy of Merce Cunningham Dance Company, 1993

This chance strategy avoids predictability, replacing it with surprise. Cunningham was curious about the mechanics of movement and the physical process of getting from one position to another. Once movement sections were constructed, they were rearranged for each performance in terms of the sequence, location, and number of dancers involved.[8]

Cunningham's artistic philosophy avoided rigidly thematic imagery, plots, and librettos, and instead focused entirely on movement for movement sake. The generated movement material retained the openness to numerous interpretations and celebrated the essential *singleness* of the moment to exist *as it is*. Cunningham's principles of *chaos* and *chance* also involve the *choice* of how movements will be sequenced. The precedent of involving *choice*, *structure*, and *construction* as processes in an outcome-driven approach to choreography make his chance techniques semi-improvisational.

In *The Impermanent Art*, Cunningham indicated, "Some people seem to think that it is inhuman and mechanistic to toss pennies in creating a dance, instead of chewing the nails, or beating the head against a wall, or thumbing through old notebooks for ideas. But the feeling I have, when I compose in this way, is that I am in touch with a natural resource far greater than my own personal inventiveness could ever be, much more universally human than the particular habits of my own practice, and organically rising out of common pools of motor impulses."[9]

The concept of randomness and the concept of disorder are linked and yet separable. Disorder seems intrinsic and lacks patterns and genesis, while randomness permits characterization and a strategy for outcomes.[10]

The Cunningham choreographic model maintains a sense of randomness; however, it excludes a total disorderliness. Choreographers can approach unpredictability and disorder by evaluating the degree to which variation occurs. A natural logarithm and use of proportion can ensure the probability of the number of possible movement configurations. This can lead to an organization of movement that *makes sense* or to a sequence containing patterns—symmetrical, asymmetrical, or a combination of the two.

Randomness could turn an unpredictable process into a controlled process by applying determination and choice to movements created by chance. Then, highly random sequences will become non-random, and vice versa. We naturally accept the idea that the observed outcomes are random. Therefore, we naturally accepted Cunningham's chance play after we were told that the movements were created by chance, even when we did not know chance play was used in the first place, because the use of chance play made visual and kinesthetic sense.

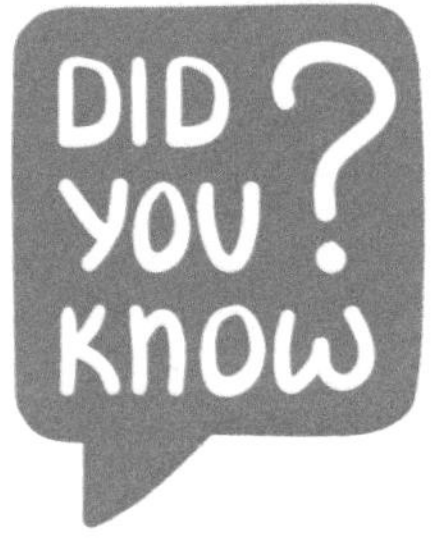

What do you think is more "structured"—ice, water, or clouds? Ice, water, and clouds are the same substance but particular conditions determine their physical forms. The molecules of ice are well structured but connected in random patterns, while liquid water and gas molecules move randomly without a set relationship—see figure to the right.

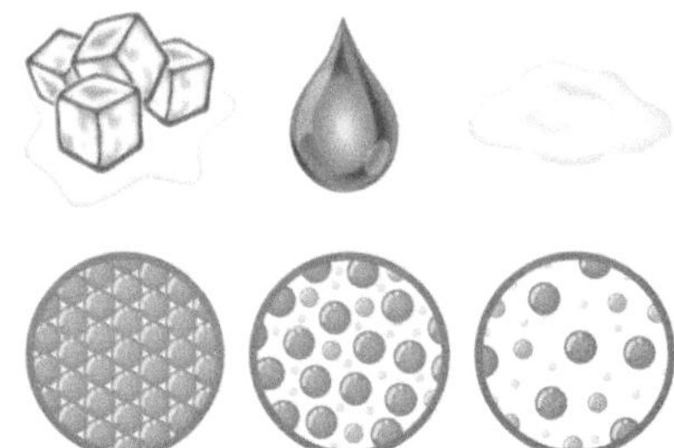

Figure 8

In comparison to spontaneous improvisation and a Zen garden, which offer an empty and open space for movement flow to occur, structured improvisation and a maze set structural limitations and directions for a movement search right from the get-go. With chance improvisation and our water example, we resolve spontaneity, chaos, and limitations by treating them as disorder and randomness. We reconfigure possibilities based on chance and choice. Returning to our initial question: Is improvisation process-driven or outcome-driven, or both? It depends on the choice you make and the chance you take—there is a wide range of nuanced options.

Finally, is there a choice-based solution about how to exit a maze? When we enter the maze, we can make a choice to turn to the right at every intersection. We might end up walking along all the possible pathways, including those not leading straight to the end. Eventually, we will exit the maze after a series of consistent turns, which solves the question of randomness. In the context of dance improvising, this means that implementing one simple principle would be enough to give us a direction in our movement research.

?

Of the various types of improvisation, which was the most appealing to you and why?

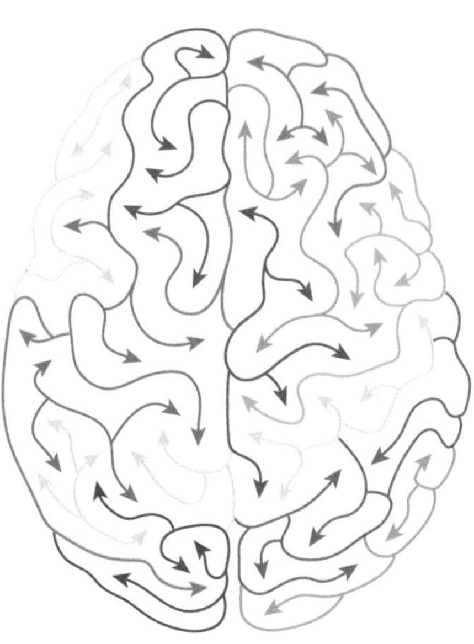

TWELVE LEADING DANCE IMPROVISATION FIGURES
– METHODS OF MOVEMENT RESEARCH AND MOVEMENT FINDING –

Improvisational choreographers often share common creative drives: to discover, embody, and enjoy new ways to approach movement and dance creation. Most improvisational practitioners work in the genres of modern and contemporary dance. This is not an accident since classical ballet operates mostly with a pre-existing movement vocabulary. In addition, the use of pointe shoes determines the specific way of approaching movements. Yet there is plenty of room to maneuver, manipulate, and modify the ballet lexicon, and several techniques are currently in use by various contemporary ballet choreographers.

In contemporary dance, the movement vocabulary is not fixed. The invention of an authentic movement vocabulary is the core of the choreographic process, with a focus on experimentation and innovation. Some improvisational artists call themselves movement practitioners rather than choreographers because their creative work is process- and practice-oriented, rather than outcome-oriented. Many improvisational artists have dedicated their lives solely to dance improvisation—either spontaneous, structured, chance, or in combinations. The following are some brief descriptions of their artistic philosophies and the branding of their practices:

01 **DANCE TASKS** was a method developed by **Anna Halprin** to kinesthetically investigate movement for generating an idiosyncratic modern dance vocabulary. Halprin used this method to incorporate modern dance improvisation into her dance performances. She also clarified the difference between *improvisation* and *exploration* by noting that exploration limits the generation of movement to those actions within a specific range.[11]

Figure 9 Photography © Ellen Crane, Anna Halprin rehearsing 'The Paper Dance' from Parades and Changes (1965), Hatlen Theater, University of California, Santa Barbara, 2017

Halprin, pictured left during one of her lectures, has been using movement improvisation as a means to bring the dance community together. She offers prompts to create a *ritual*, incorporating dance and movement to promote possible resolution of contemporary issues. The ritual of dance improvisation, the togetherness of the community, and the process of healing—all support and promote peacefulness of action in people's lives. Halprin said, "Some people do civil disobedience, protest marches, whatever—we dance!"[12]

ENVISION: The Halprin method includes written directions, symbols, and words telling the participants about the different types of activities they should perform. Her *dance tasks* bring participants and their energy together. Her signature *opening up* exercises consist of physical, emotional, and mental activities and interactions, where dancers hold and support each other while they stand in circles.

02 **CHOREOGRAPHIC IMPROVISATION**, developed by **Richard Bull**, borrowed compositional devices from other art forms such as jazz, music, and literature. Since he was a musician before starting a dance career, Bull incorporated music devices into his choreographic technique. He revolutionized dance improvisation by using existing music composition tools as choreographic tools, such as theme and variation, repetition, retrograde, canon, and fugue. Bull was also fascinated with the dialogue that takes place between two musicians during a jazz improvisation and aptly inserted *movement dialogue* as part of his dance improvisations.[13]

Bull often used formal structures or spatial configurations as part of his improvisational process. One example was his use of a diagonal pathway, to which the dancers could relate or refer while improvising. Bull also developed a movement-generating tool called "playpen," in which the dancers were encouraged to try awkward and physically challenging and unfamiliar moves so they could entertain new challenges during their exploration.[14]

In some of Bull's improvisations, verbalization also took place. The dancers would perform by creating a narrative of the dance that the audience would also read in the program brochure. Such factual information provided the audience with an alternative way to look at the dance. These verbalizations added to the performance by exploring ways the audience may have interpreted or did not interpret the dance during the performance.[15]

ENVISION: Bull's improvisational tools include: a) *allusions*—a movement reference to familiar dance material such as tango or a well-known ballet production; b) *interpolation*—a short dance inserted into a large piece; and c) *interior monologue*—where the dancers "think aloud," leading to the development of dance steps colored by the adjectives from a text.

03 **CONTACT IMPROVISATION (CI)** was introduced by **Steve Paxton** in 1972 as an avant-garde method for creating movement. Paxton has also led its development and autonomy as a sub-genre of contemporary dance into the 21st century.[16]

In classical ballet, partnering skills are usually displayed in the form of a *pas de deux*, while in modern and contemporary dance, a *duet* could be equally impressive by using physical contact and kinetically linking moving bodies. The CI dancers-artists-improvisers, also often called *contactors*, make similar physical contact, as in the tango, by moving in an ongoing, spontaneously created, and kinetically joined dialogue.

In CI there are no established dance vocabularies to be manipulated. Instead, in the CI format practitioners instantly generate fresh movement material. The absence of pre-planned choreographic instructions and guidance requires the practitioners to use intuitive and reflexive responses, although there are preliminary rules for their safety. As practitioners become familiar with the CI foundation, they master skills to maneuver each other and instantly negotiate multiple movement choices.[17]

Movement vocabulary is created instantly through body contact as the dancers play with gravity and fall into one another and to the floor. Sometimes, the dancers are on top of other rolling bodies or they counterbalance while holding or supporting each other. CI technique avoids habitual use of the hands in all pushes, touches, and holds. Contactors might share weight with head-to-head, back-to-back, or pelvis-to-pelvis contact while spiraling and circling around each other's shoulders or other body parts. Yet they maintain contact and control of the precarious dance by pressing against each other.[18]

Most contactors barely consider themselves dance professionals and have never performed in front of a paying audience or stepped onto a proscenium stage. Nevertheless, those who practice CI have identified themselves as a vibrant sub-culture with a binding communal spirit and flourishing optimism. Contact Improvisation practitioners coordinate *contact jams* as they bargain for any available wooden floor—in community centers, churches, and other improvised spaces.

ENVISION: The bodies' *weight shifts* create a certain amount of momentum that is crucial for the exploration of togetherness. *Timing* and *speed* can change while accommodating and *finding balance*. On the other hand, *sensory awareness* is the ability to feel and see multiple options and make decisions in a split second. Such awareness is *peripheral vision*, which strangely enough, requires relaxation rather than focus.

04 **THE UNDERSCORE** technique, developed by **Nancy Stark Smith**, is a longer dance improvisation structure. The Underscore format incorporates contact improvisation as a broader improvisational dance practice and also addresses a variety of kinesthetic and compositional concerns that may arise while improvising. The Underscore technique offers a long-form dance improvisation structure with guiding movement frames, maps, and a sequence *score* of how improvisation activities will unfold. Sometimes there are very small, private, and quiet internal activities. At other times, the energy is higher, with interaction incorporating contact improvisation.[19]

Figure 10 Photography © Raisa Kyllikki Ranta, pictured Nancy Stark Smith and Juha Viitamäki during an Underscore workshop, Helsinki, Finland, 2007

ENVISION: There are more than twenty phases or frames for the *Score*. Each of them has a name and a graphic symbol, which serves as a general movement map for the dancers. Within each given frame, dancers are free to create their own movements in relationship to themselves, each other, or the group. Music, images, speech, and the environment are used kinesthetically to trigger additional stimuli for improvisation.

Figure 11 Photograph © Ellen Crane, pictured Simone Forti in *News Animations* (1986–present), performed during "An Evening of Dance," Hatlen Theater, University of California, Santa Barbara, CA, 2017

05 **LOGOMOTION**, developed by **Simone Forti**, explores the relationship between movement and language. Forti, who was Anna Halprin's student, became known for her minimalist dance constructions. Her in-depth studies of animal movements, news animations, and animated dancing became the basis for the development of *Logomotion*.[20]

In the early 1960s, Forti's choice of task-based movement material for her dances was considered radical because she displayed ordinary movements onstage, rather than including stylized and technical dancing in her works. In 1980s, she began connecting movement and verbal language by having her dancers talk about events from the news. Her often humorous works juxtaposed the narrative of serious world affairs with the intimacy of the human body movements and gestures.[21] Forti encourages her dancers to explore imagery and memories through prepared instructions, from which new physical forces and movement ideas occur.

ENVISION: Stories often generate kinesthetic imagery accompanied by body language, yet the movements created do not figuratively display spoken words. Instead, Forti uses a unique communication system in which words and movement emerge together from sensations and kinesthetic imagery evoked by the words in the original story. There is a constant shifting back and forth between verbal meaning and physical action, as the dancers playfully connect the two types of language expressions.

06 **PERFORMANCE PRACTICES**, developed by **Debora Hay**, emphasize the integration of improvisations with practice by focusing on being *present*. During these improvisations, Hay's instructions could range from manipulating set choreography to a more general exploration of spatial pathways. In a documentary about her work, Hay said, "We do not have to do 'one thing at a time', when we can open up and do 'many things at the same time.'" This documentary film by Ellen Blomberg is titled *Deborah Hay, not as Deborah Hay*.[22]

During performance practice, the dancers navigate through a given choreography and engage in the presence of their performance. The effort is to involve the performers in *practicing or moving by exploring*, rather than r*ehearsing repeated movements*. Thus, the dancers are experimenting with how *to be*, rather than how *to perform*.

ENVISION: In Hay's improvisations a score and sets of directions are given to the dancers. Some of these prompts are very practical, and others are symbolic and almost impossible to follow. However, every multi-layered score aims to change the quality of the performance and explores different nuances of how performers interpret the directions in a score.

07 **COMPOSITIONAL IMPROVISATION** was created by **Judith Dunn**. She stated that choreographing, composing, and performing happen simultaneously. The improviser considers structure, order, space-time, movement material and *tone*, while making decisions quickly, consciously, and with control. Dunn was originally inspired by composition rules developed for musicians, since her collaborator, Bill Dixon was interested in mixing disciplines. In a later stage of Compositional Improvisation, she also implemented the use of text and linguistic principles. Dunn's early death prevented her further work on the method, yet it inspired a generation of improvisers to carry the torch of her legacy.[23]

ENVISION: Dunn's improvisational method fosters a unique way of nurturing artistic actions. Her analytical method supplies the dancers with visual illustrations, such as schematic drawings and diagrams, and engages the performers in map-making. Dunn's method encourages movement analysis and urges the dancers to examine what is taking place at the time. It enables participants to create an imaginative vocabulary and explore movement possibilities.

08 **TUNING SCORES**, developed by **Lisa Nelson**, investigates fundamental elements of movement behavior, performance, and communication. In addition to dance, Nelson became a videographer and taught video dance at Bennington College. Nelson was interested in creating *automated* or *cultivated* responses to given circumstances. For example, we turn our head because someone is calling our name, or we say "thanks" if someone gives us something. Further, Nelson believes that we translate perception *through* action. According to Nelson, we learn that *what* we see is actually *how* we see; therefore, we understand and react to the world through something she calls *multisensorial layers of observation*.[24]

Tuning Scores is a practice using both movement and choreographic instructions in the form of images, ideas, and memories. This method focuses on the deployment of improvisational dance practices with deeper body/mind investigations. The Nelson method suggests that movement is understood and *viewed* as a set of moving images, just like those in a film. This means some scenes could be *perceived* through the quality and changes initiated by verbal instructions, which are based on different ways of *observing*.[25] For example, when one views a picture of a banana, the questions posed might be:

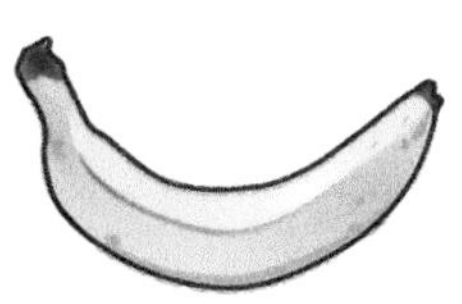

A FIGURATIVE EXAMPLE OF AN AUTOMATED RESPON

- What is this?
- The obvious answer is—*it's* a banana!
- Actually, it is not true. This is a *picture* of a banana.

Figure 12

ENVISION: Nelson frequently asks her dancers to perform in unison while their eyes are closed. Since their visual orientation and judgement are challenged in this situation, the dancers are forced to use all of their other senses. This means that sound, touch, smell, and the kinesthetic senses all come into play. Nelson's improvisational techniques also merge dance and video-editing terminology by using verbal cues such as: *pause, replay, repeat, reverse*, and *forward*.

09 » DELICIOUS MOVEMENT, created by Eiko & Koma, is an improvisation concept and a tool for teaching and community engagement. The concept functions separately from Eiko & Koma's dance technique and choreography methods, which vary widely depending on the works. Eiko uses *Delicious Movement* in teaching college courses on environmental issues and human experiences of cruelty. In their youth in Japan, Eiko & Koma studied with Tatsumi Hijikata and Kazuo Ohno, who started *Butoh*—a widely-practiced dance form that is still redefining itself today.

However, Eiko & Koma avoid using the term *Butoh* in describing their performance and teaching practices, as they are concerned about categorizing artists and limiting their development and self-curation. Since moving to New York City in 1976, Eiko & Koma have performed their interdisciplinary works at theaters, museums, and public sites worldwide.[26]

ENVISION: *Delicious Movement* starts with floor work that comfortably engages participants of varying ages, levels of experience, and skills. When lying down on the floor people are more vulnerable and less harmful to the world. By moving slowly, the participants discover poetic nuances and sensations in their bodies while engaging with time and space. In exploring the movement, participants are asked to consider the prompts below, which could be modified and the scores adjusted. Participants could also be paired and work with one another to experience and discover that kinesthetic union can be transformative.[27]

Time is Not Even | Space is Not Empty | Distance is Malleable

A Body is Asymmetrical |How to Sustain Mourning | How to Hesitate against Momentum

Figure 13 Photography © William Johnston, pictured Eiko Otake on an abandoned road, Tomioka Beach, from an ongoing choreographer-photographer collaboration project, *A Body in Fukushima*, 2014

Figure 14 Photography © Dominik Mentzos © pictured William Forsythe working with the dancers in Hellerau/ Dresden, Germany, 2013

10 **IMPROVISATION TECHNOLOGIES**, developed by **William Forsythe**, use different *algorithms* and *operations* to maneuver and play with movement material with the goal to create and discover unique vocabulary and ways of moving.[28] Although Forsythe uses the ballet lexicon, he intentionally abandons its traditional technical demands. He often directs his dancers to execute ballet positions without using traditional relationships between body parts. He believes there is nothing wrong with a conventional ballet arabesque, and yet Forsythe questions how the *arabesque* should be approached choreographically. He explores exciting possibilities by playing with the *arabesque*—tweaking, angling, contorting, and manipulating it, to the extent that the conventional *arabesque* is barely recognizable. It has become a *non-arabesque.*

Forsythe often sets specific movement phrases on dancers and then asks them to manipulate and modify these movement phrases by using his *algorithms.* His principles of transforming existing vocabulary implement movement modifications using different body parts, spatial variations, and time manipulations. He also invented stimulating exercises and tools to prepare his dancers to use his methods for generating original movement material.[29] Forsythe demonstrates these devices himself in *Improvisation Technologies: A Tool for the Analytical Dance Eye*, Book and CD-ROM.

ENVISION: In Forsythe's method, *reverse temporal order* is used when the dancers run a section of a piece and then change the direction and the spacing of the movement phrase. A different algorithm called *time compression* demands that the dancers shorten the length of time it takes to perform a phrase. Instead, the dancers abbreviate the phrase based on individual choices, which gives the dance a new look and unpredictable dynamics. *Rotating inscription* is the use of any body part to trace different abstract geometrical lines in space, including, straight, angular, and curved lines. Body parts can swish or swirl and trace three-dimensional shapes in the air from top to bottom, left to right, or by changing directions. In *room writing*, dancers use movement from memory and virtually recreate a room and its furniture. Specific points on/in their bodies can trace an imaginary sofa, table, and chairs. The dancers also use their movements to keep track of the positioning of the furniture in the space. After creating an imaginary room, the dancers navigate it for the viewer by making a new dance with unlikely parameters.

11 **GAGA MOVEMENT LANGUAGE** is an improvisational and movement research technique created by choreographer **Ohad Naharin**. Gaga operates with imagery that stimulates the imagination, as the layering of information builds into a multisensory, physically challenging experience. Gaga enables participants to connect to movement in space and in life, as well as to experience pleasure and effort while strengthening and invigorating the body. The technique investigates form, speed, and effort while responding to a range of movement qualities such as soft, delicate, and thick textures. Other devices require explosive power, understatement, or exaggeration.[30] Gaga's performance philosophy, theoretical analysis, and practical implementation also include embodied reflections, enacting, and extending receptions, dancing metaphors, mental emphases on connecting effort with pleasure, comprehending emotions and directing a mood, as well as decision making, multitasking inquiries, and the physical practice of intelligence.[31]

ENVISION: In this improvisation, the participants are positioned randomly in the space, and no mirrors are available. There is also continued movement by everybody in the group, as the leader provides words that are movement cues. The words describe images to which the participants respond spontaneously with movement. For example, what is your movement perception and response to the word *floating*? How would you respond with movement to the word skin, or to the image of *skin* stretching in different directions? The point is to embody the experience of these images and to understand how words can merely suggest what is happening physically.

12 **ILAND—THE INTERDISCIPLINARY LABORATORY FOR ART, NATURE, AND DANCE** was developed by **Jennifer Monson** to be a platform for exploring the power of dance in collaboration with other fields and to illuminate a kinesthetic understanding of the world. This improvisational and choreographic approach re-imagines our relationship to the environments and spaces that humans and all beings inhabit.

One of Monson's projects, *BIRD BRAINS*, is about the navigation routes and migration patterns of birds. It encourages social discourse about environmental issues and initiates supportive and creative interactions between movement artists, scientists, and environmentalists. Monson's dance group uses the local ecosystems as a resource and an inspiration for improvisation by engaging in conversations and research with park rangers, hikers, ecologists, and scientists so they can navigate the artists through sensory explorations and kinesthetic awareness.

Figure 15 Photography © Kenta Nagai, Performed by Charlotte Gibbons, Mariangela Lopez, Maggie Bennett, *iMAP (Interdisciplinary Mobile Architecture and Performance)/Ridgewood Reservoir*, a collaborative project between choreographer Jennifer Monson, architect Gita Nandan and landscape architect Elliott Maltby, Highland Park, New York City, 2007

ENVISION: Monson's original approach and research-based dance improvisations combine elements of environmental studies with her research and fieldwork. Monson's community improvisational classes share the same basic kinesthetic ideas found among birds, in nature, and in wilderness studies. In her improvisation, she implements *navigation exercises* such as finding north, facing toward home, remembering pathways, and flocking behaviors.

Monson shared the following comments in an artist's statement:

> *Am I compounding wilderness and nature? The usefulness of the term "nature" has become complicated for me, as I struggle with the dialectic of nature/not nature. What is not nature? Wilderness becomes a more amenable concept for me in that it alludes to something untamable, unknowable and challenging, and it is a very human concept. Wilderness as a concept seems central to human evolution. Dancing is a powerful medium for addressing our "nature" and is one of the places I experience wildness.*[33]

?

If you build an improvisation technique to serve your individual artistic and choreographic needs, what kind of content, focus, principles, and framework would you consider, and what would you name your technique?

Dance improvisation involves experimenting and exploring a variety of thoughts, feelings, and physical sensations through kinesthetic investigations. Improvisational practices require a strong mind-body connection. Being in the present moment is essential. At the same time, innovative ideas and artistic discoveries are not accessible through force, but rather by creating a supportive and inviting space for inspiration to occur organically.

Our thinking affects our actions, and our minds affect our bodies. As we look for mechanisms to minimize tension, we work to increase awareness of our surroundings and ourselves by consciously activating positive thoughts and behaviors. We rise by lifting others. A friendly mindset helps us dive into improvisation practices safely and graciously. Channel your efforts to build an affirmative attitude by embracing and enacting the following vital demeanors, helpful tips, and suggestions.

HELPFUL TIPS & SUGGESTIONS

- ~ **EXPERIMENT**
- ~ **SENSE**
- ~ **ENJOY**
- ~ **ANTICIPATE**
- ~ **CONSIDER**
- ~ **EXPLORE**
- ~ **SHARE**
- ~ **COLLABORATE**
- ~ **TRUST**
- ~ **INTEGRATE**
- ~ **EMPATHIZE**
- ~ **FORGIVE**

Figure 16 Photography © Lois Greenfield, pictured Shannon MacDowell and Kimberly Lyons, courtesy of Amy Marshall Dance Company, 2010

assignments & exercises

Interaction and feedback approaches in improvisation:

YES, describe without judgment.—Verbally
YES, analyze without expectations.—Mentally
YES, encourage without surveillance.—Socially

★ **Do experiment and explore!** Here are samples of movement research and movement finding—feel free to choose from any of the following techniques and explore them in the studio, alone or with colleagues.

➥ ***Delicious movement explorations***[34]

— Create movement based on your image of resting, sleeping, and dreaming.

— Move as if you are passing time by focusing on the image of a flower blooming, or move as though you are lingering.

— Focus on a particular taste. Then, create movements based on this taste and share them with someone.

— What does it feel like to forget or to remember? How would you move in each situation?

— Move and breathe as if you are experiencing your body as part of a landscape and then the landscape as a body that can both breathe and move.

— Look at dance as a flower that grows, blooms, and wilts as it is noticed, nurtured and savored. How would you respond with movements inspired by each stage in the life of the flower?

— Appreciate life as movement, even in relative stillness. Create movements in response to each of these images.

— Feel everyone's life as an unrecoverable, transient, precious process within a larger sense of time and space. How would you move in a way that is an abstraction of these feelings?

— Nurture and move using kinesthetic imagery to capture a feeling of kindness to oneself and others living or dead.

— Be present and loose with others, and find and a way to resolve conflicts by negotiating them.

— Move by being and feeling beautiful but not necessarily sexual. Compare the two movement styles that you create.

— Dance a solo as if you are in a duet with a shadow. Then, dance a duet as a solo while remembering the imaginary duet with the shadow.

➥ ***Contact improvisation***[35]

— *Small Dance* is an awareness exercise developed by Steve Paxton in order to focus on the minimal activities of the body noticeable during stillness, find your center and prepare for Contact Improvisation(CI) practice that will follow. Here is a brief sampling of CI terminology:

— *Weight sharing*: exploring body weight distribution and mutual physical support.

— *Counterbalance*: shared balance with partners opposing each other with equal weight or force

— *Kinesphere*: the immediate space around the body

— *Letting go*: surrendering to movement circumstances and releasing your will into the flow

— *Centering* is an integrated state of physiological and emotional balance. Once you have reached a centered state, select a contact point where a part of your body physically connects with the body of your partner.

— Explore a weight-sharing relationship with your partner where you are mutually supporting each other.

— Experiment with counterbalancing by sharing a state of balance with your partner. This can be accomplished by using an opposing but equal force as you counterbalance.

— As you counterbalance, explore the kinesphere, or the space around your bodies, by reaching out into the surrounding space. Then, let go and go with the flow.

➥ ***Improvisational technologies***[36]

POINT-POINT LINE

imagining lines

The first example describes how to construct a line from point to point. You can imagine a line between your fingers and you can recreate this line in space by moving between two set points. You can grab a line again and move it to point in any direction by re-orienting it. Using a part of your body is another simple way to construct a line because it extends between two points on the body, but the position of line is changing by moving the body part.

— extrusion +

The point-point line is a line that was inside your body and sometimes in space. The line can be also produced by extruding or thrusting a line from a point. This extruded line can collapse or extend out not only though body parts. It can also be extruded up from the floor. A line on the floor, when extruded, can produce the idea of a plane that can be flattened and/or rotated.

— matching +

Matching means simply collapsing a line. If you establish your body in a position, or when it is going through a certain number of movements, you notice that certain positions are established. You can match one of the lines that is created as you move. Now you can remove the original line or match another line.

— folding +

You can also extend the exploration by folding one of the lines in on itself to create variations of a line.

* For a video demonstration by William Forsythe including his detailed explanations of these exercises, please refer to the direct resource at: Forsythe, William, *Improvisation Technologies: A Tool for the Analytical Dance Eye*, Book and CD-ROM, Hatje Cantz, 2010.

BIBLIOGRAPHY AND REFERENCES

[1] Buckwalter, Melinda. *Composing While Dancing, An Improviser's Companion*, The University of Wisconsin Press, 2010, pp. 3–11.
[2] *Survey: Is Improvisation Choreography?*, The International Consortium for Advancement in Choreography–Dance ICONS, Inc. March 2016, http://danceicons.org/contact/debate_page.php?deb_id=6
[3] Minton, Sandra Cerny. *Choreography, A Basic Approach Using Improvisation*, Human Kinetics, 2007, pp. 10–12.
[4] The Zen Study Society. *What Is Zen?* Online article, accessed April 2017, online resource at: https://zenstudies.org/
[5] Paxton, Steve. "Small Dance" (excerpt), originally from *Contact Quarterly*, vol. 11, no. 1, Winter 1986; reprinted in CQ's Contact Improvisation, Sourcebook, Vol. 1, 1997, Source; Body Cartography Project: http://bodycartography.org/portfolio/smalldancestevepaxton/
[6] Foster, Susan Leigh. *Dances That Describe Themselves: The Improvised Choreography of Richard Bull*, 1st edition, Wesleyan University Press, 2002, pp. 99–104.
[7] The Editors of Encyclopedia Britannica. *Daedalus*, Encyclopedia Britannica, Inc., 2018, www.britannica.com/topic/Daedalus-Greek-mythology, accessed May 2018.
[8] Eagle, Antony. "Chance versus Randomness," in *The Stanford Encyclopedia of Philosophy* (Fall 2016 Edition), edited by Edward N. Zalta, First published August 2010; substantive revision, February 2012, forthcoming, http://plato.stanford.edu/archives/fall2016/entries/chance-randomness/
[9] Cunningham, Merce. "The Impermanent Art," in *7 Arts*, No. 3, Falcon's Wing Press, 1955, pp. 69–77.
[10] Eagle 2016. *Chance versus Randomness*.
[11] Buckwalter 2010. *Composing While Dancing, An Improviser's Companion*, pp. 35–36.
[12] Buckwalter 2010. *Composing While Dancing, An Improviser's Companion*, pp. 38.
[13] Buckwalter 2010. *Composing While Dancing, An Improviser's Companion*, pp. 43, 109–110.
[14] Buckwalter 2010. *Composing While Dancing, An Improviser's Companion*, pp. 22–23.
[15] Buckwalter 2010. *Composing While Dancing, An Improviser's Companion*, pp. 44–45.
[16] Novack, Cynthia. *Sharing the Dance, Contact Improvisation and American Culture*, The University of Wisconsin Press, 1990, pp. 5–12.
[17] Novack 1990. *Sharing the Dance*, pp. 6–19.
[18] Pallant, Cheryl. *Contact Improvisation, An Introduction to Vitalizing Dance Form*, McFarland & Company Inc. Publishers, 2006, Chapter 2.
[19] Buckwalter 2010. *Composing While Dancing*, pp. 80–82.
[20] Buckwalter 2010. *Composing While Dancing*, pp. 13, 139, 147–148, 196.
[21] Buckwalter 2010. *Composing While Dancing*, pp. 13, 139, 147–148, 196.
[22] *Deborah Hay, Not As Deborah Hay*, a documentary film by Ellen Blomberg, on Vimeo, Web, accessed July 2016. 22 Buckwalter 2010. Composing While Dancing, pp. 38–39.
[23] Buckwalter 2010. *Composing While Dancing*, pp. 108, 192.
[24] Buckwalter 2010. *Composing While Dancing*, pp. 122–125.
[25] Buckwalter 2010. *Composing While Dancing*, pp. 122–125.
[26] Eiko and Koma. Website information, accessed June 2016, ttp://eikoandkoma.org/home
[27] Eiko and Koma. *Delicious Movement Workshops*, online information, http://eikoandkoma.org/home, accessed June 2016.
[28] Forsythe, William. *Improvisation Technologies: A Tool for the Analytical Dance Eye*, Book and CD-ROM, Hatje Cantz, 2010, pp. 46–65.
[29] Forsythe 2010. *Improvisation Technologies*, pp. 46–65.
[30] Naharin, Ohad. *Gaga Movement Language*, online description web access, November 2019, www.gagapeople.com/en
[31] Katan-Schmid, Einav. *Embodied Philosophy in Dance: Gaga and Ohad Naharin's Movement Research*, 1st edition, Palgrave Macmillan, 2016, Table of Contents.
[32] Monson, Jenifer. *Artist Statement* by Jenifer Monson, online and web information at: www.ilandart.org/artist-biography/, accessed July 2016.
[33] Monson 2016. *Artist Statement* by Jenifer Monson.
[34] (Paraphrased short excerpt) Eiko and Koma, *Delicious Movement Workshops and Manifesto*, http://eikoandkoma.org/home, accessed June 2016.
[35] Pallant, Cheryl. *Contact Improvisation, An Introduction to Vitalizing Dance Form*, McFarland & Company Inc. Publishers, 2006 (paraphrased short excerpt).
[36] Forsythe, William. *Improvisation Technologies: A Tool for the Analytical Dance Eye*, Book and CD-ROM, Hatje Cantz, 2010, (paraphrased short excerpt).

VISUAL REFERENCES

Figure 1: Diagram © Vladimir Angelov

Figure 2: Photography © Lois Greenfield, image left pictured Karen De Luna, Victor Manuel Ruiz, courtesy of Aspen Santa Fe Ballet, 2004, image right: pictured Courtney Robinson, Tommie-Waheed Evans, courtesy of Philadanco, 2014

Figure 3: Diagram © Vladimir Angelov

Figure 4: *Zen Garden sand with stones*, stock photo, Image © Dirk Ercken, courtesy by www.123rf.com/

Figure 5: Photography © Rahav Segev, pictured Steve Paxton in the Jennifer Miller production *Cumulus Frenzy*, part of the *Brooklyn Bred* during BAM Next Wave Festival, 2012

Figure 6: Diagram © Vladimir Angelov, *Maze*, stock image, vector by pteshka, www.123rf.com/

Figure 7: Photography © Lois Greenfield, *Enter*, Merce Cunningham, pictured Michael Cole, Emma Diamond, Merce Cunningham, Patricia Lent and Carol Teitelbaum, courtesy of Merce Cunningham Dance Company, 1993

Figure 8: *Water as Ice, Liquid and Gas*, Vector © Gritsalak Karalak, courtesy by www.123rf.com/

Figure 9: Photography © Ellen Crane, Anna Halprin rehearsing *'The Paper Dance'* from *Parades and Changes* (1965) with the UCSB Dance Company during the conference *RADICAL BODIES: Anna Halprin, Simone Forti and Yvonne Rainer in California and New York, 1955–1972*, Hatlen Theater, University of California, Santa Barbara, 2017

Figure 10: Photography © Raisa Kyllikki Ranta, pictured Nancy Stark Smith and Juha Viitamäki during an Underscore workshop, Helsinki, Finland, 2007

Figure 11: Photograph © Ellen Crane, pictured Simone Forti in *News Animations* (1986–present) performed during An Evening of Dance during the conference *RADICAL BODIES: Anna Halprin, Simone Forti and Yvonne Rainer in California and New York, 1955–72*, Hatlen Theater, University of California, Santa Barbara, CA, 2017

Figure 12: Diagram © Vladimir Angelov, clip art a banana, public domain

Figure 13: Photography © William Johnston, pictured Eiko Otake on an abandoned road, Tomioka Beach, after Tsunami and Fukushima Daiichi Nuclear Plant (Japan) meltdown on July 22, 2014, a part of a choreographer and photographer on-going collaboration project *A Body in Fukushima*, 2014

Figure 14: Photography © Dominik Mentzos, pictured William Forsythe working with the dancers in Hellerau /Dresden, Germany, courtesy of Dominik Mentzos, 2013

Figure 15: Photography © Kenta Nagai, performers Charlotte Gibbons, Mariangela Lopez, Maggie Bennett, *iMAP (Interdisciplinary Mobile Architecture and Performance)/ Ridgewood Reservoir*, a collaborative project between choreographer Jennifer Monson, architect Gita Nandan and landscape architect Elliott Maltb, Highland Park on the border of Queens and Brooklyn, New York City, 2007

Figure 16: Photography © Lois Greenfield, pictured Shannon MacDowell and Kimberly Lyons, courtesy of Amy Marshall Dance Company, 2010

If you can't explain it simply, you don't understand it well enough.

Albert Einstein (1879–1955)

CHAPTER 16

CHOREOGRAPHIC PHRASE
– DIVING INTO THE MOVEMENT FLOW –

A choreographic phrase is a simple movement sentence that comprises movement ideas unified by intent. Within a phrase, a sequence of movements progresses from an initiation to a resolution. Similar to a spoken sentence that provides condensed information, a movement phrase begins, it goes somewhere, and it finds its ending.[1] Building a choreographic phrase is a fundamental skill and a basic instrument in the formalized process of dance making. A phrase organizes kinesthetic content and expresses movement ideas. A single phrase can demonstrate a choreographer's uniqueness and proficiency.

◆ **There is a difference between a *movement combination* and a *choreographic phrase*.**[2] A dance teacher compiles a variety of movement combinations for dance training. These sequences during daily dance classes aim to prepare the dancers for work. Technique combinations improve the dancers' coordination, performance skills, strength, and endurance, with a focus on expressive qualities, texture, precision, form, and style. Teachers often use movements, techniques, vocabulary, and exercises compiled from a variety of dance traditions. The goal for each dancer is to build, develop, and improve technical ability.

A choreographer, by contrast, creates choreographic phrases with the intention to convey specific kinesthetic concepts, imagery, feelings, symbols, narratives, and visions. Most importantly, a choreographic phrase has the capacity to reveal the creator's originality, uniqueness, and distinct artistic identity—see Chapter 13.

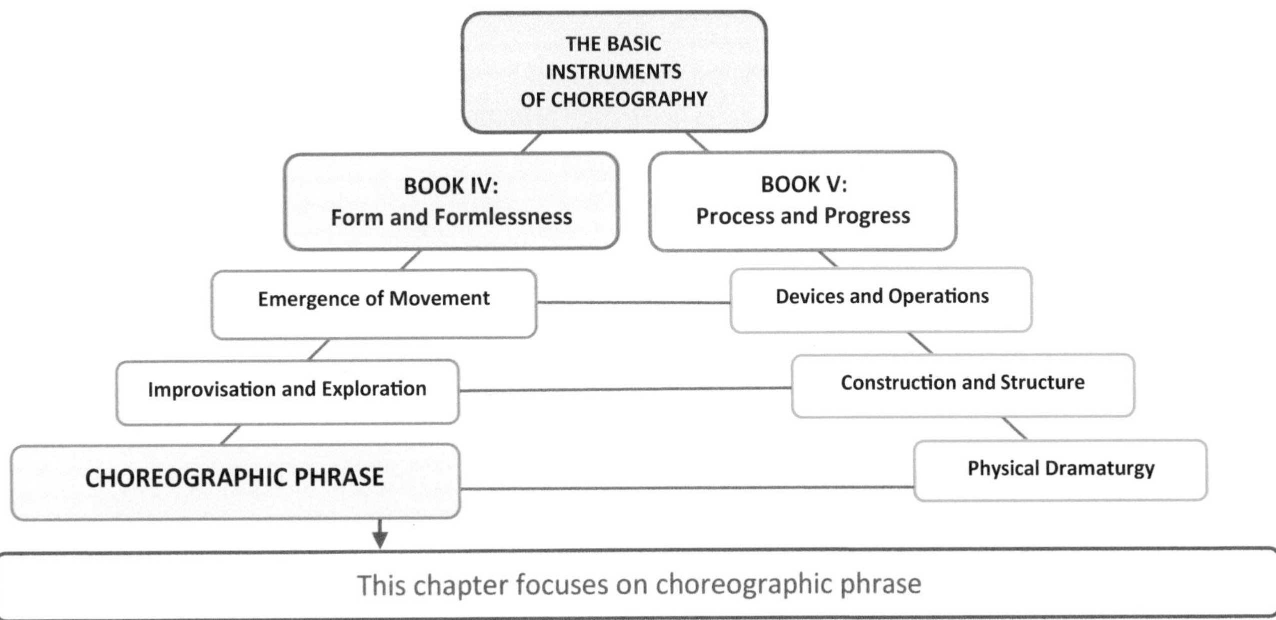

Figure 1

ASSEMBLING A SIMPLE PHRASE SEQUENCE

Let's recall the choreographer's drawer from Chapter 14 on stillness and movement. A choreographer assembles movements from different *movement categories* into a sequenced choreographic phrase. The movements, chosen arbitrarily or purposefully, could range from conventional vocabulary to newly created movement material that has not yet been stored in the drawers. The process of sequencing movement may appear simple, yet there are several conceptual lenses to consider.

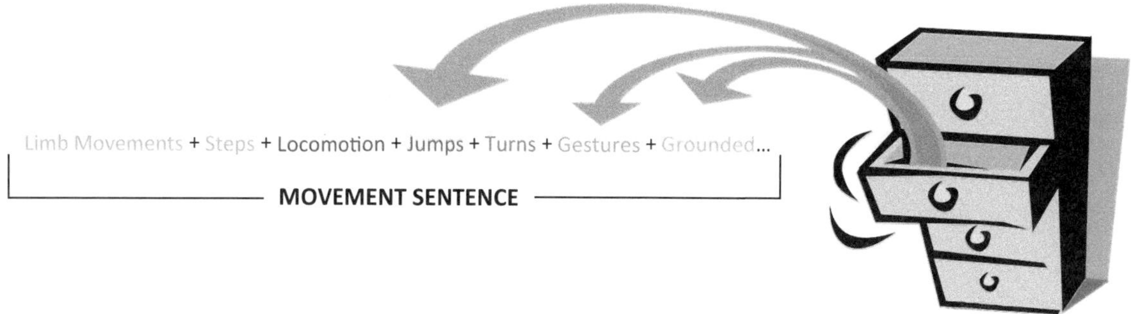

Figure 2

HOW SIZE FITS THE PURPOSE

– THE LENGTH OF A PHRASE –

Before we entertain a fashion analogy, let's get a sense of the *length of a choreographic phrase* by comparing it to spoken language. A child, for example, speaks in short sentences such as, "I'm hungry!" or "Give me the toy!" or most notably: "What is that?" Often, we have to ask questions to clarify what the child means. On the other hand, a university professor lecturing graduate students typically speaks in long and complex sentences. The students taking notes strive to capture the details of the professor's academic language, terminology, and definitions. Often, questions are asked to clarify what the professor means.

In further contrast, a poet—writing or speaking—creates metaphors, rhymes, and symbolic lines with abstract ideas that are presented in measures and stanzas. The readers are left to their own imaginations to generate interpretations or to simply absorb the sound of the words. The beauty of poetry is that it can convey rich imagery and sensations in a concise, rhythmic, and melodic flow of words.

This leads us to a fashion analogy: The size and the length of a choreographic phrase should fit the purpose—just like a good pair of jeans—pictured left. There is no standard for how long a phrase should be and how much movement material it should contain.[3] We can loosely define a phrase length as anywhere between 8 and 32 movements, including the transitions.

Figure 3

THE PROCESSES AND ELEMENTS OF BUILDING A CHOREOGRAPHIC PHRASE

The process of building a choreographic phrase consists of many smaller processes. Multiple elements are at play when composing the movement flow of a choreographic phrase, as outlined in the following summary. We examine each of these elements and processes separately in the next few pages as we dive courageously into the craft of building a phrase.

CONTENT

- MOVEMENT ORIGINS, SOURCES, AND INITIATION
- INTENT, SUBJECT MATTER, AND UNIQUE PERSPECTIVE
- KINESTHETIC IMAGERY AND VOCABULARY CHOICE

PROCESS

- CONSTRUCTING, STRUCTURING, AND ASSEMBLAGE
- SEQUENCING AS LINEAR, NON-LINEAR, AND COLLIDING
- TRANSITIONS, CROSSOVERS, AND OVERLAPS

FORM

- SPACE OCCUPATION, LOCOMOTION, AND TRACING
- TIME INTERVALS, DURATION, AND SPEED
- ENERGY SOURCES. AMOUNT. AND DISTRIBUTION

Figure 4 Photography © Lois Greenfield, pictured Nikita Maxwell, Sheila Carreras Brandson, and Terry Dean Bartlett, courtesy of STREB Extreme Action, 2002

THE CONTENT OF A PHRASE

– MOVEMENT ORIGINS, INTENT, AND VOCABULARY CHOICE –

◆ MOVEMENT ORIGINS IN THE PHRASE is the selection of movement sources and the choreographer's choice of movement vocabulary, which are related to the content of a choreographic phrase. Some choreographers prefer to use conventional movement material and traditional resources. Others prefer to modify conventional movements and to explore unique ways of moving—see Chapter 14. Ultimately, when building a phrase, a choreographer might intentionally, unintentionally, or arbitrarily use movements from one or all of the three following sources:

➢ Existing sources of traditional vocabulary refer to movements that are drawn from the choreographer's background and sources that were *given* and available, including upbringing, traditions, culture, education, and dance training. These sources have served to build and form the choreographer's artistic individuality. For example:

— **Upbringing, traditions, and cultures**—the choreographer's background and positioning as a dance artist in a certain historic, demographic, ethnographic, geo-political, socio-economic, and cultural context.

— **Accumulated dance education**—the choreographer's sustained exposure to a variety of dance genres such as classical ballet or Indian, modern dance, jazz dance, hip-hop, Afro-Caribbean, tap, ballroom, national and folk dances, cultural fusions, as well as any other movement forms from various countries and continents.

— **Approach to processing movement—**the choreographer's past and current experience in learning and engaging with movement that has been given, received, and interpreted individually—see Chapter 14.

➢ Adopted sources of modified vocabulary refer to an individual choreographer's unique approaches, instruments, and methods to manipulate movement material:

— **Individual devices** for interpreting the learned movement material and manipulating the inherited vocabulary to suit a specific purpose.

— **Creative methods** of modifying or distorting movement within the framework of specific and distinct movement categories, such as steps, turns, and jumps, as well as grounded, locomotive, gestural, and narrative vocabulary.

— **Collaboration with the performers** by setting a framework of tasks, scores, rules, and guided improvisation to generate movement material collectively, and subsequently integrate various creative perspectives.

➢ **Sources of stimuli** for generating vocabulary and sequencing of the movement phrase encompass how individual choreographers respond kinesthetically to stimuli in the environment or in their memory to tackle the subject matter in the form of a response:

— **Kinesthetic and tactile response:** Movement often springs from other movement, abstract or literal. In some instances, theatrical and literal gestures can serve as an impetus for abstraction. In addition, the physical texture of objects, props, and the physical surroundings can influence the kinesthetic response to movement.

— **Visual and auditory response:** Rhythmic- and melodic-based music, as well as sound, noise, and spoken word, are natural motivators for generating movement material. Architecture and visual artwork containing figurative lines and colors can also inspire movement imagery.

— **Emotional and intellectual response:** Individual experiences and dramatic or uplifting personal circumstances, as well as the social/political environment, can serve as emotional and intellectual sources for generating unique movement vocabulary.

◆ **SUMMARIZING INTENT, SUBJECT MATTER, AND UNIQUE PERSPECTIVE** relate to the content of the movement material in the choreographic phrase. Comparable to a spoken sentence, a choreographic phrase contains condensed information, like a proverb.[4] A proverb summarizes the essence of a general truth or provides a piece of advice. For example, "Always put your best foot forward." The content of proverbs is easy to identify, just like a motif in a melody. Proverbs are also catchy and easy to remember because they capture the *essence* of common values. Some similarities between a proverb and a choreographic phrase are:

➢ **Summarizing intent** is the purpose of a phrase in the work as a whole. Each choreographic phrase may condense the idea behind a dance to its essence through the choice of movement material and how it is crafted. For example, in gastronomy we might need just one bite of the entire dish to identify what the dish is and whether or not we like it. What do you intend to cook?

BOTH DISHES BELOW CONTAIN FISH AND VEGETABLES.

A CHOREOGRAPHIC PHRASE IS SIMILAR TO ONE BITE OF SUSHI, RATHER THAN A FULL MEAL.

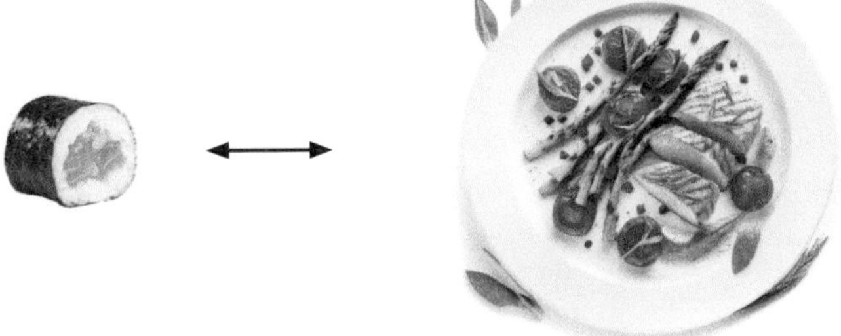

Figure 5

In contrast to the short length of a single movement, a choreographic phrase is a longer kinesthetic statement and an elaborate passage of motion. Therefore, the content of the phrase is also a summary of the underlying intentions. As the choreographer creates a phrase, a question about creative intent arises: *What does the phrase do, and what is it made of?*

For example, as part of a non-narrative dance work, a large ensemble of dancers passes across the stage behind a soloist. The phrase here highlights the contrast between the group and the individual. During a narrative dance work a phrase reveals a slow-moving group of performers carrying a motionless body above their heads, which sends a clue that perhaps this is a funeral procession.

The simplest way to identify and illustrate intent is by using verbs. Verbs could describe quiet and stationary actions, such as waiting, resting, mourning, or explicit and intense actions, such as chasing, catching, and confronting. These actions then translate kinesthetically into the movement phrase in either literal or plotless expressions.

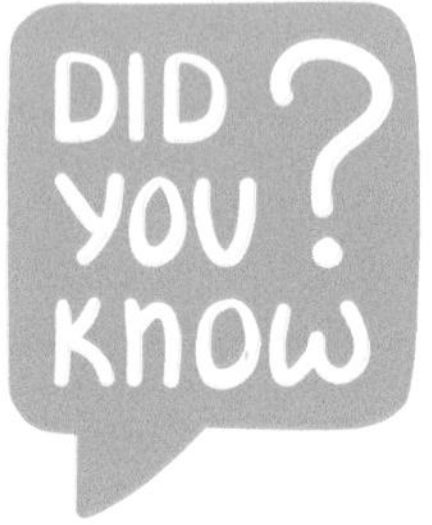

Our brains operate automatically and quickly with little or no effort and no sense of voluntary control.[5] We can instantly identify any given purpose and intent before paying attention to the details of the content. In speech, for example, when a sentence is spoken to us, we rapidly determine whether the person is asking a question, giving an instruction, or whispering a poem. Visually, we can immediately distinguish whether we are looking at a warning street sign, a banner from a political rally, or an advertisement billboard. We know what these signs are intended to do before we process the details of what they actually say.

➢ **An evolving motif** is a characteristic that summarizes the content of a choreographic phrase. In comparison to the summary of intent, which answers the question of what the phrase does and is made of, a motif manifests the key features of a phrase and answers the question of *how the phrase emerges and what its character is.* A motif can function independently and capture the essence of the entire work. Movement motifs can appear as shapes, figures, movement, and patterns. They are prone to repetition, expansion, modification, contrasting, recycling, variations, and development.

The use of motif is important not only in dance, but also in music. An excellent example is Beethoven's Fifth Symphony; the entire piece unfolds based on the development of the first four notes.[6] Also, a famous music work by Mozart or a popular song by the Beatles could be identified simply by humming the opening short, melodic motif of the piece.

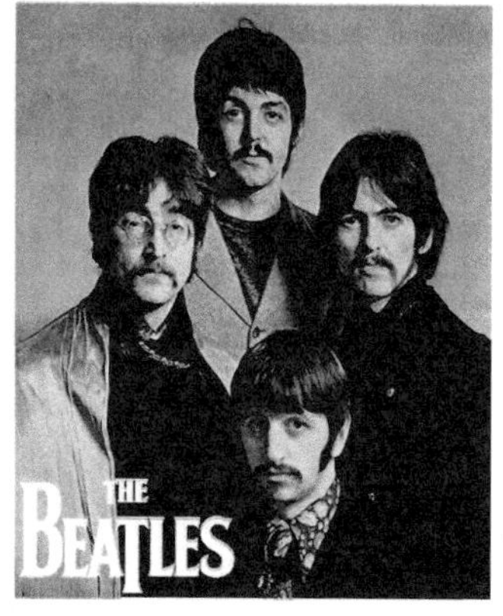

Figure 6

➢ **A unique perspective** is what makes the phrase distinct in terms of the overall content, including movement choices, appearance, and structural flow. Often, content, intent, conventionality, and originality either work well together or collide.

For example, if a choreographer chooses as content a distinctly personal experience and discreet narrative and then conveys it with traditional movement vocabulary, it might not serve the purpose well. In the reverse, a traditional concept—let's say the strength of love—might be appealing if the choreographer is able to experiment with movement material to discover evocative vocabulary. The reason is that in most cases, new movements or unique sequences are derived from choreographic vision, not the opposite.

What makes us unique is the way we see things, which is different from the way things are ordinarily presented, seen, and accepted. A unique perspective might be unusual, awkward, uncomfortable, and even provocative. Choreographers might struggle between wanting to be liked and accepted and wanting to be themselves and honest with their work. The artist's goal of truthfulness might either work well or collide with conventional expectations. Here is an unorthodox example:

HOW DO WE TRANSFORM SOMETHING ORDINARY

INTO SOMETHING UNIQUE AND INTRIGUING THAT IS ALSO TRUTHFUL?

Another way to say that it is:
1:15 PM
is to say that it is:
12:75 PM

Figure 7

◆ **VOCABULARY CHOICE, KINESTHETIC IMAGERY, AND TEXTURE** are the presence or the absence of uniformity of the movement material in the choreographic phrase. A movement sequence characterized by varying vocabulary or by the consistent reappearance of selected vocabulary determines the overall *kinesthetic imagery and texture* of the phrase. The choreographer's choice of vocabulary from various movement categories sets the initial parameters of how content will form and flow.

We determine *kinesthetic imagery and texture* by the use of a single or multiple categories of movement vocabulary that dominate the movement flow. Implementing movement from similar or different movement categories determines how the overall sequencing will appear. We can use terminology from the visual arts to describe the characteristics of kinesthetic texture and, for this purpose, we name them *monochromatic*, *polychromatic*, or *eclectic*.

➢ ***Monochromatic phrase*** is a choreographic phase that contains movement vocabulary from one dominant category, for instance: steps, stomps, tapping, walking, marching, and other movements of a chosen category.

In this case, the kinesthetic texture of the phrase might focus on virtuoso footwork. Phrases in dance genres such as American tap dance, Irish dance, Flamenco, and other regional and folk dances are sequences of complex steps in variations and deviations, with an emphasis on technique, speed, and accuracy of the feet.

The dominant movement category used in the genres is "steps." Although the phrase may contain some turns, jumps, locomotion throughout the space, and limb movements, the main emphasis is not to display high extensions of the legs or a series of virtuoso pirouettes. The one main texture and focus is the impressive movement of the feet. In this context, the phrase has one predominant movement category, while the other movement categories are supportive, supplemental, or decorative.

➢ ***Polychromatic phrase*** is a choreographic phrase that contains vocabulary from various movement categories that is treated with equal importance in the movement sequencing.

For example, in ballet, modern dance and jazz dance genres, a phrase might begin with rhythmically complex footwork, followed by leg extensions, jumps, turns, and inversions on the floor.

The kinesthetic texture and complexity of flow in a polychromatic phrase change as non-dominant movement categories are used. Vocabularies containing movements of larger size and range increase kinesthetic possibilities. The manipulations of movement no longer focus on complex steps and rhythmic patterns of the feet. Instead, the movement flow expands and uses the body's full capacity of motion, as well as the complexity of spatial interactions, locomotive patterns, and formations.

➢ ***Eclectic phrase*** is a choreographic phrase that incorporates vocabulary from any or all movement categories, as the phrase is kinesthetically integrated with any artifacts and an ongoing movement interaction with the surrounding environment.

Furthermore, the choreographic phrase combines with one or many interdisciplinary elements, including dramatic and visual arts, digital technology, and other media. Welcoming such an approach are experimental works in contemporary dance, movement theater, conceptual performances, site-specific and installation works, as well as movement performances incorporating technology.

Movements modified by the interaction with external elements affect the kinesthetic texture of the phrase. For example, a phrase can begin with a dancer's gestural movement, followed by the dancer reciting text, and then followed by a dance movement navigating a 3D projected image in the surroundings. The interlacing of human motion with non-dance elements, or with the surrounding environment creates the eclectic flow of the phrase. Such phrase might be exempt from manipulation by traditional compositional devices.

THE PROCESS OF BUILDING A PHRASE

– CONCEIVING MOVEMENT AS TOGETHERNESS –

◆ **PHRASE CONSTRUCTION, STRUCTURE, AND ASSEMBLAGE** are the processes of organizing, integrating, and bringing together movement material into a choreographic sequence by assembling it in a particular manner and with a distinct design.

Figure 8 Photography © Lois Greenfield, *Polaris*, choreography by Paul Taylor, pictured Rachel Berman, Heather Berest, Caryn Heliman, Thomas Patrick, Patrick Corbin, courtesy of Paul Taylor Dance Company, 1996

➢ ***Phrase construction*** is the strategy of compiling the movement material into a deliberate sequence. After a movement brainstorming session or a playful improvisation, a choreographer might wonder which of the generated material to use in the phrase.

While an *improvisation mindset* leads to the emergence of ideas in a spontaneous and random manner, a *construction mindset* leads to orderly placement of the ideas by their significance. By sorting and prioritizing movement ideas, the choreographer—just like a homebuilder—selects the most suitable movement material for the construction process. After the choreographer chooses movement material, questions might arise as to which key movement should begin the phrase and which will appear in the middle and at the end.

What is the process for constructing a phrase? Will an initial blueprint remain the *same* or will it be *reformulated*? The process is similar to constructing a home. When building a new house, multiple processes must occur before the brick laying begins. The owner might focus on choosing the paint color for the bedroom. However, from an engineering and construction perspective, the main goal is to use the appropriate building materials and to lay a solid foundation that is safe and functional. A house built upside down might look intriguing, but it would not be practical for daily living.

Key movement ideas can begin the phrase, appear in the middle, or come at the end, as long as the substantial material *is in* the phrase. As a construction strategy in building a *foundation*, one movement can serve as the *anchor*, with additional movements preceding and following it. Improvisation offers a spontaneous kinesthetic flow and evolving movement ideas. The goal is to brainstorm and generate new movements rather than to memorize and retain them. As choreographers generate phrases to progress toward creation of a full dance, they often return with a curious eye to what they have made. This critical strategy of "shuttling back and forth" between the generated material and nascent ideas is actually a natural process. With this backward glance, a choreographer recalls, reconstructs, and reformulates. The choreographic process of phrase construction is therefore cyclical: just like building and editing sentences in written expression, creating a dance phrase is an inner deliberation between what a choreographer has crafted and strives to craft.

➢ *Phrase structure* is the plot and the developmental framework of a choreographic phrase. Fundamentally, any plot is configured to have a beginning, a middle, and an end. Back in the 4th century BC, Greek philosopher Aristotle described this design principle in his *Poetics*. He offered an account of how a narrative unfolds and how to act it out. With this idea in mind, what is the plan for structuring a phrase?

Traditionally, an initial *exposition*, the introduction of the phrase, leads to *elaboration* of a statement, which concludes with a reconciliation and a *finale*. In many instances, there is a *climax*—a built-in accent serving as an intense culmination. In other instances, the phrase structure might be *neutral* or *fragmented*, and the movement material could be distributed evenly to intentionally avoid a climax. A variety of traditional *structural patterns* and well-known devices and strategies for manipulating movement flow are available for use during phrase construction—see Chapters 17 and 18.

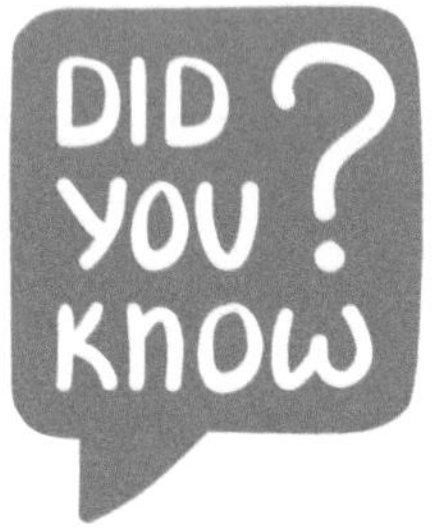

The American modern dance pioneer and choreographer Doris Humphrey was adamant about formal phrase structure: "Scientists have long noted the fact that the human mind has a proclivity for grouping experience in patterns; people are happier when a maze of sensation can be sorted out into some kind of order. The viewer of dance instinctively wants to understand the order of it, and the phrase-pattern is one thing that he can perceive."[7]

➢ *Assemblage and completion* is bringing the connected movement material to function as a standalone movement statement. Random and unstructured movement material has been selected and presented in an organized manner. Assembling and completing a movement sentence is similar to writing a sentence in verbal language. The movement sequence is subject to ongoing *editing* and *fine-tuning* to accommodate the choreographer's intent. As patterns of thought yield movement patterns, a few final details will bring the process to conclusion. In many cases, the choreographer can *emphasize* key movements by repeating them and manipulating their dynamics in space, time, and energy. Placing a *kinesthetic* accent on selected movements highlights their importance.[8] These final details might play a decisive role! As a movement phrase follows the rules of sentence construction in spoken and written language, a strategic emphasis on kinesthetic accents and *movement punctuation* can alter the meaning and the intent of a movement sentence.

COMMAS MATTER:

I love my parents Mickey Mouse and Donald Duck. (These are your parents?)

OR

I love my parents, Mickey Mouse, and Donald Duck. (In addition to your parents?)

HYPHENS MATTER:

Give me twenty–five dollar bills! (Ok. That is 25 x $1 = $25)

OR

Give me twenty five–dollar bills! (Ok. That is 20 x $5 = $100)

Figure 9

◆ **PHRASE SEQUENCING** is the particular order that movements follow. The sequencing of walking occurs when we put one foot in the front of the other, while simultaneously transferring our body weight to the leading foot. This motion accelerates the body in a forward direction. Walking is an instinctive and automatic movement sequencing as we consciously control our speed, direction, and range of motion. In choreography, the approach to movement sequencing ranges from an *instinctive and intuitive act* to a *rationally controlled formal design*, or a combination of both. How does one sequence a choreographic phrase?

In many improvisation techniques and *improvisational choreography*, movement sequencing emerges in a spontaneous, un-rehearsed natural flow. In most cases, improvisational artists are not interested in memorizing, revisiting, and reworking their choreographic material. Spontaneous and structured improvisation aim to play and experiment with movement; however, the generated choreographic sequencing might never recur in the same way—see Chapter 15.

Choreographers working in concert dance and formal dance presentations, on the other hand, might be drawn to *set choreography* and to crafting phrases in a controlled, organized, and methodical manner. In such cases, the choreographic phrase will be determined, memorized, and rehearsed. The set choreography is also subject to restaging, teaching, and transferring from one moving body to another, while the movement sequencing remains the same.

Movement sequencing in set choreography is part of implementing the choreographer's grand plan to construct a staged dance. Movements could be organized in a linear progression that leads to an expected resolution, and therefore, a satisfying and sensible outcome. The choreographer takes on a phrase as a puzzling equation, like a mathematical problem, and faces the challenge of resolving it choreographically.

Figure 10 Photography © Paul Gordon Emerson, pictured dancer Kathryn Sydell Pilkington, Company | E, 2020

Choreographers use various strategies and approaches to link movements. For instance, principles and devices from *chance improvisation*—see Chapter 15—might be useful in building a phrase sequence. Choreographers might choose to implement multiple devices separately or simultaneously. The process could be illustrated by replacing a number with movement and vice versa, as in the following samples:

➢ *Linear and cumulative:* Select a movement and let it flow into another, followed by a third one in seamless succession. Let the phrase develop incrementally on its own in a natural, cumulative progression:

1
1+ 2...
1+ 2 + 3 + 4...

Figure 11

➢ *Non-linear and random:* Select movements that did not originate chronologically and flow naturally from one into another. Connect them in ways to "make sense" of them:

3 + 7... (makes 10)
11 + 3 + 2 + 5... (makes 21)
4 + 11 + 5 + 8 + 6... (makes 34)

Figure 12

➢ *Parallel and/or colliding:* In partner dance, a phrase performed by two dancers might interconnect in a new sequence. One of the dancers (number without parenthesis) might perform a different sequencing of the same material than the other dancer (number with parenthesis). They might perform the same movement material simultaneously, but in different order, generating a parallel construction and deconstruction at the same time.

1(3) + 5 (7) + 9 (11) or 4(4) + 6(6) + 7(7) or 8 (103) + 9 (576,412) + 1(000)...
........Asymmetrical .... In-synchrony.................................. Accidental..........................

Figure 13

◆ **TRANSITIONS, LACK OF TRANSITIONS, CROSSOVERS, AND OVERLAPS** are the movement links connecting each separate motion, as they enable the phrase to flow and evolve. Transitions also allow the addition of more movements and the growth and expansion of the phrase. *Prolonged transitions* offer a lengthier period for qualitative variation to occur between movements. *Abrupt transitions* could be purposeful to cause a sense of disjuncture. *Absence of transitions* shortens the length of time between movements, causing the movements to *cross over* or *overlap*..

Transitions might emerge out of natural kinesthetic necessity. For example, after a dancer's traveling jump, transitional steps are essential to absorb the inertia before executing the next movement. Often, instinctive responses to movement generate an instant kinesthetic link. When one movement naturally transitions to another, it creates an *organic flow*. Other times, complex transitions emerge by manipulating movement dynamics to create a connection. Transitions might be *overlapping* with subtle and minimal micro-movements. Or a choreographer may use *crossover movements* by inserting additional steps, turns, and torso shifts to serve as "bridges" and proportional connection between movements.

Movement vocabulary from the same movement category and with similar characteristics is more suited to connectivity, fluidity, and speed, which allows for smooth, seamless transitions between movements. A movement sequence with minimal or no transitions is easier to execute at a fast tempo. For instance, simultaneously moving a few small red triangular figures amid white ones might be less fluid and fast than moving a red silk scarf.

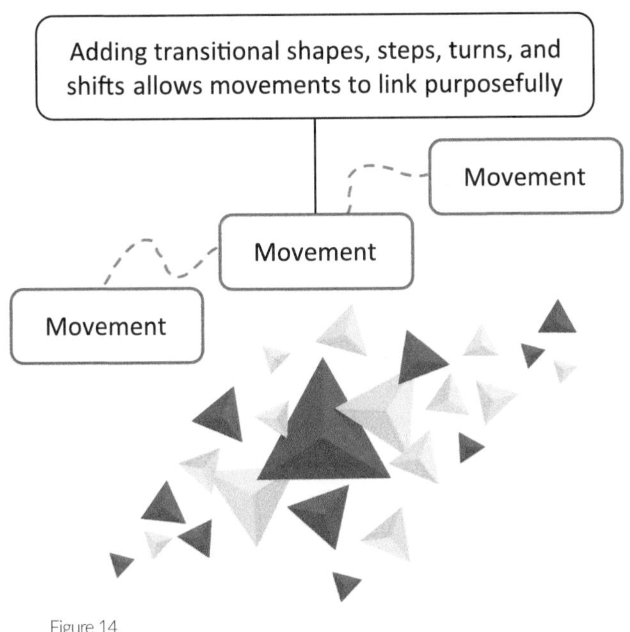

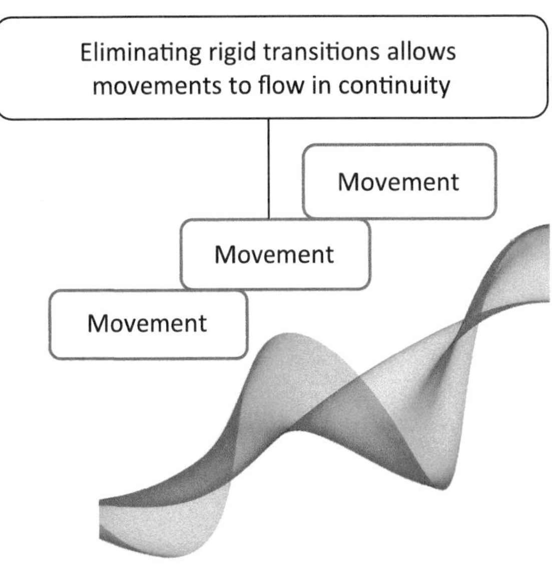

Figure 14

When choreographing long-format dance works, addressing transitions is relevant not only between movement phrases, but also between the various sections and scenes contained in a longer dance. The expandable function of links as transitions varies according to their use and can be categorized as: a) the links between movements based on kinesthetic necessity; b) the links between phrases based on the section's purpose; and c) the links between longer dance sections based on the overarching concept of the entire work and its physical dramaturgy—see the text diagram that follows and Chapter 19.

TRANSITIONS AS AN OPERATING CONCEPT

THINK OF CONNECTIVITY AND BUILDING LINKS...

between movements in a single phrase → between movement phrases → between dance sections

↓ ↓ ↓

consider kinesthetic necessity → **consider section's purpose** → **consider overarching concept**

Figure 15

?

Based on your experience in linking movement in various ways and creating transitions, what are the most exciting challenges for you, and why?

THE FORMING OF THE PHRASE
– SCOPE, TEMPORALITY, AND DEPLOYMENT –

◆ **A PHRASE IN SPACE** is the three-dimensional occupation of space by a movement sequence. The sequence has dimensional scope—height, width, and depth, as well as an observable presence and a locomotive flow in space.

➢ **Phrase observation in space.** The human eyes have a limited visual field, which makes it impossible for the viewer to have a 360-degree view of the moving body at any given moment. For example, we see only the bright side of the moon, while the dark side remains hidden. The choreographer makes artistic choices about which side of the moving dancer is visible and what elements of the choreographic phrase are accessible for observation. When the performer is dancing on a proscenium stage, the audience has a 180-degree visual field. The choreographer guides *what* the audience sees and *when* they see it by choosing a *front view* and a *focal point* to draw the needed attention. For example, there are multiple angles and viewpoints from which to observe a jumping dancer.

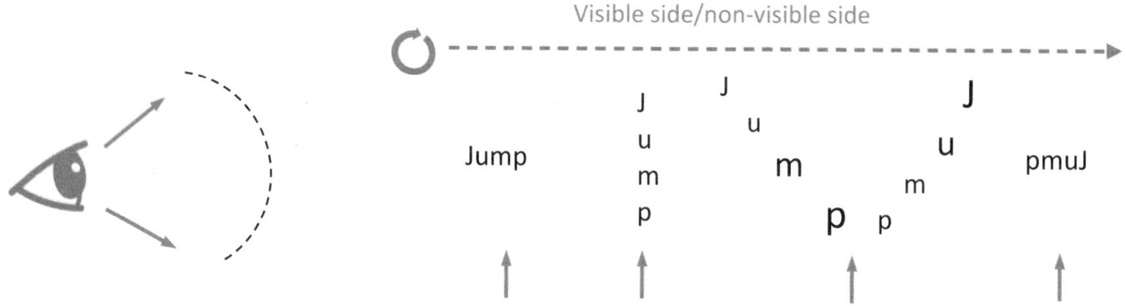

The chosen view could be ------► frontal view –► side view –► three-quarter view –► back view

Figure 16

➢ **Phrase occupation of space.** The choreographer creates the phrase in the three-dimensional performance space. Vertical, horizontal, and lateral dimensions are *spatial planes*. Each dimension allows for movement development in a *spatial design*. The phrase dynamically re-positions the dancers in different planes, directions, and dimensions.[9] Regardless of whether the dancers perform on a proscenium stage or at a site-specific location, the kinesthetic development of the phrase might unfold in multiple ways.

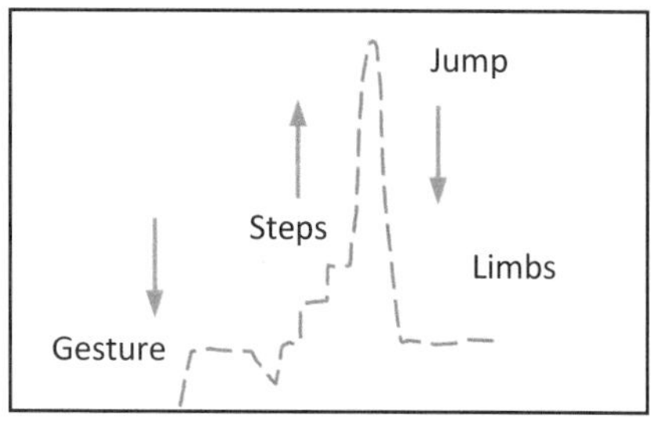

Up and down

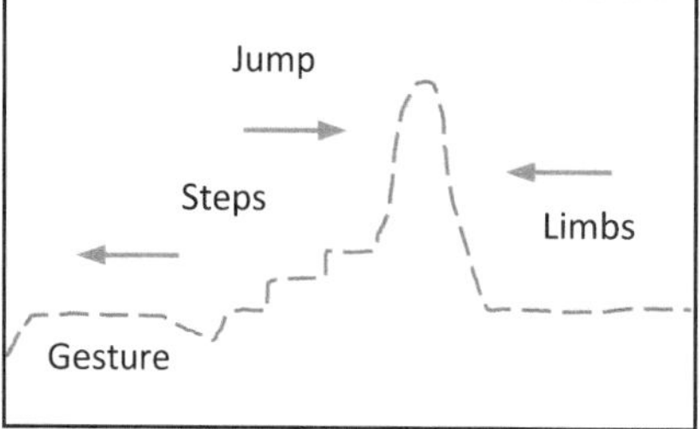

From side to side

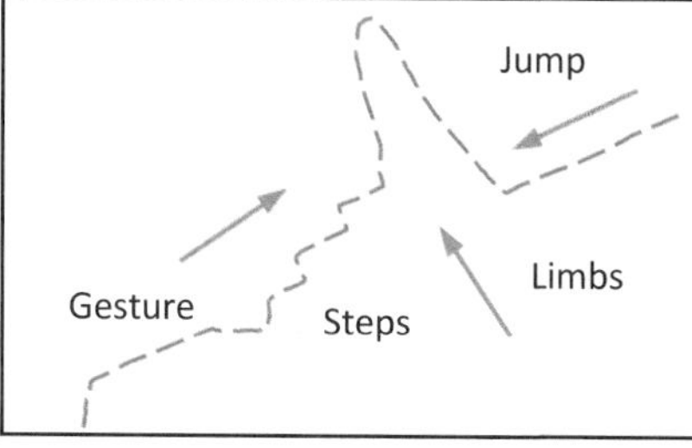

Deep and flat

Figure 17

➢ **Phrase locomotion in space.** The choreographer chooses *pathways, patterns,* and *placement* of a movement phrase in the performance space. The choreographic phrase progresses through these pathways. For example, a group of dancers might travel in a straight line across the floor to create pattern-formations and arrive at various locations and placements in space—see Chapter 18. In general, symmetrical patterns suggest calculated formality, while asymmetrical patterns might suggest intimacy and surprise or casualness and freedom. Floor patterns could be one or a combination of the following:

— *Geometrical* lines, forms, and figures such as circles, triangles, squares, and spirals, as well as locomotion in straight or curved lines;

— *Non-geometrical,* which contain a grid and instead appear in irregular and unrestricted pathways in natural forms, such as the flow of water, mountain landscape, or branches and leaves of trees;

— *Random,* occurring by chance and without a specific purpose or function.

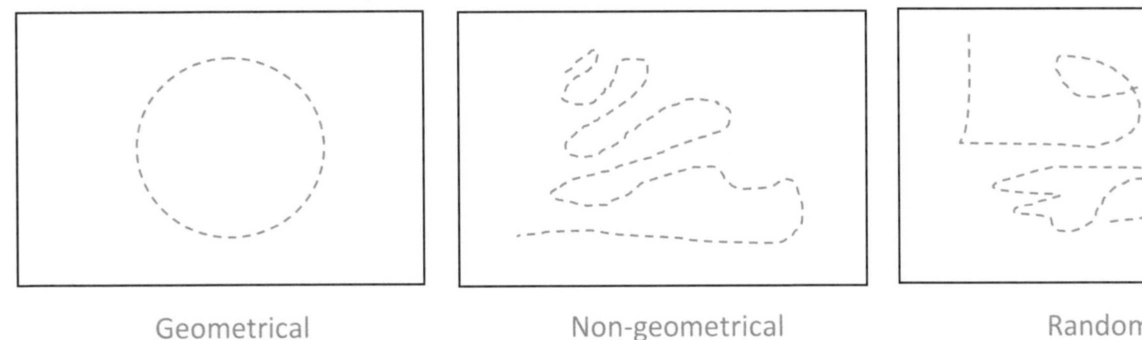

Figure 18

Two or more movement sequences of multiple performers and their floor pathways and patterns might *interact* and *share space.* These *spatial interactions* could form variable perceptions of new spaces—for example, they could express closeness by narrowing the space between them, or distance by their separation. By sharing floor patterns and spatial pathways of one or more movement sequences, multiple floor patterns might occur and interact as *parallel togetherness, in mirror symmetry,* or *by random chance.*

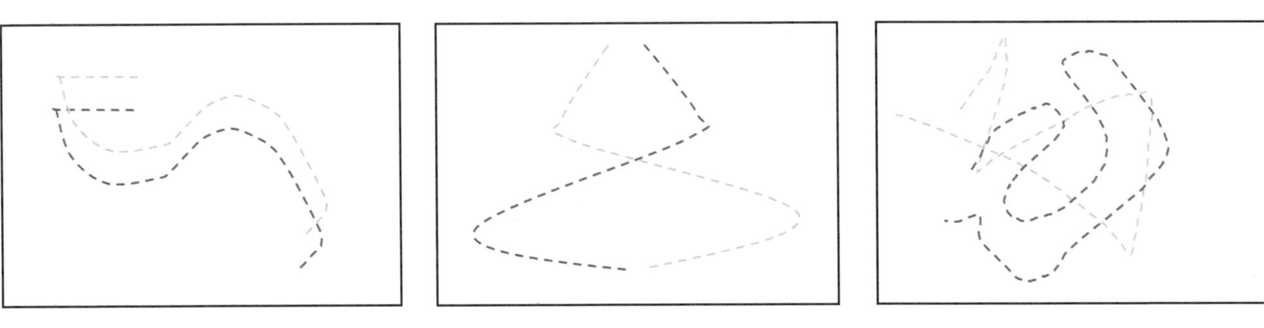

Figure 19

◈ **TIME IN A PHRASE** encompasses temporal factors such as: the clock-time length of movement sequencing and its starting and ending points, the duration of movements within the choreographic phrase, and the overall speed and pace of the movement sequence.

➢ **Time as an interval** is the clock-time distribution for certain movements in the sequence. Movements such as jumps, as well as some turns, have time intervals that are predetermined by the *force of gravity*. A jump has a consistent interval and cannot be longer than seconds. In addition, the gradual acceleration or deceleration and energy distribution—*momentum*—are important factors to consider. Some of the movements in the phrase can vary in terms of intervals, and some have consistent intervals.

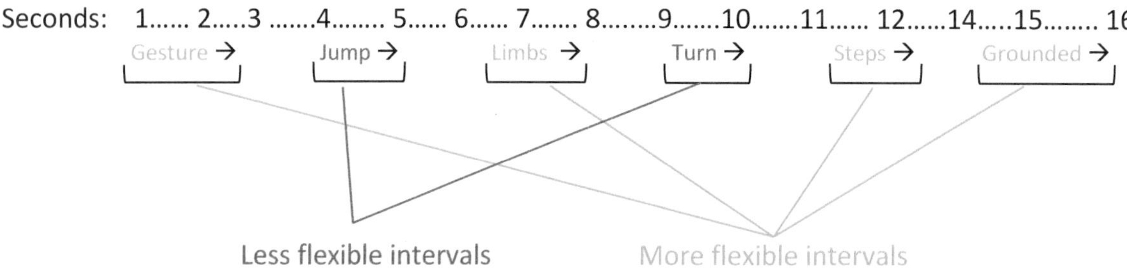

Figure 20

➢ **Time as duration** is a tool available to the choreographer to determine the preferred length of movements in the phrase. The movement duration can be shortened and/or prolonged, which might create a *movement accent* and a point of attention. The duration of movements can be used as an artistic device and support the choreographic intent in the context of the phrase.

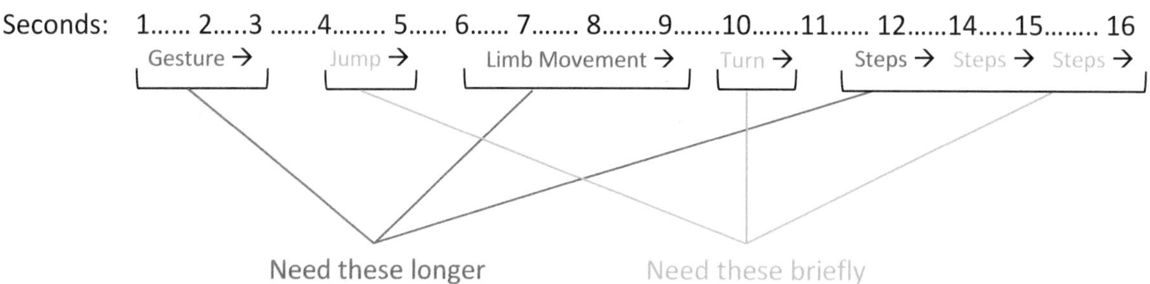

Figure 21

➢ **Time as speed** is the *pace of movement intensity*. In the choreographic phrase, the speed of movement is measured by the *beat*. The beat could have an even and steady pulse, while the *rhythm* could change in duration and pattern. Irregular rhythmic accents create *syncopations* that counterpoint the regular beat and introduce a *percussive quality*. The beat and rhythm also determine the *tempo* of movement—see Chapter 20. The tempo can increase and decrease. Slower tempos tend to convey dramatic moods, while faster tempos suggest cheerfulness. A phrase can be manipulated in various ways to fit the purpose.

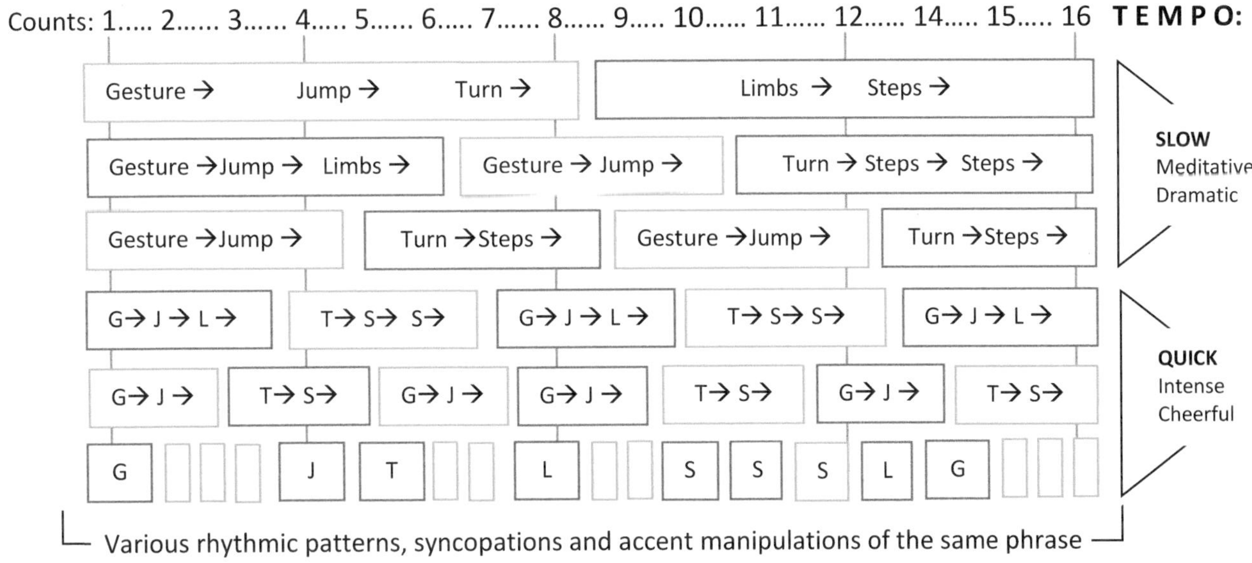

Figure 22

◆ **ENERGY IN A PHRASE** is the source, amount, and distribution of force that affects the substance, quality, and appearance of the movement material.[10] The energy deployed by internal and external sources enables the choreographer to reconfigure and kinesthetically manipulate the movement characteristics of the choreographic phrase.

➢ **Energy source** relates to the movement initiation and its intensity throughout the sequence. For example, to shift their bodies off balance, dancers might either forcefully launch their arms forward, pull their hips sideways, or arch their backs. The energy sources might vary in intensity in different parts of the body or in the whole body.

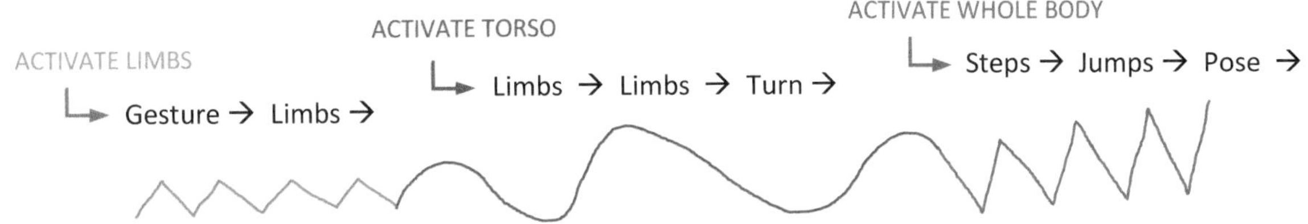

Figure 23

➢ **Energy amount** is the power needed to overcome gravity or other obstacles, which requires different amounts of physical force. Dancers need more energy to push against the floor to take off and jump into the air than to execute a minimal hand gesture. Each movement in the sequence reveals itself as energy waves and pulses of different amounts of power.

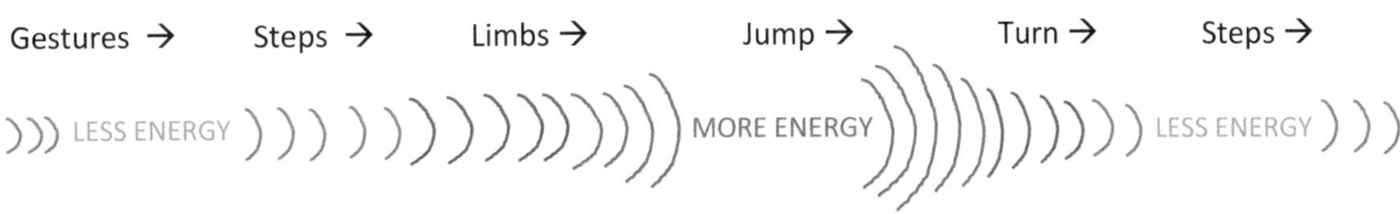

Figure 24

➢ **Energy distribution** is the allocation of force and the variability of power in a movement sequence as the energy is divided unevenly throughout the sequence. There are three separate types of energy distribution, which function simultaneously:

— *Precise energy* and force needed to accommodate the movements' needs and requirements, for example, the amount of energy and anticipated momentum needed to execute only one turn or pirouette, instead of two or many in succession.

— *Calibrated energy* and balance between the forces already at play, for example, gravity, momentum, other objects, or another body, and the additional forces needed to execute a high jump, then land and balance on one leg.

— *Nuanced energy* and scope to produce desired movement qualities in part or in the entire sequence, for example, the same movement material could appear in two opposite movement qualities, such as forceful or gentle and fluid or sharp at the same time.

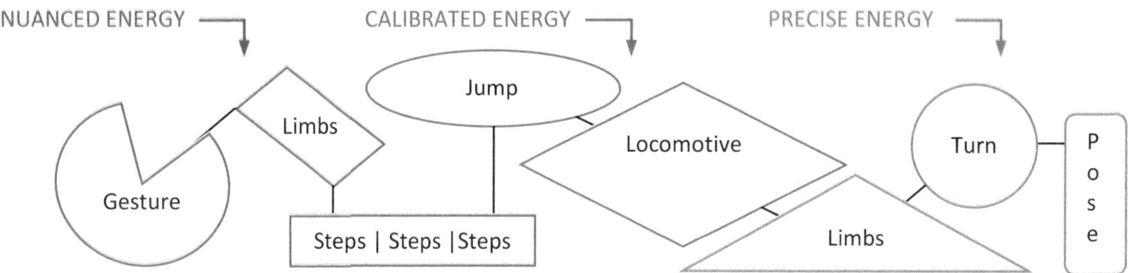

Figure 25

Finally, once a phrase has been crafted as a basic movement sequence, the choreographer can manipulate the phrase's *movement dynamics and qualities*—see Chapter 14—by using space properties—spatial occupation and dimensional patterns; time properties—duration, speed, and rhythmic patterns; and energy properties—source, volume, and distribution. More tools such as traditional choreographic devices, customized operations, and unique prompts are addressed and described in Chapters 17 and 18.

HELPFUL TIPS & SUGGESTIONS

~ Begin with what you have, instead of trying to begin
~ Rather than questioning an idea, experiment with it
~ Physicalize a thought to make it a dance
~ Vary a phrase to build a new phrase
~ Consider revising while creating
~ Implement stillness as part of movement
~ Think about the end before you get to the end

assignments & exercises

RESEARCH ASSIGNMENT:

➡ Identify a prominent choreographer who has inspired you the most in the past. Search videos online and look up a solo created by that choreographer.

➡ After looking at the dance with music, mute the music and look at the dance one more time without music.

➡ Study the content, the vocabulary used, the sequencing of the movement, the transitions between the movements, and the flow of the solo from beginning to end.

➡ Watch the work again and quickly learn, mimic, and mark the movement phrase within your own body.

➡ Analyze what makes the solo effective and why you find it impressive.

➡ Research the background of the choreographer and try to find out how the choreographer came up with the sequence, how long it took to make it, and how many drafts the dance underwent before it was finalized.

★ **CREATIVE ASSIGNMENT:**

➡ As a starter, think of *potential sources of stimuli*. What causes you to feel comfortable, excited, or intrigued to explore? Notice your internal kinesthetic response as movements emerge from other movements. Notice external stimuli, either visual or auditory, sights or sounds. Notice your emotional responses and the movement that emerges from a situation, circumstance, or past experience.

➡ Use *improvisation* to generate material. What makes you move? Use verbs such as reach, run, connect, or other well-established techniques from Chapter 15. As you improvise, pay attention to the type of vocabulary you generate. Navigate your improvisation to expand your range and use vocabulary from various movement categories. Which type of vocabulary best captures the content of your stimuli?

➡ Determine the best way of *sequencing* your solo phrase. In what order do you best express yourself? Explore guiding principles such as: a) accumulation and natural flow, b) minimal attention paid to transitions, c) random selection with greater attention to spatial and temporal relationships to generate an organic flow and a logical progression.

➡ As you construct your phrase, determine its *structure*. How do you arrange your material? Explore guiding principles such as a) How do you begin and introduce the material? b) Where is the midpoint of the phrase? c) How will the phrase lead to a conclusion, and what will the ending be—a *stop* and *pose*, an *exit*, or will it *transition* to the next phrase/section? Will you be able to present all of your material in 16 to 32 movements?

➡ Determine how your phrase is developing *spatially*. Use your sense of positioning and how much space you need to obtain and occupy. Define your sequence spatially: a) What part of the movements and sequencing are visible? b) How does the movement develop in height, width, and depth? c) What type of floor pattern is most effective?

Figure 26 Photography © Lois Greenfield, pictured Katherine Bolaños, courtesy of Aspen Santa Fe Ballet, 2008

➥ Determine how your phrase develops in *time*: Use your sense of timing as a point of attention, intensity, speed, and mood. Define your timing: a) by a clock, b) by the duration of each movement, considering the dramatic effect you aim to accomplish, and c) by the speed, beat, rhythm, and tempo, and how these elements enhance your movement material.

➥ Determine how your phrase develops in terms of *energy*. Experiment with adjectives such as light, heavy, floating, sustained, percussive and others. Determine the energy of the sequence: a) What is the intensity of the movements, nuanced or potent? b) How much pressure and force are necessary for the movement to be executed? and finally c) What are the volume, size, and range of the movements in the phrase that make them most effective to express your initial stimuli?

➥ Ask for peers' and mentors' feedback about how effectively your choices and your creative process have accomplished your initial intentions.

COMPARATIVE ASSIGNMENT:

➥ Consider the prominent choreographer of your choice in the initial research. Compare and analyze your strategies to those used by the choreographer of your choice. What was effective, and what could be improved?

➥ Analyze the similarity and/or difference between the outcome of your phrase and that of the prominent choreographer.

➥ Analyze and compare the qualities of your phrase and those of the prominent choreographer.

BIBLIOGRAPHY AND REFERENCES

[1] Bloom, Lynne Anne and Chaplin, Tarin L. *The Intimate Act of Choreography*, University of Pittsburg Press, 1996, p. 26.
[2] Bloom and Chaplin 1996. *The Intimate Act of Choreography*, pp. 29–30.
[3] Bloom and Chaplin 1996. *The Intimate Act of Choreography*, p. 29.
[4] Humphrey, Doris. *The Art of Making Dances*, Grove Press, 1959, pp. 70–71.
[5] Kahneman, Daniel. *Of 2 Minds: How Fast and Slow Thinking Shape Perception and Choice* (excerpt from book), online article, *Scientific American*, 2012, accessed 2017.
[6] Humphrey 1959. *The Intimate Act of Choreography*, p. 102.
[7] Humphrey 1959. *The Art of Making Dances*, pp. 68–69,
[8] Humphrey 1959. *The Intimate Act of Choreography*, pp. 63–67, 107.
[9] Humphrey 1959. *The Intimate Act of Choreography*, pp. 31–36.
[10] Humphrey 1959. *The Intimate Act of Choreography*, pp. 75–76.

VISUAL REFERENCES

Figure 1: Diagram © Vladimir Angelov

Figure 2: Diagram © Vladimir Angelov and chest of drawers illustration, free clip art, courtesy of http://search.coolclips.com/

Figure 3: Diagram © Vladimir Angelov, photo © Vladimir Angelov

Figure 4: Photography © Lois Greenfield, pictured Nikita Maxwell, Sheila Carreras Brandson and Terry Dean Bartlett, courtesy of STREB Extreme Action, 2002

Figure 5: *Maki sushi food*, credit: Miquel courtesy of Adobe Stock, *Grilled salmon steak with asparagus and tomatoes cherry on a white plate isolated on white background. top view. Generative AI*, credit: AkuAku courtesy of Adobe Stock

, Wirestock, royalty-free use from freepik.com, *Salmon Dinner, Grilled Salmon*, Timolina, royalty-free use from freepik.com

Figure 6: Portrait of Ludwig van Beethoven, by Joseph Karl Stieler, oil painting, 1820, public domain; posthumous painting of Wolfgang Amadeus Mozart, Barbara Krafft, 1819, public domain, edited by Charles Scheland, 2021. The Beatles—All You Need is Love & Baby, You're a Rich Man, Capitol Records, public domain, 1967, edited by Charles Scheland, 2021

Figure 7: Diagram © Vladimir Angelov, clipart: *Flat long shadow clock icon isolated on white background*, credit: dariachekman courtesy of Adobe Stock

Figure 8: Photography © Lois Greenfield, *Polaris*, choreography by Paul Taylor, pictured Rachel Berman, Heather Berest, Caryn Heliman, Thomas Patrick, Patrick Corbin, courtesy of Paul Taylor Dance Company, 1996

Figure 9: Diagram © Vladimir Angelov

Figure 10: Photography © Paul Gordon Emerson, pictured dancer Kathryn Sydell Pilkington, Company | E, 2020

Figures 11, 12, and 13: Diagrams © Vladimir Angelov

Figure 14: Diagram © Vladimir Angelov, with clip art. Left Image: *Red Triangles, Abstract Triangle Elements*, credit: Alliesinteractive, royalty-free use from freepik.com; Right image: *Abstract red wave Raster wavy pattern Copy space for text Bright ribbon on white background*, isolated. Credit: Anna Bliokh, royalty-free use, courtesy of iStock/Getty Images

Figure 15: Diagram © Vladimir Angelov

Figure 16: Diagram © Vladimir Angelov, clip art: *Eye side view*, credit: Barbulat, sourced at iStock/Getty Images

Figures 17 to 25: Diagrams © Vladimir Angelov

Figure 26 Photography © Lois Greenfield, pictured Katherine Bolaños, courtesy of Aspen Santa Fe Ballet, 2008

BOOK V

PROCESS AND PROGRESS

DEVELOPING MOVEMENT MATERIAL

At end of first spacing rehearsal on stage:

CHOREOGRAPHER: Good run-through! Thank you all. Dismissed.

DRAMATURG:...(shifts uncomfortably in his seat)

CHOREOGRAPHER: So, what do you think?

DRAMATURG: The dancing? Great energy! Yet the finale, although powerful...is a bit unclear.

CHOREOGRAPHER: Remember we also have the white dots snowfall effect behind the dancers.

DRAMATURG: Oh, yes. Without the tech crew, I forgot to imagine it. Then it's all good!

CHOREOGRAPHER: Ok. Let's get some dinner.

Excerpt from

dance DIALOGUES

An Anonymous Unpublished Manuscript, 376 BC–AD 2091

CHAPTER 17

CHOREOGRAPHIC DEVICES AND OPERATIONS

– GROWING A DANCE GARDEN –

For each choreographer, creating dance is a unique process and a personal journey that often involves a lot of guesswork and luck. When crafting and setting a dance, a choreographer might face unplanned circumstances that demand firm decisions to move the creation forward. In this often-chaotic process, the choreographer needs reliable tools and developmental principles to make the dance—from an initial idea, through construction and assembly, to tackling essential details and adding the "final touches."[1]

Although creating a dance by enduring multilayered processes might be a tedious experience, it is a rewarding one. The creative process can be compared to planting and growing a vegetable or flower garden. If movements are the seeds and phrases are the plants, then the choreographic devices are the gardener's tools that help the seeds and plants grow, along with the soil, water, and sunlight. Gardeners say that plants thrive when someone nurtures them. And if a plant dies, then a new one will be planted in its place—a dynamic process of gardening and *avant*-gardening.

> ◆ **Various choreographic tools—devices, prompts, and operations—are available to the choreographer to experiment and develop movement material.** They are the fundamental instruments of a choreographer's craft. These tools, some traditional and some new and unique, intend to stretch a movement idea outside its conventional and habitual treatment. There is no right or wrong way to implement these tools; the process is less about what the choreographer *should* do and more about what the choreographer *could* do.

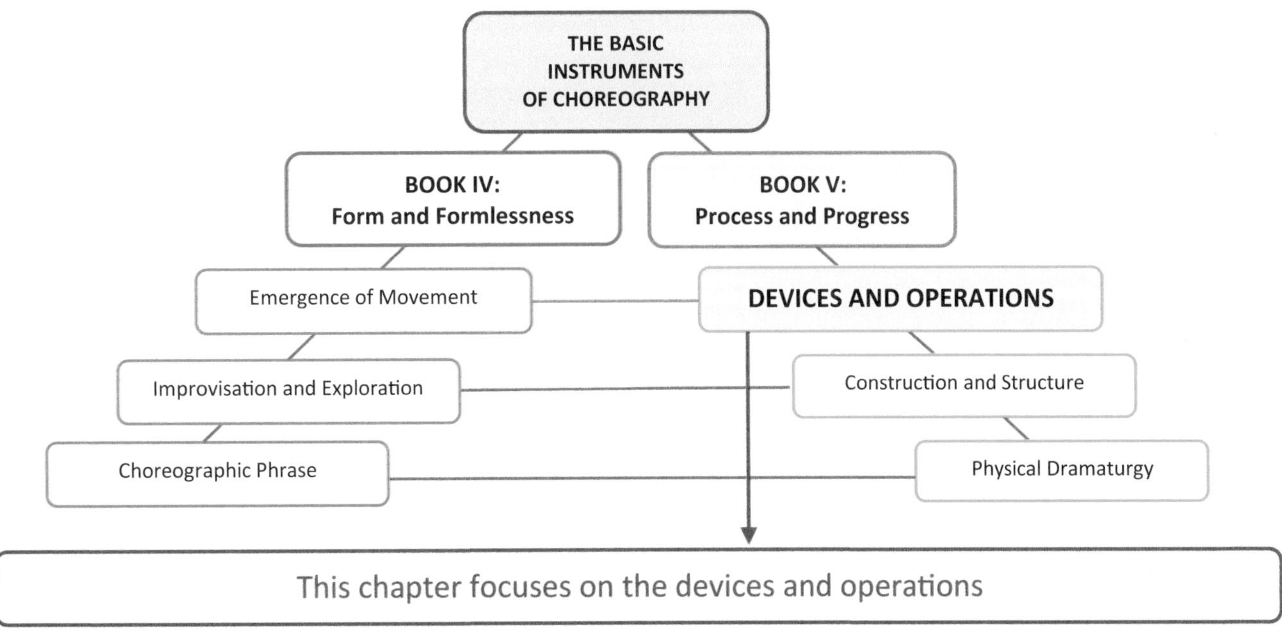

Figure 1

EXPERIMENTING AND EXPLORING, REVISITING, AND DEVELOPING MOVEMENT MATERIAL

Concert dance choreographers might be inclined to use dance improvisation and movement brainstorming techniques to generate initial movement material; then they might choose a formal approach to select, develop, and consolidate their movement ideas and findings into set choreography. Improvisational choreographers, on the other hand, might focus solely on movement research, and therefore, they might be less concerned about a formal performance outcome. For them, the instantaneous act of moving itself *is* the choreographic creation. There are variable levels of formalism and ways of manipulating and maneuvering movement material and sequencing, which can be summarized as:

IMPROVISATION

NON-FORMALIST DEVELOPMENTAL APPROACH TO MOVEMENT MATERIAL:

...Dancing while Choreographing ←→ Choreographing while Dancing...

and/or

SET CHOREOGRAPHY

FORMALIST DEVELOPMENTAL APPROACH TO MOVEMENT MATERIAL:

...Dancing and Experimenting → **Structuring and Developing** → **Constructing and Consolidating...**

Figure 2

In the first case, the choreographer's non-formalistic developmental approach shines in the designing of tasks, scores, and any directional framework that is given to the dancers to experiment with and explore. Movement spontaneity and immediate response to specific prompts, directions, and provocations are dominant tools for generating new movement material. Therefore, a traditional formalist choreographic development that requires revisiting and developing of the *same* movement material might not be a priority. For more on choreography as improvisation, see Chapter 15.

In the second case, the choreographer might choose to solicit movement material that fits their intentions and/or a particular concept. An artistic agenda might emerge not only while merely moving, but it could also be formed by the content, structure, and specific demands of a choreographic project. The movement material might be revisited, repeated, modified, developed, edited, assimilated, and consolidated before concluding as a final, set choreography.

In many instances, both approaches merge as the choreographer's mindset shifts between being an *improviser* and a *constructionist*. The *improviser* spontaneously and playfully explores random movement ideas without assessments; the *constructionist* evaluates useful ideas and implements various *choreographic devices* and *compositional structures* to *develop* the movement into set choreography.

WHAT DOES "DEVELOPING" MEAN?

Developing is a complex term with variable interpretations, especially when it comes to movement material. Emerging choreographers often hear from mentors and dance authorities: *"This dance section has great potential, but it needs developing. Go for it!"* The feedback does not provide information about what the choreographer should do exactly.

Professor Larry Lavender of University of North Carolina at Greensboro wisely wrote that "Choreographers regularly act upon their works to change expressive details or to shape particular characteristics. They *develop* in myriad ways specific aspects of material and structural/presentational frameworks for material: they may lengthen, shorten, expand, blur or sharpen material, or change its speed, direction, or location in space. They may infuse their work with a particular energy quality, or turn it backwards or upside down, and so forth."[2] In summary, to develop means to play and tweak, revisit and modify, experiment and explore, frame and reframe, manipulate and maneuver selected movement material. Furthermore, developmental actions can be grouped in two distinct processes:

- **Organizational structures** are ways for choreographers to organize large sections of material in movement formations and structural formats; to build movement elements in phrases; to divide movement phrases among different numbers of dancers and groupings; and to finally consolidate movement ideas and choreographic sections into a conceptual unity.[3] More on dance construction and structure is in Chapter 18.

- **Choreographic devices**, prompts, and operations are tools and techniques to manipulate, expand, amplify, and reshape smaller chunks of movement material.[4] The developmental process advances by continuing creative engagement such as revisiting, modifying, evaluating, selecting, and editing the choreographic material—see Figure 3.

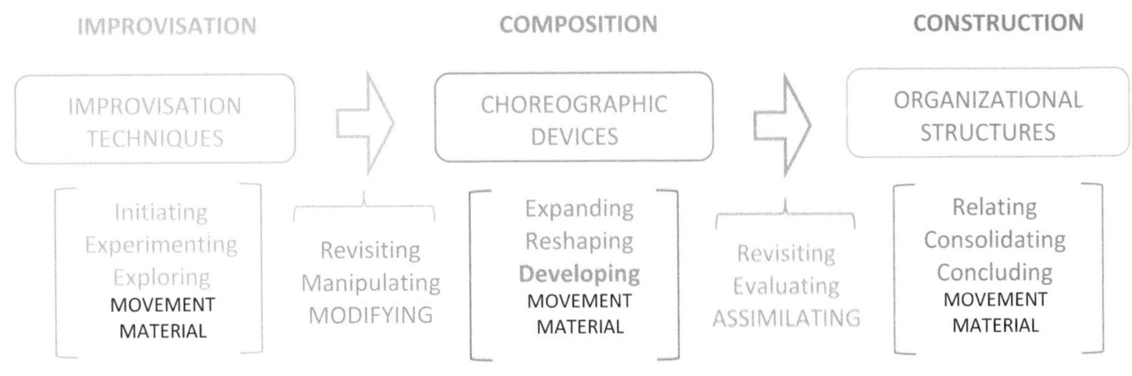

Figure 3

The *choreographic devices* and *organizational structures* are often called a ***toolbox***, as creative instruments kept "in the box" that are ready to be retrieved. Ironically, the goal of using these tools is to elaborate on movement ideas by getting the choreographer's imaginative work "out of the box." Perhaps there is a hidden paradox in using the toolbox.

EXPANDING THE AVAILABLE MOVEMENT MATERIAL
– THEME AND VARIATIONS VS. MOTIF AND DEVELOPMENT –

A choreographer often generates and handles various ideas simultaneously, while the work-in-progress develops on multiple levels and in different directions. A traditional and formalist strategy for expanding and developing a choreographic idea is movement repetition and recurrence of movement material that may shape the characteristics and the entire dance. When using this strategy, it is important to clarify the distinction between two fundamental entities: theme and variations, and motif and development. The two principles are different, yet related, and have no preferred order.[5]

Theme is an overarching, specific movement concept, composed of multiple movements in a phrase sequence, which can be conceived as the *home* (A) upon which to develop variations. Variations may maintain the sequencing of the original theme, yet vary in character, size, and flavor.[6] Once a movement theme is presented, the sequence can be repeated multiple times and the variation can be changed. Each variation can be presented simply by shifts in the quality and the interpretation of the movement material. Think of theme as something that could appear in many different versions of the general idea:

THEME AND VARIATION: A = A1, A 2, A3, A 4, A5, A 6, A 7

Figure 4

Motif is a movement feature, a decorative element, or a dominant characteristic that has the capacity to expand and evolve within a design. A motif can be related and linked to a theme, or a motif can exist independently and connect random entities. Think of motif—an *element* (A)—as a condensed idea with variable reappearances within a succession:[7]

MOTIF AND DEVELOPMENT: A = ABCDA, RAAR, ABRACADABRA...

Figure 5

In summary, theme is a concept with capacity to vary conceptually and structurally. Motif is an element with capacity to recur, adapt, and expand. While a theme is usually developed and varied within the framework of a *compositional structure*, a motif is usually manipulated and developed by using *choreographic devices*.

For instance, the **theme** of the ballet *Swan Lake* explores an archetypical metaphor that identifies the swan with female beauty and vice versa. The idea of a swan/woman appears in opposite characteristics and colors as the *White Swan* and the *Black Swan*. There are also the *Four Little Swans*. The movement **motif** of the ballet *Swan Lake* explores the fluid movements of the arms and wrists that recall swan wings, a distinctive movement element and narrative metaphor that recurs throughout the ballet.

TRADITIONAL CHOREOGRAPHIC DEVICES

Traditional choreographic devices are prescribed tools and defined tasks aiming to manipulate and develop newly generated movement material towards a specific outcome. Many traditional devices in choreography are "borrowed" from similar developmental principles used in music composition, architecture, literature, and other arts.[8] Once basic movement material has been generated and is available in the form of movement sketches and sequencing, the choreographer works with the dancers to choose one or a combination of devices to maneuver the movement material by expanding it in multiple versions. For example, the choreographer may instruct the dancers to:

"Use repetition and steadily reprise this movement."

or

"Change the speed and perform this movement faster."

or

"Retrograde and reverse this movement sequence."

Traditional devices are predetermined principles that lead to predictable outcomes. Using repetition always results in repetition. Yet being informed about the traditional devices and gaining proficiency in using them helps build craftsmanship and choreographic skills. Here is a list of the twelve most popular traditional devices:

➢ **Space manipulation:** Consider manipulating the spacing of a movement phrase: a) Change the front or the stage location of the movements. b) Use the stage space differently by changing planes and levels—up, down, and side. c) Experiment with changing the floor pattern of the original phrase and reposition it in a variety of new spots on the stage.

➢ **Time manipulation:** Consider manipulating the timing of the original movement material: a) Manipulate the duration of some or all movement—together or separately. b) Manipulate the tempo but not the rhythm. c) Manipulate the rhythm but not the tempo. d) Finally, insert occasional holds, pauses, and stops.

➢ **Energy manipulation:** Consider manipulating the energy and attributes of movement quality: a) Experiment with different pressure. b) Expand or subtract the range of force and movement volume. c) Play with qualitative aspects of movement—sharpness, looseness, strong attack, weak retreat, or with gentle or forceful qualities.

➢ **Repetition:** Consider repeating a selected movement multiple times during a movement sequence. The repeated movement may gain importance and become a *focal point* and/or a *motif* that is recalled, re-echoed, and reiterated.

➢ **Retrograde:** Select a portion of the sequence and redo the phrase backwards, imagining that you are re-winding from the end to the beginning. Allow inaccuracy when precise retrograde is physically impossible. Instead, generate a modified sequence that is possible to perform and rehearse.

➢ **Inversion/Opposition:** Consider selecting elements of the phrase and staging them upside down or moving an element that is done to the left, to the right. A jump can be turned into a floor movement, and vice versa; inversion might include *mirroring* or oppositional reflections. Turning around, over, backwards, upside-down, right side up, inside-out, or to the other side are all intriguing options.

➢ **Minimization/Maximization:** Consider manipulating the range and the size of certain movements by making them very small or very large.

➢ **Insertion/Ornamentation:** Consider inserting occasionally or repeatedly an additional single movement of the same dance genre and/or gestural and stylistic embellishments inside the original sequence and flow of the phrase. The new recurring movement could become a *motif.*

➢ **Instrumentation:** Consider switching certain movements to different parts of the body. For example, a movement with the hand will be executed with the leg; a movement with the leg can be executed by moving only the hips.

➢ **Accumulation:** Consider adding new movement material to the end of the phrase. Expand the phrase by adding at least three new movements at the end of each repetition.

➢ **Merging:** Like insertion, consider merging one phase with another phrase by de-constructing all phrases and reassembling them in a new, non-linear random sequence.

➢ **Contrasting:** Consider manipulating the movement by adding contrasting movement vocabulary from different dance genres and styles. For example, in a phrase of contemporary dance, insert a characteristic step from ballet, folklore, or ballroom dance.

UNIQUE CHOREOGRAPHIC PROMPTS

Unique prompts are specifically designed tasks, assignments, and requests that engage the dancers in creative collaboration. Prompts tend to be customized and expandable. They could be a combination of traditional devices and any non-traditional operations that are triggered and inspired by the unique movement material presented and observed in rehearsal.

Compared to traditional devices, unique prompts often lead to a less predictable outcome or even surprising versions of the existing movement material. When dancers are asked to use repetition, the execution of the repetition is the anticipated result. Therefore, traditional devices are tools for *manipulating* the movement material and generating variations, while unique prompts are tools for *engaging* and *activating* dancers' creativity and collaborative participation.[9] For example, the choreographer may ask the dancers to:

"Personalize and modify the movements in the phrase to make them your own."

or

"Dance the same phrase but use only the movements most appealing to you."

or

"Alter the movements and add new ones, as if you are suddenly feeling disappointed."

Unique prompts are adventurous. They can fundamentally alter the movements and their quality, the sequencing, and the overall look of the initial choreography. Specific or general prompts will give the dancers certain restraints or unlimited freedom. Unique prompts are an opportunity to experiment with movement material with the dancers' creative input.

EXPANDABLE CHOREOGRAPHIC OPERATIONS

Expandable operations are large-scale creative directives that invite an overarching augmentation of the movement material of the entire dance. These *choreographic provocations*[10] are meant to substantially revise the initial choreographic intent. The goal of expandable operations is not only to *manipulate* vocabulary and movement sequencing, but also to fundamentally *transform* and drastically *re-envision* the core of a choreographic idea with significant creative input from the dancers. Once the dance work has some set structure and has been rehearsed, the choreographer might experiment with radical options. This choreographer could say, "Let's try something different," thereby releasing the dancers from their duty to strictly repeat the work in its initial choreographed version.

The dancers might be allowed to make substantial adjustments and alterations to the entire movement material, as the choreographer could direct changes in the movement intention, introduce new imagery, or drastically reconfigure structural sequencing, floor patterns, and group formations. Such an approach might awaken alternative versions of the existing material by provoking the dance work as a whole. Intriguing creative alternatives may also emerge if the dancers simply get permission to transform a still shape into a movement or a jump. For example, the choreographer may direct the dancers to:

"Alter the initial movements and sequencing to make them fit this new music score."

or

"Modify your solo by relating clearly to anything or anyone nearby."

or

"Expand your solo into a duet with a person from the stage crew as they walk onstage."

Engaging in expandable operations might trigger different reactions and responses from the dancers. Possible scenarios are that the dancers could: *collaborate*, meaning accept and implement the operations; or *resist*, meaning express discomfort with execution or lack of inspiration; or *negotiate*, meaning bargain or counter-propose different ideas.

Based on the new versions of the movement material, the choreographer makes the final creative "editorial" choices. This process involves evaluating the subtleties and complexities of the newly generated movement material and then selecting and editing it to finalize the creative process. Discerning the ability of instantaneous problem-solving to retain its freshness and repeated desirability is a challenge of the provocation method. What may look more exciting and "better" the first time may lose its attractiveness as it becomes known and predictable to the dancer. Making decisions about what to change and what to keep is not simple, and yet it is more manageable once the section in question is positioned in context and as part of the work's overall content.

Figure 6 Photography © Lois Greenfield, pictured Parsons Dance Company, 2000

EVALUATING, SELECTING, AND EDITING
– FACING CHOICES, TAKING DECISIONS, AND MAKING CHANGES –

The use of various devices, prompts, and operations results in a wealth of developed material available for review, though all of it need not be kept. The choreographer speaks through movement, and movement will speak back to the choreographer. What "was good" and what "got better"? Mentors might be in the dance studio as "outside eyes" to help reveal the choreographer's "inside eyes." What response will the choreographer hear? Critical voices, praise, or silence? It may be hard for the choreographer to remain both open to critique and true to their own artistic goals. The choreographer may feel a need to either defend or justify their artistic choices, which interferes with the benefits of any feedback process. All commentary is useful; the choreographer can take it or leave it. Yet knowing what outside viewers see as choreographic intentions is very useful.

Making the right creative choices involves a delicate balance: If there is *overthinking*, the creative process may feel unnatural and the choreographer may become discouraged. If there is *underthinking*, then important details might slip away and the choreographer may wonder why the hard work did not pay off. Although the choreographer's choices in each creative journey may vary, the road ahead remains the same.

◆ **Evaluating** is *examining why* certain parts are worth keeping. Evaluations could be made as a spontaneous reaction, or a reflective conclusion, or an intuitive decision[11]—all guided by how the new versions of the old material relate to the overall concept.

◆ **Selecting** is *deciding which* parts are worth keeping, and which parts the choreographer will change, remove, or replace. This leads to the assimilation and perhaps further modification of the material to fit organically to a newly reconfigured structure and the re-envisioned concept.

◆ **Editing** is *implementing* the changes to the movement material. Some edits may alter details through *cutting and pasting*, while other edits may substantially adjust and *rewrite* the big picture.

In the center of it all is the dance still to be created and completed. The choreographer, alone or in collaboration with the dancers, is simultaneously a creator, critic, decisionmaker, and executive.

INCREASING NUMERICAL FORMATS, CAST SIZES, AND CASTING CHOICES

Choreographic devices, unique prompts, and expandable operations can lead to an increase in cast size by allowing movement material to be distributed to more than one dancer. For example, a choreographic phrase originally created as a solo could be deconstructed and then performed by two dancers as a duet involving partnering, or by a whole group in unison. Large group formations, on the other hand, may contain solos and duets or other sub-formations moving simultaneously, in contrast to one another, or in succession—see Figure 7.

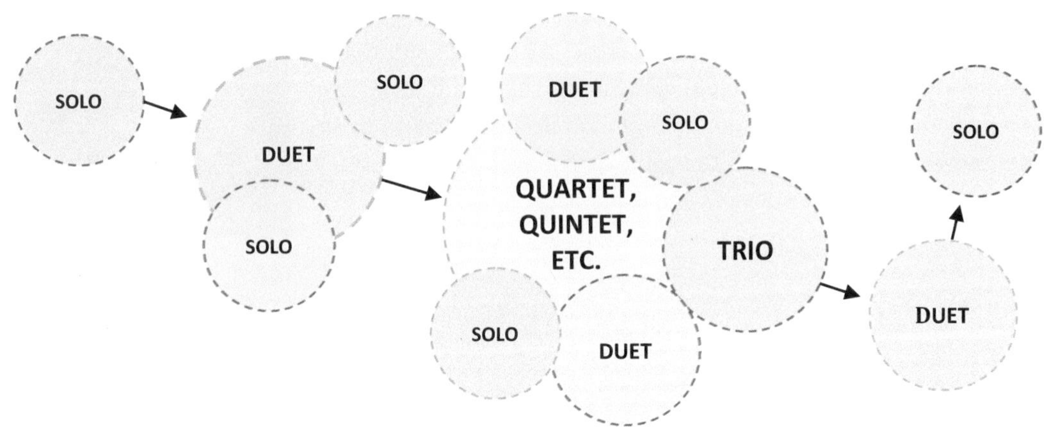

Figure 7

Cast size, casting choices, and numerical format may carry certain characteristics with artistic intent and a desired impact. A duet between dancers of the same or different gender, race, and age may be interpreted as a purposeful artistic choice and statement. The numeral grouping and the number of dancers performing may be used not only as a visual effect, but also as an integral part of the overall concept and dramaturgy.

THE SOLO

– A MOVEMENT MONOLOGUE –

With only a single body in motion, a solo has the powerful capacity to convey a wide range of movement ideas and to capture the human condition as a movement experience. A dance solo may unfold as an abstraction of an image, an interpretation of a general theme, or an illustration of a specific idea. A solo might be a candid confession about inner forces, a reflection about the outer world, or an intimate monologue where the dance tells a story about significant events, feelings, struggles, and victories. Finally, a solo could simply be a dance about dance, or movement about movement, or movement without dance.

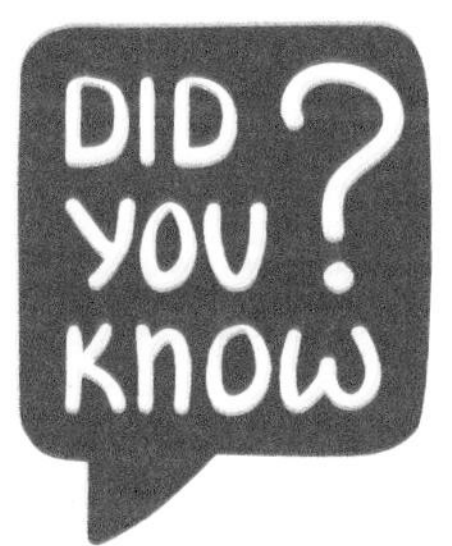

Solo choreography may embody a rich spectrum of literal and abstract concepts. For example, in many Indian classical dance traditions, a solo choreographer-performer can elaborately portray mythological tales and sacred chronicles. Complex narrative solos can depict multiple characters at the same time, including humans, animals, and natural forces. A single body may convey intricate story plots with convincing personalities and capture the complexities of a fairytale universe.

Choreographing a solo is challenging but also exciting, from developing the initial concept to finalizing the dance. This complex and delicate creation may condense movement ideas that showcase a captivating performer. In modern dance, a rich heritage traces astonishing solos by a constellation of prominent choreographers—from Loie Fuller, Ruth Saint Denis and Isadora Duncan, through Martha Graham, Merce Cunningham, Yvonne Rainer and Trisha Brown, up to the latest works by Carolyn Carlson, Anne Teresa De Keersmaeker, Kyle Abraham, and Akram Kahn. We can learn from these choreographers that a clearly defined concept makes a solo profound and that a solo needs an *anchor point* around which to evolve. In addition, a choreographer must have a fresh, innovative, and individualistic approach to invent core movement vocabulary that will be developed with various devices and expandable operations.

Figure 8 Photography © Vishal Kanwar, pictured Maya Zhalova-Kanwar as Lord Ardhanareeswara, 2011

THE DUET
– A KINESTHETIC DIALOGUE –

A duet involves a movement relationship in which two dancers share a common space or enter each other's space. Any movement material or choreographic sequence can be deconstructed and taken apart, then assigned or scattered between two dancers, who may perform it separately or together, in unison or in contrast, interactively or independently. Compared to a solo, a duet may unfold as a movement dialogue and a physical encounter involving bodily contact and partnering.

Historically speaking, couple dances have enjoyed wide popularity throughout time—from the basic dancing in pairs in folklore and social dances, to elaborately developed principles of partnering techniques used by various styles and genres, such as ballroom dancing, classical ballet, modern dance, and contact improvisation, among many others.

Two dancers could form a duet and a kinesthetic relationship without engaging in physical contact by simply being in a space at the same time. In such instances, the two dancers could move, dance, interact, and engage with the space around or between each other. They dance together but with physical distance and without bodily encounter.

A duet with physical contact, on the other hand, offers a variety of partnering possibilities that can be explored through a range of traditional and established partnering techniques or newly invented ways of kinesthetic interaction with physical contact.

Traditions and experiences in couples and duet dancing reveal three major categories of dance partnering, which are based on points of physical contact and the amount of weight shifting, sharing, and bearing:

➢ **Touching, holding, embracing, pressing** and any physical gestures such as grabbing, hugging, squeezing, brushing, rubbing, and bumping. The two dancers use their palms, hands, legs, and torsos as points of contact, while the rest of their bodies are in motion without elaborate physical engagement or lifting.

➢ **Weight sharing and shifting, rolling and rotating, and maneuvering each other's bodies and limbs** while one or both dancers remain grounded on the floor. The two dancers interact with greater physical contact and movement intensity as their bodily encounter affects one another's movement and position.

➢ **Full body lifting off the ground to the trunk, shoulder, or head level,** where one of the dancers no longer touches the floor and is fully supported in a lift by the other dancer—see figurative samples in Figure 8:

TOUCHING AND HOLDING | WEIGHT SHIFTING & WEIGHT GIVING | FULL BODY OVERHEAD LIFTING

Figure 9 Photography © Paul Gordon Emerson, image left, pictured dancers Robert J. Priore and Vanessa Owen, Company | E, 2015; image center, pictured dancers Giselle Alvarez and Maleek Washington, Company | E, 2010; image right excerpt from *ENTANGLED*, choreography by Paul Gordon Emerson, pictured dancers Elizabeth Gahl and Jerome Johnson, Company | E, 2009

A choreographer might choose to give specific directions for partnering and set the movement duet on the dancers. Alternatively, the choreographer may experiment and collaboratively work with the dancers on movement material involving physical contact and partnering options.

There are a few key factors to consider when choreographing a duet. First and foremost is safety and that the physical demands of the partnering are proportionate with the dancers' technical abilities. Another factor is the extent of physical *connectivity* between the dancers, which deals with concept and intent—why and how the dancers are present for each other. This aspect will determine movement qualities, the intensity of the couple's physical interaction, and the range of fluidity and/or the abruptness of their partnering.

The final factor is *delegating* the roles during partnering. Who is the *leader* and who is the *follower* during the duet? Who is in the *active* role and who is in the *supportive* one? Will these roles reverse, and if so, will they reverse frequently and according to a plan, or randomly? These determinations help the choreographer develop confidence in creating a duet and may foster bonding between the two dance partners.

TRIO, QUARTET, GROUP
– A CONVERGENCE IN MOTION –

A trio, a quartet, or a small or large group of dancers instantly conveys the idea of a small or a large community in motion. Dancing with others is often more fun than dancing alone. A sense of *togetherness* leads to a sense of security, affection, and pride. When the action on stage is supportive and congenial, a desire for interaction and social approval is easily satisfied, yet conflict and tension can also be conveyed within or between groups, affecting the kinesthetic experience.

When conflict is not the choreographer's vision—although this is also possible as shown in the image to the left—a dancing group, small or large, is often a convergence in motion. Humans are social by nature; they like to connect, play, collaborate, and explore their existence as a community within various harmonious relationships. People are also curious about each other and most often strive to get along, in life and during dancing.

A dancing group may change in size and numerical format and divide into smaller units. For example, a trio or a quartet already carries the origin of a solo or solos, or a duet or duets. Such expansion and reduction, reconfiguration and regrouping allow the choreographer to maneuver and explore a range of movement relationships. These may include, connect, and fuse dance monologues, dialogues, trios, quintets, and various interactions between the dancers within the group. As the number of performers onstage increases and dynamically varies in numerical format, so does the complexity in arrangement, compositional framework, and strategy for moving the group around. Working with a large cast of dancers might feel intimidating at first for an emerging choreographer.

Figure 10 Photography ©Lois Greenfield, pictured Heather Kemp, Theresa Duhon, Lauren E. Jaynes, Leslie Simpson, courtesy of KDNY Dance Company, 2005

A choreographer may handle the kinesthetic architecture of a large group of dancers by experimenting with various improvisational tasks or specific prompts triggering *group movement* actions, and then build up the large-scale group work based on how the process unfolds. Or the choreographer might choose to provide predetermined and preplanned movement and visual directives, including sketches and charts of movement arrangements.

A type of movement convergence of people and what directs and identifies group movement actions could be defined with a single word. Group movement patterns and shapes are often based on a common task and intent, which can be planned or generated spontaneously. The best strategy to identify a movement action is to think of and use verbs, for example: *gathering around, fighting, defending, supporting, disturbing, uniting, demonstrating,* and *dispersing.* WIth that in mind, the choreographer gives movement tasks, directives, and assignments leading the dance group to interact in certain ways.

For example, people could move individually and within a group, or together in synchrony as a human blanket, with a specific intent and a "choreography" based on various agendas or coordinated rules—see the sample images (Figure 9) from left to right: a scene in a ballet production enacts two opposing parties involved in argument; a military march expresses unity, pride, and commitment; a sports game evolves around a strategy of calculated tactical decisions to score winning points.

Figure 11 Image left: Photography © Theo Kossenas, *The Nutcracker*, choreography by Septime Webre, pictured performer Christianne Campbell, production of the Washington Ballet 2010; image center: Officers in a parade, dressed in a traditional uniforms of the Bulgarian Army, credit: martin-dm, courtesy of iStock/ Getty Images; image right: Soccer players, courtesy of iStock/Getty Images

There are multiple dimensions to consider when choreographing a group. For example, small or large group motion can portray still shapes and use intense movement sequences that appear dynamic or static, supportive or dominant. The group can move in various *formations*, as well as *patterns* and *pathways*, that are narrow, wide, angular, round, symmetrical, or asymmetrical. Different areas of the performance space and the group's *placement* might draw attention to important conceptual elements of the dance. Finally, choreographic decisions determine the *structural progression* of movement events. In summary, the group's *shapes and motion* could develop dimensionally and in multiple ways, by considering a) *Group Movement Formations*; b) *Group Floor Patterns, Pathways, and Space Placement*; and c) *Group Movement Structural Progression*—see Chapter 18.

?

How can solo movement material become a duet and a group dance, and what strategies are best suited to expand the cast size?

GETTING READY FOR FIRST REHEARSAL

– MAKING SENSE OF THE EQUATION 3+2=1 –

"The beginning is the most important part of the work,"[12] said Greek philosopher Plato. Nothing can be accomplished if it is never started in the first place. Let's add a prequel to Plato's words—*the most important part of the beginning is the preparation for it.*

The dancers are the choreographer's first audience and the new creation's "first responders." They will become the physical embodiment of the choreographer's idea. To be efficient and earn the dancers' trust, the choreographer must prepare in advance and manage expectations about how much can be accomplished during rehearsals.

Depending on the concept, cast size, and complexity of the dance, the time to prepare for a rehearsal and to anticipate results might vary. The average proportion of preparation time in relation to an expected outcome, brings us to the equation **3+2=1**.

3 hours for the choreographer's prep work to singlehandedly engage in artistic research, experimentation, and music/sound inquiries.

\+

2 hours for an average rehearsal length to work with the dancers by showing, teaching, or guiding movement material, experimenting, making choices, and finalizing movement material leads to:

---

1 minute of accomplished, set choreography that the dancers are expected to learn, retain, perfect, and perform.

Figure 12

PREPARING FOR THE FIRST REHEARSAL OF A NEW WORK

- ☐ **Short verbal description of the concept**—summarize the "big picture" for the dancers
- ☐ **Concept sample**—demonstrate movements or use a visual sample to illustrate the concept
- ☐ **Music choices**—bring music or sounds to experiment with, even if it is not a final choice
- ☐ **Casting flexibility**—adapt to last minute cast changes due to variable circumstances
- ☐ **Dancers' abilities**—take into consideration dancers' technical and performance skills
- ☐ **Modifying Steps**—if the movement is yours, the dancers should own it; be open to adjusting it
- ☐ **Inspiring collaboration and positive attitude**—be encouraging and engage individual personalities

INTELLECTUAL INVESTIGATIONS AND THE CREATIVE PROCESSES

– BRAINSTORM AS YOU CREATE, RESEARCH AS YOU STAGE –

Often, we move and dance before we think. And yet an efficient and meaningful process is needed to sort out various concepts and organize them into a manageable framework.

"How can I do it?" is the most common question that emerging choreographers ask when facing creative challenges and uncertainties. For a good beginning, the better way to ask the same question is: *"How can it be done?"* By taking *"I"* out of the equation, the choreographer "opens the door" to knowledge, references, and options. The *"it"* allows the work to develop naturally on its own terms with the choreographer's artistic nurturing.

To help the creative process, this book introduces a creative algorithm and functional philosophy of choreography: ***ICON***—**I**nstruments of **C**horeography, **O**bjectives and **N**orms. *ICON* elaborates on various essentials, strategies, and devices to create a dance and help identify subject matter, project-specific plans, parameters, and purposes shared among the participants in a choreographic project. Additionally, there is ***SMART***—**S**ystematic **M**ethods of **A**rtistic **R**esearch and **T**raining, with three forms of artistic research: scholastic, creative, and movement research—see Chapter 10. Once a choreographer narrows down the subject matter and a concept emerges on the horizon, a few strategies for *determining the direction of the new work* dramaturgically could help make the creative process manageable:

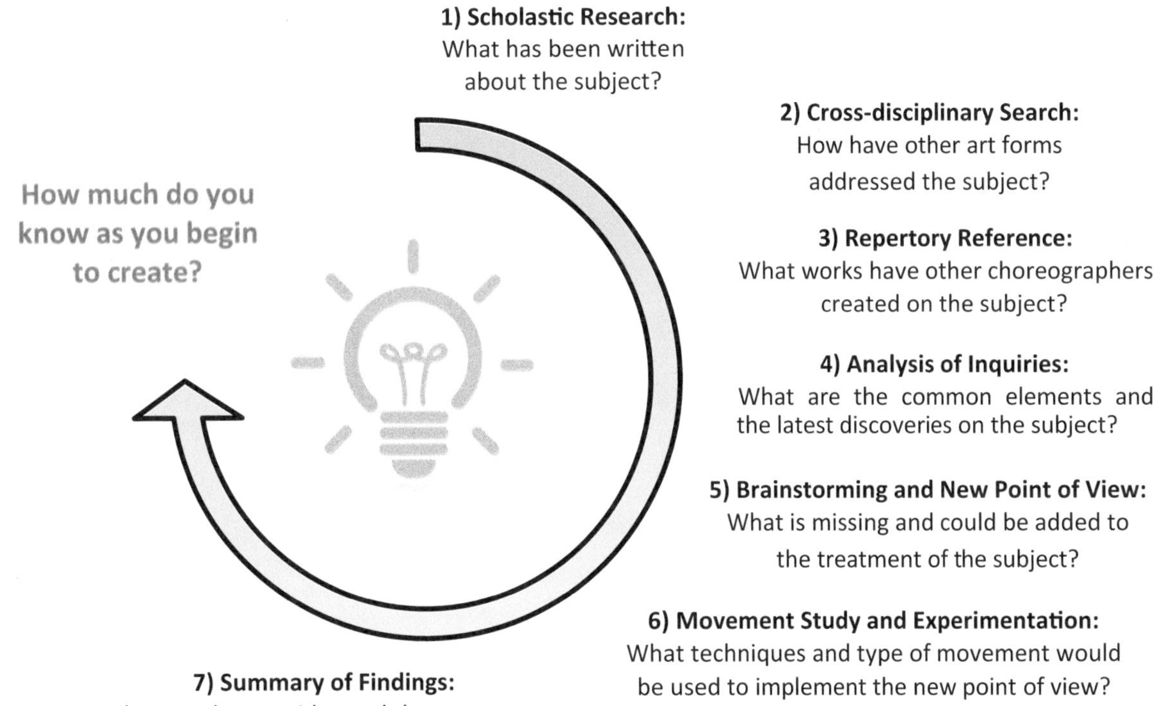

Figure 13

GROWING A DANCE GARDEN

– A SAMPLE LINEAR ALGORITHM OF CREATIVE PHASES –

Similar to a garden, a dance grows in time and develops through various phases and processes. These processes are covered separately in the chapters of BOOKS IV and V. Let's admit that it is quite challenging or nearly impossible for a choreographer to *instantly* plan, choreograph, and effectively stage a long and elaborate concert dance piece. Carving out time to brainstorm, research, and create requires advance planning.

Phasing the creative process makes it realistic, manageable, and efficient. The linearity and sequencing of the proposed phases—see Figure 14—are subject to individual preferences. A creative process can begin with Phase 4, and like a spider web, it can branch into the nearby phases. The idea is to establish a plan and *a process for how the new work will be constructed and developed.*

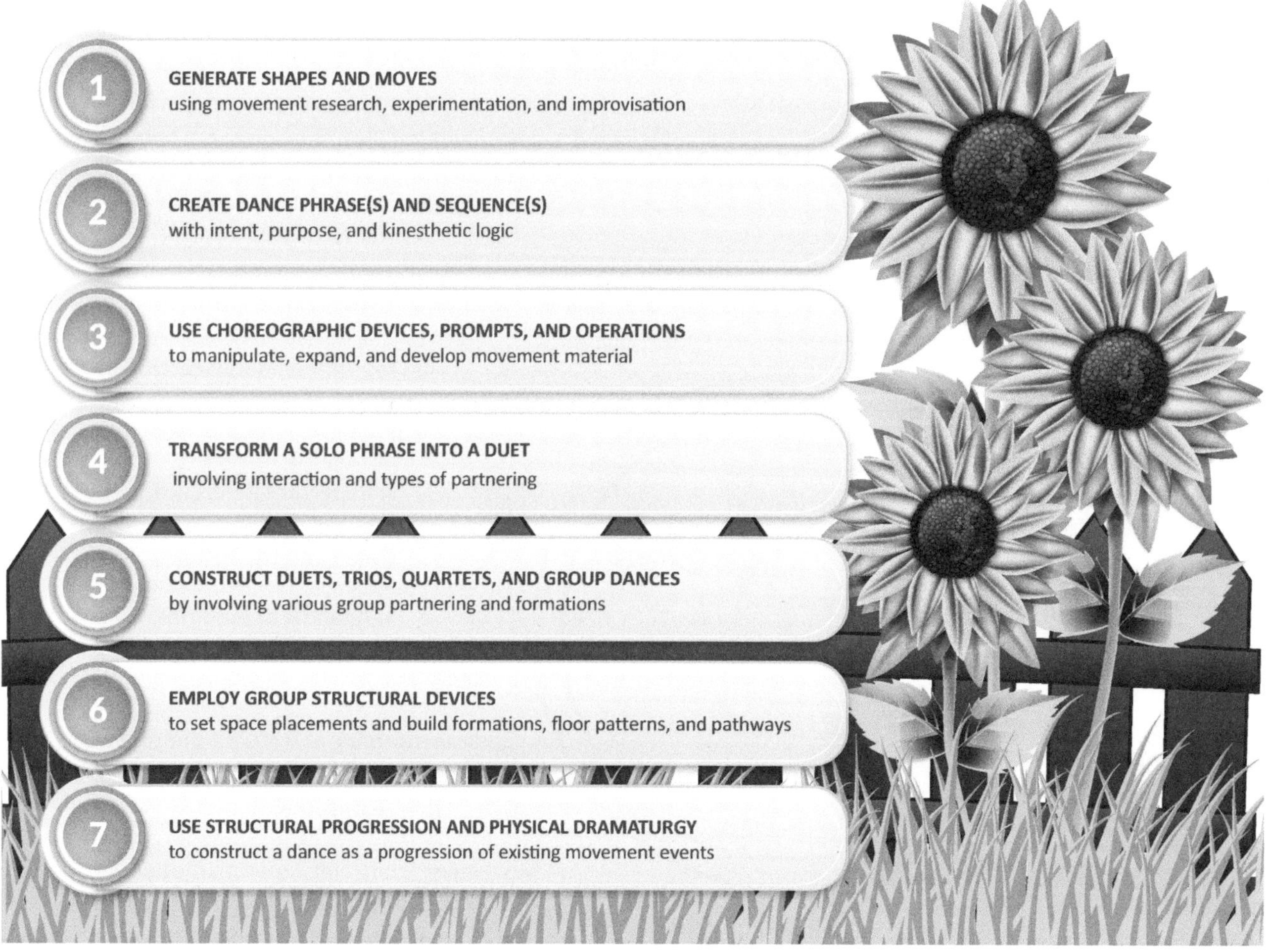

Figure 14 Diagram © Vladimir Angelov, graphic design © Vishal Kanwar

THE CHOREOGRAPHER AS MOVEMENT STAGER, ARTISTIC FACILITATOR, AND CREATIVE COLLABORATOR

One of the most exciting parts of the choreographer's creative labor is working and interacting with the dancers. The choreographer approaches the dancer's body by employing various strategies for how movement will be activated, sensed, thought about, and observed. For more on these practices see the subchapter *Body and Movement Awareness* in Chapter 8, *The Moving Body as a Work of Art—Corpus Cognitus*, in Book II.

The choreographer is in the position to lead, facilitate, and/or share creative practices in the dance studio and therefore to determine the working algorithms with the dancers.

The choreographer may propose, choose, or pursue one or a combination of the following three distinct approaches, where the choreographer acts as:

- ➢ **Movement stager**, who demonstrates and teaches pre-created movement material and provides shapes, steps, moves, and musical cues to the dancers to learn, adapt, and interpret.
- ➢ **Artistic facilitator**, who shares experiences, methods, principles, and philosophies to initiate and provoke body sensations and awaken a movement-generating process.
- ➢ **Creative collaborator**, who collaboratively invents movement material with the dancers, where the mutual goal is movement embodiment and movement ownership with skillful implementation and performative qualities.

Choreographers tend to creatively respond to what they observe dancers do. Dancers, however, tend to creatively respond to what they sense, while form-searching and/or form-fitting the movement to their bodies.

This complex, active-reactive-interactive process of generating movement material, teaching it, and performing it, narrows down to three important operations in the form of queries and actions:

DANCERS' QUERIES	⟷	CHOREOGRAPHER'S ACTIONS
What do we do?	⟷	Communicate movement concepts, provide directions, articulate intentions, demonstrate steps and moves
When, where, and with whom do we do it?	⟷	Direct, describe, and designate movement interaction between the dancers, and its timing and location
How do we do it?	⟷	Clarify performative methods, movement qualities, somatic nuances, and dance technique

Figure 15

In addition to the dynamic algorithm, there are three sublet points of tension that may arise from the dancers' further queries, and which the choreographer must address during creative work in the studio. These are:

Performance Challenges vs. Choreographic Challenges

When the choreographer and the dancers identify that certain steps and movements are challenging, there are two fundamental explanations:

➢ Performance Challenges may occur when the dancers do not comprehend how to execute the movement material. The choreographer should then elaborate on movement tasks or break down the vocabulary in slow motion and clarify the nuances and methodologies.

➢ Choreographic Challenges may occur when the dancers are struggling with the movement material caused by lack of kinesthetic logic, uncomfortable transitions, or a disagreement about the movement execution. The choreographer should revisit, restructure, and edit the movement material to an achievable and manageable scale.

Training Dancer vs. Accommodating Dancer

All dancers come with different body types, training backgrounds, technical abilities, and performance experience. Therefore, it is important to consider the dancer's education and potential, as well as the extent of their versatility. On occasions when the dancers have worked with a certain choreographer for a long period of time, they have been "trained" in that choreographic style and have a thorough understanding of that type of movement.

When the dancers encounter a *guest choreographer* for the first time, they may need more time to adapt to the new choreographic vocabulary and the demands of the style. In addition, a limited number of staging rehearsals may challenge the dancers to comprehend the specifics of unfamiliar choreographic material in a short amount of time. Alternatively, the choreographer could consider adapting or modifying the movement material to accommodate the dancers.

Executing Dance vs. Performing Dance

What happens when the choreography is completed, and yet the dancing looks dull and unengaged? In addition to creating the movement sequences, the choreographer should nurture the dancers' confidence and presence on stage. Performers always need extra help to fully embody the choreographer's intent beneath the steps so that they can deliver an in-depth *performance* rather than a mechanical *execution* of the dance. For many dancers, any amount of rehearsals is never enough.

For the performers to own the movements and the dance, it is necessary for the choreographer a) to provide sufficient information about the movement imagery, and to identify, describe, and explain *details of the movement mechanics,* experience, and execution; b) to address the necessary range of *physical and emotional commitment* to the movement material; c) to make sure that the dancers are *actively sensing, kinetically responding, and creatively adapting* the movement material.

REVERSING THE PERSPECTIVE

– IF THE DANCERS COULD SPEAK UP –

MEMO

From: United Dancers Opinion Anonymous, Inc.

To: The Choreographer Extraordinaire & the New Work

Date: Today, after warm-up dance class

Dear Choreographer,

Congratulations on your first day of rehearsals! You must be excited! As you begin and continue your work with us, please be sensitive, embracing, and humble, yet strong and assertive. Most importantly, kindly consider the following points, as you are about to create and deliver your masterwork to us—the dancers:

Please know that your artistic commitment is also ours. Please agree with us that it will take time, effort, collaboration, and coordination to perform the new work well.

- Each movement of the dance has technical demands and subtleties. Therefore, it might take us up to two hours of coaching to perfect a two-minute-long dance.
- Each second of time on stage is a gift and we work hard for it. The audience will give seconds of their lives to watch, so let's make it worthwhile.
- Each of us desires to look great on stage. The only feedback we get is from you, the choreographer. We trust you and we take your words as the absolute and the ultimate truth. Please know that when you give us feedback.

Please talk to us about movement goals, clarity, and performance quality. Please give us visual images to work with. Describe movement qualities with adjectives. Define movement energy, drive, and action with verbs. Provide us with context and even with a fictional situation to boost our imagination—just as you do! Please be patient with us.

Please be our tolerant, optimistic leader and problem-solver. If we do not correctly pick up the steps and movements right away, it is not intentional.

- Please identify our mistakes without overreacting! Please avoid saying: "That's terrible!" and instead please say, "Could you please try this." When we ask a question about a movement, please avoid saying: "I don't know," even if you do not know. It stops creative flow. Instead, please say: "Let's figure it out together."
- Please listen when we share our ideas. Often, we come up with interesting choreographic suggestions and edits that might be good enough to consider.

- Please ask us questions about how everything feels to us. For example: "What movements and transitions are you struggling with?" or "What are you feeling and thinking while you're dancing this particular section?"

And finally, when the time comes for an in-studio run-through, and major feedback will follow, please begin with compliments and acknowledgments; then give us your notes for improvement. Please avoid the opposite progression: being upset about our mistakes, barely acknowledging us, and only briefly mentioning what is working well.

Thank you, and we look forward to working with you!

Sincerely,

Your Dance Cast

Figure 16 Photography © Paul Gordon Emerson, pictured dancers Ja'Malik, Alice Wylie, Delphina Parenti, Bruno Augusto, Kathryn Sydell Pilkington, Company | E, 2008

As the staging advances, the choreographer's role of delivering the dance to the dancers decreases, while the dancers' role of delivering the dance to the audience increases. On opening night, the dancers are on stage working hard, while the choreographer becomes an audience member. But initially, wasn't this creative positioning in reverse?—see the humorous image in Figure 16 and guess who is who. On a serious note, let's keep in mind that the dance *was created* by the choreographer; however, the dance *now belongs* to the dancers.

HELPFUL TIPS & SUGGESTIONS

~ Hone traditional devices to manipulate the movement material of a new work
~ Generate unique prompts to explore the direction of the process to create a work
~ Implement expandable operations to define the direction of the work as a whole
~ Use verbs to trigger and channel dance and movement actions
~ Embrace intellectual work as part of the artistic work
~ Create an algorithm of your creative process to make it productive and efficient
~ Open conversation to understand your dancers so they can understand you

assignments & exercises

RESEARCH ASSIGNMENT: Watch dances on video from various historic periods and genres, and select three, such as a folkloric dance, a social dance, and a contemporary dance. Determine which devices these dances contain, if any, and list them.

Analyze the dance and guess the reason for using a specific device—let's say repetition. Was repetition used to create an ongoing meditative character of the dance, or was it used to emphasize a specific element of the dance? Was the reason for repetition in each dance different, and what was its purpose?

★ **CREATIVE EXERCISE:** Create a simple choreographic phrase or a movement sequence for the dancers, and practice the following devices, prompts, and operations:

√ **TRADITIONAL DEVICES:**

➥ Implement Space, Time and Energy devices in a movement phrase of a single dancer. How does the phrase change? How much does the phrase expand? How are the original idea and intent of the phrase altered?

➥ Implement Instrumentation and Insertion/Ornamentation devices and explore what the new elements add or take away from the phrase. Is the movement material enriched or diminished from the original version?

➥ Implement Accumulation, Merging, and Contrasting, and continue to manipulate and expand the phrase. How do merging and accumulation contribute to making the phrase longer? Does lengthening of the phrase contribute to the original idea? Does contrasting add a surprising element to the phrase?

√ **UNIQUE PROMPTS AND EXPANDABLE OPERATIONS:**

➥ Experiment with amplifying the overall look of the movement sequence of the group. For example, if one of the dancers moves in slow tempo, have that dancer move even more slowly, and if another dancer moves fast, have that dancer move even faster. How does the overall character of the group change, and does this prompt accentuate the initial intent?

➥ Experiment by adding an element of surprise, such as inserting an unexpected action into the phrase. For example, take a busy group dance section where the dancers have a lot of entrances and exits. Then, instead of exiting the stage, ask the dancers to gather center stage and pretend that they're off stage, only to reenter the stage from center stage.[13] How does the modification of pathways change the relationship between the dancers?

➥ Experiment with oppositions by adding new contrasting movement material and a new dramaturgical element. For example, during a slow tempo lyrical love duet at center stage, ask the rest of the cast to create a contrasting and intense atmosphere by running back and forth on stage, chasing each other, and screaming randomly. How does the impact of the lyrical duet at center stage change?

Figure 17 Photography © Lois Greenfield, pictured Adam Battelstein, John Mario Sevilla, Kent Lindemer, Vernon Scott, courtesy of Pilobolus Dance Theater, 1990

√ CAST EXPANSION

➥ Use a phrase that has been originally created for a solo and add another dancer in the space. What task would you give to engage the additional dancer in the duet without physical interaction with the soloist?

➥ Continue exploring the possibilities of the duet by engaging both dancers in contact and using the three types of partnering: a) touch and hold; b) weight sharing and weight shifting; c) full body overhead lifting. Which types of physical partnering do you feel the most comfortable with? Why?

➥ Add a 3rd and 4th dancer to the mix. Explore how their presence changes the duet. What new movement relationship opportunities are available without physical contact? What other partnering opportunities are possible in the group format of three or four dancers? How could you explore and invent group lifts involving everybody?

⤮ COMPARATIVE ASSIGNMENT: Attend a rehearsal of a choreographer colleague. Observe how the rehearsal is conducted; notice the choreographer's individual style in terms of movement material, as well as how the choreographer handles various devices, prompts, and operations; and watch how the choreographer communicates with the dancers.

➥ Analyze how the choreographer manipulates the material by using traditional devices. What criteria do you use to identify those devices as traditional in various aspects of the work, and how do you distinguish them from unique prompts and expandable operations?

➥ Observe and identify when and how the choreographer uses unique prompts and expandable operations during the rehearsal. Do you think that the tools are used effectively to change various aspects of the work? When and why does the choreographer choose unique prompts and expandable operations over traditional devices?

➥ Take notes on how feedback is given and how appreciation, acknowledgment, and instructions for corrections are communicated. Analyze what is effective and what isn't. How does this observation help you to improve the way you give feedback to the dancers?

BIBLIOGRAPHY AND REFERENCES

[1] Lavender, Larry. "Facilitating the Choreographic Process," in *Contemporary Choreography: A Critical Reader*, 2nd edition, edited by Jo Butterworth and Liesbeth Wildschut, Routledge, 2018, pp. 107–120.
[2] Lavender 2018. "Facilitating the Choreographic Process," pp. 109–123.
[3] Blom, Lynne Anne and Chaplin, L. Tarin, *The Intimate Act of Choreography*, University of Pittsburg Press, 1982, pp. 92–93.
[4] Blom and Chaplin 1982. *The Intimate Act of Choreography*, pp. 92–93.
[5] Blom and Chaplin 1982. *The Intimate Act of Choreography*, pp. 99–100.
[6] Blom and Chaplin 1982. *The Intimate Act of Choreography*, pp. 99–100.
[7] Blom and Chaplin 1982. *The Intimate Act of Choreography*, pp. 101–102.
[8] Blom and Chaplin 1982. *The Intimate Act of Choreography*, pp. 101–104.
[9] Lavender 2018. *Facilitating the Choreographic Process*, pp. 107–123.
[10] Lavender 2018. *Facilitating the Choreographic Process*, pp. 107–123.
[11] Lavender 2018. *Facilitating the Choreographic Process*, pp. 107–123.
[12] Plato, *The Republic*, Book I. 377-B. Selected quotes from various online resources.
[13] Lavender 2018. *Facilitating the Choreographic Process*, pp. 107–123.

VISUAL REFERENCES

Figures 1, 2, 3, 4, and 5: Diagrams © Vladimir Angelov

Figure 6: Photography © Lois Greenfield, pictured Parsons Dance Company, 2000

Figure 7: Diagram © Vladimir Angelov

Figure 8: Photography © Vishal Kanwar, pictured Maya Zhalova-Kanwar as Lord Ardhanareeswara, 2011

Figure 9: Photography © Paul Emerson, Banner images illustrating different types of partnering: First image of a duet—Touching and Holding, pictured dancers Vanessa Owen and Robert J. Priore, Company | E, 2015, Second image of a duet—Weight Shifting & Weight Giving, pictured dancers Giselle Alvarez and Maleek Washington, Company | E, 2010, Third image of a duet—*Full Body Overhead Lifting*, excerpt from *ENTANGLED*, choreography by Paul Gordon Emerson, pictured dancers Elizabeth Gahl and Jerome Johnson, Company | E, 2009

Figure 10: Photography ©Lois Greenfield, pictured Heather Kemp, Theresa Duhon, Lauren E. Jaynes, Leslie Simpson, courtesy of KDNY Dance Company, 2005

Figure 11: Image left: Photography © Theo Kossenas, *The Nutcracker*, choreography by Septime Webre, pictured performer Christianne Campbell, production of the Washington Ballet, 2010; images center: Officers dressed in a traditional uniform of the Bulgarian army, credit: martin-dm, courtesy of iStock/ Getty Images; image right: Soccer player in blue jersey in the air heading the ball, credit: vm, courtesy of iStock/Getty Images

Figure 12: Diagram © Vladimir Angelov *Checklist Board*, by www.clker.com/ , public domain

Figure 13: Diagram © Vladimir Angelov, light bulb isolated on white background, credit: Hendry Wijayanto, courtesy of iStock/Getty Images

Figure 14: Design © Vishal Kanwar, diagram © Vladimir Angelov

Figure 15: Diagram © Vladimir Angelov

Figure 16: Photography © Paul Gordon Emerson, Quintet about the choreographer as creator and audience member, pictured dancers Ja'Malik, Alice Wylie, Delphina Parenti, Bruno Augusto, Kathryn Sydell Pilkington, Company | E, 2008

Figure 17: Photography © Lois Greenfield, pictured Adam Battelstein, John Mario Sevilla, Kent Lindemer, Vernon Scott, courtesy of Pilobolus Dance Theater, 1990

Three rules of work:

Out of clutter find simplicity;

From discord find harmony;

In the middle of difficulty lies opportunity.

Albert Einstein (1879–1955)

CHAPTER 18

STRUCTURE AND RESTRUCTURE, CONSTRUCT AND DECONSTRUCT

– ARCHITECTING A DANCE –

Choreographers may use *choreographic devices, prompts, and operations* to develop initial movement material, while dance *construction and compositional structures* help them organize the dancing into large sections of choreography.

◆ **Structure and construction define the *kinesthetic architecture of a dance*—conceptually, visually, and dimensionally—and are the fundamental instruments of a choreographer's craft.**

Structure is a *plan*, map, and system that conceives of the whole, rather than of any single part, and it comes from the Latin word *structura*, which means "a fitting together, building," and although it originally served architecture, it is applicable to any activity, serving as a concept of organization.[1] Choreographic structure is the arrangement and placement of different dance sections, dance formations, and group designs built during the process of construction or planned to serve a specific purpose. Structures can be improvised or predetermined; yet many of them are flexible and can be altered. *Restructuring*, in this context, means to change, expand, and develop a fixed structure into a new version. Restructuring can transform an existing structure into a more efficient entity, since it is based on an existing plan that has been updated and improved.

Construction is a *process* of accumulating, gathering, and placing various elements together.[2] Construction elements are the kinesthetic images, movement events, and dance sequencing that constitute how the dancers will assemble, act, and disperse.

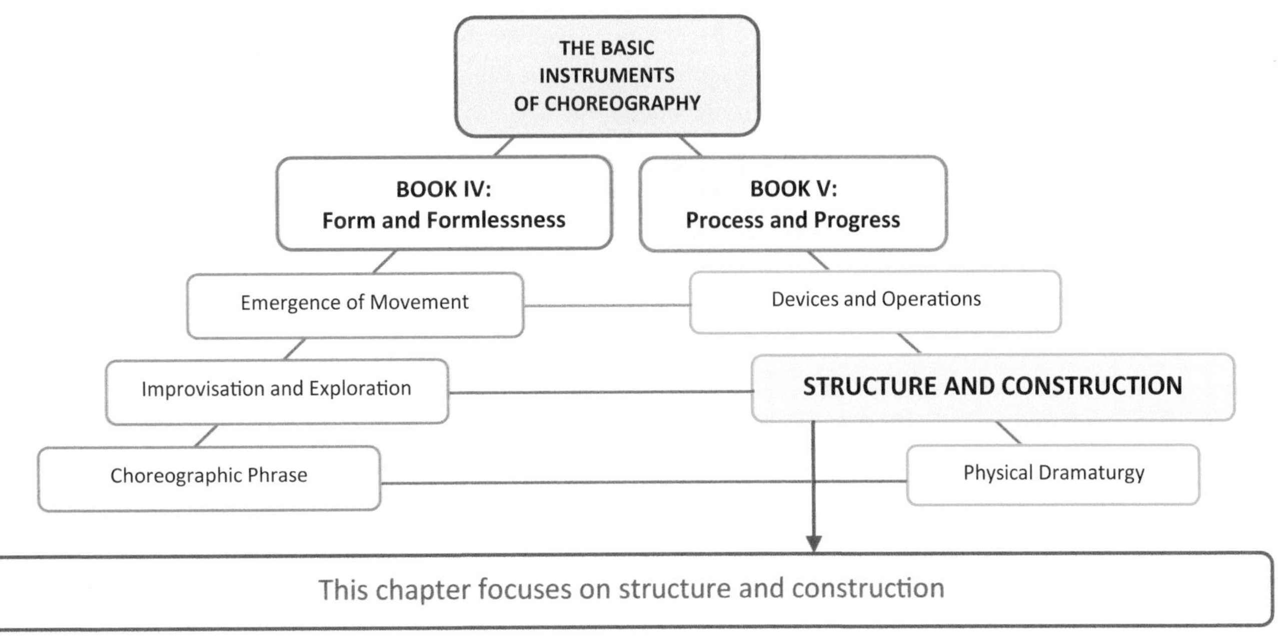

Figure 1

Constructing is building a sequence of choreographic images and the process of coordinating and controlling, organizing, and directing a three-dimensional kinesthetic progression of a moving group of performers. Moving and shaping a group of dancers and assembling them into patterns and formations evolves as a translation of physical relationships into visually articulated movement interactions. In addition, the principles, devices, and prompts used to choreograph a solo for a single performer could be applied to multiple performers or to a single group.

Deconstruction, the opposite of construction, is a general term also used in architecture and philosophy. It is the reverse of assembling, the undoing of construction, and the breaking into pieces.[3] Choreographers, however, ultimately seek a whole "work," and deconstruction becomes essentially re-assembling, re-using, repurposing, and recycling. From a philosophical and aesthetic angle, choreographic deconstruction could be the examination of the differences between form and content. Once something is constructed and broken apart, then deconstructed (not reconstructed), how does the original meaning change? Can broken cups, vases, and plates turn into a piece of clothing?

Figure 2 Images left and center: porcelain objects and broken vases, courtesy of iStock/Getty images. Image right: Art work and photography © Li Xiaofeng, *Beijing Memory*, porcelain dress, courtesy of the artist and Brian Wallace, Red Gate Gallery, Beijing, People's Republic of China, 2007

The three important processes to conceive a new dance are the intention and subject (concept), the structure (plan), and the construction (action). Without a concept, there is no reason for the structure, and without a structure, there is no plan to construct a dance. The choreographer's intentions may be the starting point for the generative process. The choreographer's actions and plans may dynamically modify the direction of the work, which may possibly result in a different outcome than the initial intent. In summary:

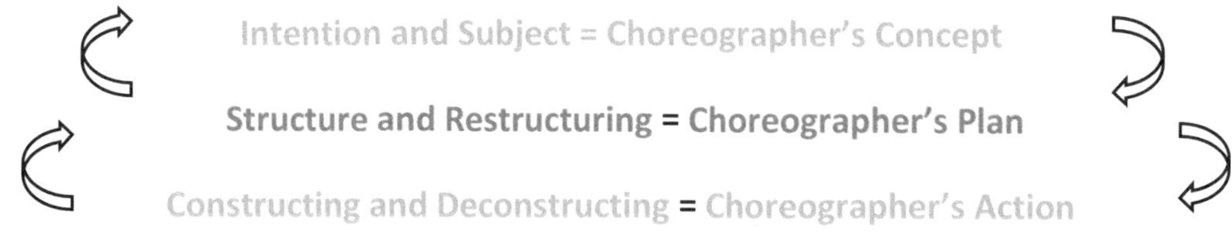

Figure 3

THE STARTING POINT: MICHELANGELO'S DAVID
– WHEN THE BEGINNING IS IN THE MIDDLE –

"Where do I begin?"—An emerging choreographer would ask. The answer is: "Begin with what you know best, then brainstorm further, and follow where the work takes you." We tend to identify the starting point in a linear progression of time and events. When we are told to start counting, we begin with 1, 2, 3, 4 . . . before we move on. But what happens if we jump to 100 before our counting gets there? A dance teacher would often count "and 5, 6, 7, 8" to cue the beginning of an upcoming sequence. It means that the *beginning* is not always at the beginning, but it can be wherever we decide to start.

Renaissance artist Michelangelo carved his 17-foot marble sculpture of *David* from a single marble block that was unwanted by other sculptors because it was cracked and severely damaged[4]—see Figure 4. The way he carved was unusual. Although his work process was in complete secrecy, it has been speculated by a biographer that he "began" working on David by drilling a single hole in the middle of the block—image 2, perfectly predicting where the figure would be—image 3. After that he began to carve the figure from top to bottom as though it were rising from the water—image 4. It took him two years to complete the sculpture—image 5.

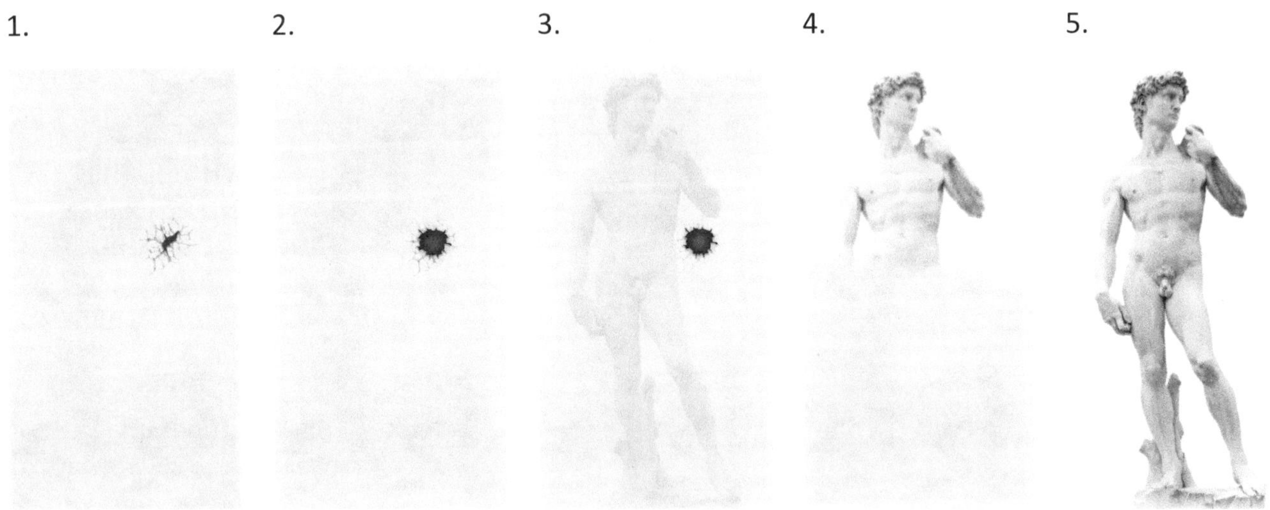

Figure 4 Images 3, 4, and 5 Photography © Jörg Bittner Unna, *David* by Michelangelo di Lodovico Buonarroti Simoni, marble sculpture, Florence, Galleria dell'Accademia, created 1501–4, public domain. Wikki Commons, 2020

The mysterious ingenuity of Michelangelo can be understood once it is placed within context; his uncanny ability to imagine a marble figure before it was created—to foresee art—is demystified. Michelangelo was an expert in human anatomy and possessed knowledge of classical literature and religion. His rigorous artistic training as a child had developed into remarkable professional skills by the age of 27. Regarding *David*, Michelangelo was able to predict proportionally where the body would be positioned inside the marble block and where to begin carving.[5]

THE THREE-DIMENSIONAL THINKING OF CHOREOGRAPHING A GROUP

During a group dance, the performers enter and exit the stage, moving from one formation to another, connecting and disconnecting individually and as a group. As audience members and spectators, we watch and perceive it in various ways. Intuitively, we may guess what the dancers are expressing or portraying. We may look at kinesthetic, visual, and conceptual cues, wondering if there is any intent, purpose, or meaning. Intellectually, we may analyze and "decode" what is beneath the dimensional movement imagery that may be unfolding with mathematical precision. We may realize that all of this dancing must have been planned as we are guided through the structure of the overall movement progression. Choreographically, we may be curious about the choreographer's structural design and even guess how the elements and layers were created and what plot was used to generate the satisfying complexity of bodies moving in space. To demystify the construction of these dancing and moving architectures, we can characterize three dynamic principles of choreographic structuring:

1) WHAT IS THE CONFIGURATION OF THE DANCING GROUP?
THINK:
MOVEMENT FORMATIONS
1) Unison; 2) Succession; 3) Contrast; 4) Divide and Differ; 5) Add and Subtract; 6) Zoom In and Out; and 7) Foreground and Background.

2) WHAT IS THE TRAFFIC AND PLACEMENT OF THE DANCING GROUP?
THINK:
PATTERNS, PATHWAYS, AND PLACEMENT
1) Patterns such as circles, diagonal lines, triangles, squares, etc.; 2) Pathways to enter, exit, and move from one pattern to another; 3) Placement of where the dancers are positioned on stage.

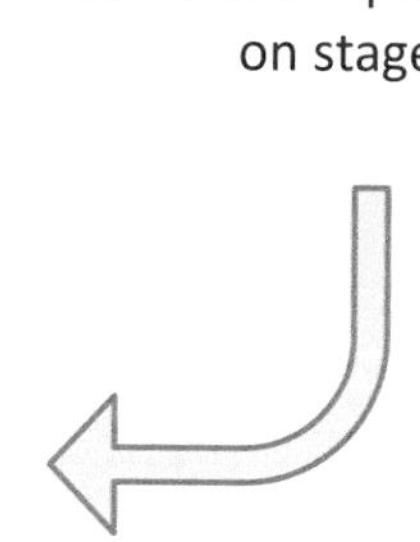

3) WHAT IS THE SEQUENCING OF THE DANCING GROUP?
THINK:
STRUCTURAL PROGRESSION
1) AB Form; 2) ABA$_1$ Form; 3) A: A$_1$, A$_2$, A$_3$ Form; 4) AB – AC – AD Form; 5) ABC – BCD – CDE Form; 6) CANON Form; 7) A, B, C, D, E Continuing Narrative Form.

Figure 5 Photography © Lois Greenfield, Eliot Feld's Ballet Tech, 1995

MOVEMENT FORMATIONS

Working with a large group of dancers is an exciting creative endeavor that offers endless possibilities of group arrangements and rearrangements. The more dancers and the more complexity in formations, the more thoughtful effort it takes to choreograph.[6] A group formation or a solo phrase may be manipulated with the basic choreographic devices such as time, space, and energy. Building group movement formations could be approached with seven primary strategies, which may be implemented separately or in combinations:

- **UNISON** is *unifying* all the dancers to perform the same movement together at the same time. Treating the dance group as a mass human blanket is impactful. IMAGINE WIND! A group dancing in unison brings a commanding effect on stage: the movement of one is conveyed by the many! Unison is a powerful formation considered by many choreographers to serve as either the climax or finale because of its bold visual impact. And yet if unison appears too often or for too long, it can lose its effectiveness. Great timing = great impact! For example, in the winter many snowflakes fall from the sky at the same time, just like snowflakes dancing in unison in the ballet *The Nutcracker*. In contemporary dance, a good example of unison is Ohad Naharin's work *Echad Mi Yodea*.

- **SUCCESSION** is *perpetuating* movement in a sequential progression from person to person, or from one group to another. IMAGINE WATER! This device could come across as perpetual, monotonous, and yet dramatically intense. A formation in succession carries the effect and the impact of continuity and endurance. One example is a scene called the "Kingdom of the Shades" from Marius Petipa's ballet *La Bayadère*. Doris Humphrey's signature piece *Water Study* is another example of composing a group in succession and the dramatic effect of sequential movement.

- **CONTRAST** is *isolating* a soloist or *splitting* a large group into opposing smaller groups. Contrast may be used to initiate disputes and clashes. IMAGINE FIRE, WATER, AND WIND. One of the groups might remain still while the other group is moving, and vice versa. The groups can enter each other's space with calm or intense energy. The groups and/or the isolated soloist may move with specific dynamics as the two or more separate units merge, oppose, or confront each other. A good example of handling oppositions of groups can be found in multiple dance scenes depicting the Sharks and the Jets in Jerome Robbins's *West Side Story*.

- **DIVIDE AND DIFFER** is *dividing* a large group into smaller groups by changing the relationships between the dancers in the group into different numerical proportions. The divisions within the group may generate geometric qualities within the movement architecture. This principle is similar to Contrast; however, the main point is to *differentiate* and *distinguish* the groupings with complementing movement material and qualities, rather than to *counterpose* and *juxtapose* them. For example, a quartet dancing in unison can turn into a trio and a solo, and then transition into two duets, after which the quartet is broken down to one duet and two solos. Each sub-group displays different spatial relationships, but with corresponding movement material that works in harmony rather than in contrast.

- **ADD AND SUBTRACT** is *expanding* and *decreasing* the dancers on stage and the size of the movement image, which is established by the dancers entering, remaining on, and exiting the stage. For example, unpredictably, single dancers may enter and exit the stage while several dancers remain on stage at the same time. Groups of dancers or a single dancer could dart across the stage or linger with their passage periodically. Movement events and actions that change the perception of the *volume of dancers in the performance space* may lead to a desired choreographic effect.

➢ **ZOOM IN AND OUT** is *condensing* and *amplifying* a focus of attention or attraction within the group. Where, who, and what should the audience watch? This technique is also called *focal point*. The choreographer decides how the point of attention shifts from one dancer or to portions of the group—either unified or divided. *Group partnering* might fall into this strategy. For example, while the group is moving in slow unison, a dancer within the group moves in more a frenetic way, which demands the attention of the group. Or a small gesture by a single dancer could be seen as motivating the group's reaction.

➢ **FOREGROUND & BACKGROUND** is *emphasizing* and *prioritizing* the movement or dimensional placement of the group(s) to define relative proximity and distance. Similar to the *perspective* technique in Renaissance paintings, a dance formation may be positioned with deliberate use of the stage depth, guiding the eye toward a center of attention and to what needs to be seen in the front or the back—see Figure 6. Foreground and background can also be determined by different rhythmic and spatial patterns, as well as "active" and "non-active" group tableaus.

For example, in many classical ballets a large group of dancers forms the essential background—the *ensemble or corps*—serving as an active or passive human backdrop. On the other hand, a few selected dancers could be positioned exclusively in the foreground—the *soloists* and the *principals*. The distinctions between the members of the cast and their importance on stage originated in the hierarchy of royal court society where ballet was born as a dance genre.

The Paris Opera Ballet's *Défilé*, image bottom left, shows the hierarchy in casting with the principal dancers in front. In *Giselle*, image bottom right, the opposite perspective technique shows the dancers at front center stage, serving as background, while the cross in the back is the center of attention.

Figure 6 Image left photography © Julien Benhamou, *Défilé*, Paris Opera Ballet, 2016; image right: photography © Yonathan Kellerman, *Giselle*, Paris Opera Ballet, 2020

SPATIAL PATTERNS, PATHWAYS, AND PLACEMENT

A well-choreographed group dance may contain the movement of individual dancers or a group formation of dancers moving through various *spatial patterns, pathways,* and *placements*—all together known as the creating of dynamic ***spatial designs***. These important aspects may guide the choreographer to determine how the dancers may move dimensionally:

➢ **SPATIAL PATTERNS** are formational arrangements that can be 1) *geometrical,* with such lines and forms as circles, triangles, squares, and spirals, as well as locomotion in straight or curved lines; 2) *non-geometrical*, which presents irregular and unrestricted shapes in natural forms, such as the flow of a river, landscape, or branches of trees; or 3) *random*, where patterns are made by chance and without a predetermined function. For example:

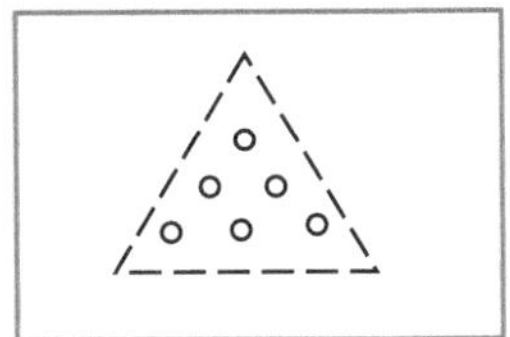
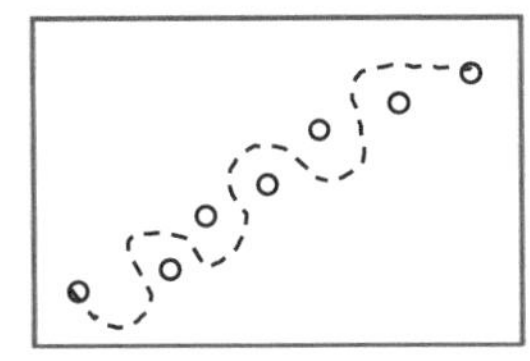
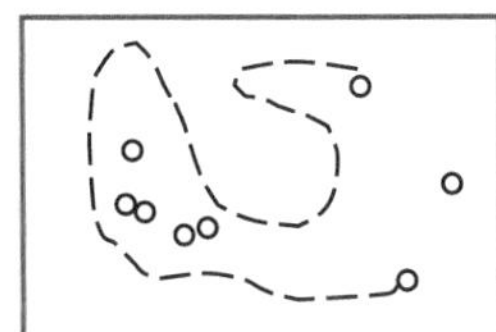

Figure 7

➢ **SPATIAL PATHWAYS** are the spatial trajectories and locomotive manner of the dancers' movement from one place to another. They might enter, exit, reenter, and move around randomly as a crowd, or in arranged formations, or appear scattered in different locations. Changes in *spatial directions, interactions*, and *relations* throughout a dance create perceptions of intimacy and distance between dancers. A dancer could appear from different *entry points* to the performance space and move from one formation to another with a direct spatial transition, or through complex patterns. For example:

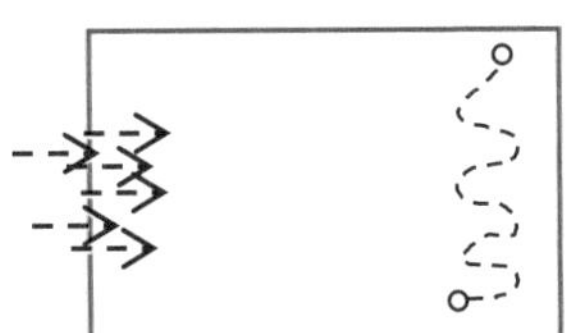
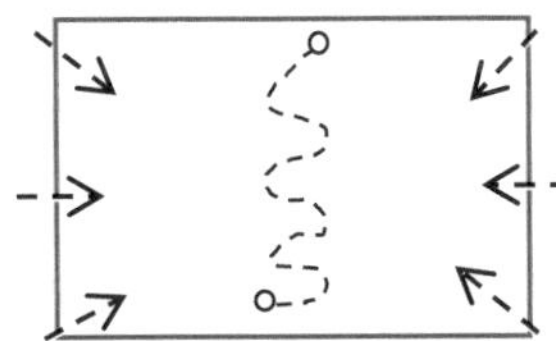
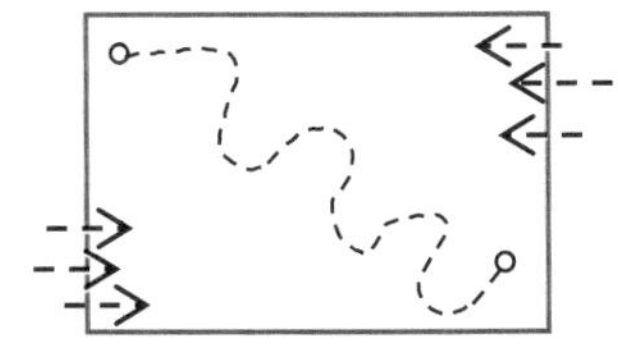

Figure 8

➢ **SPATIAL PLACEMENTS** are the locations of the dancers in the space within a rectangular proscenium stage space—the dancers could be center stage, down stage, or within any planes of the *three-dimensional performance space*. Vertical (up and down), horizontal (side to side), and sagittal (forward and backward) are spatial planes of the performance space. Dancers may move in different directions and dimensions at the same time. The understanding of spatial *placement and dimensionality* develops a sense of *spatial awareness*. A dance unfolds into the three fundamental spatial dimensions: *height, width*, and *depth*. For example:

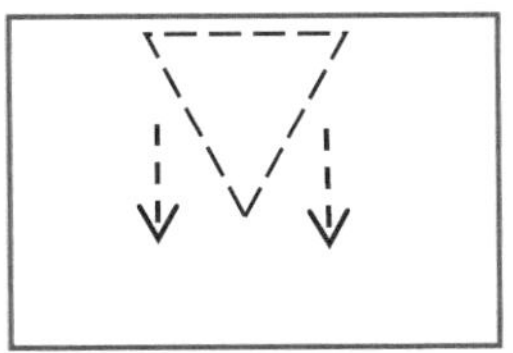
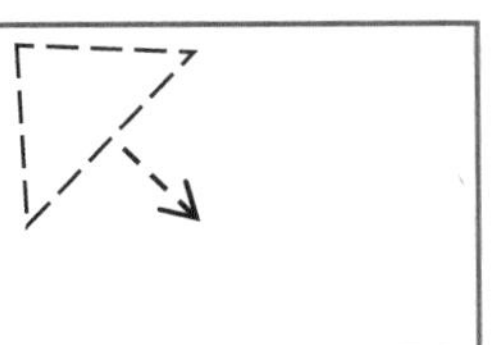
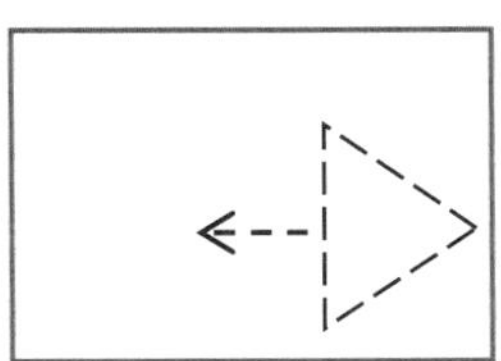

Figure 9

➢ **SPATIAL PATTERNS** are the "maps" and "roads" in the space where the dancers are or will be positioned to stand or move. Patterns enhance the conceptual and visual impact of the dance and influence its structural progression. Patterns can change shape and form at any given moment. Patterns are often drawn and identified from a bird's eye view—a *view from above.* Once the dancers are inside the patterns, however, their floor placement is most often *viewed from the front.* The choreographer designs the spatial relationships between the dancers and determines how they occupy the space.

Patterns exist two- and three-dimensionally. For example, symmetrical floor patterns with the dancers standing on stage could be combined with asymmetrical shapes and forms that the dancers go through while either static or moving. A pattern is three-dimensional and may include multiple visual perspectives at the same time—a bird's-eye view from above and a view from the front. For example, in Alexei Ratmansky's *Seven Sonatas*—see Figure 10—the dancers are positioned at equal distances in a diagonal floor pattern, while also forming a diagonal spatial design with their poses.

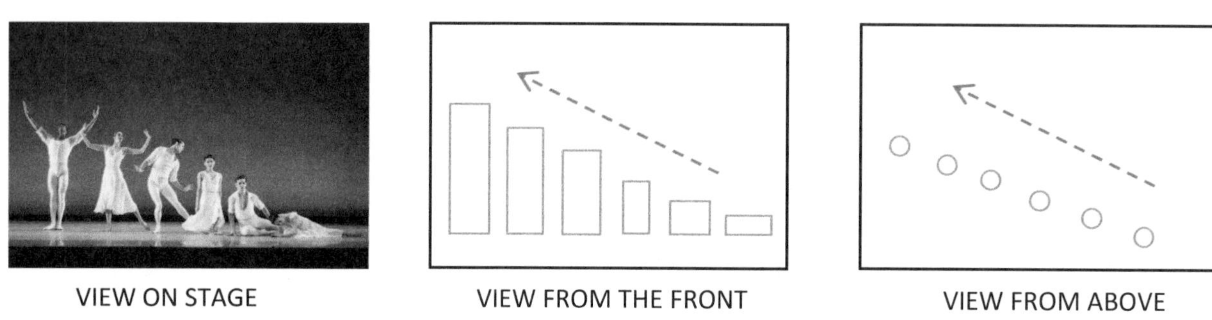

Figure 10 Photography © Theo Kossenas, *Seven Sonatas* (2009), choreography by Alexei Ratmansky, pictured dancers of the Washington Ballet, 2017

Geometrical, non-geometrical, and random patterns in dance, and also in nature, can originate and form deliberately or accidentally. Such patterns exist in nature as a mathematical embodiment of functionality, growth, and sustainability. For example, an orange's radial symmetry allows the maintenance of water and nutrition; seashells grow in spirals to protect the mollusk within; honeybees construct hexagonal cells to efficiently hold and store their honey. These occurrences of nature can also be found in the floor patterns of the Maypole dance, in the works of the iconic choreographer Busby Berkeley's lavish dance formations, and in dancing couples as human nuclei of procreation—see Figure 11 with samples of *biological-architectural patterns* and those in dance:

Figure 11 Sample images courtesy of iStock/Getty Images and archival dance photography—see bibliography references

Intriguing new patterns may be devised as variations of an existing pattern. Choreographers may modify patterns to fit practical purposes and to convey certain ideas. For example, in the past, many geometrical forms had spiritual meaning. *Sacred geometry* was implemented with the conviction that God as the creator of the Universe was the geometer in charge. Specific geometrical shapes and purposefully formed symmetrical designs carried symbolic messages and had to be taken into consideration when constructing sacred buildings such as churches, mosques, and temples, as well as special monuments and government buildings.[7]

The symbolic meaning of patterns comprises various philosophies, myths, and ideologies, which suggests that geometrical patterns have a cognitive and emotional impact on humans. In summary, patterns can be treated as the mathematical expression of symbolic ideas.

○ **The circle is a symbol of the cosmic and celestial. The shape of the sun, the moon, the planets, and their orbits figuratively capture the universe, the divine, and the continuation of existence. The circle represents totality, wholeness, perfection, the infinite, and timelessness.**

△ **The triangle is a symbol of wisdom, ambition, and advancement. Additionally, the direction of the triangle point has represented gender in certain cultures and beliefs. Traditionally, when pointed upward it has symbolized the power of the male, and fire, and when pointed downward—the power of the female.**

□ **The square is a symbol of stability. Its straight lines and sharp corners represent laws and regulations, competency, and intellectualism. The four sides of the square connect with the compass points and represent the four main directions of north, east, south, and west. The square also symbolizes unity.[8]**

Patterns were used in dance and the arts as ways of understanding the forces of the Universe and to manifest control over society at large. Cave art of the oldest lunar calendars found in France and Germany displayed patterns of interplay between the moon's annual cycle, the ecliptic, the solstice, and the seasonal changes on Earth.[9] These patterns were part of early ritual dance. Nicolaus Copernicus' astronomic model of 1543 positioned the Sun at the center of the Universe, with Earth and the other planets rotating around it in circular paths at uniform speeds—orbits.[10]

Circular dance floor patterns were drawn on the floor to direct English country dancers and early Baroque dancers to "orbit" around someone else as part of the basic dance technique introduced at social celebrations and theatrical court events[11]—see Figure 12.

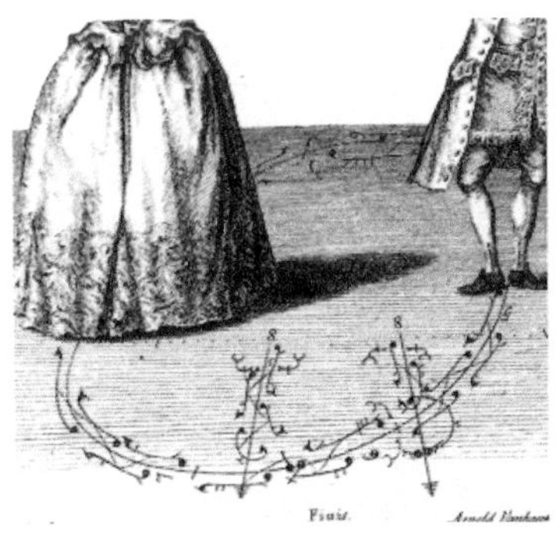

Figure 12 Copernicus's astronomic model and Baroque couple dancing floor patterns: Copernicus, Nicolaus, and Johannes Petrejus *Nicolai Copernici Torinensis De revolvtionibvs orbium cœlestium*, courtesy of Library of Congress

Figure 13 Photography © Therese Gahl, *Choreographer's Note Book*, 2020

THINKING ABOUT CHOREOGRAPHING FLOOR PATTERNS AND PATHWAYS WITHOUT THE DANCERS PRESENT?

Candy can help. ☺

Colorful candies can do double duty: as fun snacks to cheer up choreographers and as stand-ins for the dancers to be maneuvered on a flat surface though potential patterns. Choreographers can also happily experiment with various formations and movement pathways—see the image left.

➢ **SPATIAL PATHWAYS:** Pathways are movement trajectories and locomotive patterns that allow dancers to travel through the performance space. Although there might not be a coded symbolic message in a pathway, the dancers' journey within the performance space may result from the choreographer's careful guidance and directives—how to move, where to go, when to enter and exit, where to start, and where to end.

– OCCUPYING SPACE: Pathways are three-dimensional and define stationary and moving configurations. In the space above the floor, the dancers push the air; they move through space by drawing lines and tracing forms and shapes. Dancers make the space appear larger by "moving bigger," extending lines and motions beyond their limbs, and taking up more space with their movement than they appear to have.

– SPATIAL PASSAGES: Pathways are either symmetrical or asymmetrical. Traditionally, symmetrical designs often suggest formality, balance, and neatness, while asymmetrical designs tend to suggest spontaneity, liberation, or fragility.

– DIRECTION OF LOCOMOTION: Pathways appear in straight lines and curved lines, denoting where and how the dancers travel from one place in space to another. The dancers may move in random and arbitrary paths, or with clear directions in space. Figure 14 depicts a frontal view of dynamic spatial designs and directions in combination with different paths. All of these possibilities may change or repeat in a matter of a few seconds.

Figure 14

➢ **SPATIAL PLACEMENT** is the location within a particular performance space where a dancer or a group of dancers is positioned, or where they are moving through determined or random patterns. Making calculated or intuitive decisions of positioning and placement of the dancers in space will influence the visual and dramatic effect of a dance. Theatrical conventions for the proscenium stage divide the space into nine focal points, presuming that dancers exit only stage left and right, and a seated audience views the dance from across the proscenium line. For centuries, traditional rules anticipating the effects of each portion of the stage were followed dutifully. However, nowadays choreographers may reject theatrical conventions to disrupt expectations or to suggest deviance.

The proscenium stage is one of the most common in Western performance tradition. Other types of stages are thrust stage and arena/round stage, which allows multiple angles of observation. Blackbox theater is a flexible stage configuration allowing adaptable arrangements of the seating and performance areas. Non-traditional performance spaces include site-specific locations such as galleries, churches, and various outdoor sites. Any possible space could be a performance space.

STAGE AREAS

Upstage Right	Upstage Center	Upstage Left
Center Right	Center Stage	Center Left
Downstage Right	Downstage Center	Downstage Left

Figure 15

Typically, *center stage* is the area of dominance and main focus. Any action moving toward *downstage center* progressively increases the potential for impact due to its closeness to the audience. *Upstage corner* areas and the side-curtain areas are traditionally used as entry points. Patterns often progress towards *center stage* and *downstage. Diagonals,* on the other hand, stretch from upstage to downstage left or right, and vice versa. These pathways tend to be used dynamically since they offer the longest "runway" on stage, providing more space for leaps, athletic partnering, and traveling moves, steps and jumps. The areas "in-between" and within the corners and the edges of the stage are all considered "neutral" or *midsection*, where traditionally most of the dancing transpires.

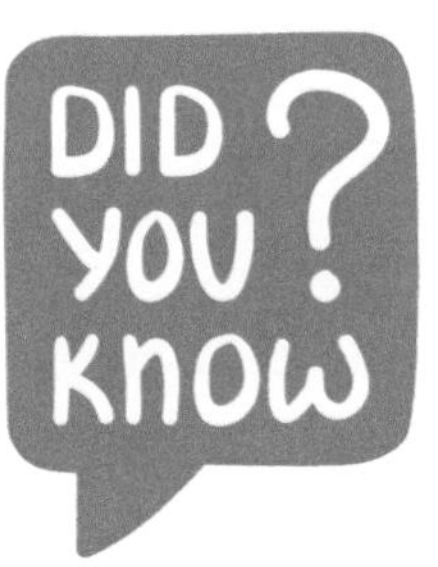

Different treatment of stage space can be traced in history within a few generalized concepts: The 16th–19th-century classicism: **The stage space is topography with spots of attention, meaning center stage is most "important"; upstage is "shy"; downstage stage could mean "sharing with the audience."** The 20th-century modernism: **The stage space is a dynamic place, meaning in the words of Martha Graham: "The center of the stage is where I am."[12] The attention is on the dancer, no matter where they are located.** The 21st-century conceptualism: **The stage space is an equal visual field, meaning that multiple events may take place at the same time, such as video displays, three-dimensional projections, installations, and various movement events. The attention is on all elements, which are treated with equal importance and perceived at the same time.**

STRUCTURAL PROGRESSION

Formal compositional structures used in dance have been borrowed from similar compositional forms, and the *terminology* used has been applied in Western music, as well as in literature, architecture, and the other arts. However, the core concepts of these structural models can also be found in *ordinary patterns of living* and in the experiences of people and cultures anywhere in the world, as the examples below reveal.

Compositional structures are used to organize and unify movement material.[13] They also determine the *structural progression* of a dance. A complete dance, a section of a dance, or a single dance phrase could incorporate one or more compositional structures or a combination of structural forms, all at the same time. Although these structural models seem to be "set and solid" prototypes, they are in fact expendable and dynamic. They can be modified, *restructured*, and *deconstructed* to accommodate the choreographer's creative inquiry. The following is a description of seven traditionally used structures:

➢ **BINARY—AB Form** is a structural form operating with two different subjects or entities. These entities could function in unity or separately, by complementing each other or operating in opposition. Artistic compositions often capture surrounding experiences—opposition and contrast are embedded in human nature and in ordinary events in life. Day is replaced by night; fire is extinguished by water; and sadness is followed by happiness.

Binary form is the most basic form of composition. It offers a suitable creative framework to explore the relations between two entities and the dynamics of action and reaction. A choreographer could choose to depict the tension between two forces: how they differ and oppose each other, while also overlapping and merging into each other. Discovering the dynamics and the connection between the two entities may be the key that drives the dance to a resolution. For example, the destruction of something can lead to a change that brings something new to life.

➢ **TERNARY—ABA$_1$ Form** is another formal choreographic structure. This form delineates three sections—1) an exposition, followed by 2) a distinct new entity, and concluding with 3) a repetition of the introductory exposition, which contains an element of the new entity.

This three-part form could be a simple symmetrical structure when the final portion is a straightforward repetition of the first part. The conceptually expanded and advanced version of the ternary form (in music known as *sonata* form), however, will likely contain the three distinct sections of exposition, development, and recapitulation. In the last case, three main sections could be subdivided as A (aba) → B (bcb) → A_1 (abc), where the recurring A_1 section and the subdivisions provide an overall sense of unity and balance.

The ABA_1 form is suitable for examining a state of change within steadiness in life. The form provides a sense of upward spiraling rather than circling. For example, looking at something from the past but with fresh eyes and a new perspective, or having a journey-like experience by going to a new place only to return back home.

➢ **THEME AND VARIATION—A: A_1, A_2, A_3** is a compositional structure that first introduces a subject or a concept in its original unadorned form—a theme—which is then repeated with varied treatments that alter the original theme. Variations are different than repetitions, which lack modifications. Variations contain changes and deviations, while the core ideas of the original theme remain.

Variations may vary. They could be *strict* and within the length of the original theme; *flexible* and without a duration limit; *sectional* with a clear ending; *continual* with a transition into other variations; *contained* with a gravitational enclosure to the center of the theme; or *free* with wider deviations and dramatic departures from the main theme.

Although variations seem decorative in function, they are different than a *motif*—see Chapter 17. While a motif is a recurring and distinct decorative element, variations may branch progressively in different directions. A motif can have a variation, and that variation could have a sub-variation—a *coda*—which could be either the *introduction*, the *expansion*, or the *recapitulation* of that variation. This structural format is suitable to explore certain variant aspects of sameness. Something may look the same, but it is never exactly the same, for example, observing the same landscape during different seasons or seeing the sunset in different locations.

➢ **RONDO—AB–AC–AD** is a structural form that establishes an initial concept or a subject, followed by alternating new and contrasting parts, and then returns repeatedly to the initial subject. Rondo, which also means *round*, uses a *refrain* or a *recurrence* as the main technique in this structural form. A similar technique in Baroque music was first conceived as *ritornello*, which consists of a few small units that reappear in a composition as a recurring passage.[14]

Once a rondo establishes its *center* as a statement of the theme, or *refrain*, there are *episodes* and *occasions* that introduce new material, subjects, and elements that are different from the theme. This form is suitable for exploring repetition, and yet it allows the introduction of new material by juxtaposing it with the returning *themes* or *motifs*. For example, on a spinning carousel, a mythological Fire Horse figure is the central subject in the dance, and as other animals and creatures appear, the Fire Horse periodically returns.

➢ **FUGUE—ABC – BCD—CDE** is a structural form that introduces and establishes a concept, a subject, or a theme, followed by occasional recurring thematic elements, which are developed progressively, causing substantial alterations of the theme during the overall work. Fugue initially seems similar to Rondo.

The repetitions used in a Fugue, however, are less insistent: emphasis is on accumulating new material. Additionally, the Fugue's new material is often *counter-punctual*, as certain elements and parts can *go against each other* but may simultaneously work in harmony.

While Rondo is always thematically associative, Fugue can be dissociative. The Fugue is suitable for exploring concepts where the goal is to reveal how a theme or subject matter is taken to a new place. For example, a person confronting unfavorable living circumstances relocates geographically in hope of a better life. The person is the same yet moving in a new direction to function in a new environment.

➢ **CANON—ABC**

ABC

ABC—is a form, sometimes called a "round," where an overlapping, recurring movement sequence runs parallel to the same sequence that begins at a later starting time. The canon is a combination of repetition and overlap, where a purposeful delay creates an *echo*—waves bouncing and reflecting back.

Canon is *chance harmony*. As the same theme is performed simultaneously but with delayed timing, it creates a natural juxtaposition that matches harmonically. This form is suitable for exploring similar experiences that repeat and overlap in time. For example, an older sister looks after her younger sister and naturally connects with her, not only because they are relatives, but also because the older sister can relive the age of the younger.

➢ **RHAPSODIC/NARRATIVE FORM—A, B, C, D, E ...** is a compositional structure built by a series of independent movement events deliberately arranged to reveal the dramatic, thematic, or emotional significance of a narrative. A narrative could magnify a story, legend, or news report, where events are in chronological order. In addition, a narrative could zoom-out and broadly handle a subject matter, plot, statement, or situation.

In music, a rhapsody is a one-movement, episodic work that integrates multiple sections with highly contrasting moods and is compiled in a free-flowing structure. The word rhapsody comes from a *rhapsodist*—a reciter of epic poems in ancient Greece.[15] What makes this format attractive to composers is its structural irregularity, non-symmetrical framework, and often highly emotional narrative characteristics.

There are multiple degrees of *literal representation* of a narrative, a plot, or a subject matter. A plot could be a direct and accurate portrayal of specific events, or it could reveal a semi-narrative, abstract, and alternative interpretation of the narrative. This form is suitable for organizing a sequence of events or to capture a storyline. For example, when asking a married couple how they met and what led them to fall in love, their response might naturally reveal a romantic narrative containing multiple independent episodes based on relived memories, shared with a dose of emotionality.

?

These structural forms are linked with real life examples—which one of them is the most appealing to you, and why?

Figure 16 Photography © Lois Greenfield, pictured Aaron Ashby, Andrew Claus, Cornelius Brown, Colleen T. Sullivan, Sarah Wagner, Vanessa Lynn Campos, courtesy of Dodge Dance Company, 2005

ACCESSORIES, PROPS, SETS, AND SCENERY
– BRINGING OBJECTS INTO THE DANCING ARCHITECTURE –

Usually, a dance production incorporates far more than human movement. Production design elements such as accessories, props, sets, and stage scenery may be an integral part of the structure and the construction of a dance – see Chapter 24. If various stage objects are part of the concept, it is essential to integrate them early in the rehearsal and staging process.

An introduction to accessories, stage objects, and props provides the dancers with ample time to interact and get used to them. If there will be a white elephant on the stage, let's bring it in soon and use it to the fullest. Various stage objects used in performance may be grouped, categorized, and characterized as the following:

- **Small props and portable accessories** are any objects that can be maneuvered with one hand. These include small or large removable pieces of clothing and stage costuming such as scarves and ponchos, as well as maneuverable objects such as hats, gloves, cigars, glasses, bags, umbrellas, canes, weaponry, flags, flowers, and others. Small props and accessories could be incorporated creatively as part of the movement and dance. For example, a suitcase might become a sitting prop, or an "umbrella" that is carried over the head. A large empty picture frame may be choreographed around the dancer's body to represent a portrait coming alive. Certain accessories, such as monocles or a period smoke pipe, may become instrumental in determining a stage personality or in developing a role or character. Accessories can also serve a purely kinesthetic purpose without a narrative context, for example, dancing with and tossing a long, light scarf into the air and catching it with fluid hops and spins.

- **Mid-size props** include any objects that can be moved and maneuvered by one or two individuals. Stage objects can include small furniture such as wooden boxes, chairs, tables, podiums, and portable platforms. They can be placed and moved on stage by the stage crew or by the performers as part of the choreography. For example, a bed with casters can turn into a driving device traveling around the space. Several stacked chairs could turn into an improvised house for "hide and seek," or chairs placed in a round formation could become a sitting circle game. A few portable wooden boxes can be stacked on top of each other for a dancer to climb and "freeze" on top of, like a sculpture.

- **Large props, stationary sets, and scenery** are large objects, decorations, and scenery that require a stage crew and technical equipment to be positioned, assembled, and installed. Such items include platforms of different sizes and on multiple levels, staircases, sculptures, draperies, stage legs, hanging screens, backdrops, cycloramas, projection screens, large pieces of furniture, mobile or stationary vehicles, as well as stationary architectural structures such as oversized plants, walls, bridges, buildings, etc. Large and special scenery might also include, for example, a dance installation of hanging ropes or fabric strips of assorted sizes and colors scattered across portions of the stage or covering it. Special gymnastics equipment for aerial dancing, including bungee cords, might require scenery construction and field specialists.

A considerable challenge for dancers is the handling of unorthodox dance surfaces that are elevated above the standard floor level of the stage. In addition, stairs, ramps, unusually shaped sets, and eccentric three-dimensional structures may be difficult to dance on, around, or with if not included in the rehearsal process from the start. Choreographers may need to plan in advance to work through these complexities with the dancers.

Under the guidance of the choreographer, the performers may interact choreographically with accessories, props, sets, and scenery. While in the process of staging the work, the choreographer should take into consideration any requirements of the performers to maneuver large or small objects as they dance.

The dancers' interactions with the objects might include incorporating them into the choreography by lifting them, moving them, placing them, and repositioning them. Choreographers may effectively use accessories, props, and scenery in various ways—see Figure 16:

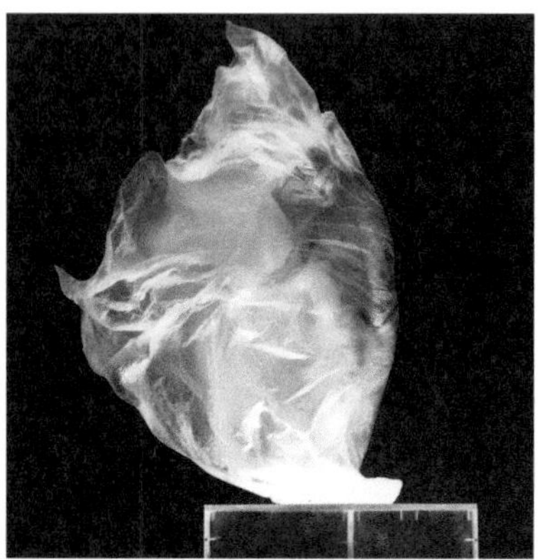

Figure 17 Photography © Lois Greenfield, image left pictured performer Wu-Kang Chen, Ballet Tech, 2007; image center pictured performers Clint Lutes, Daniel Jaber, Australian Dance Theater, 2018; image right pictured performer Fang-Yi Sheu, Ballet Tech, 2008

In ordinary life an ongoing interaction between objects and humans occurs naturally. Therefore, it may seem logical and even advantageous for choreographers to consider exploring and incorporating in their dances various types of material items that may combine reality and the arts. Ordinary objects, works of fine art, visual installations, stage design, and scenery may not only link the stage environment with distinct life experiences but may also enhance a dance's impact.

HELPFUL TIPS & SUGGESTIONS

~ Construct with your brain, create with your heart
~ Use movement formations as tools to build up and pare down
~ Use floor patterns to direct and re-direct action
~ Use spatial placement to narrow focus and widen viewpoints
~ Choose clear pathways or create new paths for moving or detouring
~ Treat compositional structures as a part of life instead of art dogma
~ Approach accessories, props, and sets as active tools, not passive objects

assignments & exercises

RESEARCH ASSIGNMENT: Investigate various construction and structural techniques used by historically renowned choreographers in the United States. Research online video materials that contain samples of techniques in the following famous works: for **Succession**, see Doris Humphrey's *Water Study*; for **Unison and Contrast**, as well as **Divide and Differ**, see Jerome Robbins' *West Side Story*. Pay particular attention to the scene entitled "The Gangs Fight in the Street"; for **Canon and Rondo**, see Mark Morris' work *Spring, Spring, Spring*. Analyze and discuss how the choreographers use these techniques.

Research online video materials to explore samples of dance works that extensively use **accessories**, **props**, and **sets** as part of choreographic construction and structural development. For the use of the tables as part of the choreography, see William Forsythe's work *ONE FLAT THING, REPRODUCED*; for use of wooden boxes as part of the choreography, see Sidi Larbi Charkaoui's work *SUTRA*; for use of small green balls and various accessories, props, and sets, see Alexander Ekman's work *PLAY*.

★ **CREATIVE ASSIGNMENT:** Explore creatively various aspects of:

√ **Movement formations:**

➥ Create a short movement phrase and teach it to a few dancers. Explore the same phrase by using the first three major formations: *Unison*, *Succession*, and *Contrast*. Then, add some additional formations such as *Divide and Differ*, *Add and Subtract*, *Zoom In and Out*, and *Foreground and Background*. How does the impact of the same phrase change within each formation?

√ **Floor patterns, pathways, space placement and displacement:**

➥ Practice moving a few dancers from one floor *spatial pattern* to another. For example, form a straight line and then transfer it to a diagonal line, then form a circle, then a triangle, then a square, then two parallel lines, and finally, form a non-symmetrical cluster of dancers. What visual impact do these geometrical configurations have?

➥ Explore a variety of pathways and focus on *spatial direction* to move the dancers from one floor pattern to another. Do you implement a short traveling trajectory, or do you prefer to use transitional pathways to get from one pattern to another? How frequently do your designs change and how do they affect the content of the overall motion?

➥ Create a simple still shape for a few dancers and place it in different stage locations. In addition, experiment with changing the front and the direction that the dancers face during the (dis)placement of the group shape, as well as distance between the dancers—*spatial design*. How do these experiments affect the original shape? What impact do they have on the viewer?

√ **Structural progression of dance sequencing:**

➡ Take one of the structural development principles—let's pick *Canon*—that is similar to "voice and echo," and explore different versions of overlapping techniques. For example:

1 2 3 4 5 6 7 8	or	1 2 3 4 5 6 7 8	or	1 2 3 4 5 6 7 8
1 2 3 4 5 6 7 8		1 2 3 4 5 6 7 8		1 2 3 4 5 6 7 8

➡ Use *Narrative and Rhapsodic form A, B, C, D . . .* to develop a movement sequence for the group dance. Begin by choosing a subject. The subject could be a specific image or a particular story. Next, decide how literally and realistically this subject or the story will be presented. For example, would you choose to portray specific actions or to present a semi-narrative and semi-abstract version of the subject matter? Finally, create a brief outline of movement actions and give the "itinerary" to the dancers; ask them to play with the idea by modifying the initial choreography on their own terms. How accurately do the dancers follow your outline, and what did they choose to modify? Did they propose an alternative interpretation of the narrative? Why?

➡ Choose small portable accessories and/or available portable props. If you have already choreographed a phrase for your group and have used some of these techniques, ask the dancers to use elements of the choreography that they have practiced, but now add accessories and props and decide how you want to use them in the dance. How does use of these props change the choreography and the initial concept? What works and what does not work? Why?

COMPARATIVE ASSIGNMENT: Explore and compare one or various development devices from Chapter 17—for example, *repetition*—and identify how it may be used and implemented in movement compositions of structural progressions such as *succession*, *canon*, and *rondo*. What are the differences and the similarities in the use of *repetition*? How do the visual impact and the movement flow change when *repetition* includes all of these structural progression techniques?

Figure 18 Photography © Lois Greenfield, pictured Nick Dinicolangelo, Anthony Morigerato, Jason Luks, Matt Boyce, Michael Minery, courtesy of Tapaholics, 2005

BIBLIOGRAPHY AND REFERENCES

[1] Editors. *Structure*, Online etymology dictionary, www.etymonline.com/word/structure, accessed May 2019.
[2] Editors. *Construction*, Online etymology dictionary, www.etymonline.com/word/structure, accessed May 2019.
[3] Editors. *Deconstruction*, Deconstruct, Online etymology dictionary, www.etymonline.com/word/structure, accessed May 2019.
[4] Vasari, Giorgio. Editors. *Michelangelo's David*, online article, Guide to the academia Gallery in Florence, Italy, www.accademia.org/, accessed May 2019.
[5] Stone, Irving. *The Agony and the Ecstasy: A Biographical Novel of Michelangelo*, Reissue edition, Berkley Press, 1987.
[6] Blom, Lynne Anne and Chaplin, L. Tarin. *The Intimate Act of Choreography*, University of Pittsburg Press, 1982, pp. 178–189.
[7] De León, Carlos Arturo Alvarez Ponce. *Sacred Geometry and Architecture*, Architectura Bilogica, 2017, 2019.
[8] Beyer, Catherine. "Geometric Shapes and Their Symbolic Meanings, Forms Ranging from Circles to Dodekagrams Have Significance in Many Philosophies," *Learn Religion*, online article: www.learnreligions.com/geometric-shapes-4086370, accessed July 2019.
[9] Editors. *The Oldest Lunar Calendars*, Solar System Exploration Research Virtual Institute, formerly NASA Lunar Science Institute, online article: https://sservi.nasa.gov/articles/oldest-lunar-calendars/, accessed May 2020.
[10] Westman, Robert S. *Nicolaus Copernicus*, online article, Encyclopedia Britannica, Inc. May 20, 2020, www.britannica.com/biography/Nicolaus-Copernicus, accessed June 2020.
[11] Foster, Susan Leigh. *Choreography Narrative: Ballet's Staging of Story and Desire*, Indiana University Press, 1996, pp. 20–27.
[12] Teachout, Terry. "The Dance MARTHA GRAHAM," article, *Time Magazine*, online article, June 1998, http://content.time.com/time/magazine/article/0,9171,988513,00.html, accessed 2019.
[13] Blom and Chaplin 1982. *The Intimate Act of Choreography*, pp. 93–101.
[14] Editors. *Rondo Form in Music: Definition & Examples*, Study.com, 08.04.2015, study.com/academy/lesson/rondo-form-in-music-definition-examples-quiz.html
[15] Editors. *Rhapsody: Merriam-Webster.com Dictionary*, Merriam-Webster, www.merriam-webster.com/dictionary/rhapsody, accessed July 2020.

VISUAL REFERENCES

Figure 1: Diagram © Vladimir Angelov

Figures 2: Image left and center: Porcelain objects, credit: aluxum and broken vases, credit: bizoo_n, Courtesy of iStock/Getty images, image right; Artwork and photography © Li Xiaofeng, *Beijing Memory*, porcelain dress, courtesy of Brian Wallace, Red Gate Gallery, Beijing, People's Republic of China, and the artist, 2007

Figure 3: Diagram © Vladimir Angelov

Figure 4: Photography © Jörg Bittner Unna, *David* by Michelangelo, Florence, Galleria dell'Accademia, 1501–4, public domain, Wiki Commons, image edits by Elizabeth Gray

Figure 5: Photography © Lois Greenfield, Eliot Feld's Ballet Tech, 1995

Figure 6: Photography © Julien Benhamou, *Défilé*, Paris Opera Ballet, 2016, and photography © Yonathan Kellerman, *Giselle*, Paris Opera Ballet, 2020

Figures 7, 8, and 9: Diagram © Vladimir Angelov

Figure 10: Photography © Theo Kossenas, *Seven Sonatas* (2009), choreography by Alexei Ratmansky, dancers of the Washington Ballet, 2017

Figure 11: Images from left to right: 1A: Sliced half of orange fruit, credit: vmenshov, courtesy of iStock/Getty Images; 1B: Photography © Harris & Ewing, *Friendship charity fete, maypole dance*, Public domain, Library of Congress, 1915; 2A: Ammonite—ancient mollusk fossils, Credit: dja65, courtesy of iStock/Getty Images; 2B: Frame from public domain trailer for 1933 Warner Bros film *Gold Diggers* (1933), showing musical number "Waltz of the Shadows" by Busby Berkeley, courtesy of Wiki Commons; 3A: Bee on honeycomb, Credit: Filip_Krstic, courtesy of iStock/Getty Images; 3B: Couples dancing at the Majestic Ballroom, Pier Parade, South Shields, February 1952, courtesy of Tyne & Wear Archives & Museums

Figure 12: Copernicus' astronomic model and Baroque couple dancing floor patterns: Copernicus, Nicolaus, and Johannes Petrejus. *Nicolai Copernici Torinensis De revolvtionibvs orbium cœlestium, libri VI*. Norimbergæ, apud Ioh. Petreium, 1543. Pdf. Retrieved from the Library of Congress, and Kellom Tomlinson, author, plate from dancing manual *The Art of Dancing Explained*, published in London, 1735. Library of Congress, Washington, D.C.

Figure 13: Photography © Therese Gahl, Choreographer's Note Book, 2020

Figures 14 and 15: Diagrams © Vladimir Angelov

Figure 16: Photography © Lois Greenfield, pictured Aaron Ashby, Andrew Claus, Cornelius Brown, Colleen T. Sullivan, Sarah Wagner, Vanessa Lynn Campos, courtesy of Dodge Dance Company, 2005

Figure 17: Photography © Lois Greenfield, image left pictured performer Wu-Kang Chen, Ballet Tech, 2007; image center pictured performers Clint Lutes, Daniel Jaber, Australian Dance Theater, 2018; image left pictured performer Fang-Yi Sheu, Ballet Tech, 2008

Figure 18: Photography © Lois Greenfield, pictured Nick Dinicolangelo, Anthony Morigerato, Jason Luks, Matt Boyce, Michael Minery, courtesy of Tapaholics, 2005

Plan for what is difficult

while it is easy,

do what is great

while it is small.

Sun Tzu (544 BC–496 BC)

CHAPTER 19

PHYSICAL DRAMATURGY

– MAKING A MONUMENT OUT OF MOVEMENT –

We never know what to expect when we are about to see an original dance performance on opening night. We voluntarily agree to journey inside a dance work, expecting the choreographer's guidance. We enter a monument made of movement—just like walking into a memorial tomb, mysterious temple, or shadowy cathedral. We hope to be handed a lighted candle to avoid getting lost, to find our way around, and leave enlightened by the experience. That candle is not only a guiding glow in the dark, but also a deliberate navigation tool to explore a monument of motion.

◆ **Physical dramaturgy navigates and sculpts movement content.** While the choreographer's *movement mind* produces bodily motion, the *dramaturgical mind* explores various working strategies and defines the direction of the creative process, and therefore, the direction of the work. The dramaturgical mind engages in multiple operations—to initiate artistic research, formulate concepts, and determine how these concepts will be revealed. Dramaturgical skills help build the skeleton of a dance—its sequencing and architectural appearance—by breaking down ideas and putting them back together to make sense.[1]

Choreographers of concert dance often act as their own dance dramaturgs. Therefore, learning about key dramaturgical principles and how they function in a wordless physical art form can be helpful. Physical dramaturgy is one of the fundamental instruments that a choreographer uses in crafting dance.

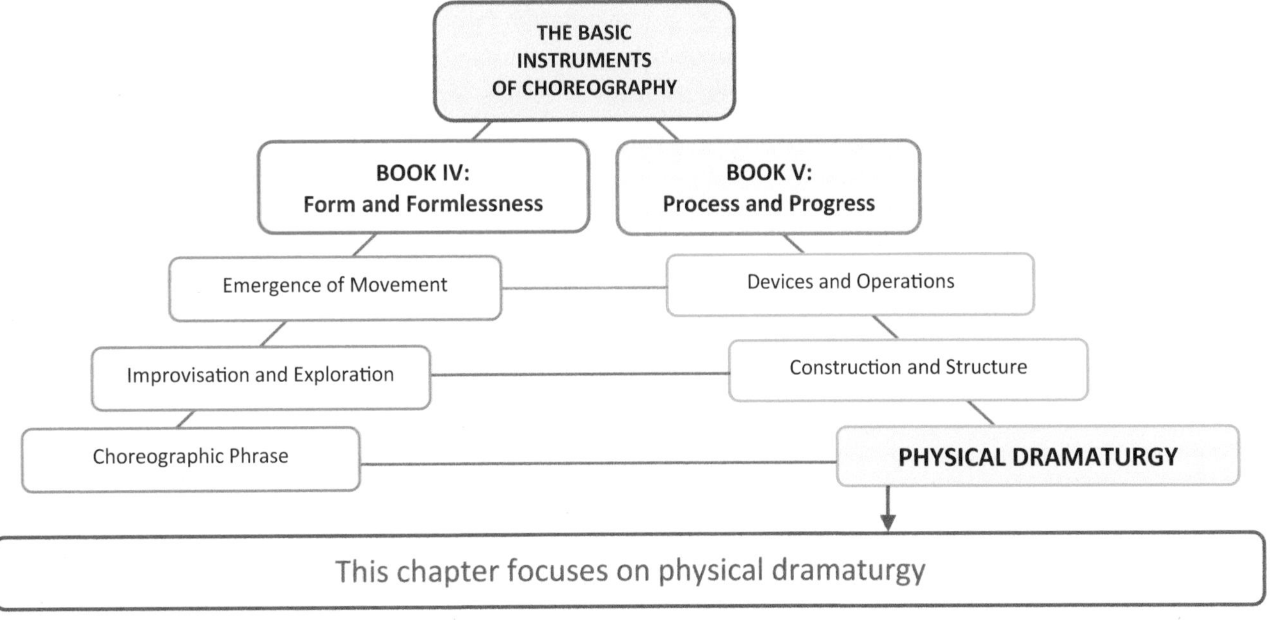

Figure 1

Some historical context: The foundation of Western theatrical dramaturgy can be traced to Aristotle's *Poetics*, which was written circa 335 BC. However, dramaturgy as a formal profession began in the mid-18th century with the German playwright, critic, and philosopher Gotthold Ephraim Lessing (1729–81). Lessing analyzed theatrical texts for quality and sustainability and then decided on staging options in original or adapted forms. In the first half of the 20th century, Bertolt Brecht introduced a new kind of dramaturgy that defined the performance's ideological objectives: Brecht determined what was relevant to the stage production by engaging in background research and evaluation.[2]

In classical ballet, a *librettist* was assigned to develop a dramaturgical outline of a large body of narrative ballet productions driven by elaborate story plots. The librettist focused on adapting and re-writing a literary work to fit a coherent libretto with scene sequences in a logical progression and clear narration expressed through mime and physical theater. Although ballet librettists (from Italian—*libro*, meaning book, and *libretto*, meaning booklet)[3] had to maneuver words and texts, they had to prioritize movement and dance.

In contemporary dance, the concept of professional dramaturg emerged in 1979 with Raimund Hoghe, who worked with renowned choreographer Pina Bausch. At that time, choreographers sought to avoid self-critical observation by assigning a feedback peer, artistic confidant, and intellectual collaborator. Hoghe's new model drew dance and theater dramaturgy together and included critical evaluation and the framing of performance philosophy, to help choreographers better articulate their movement ideas.[4]

Besides literature, language also operates across disciplines and specifically in dramaturgy for theater, opera, and film. Can language's text-bound dimensions still function in a predominantly wordless physical art form? The challenges are not to flip dance and physical dramaturgy to serve movement over words by physicalizing text, but to find and build a relationship between movement and words.[5] Exploring such an idiomatic connection and inter-disciplinary approach between semantics and dance may transform a literary text into a movement text, and a written script into physical dramaturgy.

Many choreographers develop dance works that are not text-based; rather, these works spring from other primary sources such as images, music, physical senses, and movement. Whether a professional dramaturg steps in to collaborate or a choreographer acts as a dramaturg, the main objectives of physical dramaturgy are:

- **DEFINING INTENTIONS, SUBJECT MATTER, CONCEPTS, AND APPROACHES:**
  What is the work about? What will it capture with motion, and what will it do?

- **FRAMING DIRECTION OF THE CREATIVE PROCESS AND BUILDING THE WORK STRUCTURALLY:**
  How does the dance work emerge, develop, and expand in response to its dramaturgical components?

- **ENSURING COHESIVENESS AND DRAMATURGICAL DIMENSIONALITY:**
  How do auditory, visual, and other core production elements bind the work together, and how does this nexus influence the dance work as a whole?

DRAMATURGICAL MODALITIES IN DANCE
– LITERAL OR FIGURATIVE, DESCRIPTIVE OR EMBODIED –

Creating a new dance rarely begins with a calculated plan and a written outline. Instead, a dance might emerge from a choreographer's random physical encounters and intuitive responses. In other instances, the choreographer might use a literary work or a visual image, music, or sound as a starting point. As the dance evolves, the choreographer begins to crystalize, justify, and verbalize numerous intentions and concepts. The question is: In which modality will these ideas be expressed—*linguistic, illustrative*, or *kinesthetic*? To examine the difference between *written description, visual image*, and *physical action*, let's imagine reading a novel where the first sentence is:

"The two sisters joined hands and whirled with joy."

How accurately can this sentence be *translated* kinesthetically into its movement and dance equivalent? A dance can capture the physical action of *two girls whirling* with *joy* while holding hands; however, pure dance may obliterate any effort to represent the *two girls* as *two sisters* because dance as an art form is always *figurative* but not always *literal*. To hint and communicate...*two sisters*..., the choreographer may add gestures, mime, spoken word, supplemental narrative, and theatrical devices to establish that the girls are closely related. Even then, the specificity of...*two sisters*... might still be kinesthetically interpreted as...*two joyful girls*....Let's put linguistics and written description to the test:

WHAT DO YOU SEE IN THE PICTURE BELOW? – Please check boxes of all the possible options

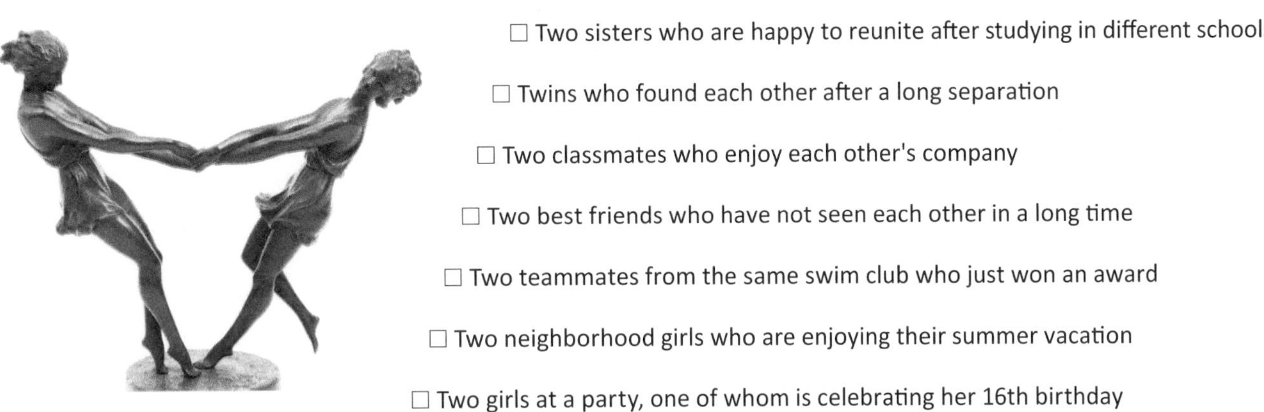

Figure 2 *Whirling–A Dance of Spring*, by Andre Gilbert, Art Deco bronze sculpture, France, 1925 © Image courtesy of Woolley and Wallis Salisbury Salerooms Ltd., 2020

All of the options listed earlier are quite distinct. Yet all of them could be absolutely correct and absolutely wrong—simultaneously. This paradox proves that the *descriptive* nature of words may not be applicable to the physical expressiveness of dance, where content and meaning are *embodied*. We learn about the girls based on what they do. Physical dramaturgy instantly captures an emotional state better than words—in this case, it is *joy*.

Adapting a literary work into a physical performance and effectively transforming the meaning of text and words into dance and movement is dramaturgical craftsmanship in its own right. A novel serving as the foundation for a story ballet or a narrative dance-theater work may be substantially rewritten, restructured, and modified in terms of the plot. This leads us to the question: How can complex linguistic communications and nuanced verbal interactions *be translated* into dance and movement without losing substance and content? Important points to consider about how dance and literature operate are:

➢ **In literature, the action unfolds in the mind.** Written text builds semantic imagery with internal visual impact. As we read a novel, we imagine and cognitively grasp the action and then deduce what is happening.

➢ **In dance, the action takes place with performers on stage.** Physical behavior and interaction build movement imagery of external visual impact. As we watch a dance, we directly observe the action, and then we deduce what is happening.

➢ **In choreography, a plot from a novel might be modified into a dance plot.** A few tips are: a) simplify elaborate plots, b) translate internal feelings into figurative kinesthetic actions, c) turn nuanced and narrative interactions into uninhibited physical encounters.

Great classical works of literature are often substantially modified for the stage to accommodate a dance narrative. For example, the novel *Don Quixote*, by Miguel de Cervantes, focuses exclusively on the adventures of Don Quixote and accomplice Sancho Panza in their efforts to bring justice to the world. By contrast, the ballet production with the same name and based on episodes from the famous novel focuses on the love relationship unfolding between Kitri and Basilo. Don Quixote and Sancho Panza are peripheral characters appearing in the ballet production.

The ballet libretto of *Don Quixote* has reconfigured the plot and the importance of the characters from the novel, shifting the emphasis from a drama about an aging gentleman to the drama between two young lovers. Similar to the novel, the narrative of the ballet is also about curiosity, adventure, justice, love, and overcoming struggles. Therefore, by keeping the same characters and morals of the novel in place, the modified ballet plot retains the substance of Cervantes' classic.

EL INGENIOSO
HIDALGO DON QVI-
XOTE DE LA MANCHA,
Compuesto por Miguel de Ceruantes Saauedra.
DIRIGIDO AL DVQVE DE BEIAR,
Marques de Gibraleon, Conde de Benalcaçar, y Bañares, Vizconde de la Puebla de Alcozer, Señor de las villas de Capilla, Curiel, y Burguillos.
Año, 1605.
CON PRIVILEGIO,
EN MADRID, Por Iuan de la Cuesta.
Vendese en casa de Francisco de Robles, librero del Rey nro señor.

Figure 3 Image left: *El ingenioso hidalgo Don Quixote de la Mancha*, libro de Miguel de Cervantes. Publicado en Madrid, en 1605, en la imprenta de Juan de la Cuesta. Image © Raimundo Pastor, source Wikki Commons; Image center—*The Ingenious Gentleman Don Quixote of La Mancha*, source iStock/Getty Images; Image right—Photography © Johan Persson, Carlos Acosta as Basilio and Marianela Nuñez as Kitri in *Don Quixote*, The Royal Ballet, Royal Opera House, 2013

DETERMINING INTENTIONS AND SUBJECT MATTER, FORMULATING CONCEPTS, AND CHOOSING APPROACHES

One of the exciting tasks of dance and physical dramaturgy is to formulate a summary of choreographic intentions and concepts orally and in writing. Basically, this is the crafting of a *synopsis* of a dance project. The critical question pending an answer is: "What is the *dance about*?" Similar to the activities of a publicist, a dramaturg will inquire about and weigh in on the project's subject matter and the creative approaches a choreographer has chosen. These are the first steps towards formulating the *aboutness* of a dance.[5]

But how can one dramaturgically formulate with words the content of an art form that is meant to be wordless? Choreographers predominantly explore the body's possibilities for bold and nuanced physical expression. Yet a dance performance might be experienced in many ways—as narrative, thematic, or abstract.[6] A dance at its core might tackle *subject matter* by focusing on a specific topic and by engaging in a certain *approach*, as choreographers define and redefine their *intentions* and *concepts*. As the choreography takes physical shape, the dance also positions itself within one or multiple conceptual frameworks—see Chapter 12.

An *approach* activates various treatment strategies of the *subject matter*, ranging from illustrative and referential, to interpretive and investigative. However, these determinations do not immediately guarantee potent choreographic imagery, and the work will continue to situate itself somewhere in the range between literal meaning and evocative meaning.[7] A visual illustration offers a short list of verbs defining various *approaches* and another list of general categories of *subject matter*:

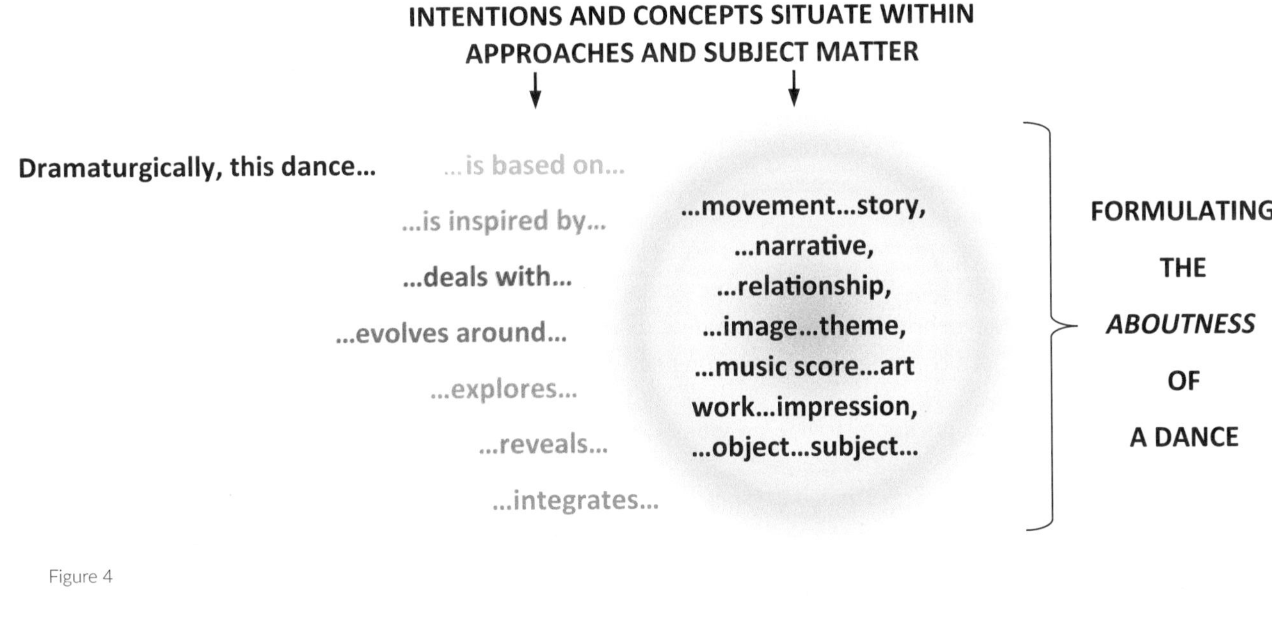

Figure 4

?

In your opinion, considering any similarities, was the film-musical *West Side Story* "inspired by" or "based on" Shakespeare's play *Romeo and Juliet*?

[NEW] DIRECTION OF THE WORK AND A POINT OF REFERENCE
– THE ORIGINALITY AND THE FAMILIARITY OF A DANCE –

Naturally, we want to quickly understand what we see and experience. We feel more confident when we find the reasoning behind everything and can make sense of the world. The same applies to dance. Does a dance look familiar or unfamiliar? Is it difficult to understand, watch, and enjoy? Do we need to *unravel* and *decode* its meaning? Or do we *assign* and *attribute* our own meaning to it? We may apply what we already know or make a guess about what we do not know. We may search for clues to uncover an *interpretation* or look for a *point of reference*.

While *interpretation* is a particular adaptation or a substantial re-envisioning of a work, *point of reference*, on the other hand, is the intentional use of one thing to indicate something else.[8] What makes a dance recognizable is the link between the dance and a familiar content, as well as the strength of that link. Naturally, choreography based on a well-known work of literature may lead to the anticipation that the dance will adapt, interpret, or reference its primary source.

For example, there are striking similarities between the play *Romeo and Juliet*, by William Shakespeare, and the musical *West Side Story*, by Jerome Robbins and Leonard Bernstein. The love story between Romeo and Juliet parallels the romance between Tony and Maria. The dramatic tension between the Montague and Capulet families in *Romeo and Juliet* is mirrored in *West Side Story* by the fights between the Sharks and the Jets. The new socio-cultural lens of *West Side Story* takes the well-known love drama to New York during the mid-20th century. Therefore, it is fair to say that the musical *West Side Story* was not based on (interpretation) Shakespeare's *Romeo and Juliet* but was inspired by (point of reference).

Dramaturgically speaking, not all dances need to be illustrative and *based on* something or have an interpretive *point of reference*. As a matter of fact, radical dance experimentation seeking new direction may not have any prescribed interpretive nature or intended point of reference. In these instances, the audience is liberated to come up with their own interpretations and freely attribute various points of reference. The role of the audience also transforms—from less passive observers to more active participants.

There are three major criteria to distinguish the new adaptation, interpretation, and referencing of a traditional dance work from the experimental innovation of a new, original dance work heading in a new direction. To strive towards genuine originality, a choreographer may consider at least two of these three criteria:

- Genuinely original concepts not related to previously known literary or other works.
- Genuinely original music scores created for specific dance works.
- Genuinely original movement vocabulary and unique kinesthetic systems of expression.

ASSIGNING AND ATTRIBUTING MEANING, INTENDED AND UNINTENDED OUTCOME

Choreographers generally desire to communicate and connect with their audience through their dances, and most choreographers want their dances to be understood and enjoyed. However, seemingly recognizable subject matter and movement material might be difficult for the audience to *read* and *translate* and, consequently, difficult for the audience to understand.

The *aboutness* of a dance may involve assigning and attributing meaning. The choreographer, engaging as a physical dramaturg, may assign meaning by:

➢ **Exploring opportunities** in which *aboutness* is the process and approach to the creative act, revealed as documented research, exploration, and findings on how the dance was created.

and/or

➢ **Disclosing narrative** in which *aboutness* is the subject matter of the dance, where a dance neutrally reveals to the audience the specificity and the complexity of a particular topic.

and/or

➢ **Taking a stand** in which *aboutness* is the choreographer's unique view, interpretation, position, and artistic commentary about subject matter that are revealed in a dance.

Assigning and attributing specific meaning to the content, concepts, and movement material may go off course and alter the choreographer's predictions about the outcome. The audience may inaccurately *read* or simply misunderstand the attributed meaning that the choreographer thought had been successfully communicated. This is no one's fault because the audience sees only the result of the choreographer's process, but not the actual process. Appropriate edits and adjustments can be made during the *work-in-progress* stages.

While the *aboutness* is still taking shape and the work's structure is unsettled, the choreographer may solicit feedback from a trusted peer-dramaturg and pursue a critical mid-point evaluation. Physical dramaturgy engages choreographers and their artistic associates to act as *editors*, *facilitators*, and *moderators*. Reframing imagery, reconfiguring movement material, and dramaturgically restructuring the work may help bridge the choreographer's goals for an anticipated outcome with the audience's *reading* of the work, as indicated in the following meme:

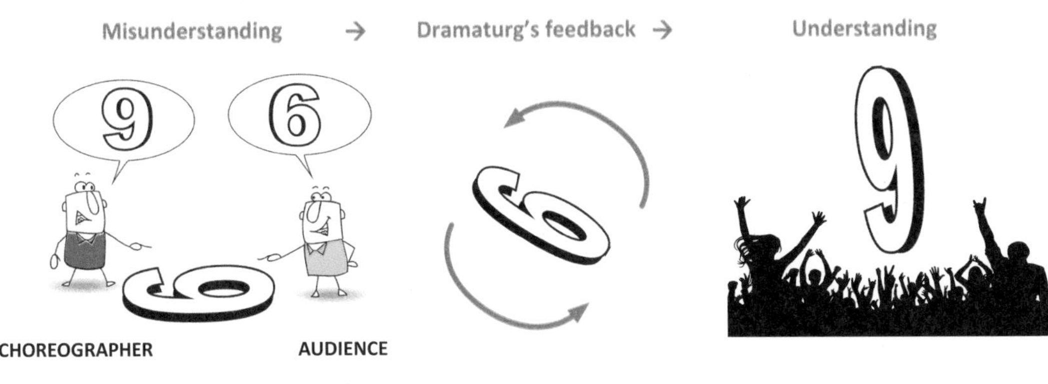

Figure 5 Image © Christophe Boisson, *9 vs. 6 Misunderstanding, Two Points of View*, illustration, 2020

When choreographers are in the middle of their creative process and deeply involved in juggling and balancing the multiple facets of the work, it might be challenging for them to step back and observe their own work from a distance. Choreographers acting as dramaturgs are generally expected to maintain a certain level of *neutrality* in order to self-produce an objective evaluation of their subjective processes. Is it possible to properly process a process while being in the process?

One option is to bring in trusted dramaturgical eyes for ongoing or occasional feedback. Another option is to seek the opinions of artists collaborating on the project. A third option is to solicit the audience's response to the outcome and the impact of the work. However, the latter might lead to a broad spectrum of reactions, and at some point, the choreographer might no longer care what others think and say—see Figure 6.

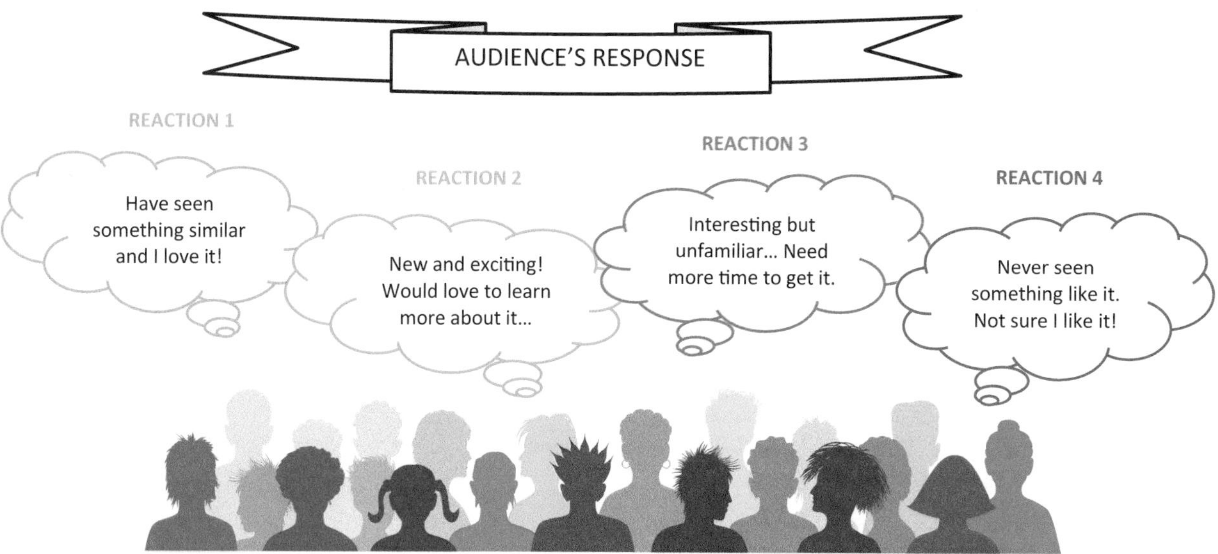

Figure 6

Further complexities in audience feedback may arise if the choreographer forgoes stage adaptations and familiar subject matter and instead courageously explores new directions. Groundbreaking choreographers strive for experimentation, innovation, and uniqueness, and yet creating new content and original choreography is always a risk-taking enterprise.

The choreographer and audience may have varying levels of tolerance for experimental work. All parties involved may push each other's boundaries while anticipating the same outcome—the experience of a new, well-crafted, unique dance. Assigning and attributing meaning might even take a back seat because meaning is subjective, especially when looking at experimental work—see sub-chapter *Does Movement Have (to have) Meaning*, as part of Chapter 14.

Although the intended outcome and perception of a dance are always pure guesswork, what has proven helpful is *educating* the audience by moderating the work with pre- and post-performance discussions. On these occasions, the descriptiveness of words can assist and support the figurativeness of dance and its physical dramaturgy.

BUILDING DRAMATURGICAL SEQUENCE AND ITS STRUCTURAL COMPONENTS

A key aspect of physical dramaturgy is determining the structure and construction of a dance, which include: 1) the sections and scenes as autonomous events; 2) the transitions between scenes and the relationships between the various sections; 3) the sequencing as the dance occurs in time progression. A dance is generally structured with a beginning, middle, and ending. These parts of a dance, often created independently, are assembled during the rehearsal process under what one might call the conceptual umbrella of the choreographer's intentions, concept, and approach to the subject matter—see Figure 7.

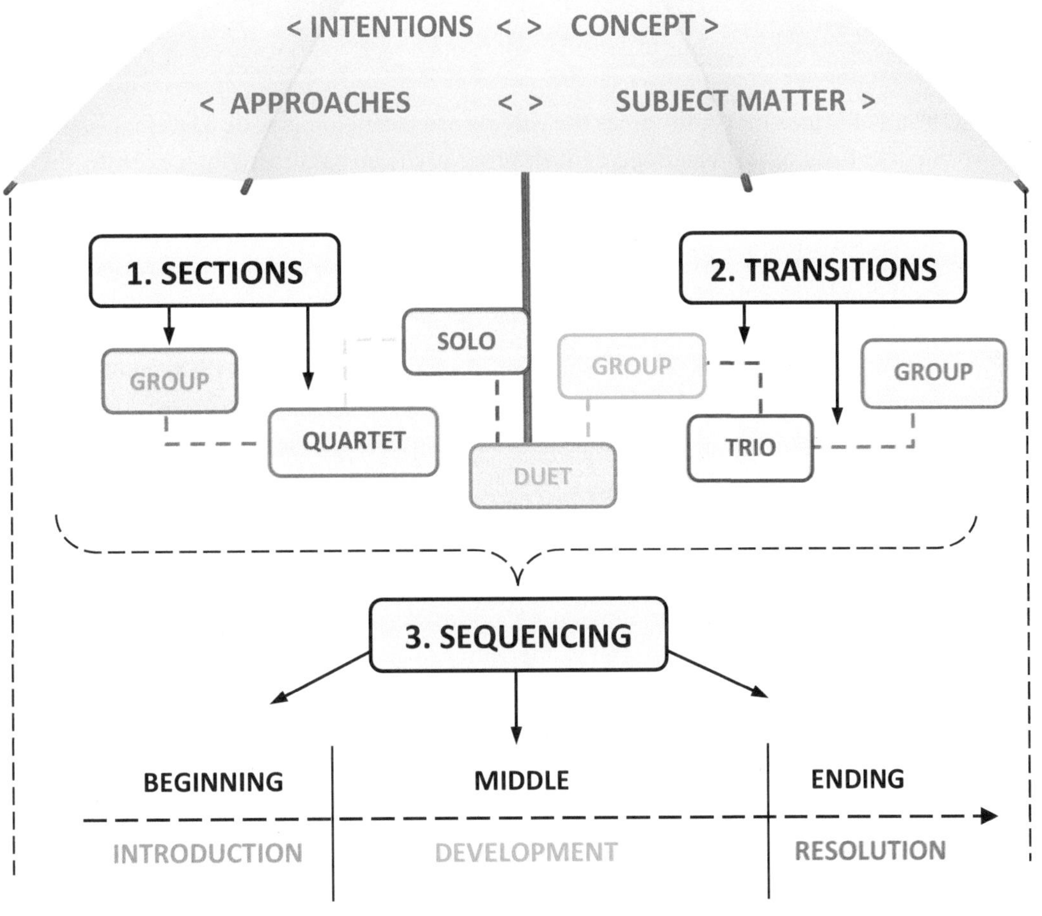

Figure 7

A single dance section or scene serves as a dramaturgical unit of a mid- to large-scale performance format. Sections may also be divided into sub-sections, each having distinct characteristics. There are various ways to distinguish, identify, and name a section. Choreographers have individual preferences for indicating the various sections, which may be based on the number of dancers—for example, *Duet*, as in Figure 7; or based on a distinct image, action, or narrative of the dance section—for example, *Love Scene*; or based on the corresponding musical equivalent of the dance section—for instance, *Adagio*.

1 **SECTIONS**: Key factors to consider when building dance sections are:

➢ Content of the dance scene: a) *Movement intentions*, which may be exploratory, interpretative, or suggestive; b) *Kinesthetic actions*, which may be narrative, plotless, or task-oriented; and c) *Mood or emotions, if any*, which may be cheerful, optimistic, dramatic, sad, intense, calm, or neutral.

➢ Numerical range and how many dancers are in each dance section: for example, a solo, a duet, a trio, and others, and how and why their numerical configuration changes or not. An independently crafted short chamber dance section could expand and become an integral element of a larger group section.

➢ Relational complexity and interactions between the participants, revealing the movement relationships among them and with one another. Different groupings of bodies may exist and interact to create static and dynamic patterns which expand, shrink, or open up the perceived focus of the performance.

2 **TRANSITIONS:** Key factors and options to consider when building transitions are:

➢ Connecting strand or bridge that determines the volume of a transition may be a brief reccurring movement motif, a short theatrical gag, or a longer segment in other art forms and activities, such as the performers rearranging the stage scenery, spoken word, a musical interlude, or a multimedia event.

➢ Overlapping or coinciding, where the lack of formal transitions leads to the merging of one section into another or sections unfolding simultaneously.

➢ Momentum and pacing, which focus on timing and tension-building, as well as the temporal development of the dance with emphasis on how slowly or quickly one event or action leads to the next.

3 **SEQUENCING:** Key factors to consider when building a sequence are:

➢ Linear or Nonlinear, which refers to the order of the sections and how they are assembled. A sequencing may be *linear* and follow a chronological succession of events or *nonlinear* with intentionally crafted distortions of the narrative arc, purposeful fragmentation, and juxtaposition. A sequencing may rely on traditional structural progression formats such as AB, ABC, or it may reveal a random series of unrelated events.

➢ Purpose, which is the reason for the specific placement of a dance section within the sequence, and the role it is intended to serve—for example, to drive a narrative action forward or to elaborate figuratively on a specific event.

➢ Causality, which is the effect a particular dance section has on the surrounding sections and on the overall sequencing.

SECTIONAL DEVELOPMENT WITHIN THE DRAMATURGICAL SEQUENCING

Although a dance traditionally has a *beginning*, *middle*, and *ending*, choreographers do not necessarily begin their creative work by choreographing the beginning. Often, choreographers multitask as physical dramaturgs and develop various sections simultaneously. They may randomly explore multiple options of sequencing and connections before determining the most effective dramaturgical chronology and the final order of the scenes.

Choreographers often envision the entirety of a dance by *foreseeing the totality of the work* before all the details, sections, and final sequence have been determined. The section the choreographers build first may differ based on personal strategy. However, the end goal is the same—to craft and implement the dramaturgical sequence of the new dance, which may follow one of the most conventional of all patterns—see Figure 8.

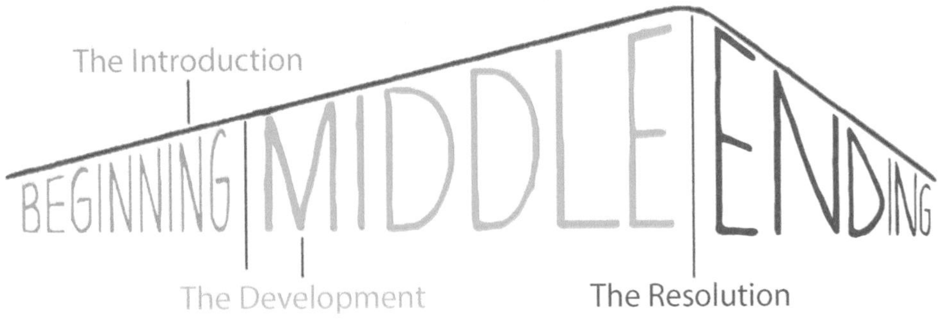

Figure 8

Some choreographers prefer to ***begin at the*** *beginning*, considering it the most straightforward starting point. The origination of an idea and its circumstances provide an inspiring opening narrative to serve as the beginning of a dance.

Other choreographers prefer to ***begin with the end*** by looking at the conclusion of an event and exploring how we got there. An ending point doesn't instantly describe or justify the beginning. How did we arrive where we are now? Many screenplay writers work on their film scripts by creating the story backwards by using *reverse engineering*. This strategy is effective when a narrative is told in a non-traditional and non-linear way.[9]

Another approach is to ***begin in the*** *middle*. This strategy helps explore and develop the work in two opposite directions—toward the beginning and end. At first, this approach might seem counter-intuitive; however, it can be fun and worth exploring.

For example, let's imagine arriving in the middle of a group conversation; suddenly, we're in a situation where we must quickly predict what happened before we arrived and where the conversation is headed. We must not forget that life on Earth was in full swing when we were born—things were happening before we arrived and will continue happening after we are gone. The same point could apply to choreographing by beginning in the middle. For more about this strategy, see *Michelangelo's David—The Beginning is in the Middle*, which is part of Chapter 18.

CRAFTING THE BEGINNING

Conventional wisdom has it that we get one chance to make a good first impression. Similarly, the beginning of each dance prompts the first impression of what will follow. The beginning is often an introduction that may summarize the entire dance. A catchy and exciting opening attracts attention and draws the audience into the work. The beginning may implement a single but powerful movement or visual image, sound or music offering, ritual, event, or action. A few strategies for developing a beginning are:

- **The *Fade-In*** is a descriptive introduction using a soft prologue that sets forth the theme of the performance. Classical ballet often uses so-called *music overtures* to set the mood before the curtain rises, and this type of beginning is widely used.

- **The *Hook*** is an intriguing introduction that could be dramatic action, a movement element, a sound bite, or a mysterious visual effect that sparks curiosity and increases interest in learning more. Such a beginning may be approached by "asking a question" rather than "making a statement."

- **The *Surprise*** is an unexpected introduction of unpredictable nature. The goal is to shock, and therefore, to sharpen the audience's attention quickly. One may think of the most outrageous element in the concept of the dance and use it as a starting point. Various devices may include noise, sound, music, visuals, a shocking movement activity, or an unusual act that draws immediate notice.

CRAFTING THE MIDDLE

The middle, the longest part of the dance, is where the substance of the work is unveiled. One can think of the middle section as a "travel itinerary" with a list of numerous adventures, where things may or may not go smoothly, but all will end just fine—hopefully. The middle section unpacks and explores the situation introduced during the beginning through additional dancing, movement, and dramatic action. A few strategies for developing the middle section are:

- **Introduce complexity, explore contrast, and create tension** by adding new participants with different agendas, new dramatic situations, and movement elements, and by revealing how they encounter, act, and interact with each other and the surroundings.

- **Expand and elaborate** by providing supplemental figurative material and details about the participants and their kinesthetic interactions and/or dramatic relationships.

- **Propose and display multiple options** for how the existing complexities might unfold, why tension is building, and what the possible resolutions are.

Traditionally toward the end of the middle section, the movement and mounting dramatic action arrive at a high point—*climax*. The climax is the most intense subsection in a conventional dramaturgical sequence. A wavy line of buildups reaches a *turning point*, where dramatic *tension and conflict* are finally about to be resolved. A climax, or multiple climaxes, may figuratively spark questions: if there was an argument—will it be settled? If there is a longing—will it be fulfilled? If there was a misunderstanding—will the truth come out? The climax is the final push as the effort and the tensions in the plot are settled.[10] Key strategies for developing the middle sections are avoiding monotony by exploring movement and dramatic tension and dynamically altering the moods within the middle sections. Climax does not mean crowding the stage with more dancers, louder music, and visual effects, but instead crafting a gradual and intense buildup and then a release.

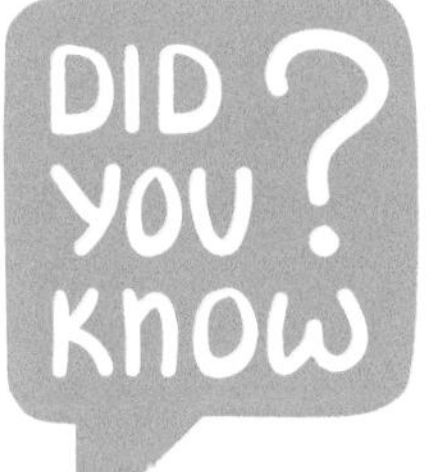

If we naturally avoid conflict in life, why do we need it in art? Because when we witness a resolution to a conflict, we feel relieved and liberated. Conflict often emerges from the tension between contrasting ideas that are fundamental in art. And obviously, we do not mean tension between the choreographer and the dancers. Contrasting ideas can be found within the body and movement, as in Martha Graham's technique of *contraction* and *release*.

According to choreographer Crystal Pite, many contrasting situations and qualities carry tension and conflict, such as recklessness and vigor, confinement and freedom, chaos and control, or a conflict between intellect and instinct. Exploring such conflicts is vital![11] Tension also exists when we strive to achieve something difficult. Appealing work contains *contrast*, *conflict*, and *tension*, which unfold and come to a resolution during the performance.

CRAFTING THE END

Following a climax as the highest point of dramatic progression, a moment of calm may follow organically. Such a transition may then lead to the resolution and the finale of the performance—basically, its end. The best ending is a satisfying ending—whether it is happy, sad, or neutral! An ending may contain only the climax or a *resolution*—a decisive settlement or a reflective grand *finale* that hints at the takeaways. Types of ending are:

➢ **Happy, sad, or bittersweet endings:** Often the story itself dictates the ending. A happy ending may be expected if the dance is an adaptation based on a children's book. A classic Greek tragedy would logically lead to a sad ending, while a contemporary narrative might end with a bittersweet finale. A learning experience or a moral is always the pivotal point at the end of narrative plots in dance, theater, and literature.

➢ **Accumulative, de-accumulative, or ambiguous endings:** Semi-abstract works and those in contemporary dance genres might not carry emotionally charged narrative dramatic endings. Accumulated or de-accumulated endings trigger feelings based on the physical performance, such as when watching a game between unfamiliar sports teams where the winner is irrelevant. The physical performance of the game itself could be appreciated without emotionally charged anticipation.

➢ **Continuing "open" ending, or fading to "still pose" ending, or neutral "is-that-the-ending?" finale.** The descriptions of these endings speak for themselves: In the first case, a repetitive action is used. In the second case, dance is brought to a still shape, bringing the work to its conclusion. In the third case, the dancers might exit, leaving the stage empty; this is a neutral ending that could match the end of the music but might not deliver a bold visual statement or a dramatic resolution.

How long and complex can an ending be? Well . . . as long as necessary, and hopefully the ending leads to a great grand finale. Let's look at Shakespeare's *Romeo and Juliet*, a dramatic play with various dance adaptations and many staging versions. The story is well known for its multiple dramatic resolutions that serve as "deceptive" finales. For example:

...**Finale 1:** Juliet dies, or at least it seems that way, but wait—the drama continues...

......**Finale 2:** Romeo dies next to Juliet, but wait—the drama continues...

........**Finale 3:** Juliet wakes up, realizes Romeo is dead, and this time she really does die. Romeo and Juliet's deaths ultimately reconcile their feuding families. Most of the ballet productions finish with this scene.*

*Finale 3 still serves only as a *resolution* and not a *denouement* and a *grand finale*. Why? Death is not necessarily an inspiring takeaway. A better grand finale would convey a message to all of us to become better people and strive for understanding, tolerance, and respect. Here is a suggestion for a grand finale:

............**GRAND FINALE:** The two families enter the scene and realize their children are dead. In a moment of deep grief, the families gently sway toward each other, sharing the mutual struggle and wiping their tears on each other's shoulders. The tragedy brings them together for the first time and makes them realize that the situation was preventable. If they had overcome their hate, the lives of their children could have been spared.

The tragedy with such a grand finale could suddenly be viewed as optimistic in a sense—it gives us hope that we are in control of our lives and that our actions can lead to unnecessary heartache and grief. The tragedy is a moral tale and a learning experience that elevates our spirits and teaches us a life lesson.

Figure 9 Photography © Theo Kossenas, *Romeo and Juliet*, choreography by Septime Webre, performers Elizabeth Gaither and Jared Nelson, a production of the Washington Ballet, 2010

Many notable choreographers have tackled the famous love story, among them;

1940: Leonid Lavrovsky
1955: Frederick Ashton
1962: John Cranko
1965: Kenneth MacMillan
1971: John Neumeier
1979: Yuri Grigorovich
1996: Jean-Christophe Maillot
2008: Krzysztof Pastor
2010: Septime Webre *(image left)*
2011: Alexei Ratmansky

DRAMATURGICAL DIMENSIONALITY AND COHESIVENESS

– VARIOUS DISCIPLINES AND ART FORMS SPIRALING TOGETHER –

In addition to creating bodily movements, the choreographer as a physical dramaturg may invite collaborators and incorporate multiple art forms and disciplines into the spiraling DNA of an emerging work —Figure 10. A choreographer may choose one or more of the following approaches:

- ◆ ***Multidisciplinary***, when a main discipline engages with a contributing discipline in a particular function and purpose, within the boundaries of that discipline, or engages across disciplines, also known as *cross-disciplinary*, where one discipline reaches out to the other.

- ◆ ***Interdisciplinary***, when ideas and concepts from different disciplines integrate into new structural patterns that organically connect all of the disciplines.

- ◆ ***Transdisciplinary***, when different disciplines work jointly to create new conceptual integration that *moves beyond* a discipline-specific field.[12]

A dance performance then may emerge as a multi-, inter-, or transdisciplinary work that is complexly layered with the figurative dynamics of dance, the sonic motion of audio and acoustic arts, the dramatic encounters of theater art, and the sculpting of the space by visual arts, lighting, and scenic design. These layered *events*, intended to occur simultaneously under a unifying concept, form the work's dramaturgical dimensionality and cohesiveness:

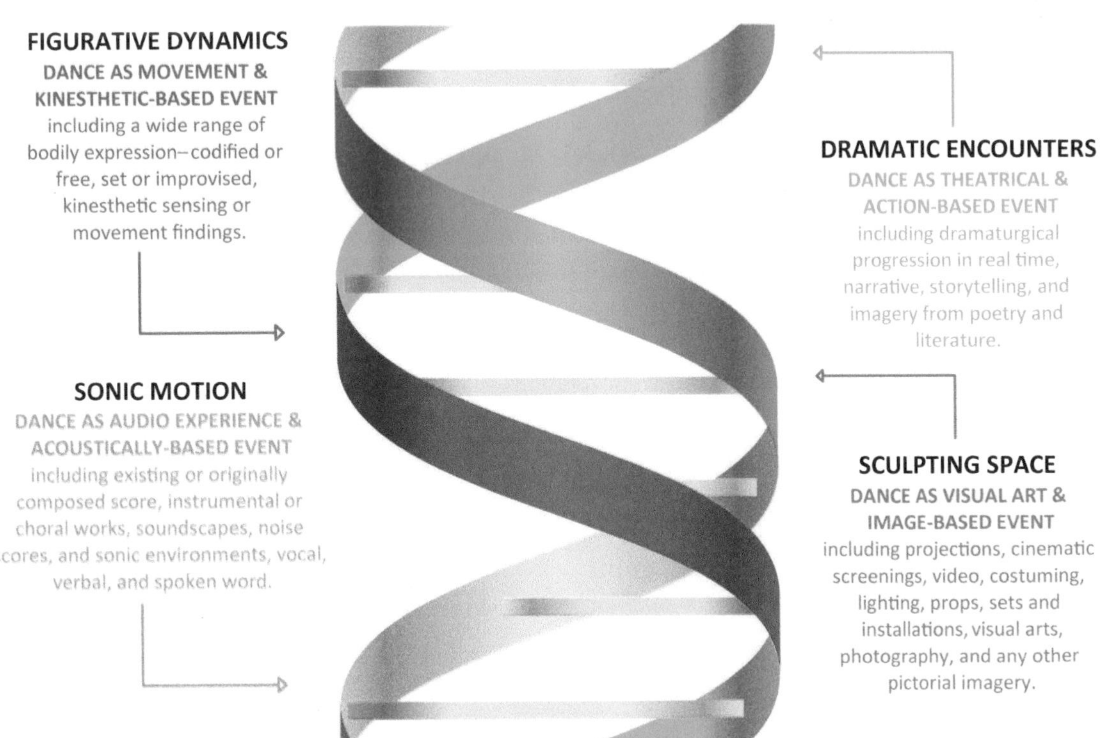

Figure 10

DRAMATURGICAL TEAMWORK
– ARTISTIC FRIENDSHIPS, PARTNERSHIPS, AND COLLABORATIONS –

Choreographers express and materialize their ideas with the vital help of collaborators—dancers, composers, designers, visual artists, actors, singers, architects, and others. And if sometimes the people are the challenge, usually the people are also the solution. Therefore, a good choreographer must strive to be a good collaborator!

Collaboration is a joint creative act where individuals agree to establish artistic relationships and dedicate time and effort to create and craft something together. The point of collaboration is to integrate the most valuable ideas, even if the choreographer did not originate them. Leveling the playing field with a focus on mutual goals and openness to contributions nurtures the emergence of fresh perspectives. The combined creative eagerness of participating collaborators to work together provides the choreographer with an additional boost of creative energy, personnel, and resources. If a dance is a song, perhaps it would be impactful to perform it as a chorus rather than as a single vocalist. *You, the choreographer*, will always be alone, and yet you will never be alone!

There are different *types of collaboration* involving interaction in the short-term or long term, working remotely or in-person and creating in similar fields or unrelated fields.[13] The *team of collaborators* may be composed of friends, colleagues, artists, and creative partners, as well as communities and institutions with established infrastructures, cultures, and traditions to be taken into consideration.[14]

Understanding the working dynamics of individuals and institutions will help the choreographer successfully lead and accommodate the dramaturgical demands of the performance. The choreographer's collaborative approach and role in the creative process demand a transformation—from being a *frontrunner* to being a *facilitator*, and from acting as a *self-reflective mind* to activating a unified *collective mind* by opening up space for others to contribute ideas.

A new monument made of movement could be as big as a Gothic cathedral with giant pillars, glorious arches, and whimsical gargoyles. Or it could be as small as a tiny tower of a few rocks stacked vertically in perfect balance. Only a dance—whether large or small—crafted with passion and thoughtfulness will be worth watching.

HELPFUL TIPS & SUGGESTIONS

~ Transform words into motion and narrative into action—use verbs with adverbs
~ Explore contrast, reveal conflict, create tension, find harmony
~ Construct and deconstruct, structure and restructure, edit and rearrange
~ Analyze, intellectualize, and verbalize
~ Articulate, moderate, and educate
~ Integrate various art forms and a wide range of disciplines
~ Identify and mobilize artistic allies and collaborators—experiment open-mindedly

assignments & exercises

RESEARCH ASSIGNMENT: Explore and research before drafting a synopsis of a few sentences. Refer to well-known works to identify how the skeleton of the entire production has been built. This is a crucial dramaturgical step to prevent inadvertent duplication of other's ideas. For example, research various ballet versions of *Romeo and Juliet* to the music score by Sergey Prokofiev—see list in the chapter. Analyze how Shakespeare's play has been modified as a plot for dance, and what the structure of the dance production is as a whole.

★ **CREATIVE ASSIGNMENT:** Build your own synopsis or dramaturgical summary of a new original work of yours. Write paragraphs based on the following questions:

√ **Selecting subject matter:**

- What subject matter are you familiar with and in what areas do you have in-depth knowledge?
- What subject matter have you always wanted to explore but never had the chance?
- What subject matter makes you feel intimidated but curious to explore?

√ **Illustrating intentions:**

- What will the subject matter be if you give a visual sample of it?
- What exactly will the subject matter be if it has to be described in one sentence?
- What are the kinesthetic characteristics of the subject matter—how does it move?

√ **Referencing the concept:**

- What personal experience do you have related to this subject?
- What has been choreographed previously about this subject?
- What level of familiarity with the subject does the general public have?

√ **Creating a scene description sheet and outlining the process for generating movement:**

- **Crafting scenes and sections:**

  —If you create new movement vocabulary about the subject within a single movement phrase, what will that movement summary look like?

  —If you create a movement section, how will you structure it with its own nucleus, beginning, middle and ending?

  —How did the entire scene start and end in time progression? What will happen before and after the dance section begins, and how will it end?

➥ **Crafting transitions: Experiment with the following strategies to bridge scenes:**

– Use of movement elements—a motif or a variation of a subject that "travels" from one dance scene to the next, and so forth.

– Use of overlapping or coinciding scenes, abrupt changes, or flowing shifts.

– Use of cross-disciplinary bridging elements such as video, text, short song, music interlude, or prop placement.

➥ **Crafting Sequencing: Experiment with different starting points to build various types of sequencing:**

– Linear sequencing, by starting from the beginning and progressing chronologically to the end.

– Non-linear sequencing, by starting from the middle of the piece and then moving toward the beginning or the end, or in any unpredictable and out-of-order sequencing.

– Backwards, by starting with the ending in the form of a "flashback," after which, narrate from the beginning how the whole story unfolds.

√ **Create structure and construction with the main building blocks:**

➥ **Experiment with the beginning:** Create multiple beginnings of your dance piece. Explore these strategies: The *Fade-In*, the *Hook*, and the *Surprise*. Improvise several beginnings and get feedback from peers about what is best and why.

➥ **Experiment with the middle:** Expand the dance by adding new participants/characters and additional information to add to the complexity of the narrative. Create new streams of how situations could develop in multiple versions.

➥ **Experiment with the ending:** Explore variations of an ending by making it happy, sad, or bittersweet, or endings that are cumulative and neutral. Think of surprising endings, and what would be unusual, unexpected, and provocative.

INCORPORATING AND WORKING WITH COLLABORATORS:

➥ **Select your collaborators:** How well do you know the work of your collaborators? Why do you feel that their contributions will be valuable? Are you confident that you can manage any potential disagreement and miscommunication?

➥ **Inspire your collaborators:** How will your idea motivate others and inspire them to contribute? What energizes your collaborators? Are you drawn to like-minded ideas or to contrasting ideas? How flexible are you? Are you willing to accept that someone else's ideas may be more effective than yours?

➥ **Integrate your collaborators' work:** How much are you asking for, and how much can you take in? How firm are you about keeping the integrity of the original idea? To what extent are you willing to negotiate, compromise, and adapt?

BIBLIOGRAPHY AND REFERENCES

[1] Wildschut, Liesbeth. "Reinforcement for the Choreographer: The Dance Dramaturge as an Ally," in *Contemporary Dance: A Critical Reader*, edited by Liesbeth Wildschut and Jo Butterworth, Routledge, 2010, pp. 383–398.

[2] Wildschut 2010. "Reinforcement for the Choreographer," pp. 383–398.

[3] Editors. *Libro, Libretto*, Online etymology dictionary, www.etymonline.com/, accessed May 2019.

[4] Profeta, Katherine. *Dramaturgy in Motion: At Work on Dance and Movement Performance*, University of Wisconsin Press, 2015, pp. 24–51.

[5] Lavender, Larry. "Facilitating the Choreographic Process," in *Contemporary Choreography: A Critical Reader*, 2nd edition, edited by Jo Butterworth and Liesbeth Wildschut, Routledge, 2018, pp. 107–123.

[6] Wildschut 2010. "Reinforcement for the Choreographer," pp. 383–398.

[7] Lavender 2018. "Facilitating the Choreographic Process," pp. 107–123.

[8] Editors. *Point of reference*, Merriam-Webster.com Dictionary, Merriam-Webster, www.merriam-webster.com/dictionary/, accessed July 2020.

[9] Frensham, Raimund G. *Screenwriting*, Teach Yourself Books, 1996.

[10] Frensham 1996. *Screenwriting*, various pages.

[11] Pite, Crystal. "Between Rigour and Recklessness," Crystal Pite speaks at *Creative Mornings Vancouver*, TV program. Published and released as online video on August 21, 2013, http://creativemornings.com.

[12] Aboelela, S. W., Larson, E., Bakken, S., et al. "Defining Interdisciplinary Research: Conclusions from a Critical Review of the Literature," *Health Serv Res*, vol. 42, no. 1 Pt 1, 2007, pp. 329–346.

[13] Tharp, Twyla. *The Collaborative Habit, Life Lessons for Working Together*, Simon and Shuster, 2009, multiple pages.

[14] Vass-Rhee, Freya. "Distributed Dramaturgies: Navigating with Boundary Objects," in *Dance Dramaturgy: Modes of Agency, Awareness and Engagement*, edited by Pil Hansen and Darcey Callison, Palgrave Macmillan, 2015. pp. 87–105.

VISUAL REFERENCES

Figure 1: Diagram © Vladimir Angelov

Figure 2: Gilbert, Andre. *Whirling—A Dance of Spring*, Art Deco bronze sculpture dancing girls modeled holding hands, wearing swimming costume, on circular base, signed in the cast, 37 cm. 1925, France © Image courtesy of Woolley and Wallis Salisbury Salerooms Ltd., 2020

Figure 3: Image left: *Portada de la primera edición de la primera parte de El ingenioso hidalgo Don Quixote de la Mancha*, libro de Miguel de Cervantes. Publicado en Madrid, en 1605, en la imprenta de Juan de la Cuesta. image © Raimundo Pastor, source Wiki Commons; Image center—*The Ingenious Gentleman Don Quixote of La Mancha*, image © aluxum, source iStock/Getty Images; Image right—Photography © Johan Persson, Carlos Acosta as Basilio and Marianela Nuñez as Kitri in *Don Quixote*, The Royal Ballet, Royal Opera House, 2013

Figure 4: Diagram © Vladimir Angelov

Figure 5: Image © Christophe Boisson, *9 vs 6 Misunderstanding, Two Points of View*, 2020, content and design by Vladimir Angelov ©

Figure 6: Diagram © Vladimir Angelov, clipart audience Image by ilyaka1972, source www.123RF.com

Figure 7: Diagram © Vladimir Angelov, clipart *Umbrella*, credit: byzonda, source www.123RF.com

Figure 8: Diagram © Charles Sheland, *Beginning, Middle, and End*

Figure 9: Photography © Theo Kossenas, *Romeo and Juliet*, choreography by Septime Webre, pictured performers Elizabeth Gaither and Jared Nelson, a production of the Washington Ballet, 2010

Figure 10: Copyright Vladimir Angelov, vector by Gines Valera Marin, source www.123RF.com

BOOK VI

SONIC SWING

DANCE THE MUSIC, MUSIC THE DANCE

At the dance studio. In corner, next to the piano and the musicians:

CHOREOGRAPHER: So...What is the status?

COMPOSER: We made some changes. Here is how it sounds now...(playing...)

CHOREOGRAPHER: Great! Except...Can we speed up the tempo a bit?

COMPOSER: Hmmm...All the parts? For the piano and for the trumpet?

CHOREOGRAPHER: Yes, the overall tempo. When the dancers jump, they can't hang in the air.

COMPOSER: Oh...Sure. We can accelerate the pace a bit.

CHOREOGRAPHER: Thank you. More coffee, everyone?

Excerpt from

dance DIALOGUES

An Anonymous Unpublished Manuscript, 376 BC–AD 2091

CHAPTER 20

MELODY IN MOTION
– ARE MUSIC AND DANCE BEST FRIENDS FOREVER? –

In the presence of music, dance occurs naturally. Since ancient times, music, dance, and poetry have coexisted in harmony and friendship—from Greek drama to modern-day rock concerts and dance music videos. Looking back in history, it is fair to state that dance needed music more than music needed dance. Music enhances dance, and in most instances, music elements may contribute to the expressiveness of movement.

Motion and pulse, flow and rhythm exist in both dance and music. Whether music serves as a background, accompaniment, counterpoint, or dramatic integral component, music provides dance with an inviting canvas. Music offers a stimulating environment that inaugurates dance.

Dance is the artful expression of movement, just as music is the artful expression of sound. But what comes first, the music and then the dance, or the dance and then the music? Some choreographers are inspired by music; others seek out music to enhance their movement ideas. And for some, the process is mutually creative, where the choreographer and the composer create music and dance synchronously or asynchronously.

Music and dance relate and converge in a variety of ways. Composers create music by integrating three major elements that form tonal music: *rhythm*, *melody*, and *harmony*. On the other hand, choreographers use and *physicalize* the same elements by interpreting them as *drive*, *mood*, and *ambience*—see Figure 1. When choreographers seek music for dance, drive, mood, and ambience are key factors. These elements will be discussed separately later in the chapter.

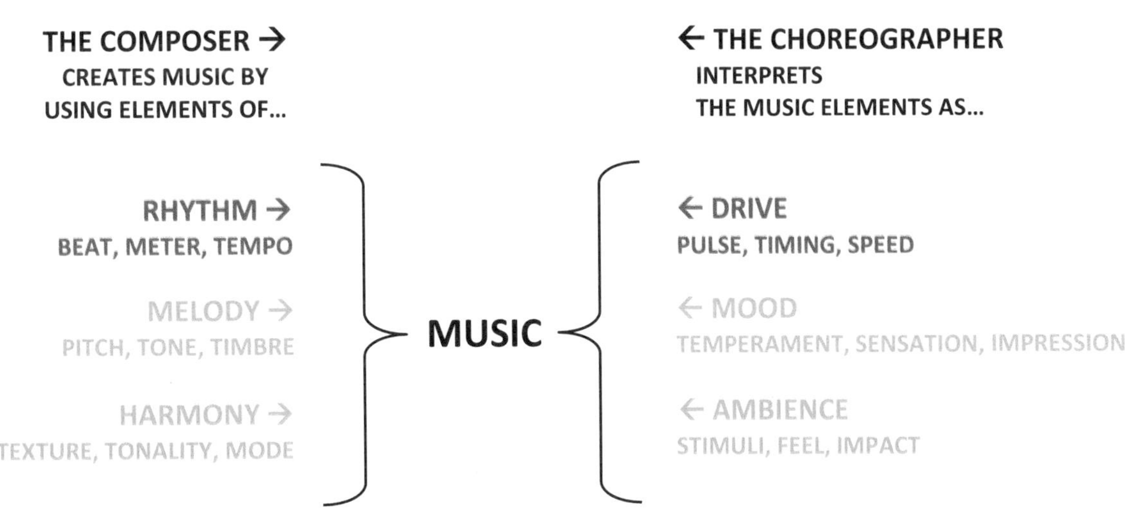

Figure 1

There are many ways in which music and dance integrate. Yet music and dance do not have to express the same thing in the same way. Sound and movement, music and dance, can complement each other in an artful expression. The interactions between sound and movement, the music score and the choreography, the composer and the dance maker could be very dynamic with planned or unexpected changes in who leads and who follows.[1] For choreographers working with music, the certainties needing attention are:

- **Choreographers become better at their craft by learning how music is made and how it works.** Music history and music theory will help the choreographer understand the content, the context, and the construction of any given music work. Also, it is helpful to learn and use music terminology when communicating with a composer.

- **Choreographers adopt music as part of their artistic expression.** Once a choreographer chooses a music piece for a dance or a composer to collaborate with, the choreographer commits to a creative partnership and develops strategies for integrating music and dance.

- **Choreographers approach music differently than composers and musicians.** A variety of music elements and terminology used by composers might have different meanings and use by choreographers. For example, when a choreographer says to the dancers, "follow the rhythm," that usually means in music language to "keep a steady beat."

Is music dance's best friend forever? A choreographer as the host at the House of Dance may treat the music in various ways—as a visiting comrade, a new roommate, a formal guest, or the landlord. Let's explore these types of relationships in this chapter and the following two. For starters, how is music made and how does it relate to dance?

THE BUILDING ELEMENTS OF MUSIC AND THEIR USE IN DANCE

Music can be understood by looking at how various elements and features function individually and together. The following is a list of the "raw materials" of music and how choreographers might interpret and use these elements when they incorporate them in dance.

RHYTHM organizes time in music and it contributes to the arrangement of sounds and musical tones with regard to their duration. Rhythm can occur in repetitive symmetric or asymmetric patterns, as an interplay of short and long sounds and silences. A rhythmic sequence performed by various percussion instruments can be satisfying without adding any melody or harmony. Rhythm is primal and fundamental.[2]

Beat is the basic unit that measures the time in music. It organizes, groups, and unifies the various sounds and periodic rhythmic patterns. Beats, rhythmic patterns, and note values are organized into *measures*. Measures are vital to identify so choreographers can orient themselves musically. In music, there are strong and weak beats. In addition, some beats can be accented.[3] During preparations and staging rehearsals, a choreographer may indicate, implement, and vocalize a more or less prominently accented pulse called *downbeat*, for example—**1**-2-3; **1**-2-3; or **1**-2-3-4; **1**-2-3-4; or **1**-2, **1**-2.

Meter represents the beat and the pulse in music, or the grouping of beats and accents within a measure. Meter is indicated by a *time signature*—two numbers placed at the beginning of a piece of music. The upper number of a time signature indicates the number of beats in each measure. The lower number tells us which note gets the beat (quarter note or eighth note, etc.). For example, *waltz* has three beats per measure, with a time signature of 3/4 (triple time), a relatively strong downbeat (first beat of the measure), and two weak beats (second and third beats). However, many other meters have either two or four beats per measure—2/4 (duple time), and 4/4 (quadruple time).[4]

SAMPLES OF COMMON MUSICAL TEMPI

ADAGIO - LEISURELY, COMFORTABLE
ALLEGRO - QUICK, EXCITED
ANDANTE - AT A WALKING PACE
LARGO - SLOW, STATELY
LENTO - SLOW, HEAVY
MODERATO - AT A MODERATE PACE
PRESTO - VERY QUICK, FAST

Tempo comes from the Latin word for "time." The tempo in music could be the speed keeper in dance, and therefore it defines the speed of the dance and the music. The tempo in a single music piece can vary. Choreographers determine how the dance steps and rate of movement will match and reflect the rhythm, meter, and tempo of the music. Specific music terminology, originally from the Italian language, indicates the overall and the relative *rapidity* in classical music compositions, for example, *adagio*, *allegro*, *moderato*, and others.[5]

Figure 2

◆ **For the choreographer,** the **DRIVE** of the rhythm and its components—the beat, meter, and tempo—can determine the pulse, speed, and timing of motion, as well as the regularity or irregularity of movement. The steadiness of rhythm, for example, can be incorporated in dance by maneuvering the movements' momentum, acceleration, and suspense. Beat, on the other hand, can serve as a guide to determining movement speed. For instance, a choreographer could playfully insert unexpected movement accents in conversation with the beat, which would change the movement speed. The meter can be a constant to follow or to contrast, and so can the tempo. Some dance movements have natural kinesthetic timing that corresponds to a certain rhythm. For example, a deep body swing leading to a suspended balance in a pose might take twice as much time as a quick drop to the floor. Similarly, a complex partnering between two dancers might require slowing down the overall speed of movement execution. In contrast, a few small hand gestures could be performed very quickly.

Pitch is the perceived highness or lowness of a sound. Sounds are higher or lower in pitch, according to the frequency of vibration of sound waves. For example, a high frequency of 880 Hz and above is perceived as a high pitch, while a low frequency of 55 Hz or below, as a low pitch.[6] The complete collection of possible pitches in music produced by a human voice or an instrument is known as *range*.

Pitch distinguishes a musical tone from a noise. Whether the tone is produced by a vibrating string or the vibration of the vocal cords, higher tones involve more vibration per second. Every melody is made up of a group of tones of different pitches.

Notes are symbols used in musical notation to represent the duration of a sound.[7] Notes are named after the first seven letters of the alphabet, with C at the beginning of a seven-note scale—see the piano keyboard in Figure 3. Between some of those notes, there is an extra note in black. The black note between C and D is called either C *sharp*, meaning a half step higher than C, or D *flat*, meaning a half step lower than D. An octave (the distance from C to C, or D to D, etc.), is divided into 12 half steps. A half step is the shortest distance between two notes on the keyboard, and it is the distance from one key to the next key—black or white. A whole step is made up of two half steps. This system of naming sounds and notes has been used in Western tonal music for a several centuries.[8]

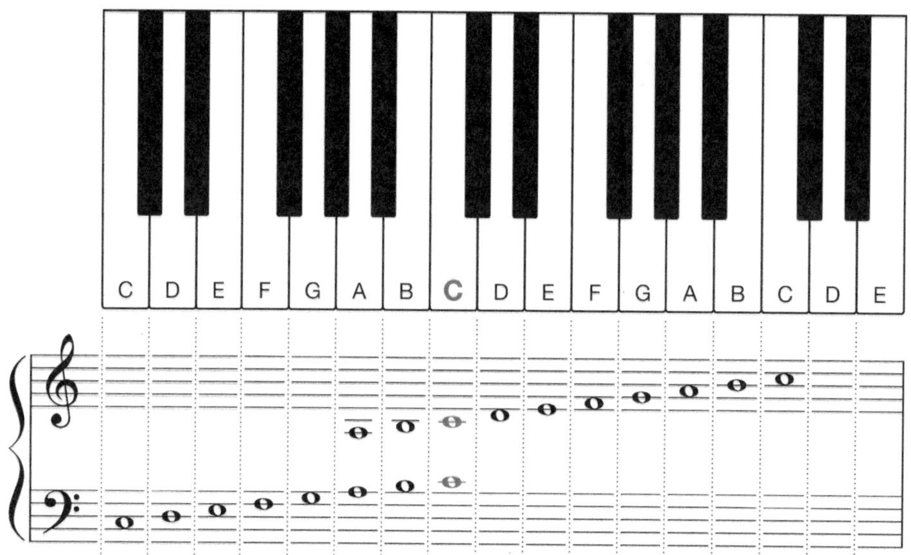

Figure 3

Tone color—timbre, dynamics, and sound source: Tone color, also known as timbre, is the perceived sound quality of a musical sound or tone. The same note might have a different sonic characteristic depending on the sound source and the musical instrument.[9] For example, the same note or melody produced by a flute will sound distinctive when played by a saxophone or a xylophone. The notes and their frequency remain the same, but the timbre varies.

A tone can be played with different *dynamics*, determined by the gradation of loudness ranging from very soft to very loud. Dynamic signs in music indicate how loudly or how softly to play: *piano pianissimo (ppp)*—extremely soft, *pianissimo (pp)*—very soft, *piano (p)*—soft, *mezzo piano (mp)*—medium soft, *mezzo forte (mf)*—medium loud, *forte (f)*—loud, *fortissimo (ff)*—very loud, *forte fortissimo (fff)*—extremely loud.[10]

Based on the size, shape, material, and sound produced by various musical instruments, the timbre of a single note varies in its color, loudness, and quality. In the modern world, musical instruments are often divided into two broad categories: *acoustic instruments*, which usually require nothing more than a player to produce the sound, and more recent *electronic instruments*, which need electrical power, electronic technology, and digital equipment to produce the sound and music.

Acoustic instruments are primarily associated with classical music and are made of materials that can be found in nature. On the other hand, electronic instruments are associated with modern technology, producing more artificial sounds with a synthetic quality. There is an endless number of different timbres and sound effects offered by electronic instruments.

Musical instruments of different families are put together to form a music ensemble, a band, or an orchestra. Sizes and types of orchestras can vary—from a few instruments and musicians forming either a chamber music group or a rock and roll band, to a full-size symphony orchestra, which could employ over one hundred musicians.

There are various methods of *musical instrument classification*. The most commonly used system divides instruments into *String*, *Woodwind*, *Brass*, and *Percussion* instruments. Other categorizations have been devised as well. The unique characteristics of each instrument are size, shape, the material of construction, and the way sound is produced.[11]

a) SIZES AND SHAPES:

- Small
- Medium
- Large
- Spherical
- Trapezoidal
- Rectangular
- Asymmetrical

b) MATERIAL OF CONSTRUCTION:

Wood, **Metal**, and/or **Skin**

- Voice
- Woodwinds
- Strings
- Keyboard
- Brass
- Percussion

c) WAYS OF PRODUCING SOUND:

- Exhale
- Blow
- Stroke
- Pluck
- Squeeze
- Press
- Beat

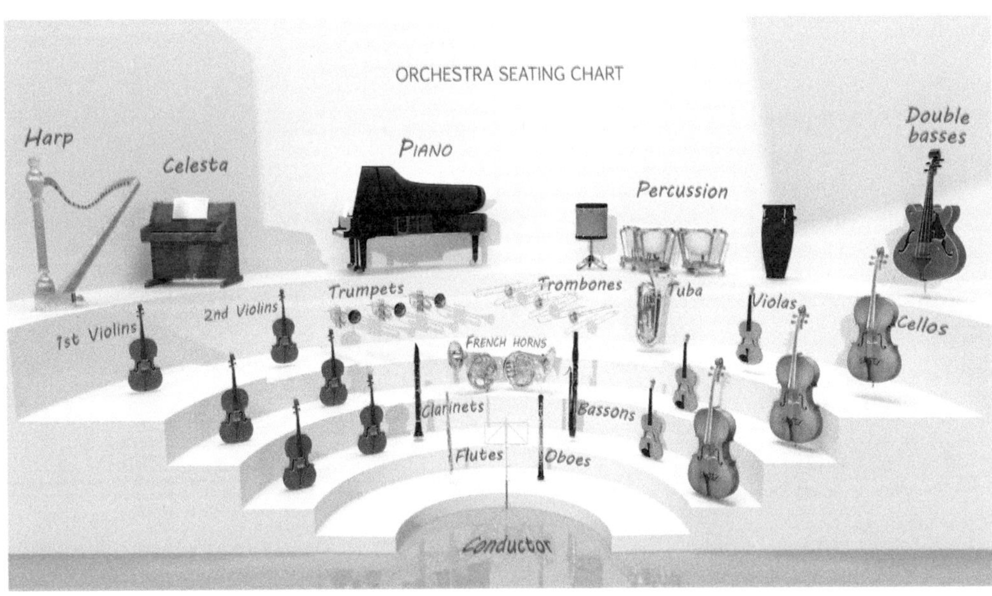

Figure 4

MELODY is a series of tones with an implied rhythmic organization and contour. Historically, melody is far older than harmony. The single melodic line was highly developed in musical history; it can be found in the ragas of Indian and Arab music and the troubadour songs of medieval Europe.[12] Melody contains several key characteristics and grows in multiple dimensions:

➢ Melody consists of notes emerging from a specific scale. In certain musical cultures, scales are formally recognized as systems of tones from which a melody can be built. Melody, however, predates the concept of scale, which is a line of notes ascending or descending by step. Scales may be abstracted from their melodies by listing the tones used in order of pitch. There are several types of scales such as major, minor, modal, etc. Each scale has a specific combination of half steps and whole steps. The intervals of a melody's scale contribute to its overall character.[13] The children's song "Twinkle, twinkle little star" is an example of a melody that begins with three tones and ends with a descending scale.

➢ Melody consists of motifes, phrases, and themes, which are the essence of a melody. Motive is a short melodic idea expressed with as few as two or three notes. A short motive, such as "da-da-dam," could be repeated and could expand by adding more notes and new melodic shapes. A *phrase* is a musical sentence; it is a section of a melody forming a recognizable unit. Phrases can vary in length but usually include 2, 4, 6, or more measures. *Theme* is a series of tones establishing the foundation in the construction of a musical composition. A theme could serve as a single exposition—a base for a set of variations or a subject in episodes combined in a group of themes.[14]

➢ Melody has *contour*, *sequence*, and *ornaments*. *Contour* is the movement of the overall melodic line that rises, falls, arches, undulates, or moves in various ways. The melody's contour is formed when melodic motion is divided by using leaps or conjunctions. Some melodies have big jumps in the melodic line, while others glide between close tones and intervals. Interval is the distance between two notes, while duration (or note value) is the length of a note.[15] A clear melodic line may be perceived as a distinct geographical landscape—one can compare it to the sunset silhouette of a city, or the calming topography of a mountain in the morning, for instance:

Figure 5

Sequence is a short melodic figure or phrase repeated at different pitch levels. *Ornaments* are small melodic devices such as grace notes, appoggiaturas, trills, slides, tremolos, and slight deviations from the standard pitch. Ornaments are often used to embellish a melody. Melodic ornamentation is present in most Western music and is essential to Indian, Arabic, Japanese, and much other non-Western music.[16]

Modes are structures of sequencing the tones of a scale in a particular way. In addition, modes are sets and groupings of melodic characteristics and harmonic behaviors. These structures apply to pitch relationships and their organization and the emotional effect and character of the melody. These sequences of tones identify any given melodic lines, such as lyrical melody, angular melody, or ornamented melody.[17] Modes and their melodies and sound waves can be visualized with particular shapes and motion characteristics—see Figure 6.

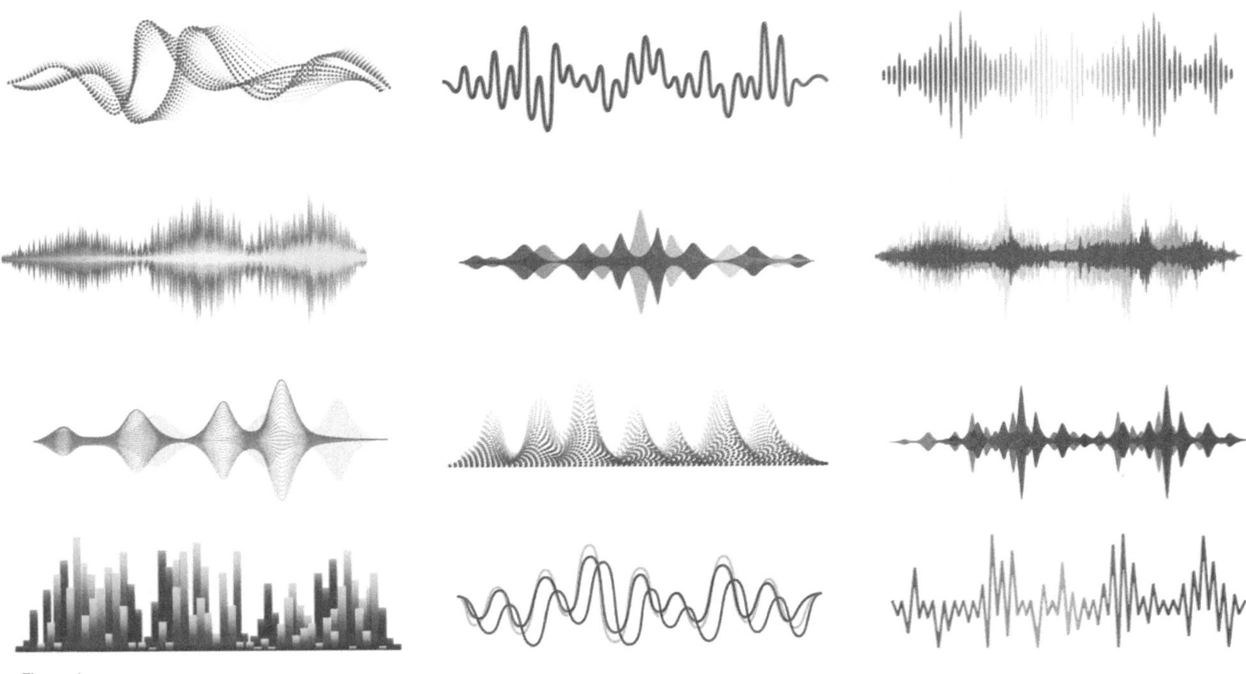
Figure 6

◊ **For the choreographer,** the **MOOD** of the melody is revealed by the mode, melodic line, timbre, dynamic, rhythm, and tempo. Mood is a determining factor in how music and dance will relate to one another. Melody, in particular, has a certain *emotional impact* that might also affect the type of movement material and dramaturgical effect of the choreography.

For example, a melody written in a major key sounds brighter and happier, while a melody composed in a minor key has a melancholic feel. A melody increasing in tempo, volume, and pitch often has a stimulating effect, while its decreasing version has a calming effect.

Finally, melody containing repetition can build anticipation that something is about to happen in the dance. A melody may gradually lead to a dramatic effect or climax. In summary, the choreographers determine and identify the mood of music (melody, timbre, dynamics, and modes) as a particular melodic behavior that might affect movement behavior during the dance creation.

HARMONY is the simultaneous sounding of two, three, or more musical tones. The result is a *chord.*[18] Harmony is the opposite of cacophony.

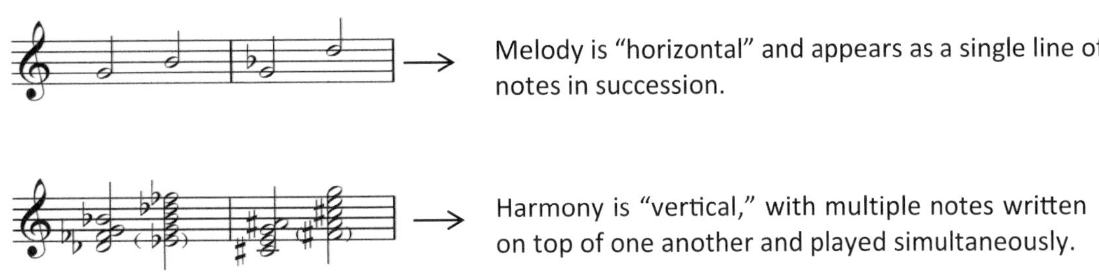

Figure 7

Combinations of notes that sound pleasant are called *consonant*, while those that sound tense are called *dissonant*. Harmonious or consonant chords dominate the music landscape in tonal music. Chords and harmonies often form the background for the melody and support the punctuation of the phrasing of the music.[19] In addition, *consonance* and *dissonance* are categorizations of intervals and chords in tonal music. Consonance can be associated with sweetness, while dissonance is often associated with harshness.

Texture in music is characterized by sound rather than tactile feel. Texture is the character of a composition or passage, as determined by the relationship among the sound from within. There are four prominent textures in Western Music. *Monophony* is a single melodic line played by one or many instruments; *homophony* combines melody and chords; *heterophony* varies a melody in simultaneous performance; and *polyphony* combines several independent melodic lines at once.[20]

Tonality or Key is an organized system of tones, where one tone becomes the central point for the remaining tones. Tones and chords are arranged in a hierarchy of perceived relations, stabilities, attractions, directionality, and resolution.[21]

Tonal music gives priority to a single tonal center, called *tonic*. The larger portion of the world's folk and art music can be categorized as tonal. All of the constituent tones and resulting tonal relationships are heard and identified relative to their tonic center in this kind of music. Music that centers "around" a "home" pitch is described as tonal.

Atonal music, on the other hand, lacks a tonal center or a key. Why avoid tonal hierarchies? Most atonal composers did not intend to write unpleasant-sounding music. Instead, they challenged traditional tonal structures and the general assumptions about what music should be. By implementing the *twelve-tone serialism*, introduced by Schönberg, Berg, and Webern, a composer uses a series of 12 notes and doesn't repeat any note until all twelve have been used. This practice organizes all twelve notes of the Western musical system into a *tone row*. The composer then writes music using only modifications of the tone row, including backward and upside-down variations.[22]

> For the choreographer, the AMBIENCE of music, which often relates to harmony, determines the interaction between the sound environment of music and the movement environment of dance. For example, the presence or the lack of a tonal center and the tension of dissonant harmony could translate as tension in the movements. Dominant sounds in the music texture might trigger particular accents in the phrasing of dance.

The harmony and chords from the orchestra in the background, against the melody of a solo instrument, could be represented on stage with a large dance ensemble confronting a solo performer. Polyphony created by several independent melodic lines and played simultaneously could be choreographed as several dance solos performed simultaneously.

The choreographer might use the features of tonal music to provide musical cues for when movements should be executed. Atonal music, on the other hand, might serve as a sonic background for the dance. Choreographers may use music ambience to enhance the buoyancy of dance without the need to interpret or mimic the music through movements.

?

When you listen to an appealing piece of music, can you identify which elements make it attractive to you: a) the *drive*, rhythm, and beat; b) the *mood*, melody, and timbre; or c) the *ambience*, harmony, and texture?

STRUCTURES AND FORMATS IN MUSIC

Music structures feature various compositional formats. Similar to an architect, the composer uses the music material to design and construct the musical work. The composer also activates creative devices to engage with the musical elements and organize them in traditionally known or newly invented compositional formats.

For small-scale structures, the composer may use a range of devices such as motives, repetition, rhythmic patterns, ascending/descending progressions, open-close melodic phrases, call-and-response, antiphony, chord progressions, ostinato, accompaniment figuration, and others.

For large scale structures, the composer may use typical formats such as sonata form, binary form (AB), ternary form (ABA), rondo (ABACABA), theme and variations, 12 bar blues, strophic, minuet and trio, fugue, and others—see also Chapter 18.

For unity and contrast, the composer may use and manipulate a mixture of musical elements. Some of these elements remain constant and recur throughout the piece; other components create contrast and bring change, variety, and dramatic intensity.

◆ **For the choreographer**, identifying **STRUCTURE AND FORMAT** of a work of music and its organization of elements is essential. The structure of music may potentially be incorporated into the construction of the dance. Therefore, when searching for and considering music for dance, choreographers may take into account the following suggestions to help them recognize and distinguish key structural features:

➢ **Identify the format, genre, dominant sound, mood, and overall scope of the piece.** While *Vocal Music* is dominated by the human voice, *Instrumental Music* excludes singing and lyrics. Also, operas and Broadway musicals are made up of vocal numbers with instrumental accompaniment. There are orchestral overtures and additional large instrumental sections accompanying the action on stage and the dance scenes. The main characteristics to identify formats are:

— SCOPE: size, performance duration, number of movements, structural elements, and others

— VOCAL music formats: song, aria, duet, motet, cantata, oratorio, madrigal, hymn, and others

— INSTRUMENTAL music formats: etude, prelude, overture, sonata, concerto, symphony, dance suite, theme and variations, fugue, and others

➢ **Analyze the overall musical structure and how it has been developed.** The choreographer should be able to identify how the different sections in a music piece are positioned together to form the architecture of the work. The three key concepts for the choreographer to look for are:

— Rhythmic, melodic, and harmonic statements

— Repetition, variation, and contrast

— Progression, continuity, and development

➢ **Characterize the specific features of different musical sections and transitions.** A composer creates bridges and transitions between sections and uses various musical features to introduce new melodic ideas. A choreographer should be able to identify the overall structure, intended unity, and contrast between various parts of a musical work. Changes between sections may be distinguished by the introduction of:

- New melodic idea, key, mood, and dynamics
- New rhythm, tempo, and meter
- New instrumentation, voice(s), and lyrics

Finally, vital musical features, formats, and structures are determined and characterized by the historical period when a work of music was created. A concise chronology of major historical periods and the key composers who contributed to the development of music through the ages can be seen in the diagram below.

BRIEF OVERVIEW OF HISTORIC PERIODS AND KEY COMPOSERS

Choreographers are the driving force in the development of dance as an art form. Composers are the driving force in the development of music as an art form. Throughout the ages, many composers have made enormous contributions to the advancement of music, and choreographers have benefited from using celebrated music works for their dances. Let's first look at the development of music chronologically. The historic periods listed in Figure 8 may overlap with one another and transfer fluidly from one into another.

PERIOD	TIME	REPRESENTATIVE COMPOSERS
EARLY MUSIC	500 BC–5 BC	No records
ANCIENT	5 BC–5 AD	Sappho, Limenius, Mesomedes of Crete
MEDIEVAL	500–1400	Hildegard von Bingen, Guillaume de Machaut
RENAISSANCE	1400–1600	Claudio Monteverdi, Thomas Tallis, William Byrd
BAROQUE	1600–1750	Jean-Baptiste Lully, Jean-Philippe Rameau, J. S. Bach, George Frideric Handel, Antonio Vivaldi, Henry Purcell
CLASSICAL	1750–1800	Wolfgang Amadeus Mozart, Ludwig van Beethoven, Franz Joseph Haydn, Luigi Boccherini, Christoph Willibald Gluck
ROMANTIC	1800–1900	Hector Berlioz, Franz Schubert, Felix Mendelssohn, Frédéric Chopin, Robert Schumann, Richard Wagner, Pyotr Ilyich Tchaikovsky, Johannes Brahms, César Franck, Bedrich Smetana, Antonín Dvořák, Modest Mussorgsky
MODERNISM	1900–2000	**Impressionism:** Claude Debussy, Maurice Ravel, Erik Satie, Ottorino Resphigi **Nationalism:** Isaac Albeniz, Manuel de Falla, Enrique Granados **Neo-Classicism/Post Romanticism/Jazz/Contemporary/ Avant-Guard, Minimalism:** Alexander Scriabin, Sergei Prokofiev, Sergei Rachmaninov, Igor Stravinsky, Jean Sibelius, Samuel Barber, Nicolas Flagello, Vittorio Giannini, Ernst Bloch, Aaron Copland, George Gershwin, Duke Ellington, Arnold Schönberg, Alban Berg, Anton Webern, Béla Bártok, Dmitri Shostakovich, Gustav Mahler, Carl Orff, Leonard Bernstein, Benjamin Britten, Olivier Messiaen, John Cage, Pierre Boulez, Eliot Carter, Toru Takemitsu, Arvo Part, Ralph Vaughan Williams
CONTEMPORARY	2000–now	**Established:** John Adams, George Crumb, Philip Glass, Henryk Górecki, Michael Gordon, John Corigliano, David Lang, Gyorgy Ligeti, Michael Nyman, Steve Reich, Max Richter, Peteris Vasks, Julia Wolfe **New Voices:** Mason Bates, Missy Mazzoli, Dobrinka Tabakova, Cheryl Frances-Hoad, Ann Cleare, Angélica Negrón, Nico Muhly, Daníel Bjarnason, Judd Greenstein, Thomas Adès, Mikael Karlsson, Owen Belton, Joby Talbot, Keaton Henson, Greg Haines, Sufjan Stevens, Bryce Dessner, Vincenzo Lamagna, Ben Frost

Figure 8

CONTENT, GENRES, AND COMPOSER'S STYLE IN MUSIC FOR DANCE

Music can be based on nonmusical subjects—stories and librettos from literature, poetry, folklore, history, and visual arts. For example, 19th-century Romanticism provided a world of fairy imagery, and many composers desired to integrate music with the other arts. Music drama became a new outlet of expression, where composers tackled how to narratively portray different events and characters in musical terms. Music can also be non-narrative.

◆ **Programmatic Music and Absolute Music** are two categories that differentiate narrative-based from nonnarrative music content. *Programmatic music* typically follows the order of a story, poem, painting, patriotic subject, historical event, dramatic action, mood, and imagery often adapted from literature, poetry, to visual art. Most of the music for the well-known Classical Ballet repertoire is *programmatic music.* It was written to support a narrative and provide direct correlation between the dance and the music.[23]

Absolute music is instrumental music composed for music's sake. Such music is free of nonmusical associations. Absolute music, also known as abstract music, is not intended to represent a story and is not based on anything specific. The content offers freedom to fully explore musical expression based on the aesthetic of sound. Absolute music is abstract in concept and without relationship to narrative circumstances.[24]

While listening to a music piece, choreographers might have a range of responses as to whether a piece is programmatic or abstract. A music piece can trigger varying interpretations in different circumstances and it can be treated choreographically as either abstract or programmatic music.

◆ **Music genres** are categories of large bodies of music works that either belong to a specific historic period or that are formed in a particular style by shared traditions and commonalities, such as *secular* vs. *sacred music.* Genres are also categorized in groups by similar characteristics, forms, structures, and compositional techniques. A traditional and broad spectrum of classifying genres can be defined in categories such as:

- *Art Music* emerges from the Western classical tradition and is often associated with the royal courts and performing arts institutions. Art music is associated with the composers rather than the performers, and it has high artistic and aesthetic value.
- *Popular Music* emerges from the entertainment industry. Popular music is easily accessible and accommodates the taste of the populace. It is intended for the broadest possible audience by aiming to please and amuse; therefore, it often contains casual content with widespread appeal.
- *Traditional Folk and Indigenous Music* emerge from regional historic music traditions handed down and learned through singing, listening, and sometimes dancing.

A *genre division* can be strict but also fluid. *Folk* and *Popular* music are two different genres that could also merge. *Art Music* is by nature complex and sophisticated, while *Popular Music* is defined as simple and accessible. However, some Art Music compositions, such as *The Nutcracker*, could be referenced as popular music and used in pop music.

A composer's individual style is the artistic approach by which the composer creates music. Individual style in music is unveiled through a variety of factors. It is associated with: a) the creative environment and the era in which the composer is situated, the dominant aesthetics of that historical period, and the composer's artistic interests; b) the creative influence and how the composer uses existing and newly found resources, artistic references, inspiration, and collaboration; and c) the creative devices, and how the composer uses musical elements, compositional techniques, and principles of musical construction.

The individual artistic style could also incorporate the artist's research and references—for instance, *Appalachian Spring* composed by Aaron Copland. The American patron of the arts Elizabeth Sprague Coolidge requested a new ballet for the dancer and choreographer Martha Graham, so she commissioned the music score in 1942. The dance tells the story of a young frontier couple on their wedding day. As the war in Europe was ending, the dance captured the imagination of Americans who were beginning to believe in a more prosperous future. Letters between Graham and Copland revealed artistic negotiations about the project, and Graham ultimately supplied the initial storyline and the libretto.[25]

In his music for the dance, Copland integrated various resources that helped him create initial melodic material, outline the format of his work, and make important choices about the particular instrumentation of the music score for the dance—Figure 9.

COMPOSER'S STYLE AND HIS INSPIRATIONS, RESEARCH, AND REFERENCES LEADING TO A NEW WORK

- European motivic development, counterpoint, and harmony
- American popular songs and sacred folk melodies
- Anglo-Celtic songs, prayers, and secular dances
- 19th Century life in the Pennsylvania mountains
- Programmatic music, regional styles, and nationalism
- Modern orchestra with acoustic instruments
- Narrative dance drama proposed by the choreographer

Figure 9 Top image: Composer Aaron Copland at Rock Hill. Photograph retrieved from the Library of Congress; Bottom image: Photography © Lois Greenfield, *Appalachian Spring*, choreography by Martha Graham, pictured Miki Orihara, Elizabeth Auclair, Rika Okamoto, Camille Brown, Pascal Rioult, courtesy of Martha Graham Dance Company, 1994

CHOREOGRAPHER AND COMPOSER
– A CREATIVE COMPANIONSHIP AND COLLABORATION –

Commissioning and creating original music work for a new dance is a special privilege a choreographer can acquire. A creative collaboration between the choreographer and the composer is fertile ground for innovation, progressive ideas, and advancing choreography as an art form. A composer may identify the difference between composing concert music and composing music for dance. A choreographer may identify the difference between staging dance on a pre-created music score and working with a live composer on an original composition. The choreographer-composer collaboration invites both artists to immerse themselves in one another's forms of expression. This new artistic partnership offers a range of exciting creative experiments!

There are infinite freedoms and complexity in music, which can be expressed with the human body. Music also offers structural patterns, rhythms, and pulse for the choreographers to work with and embellish the dance. For instance, there is repetition in music, and likewise there is repetition in dance. Music also helps dance with the emotional undertones of the movement and the steps through dynamics and timbre. These elements can enhance the expressiveness of dance.

While music is an auditory expression of sound and noise, dance is a visual expression of human motion. Since the medium is different, it is helpful for composers who create for dance to learn about dance as an art form and the possibilities and the limitations of human movement. The composer may see the music as physicalized motion and kinesthetic illustration through the choreographer's eyes and craft.

Important to note is that physical timing in dance is perceived differently than in music. Often, choreographers and composers do not count time and mark structure in the same way. Composers might even be critical of choreographers on this account. However, it may not be in a choreographer's best interest to count like a composer or use music terminology with the dancers. Productive collaboration occurs and unfolds when that professional lingo barrier is overcome. Both artists develop a mutual understanding of how they need to communicate with their constituents—the musicians and the dancers.

Both collaborators may need adequate time to synchronize artistic efforts and manage their expectations. Initially, the composer may expect limitlessness in music expression. Choreographers may expect the music score to support the dance fully, or they may be concerned that the music elements draw too much attention by becoming a foreground instead of being equal to the dance. Modifying and satisfying expectations is a balancing act requiring sensible compromises from the composer and the choreographer. Logistically, creative planning and collaboration may unfold as follows:

INITIATING CREATIVE COLLABORATION: The setting up of new and original collaborative projects can be initiated by different artistic and administrative divisions to accommodate the specific artistic needs of a dance commission or the goals of artistic experimentation. The collaboration could be:

— *Artist-initiated collaborative project:* A choreographer or a composer is in the commissioning role to maximize freedom of creative choices.

— *Producer-initiated collaborative project:* An impresario, a presenter, or a producing individual tailors a project to satisfy specific criteria for an occasion.

— *Institutionally-initiated collaborative project:* An administrator or an art institution puts together a choreographer-composer team to create a particular project for a performance series, festival, themed celebration, or other specific purpose.

◆ **CREATIVE APPROACHES AND WORKING INTERACTIONS:** During a composer-choreographer collaboration, various working interactions and creative approaches are in practice. A composer may be brought into a project to create music for a new dance specifically, or a composer may ask a choreographer to make a dance to new music. There are a few types of approaches and interactions that may unfold during the collaboration:

➢ **Directive approach:** Music is composed by considering a specific idea, libretto, or preconceived choreography. The choreographer may give the composer overall directions or specific instructions about the length of the music, the mood, the character of the melodic line, and even the rhythm and tempo of certain sections.

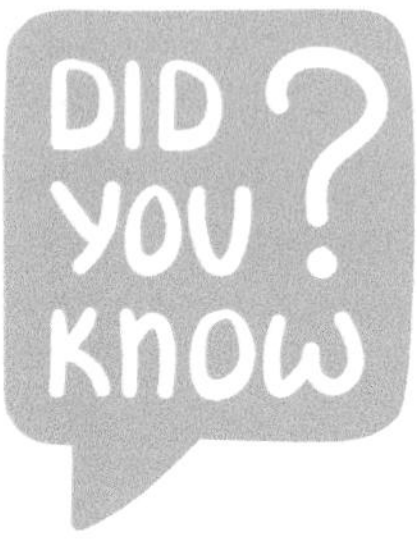

The foremost classical choreographer, Marius Petipa, (pictured left) was adamant in his instructions to Tchaikovsky (pictured center) while the composer was writing the music for *The Nutcracker* (pictured right). Petipa had simple directions and outlined the structure and scenarios in the style of a "wish-list."[26] Petipa might have said: "A march for 64 bars and a short rococo for 16 bars. A gallop. Drosselmeyer, a magician, enters. Awe-inspiring but comic music—16 to 24 bars. That music changes character during 24 bars; it becomes lighter but also grave. Grave music for 8 bars. A pause. Repeat the 8 bars. Another pause..."[27]

Figure 10 Image left: *Portrait de Marius Petipa*, photographer unknown, 1898; Image center: *Portrait of Pyotr Ilyich Tchaikovsky*, Evans, Edwin, E. P. Dutton & Company, 1906; Image right: Scene from the ballet *The Nutcracker* in St. Petersburg, photographer unknown, Mariinsky Theatre Archives, 1892

➢ **Interactive approach:** Music is created while the conceptual framework of the dance is still forming and the choreography is emerging. The composer and the choreographer contribute equally to the core ideas of the project. The composer and the choreographer may improvise together, generate ideas, and create sketches, drafts, and temporary versions, as well as make modifications and changes. They decide collectively on the total length, structure, mood, tonality, rhythmic patterns, and melodic lines of each music section and the music work in its entirety.

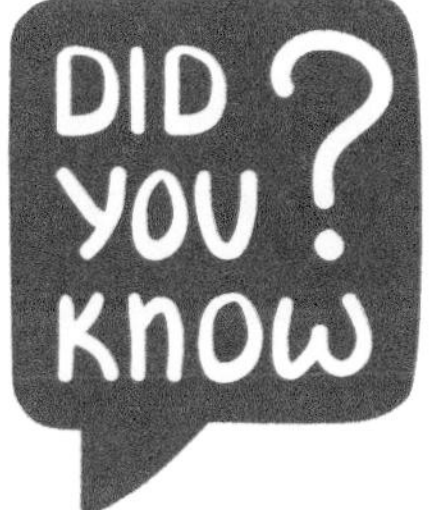

For nearly four decades, Stravinsky and Balanchine had an interactive collaboration fed by the composer's deep interest in dance and the choreographer's impeccable musicianship—pictured in Figure 11, left and center. Their artistic partnership gave birth to many signature works, among them and still performed today, the ballet *Agon* (1957), pictured in Figure 11 on the right.[28]

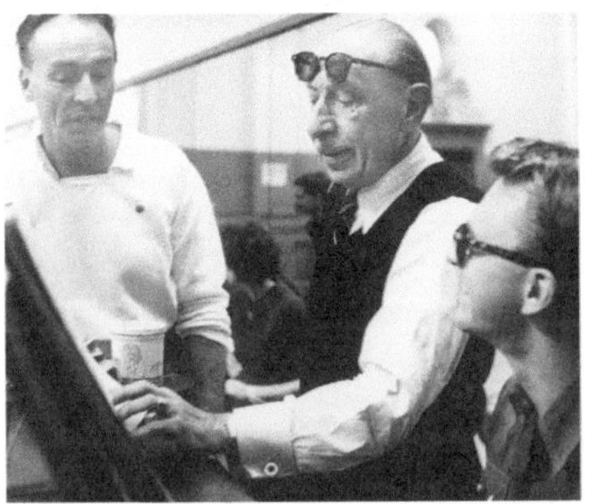

Figure 11 All photographs © Martha Swope. Image left: Choreographer George Balanchine, left, and composer Igor Stravinsky, right, 1957; Image center: New York City Ballet in rehearsal, left to right: Arthur Mitchell, Diana Adams, George Balanchine, and Igor Stravinsky, 1957; *Agon*, choreography by George Balanchine, left to right: Richard Rapp, Gloria Govrin, and Earle Sieveling, New York City Ballet, The New York Public Library for the Performing Arts, 1970

➢ **Relative Approach:** Music and dance are created as conceptually independent, yet they relate when performed together. The composer and the choreographer work separately but in coordination, emphasizing the independence of creative processes and the sovereignty of each art form. Dance and music are integrated purposely, by planning, chance, or circumstance, as *relative* to one another.

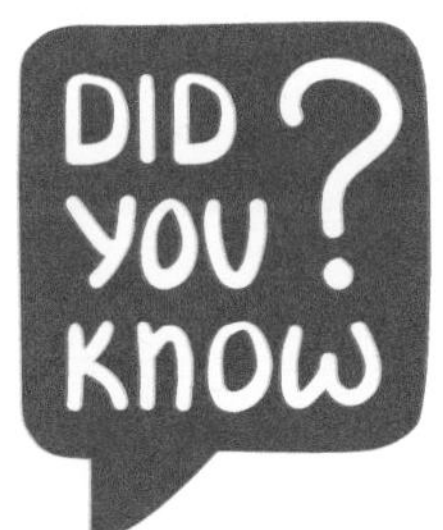

Choreographer Merce Cunningham was concerned only with movements; composer John Cage was concerned only with sound. Their work together led to collaborations in which both artists created in coordination but separately. In this type of collaboration, dance, music, lighting, costumes, and sets were developed independently and in isolation, but came together at the last minute before the curtain rose, such as in their collaboration *Roaratorio* (1979), pictured in Figure 12.[29]

Figure 12 Image left: photography © Lois Greenfield, *Rhythm in Motion*, Merce Cunningham, left, and John Cage, right, 1982; Image center and right: photography © Tom Brazil, *Roaratorio*, choreography by Merce Cunningham, Merce Cunningham Dance Company, BAM Next Wave Series, 1986

◆ **LIVE OR RECORDED, COMPOSED OR IMPROVISED MUSIC AND CHOREOGRAPHY.** Once a choreographer and a composer agree to collaborate, how will the logistics and sequencing of the project unfold? In *A Study of the Choreographer/Composer Collaboration*, the American composer and educator Van Stiefel describes several scenarios of sequencing and integration between a set or improvised choreography, composed or improvised music, and music played either live or as recorded.[30] Here are some possible combinations of composed versus improvised and live versus recorded music:

- Music composed prior to choreography and performed live with dance
- Music composed and recorded prior to choreography
- Music composed alongside the creation of choreography and performed live
- Music composed and recorded alongside the creation of choreography
- Music improvised to choreography and recorded or performed live
- Dance performed to live music
- Dance performed to recorded music

On many occasions, composers and musicians, choreographers, and dancers can all perform together and interact. Choosing live music for a dance performance, for instance, could be the signature element of an artist's aesthetic, or it could simply accommodate the demands of a particular work.

In summary, a choreographer-composer collaboration may occur in various circumstances and manners. The common goal is to reach an artistic equilibrium, where the artists share ideas and learn from each other while balancing creative freedom and artistic coordination. Developing an understanding of each art form only benefits the choreographer and composer's teamwork. Music and dance use similar terminology and share common vocabulary such as duration, tempo, rhythm, dynamics, texture, phrase, format, and style, among many others.

Let's end with the question posed at the beginning: Are music and dance best friends forever? Whether they are "best" or "friends" or "forever"—it has been proven historically and statistically that music complements dance very well. Therefore: "Hey dance, you better be nice to music!"

HELPFUL TIPS & SUGGESTIONS

~ Think of music as an escape; think of dance as a compass
~ Don't be afraid of new ideas in dance and music, but rather of old ones
~ Know that when your words fail, music speaks and dance captures
~ Consider making music sound better when you choreograph a dance to it
~ Create dances to the rhythm of your life and the beat of your heart
~ Keep dancing and singing, no matter who listens or watches
~ Remember that dance and music make the rules, and not the other way around

CHOREOGRAPHING TO NEW MUSIC, COMPOSING FOR NEW DANCE

Original Concept + Original Music + Original Choreography = Innovative Work. It is a dream come true when choreographers and composers form an artistic partnership. Together, they can invent, discover, and create an original work, advancing the art of dance and choreography.

Throughout the centuries, many prominent choreographers have collaborated with respected renowned composers. Complementing abilities of talented artists galvanize both art forms. Historically, countless artistic partnerships have resulted in masterworks that are still performed today. The following is a partial list of well-known collaborations between choreographers and composers. Their teamwork has made an impact on the development of choreography and music. Sometimes the choreographer can also be a composer, like Hofesh Shechter:

PERIOD	CHOREOGRAPHERS	COMPOSERS
17th–19th Century	Pierre Beauchamp	Jean-Baptiste Lully
	Jean-Georges Noverre	Wolfgang Amadeus Mozart, Christoph Willibald Gluck
	August Bournonville	Severin Løvenskiold
	Arthur Saint-Léon	Leo Delibes, Ludwig Minkus, Cesare Pugni
	Marius Petipa	Pyotr Ilych Tchaikovsky, Ludwig Minkus, Cesare Pugni
Early 20th Century	Michel Fokine	Maurice Ravel, Igor Stravinsky,
	Vaslav Nijinsky	Claude Debussy, Igor Stravinsky
	Bronislava Nijinska	Francis Poulenc, Igor Stravinsky
	Leonid Massine	Manuel De Falla, Erik Satie
Mid 20th Century	Ruth St. Denis, Martha Graham	Louis Horst, Aaron Copland, Samuel Barber
	Doris Humphrey, Agnes de Mille	Louis Horst, Kurt Weill, Morton Gould
	Leonid Yakobson	Aram Khachaturian
	George Balanchine	Igor Stravinsky, Paul Hindemith
	Jerome Robins	Leonard Bernstein, Robert Prince
	Merce Cunningham	John Cage, Lou Harrison
Late 20th Century	Laura Dean	Steve Reich
	Twyla Tharp, Molissa Fenley	Philip Glass
	Trisha Brown	Laurie Anderson
	Lucinda Childs	John Adams, Philip Glass
	Jiří Kylián	Toru Takemitsu, Arne Nordheim
	William Forsythe	Thom Willems
Early 21st Century	David Dawson	Gavin Bryars, Szymon Brzóska, Greg Haines
	Wayne McGregor	Max Richter, Joby Talbot
	Alexei Ratmansky	Leonid Desyatnikov
	Christopher Wheeldon	Joby Talbot, Keaton Henson
	Crystal Pite	Owen Belton
	Alexander Ekman	Mikael Karlsson
	Edward Clug	Milko Lazar
	Justin Peck	Sufjan Stevens, Bryce Dessner
	Akram Kahn	Vincenzo Lamagna, Nitin Sawhney, Ben Frost
	Annabelle Lopez Ochoa	Peter Salem
	Hofesh Shechter	Hofesh Shechter

Figure 13

assignments & exercises

RESEARCH ASSIGNMENT: How did a collaboration take place?

➡ Research and choose a well-known work of dance, where a choreographer and a composer collaborated to create a new original work. Make sure that your selection originates in the 19th, 20th, or 21st century. What is the genre of music and dance of your choice? Why did you pick this particular music and dance? How does your choice of work relate to you as an artist?

➡ Use library and online resources to learn how the composer and the choreographer collaborated on this original work. Who initiated the collaboration? Which artist was in a dominant position during their collaborative work? How did their collaborative process evolve? How long was the collaboration? What were the outcomes and the feedback when the piece premiered?

➡ Expand your research and find out whether the choreographer has collaborated with other composers. What was the choreographer's process when working with other composers, and what kind of work was created? Were there any differences between the processes? Research the composer: Did the composer work with any other choreographers? Who were they? Was the process similar or different? Was other music by the same composer more successful than the music you have researched, and why?

EXPLORATORY ASSIGNMENT: Can you identify the elements of a music piece?

➡ Select a piece of music randomly and listen to it in its entirety. Identify the mood of the piece as you hear it. What emotions, images, and actions does it evoke? Draw a picture—narrative or abstract —illustrating how you feel about this piece of music!

➡ Identify the rhythm, tempo, and beat, as well as the melodic line, harmony, tonality, texture, and the instruments used. Identify the format and the structure of the piece and how it progresses. What musical elements are the most engaging for you, and why?

➡ If the music piece has lyrics, is the text connected with the character of the melody? Does the narrative present a story and address an emotional state? Research the background of the music composer and identify why this piece was created. What was the inspiration behind the work?

★ **CREATIVE EXERCISE:** Can music and dance relate randomly, and what does it take to make them fit?

➡ Ask a friend to pick three different random musical selections from various historical periods and styles. These could be Baroque and a classical instrumental music piece, a contemporary 20th-century instrumental piece, and a recent 21st-century instrumental piece that might use various electronic instruments and sound effects. Ensure that all selected works are written in short formats and are no longer than five to seven minutes each.

➡ Create a short choreographic phrase in complete silence and unrelated to any music. Ensure that your choreographic phrase contains a movement concept evolving around a particular image, feeling, action or narrative. Practice your phrase independently of any music, and make sure that it is ready to be performed either by you or by a dancer.

➡ Use the accompaniment of the randomly selected pieces of music and perform the newly created choreographic phrase separately on each one of them. While performing the dance phrase, try to instantly match the movement sequence to the rhythm of the music and its melodic line. You can also slightly modify the movement phrase to fit each music piece, just as it seems that those movements have been created to fit each particular piece perfectly.

➡ Analyze and discuss with your peers and mentors how the music piece affected the choreographic phrase's quality, timing, and performance. To what extent does the choreographic phrase become different because of the music? Did the mood and the quality of the movements change? How much modification was needed to adapt the movement to the music?

➡ Which of the music choices best fits the idea of the choreographic phrase and why? If you are free to make a completely new music choice to match the original choreographic phrase, what kind of music would you pick and why? Will the difference be in rhythm, tempo, beat, melody, timbre, musical instruments, texture, format, or structure?

➡ When you have the opportunity to collaborate with a living composer, would you begin with sharing musical, movement, or philosophical ideas? What would you ask or instruct the composer to consider while you are preparing for the collaboration?

➡ How do you envision the process and interaction between you and your collaborating composer? How specific and engaging do you see your collaborative process with the composer? Would you engage in spontaneous improvisation between dance and music? Would you narrow it down and suggest using specific musical instruments, rhythmic patterns, beat, tempo, melodic line, and a particular progression of music sections? How would you determine and define your overall approach with the composer? What type of interaction would you propose to make sure that there is equal and mutual collaboration?

BIBLIOGRAPHY AND REFERENCES

[1] Teck, Katherine. Editor. *Making Music for Modern Dance, Collaboration in the Formative Years of New American Art*, Oxford University Press, 2011, p. 46.
[2] Straub, Brandon. *Lectures on Music Theory* (live), ICONS Choreographic Institute at the Dance Loft on 14, Washington DC, USA, February 2017–2019.
[3] Manoff, Tom. *Music: A Living Language*, W.W. Norton & Company, 1982, pp. 10, 11, 83.
[4] O'Brian, James Patrick. *The Listening Experience, Elements, Forms and Styles in Music, Schirmer Books*, 1995, pp. 44–48.
[5] O'Brian 1995. *The Listening Experience*, pp. 49–56.
[6] Randel, Don Michael. Editor. *Harvard Dictionary of Music*, The Belknap Press of Harvard University Press, 2003, pp. 661–663.
[7] Randel 2003. *Harvard Dictionary of Music*, pp. 571.
[8] Randel 2003. *Harvard Dictionary of Music*, pp. 443–444.
[9] O'Brian 1995. *The Listening Experience*, pp. 105–107.
[10] O'Brian 1995. *The Listening Experience*, pp. 90–103.
[11] O'Brian 1995. *The Listening Experience*, pp. 116–142.
[12] Rogers, Kara. "Melody," article, in *Encyclopedia Britannica Online*, 2017, edited by Parul Jain, 2012 and Yamini Chauhan, 2010, accessed February 2019.
[13] O'Brian 1995. *The Listening Experience*, pp. 82–86.
[14] O'Brian 1995. *The Listening Experience*, pp. 66–76, 80–82.
[15] O'Brian 1995. *The Listening Experience*, pp. 75–77.
[16] Randel 2003. *Harvard Dictionary of Music*, pp. 617–622.
[17] Randel 2003. *Harvard Dictionary of Music*, pp. 499–502, 521–522.
[18] Randel 2003. Harvard Dictionary of Music, pp. 379.
[19] Randel 2003. *Harvard Dictionary of Music*, pp. 209.
[20] Randel 2003. *Harvard Dictionary of Music*, pp. 877–878.
[21] Randel 2003. *Harvard Dictionary of Music*, pp. 898.
[22] Randel 2003. *Harvard Dictionary of Music*, pp. 898–899, 926–928.
[23] Randel 2003. *Harvard Dictionary of Music*, pp. 680–683.
[24] Randel 2003. *Harvard Dictionary of Music*, p. 1.
[25] Allen, Erin. *Documenting Dance: The Making of "Appalachian Spring"*, article, Library of Congress Blog, 2014, https://blogs.loc.gov/loc/2014/10/documenting-dance-the-making-of-appalachian-spring/, accessed February 2019.
[26] Anderson, Jack. *The Nutcracker Ballet*, Mayflower Books, 1979.
[27] Wiley, Roland John. *Tchaikovsky's Ballets*, Oxford University Press, 1985, pp. 321–341.
[28] Alm, Irene. "Stravinsky, Balanchine, and Agon: An Analysis Based on the Collaborative Process," journal article, *The Journal of Musicology*, vol. 7, no. 2, Spring, 1989, pp. 254–269.
[29] Weinstein, Beth. "The Collaborative Legacy of Merce Cunningham: A Rich Look at an Unrecognized Architectural Genre: The Diverse Collaborations between Major Choreographers and Eminent Architects," journal article, https://placesjournal.org, accessed March 2011.
30 Stiefel, Van. *A Study of the Choreographer/Composer Collaboration*, Princeton University, Center for Arts and Cultural Policies Studies, 2002.

VISUAL REFERENCES

Figures 1 and 2: Diagrams © Vladimir Angelov

Figure 3: *Middle C on a piano keyboard, learning aid and cheat sheet.* Diagram of two octave sections, for treble clef and bass clef, on keyboard and grand staff, Middle C in red color. Illustration, Credit :PeterHermesFurian, courtesy of iStock/Getty Images

Figure 4: Illustration ©Vikto_r_LA/Shutterstock. Orchestra Seating Chart, purchased from Shutterstock 05/27/21, created in 2019

Figure 5: *Watercolor illustration of mountain landscape*, credit: keiko takamatsu, courtesy of iStock/Getty Images; music measure © Wagner, Tristan & Isolde, "Liebestod Closing Bars," 1865, public domain, edit and graphic design © Charles Scheland, 2021

Figure 6: *Sound waves.* Frequency audio waveform, music wave HUD interface elements, voice graph signal. Vector audio wave set, Credit:SpicyTruffel, courtesy of iStock/Getty Images

Figure 7: *Sample of melody harmony measure* © Hyacinth, *Diminished Seventh Modulation*, non-copyright eligible, 2011, edited by Charles Scheland, 2021

Figure 8: Diagram © Vladimir Angelov

Figure 9: Top image: Composer Aaron Copland at Rock Hill. Photograph retrieved from the Library of Congress; Bottom image: Photography © Lois Greenfield, Appalachian Spring, choreography by Martha Graham, pictured Miki Orihara, Elizabeth Auclair, Rika Okamoto, Camille Brown, Pascal Rioult, courtesy of Martha Graham Dance Company, 1994

Figure 10: Image left: *Portrait de Marius Petipas*, photographer unknown, 1898, public domain; Image center: *Portrait of Pyotr Ilyich Tchaikovsky*, Evans, Edwin, E. P. Dutton & Company, 1906, pp. Frontispiece Retrieved on 27 March 2009, public domain. Image right: *The Nutcracker* in St. Petersburg, photographer unknown, Mariinsky Theatre Archives, 1892, public domain

Figure 11: All photographs © Martha Swope. Image left: Choreographer George Balanchine, left, and composer Igor Stravinsky, right, 1957; Image center: In rehearsal, left to right: Arthur Mitchell, Diana Adams, George Balanchine, and Igor Stravinsky, 1957; *Agon*, choreography by George Balanchine, left to right: Richard Rapp, Gloria Govrin, and Earle Sieveling, New York City Ballet, The New York Public Library for the Performing Arts, 1970

Figure 12: Image left: photography © Lois Greenfield, *Rhythm in Motion*, Merce Cunningham, left, and John Cage, right, 1982; Image center and left: photography © Tom Brazil, *Roaratorio*, choreography by Merce Cunningham, Merce Cunningham Dance Company, BAM Next Wave Series, 1986

Figure 13: Diagram © Vladimir Angelov

To lead an orchestra you must turn your back on the crowd.

Aristotle (384 BC–322 BC)

CHAPTER 21

ATTRACT AND RETRACT
– SEEKING, CHOOSING, AND WORKING WITH MUSIC –

When choreographers find a piece of music for their dance, they better like it because they will hear it many times. Choosing music is just like choosing a new companion. The dance and the music will share artistically common spaces—the dance studio, the stage, and ultimately, the completed dance work. The relationship is one of attraction and retraction.

While music might drive movement and dance, music does not necessarily create movement and dance. Music might inspire and enhance a dance created by the choreographer, who reflects on the human condition and captures it through motion.

A skillful choreographer should be able to create movement and dance even without music, as the choreography stands on its own. Often music is there only to support the dance. The simplest way to test the impact of choreography is to turn the music off when watching the choreography on video. Does the choreography hold its artistic merit and impact during silence and without any sound? When using music, how does a choreographer engage and work with the music and sound in the first place?

There are three possible options for initiating a relationship between dance and music, movement and sound—as illustrated in Figure 3. They are: the choreographic idea comes first, and then the music and sound; the music and sound come first, then the choreography; or the choreography and the music and sound emerge simultaneously and in collaboration:

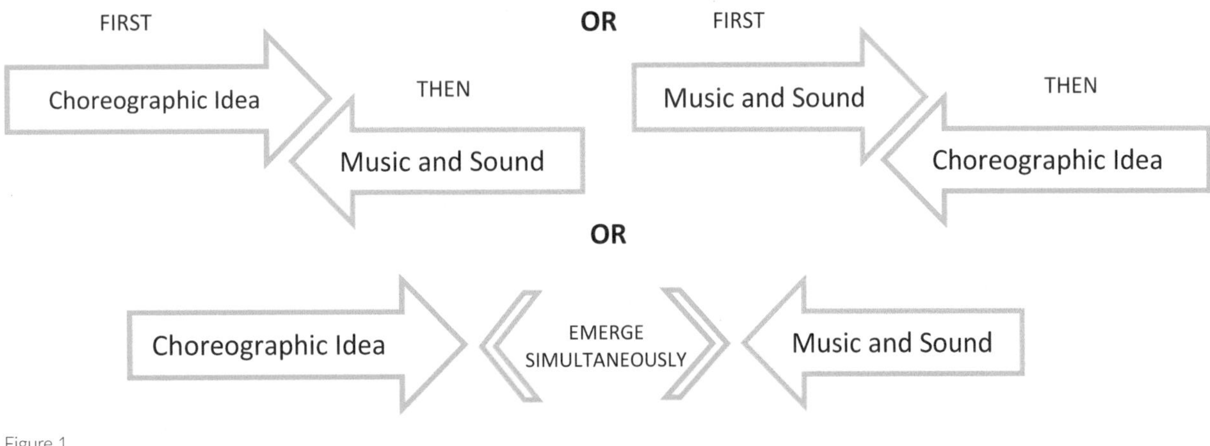

Figure 1

?

What comes first in your choreographic work—the music or the dance?

WHY DO WE NEED MUSIC FOR DANCE?

In the presence of music, dance occurs naturally. Everybody has experienced it, especially in a casual setting—during a party, a celebration, a gathering, a dance lesson, an interactive movement event, or a fun time at a dance club.

We first hear the music, and the rhythm and the melody "get into our body." Then we gradually begin to move under the beat. With the music stimulation and the passage of time, we become increasingly comfortable moving and dancing.

> If we *enjoy dancing to music*, our urge to move may feel natural. It is fair to suggest that *certain music inspires us to dance spontaneously.*
>
> If we *need music* for concert dance, our approach may change. Music becomes a collaborative medium in our artistic work and part of a bigger picture. Then it is no longer about the music enjoyment and the emotional effect of the music. One may engage more thoughtfully when seeking and choosing music to accompany artful movement. It is fair to suggest that *certain music inspires one to create and choreograph a new dance.*

As active music listeners, choreographers are often attracted to and inspired by particular musical works and composers. Many choreographers already have a playlist of favorite music works that they feel connected to in specific ways. Therefore, the choreographer's initial response, preference, and choice of music might begin with one or a combination of the factors outlined below. Which of them are most common for you?

- ☐ I have heard a piece of music, and I wonder if I should choreograph to it.
- ☐ I have improvised to a random music piece that perfectly suits my movement.
- ☐ I always liked a music piece, yet I do not feel ready to choreograph to it.
- ☐ I have found a piece of music that I love, and I cannot wait to choreograph to it.
- ☐ I have seen this music piece choreographed, and I can choreograph it my own way.
- ☐ I have been following a few composers, and I wonder what else they have written.
- ☐ I was given a music piece to choreograph, and I am beginning to like it.

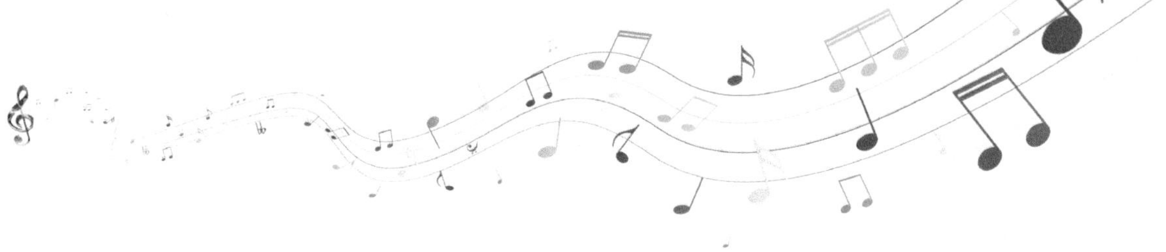

Figure 2

CHOREOGRAPHIC APPROACHES TO RELATE MUSIC AND DANCE

The relationship between dance and music can be simultaneously dynamic and restricting. Ultimately, it is the choreographer's artistic choice as to how music and dance will relate.

Sometimes choreographers have decisive artistic philosophies for approaching music before they have even selected the music piece. Other times, according to each project, choreographers make strategic decisions on how to operate with the music. In general, there are multiple ways in which music and dance relate and integrate—a non-hierarchical range of choreographic approaches is summarized in Figure 3:

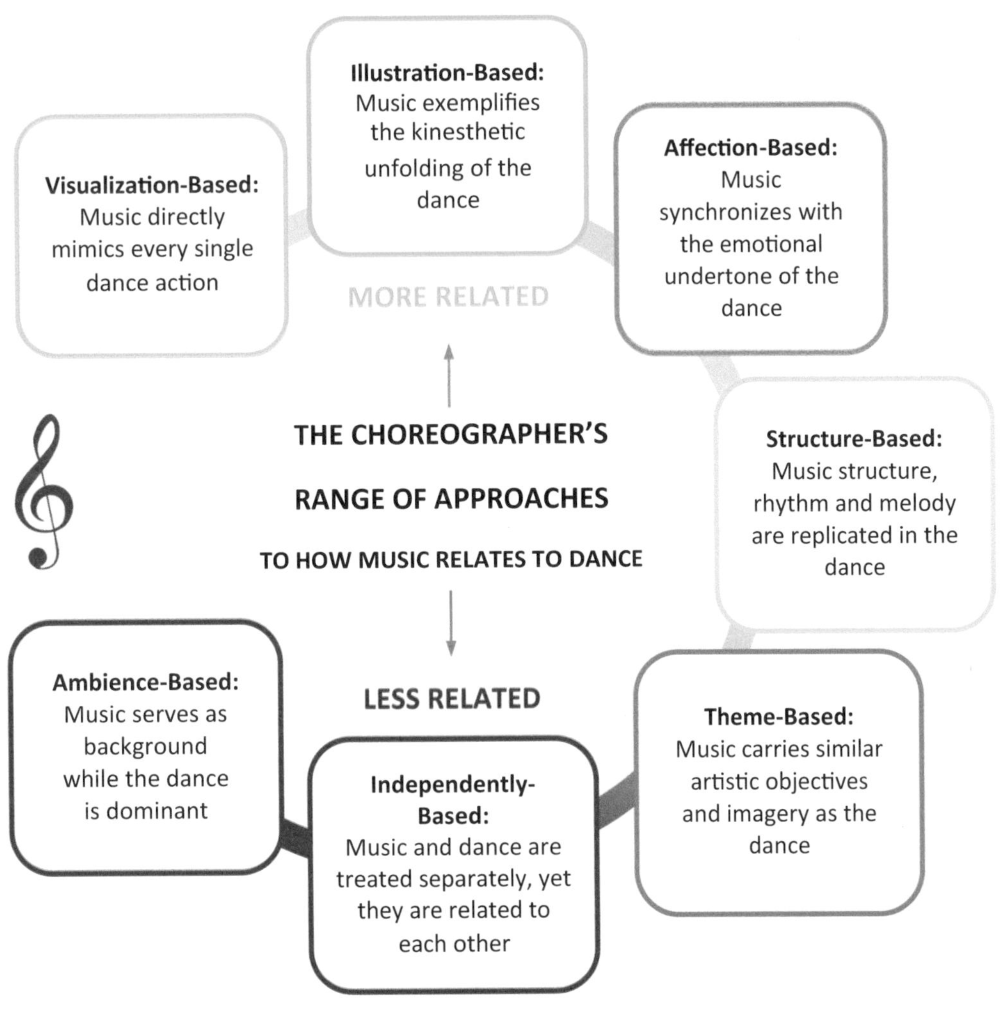

Figure 3

Several of these approaches can be seen within a single short dance piece or during an extended full-length dance performance. These possibilities, choices, and combinations could be implemented in the dance within each music movement, section, and even a particular measure of music.

For example, in the traditional Petipa version of the ballet *The Nutcracker*, the staging relates to the music as *Ambience-based* during the Party Scene in Act I. During the battle between the Nutcracker and the Mouse King, the choreography refers to the music as *Illustration-based.* When the nutcracker doll has been broken and Clara's solo follows, the music treatment is *Affection-based.* And finally, during the *Waltz of the Snowflakes*, the choreography simultaneously relates to the music as *Theme- and Structure-based.* In summary, a specific approach might better suit a particular dance scene.

This mixed-approach strategy is mainly used in large dance works with narrative plots. Plotless dance works are commonly less inclined to visualize and illustrate music than more theatrical and narrative works. Also, shorter dance formats such as one-act ballets and chamber contemporary dance pieces invite a one-approach strategy, which seems to dominate throughout the space of chamber format works.

Finally, based on aesthetic preferences and particular movement ideologies, certain choreographers might decide to apply a single approach to an entire dance or implement a combination of processes into a unique merger. Some of these approaches can be grouped with the following characteristics:

➢ The **more-related-to-music** approaches—*Visualization-* and *Illustration-based* treat the music as subordinate to the dance. The movement mimics various descriptive musical characteristics through the dance action, leaving very little space for the musical composition to stand on its own as an independent work of art.

➢ The **less-related-to-music** approaches—*Independently-* and *Ambience-based* treat the music as an independent entity related to the dance without any conformity. The composer and the choreographer might even have very different intentions when creating and approaching the work. Therefore, moments of contrast and randomness might be expected. The two art forms—music and dance—might collide unpredictably, especially if there is no pre-conceived coordination between movement and sound.

➢ The **equally-related-to-music** approaches—*Affection-*, *Structure-*, and *Theme-based* treat the music and dance as conceptually integrated. The music and the dance are positioned in an equal relationship and in harmony. Subtle parameters of balance are intuitively found, as dance and music assimilate organically. In many cases, the choreography results in a "music-driven dance." The choreographers feel the music expresses an inspiring idea to capture with movements. Many dancemakers have been inspired by music as a driving force for their dances. For example, in neo-classical ballet, the most prominent "equally-related-to-music" choreographer was George Balanchine.[1] In late 20th-century modern dance, one choreographer whose work is predominately inspired by music is Mark Morris.[2]

?

In your work, what is the relationship between music and dance?
What approaches have you used, and how?

GRAVITATING TOWARDS WELL-KNOWN DANCE MUSIC

– SAME MELODY, BUT DIFFERENT MOVES –

A large body of musical works has been composed specifically for dance or used extensively for dance. Many choreographers are inclined to tackle and interpret the rich heritage of music that has endured the test of time. The most commonly restaged music scores in classical ballet are *The Nutcracker, Swan Lake, Sleeping Beauty*, and *Don Quixote*. Over the past couple of centuries, popular musical works used by choreographers are *Rite of Spring, Bolero, Carmina Burana, Carmen*, and *West Side Story*, among many others.

Well-known music sounds familiar, and the spectators might have certain expectations. The choreographer might consider either a new treatment and original libretto, or changing only certain aspects of the initial dance and music concepts. The music could also have an unconventional rendering when the music score is initially written for a symphony orchestra, but is performed, let's say—by a jazz ensemble.

***Rite of Spring*, originally named *Le Sacre du printemps* in French, is a ballet and symphonic work by Igor Stravinsky, written for Ballets Russes. It was originally choreographed by Vaslav Nijinsky and first performed at the Théâtre des Champs-Élysées, on May 29, 1913. The libretto is simple: during a tribe ritual, a Chosen Maiden must die to save the earth, and she dances herself to death.[3] In 1987, the Joffrey Ballet reconstructed the 1913 original production of *Rite of Spring* (Figure 4, left panel). Other interpretations of the same work have been created by Leonide Massine in 1920, Mary Wigman in 1957, Kenneth MacMillan in 1962, Maurice Béjart in 1959, Pina Bausch in 1975 (Figure 4, center panel), Glen Tetley in 1974, John Neumeier in 1972, Hans Van Manen in 1974, Paul Taylor in 1980 (Figure 4, right panel), Martha Graham in 1984, Angelin Preljocaj in 2001, Shen Wei in 2003, Jorma Elo in 2009, and Wayne MacGregor in 2018, among many others.**

Figure 4 From left to right: Photography © Herbert Migdoll, *Rite of Spring*, 1913, choreography by Vaslav Nijinsky, performed by The Joffrey Ballet, 1987; Photography © Sasha Gouliaev, *Rite of Spring*, 1975, choreography by Pina Bausch, center performer Tsai-Wei Tien, surrounded by performers of Tanztheater Wuppertal Pina Bausch, 2018; Photography © Tom Caravaglia, *Le Sacre du Printemps (The Rehearsal)*, 1980, choreography by Paul Taylor, Paul Taylor Dance Company, performed by Annamaria Mazzini and Michael Trusnovec, 2008

A choreographer may face three exciting challenges when using well-known dance music: a) What is your unique interpretation? b) What is your new context and movement vocabulary? c) What is your artistic statement about the work's relevance today? The answers to these questions and the implementation of your vision may lead to an innovative treatment of the initial libretto and the music score.

ADVENTURING AND HUNTING FOR DANCE MUSIC

Choreographers usually seek music that connects with their movement concepts. Various musical features such as a clear perceptible beat, memorable melodic line, or sonic landscape with texture are often desirable. How does the music hunt begin?

HELPFUL TIPS & SUGGESTIONS

N
NW NE
W E
SW SE
S

NEED A COMPASS? Establishing search criteria and key Q & A's helps navigate through a vast space of available music choices. The following meridians could be implemented in a non-linear order:

- **Duration:** How long is the music? Choreographers working on a particular project might be given a specific length for their choreography. In some cases, the length of the music might be a crucial factor in choosing a music piece. The lengths of silence count too.

- **Full length, excerpt, or a collage:** Does the music piece need to be used in its entirety? Choreographers might be attracted to segments of an extended musical work, for instance, only an *Adagio* or an *Andante* as part of a concerto. Then the sections could be repositioned to serve the dance, rather than using the entire concerto in the original sequence.

- **Historic Origin:** Should choreography illustrate period music, and vice versa? Dance doesn't need to mimic the historical origin of the music piece unless it is intended to do so. Often, an eclectic collision between music of different ages and modern dance genres is innovative.

- **Genre:** Should genre references in the music be captured in the choreography? Not necessarily. Classical music and contemporary pop music, for example, are distinct genres. Yet they could be integrated into a single musical piece. Music and dance are adaptable and can easily develop into inventive hybrids of multiple kinds of music and dance styles.

- **Content & Composer's work:** Do the reasons behind writing a music piece impact the content of the choreography? Not always. However, research and information about the origins of the music work and the composer's intentions help the choreographer to understand better why this work came to exist in the first place.

- **Music Elements:** Do music elements need to relate to dance elements? A common expectation is that the music's beat, tempo, rhythmic patterns, and melodic line will connect to the dance. If music is the drawing canvas, then dance may emerge from it.

- **Structure:** Should dance comply with the structural features of the music? Not necessarily. It depends on the musical format and genre—whether it is a song, an instrumental solo, or a symphony. Understanding the form and the structural development of the music could be advantageous in crafting the choreography—if not always, then perhaps occasionally.

THREE QUESTIONS BEFORE BONDING WITH A MUSIC CHOICE

The choice of music is a choice that will affect the dance. The music, to a certain degree, will impact how the choreographed movement is perceived. For example, "furious" music usually sounds fast and intense, while "peaceful" music sounds slow and meditative. The same movement phrase performed to furious or peaceful music will be perceived differently by the audience. Music qualities and emotional drive may impact movement qualities and kinesthetic flow. The overall choreography might transform because of the music—intentionally or unintentionally.

From the audience and spectators' viewpoint, there is an organic connection between the sound of the music and the response of the human body in motion. There are even semantic similarities, where the word "emotion" has "motion" in it.

Choreographers often debate whether they like, love, or are just curious about a pending music selection for their dances. The following three questions can help guide a choreographer through the process of potential attraction and attachment to a music choice:

REFERENCING: Is the music appealing and engaging on first impression?

The mind responds to music in multiple ways. Music can awaken certain impressions and images; it may stir emotions about memories or life experiences. Or certain music elements may be organically "in-tune" with the choreographer's sensibility. If such responses to the music come across as appealing and engaging, then working with and creating movement to such music is assured to emerge naturally.

PROPORTIONALITY: Should three dancers equal three musicians?

The panoramic scale of a symphony could fit with the intimacy of a dance solo, as long as the music does not "speak louder" than the dance. A specific dance scene may have its music demand, for instance, a choreography portraying a funeral procession with a large cast of dancers accompanied by a single trumpet. There is no rule about accommodating proportionality, yet one can look for why certain choices are better than others.

CONNECTIVITY: Is it a matchmaking commitment or a willingness to fall in love?

When watching a dance performance, spectators comprehend music and dance together, not separately. Regardless of the choreographer's approach towards music, the common perception is that music and dance complement each other. Through the work, the audience may sense the choreographer's relationship with the music: Is it true love or only commitment? As when observing a newlywed couple, it is magical when dance and music immerse themselves into oneness—without fear to explore the complexity of a relationship!

MUSICALITY IN DANCE
– INHERITED OR TRAINED –

Musicality is the response and receptivity to music. Musicality is a widely valued quality among musicians. Many choreographers also strive to develop abilities to sense, comprehend, and demonstrate a working knowledge of musical concepts such as rhythm, tempo, melodic line, phrasing, structure, and overall sound.

Can musicality be taught, or is it about being born with a musical gene? In most instances, it is a combination of both. It is commonly perceived that musicality is something that we inherit as a natural talent. There are always degrees of musicality potential, which may be either natural or nurtured early in childhood. However, there are also multiple ways to train sensibility and receptivity to music.[4] A choreographer does not need to play a musical instrument to be musical. Musicality can be taught through *ear training*, where choreographers and musicians learn and develop skills to identify essential elements of music. Studying *ear training and musicality* are similar to the skill of quickly taking dictation in written and spoken language.[5]

◆ **BASIC MUSICALITY** training begins with: a) *clapping hands, skipping, jumping, and moving* while following the tempo, pulse, and basic rhythm. The next step is: b) *developing an awareness of repetitive music patterns.* The following step is: c) *counting the music's beats and rhythmic variety by developing a sense of mathematical concepts in music.* Hearing all of these initial music elements cultivates the ability to connect with music.

◆ **ADVANCED MUSICALITY** training can develop a deeper comprehension of music. More involvement may also spark more fun, where one can play an "imitation game" of sensing music by exploring and taking on different "roles." For instance: a) *Being a musician*, who identifies the musical instruments as they play different parts, either separately or at the same time; b) *Being a composer*, who identifies changes in the rhythm, melodic line, the sections and their transitions, the structure sequencing, and the overall architecture of the work; c) *Being a conductor,* who identifies how all of the instruments come together as unified sound, and how the performance of the whole orchestra involves and brings together all of the components happening at once. Hearing these complex musical elements enables one to better understand music. In a humorous analogy, developing musicality is similar to understanding the instrument parts played by every musician in a marching band:

Figure 5 Children playing instruments in a marching band parade, illustration by Aleutie, courtesy of iStock/Getty Image

BEFRIENDING A MEASURE AT THE BAR, AND MAKING AN IMPERFECT PROMISE TO COUNT

The fundamental components of music cannot only be heard, but also notated. Written music is called a *score*. A choreographer doesn't need to read musical scores. However, learning the basic elements of music is essential: how music is organized in measures, what the score looks like, and how to count music. For starters: A music *measure* or *bar* is the rudimentary guide for choreographers to navigate through the sonic landscape of the score. *Measure* is used more commonly in American music, while *bar* is preferred in other English-speaking countries. The basics of musical notation are described below.[6]

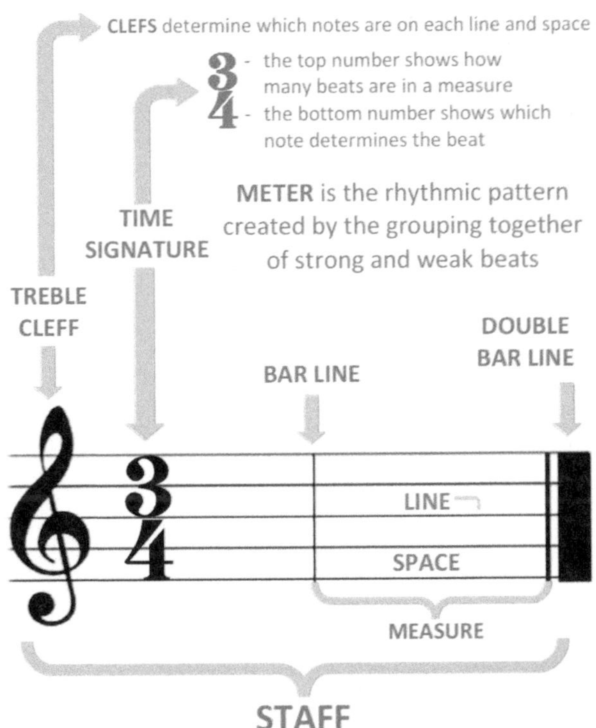

Figure 6

If you look at the *staff* to the left, the treble *clef* is followed by the time signature of 3/4. It tells us that the meter of the music has a *three-beat* pulse, where the length of each beat is a quarter-note. If we add up the lengths of the notes in each music bar, we will get a total value of three quarter-notes. Not every measure begins with the clef—see the diagram on the left illustrating the beginning portion of a music bar of a music score with several guiding symbols and their brief descriptions.

Bars are filled with various music symbols, which help one understand musical fractions. Two of these symbols are *notes* and *rests*—see the diagram on the right. Rests are silence and pauses in the music, which are notated differently depending on the length. Music notes indicate the length of the pitch—the rhythm fits into fraction bars, as a mathematical expression of the rhythmic measurement. When we have a sequence, we can write it, sing it, or play it on an instrument.

NOTE

REST

WHOLE NOTE

HALF NOTE

QUARTER NOTE

EIGHTH NOTE

SIXTEENTH NOTE

THIRTY-SECOND NOTE

Figure 7

A music *measure* or *bar* is a fragment of time corresponding to a specific number of beats. Staff notation is not written as one long stream of musical note symbols. Instead, it is divided into equal chunks—bars or measures, each containing a certain amount of time.

Most music styles have a *regular beat* (or pulse) that can be felt. Each bar usually has the same number of beats in it. Music that feels like 1-2-3-4...1-2-3-4...will be divided into bars with four beats in each bar.[7] For example, the *Frère Jacques* tune has four beats per bar, and one quarter note equals one beat. In the melody, each beat is represented by a particular note value, and vertical bar lines indicate the boundaries of the bar.

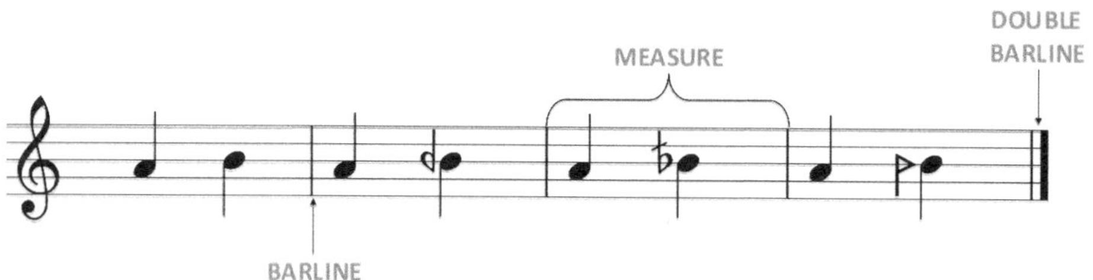

Figure 8

For instance, the beats in the measures may recall a waltz when the body begins rocking gently to the left and to the right. One might count it out like this: 1-2-3...1-2-3, and so on. That's 3/4 time; each measure could be three quarter-notes/rests long, or the equivalent number of notes/rests of other lengths. Or it could be 4/4—as shown in Figure 9.

Figure 9

Various types of artists use and adopt music terminology according to their needs. A choreographer might notice that composers, musicians, and conductors prefer to use the term *bar* to indicate the position of a music cue in the score. For example, "Let's play it from bar 36, or Letter B." At the same time, when indicating the amount of music needed, dance artists, teachers, and choreographers prefer to use *measure*. For example: "I need 16 measures of mazurka."

In addition, the same beats in a single measure could be counted differently by a choreographer than a musician. A musician, for instance, would count a bar of a waltz in 3/4 time as "1-2-3...1-2-3...," while a choreographer could count it as "1-and-2, 1-and-2," where the "and" *is* 2, and the 2 *is* 3. The total beat count in the bar is the same. Semantically, it is expressed differently by suggesting a kinesthetic change during the "and." The choreographer is not making a mistake but adopting the verbalization of the counts to articulate and demonstrate how *two* legs can dance *three* beats.

COUNTING THE MUSIC VS. FOLLOWING THE MUSIC

– DANCING ON COUNTS VS. DANCING ON MUSIC CUES –

Before incorporating existing music and dance together, choreographers traditionally seek to establish a clear sense of the landscape of the music work. Many strive to immerse themselves in the music to the extent that they feel they have *co-created* and *own* the music. A primary choreographic practice is to count and map the music score. However, not all music pieces have a distinct beat to count and an obvious melody to follow.

Twentieth-century contemporary composers such as Arnold Schoenberg and Alban Berg have created complex atonal musical pieces that choreographers might find challenging to count. Baroque composer Antonio Vivaldi, on the other hand, wrote works using mostly simple, repetitive rhythmic patterns that are easier to hear and follow. Some music is challenging to count, and some is not.

Even if choreographers are not able to read a musical score, they can use helpful strategies to work with the music while listening to it many times. They include: "Active Listening" to understand the piece's mood, "Attentive Perception" to repeatedly hear a music piece and grasp the structural flow, and "Accumulative Understanding" to comprehend all of the subtle details of the musical piece.[8]

THE CHOREOGRAPHER'S ENGAGEMENT WITH THE MUSIC

ENCOMPASSES

ACTIVE LISTENING → ATTENTIVE PERCEPTION → ACCUMULATIVE UNDERSTANDING TO ↓

- understand the composer's intentions and the content of the music
- recognize the rhythm, pulse, melodic line, and texture
- comprehend the architecture and structural flow of the piece
- identify the length of sections and transitions
- count measures and duration of rhythmic and melodic phrases
- create choreography that integrates the music
- work with the dancers to form ↓

MUSIC MEMORY → MOVEMENT MEMORY → MUSCLE MEMORY

Figure 10

As a choreographer gradually integrates the music with the choreography, the performers begin to articulate the music-dance relationship more productively. It is essential that the dancers eventually stop counting the music and instead dance on the music cues. Therefore, choreographers should consider facilitating a transition from *dancing on the music counts and beats, to dancing on the music cues and landscape.*

By opening night, the performers should no longer deal with the musical features but instead give their full attention to the movement work. Integrating movement and music could be a back-and-forth process, requiring patience and diligence. Therefore, choreographers may experiment with different methods of integrating the movement phrasing with the musical phrasing. Some valuable practices are:

◆ **Mapping Music Sequencing** is a tool to identify and outline the beats, counts, and measures of music. Mapping could be implemented without looking at an actual musical score but by *active listening, attentive perception,* and *cumulative understanding.* Before walking into the dance studio to work with the dancers, a choreographer may consider mapping the musical score by indicating the measures of rhythmic and melodic elements, time signature, accents, structure, and transitions. Converting the music into a visual grid and *mathematical notation of measures and counts* helps the choreographer easily maneuver through the musical landscape. For example, eight beats in one measure are:

1 2 3 4 5 6 7 8–Sequencing of **1 measure of 8 beats, or 1x8**

Figure 11

Choreographers may create their individual and personalized ways to group the musical counts into measures by counting and notating the mathematical division of beats. For instance, the first beat of each measure, called the downbeat, emphasizes the strong beat and could be highlighted in the choreographer's music mapping, which might look as follows:

(**1**) 2 3 4–5 6 7 8, (**2**) 2 3 4–5 6 7 8
(**3**) 2 3 4–5 6 7 8, (**4**) 2 3 4–5 6 7 8 } Introduction section with base: 4 measures of 8 beats or 4x8

1 2 3 4–Transition/Bridge

(**1**) 2 3 4–5 6 7 8, (**2**) 2 3 4–5 6 7 8
(**3**) 2 3 4–5 6 7 8, (**4**) 2 3 4–5 6 7 8 } 1st theme with piano in slow tempo: 4 measures of 8 beats, or 4x8

1 2 3 4–Transition/Bridge

1 2 3–**1** 2 3–**1** 2 3–**1** 2 3–**1** 2 3–**1** 2 3
1 2 3–**1** 2 3–**1** 2 3–**1** 2 3–**1** 2 3–**1** 2 3 } 2nd theme with percussions in fast tempo: 12 measures of 3 beats, or 12x3

Figure 12

◆ **Mapping Dance Sequencing** is a tool for creating an initial blueprint of the chronology and the progression of dance sections, which may be drafted prior to using the music—a map of dance sequencing. The goal then is to merge both—the music and dance maps.

Choreographers may consider using a notebook to outline and notate a map of the music on one page, and a map of the dance sequencing to the corresponding music bars, on the opposite page.

The diagram in Figure 13 summarizes the basic features of the music and the dance alongside each other. Such mapping displays the simultaneous progression of the dance and the music, how they will integrate with one another, and how a particular dance sequence will synchronize with a particular section of a musical structure.

Alternatives might emerge, and decisions could be made, for instance, on which measure and beat the dancers will position themselves on stage, when they will begin to dance, and when they will enter or exit the stage. Modifying each dance phrase and adding various movement accents corresponding to musical accents could happen spontaneously or purposefully at any time while positioning the dance to the music.

Dance sequences, movement qualities, and timing may continue to evolve as choreographers experiment with how the concept of the dance fits the music, and vice versa. Ideally, choreographers will gradually *embody* the music score to reach the dance's desired movement and dramatic effect. A sample mapping follows:

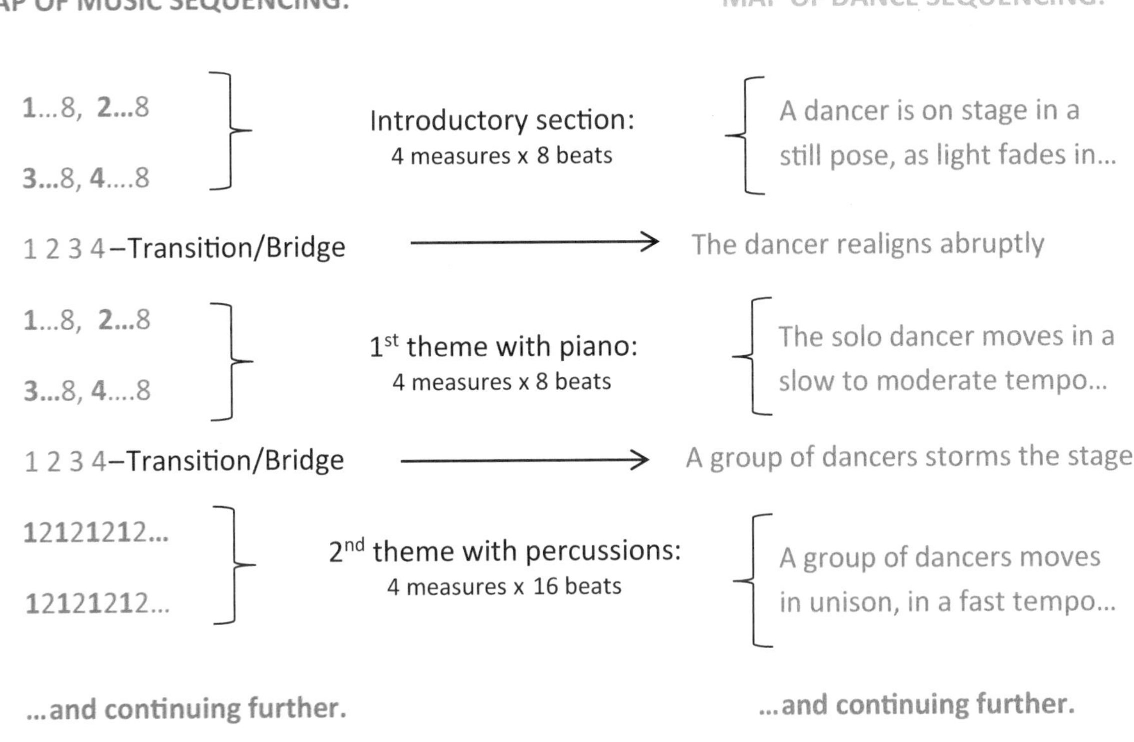

Figure 13

◆ Integrating features of choreographic phrasing with features of music phrasing:

As choreographers merge the music map with the dance map, and the movement material with the music material, there might be a few exciting challenges: Various features such as *tempo*, *articulation*, and *rhythm* may often be treated similarly and differently in music and dance. For example, the tempo of the music and the tempo of the dance might not immediately go hand-in-hand. The choreographer might consider the multiple strategies offered further along in this chapter to handle the similarities and the differences; either music or dance will mirror and relate to each other, or they will juxtapose and disregard each other. Or a choreographer may use a combination of multiple options.

SIMILARITIES AND DIFFERENCES OF USING TEMPO, ARTICULATION, AND RHYTHM IN MUSIC AND DANCE

Multiple established devices and terminology that originated in music are also used in dance, as various types of music and dance features are applicable to both art forms—see Figure 14. However, depending on the context and the choreographer's intentions, the tempo, articulation, and rhythm of music and dance can be treated similarly or differently as they are about to engage and integrate.

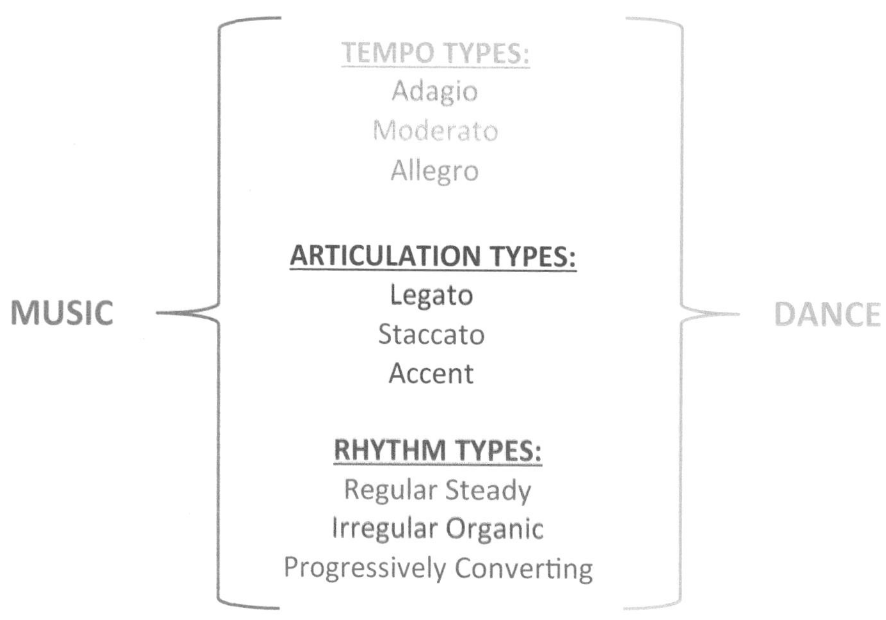

Figure 14

➢ **Tempo in music** is defined by how fast a piece of music is performed.[9] Tempo can change during a piece of music just as it can change in a dance. Music scores for classical ballets often feature tempo changes during a long piece to add to the dramatic effect. Classical music, in general, tends to have steadier speed, but it is common to use a gradual slowdown of the tempo—*ritardando*.[10] The opposite effect is *accelerando*, when the tempo gradually increases. Classical music may also be used in contemporary dance, an open-ended genre that may not always follow the tempo changes in music. In those instances, music and dance might often integrate by revealing a contrast.

TEMPO IN DANCE is defined by how fast the movements are performed. There are specific categories of movement vocabulary suitable for a slow or fast dance sequence. Such movement vocabulary includes full body poses and shapes, limp motions that are performed in a slow tempo, and usage of floor and grounded partnering sequences, which might include lifting and supporting the partners. Movement vocabulary such as big jumps and turns have consistent timing and energy related to gravity and acceleration. Therefore, their tempo cannot be altered as in music. For example, a particular dancer in a jump always lands at the same specific speed. Other types of dance vocabulary, such as steps, walks, runs, hops, and slips, are adaptable to tempo alteration.

Although a piece of music may be written and performed in a slow tempo—*Adagio*, for example—the choreography may not unfold in a consistently slow tempo. The human body offers a more dynamic kinesthetic range in tempo manipulation than the music offers sonically. Even in early dance, the entire body can move by switching tempos instantly, as different body parts can also move in *different tempos* simultaneously. The latter would be difficult to accomplish with the melodic line of an early musical instrument, such as a wooden flute.

➢ **Articulation in music** refers to how music notes should be played. *Legato* requires notes to be played or sung smoothly and in a connected manner. The player makes a transition from note to note without interrupting the sound, and with no intervening silence. *Staccato* means a detached manner of performing the music. *Accent* is an emphasis, stress, or a purposeful attack placed on a particular note or set of notes.[11] The different types of articulations in music might be aligned to correspond to the dance's movement quality and dynamics.

◆ **ARTICULATION IN DANCE** is the kinesthetic equivalent of physically handling energy allocation within the dancing body—it is the source, amount, and distribution of power when executing a given movement. Articulations may be revealed in various movement qualities and dynamics—see Chapter 14. The moving body can perform multiple dynamic articulations at the same time. For example, in Flamenco, the hands might move very slowly in *legato*. At the same time, the feet engage in rhythmically complex steps in *staccato* while juxtaposed with the fluid movement of the hands. The Flamenco dancer could also "storm" into a sequence of still shapes and poses with syncopated *accents*. Such articulations aim to kinesthetically highlight a range of a range of distinct rhythmic inflections and to display the passion and intensity of the moving body indulging in a percussive accompaniment.

➢ **Rhythm in music** is the placement of sounds in time in a repeated regular or irregular pattern of pulses. The occurrence of strong and weak beats can produce a particular form of meter and rhythm:[12]

In a broader context, rhythm is the drive, pulse, beat, momentum, emphasis, accents, and syncopations used in music and dance, poetry, speech, writing, visual art, design, and even biology and nature. Prominent designer and web developer Steven Bradley has characterized three distinct *visual and environmental rhythms*.[13]

— *Regular Steady Rhythm* is when rhythmic elements are similar in size or length. They repeat over a predictable interval of time and in a linear path—for example, the steady beat of raindrops on the roof.

— *Irregular Organic Rhythm* is when the rhythmic elements and intervals are organic and unique, though similar, over each interval of time. For example, when ocean waves brush the beach, there are no two alike. However, seen together in a sequence, they create a rhythm of natural movement and flow.

— *Progressively Converting Rhythm* is when the elements repeat over an interval of time, but with variations and modifications. Gradual increases or decreases create a sense of direction over the sequence. Rhythmic pulses might emphasize, contrast with, or interrupt the rhythmic pattern. Combinations might include *regular steady* and *irregular organic* rhythms. For example, the beat of the human heart can accelerate and decelerate organically and change rhythmic patterns due to physical activity.

◆ **RHYTHM IN DANCE** is the interplay between movement and stillness in regular or irregular patterns. The number of movements or steps per given time period may be organized in a rhythmic occurrence and defined metrically by the beat. In dance, rhythms have a vast range and complexity, which are also related to the anatomical and kinesthetic capacity of the human body.

American tap dance, for instance, especially rhythm tap, focuses on musicality. Tap is a hybrid dance form combining moves with rhythmic sound produced by the dancer's shoes, which are equipped with metal "taps" on the heel and the toe. The performers use their bodies not only to dance, but also as musical instruments capable of producing percussive sounds. Instead of moving to someone else's musical accompaniment, tap dancers instantly create their own original rhythms and "speak" musically in their own ways. Tap dancers are not only dancers but also composers and musicians—all at the same time.

Figure 15 Photography © Lois Greenfield, pictured Defne Enc, Antonio Hidalgo Paz, courtesy of Flamenco Vivo Carlota Santana, 2006

Flamenco dance also involves extensive use of percussive footwork as a dominant characteristic of the form. Rhythmic stomping of the feet is often combined with staccato hand-clapping or the use of castanets, which could accompany the complex footwork in regular rhythm or in counter time. Encouraging words and sounds are often shouted by flamenco performers to other participants or by observers, such as:... ¡Olé!, anda, vamos, etc.

In summary, both music and dance use similar terminology and expressive tools. However, which art form came before the other? While dance traditionally may need music more than music needs dance, then does movement precede music, or does music precede movement? A musician first needs to move in order to produce sound and music. A dancer unquestionably needs to move in order to produce physical artistry. Therefore, from a purely kinesthetic standpoint, human engagement in movement and dance is more primal than human engagement in sound and music.

TO BE OR NOT TO BE? [...ON MUSIC]

Dance and music treat tempos, articulations, and rhythms in distinct ways. As dance and music occur on stage simultaneously, a choreographer serves as a conductor and a "merger in charge." Artistic decisions are made about whether the dance will be subordinate to the music, and if so, to what extent. Will the dance subserviently visualize the music? Will the music be used as an accompaniment to the movement? Or will the music be a supportive background?

The choreographer's approach to the music might change randomly or deliberately, within one single dance phrase of eight to 16 movements or a few music bars. For example, during a particular dance phrase, the choreography may require the performers to stand still on stage while the music is playing. Then, the performers might move abruptly in contrast to the rhythm. A section may follow where the performers dance undoubtedly according to the music beat.

The choreographic treatment of the music could be definitive or dynamic, where the choreography may ***follow*** and ***mirror*** the music or ***be juxtaposed with*** and ***detached from*** certain musical elements—see Figure 16. Illustrated by the connecting arrows, the choreographer's approach and maneuvering could switch at any time and entertain explorations in the same direction, similar directions, or opposite directions. Pairing these approaches is also possible: for instance, a dance phrase could follow *without* mirroring the rhythm, or it could follow *and* mirror the music beat.

With all options available, the choreographer has the artistic control to choose how dance and music will integrate and merge.

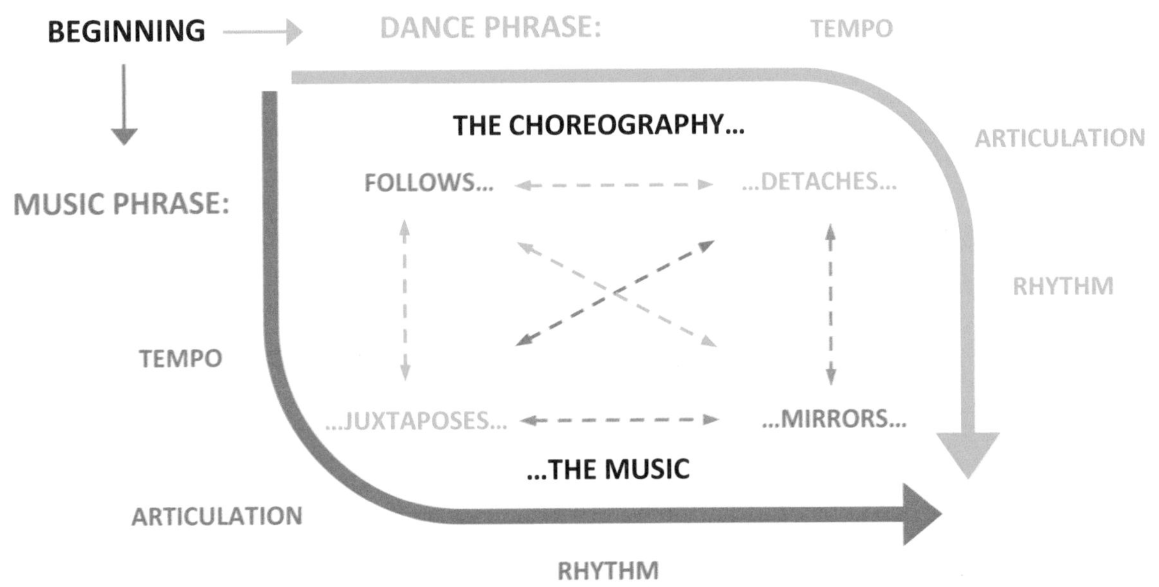

Figure 16

DANCE FOLLOWS AND/OR MIRRORS MUSIC—ATTRACT!

Following and/or mirroring the music means the choreographer will create movement vocabulary and sequence movement patterns that closely correspond to or directly mimic specific musical features, such as structure, melody, mood, tempo, and rhythmic characteristics. This approach is a common artistic practice.

By studying the music in advance, the choreographer may explore how the details and the overall organization of the dance material will relate to the music based on determining their *points of attraction*. The choreographer may also consider choreographing and teaching dance phrases before playing the music. This strategy helps performers become familiar with the dance moves, kinesthetic flow, and rhythmic patterns of the dance phrase prior to hearing the music. Then the dance phrase will merge more smoothly with the musical phrase.

Subsequent mapping of the music and dance sequencing also helps. Measures in most conventional music compositions typically begin with a downbeat, which makes it easy to count and map the musical phrasing. A strong downbeat may appear consistently in the following measures in a recurring rhythmic pattern. Following the downbeat is usually called *following the music*.

However, the counts in the music measures may not always correspond to the counts and length of specific dance moves. In these instances, the choreographer can assist the performers in identifying strategic features in the musical landscape and how these features integrate with the dance phrases.

Alongside the rhythm, melody, and musical structure, the choreographer also determines to what extent dance features will parallel music features. When dance features directly mimic musical features, the approach is usually called *mirroring the music*—see Figure 17:

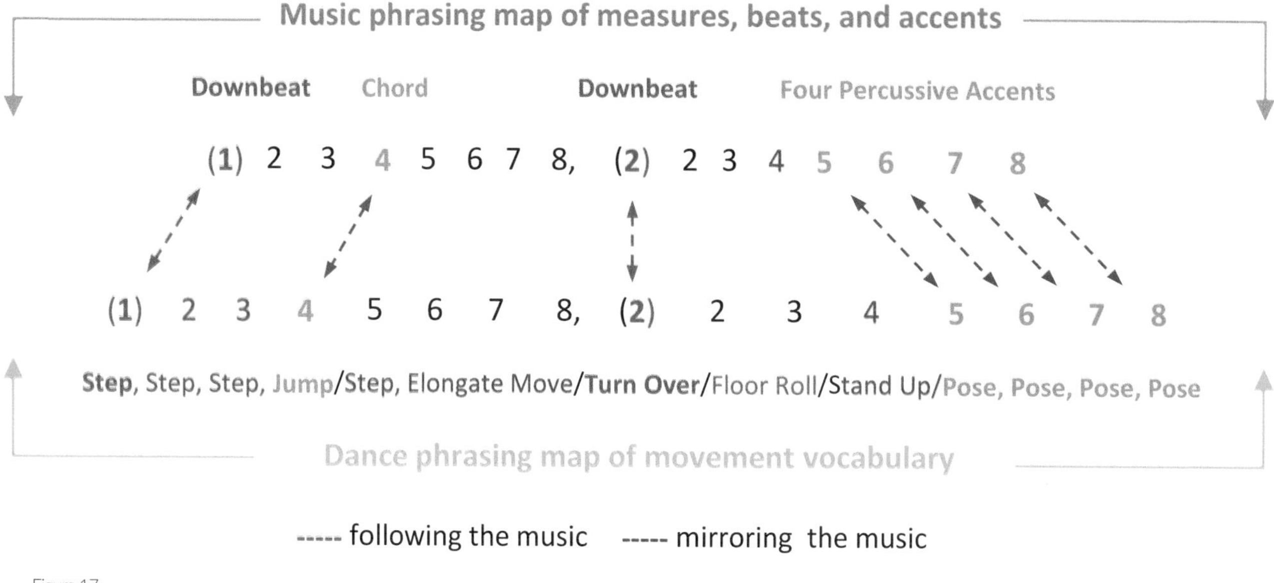

Figure 17

DANCE JUXTAPOSED WITH/OR DETACHED FROM MUSIC—RETRACT!

Choreographers may deliberately choose to retract from mirroring or following musical features and instead contrast or differentiate the features of dance from those in the music. This strategy is not to be confused with "not dancing on the music," where music happens to be present without a conceptual and kinesthetic connection to the dance.

Detaching dance from music is a strategy to reframe and experiment with how dance and music can correlate by separating and differentiating them. It is essential to clarify that the choreographer chooses this approach not because of a dislike of the music. Instead, the reason to retract is to create contrast and calculated tension between music and dance without diminishing the music's importance.

A popular device to create a contrast and a satisfying juxtaposition is syncopation. Syncopation is a purposeful interruption, an intended or unexpected disturbance of the regular rhythmic flow.[14] Syncopation creates displaced accents where they would not typically occur—it is often used in jazz. In dance, for instance, a few music measures which go **1-2-3-1-2-3-1-2-3-1-2-3** can be combined with short dance skips and beats which go on **1-2-1-2-1-2-1-2-1-2-1-2**. The dance on 1-2 will appear faster than the music on 1-2-3.

The dance skips will contrast, yet they will complement the music because the total beats and measures of music will match accordingly with the total beats and measures of dance. If the time signature is 6/4, there will be two measures with six beats in each measure, or if the time signature is 3/4, there will be four measures with three beats in each one. Therefore, in both of these scenarios, every first count of dance and music phrase—the downbeat—will fit with mutual accents, while the rest of it will *appear* as syncopated:

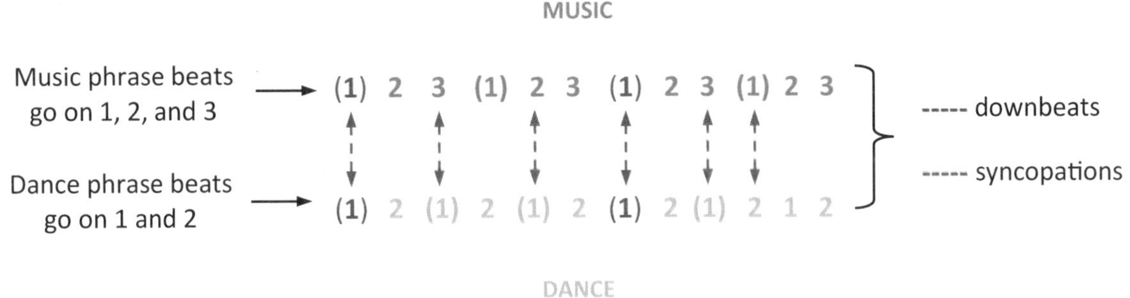

Figure 18

In summary, a slower pace of music does not necessarily dictate a slower pace of dance. Similarly, distinct musical accents and rhythm do not necessarily dictate corresponding dance rhythms and downbeat accents. Juxtaposition, contrast, and pairing of opposites side by side, as a way of highlighting their differences, are exciting devices that compare and explore the distinctions of polarities. Elements that are vastly different or in reverse of each other can still coexist harmoniously. The choreographer may use these available tools to explore and discover new, dynamic interactions between music and dance.

WORKING WITH THE MUSIC
– MUSIC-DRIVEN DANCE OR DANCE USING MUSIC –

In summary, the seven nuanced choreographic approaches to how music relates to dance in Figure 3 of this chapter can be pared down to two distinct strategies for *connecting* music and dance when working with the music. They are:

Music-Driven Dance is when dance features are emerging in correlation with the music features. The music may be the inspiration for a dance to take shape in the first place. Music may inspire movement imagery and influence the flow of the dance. Dance could still be created independently of the music and then merged with selected features of the music. The music-driven dance offers a wide range of options for how music and dance could relate. Rotation of choreographic devices outlined previously, such as *following, mirroring, juxtaposing,* and *detaching,* could still be incorporated.

Dance Using Music is when the music and dance emerge or occur in parallel; however, they transpire independently and without relation to one another. Music and dance features may have very little in common or nothing at all. Music is simply present alongside the dance. Both constructs are summarized in the following diagram:

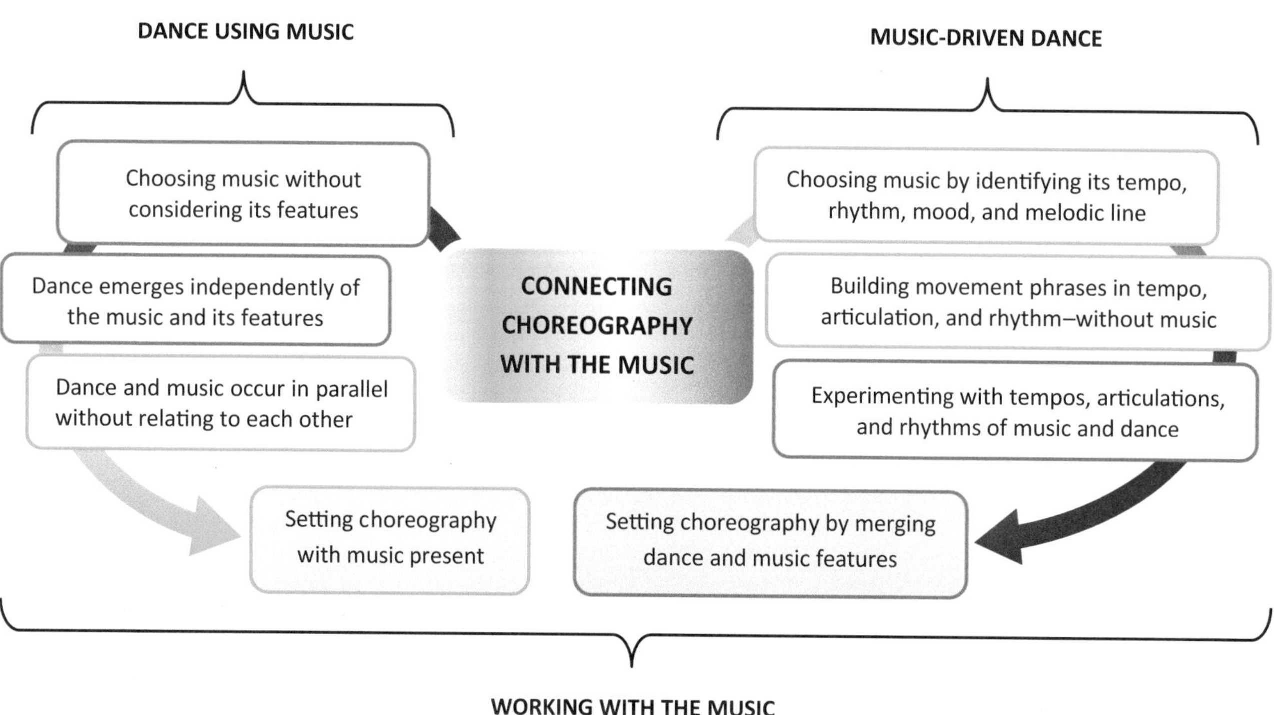

Figure 19

Creating dance and setting choreography with/on/to the music entails a broad spectrum of creative processes and artistic options. As music and dance share a common space, choreographers define their unique approaches and strategies for connecting music and dance in a dynamic relationship of attraction and retraction.

assignments & exercises

RESEARCH AND EXPLORATORY ASSIGNMENTS:

➡ Research dance works created to well-known dance music, such as *Rite of Spring*. Take a look at short segments from at least three versions created by prominent choreographers such as Maurice Béjart, Pina Bausch, Paul Taylor, Mark Morris, and others.

— What are the individual style elements, modern interpretation, and new meaning?

— Describe which interpretation is most appealing to you and why.

— If you were about to improve one element in that production, what would it be?

➡ Research music and listen to several music pieces. Pick your top three choices:

— Why do the music works you chose appeal to you emotionally?

— What do you imagine happening while you're listening to those music pieces?

— What is the one specific music element that makes you relate to the piece of music?

➡ Explore and examine whether you can instantly recognize the music elements of the music you have selected:

— Can you identify the tempo, beat, and rhythm of the music?

— Can you identify the melodic line and the key in which it was written?

— Can you identify the music sections and the transitions, as well as the overall structure?

★ COMPARATIVE, INVESTIGATIVE, AND CREATIVE ASSIGNMENTS:

➡ Create a movement phrase of up to 16 movements. Perform the phrase three separate times under three different music choices, randomly selected, but in specific music genres: for the first, pick a classical music selection; for the second, pick a contemporary orchestral music piece; for the third, pick an electronic music composition.

— How do the different music selections change the perception of the movement phrase?

— Do the music choices affect the movement quality and the choreography, and how?

— Discuss with your peers and colleagues which of the three music pieces best fits the dance, and why.

➡ Return to your initial movement phrase: describe the inspiration for your movement imagery. Based on your description, search for, investigate, and find music that fits your movement with similar images and inspirations:

— What specific search criteria would you set forth to select music that matches your movement?

— What composers who have written music reflecting your imagery and inspiration would you include in your search?

— In your investigation, would you consider music of different historical periods, world locations, and genres that are less familiar to your culture and to you?

➥ After choosing one piece of music, preferably no longer than three minutes, map the score by identifying repeating patterns, counting the measures/bars, and determining how they are grouped in sequences:

— Align your movement phrase to the map of the music score and see how your movement material fits the length of the music. Is the music too short or too long?

— Use the choreographic devices, manipulation, and alterations in tempo, articulation, and rhythm to fit the movement phrase in the mapped music length. What are the biggest challenges?

— To what extent was the movement phrase completely altered by complying with the music structure, and did the movement phrase become more or less effective when adapted to the music map?

CREATIVE AND EXPLORATORY ASSIGNMENTS IN THE FORM OF PLAYFUL GAMES:

Figure 20 Photography © Lois Greenfield, pictured David Pakenham, Ramona Staffeld, courtesy of Vanaver Caravan, 2006

➥ **GAME 1:** Look at a fragment of a dance piece created by a prominent choreographer online, on video, or on TV. Then, look at the same piece again while muting the sound. Do the movement language and the overall choreography hold their artistic merit and impact while the music is muted and with ambient sound absent?

➥ **GAME 2:** Imagine that the dance music you just heard is composed for a movie, and you are about to create a dance to it. What actions do you imagine on the screen? What would you say if the music is poetry or text in the background?

➥ **GAME 3:** Pretend you are a composer and think of a simple melody. Think of a simple regular or irregular rhythm and merge the melody with your rhythm. Record it on a sound device and ask your peers what they think of your creation, what kind of emotion and movement it evokes, and what type of dance they could imagine and create.

BIBLIOGRAPHY AND REFERENCES

[1] Editors. *Physical Musicality and the Balanchine Tradition*, article, March 2019, online resource: www.interlochen.org/story/physical-musicality-and-balanchine-tradition, accessed May 2019.
[2] Kaderlan, Alice. "The Meticulous Musicality of Mark Morris," article, *The Seattle Times*, November 13, 2015, online resource: www.seattletimes.com/entertainment/dance/the-meticulous-musicality-of-mark-morris/, accessed May 2019.
[3] Schwarm, Betsy. "The Rite of Spring," in *Encyclopedia Britannica, Inc*., article, December 11, 2014, online resource: www.britannica.com/topic/The-Rite-of-Spring, accessed May 2019.
[4] Levitin, Daniel J. "What Does It Mean to Be Musical?" *Neuron Magazine, Science Direct*, vol. 73, no. 4, February 23, 2012, pp. 633–637.
[5] Wolf, Anna and Kopiez, Reinhard. "Development and Validation of the Musical Ear Training Assessment (META)," *Journal of Research in Music Education*. First Published February 6, 2018, research article: https://doi.org/10.1177/0022429418754845.
[6] Bent, Ian D. "Musical Notation," in *Encyclopedia Britannica, Inc*. Published December 18, 2019, online article, resources: www.britannica.com/art/musical-notation, accessed May 2019.
[7] Manoff, Tom. *Music: A living Language*, W.W. Norton & Company, 1982, pp. 10, 11, 83.
[8] Lilliestam, Lars. "Research on Music Listening: From Typologies to Interviews with Real People," *Volume! Magazine*, vol. 10, no. 1, 2013, online since 30 December 2013, http://journals.openedition.org/volume/3733; https://doi.org/10.4000/volume.3733, accessed May 2019.
[9] O'Brian, James Patrick. *The Listening Experience, Elements, Forms and Styles in Music*, Schirmer Books, 1995, p. 49.
[10] O'Brian 1995. *The Listening Experience*, pp. 54–55.
[11] O'Brian 1995. *The Listening Experience*, pp. 78–80, 98–99.
[12] O'Brian 1995. *The Listening Experience*, pp. 33–49.
[13] Bradley, Steven. *3 Types of Rhythm You Can Create Visually*, October 22, 2012, Web article: http://vanseodesign.com/web-design/visual-rhythm/ , accessed May 2019.
[14] O'Brian 1995. *The Listening Experience*, pp. 58–59, 370.

VISUAL REFERENCES

Figure 1: Diagram © Vladimir Angelov

Figure 2: Diagram © Vladimir Angelov, Clipart: *Vector illustration of colorful music notes background, abstract sign and symbol*, Credit: radenmas, courtesy of iStock/Getty Image

Figure 3: Diagram © Vladimir Angelov

Figure 4: Image right: Photography © Herbert Migdoll, *The Rite of Spring* (1913), choreography by Vaslav Nijinsky, performed by The Joffrey Ballet, 1987; Image center: Photography © Sasha Gouliaev, *Rite of Spring*, 1975, choreography by Pina Bausch, center performer Tsai-Wei Tien, surrounded by performers of Tanztheater Wuppertal Pina Bausch, 2018; Image left: Photography © Tom Caravaglia, *Le Sacre du Printemps (The Rehearsal)*, 1980, choreography by Paul Taylor, Paul Taylor Dance Company, performed by Annmaria Mazzini and Michael Trusnovec, 2008

Figure 5: *Cute children playing instruments in a marching band parade*, illustration by Aleutie, courtesy of iStock/Getty Image

Figure 6: *Musical bar/measure*, diagram and design © Charles Scheland

Figure 7: *Notes and rests, diagram and design* © Charles Scheland

Figure 8: *Bar line and double bar line*: Image © Huji, *Microtonal Accidentals in Different Music Systems* (CC BY-SA 4.0), 2017, public domain, edited by Charles Scheland, 2021

Figure 9: *Measure 1, 2, 3*: Image © Thepriest75, Hauptthema 1. Satz, *Hummel Trompetenkonzert* (CC BY-SA 4.0), 2020, public domain, edited by Charles Scheland, 2021

Figures 10 ,11, 12, 13, and 14: Diagrams © Vladimir Angelov

Figure 15 Photography © Lois Greenfield, pictured Defne Enc, Antonio Hidalgo Paz, courtesy of Flamenco Vivo Carlota Santana, 2006

Figures 16, 17, 18, and 19: Diagrams © Vladimir Angelov

Figure 20: Photography © Lois Greenfield, pictured David Pakenham, Ramona Staffeld, courtesy of Vanaver Caravan, 2006

Not everything that counts can be counted,

and not everything that can be counted counts.

Albert Einstein (1879–1955)

CHAPTER 22

BODY OF SOUND
– DANCING SILENCE, NOISE, SOUNDSCAPE, AND SPOKEN WORD –

In addition to creating traditional music-based dances, many choreographers in the past and present have been interested in using various sonic elements to create sound-based dances. An extensive dance heritage has integrated human movement with sound. In many instances, dance can produce both sound and music. With the development of digital sound technology, more resources are available for such artistic endeavors.

Music, as mentioned in the previous chapter, triggers a range of conceptual and aesthetic responses. Sound and noise may trigger a range of instinctive responses. For example, the opening music sequence in Act One of Richard Wagner's *Die Walküre* (The Valkyrie), as part of The Ring cycle, depicts a raging storm that builds a sense of fear and impending destruction—powerful, harsh, and almost militaristic.[1] Similarly, during a real military offensive, the noise of explosions and the sounds of the military sirens produce a sensation of anxiety, the urge to escape, and the lookout for safety. While music is primarily abstract, sounds and noise are primarily specific.

As part of the choreography, speaking and speech—verbalization and spoken word— effectively enhance movement with thought-provoking imagery. Envision reciting excerpts of commanding poetry ranging from Shakespeare to Maya Angelou. Silence in dance is a powerful tool to emphasize the intensity of movement by eliminating auditory references.

These sonic elements —silence, noise, sound, music, and speech—used separately or in various combinations, could physicalize distinct sonic bodies available for choreographic exploration:

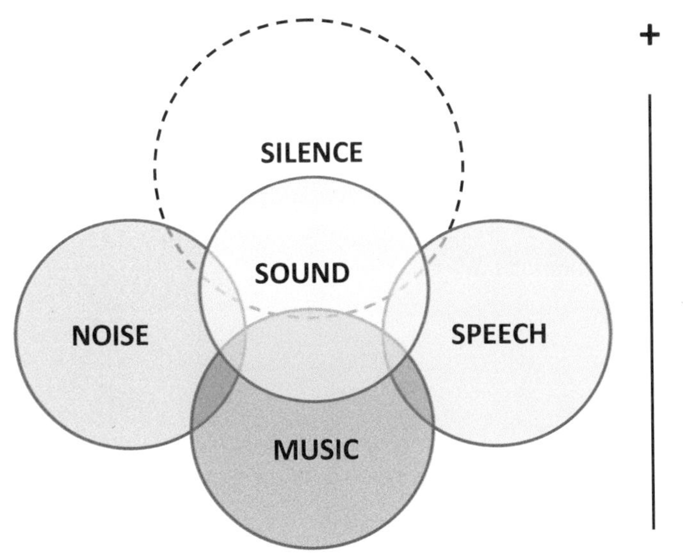

Figure 1

+ DANCE:

Silence + Silence = Quiet Body

Silence + Noise = Breathing Body

Noise + Sound + Music = Sounding Body

Sound + Speech + Noise = Vocalizing Body

Speech + Sound + Noise = Verbalizing Body

Sound + Music + Speech = Singing Body

Noise + Sound + Music + Speech = Soundscape Body

Let's begin with the descriptions and the functions of the primary sonic elements, then explore how they interact with the creative process of choreography.

Noise and sound result from *air vibrations* in the surroundings creating different levels of air pressure through higher and lower compression and decompression. The vibrations travel across the air in waves and create sounds perceived by the sense of hearing.[2]

The physical properties of sounds, noise, music, and speech and their intensity, strength, and loudness are measured in decibels (dB). Sounds with a higher dB value are louder. More robust sounds starting from 120 dB can be considered as noise. Hertz (Hz) is a unit measuring sound frequency. The higher the frequency, the higher the pitch, and the more disturbing the sound becomes.[3] Below are other definitions for this chapter:

➢ **Silence** is a purposeful absence of sound, noise, and music. The presence of silence is a powerful device to frame what happened before or after the occurrence of sound. When silence is used with explicit intention and calculated timing, it might imply a particular purpose and importance. We could refer to it as the *loudest silence.*

➢ **Noise** is chaotic, sporadic, and uneven, with irregular quality of constantly fluctuating vibrations in a seemingly uncontrolled manner.[4] Noise can originate in the environment—from nature, with its gentle forest sounds, to the big city, with its traffic jams and bustling industries. If there is too much noise from many sources simultaneously, we could refer to it as *noise pollution.*

➢ **Sound** is more organized and periodic than noise, and it has regular vibration characteristics.[5] Sound is figurative. One can hear and envision something without seeing it. Sounds give clues about place and space, distance and origin. Sound can have a specific pitch that is pleasing to the ears. There is an intimate connection between the sound source and the sound recipient.[6] We could refer to this sound bonding as *sound figures.*

➢ **Spoken Word** is verbal communication that expresses thoughts in semantic sounds—the spoken word. While a notated text provides content in writing, speaking is always vocal. Historically, spoken words preceded written text. Spoken language enables us to understand, communicate and handle the complexity in the world. Spoken words are similar to a "verbal photo lens," which can capture reality and its meaning. We could refer to spoken words as *sound images.*

➢ **Music** is an artistic representation of sound. Music is organized in time and contains expressive elements and intentional patterns. Random sounds might become music when one or more music elements are present, such as rhythm, pitch, melody, harmony, and dynamics, as well as sonic qualities, such as timbre and texture[7]—see Chapter 20. Innovative combinations of the musical elements are arranged in compositional structures with mastery and the purpose to capture ideas, impressions, and emotions. We can refer to music as an assembly of *sound symbolism.*

CHOREOGRAPHING SEVEN SONIC BODIES

Choreographers use different sound sources and ways of movement to produce sounds, which can appear separately or in combinations to reach a desired artistic effect. Sonic events in choreography can be described in a few significant categories—see Figure 2. In addition to the sound's intensity, strength, and frequency, choreographers might consider how *volume* and its range will appropriately relate to the surroundings. Sound waves travel differently during an outdoor performance than in a concert hall, museum, or small intimate dance space. Therefore, consideration of the architecture and the properties of the performance space where a sound-based dance will occur is essential for the quality, control, and transmission of sound—the *acoustic environment*.

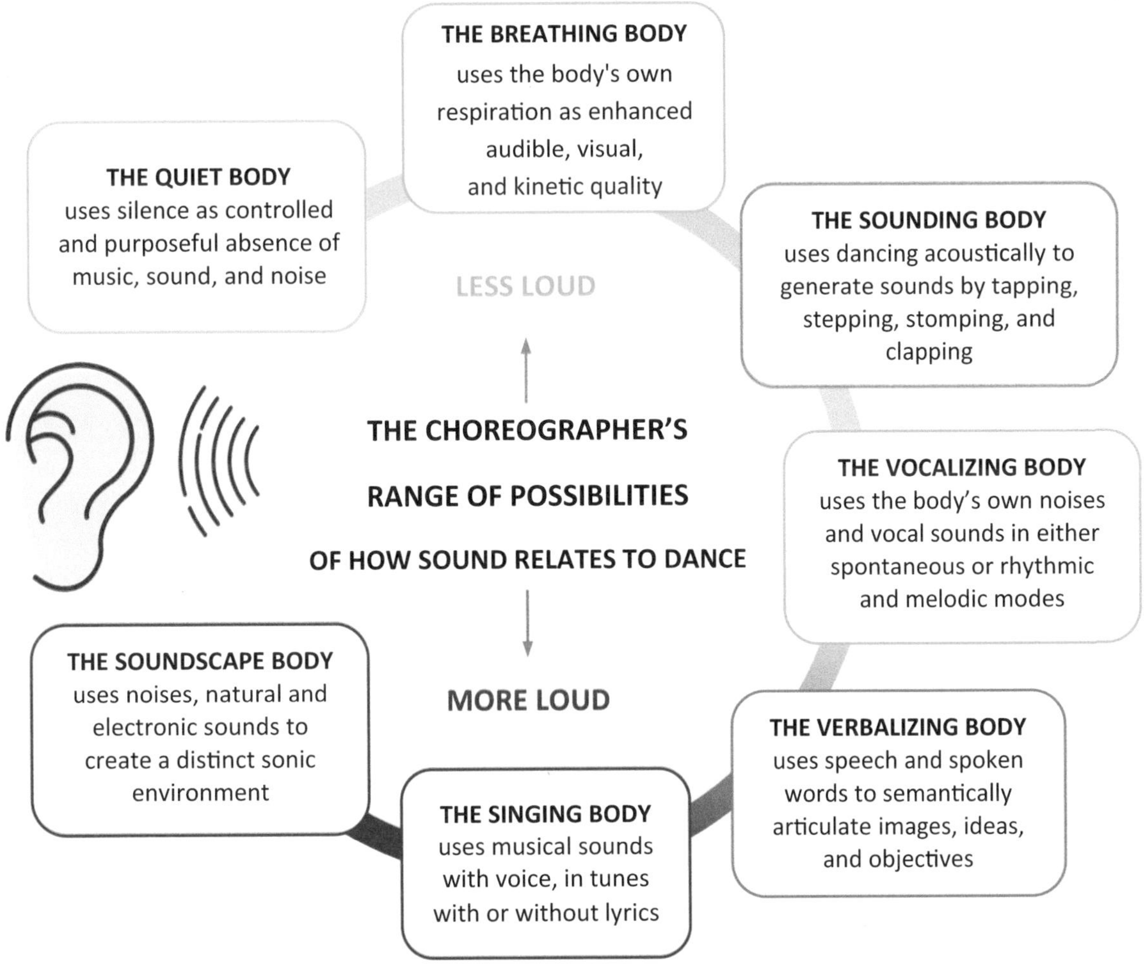

THE BREATHING BODY uses the body's own respiration as enhanced audible, visual, and kinetic quality

THE QUIET BODY uses silence as controlled and purposeful absence of music, sound, and noise

THE SOUNDING BODY uses dancing acoustically to generate sounds by tapping, stepping, stomping, and clapping

LESS LOUD

THE CHOREOGRAPHER'S RANGE OF POSSIBILITIES OF HOW SOUND RELATES TO DANCE

MORE LOUD

THE VOCALIZING BODY uses the body's own noises and vocal sounds in either spontaneous or rhythmic and melodic modes

THE SOUNDSCAPE BODY uses noises, natural and electronic sounds to create a distinct sonic environment

THE VERBALIZING BODY uses speech and spoken words to semantically articulate images, ideas, and objectives

THE SINGING BODY uses musical sounds with voice, in tunes with or without lyrics

Figure 2

?

Which of these approaches are most appealing to you and why?

THE QUIET BODY

– MOTION IN SILENCE–SILENCE IN MOTION –

There is an assumption that dance should always be paired with music. However, the foundation of dance—human movement—occurs without music. We wake up in the morning and go to work. We speak with friends and family without music accompaniment. We also do not need corresponding sound and matching noise to accomplish our goals.

In dance, silence is the purposeful absence of music, sound, and noise. Choreographers use silence as a *controlled sonic strategy* to let movement emerge in the negative space of a predictable sound experience. Dancing in silence eliminates any explicit or implicit audible framework. Silence seems to pause time, and it provides a chance to rest, breathe, meditate, think, and concentrate; it opens space for a new interpretation of a movement event.

But is there *true silence*? A conceptual work of music by John Cage entitled *4' 33"*, for example, did not have a single musical tone. The pianist sat at the piano and closed the keyboard lid. Instead of music performed in a traditional concert setting, the initial impression was that the audience had been subjected to silence. The audience became aware of the existing sounds around them. No matter how quiet it was, one began to hear a "symphony" of accidental sounds that occurred in the surroundings after a while.[8]

Dancing in silence is unusual; it might feel awkward and uncomfortable for the performers and the audience. One might wonder how dance is possible without a guiding rhythm and melody. The truth is that movement has its internal energy, pulse, and rhythm. We can *hear dance* without its music.

Dancing in silence amplifies the dance and the movement, and therefore, only exceptionally powerful dance can be effective in silence. The choreographer is no longer focused on creating a dance without music but on creating a dance in silence.[9] Therefore, dance in silence is power and burden. Dance in silence is about finding inner music: What do you feel when you move? What do you hear when you feel? How do you move to what you hear? Many choreographers create material first in silence before implementing music. Purposeful avoidance of music helps dance makers focus entirely on the choreography.

Figure 3 Photography © Costas, *Moves* (1959) choreography Jerome Robbins, performed by members of the New York City Ballet, NYC, courtesy of Costas, 2010. *Moves* is ballet without music accompaniment, which explores various moods, dynamics, formations, and relations between the dancers

THE BREATHING BODY

– DANCING WITH THE FLOW AND ACCENTS OF THE AIRSTREAM –

Breathing is an organic part of life and dance, and it occurs whether we think about it or not. Efficient breathing is also integral to a choreographer's work. Breathing normally, or holding, controlling, and channeling breath in specific ways, has been implemented in various techniques that are often used during training and choreographic practices. In concert dance, forms of audible and visible breathing have been increasingly accepted and embraced in recent times.[10] However, that has not always been the case.

During the 18th and 19th centuries, breathing in ballet choreography had a supportive rather than fundamental role. Breathing was "hidden" inside the bodies of otherworldly stage creatures, such as sylphs and swans. Sustained breath accommodated higher jumping, while a controlled diaphragm helped multiply pirouettes. Audible breathing on stage was unacceptable and perceived as unsophisticated. Performers quietly endured strenuous dancing until they exited the stage, where they could catch their breath behind the curtains.

During the early 20th century, Duncan, Graham, and Humphrey developed modern dance techniques that implemented breathing as a part of their dance aesthetic and training. Artistic philosophies emerged that embraced breathing and movement as naturally connected, sustaining elements of dance and life. Articulated and audible breathing became a kinesthetic doctrine that all movements *emerge* from inhaling and exhaling.

During the early 21st century, contemporary choreographers began to use breath as a purposeful demonstration of the act of breathing. Audible and visible breathing were often implemented to emphasize movement intensity and physical sensation, bring attention to bodily rhythms and locomotive accents, and articulate the organic connection between movement and breath as part of the often extreme physical act of dancing.

Contemporary choreographers working today are attracted to how breathing affects the quality of a movement. Inhalation is often used to emphasize expansive movements and exhalation to extend contracting movements. Anticipated, coordinated, and calculated use of breath provides greater fluidity of movement, emphasizes physicality, helps dancers endure movement dynamics, and improves stamina. Breathing while dancing is healthier.[11]

Intentional breathing during dancing is a movement within a movement. Breathing follows movement, and movement follows breathing—they can work in sync or in contrast. Breathing has its biological rhythm, which the choreographer can tune in to. Dance causes our breathing patterns to change when movement accelerates in intensity and speed.[12] Choreographers can cultivate and implement a variety of breath-phrasing technical elements. For example, a deep and short breath, a sustained inhale, and a sudden exhale like a quick staccato burst to blow out a candle—are all examples of breathing qualities to which dancing bodies have instant access. Audible inhaling and exhaling can become an organic part of the dance.

THE SOUNDING BODY

– GENRES AND INSPIRATIONS IN PERCUSSIVE DANCING –

The moving human body is a musical instrument capable of creating sounds and rhythmic patterns. The hands, arms, legs, feet, torso, voice, and tongue can generate an acoustic range of sounds and percussive rhythms as the sole sound score of a dance. A sounding body can also enhance rhythmic and vocal accompaniment to dance music.[13] There is a rich heritage of choreographic forms that produce percussive noises and sounds as their signature element. These dance forms can be classified historically, geographically, stylistically, or by their rhythmic characteristics and by how percussive sounds are produced. The choreography employs either singularly or in combination:

- **Tapping and stomping feet**, including bare feet, feet with ankle bells, or specific customized footwear, clogs, boots, and other footwear.
- **Clapping and slapping hands against the body**, including bare hands or using various accessories such as castanets, wooden boxes, and other noise-making objects.
- **Rhythmic vocal accompaniment**, including shouting, screaming, vocalization, verbalization, chanting, and acoustic integration of the tongue.

Figure 4 Photography © Matthew Murphy and Ken Tam, pictured tap dancer and choreographer Michelle Dorrance, 2013

For example, English, German, Scottish, and American Clog-Dancing produce sounds against the floor surface. However, producing sounds in Kathak, Haka, Flamenco, and Step Dance is different. What is behind the percussiveness of a dance?

- **Kathak**, for example, is an Indian storytelling-based dance that employs fast and syncopated footwork. The calculated rhythmic sequences depict emotions such as love and anger, illustrate soundscapes of blowing wind and raging river, and portray acoustic characteristics of the unfolding action throughout the dance.[14]

- **Haka** is a New Zealand war dance, originally performed by warriors before a battle, proclaiming their commitment to fight and demonstrating their strength to intimidate the opposition. Employed are vigorous rhythmic body actions, such as stomping feet and slapping hands against the torso and legs, chanted words, and various cries and grunts.

➢ **Flamenco** originated in Southern Spain and was associated with influences of the Romani people. The proud carriage of the overall body, the expressive use of curved arms, and the virtuoso rhythmic stamping of the feet portray inner emotional intensity, existential struggle, and yet control.[15] The clapping hands and vocalization encourage interactions with fellow performers, leading to a joint meditative trance and communal percussive dance prayer.

➢ **Irish Stepping** is related to traditional Gaelic arts and European folk dance jigs. It is characterized by a contained upper body and precise movements of the feet to the music accompaniment. In addition to soft shoes, "hard shoes" with metal elements enhance the sound with rapid, complex percussive rhythms and accents.[16] The genre intends to capture and demonstrate national identity. A sporting spirit drives the participants to out-dance one other's percussive virtuosity while competing as soloists or in groups.

➢ **American Tap Dance** is rooted in the fusion of several ethnic percussive dances, including African tribal dances, English clog dancing, and Irish jig. Syncopated footwork occurs in combination with sound produced by a metal "tap" on the heels and the toes of the shoes as they strike the floor. There are two major variations in tap dance: Broadway tap focuses on dancing to music and songs, and it is widely popular in musical theater. Rhythm tap focuses on musicality, where most tap artists consider themselves dancing musicians and part of the jazz tradition.[17]

➢ **Stepping or Step Dancing** draws movement influences from African foot dances, such as Gumboot, which was originally conceived by miners in South Africa as an alternative to drumming to communicate allegiance to a group. Sound is produced by synchronized rhythmic movement with a cappella percussive patterns of/on the entire body.[18] Influences from the United States date back to when enslaved Africans were forbidden to own drums, so they started slapping their hands rhythmically against their bodies.[19] The human body became the drum.

➢ **Stomping**, after the group "Stomp," is a joyful, witty, and wordless contemporary rhythmic expression capturing the noises of today's urban society, and it is a social commentary on consumer drive. Everything around us can produce beat and rhythm. Percussion sequences are humorously performed with found objects such as push brooms, wooden poles, hammer handles, garbage cans, inner tubes, Zippo lighters, and even a kitchen sink.

➢ **Percussive dance** in contemporary choreography and performance art continuously explores new expressive tools. In 1998, Sarah Rudner choreographed *HeartBeat:mb*, a solo performed by Mikhail Baryshnikov, who also had an improvisational impact on the choreography.[20]

In *HeartBeat:mb*, Baryshnikov wears wireless electrodes taped to his chest, which transmit his heartbeat live and directly to onstage loudspeakers. As the dancer engages aerobically, the heartbeat increases and he continues to dance to the beat of his own heart. The work is a fascinating artistic and conceptual experiment where the dancer is a percussionist, the percussionist is a heart, and the heart is a dancer.[21]

?

Have you trained in any of these dance genres and have you used any of these techniques in your choreography? If so, what kind of enjoyment and challenges have you experienced?

THE VOCALIZING BODY
– THINKING OUTSIDE THE [VOICE] BOX –

The human voice is as fundamental as breath and movement. The voice is a powerful instrument that is able to generate sounds of healing and reassurance, unity and emotion. The brain receives and evaluates the voice's resonance, rhythm, range, register, inflection, and volume, recognizing the vocal source's identity and intentions.

The voice is communicative and connective. When babies are just born and before they can see, they first hear their mother's voice. Speech and words are irrelevant at this moment. It is the timbre and the softness of the mother's voice that calms the crying newborn. A gently sung lullaby portrays a sonic flow of descending and rising tones, painting a comforting view of a fairytale soundscape.

The voice is fragile yet painfully truthful. Psychoanalytic expert Sigmund Freud sat his patients on a couch facing away from him. Such positioning was intentional, enabling the doctor focus on the voice to identify key emotional nuances: from suicidal tendencies and neuroticism to aggression and anger. Voice sincerely reflects the stored information the patients have taken in from a variety of life experiences.[22]

Voice, movement, and dance are organically related to bodily activities and range from running daily routines to creative movement practices. A group of Yoga practitioners will chant a meditative and prolonged "OM" to bring together the physicality of movement and the power of sound, body, and voice. Spanish Flamenco ensemble performers will rhythmically shout "¡Olé!" at the soloist during her passionate dance routine. Bulgarian folkloric dancers holding each other's hands in a Horo-group serpentine formation will jointly roar a percussive vocalization of "Ha-ta-ka!" to emphasize energy in unison.

Figure 5 Photography © Jaclyn Borowski, *The Matter of Origins*, choreography by Liz Lerman, The Liz Lerman Dance Exchange, 2010. Choreographer Liz Lerman extensively uses vocalization, verbalization, singing, spoken word and written word in her dance works

Nonverbal vocalization in dance is primal and intuitive and could be visceral and emotional. Choreographers may organically vocalize when they generate movements and demonstrate steps to the performers. Such raw vocalizations emerging during the creative process range from meditative concentration to expressing ecstasy, or both at the same time.

The organic voice-body connection naturally leads to the use of vocalization in any dance. The choreographer creates and encourages performers to produce *spontaneous or purposeful vocalization* with the intention to: a) convey emotions vocally during a dance; b) link a sound expression to a movement articulation; c) emphasize a dramatic element of the performance loudly or use a vocal cue to change a dance formation.

Vocalizing during movement puts extra pressure on the dancers. The cardiovascular nature of movement affects breathing patterns, which are essential to produce effective vocalization. Complex movement material could interfere with the effective use of voice and might require rearrangements in the choreography. Therefore, establishing an organic connection and synchronization between the use of movement and voice is essential.

Contemporary choreographers have access to a variety of vocalizing techniques. Whether the vocalization is prerecorded or performed live by the dancers, the choreographer undertakes the role of both composer and voice teacher. There are a few approaches that are used often.

Extended vocal techniques in music for dance are unconventional, unorthodox, or non-traditional approaches to produce and manipulate sounds or unusual timbres by using the human voice.[23] A summary of these techniques includes, but is not limited to, the following categories:

➢ **Speech-singing** is a technique that is a cross between singing and speaking. There is also *speech level singing*, which produces tones at speech level. Some pitches are sung, but the articulation is rapid and loose like speech. The non-intelligible language might be used purposely to emphasize sound quality rather than to verbally communicate a narrative.

➢ **Vocal multiphonics and polyphonic overtones** are singing similar to chanting, or harmonic and throat singing. This vocal technique, believed to originate in Mongolia, allows the human voice to produce two sounds at once. The sound is characterized by piercing, flute-like harmonics similar to whistling; however, one can hear the extra sounds in the single one.

➢ **Ululation** is a long, wavering, high-pitched, and usually protracted vocal sound resembling a howl. Ululation is often full of emotion and it is a common vocal expression of sorrow, joy, celebration, or reverence in many cultures. Humming, by contrast, is a neutral, steady, and continuous sound.

➢ **Vocal percussion, beatboxing, and tongue clucking** involve vocal and mouth sounds that imitate percussion instruments and drumming. Vocal percussion in Western music, known as *beatboxing*, originates in hip-hop, while in ancient music traditions of India, for example, a percussionist recites the composition about to be played.

➢ **Growling, screaming, and shouting** are produced by using extra pressure on the throat. The vocal cords produce loud noises and sounds of high intensity and pitch. Screaming is a loud, piercing cry or cries expressing emotions such as joy, excitement, anger, grief, or pain. Shouting is vocalizing or verbalizing loudly and it is traditionally used to get someone's attention.

➢ **Whispering and whistling, panting and sucking** are created by alternating breathing and manipulating the sonic space between sound, voice, and voicelessness. In whispering, the voice volume changes, leading to voiceless speech. In whistling, the air is blown or sucked through a small lip opening, creating sound by a mini-turbulence; it could also be assisted by a curled tongue, teeth, or fingers placed over the mouth.

➢ **Barking, roaring, and chirping** are initiated by mimicking animal noises, living creatures, and sound phenomena originating in nature or humans. These sounds can be vocally reproduced in a direct and literal manner, in a variety of modifications. Noises could be formed as a naming interpretation, for example, in *onomatopoeia*.

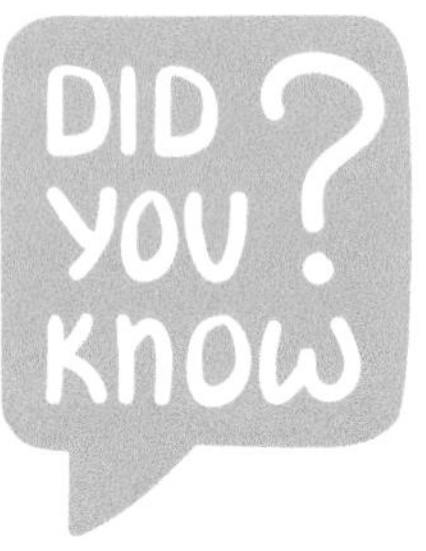

***Onomatopoeia* is the formation of a word by imitation of a sound made by or associated with its referent.[24] Common occurrences of onomatopoeia include the noise of a large dog—*wuff, ruff, arf, au au, borf, bow-wow*, and for a small dog—*yip*. Other transliterations could include: *Honk! Boom! Bang! Crash! Onomatopoeia* can differ between languages, and it conforms to the broader linguistic system. For example, the sound of a clock may be expressed as *tick tock* in English, *tictac* in Spanish, *dī dā* in Mandarin, or *katchin katchin* in Japanese. It seems that a clock speaks many languages.**

THE VERBALIZING BODY

– WHEN MOVEMENT AND TEXT COME TOGETHER OR FALL APART –

Movement and dance are non-verbal languages, while text and speaking are semantic communication. During daily rehearsal, the choreographer describes movements and verbalizes musical features while counting measures. Movement nuances are explained verbally to provide the performers with content, context, and intent.

Text and movement are related, and so are speaking and dance. Dancers might be asked to vocalize and verbalize text on stage as part of the dance. The choreographer's artistic interest in verbal and linguistic investigations might vary widely in complexity and range.

Vocalization and verbalization differ in substance. Vocalization operates with noises and sounds, while verbalization operates with text that is spoken. Under the direction of the choreographer, dancers might use noises, sounds, single words or short phrases, descriptive paragraphs, literary quotations, or poems.

Words can be spoken live or prerecorded. A recording by a professional actor reciting an existing or original script could be more effective than a dancer struggling to pronounce the same text. On the other hand, a heartfelt prayer whispered live and reenacted by the dancer's movement could be more impactful than recording it.

The process of text-to-body and speech-to-movement is fundamentally natural. Text and speech are processed differently by the brain than movement, yet they are organically connected. For example, when we talk about how we feel, we also spontaneously gesture with our hands. In a certain way, our body motion fills the gaps left by the speaking.

Speaking can comfortably exist in a dance performance. The audience will realize that the dancers are humans who can talk, joke, and giggle, or be verbally informative about their intentions of a nonliteral movement, for example. Much dance vocabulary comprises synonyms of spoken words. As written by choreographer Liz Lerman in her 1994 essay *By All Possible Means: A Look at the Relationship Between Words and Movement*, when the spoken word is used during movement, dance becomes not only "presentational," but also "conversational."[25]

◆ **CHOREOGRAPHING TO SPOKEN NARRATION** is using spoken word as semantic envelopment for dance. Narration could include prose works of literature; formal or informal announcements; explicit or rhetorical statements; lectures; speeches; homilies or storytelling; monologues or dialogues; group discussions or debates; and elements of dramatic plays. The choreographer might experiment with various ways to integrate speaking with movement. For example, the dancers could talk while dancing, or stop dancing and start talking; or some could talk while other cast members move speechlessly, etc. Other essential components of spoken narration in dance are:

➢ **Authoring and/or quoting words?** Spoken words might originate from an intellectual source—a text generated by the author, who could be a writer, a choreographer, or the performers. As that text is meant to be spoken, it turns into a *script* of a verbal narration, a speech score, or a verbal collage. The text could be written, read, memorized, or improvised. It could be spoken live or prerecorded, or a combination of both.

While it is less demanding to repeat something written by someone else—a *quotation*—it is more challenging for the choreographer to become the *author* of the original text. The choreographer becomes a writer by entering a new art form that uses words with unique ideas and an authentic voice. Good writing skills involve reading, writing, describing, editing, and rewriting, in addition to observation, exploration, and imagination. Other nuances are text and sub-text, written words versus spoken words, casual speech versus formal speech, etc.

In some cases, quoted and original wording might co-exist and interact. For example, the choreographer might use the well-known "I have a dream..." speech by Dr. Martin Luther King, Jr., and then insert their verbal commentary and additional narration.

➢ **Talking and/or saying words?** Talking in daily life is different from speaking on stage, especially for dancers, who are predominately trained to use their bodies. However, speaking on stage requires a new set of performance skills. Simply talking while dancing might not always be effective. The choreographer is already a public speaker by talking to the dancers in rehearsal. Yet speaking in a casual or work setting is not the same as speaking on stage and acting on the words.

Spoken language on stage is about *how something is said*, including word articulation, accentuation, pronunciation, amplification, voice modulation, emotional charge, breathing (or taking breaths), regional or foreign accents, and cultural connotations. For example, depending on the nuances of the voice, the question "Are you serious?" could mean "Now you made me pay attention." However, it could also mean "It sounds too good to be true" or "This is impossible." The *text* is the same, but the *meaning* is different depending on the manner in which the words are *spoken*.

➢ **Speaking and/or visualizing words?** Using spoken word in dance comes with greater complexities than setting movements to instrumental music. Proportionality and balance are needed for verbal and nonverbal languages to merge into a single language.

The audience responds differently to the meaning of words and movement. A verbal statement relates to a movement statement in various ways: a) the meaning of the spoken words may be unrelated to the dance, b) the spoken words may be conceptually/thematically connected to the dance, or c) the spoken words may be visualized/mimicked by the dance.

Speaking and dancing co-exist most effectively when they are bridged out of necessity. When the movement language cannot clearly express all thought, a verbal narration can provide context and semantically convey the content.

At the same time, spoken words tend to be overwhelming. The choreography becomes almost subservient to spoken words when the narrated text is more exciting and engaging than the dance. The objective is to strike a perfectly balanced trajectory between speaking and moving—like a pendulum, which swings equally in two opposite directions without prioritizing either of them—see Figure 6.

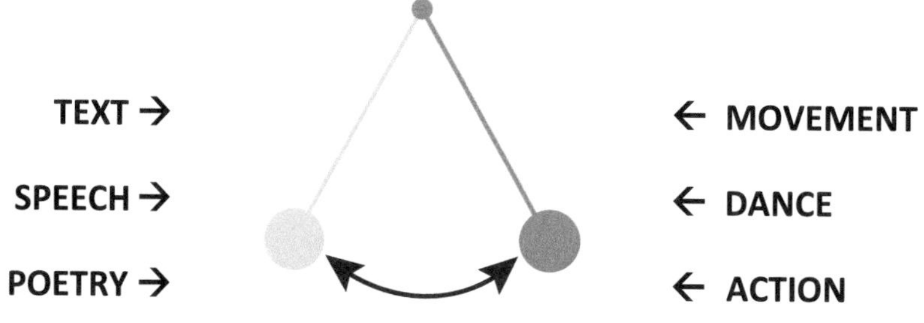

Figure 6

◆ **CHOREOGRAPHING TO POETRY** uses poems as spoken words to create the environment for dance. While verbal narration is geared toward providing narrative and information, poetry is an art form with attention to the intense expression of feelings and ideas in a distinctive style. Poems are like musical scores, and the choreographer might consider treating them as musical works.

Poetry is meant to be spoken or sung, not read. The choreographer can think of it as the music of the mind and soul. Similar to dance and music, poetry contains *patterns, rhythm, pulse, and rhyme*, which in dance is equivalent to symmetry. Basic poetry is written in verse form called *stanzas*, and it is made up of *meter*, organized in a *chorus* and *refrain*. The stanzas could also be *blank verse*—verse without rhyme—yet have rhythm established by the words in that line.

Poetry uses sound and linguistic imagery. Poetry functions independently of movement but can harmoniously interact with movement and dance on multiple levels:

➢ **Kinesthetic use:** Certain words appear to cause the poet's mouth to imitate the described objects. Diminutive words like "teeny weeny" describe something small, while "large" and "huge" describe big things. Such characteristics can affect dance vocabulary.

➢ **Qualitative use:** While choreography uses "speedy" and "staccato" devices to manipulate and emphasize certain movement qualities, poetry also uses "sharp" and "cutting" phonetics of spoken words to describe certain linguistic qualities. In this context, dance and poetry share cross-modal abstraction, and could achieve the same effect by using different ways of expression.

➢ **Integrative use:** Poetic imagery captured in sounds and semantics can be imitated by bodily motion and physical actions, which can be a literal or non-literal portrayal. The choreographer decides if what we hear is what we think and what we see.

The most successful choreographic works set to verbal scores occur when spoken text and movement act as partners. The key challenge for choreographers is to define their own "when," "why," and "how" when connecting speaking and dancing.

Movement-text-speech choreographic explorations may always be trending, inviting, and exciting. Let's remember, however, that historically, movement comes before spoken word. Spoken word is revealed as a rational and cerebral expression, while dance is revealed as an intuitive and kinesthetic expression. Dance as an art form is meant to be speechless and wordless: it is all about physical movement. Dance by nature is *preverbal* and *postverbal* and as such, it operates within the *transverbal* space. A true choreographic genius transmits wordless expressions and powerful movement ideas from body to body, mind to mind, and heart to heart.

THE SINGING BODY
– MAKING LYRICS DANCE –

Vocal music or singing incorporates a solo voice or multiple voices, with or without instrumental accompaniment. Singing and dancing are separate art forms, yet they are integrated organically in concert dance, operas, and musical theater productions—on or off-Broadway—as well as in music concerts and TV music videos. Dance often plays a supporting role in singing, requiring the choreographer to accommodate the vocal work.

The choreographer's creative relationship with choral music constantly evolves, especially when the choreographer has to consider (or not) the original content, lyrics, and libretto of the vocal music work. Operas have dramatic vitality—the plots are passionate, and the music is expressive and powerful. Choreographers do not always conform to vocal librettos and frequently transform operas into pure dance.

Carmen, a popular opera by George Bizet, has often been modified into ballets with a similar plot but without the singing. George Balanchine used some of Bellini's opera music for the ballet *La Sonnambula*. Music by Massenet accompanied Kenneth MacMillan's ballet *Manon*. Instead of applying the original music from the opera *Manon* for the ballet with the same name, MacMillan used other works by Massenet such as *Elegy* and *Meditation*.

Opera plots and musical lyrics can be presented more economically through dance. By using moving bodies, choreographers can create emotional effects with remarkable speed. A few carefully chosen gestures can condense complex feelings and powerful content. On the other hand, opera expresses certain dramatic scenes more easily than dance, such as when the performers sing the words and the dancers simply serve as a supportive background.

Choreographic integration between singing and dancing began when large dance numbers shared the stage with a singer or a group of singers and accompanied them with movement. The supplemental function of dance in the traditional European opera was replaced by the merger of song and dance in America, giving birth to *musical theater* and show business.

Historically, a long choreographic evolution took place: from minstrel shows to comique burlesques on stage, from vaudeville shows as a series of separate and unrelated acts grouped together, to the development of simultaneous dancing and singing at nightclubs and cabarets—all of which contributed to and defined musical theater in the last century. In the early 20th century, dance in musical theater was simply a diversion, serving as a break from the storyline to show off fancy moves performed by attractive dancers. By the mid-20th century, George Balanchine brought a more classical aspect to the Broadway stage and opened the door for other classically trained choreographers. Agnes DeMille became the first significant female Broadway choreographer. She transformed the importance of dance scenes from playing an incidental role to being a major plot device. A pivotal work at that time was *West Side Story*, with "dance-as-action" choreography by Jerome Robbins.

By the second half of the 20th century and the early 21st century, dancing, singing, and acting became equally important and dependent on each other.[26] Bob Fosse's *Chicago*, Twyla Tharp's *Movin' Out*, and Christopher Wheeldon's *An American in Paris* were all "dance-heavy" musical productions that demanded extraordinary ability of the performers.

Choreographing dances to and with live singing continues to be an exciting challenge for choreographers today. Good singing, acting, and dancing require extra practicing to organically connect the vocal and the acting work with the dance moves. Even when dancers have mastered singing and acting separately, choreographing them in sync could be an intense experience. The following is a list of a few helpful tips and suggestions:

HELPFUL TIPS & SUGGESTIONS

~ Choose shapes that allow the free flow of breath in the diaphragm and lungs
~ Anticipate the moments needed for breaths by inserting dance poses and pauses
~ Consider that singing longer notes requires deeper breath and longer inhalation
~ Minimize movement complexity when there is complexity in the vocal work
~ Create movements to accommodate articulation of the lyrics and the vocal work
~ Use movements to accent certain lyrics or musical phrases
~ Connect the movement flow with the vocal flow

THE SOUNDSCAPE BODY

– DANCING TO NOISE AND SONIC AMBIENCE –

Hearing often precedes seeing. Sounds and noises can have a significant impact on thinking and feeling. A sonic environment of random sounds and noises has the power to tell a story. Why? Because the memory develops and stores an extensive collection of sounds and noises with cognitive links to references and images, called sound triggers.[27]

Our auditory sensors help us identify the origins of the sounds. Sound triggers allow us to recognize the source and type of sound and noise and link them to specific references, memories, and emotions. We continuously update our psychological responses to sound and noise imagery, whether it's the phone's ring tone, the crying baby in the house next door, or the soothing jazz music playing in the bar. Identifying the sonic environment makes us decide how to react, respond, and engage. For example, choreographers are often emotionally attached to the noise of the audience's energetic applause at the end of their performance. The longer and the louder the applause, the better. Humans organically make sounds and noises—having them as part of dance is natural.

Sounds and noises can be assembled, manipulated, and devised like dance movements. In comparison, traditional composers create *musical scores* by engaging the elements of music by contemporary sound artists to explore, group, and utilize occurrences and progressions of sonic events. A *sonic score* is the organization of a soundscape. *Sonic scores* can be used for dance instead of music or in combination with music. Noises and sounds can also be produced live by the dancers on stage or prerecorded.

Soundscape is an acoustic environment of sonic resources or a combination of sounds and noises that arise and take shape from an immersive sonic setting. The term was first described by Canadian composer and environmentalist Raymond Murray Schafer.[28] He indicates three main elements of the soundscape referring to the acoustic environment:

Figure 7

- ➢ **Natural sounds created by nature**, including animal vocalizations and, for instance, the sounds of weather and other natural elements.
- ➢ **Environmental sounds created by humans** through musical composition, sound design, and other ordinary human activities including conversation and work.
- ➢ **Industrial sounds of mechanical origin** created by use of technology, manufacturing, and artificial intelligence.

Soundscape for dance also refers to an audio recording or performance of sounds that create the sensation of experiencing a particular acoustic environment. Soundscape compositions for dance are often in electronic or electroacoustic music or created using *found sound* drawn from ordinary objects that are generally not considered "musical." Soundscape can be an exclusive acoustic environment, or it can occur in conjunction with musical performances. An unconventional way to produce sound and to create *sonic textures*, for instance, is by rubbing or scratching a string inside the body of a piano or other acoustic instruments.[29] Soundscapes can also be produced artificially and electronically through digital technology. Sonic textures and found sound may originate from different sources—existing or built systems in Nature or human environments—see Figure 8.[30] Unique sound and noise interactions may also trigger unique movement interactions in dance.

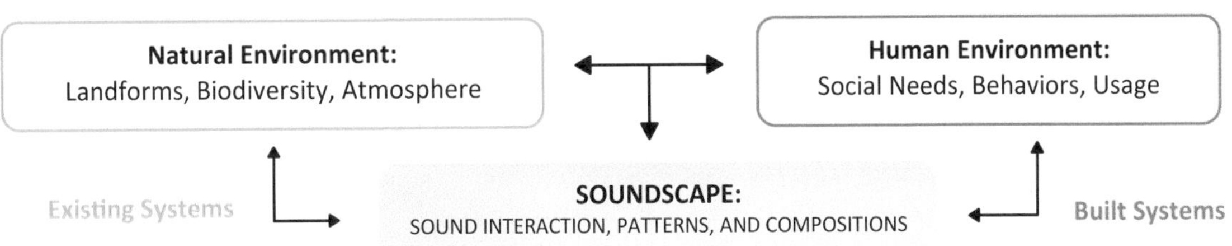

Figure 8

ALL SOUNDS AND NOISES AT ONCE

For a concluding example, let's look at a cultural heritage that implements various sounds and noises at once. Haka is derived from New Zealand's ancient war rituals and was initially performed before a battle by warriors proclaiming their strength to intimidate the opposition. Haka includes strong hand movements, foot-stamping, thigh-slapping, and loud chanting. Performers may incorporate traditional weapons, such as *taiaha* (spear-like weapons) and *patu* (clubs) into their haka. Haka is always performed in total unison; otherwise, it was regarded as a bad omen for the battle. Often, there is a ringmaster who leads the routine.[31]

In addition, the choreography involves *Pūkana*—fierce facial expressions and ritual grimaces, poking out of the tongue, and eye-bulging to help demonstrate passion and fearlessness. Although these expressions might look intimidating, they are not necessarily a sign of aggression but simply serve to demonstrate strong emotions.

Haka is performed today in its cultural dance heritage form and as a contemporary expression at various events such as birthdays, graduations, weddings, funerals, anniversaries, sporting events, and other important occasions to demonstrate commitment and unity. Most of the sonic elements discussed in this chapter can be seen at once in a single Haka:

Silence is used for meditation before Haka, as the participants might kneel and pause for a moment to concentrate. Silence is used also before a responding Haka is offered back in a form of a dialogue.

Breathing in Haka is audible and often includes loud and purposeful inhalation and exhalation to accelerate the breath.

Sound and noise are produced by vigorous foot-stamping, rhythmic hand clapping, body slapping, and tongue protrusions to create group unison percussive rhythms.

Vocalization includes grunts, cries, shouting, and screaming in a variety of vocal pitches, as well as vocal signals and instructional yelling of cues for the singing progression.

Verbalization captures text related to the occasion, or key phrases of wisdom such as "What is right is right" (Be true to yourself!) or "The answer to your struggle is inside of you."

Singing evolves around sequences of prolonged sung notes, chanted lyrics, and graceful choral or action songs.

Soundscape is present as an environmental background to the outdoor performance, including noises in nature like wind, moving branches, the raging river nearby, and the singing birds.

Figure 9 Photography © Andrew Turner, *Young Maori man performing in a kapahaka group, during a Maori dance troupe event in Rotorua*, 2006, courtesy of Wikimedia Commons

assignments & exercises

RESEARCH ASSIGNMENT: Research and look at well-known choreographic works which utilize silence, noise, sound, and speech. Explore and analyze the following elements:

➡ How has the choreographer used and synchronized movement ideas to organically fit silence, noise, sound, and speech, making them a sonic component of the dance?

➡ How and when does the discomfort of watching movement without music gradually transform into an acceptance and appreciation of moving in silence, noise, sound, and speech?

➡ How do silence, noise, sound, and speech patterns emphasize movement patterns? Do they help accelerate rhythmic physicality and dynamics?

★ **CREATIVE AND EXPLORATORY ASSIGNMENTS:**

➡ SILENCE AND BREATHING: Imagine you want to communicate with an individual who can't hear: a) Create a movement phrase that describes and captures who you are as an individual. b) Avoid pantomime and instead incorporate elements of sign language and gestures. Most importantly, use movement abstraction to describe who you are, including your name, personality, and what you do. c) Use your breath naturally, audibly, and visually to accompany and support your movement kinesthetically.

➡ RHYTHMIC SOUND: Make sound and music with your body: a) Create a rhythmic movement phrase that incorporates sounds made by different parts of the body by using them as instruments—for example, tapping and stomping feet, clapping hands, and slapping hands against the body. b) Add an additional sound layer by using accessories and props such as castanets, wooden boxes, plastic objects, tubes, containers, or small portable furniture. c) Explore ambient sounds, create sound, and search for found sounds by interacting with objects in the immediate surroundings and incorporate them in the phrase.

➡ VOCALIZATION: Link voice with movement: a) Create a movement phrase with various elements such as gestures, jumps, turns, and rolling on the floor. b) Use and assign your own made vocal noises and a variety of vocalizations to accompany each of the movement vocabularies in a way that reflects and affects the quality of each movement. c) Perform the phrase for peers and ask for feedback on whether the vocalization is related to and matches the movement, why, and how.

➡ QUOTED SPOKEN WORDS AND POETRY: Dance to spoken words: a) Choose a favorite personal story or a poem you're very attached to, and ask a colleague or friend to read it. b) Create a movement sequence that captures the emotion and the images of the text. c) Perform the text/movement sequence together in front of trusted peers and ask for feedback about how the movement and text relate.

➡ ORIGINAL SPOKEN WORDS AND POETRY: Create dance to your text: a) Choose an important personal moment in your life that has impacted you as an individual. b) Write a few sentences or poetic lines describing the episode, making sure to narrate what happened and capture the feelings involved. c) Ask a close friend to read the text out loud while you create a movement phrase based on that original writing by capturing its essence without illustrating it with mime or literal movements.

➥ SINGING: Sing the dance and dance the song: a) Pick a song that you like very much that you can easily sing without stumbling on the lyrics or the melody. b) Create a short movement phrase that fits the song's mood, melody, rhythm, and lyrics. Consider incorporating moments of breath and rest that will accommodate the complexity of vocal work. c) Demonstrate your work to peers and ask for feedback on whether the movement sequence captures and articulates the musical phrasing and the lyrics, and if the movement flow follows and matches the song's flow.

➥ SOUNDSCAPE: May the noisy dance be with you: a) Explore and identify different ambient noises and sounds in your daily life that bring reference images and a so-called sound trigger. b) Use your phone or another recording device to capture some of these sounds. Create an original sonic score—a soundscape based on the noises you have collected. c) Create a movement phrase based on the soundscape you have assembled. Make choices about the relationship between sounds and movements. Could sound waves and shapes become movement waves and shapes?—see figure below. To what extent are they related and how do they complement each other?

Figure 10 Photography © Lois Greenfield, pictured Sara Joel and Anna Venizelos, 2008

BIBLIOGRAPHY AND REFERENCES

[1] Smith, Brandon Michael. "Wagner's Philosophy, Music, & Siegfried-Idyll," *Papers & Publications: Interdisciplinary Journal of Undergraduate Research*, vol. 3, Article 2, 2014, http://digitalcommons.northgeorgia.edu/papersandpubs/vol3/iss1/2, accessed December 2019.
[2] Berg, Richard E. "Sound," in *Encyclopedia Britannica*, 2019, online article: www.britannica.com/science/sound-physics/The-ear-as-spectrum-analyzer, accessed December 2019.
[3] Berg 2019. "Sound."
[4] Berg 2019. "Sound."
[5] Berg 2019. "Sound."
[6] Rabinowitz, Neil C. and King, Andrew J. *Auditory Perception: Hearing the Texture of Sounds*, National Center for Biotechnology Information. Article published online on December 5, 2011: www.ncbi.nlm.nih.gov/pmc/articles/PMC4353848/, accessed December 2019.
[7] Rabinowitz and King 2011. *Auditory Perception: Hearing the Texture of Sounds*.
[8] Reilly, Lucas. *The Story behind John Cage's 4'33"*, 2017, online article: www.mentalfloss.com/article/59902/101-masterpieces-john-cages-433, accessed December 2019.
[9] Blom, Lynne Anne and Chaplin, L. Tarin. *The Intimate Act of Choreography*, 1st edition, University of Pittsburgh Press, June 30, 1982.
[10] Melton, Joan. "Dancers on Breathing—from Interviews and Other Conversations," article published 2012 in *New Zealand Association of Teachers of Singing*, accessed in December 2019.
[11] Sirico, Angela D'Valda. *The Use of Breathing in Dance*, Dance Teachers, online article, Web accessed April 2019.
[12] Bradley, Chelsey, "Teaching Students to Use Breath to Enhance Their Dancing," *Dance Advantage Net*, online article, accessed December 2016.
[13] Gritsch, Anita. *Percussive Dances*, Dance researcher, online article of a thesis summary, University of Music and Performing Arts, Vienna, Austria, 2012, www.anitagritsch.weebly.com, accessed December 2019.
[14] Gritsch 2012. *Percussive Dances*.
[15] Gritsch 2012. *Percussive Dances*.
[16] Gritsch 2012. *Percussive Dances*.
[17] Hill, Constance Valis. *Tap Dancing America: A Cultural History*, Reprint edition, Oxford University Press, 2014.
[18] Brown, Camille A. *A Visual History of Social Dance in 25 Moves*, TED Talk, TED Studios, 2016, Online video resource: www.ted.com/talks/camille_a_brown_a_visual_history_of_social_dance_in_25_moves?language=en, accessed December 2019.
[19] Brown 2016. *A Visual History of Social Dance*.
[20] Angelov, Vladimir. "Mikhail Baryshnikov: Heartbeat," article and performance review, *Tanz Archive Magazine*, Vienna, Austria, 1998, online: http://dancingangel.net/past-publications/baryshnikov#!Front_Page, accessed December 2019.
[21] Angelov 1998. "Mikhail Baryshnikov: Heartbeat."
[22] Lagaay, Alice. *Between Sound and Silence: Voice in the History of Psychoanalysis*, Freie Universität Berlin, 2008, online article, accessed March 2018.
[23] Jackson, Paul. *Developments in Extended Vocal Techniques: Music-Text-Voice, Intertextuality in Music*, online article, web, accessed January 2019.
[24] Bredin, Hugh. "Onomatopoeia as a Figure and a Linguistic Principle," article, *New Literary History*, vol. 27, no. 3, 1996.
[25] Lerman, Liz. "By All Possible Means: A Look at the Relationship between Words and Movement," article, *Movement Research Magazine*, Fall/Winter 1994/95 issue.
[26] Robinson, Mark. The Great Broadway Choreographers, 2019, online article: www.markrobinsonwrites.com/, accessed December 2019.
[27] Beckerman, Joel and Gray, Tayler. *The Sonic Boom, How the Sounds Transforms the Way We Think, Feel and Buy*, Houghton Mifflin Harcourt, 2014.
[28] Schafer, R. Murray. *The Soundscape, Our Sonic Environment and the Tuning of the World*, Original edition, Destiny Books, 1993.
[29] Filatriau, Jehan-Julien and Daniel, Arfib. *Instrumental Gestures and Sonic Textures*, Semantic Scholar, 2019, online article: https://pdfs.semanticscholar.org/cf88/dc798b38f86c4c3068bfd7481df598428984.pdf, accessed December 2019.
[30] Chattopadhyay, Budhaditya. "Reconstructing Atmospheres: Ambient Sound in Film and Media Production," online article, *SAGE Journals*, 2017, accessed December 2019.
[31] Smith, Valance. "Kapa haka—Māori Performing Arts," in *The Encyclopedia of New Zealand*, online platform, accessed April 2019, https://teara.govt.nz/en/kapa-haka-maori-performing-arts, accessed December 2019.

VISUAL REFERENCES

Figure 1: Diagram © Vladimir Angelov

Figure 2: Diagram © Vladimir Angelov, clip art: *Sound signal color icon. Audible soundwave idea. Listening ear.* Credit:bsd555, courtesy of iStock/Getty Images

Figure 3: Photography © Costas, *Moves*, choreography Jerome Robbins, performed by members of the New York City Ballet, NYC, courtesy of Costas, 2010

Figure 4: Photography © Matthew Murphy and Ken Tam, pictured tap dancer and choreographer Michelle Dorrance, 2013

Figure 5: Photography © Jaclyn Borowski, *The Matter of Origins*, choreography by Liz Lerman, The Liz Lerman Dance Exchange, 2010

Figure 6: Diagram © Vladimir Angelov, clip art: *pendulum*, design by Charles Scheland

Figure 7: *Lake, Dawn, Summer, Sunrise—Dawn, Two Medicine Lake*, photography credit: Haizhan Zheng, courtesy of iStock, Getty/Images, Graphic design © Charles Scheland

Figure 8: Diagram © Vladimir Angelov

Figure 9: Photography © Andrew Turner, *Young Maori man performing in a kapahaka group*, apparently (based on Flickr tags) taken during a Maori dance troupe event in Rotorua, 2006, courtesy or Wikimedia Commons, public domain

Figure 10 Photography © Lois Greenfield, pictured Sara Joel and Anna Venizelos, 2008

BOOK VII

PICTURE PERFECT

VENTURE FOLLOWS VISION

Wednesday evening at the bar in a mixed gathering:

RANDOM CITIZEN: So, what do you do for a living?

CHOREOGRAPHER: I am a choreographer.

RANDOM CITIZEN: ...*(awkward silence)*

Days later. Sunday afternoon at a park fair. Same choreographer, different citizen:

RANDOM CITIZEN: So, what do you do for a living?

CHOREOGRAPHER: I explore how the body in motion captures different ideas. Also . . . how we connect with ourselves, nature, and each other—without speaking.

RANDOM CITIZEN: Wow...This is so interesting, because...yesterday when I was taking a walk in the park, I felt so refreshed, and happy and elevated. Then...something very unusual happened with my red silk dress and the wind...*(continues talking affectionately about a personal experience).*

Excerpt from

dance DIALOGUES

An Anonymous Unpublished Manuscript, 376 BC–AD 2091

CHAPTER 23

NURTURING SEMANTICS
– NAMING A NEWBORN DANCE AND RAISING A BRAND –

The title of a dance influences the audience's first impression of the dance. Even before the dance unfolds, a word or a phrase can semantically reveal the core concept of a choreography. The title is like the name of a person: good to know and nice to remember. A repertoire of great dances is similar to an address book of great friends—a list of important names and titles. However, giving a name to a person, a title to a dance, and a brand to a dance company involves some work—finding or creating a fascinating match between an intriguing semantic expression and its physicalized equivalent.

A letter, a word, a number, or a series of words and symbols becomes an instant synthesis of meaning, characteristics, and labeling. Titling and branding can range from naming a person, project, and product to naming entire generations in historical progression: Generation X (approximately 1966–80), Generation Y/Millennials (approximately 1981–96), and Generation Z (approximately 1997–2012), and so forth. How do we decide what to call things?

Imagine you are at a lively party, having a good time and meeting new people. Then you meet a somewhat quiet person. You ask, "What is your name?" The answer you get is: "I have never had one." You would be shocked, but the person continues, "Why don't you give me a name? What would you call me?" Often, the best action is a reaction. There are a few choices: a) instantly come up with an improvised name based on your intuition, b) request more information about the person's background, or c) kindly ask for the time and opportunity to get a sense of the person's individuality before assigning a name.

This chapter addresses how names emerge and how a name can be perceived semantically in various contexts. When it comes to names, titles, and branding, choreographers might consider capturing the specifics of a single dance work and the big picture of branding: *frame of reference* and *branding bundle*. As discussed at the end of this chapter, *a frame of reference* and *branding bundle* refer to the grouping of name, title, and brand, which encapsulate identity, representation, and symbol. They, in turn, frame a purpose, vision, and mission. All of these aspects are related and integrated—see Figure 1:

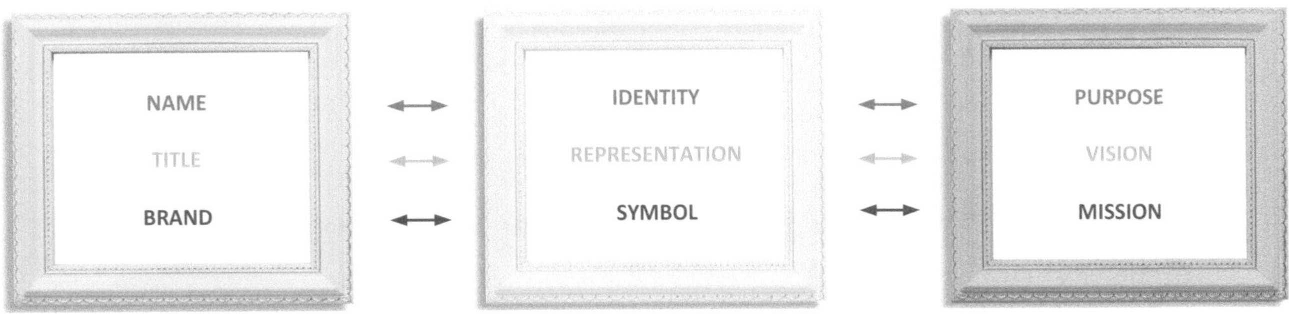

Figure 1

The name- and title-giving process can be approached in different ways at the same time: *causal*, *intuitive*, and *creative*. In most instances, names and titles are constructs of assigned and attributed meaning serving as references to particular things. They may be in the form of spoken word, writing, sound, or visual signature—they may engage the perceiver's attention with an informative association.[1] Like the name of a person, the title of a dance or a brand's name instantly generates a first impression about purpose, origin, features, and significance. Let's review some common practices for naming in the arts and humanities, and for naming people.

➢ **Naming causally based on tradition and origin:** Names in this category are based on well-known stories. For example, the Greek myth *Orpheus and Eurydice* takes its name from the leading characters in the story. But what are the origins of people's names? What traditions influence naming?

Names can be new creations or linked to genealogy and family history, such as the family dynasty names Rockefeller and Vanderbilt. Geographical, cultural, and ethnic heritage can play a role in naming, either through maintaining an established name or by manipulating existing names that are linked to one's ancestry. For example, if the grandmother is Maria and the mother is Elene, the newborn girl's name might be a combination of the names: Maria + Elene = Marlene.

➢ **Naming intuitively based on matching representation:** Names in this category may include, for example, a musical work called Bolero, which led to the creation of the dance with the same name. Another example involves the Western diatonic music scale. The syllables "do, re, me..." correspond to notes in the scale and provide an easy and intuitive way to remember the corresponding pitch of a song. Rodgers and Hammerstein borrowed the syllables to name their popular show tune "Do-Re-Mi" in their 1959 musical *The Sound of Music*. Another example is the name Wolfgang Amadeus Mozart, with *Amadeus* translating as "loved by God"—and he surely was a composer blessed by God. His parents made a good intuitive prediction.

➢ **Naming creatively based on corresponding narrative and identical features:** Names or titles in this category capture specific characteristics, events, or locations. For example, *Swan Lake* suggests that the plot will most likely contain interaction between nature, swans, and humans. In geography, Iceland means "snow land" and France means "land of the fierce," while China means "the middle kingdom." In astronomy, Mars is a red-colored planet named after the Roman god of war, while Venus, the brightest planet, is named after the Roman goddess of love and beauty.

Native American tribal names refer directly to characteristics of nature: Red Fox and Black Hawk. On the other hand, Biblical names have literal translations: Gabriel means "God is my strength," while Sarah means princess.[2]

?

What does your name mean semantically, and does it match your personality? In what ways?

HELLO NEW DANCE, WHAT IS YOUR NAME?

The moment a new dance is titled, the dance gains its own identity and autonomy. The new dance is similar to a child who is a descendant of a creative family. The new dance will grow and gain more independence and ownership, yet it will always carry its parent choreographer's DNA. Titles are names, and names are important. And yet can all words be used as titles of dances?

◆ **Good news: Dance titles are not subject to copyright law!**[3] Using similar wording in dance titles is relatively common. Often dances dealing with the same subject matter and narrative carry the same name as dances created before by someone else. It is a fact that there are many *Nutcracker* productions with the same name, ranging from traditional restaging to contemporary interpretations. Choreographers generally do not face legal ramifications for using previously-established names.

Whatever the chosen title, it needs to be a good fit for the dance. A dance's title establishes an immediate communication between the dance and the observers: audience members, journalists, critics, scholars, historians, and others encountering that dance. Therefore, choosing a proper dance title is crucial because it:

PROVIDES INITIAL CONDENSED INFORMATION
Observers may predict the concept of the dance.

PROVIDES A REFERENCE AND CREATES ANTICIPATION
Observers may contemplate how the title is revealed in the dance.

PROVIDES A TRADEMARK OF THE DANCE AS AN ARTIFACT
Observers may remember and refer to the dance by its title.

In summary, a dance title is a formulated expression that functions to represent the dance semantically. That expression may be framed as predominantly abstract or narrative, specific or general, or containing multiple nuances at once[4]—see Figure 2.

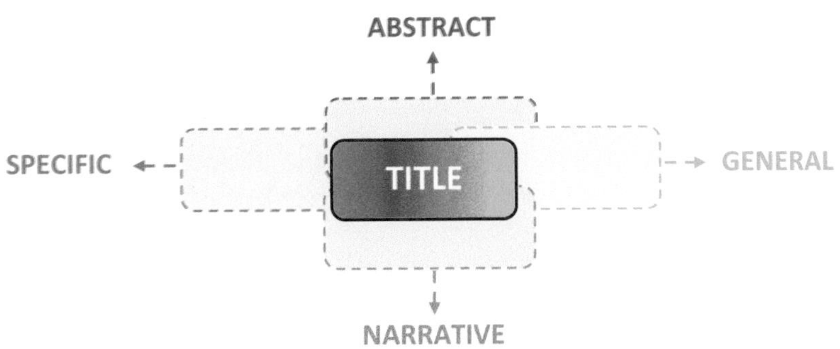

Figure 2

A RAINBOW OF DANCE TITLES

The titles of a few 19th-, 20th-, and 21st-century master dance works can be classified in a range from ordinary to unusual and from traditional to innovative. The following list aims to formulate distinct categories, provide samples, and sort out colorful dance titles, which could be specific, general, narrative, abstract, or any combination of these:

A TITLE CAN BE...

THE SAME AS THE MUSIC WORKS:
Serenade, *Allegro Brillante*, and *Symphony in C*, by George Balanchine
Boléro, by Maurice Béjart
The Four Seasons, by Roland Petit

THE SAME AS WORKS OF LITERATURE AND ART:
Prodigal Son and *Midsummer Night's Dream*, by George Balanchine
Guernica, by Roland Petit
Mona Lisa, by Itzik Galili

A PERSON'S NAME:
Giselle, *Coppélia*, and *Don Quixote*, by Marius Petipa
Apollo, by George Balanchine
Clytemnestra and *Phaedra*, by Martha Graham

CHARACTERS OR OBJECTS:
Le Corsaire, *Sleeping Beauty*, and *Nutcracker*, by Marius Petipa
Diamonds and *Four Temperaments*, by George Balanchine
Green Table, by Kurt Joss

PLACES AND SPACES:
Swan Lake, by Marius Petipa
Uncle Tom's Cabin, by Bill T. Jones
In the Upper Room, by Twyla Tharp

POSSESSIVE FORMS:
The Pharaoh's Daughter, by Marius Petipa
Limb's Theorem, by William Forsythe
Winter's Tale, by Christopher Wheeldon

EVENTS AND ACTIVITIES:
The Rite of Spring, by Vaslav Nijinsky
Night Journey, by Martha Graham
The Statement, by Crystal Pite

DESCRIPTION AND ASSOCIATION OF IDEAS:
Water Study, by Doris Humphrey
Letter to the World and *Acts of Light*, by Martha Graham
In the Middle Somewhat Elevated, by William Forsythe

Figure 3

SYMBOLIC, HIDDEN, OR MULTIPLE MEANINGS:

Petite Mort, by Jiří Kylián, meaning the "little death"—a climax during love or loss
Flight Patterns, by Crystal Pite, meaning refugees "fleeing," as revealed in the plot
Endless House, by William Forsythe, meaning to expand the definition of home

PLAY ON WORDS OR MADE-UP WORDS:

Atomus, by Wayne McGregor
Steptext, by William Forsythe
Velox, by Deborah Colker

The last category uses an innovative strategy often seen in the branding and re-branding practices of contemporary businesses and industries. Creatively made-up words in titling and branding are trending widely today. For example, the name of the popular navigation phone app *WAZE* is a combination of [finding] Ways + Ease. The name of the online travel booking agency *Trivago* comprises parts of the words "trip" and "vacation," plus the word "go"—Tri + va + go.

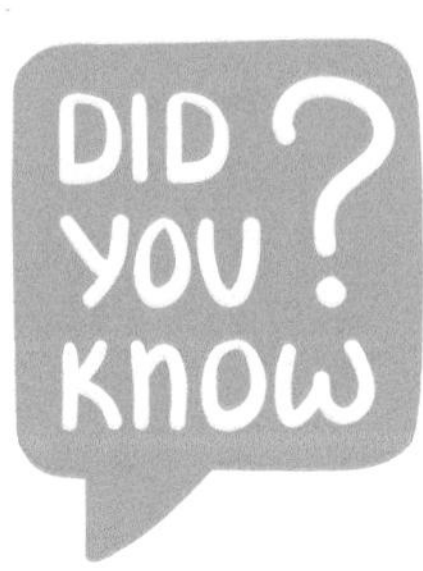

The point of wordplay is not only to craft a clever brand name related to the service or product offered but also to trigger an emotional response. The pharmaceutical industry has used this creative strategy to come up with evocative names for new drugs. For instance: the drug called *Prevagen* improves memory loss associated with normal aging, and the name might suggest that it helps prevent aging. The drug *Allegra* treats allergy; the name brings to mind an upbeat music tempo and is the word for cheerful in Italian. *Celebrex*, a drug to control pain and swelling, might be effective enough to "turn discomfort into a celebration." Could similar business and branding strategies be useful and feasible for choreographers?

What does a single dance title have to do with the overall branding of a choreographic philosophy and a dance company's name? A title or group of titles organized in a repertory of dance works sets the tone for how the work will be branded. For example, a repertory containing titles such as the *Songs of the Soul*, *Dances from Within*, and *Landscapes in Motion* may lead to a different company branding strategy than a repertory with dance titles such as *Spectra*, *Aperture*, and *Fracture*.

Before looking at the larger context of branding and how a single dance title may become part of a bigger branding picture, let's first look at the process of creating a title for a single dance. The following systematized approach proposes a three-step algorithm:

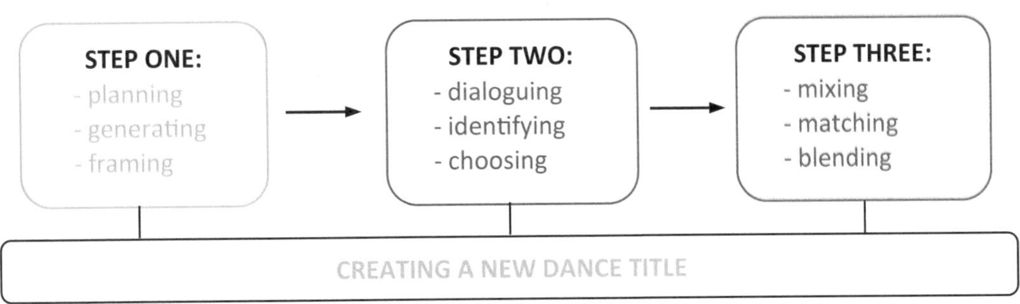

Figure 4

STEP ONE: PLANNING, GENERATING, AND FRAMING

– FITTING AN OCEAN INTO A DRINKING GLASS –

Often, a choreographer will have a *working title* in mind for the dance even before the actual creation begins. Other times, the title emerges in the middle of the creative process and must await validation. Still, other times one comes to mind when the choreographer must finally provide one for the program information. There is no pressure to immediately title the dance: the best strategy for generating a title is the one that works best. The creative challenge of choosing the title is synthesizing the inspiration, research, and content of the dance into just a few words. But how do we fit an ocean into a glass?

Good news: the title of a new dance has already been forming "behind the scenes." It is embedded within the creative process, and the choreographer just needs to find it. Before the search begins, and for those who encounter challenges with creating titles, let's consider a gradual multi-step process to generate creative and satisfying options:

◆ PLANNING: Dances can be long, while titles are usually short and concise. Concise titles, however, are challenging to create. As we dive into the process, let's use a few helpful techniques:

- ➢ Think of single words and phrases describing the initial inspiration.
- ➢ Anticipate generating a large pool of words and phrases about the creative process.
- ➢ Plan to open-mindedly play with the wording of these phrases.

◆ GENERATING AND DESCRIBING: This process can begin with reviewing information about the dance that is already available: ongoing or completed artistic research, gathered resources, the progress during the rehearsal process, and any other references that are immediately accessible to streamline potential titles.

Think of visual or *semantic imagery* that expresses the choreographic content and concepts: the *aboutness* of the dance, which includes describing the initial inspiration, intentions, and subject matter of the dance. Also, think of the creative process and how the dance work has emerged. For a refresher on these topics, please review *Framing Content and Sorting Concepts: Logistics of the Unlimited*, Chapter 12.

Write three paragraphs describing and synthesizing the inspiration, concept, and creative process of your dance. Use an informative and personal tone, as well as poetic language. The text's goal is to inform and enlighten someone who does not know anything about your choreographic work and creative process. A synopsis of the dance will emerge that can be used later in promotional materials, advertisements, press releases, and interviews. The descriptive paragraphs may answer the following questions:

➢ **Paragraph 1: What inspires you to create this dance?** What is your initial reason for making this dance? What do you find fascinating about it, and what are you drawn to? During your preparation and research, what kind of music, video clips, visual art, or quotations from literary works did you use?

➢ **Paragraph 2: What is the dance about?** If the work is narrative, what is the dramatic plot? If the work is abstract, what type of imagery and impressions do you intend to convey? What do you want the audience to *see*, and how do you want them to *feel* about the dance? What is the progression of the dance in terms of scenes and names of sections?

➢ **Paragraph 3: What is your creative process?** How do you create movement and engage creatively with the dancers? What was the most exciting moment in the creative process? If you have discovered something new, what is it? Have you incorporated elements into your new work that you have never considered before? What are they?

◈ FRAMING CREATIVE AESTHETIC/GOAL AND TYPE/TONE OF TITLE: There is an intuitive connection between how something appears and how it is named. The same principle applies in dance. There is an instinctual reference between the type of dance and the *type* of title, between the choreographer's aesthetic and creative goals and the *tone* of the title.

As the choreographer implements a particular type of aesthetic throughout the dance, the type and tone of the title emerge. For example, a dance about "lost love" might use titles capturing the same subject matter but in different tones according to the dance's aesthetic. A potential dance title could be the name of a song, such as *I Can't Stop Loving You*, which may sound accessible; or *Troubles in Paradise*, which may sound intriguing; or *Inverse*, which may sound provocative. In summary, a dance title carries a semantic context that captures the content of the dance and a sound with an emotional undertone.

The purpose of the dance could be to entertain and appeal to the mass taste, or to experiment and investigate certain phenomena, or to make an intimate artistic statement, or to frame and convey a particular dance aesthetic. Ultimately, the choreographer's agenda will also include the task to formulate a *title* that aligns with the *corresponding tone* of the work's aesthetic and the choreographer's creative goals—see Figure 5.

AESTHETIC AND CREATIVE GOAL		TYPE AND TONE OF TITLES
...conformity... entertainment...	← DANCE WORK →	...pleasant... appealing...
...uniqueness... authenticity...	← DANCE WORK →	...intriguing... candid...
...experimentation... radical view...	← DANCE WORK →	...rebellious... provocative...

Figure 5

STEP TWO: DIALOGUE, IDENTIFY, AND CHOOSE
– PARTLY CLOUDY OR PARTLY SUNNY –

Listening to a choreographer's conversations with the dancers in rehearsal is like listening to a passionate scientist during a breakthrough experiment. In addition to arbitrarily shouting corrections and a barrage of technical notes, choreographers use poetic allegories, vivid imagery, and analogies to direct the dancers and convey certain movement qualities. Simply listening is a great strategy to gather potential titles.

It's magical when choreographers can hear themselves speaking—when they tune in to their own dance to discover what has not yet been revealed. Like poets, choreographers use language as *figurative hints* to describe movement dynamics, images, and intentions. Using a phrase for a title is not only about *what* is said but also *how* it is said. In a weather forecast, partly cloudy and partly sunny describe similar weather in two contrasting ways.

◆ **DIALOGUING:** Choreographers can converse with their dances just as they speak and listen to dancers. An expectant mother speaks to her unborn baby. The baby kicks in response, and the mother reacts. A dialogue is established. Similar conversations occur as the choreographer is about to give birth to a new dance. Here are a few questions:

➢ **How does your dance appear conceptually?**
Describe how the dance emerges and what you see.

➢ **How does your dance *speak* back to you?**
Explain what is happening unexpectedly as the dance emerges.

➢ **What does your dance convey beyond your intentions?**
Listen to what others say about the dance and how they interpret it.

The answers will add to the list of possible titles, even if they aren't a close fit. Here is another practical tip: There is no need to discard unused titles. Instead, you can use and reuse titles for other purposes, such as for a *sub-title*—a secondary or explanatory title—if a title is unsuitable as the *main title* of a particular dance.

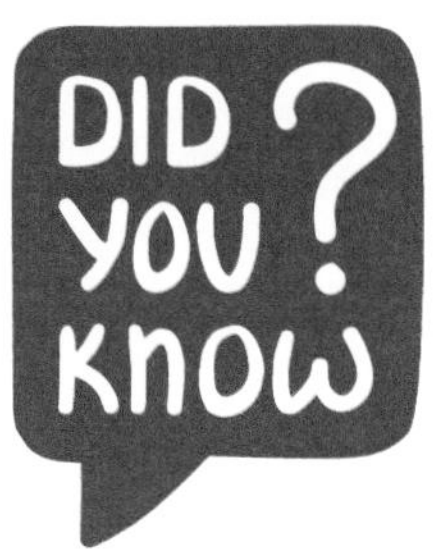

Beneath a main title one can sometimes find more titles of smaller sections of a large dance and names of multiple characters in that dance. Although *Serenade* (1934) was a plotless ballet, its choreographer, George Balanchine, assigned the leading soloists names that suggested an undisclosed narrative and dramatic plot. Such characters included the Waltz Girl and Waltz Boy, the Russian Girl, the Elegy Boy, and the Dark Angel. Composer Tchaikovsky also gave titles to different sub-sections of *Serenade*, such as *Pezzo*, *Walzer*, *Elegy*, and *Finale*.[5]

◆ **IDENTIFYING THE KEY IDEAS OF CONTENT:** After you complete the previous tasks, you might discover a waterfall of words and phrases! However, which title will best describe the dance content? Identifying content is often about identifying *key phrases* and *keywords*. A *key phrase* is usually a few words in the form of an encrypted announcement or statement containing brief content, such as "Dance for Sale." A *keyword* is a word that includes the main idea, such as "jumping." A *keyword* could also be a *tag*: a piece of information that defines a category and is used to classify content. For example, the word "jazz" could be a tag. The internet uses tags to optimize a search. As illustrated in Figure 6, the point of keywords and key phrases for a dance title is to...

...INFORM...
...REVEAL...
...IDENTIFY...
...CAPTURE...
...SUMMARIZE...
...SYNTHESIZE...
...HINT...

... THE IDEA OF THE DANCE

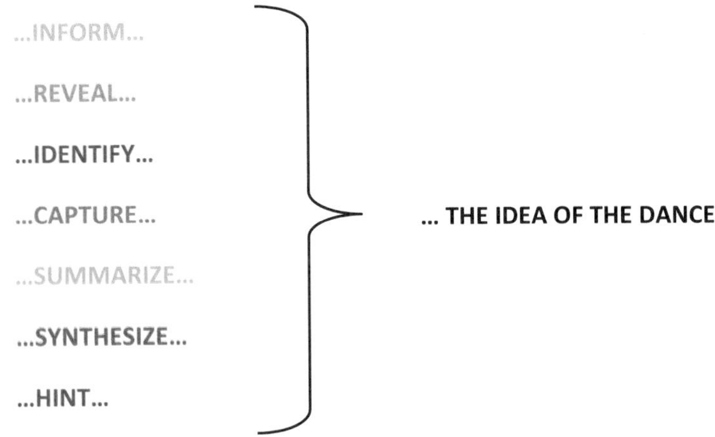

Figure 6

◆ **CHOICES AND VARIETIES:** Let's assume that rehearsals have started. Movement steps and dance imagery are evolving at the studio, and a few sections of the choreography are already complete. As the dance takes shape, it begins to speak to the choreographer. Maybe there is no need to *create* a title, but to just *find it* and use it.

In the meantime, the three-paragraph description is evolving into a more elaborate text as you identify *keywords* and *key phrases* and add entries from your *dialogue* with the dance. It's time to organize the pool of generated words and begin sorting the content:

1. Mark or circle keywords and key phrases that are significant to your dance. The words can be nouns, verbs, adjectives, pronouns, etc.

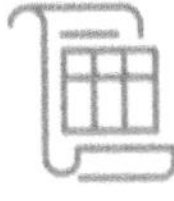

2. Create a table consisting of three columns. List verbs in the first column, adjectives in the second, and nouns in the third.

3. Add a note about creative techniques and strategies as a reference, and list names of people, places, movement, terminology, etc.

Figure 7

STEP THREE: MIX, MATCH, AND BLEND

– LOVING A [BRAIN] STORM OF WORDS –

How about working on *working titles?* Once plenty of raw material is available, creating an assortment of new titles can be a playful exercise. Instead of focusing on specific dance titles, let's illustrate how this could play out by using a generic pool of words.

◆ **MIX:** Imagine a mini-storm of words. One can randomly choose words from the different columns and arrange them in short phrases.

◆ **MATCH:** First, refer to a section of this chapter called *A Rainbow of Dance Titles*. Using the last four creative categories in the section, arbitrarily connect the compiled words with other words in the same column or across different columns. For clarity, the diagram in Figure 8 uses different colors for the words and connecting lines:

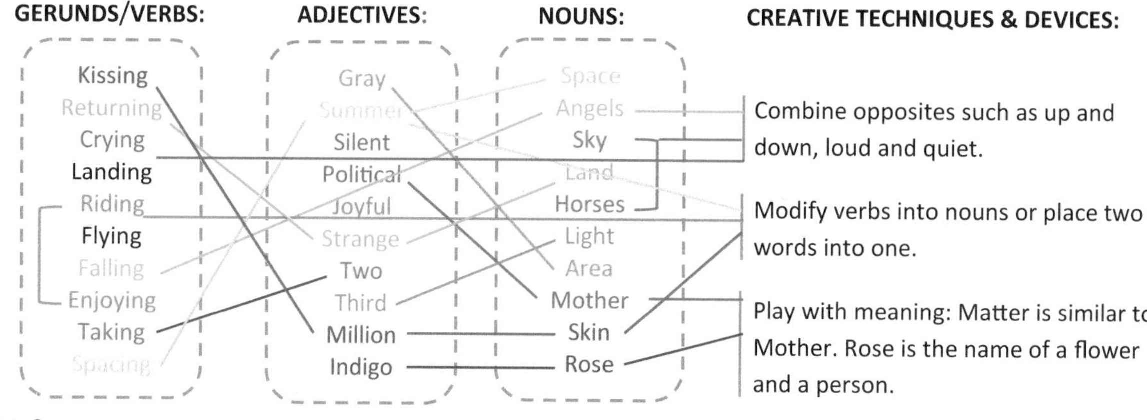

Figure 8

◆ **BLEND:** When combined in phrases, these words formed the following dance titles, which happen to be titles of some outstanding contemporary choreographic works created within the past couple of centuries.[6] See the diagram in Figure 9:

→ ***It Takes Two***
→ ***The Third Light***
→ ***A Million Kisses on My Skin***
→ ***The Gray Area***
→ ***Summer Space***
→ ***Silent Cries***
→ ***Return to a Strange Land***
→ ***Fallen Angels***
→ ***Indigo Rose***
→ ***Joyride***
→ ***Political Mother***
→ ***Horses in the Sky***

Figure 9

?

Can you create more new titles by using these same words?

FINAL EXTRA STEP:
EXPAND AND CONDENSE, PLAY AND MODIFY
— MORE IS BETTER, AND LESS IS MORE —

More creative devices could be used to expand the initial list of working titles:

◆ CREATE TITLES OF DIFFERENT SIZES AND USE PUNCTUATION: Mix and match keywords with key phrases. Titles can be short or long: one word, two words, three words, or more. Before making a final decision, experiment and consider a few more approaches. In generating working titles—the more options, the merrier! In terms of elaborately describing the core content of a dance—the less detail, the better! A title is just a hint.

Consider that titles may be composed of two titles next to each other, or a title followed by a sub-title, or a title connected with another title that is divided by comma (,) semicolon (;) hyphen (–), slash (/) or triple dots (...). Consider that longer titles might begin with or contain a question: *How/ When/Where/What/ Why*...or include verbs such as *Is/Are/Will/Do*, followed by a phrase. Longer titles tend to be more descriptive and informative, such as those of many notable dance works.[7] See the following samples:

Last Supper at Uncle Tom's Cabin/The Promised Land

Fondly Do We Hope...Fervently Do We Pray

How We Got to Now

◆ PLAY WITH EXISTING WORDS BY CREATING A PUN: Let's play with the word *choreography* and illustrate three sample titles with different tones—see Figure 10. Each title uses different keyboard symbols and punctuation to create a catchy play on words:

~ **chŎreŎgraphy** ~   %#$... **CHOREO-GRAFFITI**... &*@   ...! **Choreo*GRAPHIC* !...**

Figure 10

◆ CREATE NEW WORDS BY BLENDING AND MODIFYING EXISTING WORDS: In addition to *neologisms*, which are invented words that are still new to the mainstream language, a few devices to invent new words include changing nouns into verbs, transforming verbs into adjectives, adding prefixes and suffixes, and connecting parts of words to create new words. For instance:

Multiple + Versatility = ***Multiverse***

Love + Velocity = ***Lovelocity***

(Prefix) + Dance = ***Undance***

Get + On Board + Now = ***Onboarding***

Vase + Available = ***Vasable***

Comedy + (suffix) = ***Comedize***

Brifect = Brief + effective AND/OR brief + perfect = ***Briefect***

OPTIONS AND DECISIONS
– THE ART OF INTUITIVE INTELLIGENCE –

Various algorithms can generate options and engage choreographers in making deliberate choices to reach a final decision. Sometimes, however, choreographers might become so profoundly occupied with the creative process that thinking algorithmically about a dance title becomes burdensome. Are there other available strategies for using intelligence intuitively?

Intuitive intelligence is knowing something without concrete evidence and perceiving it correctly by instinct. Accurate decisions can be made when one absorbs only useful bits of information and applies or adapts them intuitively to resolve a dilemma. Intuitive intelligence overrides the rational mind to make sense of elusive details. Albert Einstein said: "The intuitive mind is a sacred gift, and the rational mind is a faithful servant. We have created a society that honors the servant and has forgotten the gift." Instead of making a deliberate choice and a rational ruling, one can intuitively sense which title *feels right.*

Often the dance itself selects the title. Keeping an open mind will facilitate the process. Outside feedback from peers, colleagues, mentors, and trusted friends may be helpful too. The *generating process* leads to a list of multiple options for titles, though intuitive intelligence is vital in the final two stages—the *incubating* and the *decision-making processes.* A few last tips will help guide you to a final determination—see Figure 11.

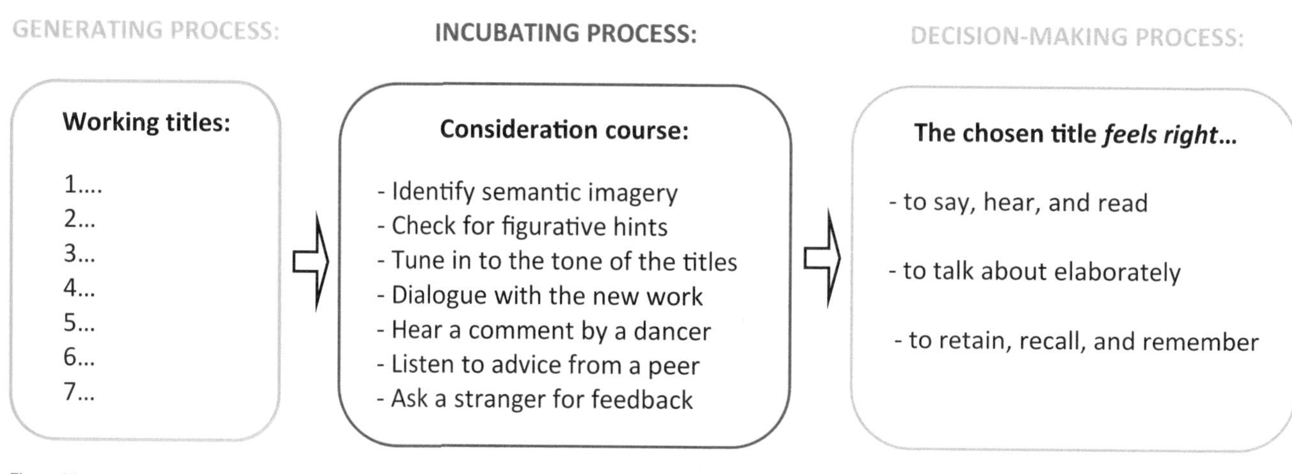

Figure 11

HELPFUL TIPS & SUGGESTIONS

~ Avoid the use of *Untitled* as a title—it suggests your work is *Incomplete*
~ Treat your *work in progress* as a piece deserving a *working title*
~ Think of any name serving as a title, as long as the title is serving a purpose
~ Recognize that names are linked to things just as ideas are linked to beliefs
~ Remember, a name is not owned but only in possession of the choreographer
~ Agree that even the best dance title is still the menu, not the meal
~ Consider that if you name *it*, then *it* exists because you named *it*

NAMING AND BRANDING A VISION

– CHOREOGRAPHIC PHILOSOPHY, MOVEMENT SYSTEM, AND SCHOOL OF THOUGHT –

A newly discovered planet, a physics law, a rare disease, a volcano, or a hurricane might be named after a person or named based on a description, an association, a random word, or coded letters and numbers. However, the most significant discoveries and new scientific theories are memorable not only for their impact but also for the scientist's name.

In dance, a distinct choreographic idea can operate within the construct of a single work or expand aesthetically within an extensive repertory. That same distinct choreographic idea may lead to an authentic approach, method, or system—a framework for other dance creators to use. It could continue to grow into a fundamentally new vision of dance as art. Let's explore how choreographic ideas, visions, and practices are organized to operate and expand within three distinct frameworks: *Choreographic Philosophy, Movement System, and School of Thought*—see Figure 12.

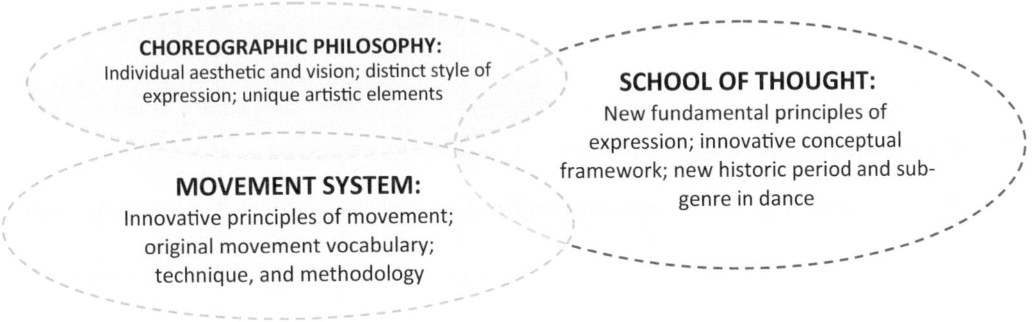

Figure 12

◆ ***Choreographic philosophy*** refers to a unique choreographic ideology, aesthetic, style, practice, and approach to dance, which could be formulated in a *dance manifesto*—see the *Prologue* of this book. Semantically, philosophy means love of wisdom, and choreography means writing or creating dance and movement. A choreographic philosophy, therefore, generally means reaching *unique individual wisdom about dance*. An individual artistic point of view gives rise to the organization and formulation of distinct *means* and *tools* of expression—that is how a choreographer: a) thinks of dance and movement, b) approaches the body kinesthetically, and c) operates creative devices to make a dance—see also *Choreographic Individuality and Artistic Identity—the Search for Who I am*, Chapter 13.

A choreographic philosophy could be traditional or innovative. For example, ballet has a predetermined movement vocabulary that can be modified to express a distinct choreographic vision. The names of choreographic styles and philosophies may be named after their founding creators, such as Bournonville Style, Balanchine Style, and so forth.

◆ ***Movement system***, on the other hand, determines and offers *uniquely framed principles for how to create* dance and movement. A movement system usually establishes and maps a new set of rules to generate and capture movement ideas. In contrast to a choreographic philosophy that is centered on an individual's unique creative identity, a movement system is an open-ended framework that can be used by other choreographers, who may in turn modify it to suit their artistic needs.

A movement system contains one or all of the following key aspects: a) new doctrine about how movement may originate, b) new systematized directives to generate authentic and unique movement, and c) new principles of organizing and structuring choreographic material. These newly formulated algorithms are often followed by stated methods of teaching and sets of creative operations. While a movement system usually emerges from a distinct choreographic philosophy, not every choreographic philosophy produces a system.

In some instances, a codified educational method, performance training technique, and creative style are titled and branded after the creator. In other cases, the name of a choreographic movement system does not use the creator's name. For example, the first half of the 20th century was heavily influenced by the Graham Technique, Horton Technique, and others. Subsequently, systems and techniques were named for their fundamental principles, not their creators. In the late 20th century, choreographers Paxton, Forsythe, Rudolph, and Shaw, among others, originated movement systems without using their names—see Figure 13.

CHOREOGRAPHER	NAME OF MOVEMENT SYSTEM	BRIEF DESCRIPTION
Steve Paxton	**Contact Improvisation**	Principles of spontaneous dance with connected bodies, touching, and sharing weight.
Nancy Stark Smith	**Underscore**	Principles of structured improvisation integrating contact and progressive compositional forms.
William Forsythe	**Improvisation Technologies**	Principles to organize temporal and spatial dance geometries and architecture of bodies in space.
David Belle	**Parkour**	Principles of movement sequencing developed from military obstacle course training.
Ohad Naharin	**Gaga**	Principles of improvisation based on imagery to foster the invention of unconventional movement.
Amelia Rudolph	**Vertical Dance**	Principles of integrating climbing techniques with contemporary dance and other movement forms.
JoAnna Mendl Shaw	**Interspecies Dance**	Principles of physical listening merge dance with horsemanship and transform animal behavior into movement forms.

Figure 13

◆ ***School of thought, new movement, and sub-genre*** refer to a *cluster of groundbreaking principles* introduced by a group of innovative artists when a new progressive construct of creative practice is assimilated as a historical stage in the development of the art form. The term *school of thought* is usually applied to philosophy, psychology, linguistics, social and political sciences, economics, and the arts. *Schools* can be "old" or "new," classical or modern, conformist or avant-garde, etc.

Choreographers creating during a particular historical period tend to artistically capture the typical characteristics of their environment—see Chapters 1–7, Book I . The world evolves continuously, and choreographers' work changes as well. Current conventional principles of dance making may be revised or radically transformed. While many choreographers may still embrace traditional principles, the emerging innovative options may challenge those conventional principles. A cumulative number of new visions could contest the dominant conventions, which, as a consequence, may cease to exist as practice. Not all dances created in the past will "survive." This discord opens up space for the new principles to gain traction and become mainstream over time. This process is ongoing.

Naming and branding a significant school of thought in choreography relates mostly to historical periods, context, and terminology. Names of these emerging "sub-genres" are usually assigned in consensus with artists, scholars, historians, critics, and dance observers. Although the branding names of these "sub-genres" may not demonstrate striking originality, they are sufficient to label a school of choreographic thought. The table in Figure 14 is an example of a few key figures in ballet and modern dance whose works did or might "survive" and who have contributed to a school of thought, historical period, or sub-genre:

GENRES	SCHOOLS OF THOUGHT PERIODS & SUB-GENRES	KEY CHOREOGRAPHERS
BALLET	Romantic Ballet	Bournonville, Coralli, Perrot
	Classical Ballet	Saint-Léon, Petipa, Ivanov
	Modern Ballet Theater	Fokine, Nijinsky, Nijinska, Massine, Balanchine
	Neo-classical Ballet	Balanchine, Tudor, Ashton, Robbins, Van Manen
	Contemporary Ballet	Forsythe, McGregor, Dawson, Wheeldon, Peck
MODERN DANCE	Early Modern Dance	St. Denis, Shawn, Fuller, Duncan, Wigman
	Modern Dance	Graham, Humphrey, Dunham, Limón
	Post-Modern Dance	Cunningham, Rainer, Paxton, Brown
	Contemporary Dance Theater	Bausch, Kylián, Ek, Naharin, Pite, Kahn, Cherkaoui

Figure 14

HOW DID ART MOVEMENTS GET THEIR NAMES? The French artist Edgar Degas, who painted dancers in dynamic compositions, joined a group of artists, among them Monet, Renoir, and Cézanne, who initially called themselves the *Société Anonyme des Artistes*. After moving through names such as the *Independents* and the *Intransigents*, the group formally adopted the label of *Impressionists*, leading to the art movement known today as *Impressionism*. The phrase *Abstract Expressionist*, on the other hand, was introduced by American critic Robert M. Coates. The term later became a household name for the *Abstract Expressionism* movement that included artists such as Jackson Pollock, Mark Rothko, and Barnett Newman.[8]

INSTITUTIONAL TITLING AND BRANDING

– THE NAMING OF WE AND US –

In the field of choreography, it takes a village to create, facilitate, and present dance. Except for solo and chamber works, most professional choreographers need institutional infrastructures to produce large and expansive works. Choreographers might choose to work freelance on a one-time project or find ongoing employment at existing dance institutions as affiliate or resident choreographers. Choreographers might be hired to run established dance companies as artistic directors or they might consider establishing their own dance company or institution. Combinations of these choices are also possible—see *A Career in Choreography—Dancing Decisions Moving Forward*, Chapter 25.

There is a competitive advantage for choreographers who form institutions and build new communities. However, starting a new institution is challenging for a variety for reasons. Incorporating a dance company requires compliance with regional government policies. A structure of leadership should be established to foster its success. Funding must be secured, a physical facility selected, artists and staff hired, and the programming and schedule preplanned and agreed upon. The most important factor is the choreographer's artistic vision, which will define the institutional mission of the new dance company.

Instituting a dance company could be initiated by a) a government entity: local, city, state, or country, which establishes a dance institution that employs choreographers affiliated with its cultural mission, b) a single visionary choreographer who establishes a dance institution that acknowledges its founder in the name of the dance company, or c) an individual or group of visionary choreographers established under an "umbrella" dance institution with an artistic vision and unique name that serves as a creative engine for one or several choreographers. Overlap can exist among these strategies. Samples of company brand names could be first distinguished in three separate categories:

CONVENTIONAL COMPANY NAMES	CHOREOGRAPHER'S COMPANY NAMES	CREATIVE COMPANY NAMES
Ballet Russes	Martha Graham Dance Company	Pilobolus
Royal Ballet	Rennie Harris Puremovement	Kidd Pivot
New York City Ballet	Stephen Petronio Company	Black Grace
Dance Theater of Harlem	Camille A. Brown and Dancers	Carte Blanche
Nederlands Dans Theater	Alvin Ailey American Dance Theater	New Adventures
Sydney Dance Company	Alonso King LINES Ballet	Urban Bush Women
Beijing Dance Theater	Joffrey Ballet	La La La Human Steps

Figure 15

Incorporating, naming, and branding a dance institution defines artistry within a chosen context. Although branding is an act of framing a specific identity, multiple creative lenses can be unified under a sole distinct vision. An institutional choreographic identity might also reflect regional and national values and unique traditions and cultures. Such establishments provide a sense of belonging and purpose to serve the community at large.

There are many examples of well-functioning institutionalized dance. George Balanchine and Lincoln Kirstein co-founded a company and named it the New York City Ballet (NYCB) instead of Balanchine Ballet Company. Yet to this day, NYCB carries the authentic Balanchine style and a distinct choreographic identity. Ohad Naharin has created a unique choreographic philosophy, an extensive repertory, and the Gaga movement language. He was also the chief choreographer of Batsheva Dance Company, named after its founder. Kyle Abraham established and named his own company Kyle Abraham/Abraham.In.Motion (A.I.M) by abbreviating the name to emphasize the progressive mission of the company.

An inspired and organized group of people is more powerful than a single individual. Either an assembly of *like-minded supporters or a board of directors* should serve as the engine for the instituting process. The new dance company's distinct *purpose*, *vision*, and *mission* and how it benefits society and culture should be reflected in the title and brand—a semantic and visual symbol (name and logo) encapsulate the institution's identity. There are branding *frames of reference* crafted in collaboration between the choreographer, the artistic team, and the public relations and advertising team. The implementation of the branding demands a *branding bundle* to help present and communicate the newly created content through various engagement aspects—see Figure 1 at the beginning of this chapter.

These aspects include articulating the uniqueness of artistic innovation, the targeted audience, and crafting the strategies and means of delivering the message. A touching story behind the mission could provide an appealing element of *human connection* and explain the reasons for forming the organization. Branding should also raise awareness about the form of cultural contribution and ensure artistic quality. Branding narrative can likewise be considered in various *educational opportunities* to convey distinctly organized artistic principles and provide new knowledge and experiences to communities, audiences, and presenters. A summary of a branding bundle is shown in Figure 16.

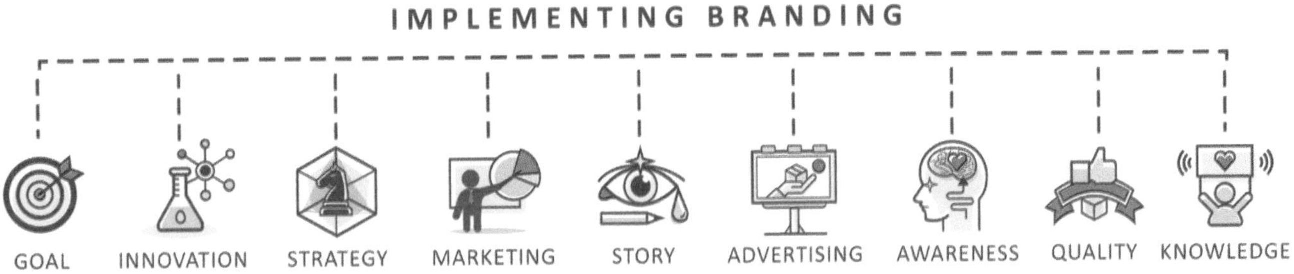

IMPLEMENTING BRANDING

GOAL INNOVATION STRATEGY MARKETING STORY ADVERTISING AWARENESS QUALITY KNOWLEDGE

Figure 16

In summary, institutional branding is about the framing of an institutional identity while nurturing unique content. One could ask: Are we framing creative freedom and therefore limiting it? Well, freedom is not chaos, anarchy, or dysfunctional entropy, but the liberty and power to simultaneously create with and without restraints. Creative freedom and ingenuity can fully flourish in an organized environment when channeled toward a purpose and mission, as generously determined by the artists and the institution's founders.

assignments & exercises

RESEARCH ASSIGNMENT: Use library, digital, and online resources to gather and collect background information about the following questions:

➥ What are the names of three of your favorite dances by different choreographers whose work you admire? Are the titles of these works as attractive as the actual dances?

➥ When and why did the choreographers of these works title their dances in these particular ways?

➥ To re-envision the content and the working title of your new dance and see it from different perspectives, research works with similar content that exists in other art forms—music, literature, theater, and film. Are the titles you found relevant and applicable to your new dance piece? How and why?

★ **CREATIVE EXERCISE:** Practice various improvisation and brainstorming techniques with a series of questions. Experiment with different devices to compose a dance title. Formulate an artistic statement and a branding bundle.

➥ **Brainstorming in The Search for a Title:**[9] You have a new dance that needs a title. Be spontaneous and write down what first comes to mind:

- What emotions and physical actions do you associate with your dance?
- What are some of the goals for the dancers?
- What images does the music of the dance bring to your mind?
- If your dance is a gift, to whom or to what event would you dedicate it?
- If your dance were a rock band or a computer game, what would you name it?
- If your dance were a person or a thing, what name or word would you expect to hear?
- Hypothetically, what was the initial impetus for this dance?
- If your dance were to appear on a vintage ad poster, what image do you envision?
- If your dance will be on a futuristic digital ad, what image would you want to see?
- If you used one word to describe the dance, what would it be?

➥ **Using Devices to Compose a Title:** Practice techniques to generate, accumulate, improvise, organize, play, combine, and rearrange:

— Generate and accumulate: Based on your early research of titles of works related to your dance content but in other art forms—music, literature, theater, and film—generate and accumulate lists of words, as described in the chapter.

— Improvise and organize: Select keywords closely related to your dance content. Create a table with columns of verbs, adjectives, and nouns.

— Play, combine, and rearrange: Play with connecting the words you have generated to create combinations of different sizes, arrangements of words with contrasting meaning, modifications, puns, variations, and unusual blends.

➥ **Formulating an Artistic Statement and Branding Bundle for Publicity/Marketing Purposes and Commissioning Proposals/Arts Funding:** Choreographers are always asked to prepare a written or verbal presentation to describe the new work for the advertisement materials and interviews with the press. Project applications for funding, grants, sponsorship, and producing and presenting venues also require written statements and summaries about creative processes, and past and current work. For instance:

✓ About your new work:

— What is your new dance about in terms of content, process, and movement form?

— What is the background of the work, and what are your intentions?

— What purpose does the work serve, and why is it essential to create it?

✓ About you, the choreographer:

— What is dance for you—your dance manifesto and choreographic philosophy?

— Why do you create dances?

— What has shaped you as an artist?

⤮ **COMPARATIVE ASSIGNMENT:** When a dance company and artistic entrepreneurship have been newly formed, more questions will be asked by a publicity team about what distinguishes the brand. Some of them might be: What is always consistent and what is always changing in your work? In what ways will your work and your dance company contribute to the dance field's current state and to the art form over time? How do you describe your institution's vision and mission in comparison with others in the field? What distinguishes your dance company from others?

BIBLIOGRAPHY AND REFERENCES

[1] Puzey, Guy and Kostanski, Laura. *Names and Naming: People, Places, Perceptions and Power*, Multilingual Matters, 2016.

[2] Hough, Carole. *The Oxford Handbook of Names and Naming*, Reprint edition, Oxford University Press, January 9, 2018.

[3] *What Does Copyright Protect?* US Copyright Office: www.copyright.gov/help/faq/faq-protect.html.

[4] Leahy, Richard. "Twenty Titles for the Writer," *College Composition and Communication*, vol. 43, no. 4, 1992, pp. 516–519. JSTOR. University Libraries, U of Minnesota, 19 July 2007.

[5] Editors. The George Balanchine Trust: http://balanchine.com/serenade/ and New York City Ballet: www.nycballet.com/ballets/s/serenade.aspx.

[6] Sample titles of notable works by notable choreographers, are: *It Takes Two*, choreography by Rob Base & DJ E-Z Rock, among many others using the same popular title for dance: *The Third Light*, *A Million Kisses on My Skin*, and *The Grey Area*, choreography by David Dawson; *Summer Space*, choreography by Merce Cunningham; *Silent Cries*, *Return to a Strange Land Falling Angels*, and *Indigo Rose*, choreography by Jiří Kylián; *Joyride*, choreography by Mark Morris; *Political Mother*, choreography by Hofesh Shechter; *Horses in the Sky*, choreography by Rami Be'er.

[7] Sample titles of notable works by notable choreographers: *Last Supper at Uncle Tom's Cabin/The Promised Land*, and *Fondly Do We Hope...Fervently Do We Pray*, choreography by Bill T. Jones; *How We Got to Now*, choreography by Bre Seals.

[8] Hart, Kim. *Giving Name or Getting Name?–From Dada to Bauhaus, How 14 Art Movements Got Their Names*, online article: www.artsy.net/article/, accessed December 2017.

[9] Editors. Center for Writing, University of Minnesota, *Writing an Effective Title*, online article: http://writing.umn.edu/sws/quickhelp/process/titles.html, accessed June 2020.

VISUAL REFERENCES

Figure 1: Diagram © Vladimir Angelov, clip art: *Old picture frame isolated on white background*, credit: 乐缘, courtesy of Adobe Stock

Figure 2: Diagram © Vladimir Angelov

Figure 3: *Colorful Pencil on a White Background*, clip art, credit: skalapendra, courtesy of iStock/Getty Images

Figures 4, 5, and 6: Diagrams © Vladimir Angelov

Figure 7: Diagram © Vladimir Angelov, *Documents Line Icon Set*, clip art, credit: SurfUpVector, courtesy of iStock/Getty Images

Figures 8, 9, 10, 11, 12, 13, 14, and 15: Diagrams © Vladimir Angelov

Figure 16: Diagram © Vladimir Angelov, and *Branding banner web icon: target, social media, storytelling, awareness, customer service, quality and brand loyalty, clip art*, credit: PlagueDoctor, courtesy of iStock/Getty Images

CHAPTER 24

PIECING A PRODUCTION TOGETHER – THINK COSTUMES, LIGHTS, AND SCENIC DESIGN –

Dance is visual art in motion. While choreography is an act of creating movement, a concert dance performance is also the *artistic unity* of other contributing arts. These may include music, visual arts, scenic and costume design, as well as other supporting disciplines that bring a dance spectacle to a complete and final appearance.

Dance production is an expression describing not only the dancing, but also important features such as costumes, lights, scenic design, and other available independent mediums. These *production aspects and elements* can organically influence and substantially impact the theatrical performance when the choreographer considers integrating them creatively.

Production team is a term describing a group of collaborating artists and designers who help to effectively conceive the production aspects of a dance performance. On some occasions, choreographers can assemble their own production team of long-term close collaborators. On other occasions, collaborators are newly invited and perhaps unfamiliar with the choreographer's creative process. Engaging other independent artists in the choreographer's work, building trust, facilitating honest conversations, and collaborating effectively often require additional effort and attentiveness.

Artistic teamwork and creative collaboration with other artists and technical specialists are vital to the success of a dance production. Usually, the planning for integrating the production aspects and elements begins early in the rehearsal process and performance planning. Therefore, the choreographer may consider some advance preparation by expanding knowledge and gaining skills, such as:

- ➢ Developing a basic understanding of how different mediums work
- ➢ Communicating truthfully all artistic intentions and content with the production team
- ➢ Collaborating respectfully and approaching the production team with an open mind

Dance production elements are instrumental in how the choreography and the completed dance work will be perceived. When the choreographer is upfront and truthful with the production teamsters, they in turn will collaborate and support the genuine vision of the dance work. Communication—both artistic and interpersonal—is key to team building among the artists and connecting the work with the audience.

An unbiased dance audience is always the holder of the truth—the spectators have nothing to lose by being honest. A personal perspective and individual interpretation are embedded in every person. In addition, the collective experience and the audience's reaction as a unified body of spectators mostly end up being straightforward.

This leads us to the vital link between intentions and realization, desires and appearance, and expression and truthfulness. All of these themes can be found in a tale familiar to most kids and adults.

The Emperor's New Clothes is a short tale written by Danish author Hans Christian Andersen. The story unfolds as two alleged weavers promise an emperor that they will make him a new suit that is invisible to those who are unfit for their positions, stupid, or incompetent. At the same time, the weavers make no clothes at all, while convincing everyone that the clothes are visible.

When the emperor finally parades in front of everybody in his new "clothes," no one dares to say that they do not see any clothes on him, fearing they will be seen as stupid. Finally, a child in the crowd cries out: "But he isn't wearing anything at all!"

The Emperor's New Clothes has acquired global iconic status while migrating across various cultures and being reshaped when retold. There are also multiple layers of meaning and ways of interpretation. Should we applaud the imagination of those who "see" the emperor's new clothes? Should we value the "artistic invention" of the two weavers separately from its material appearance? Should we sympathize with those who use self-deception as self-protection?

Figure 1 Illustration © Ann Mei, *The Naked King and his clothes*, courtesy of iStock/Getty Images

Declassifying the truth about the emperor's new clothes raises an important question about production values in choreography:

Do we *see what it is,*

or *what we want to see,*

or *what we are led to see*?

In addition to the tale's critique of pretentiousness and social hypocrisy, the most important takeaway is clearly applicable to a choreographer who is working with collaborators in other artistic mediums: Have the courage to stand up for one's convictions and the truth, no matter how humiliating it is.

Good choreography can be very well supported and presented, or totally misunderstood and incorrectly interpreted by the use of the production elements. Therefore, the choreographer develops interest, compassion, and an understanding of how to use those mediums; how to work with and talk to the designers; and how to bring the artistic team together so they can explore and develop ideas in coordination.

[UN]COVERING THE MOVING BODY

– THE BASICS OF COSTUME DESIGN FOR DANCE –

Dance costuming is the functional wear and visual appearance of the dancers while they are still and in motion. A costume designer works with the choreographer to create the most suitable garments for the performers in relation to the concept of the dance. Based on the choreographer's vision and the range of movement vocabulary, the costume designer determines whether the dance costumes should be custom-made, or if they should be obtained from a dance attire company in commercial production, or a combination of both.

Compared to costumes for drama, opera, and music, where the performers' mobility may be limited, dance costumes must endure the dancers' constant and often extreme physical actions. Dance costumes are subject to intense activities that include an enormous amount of pulling, stretching, and rubbing against the body. The costumes for dance need to be comfortably lightweight, kinesthetically functional, and exceptionally durable to withstand rigorous body motion.[1]

Effective costumes contribute to the overall look and impression, whether the dance is dramatic or neutral, classical or avant-garde, narrative or abstract. Finally, the designer should reach an optimal decision on how much of the dancer's body will be (un)covered, and whether the garment's tailoring will be *form-fitting*, *close-fitted*, or *loose*.

WHAT DO CHOREOGRAPHERS NEED TO KNOW ABOUT HOW COSTUME DESIGNERS CREATE?

The choreographer develops an understanding of how a costume designer thinks and what resources and information are necessary for the costume designer to contribute creatively to the process. Similar to choreography, costume design has its own creative foundation, tools, devices, and techniques. They can be summarized in the following **three-dimensional thinking** diagram that serves as the base of any costume design:

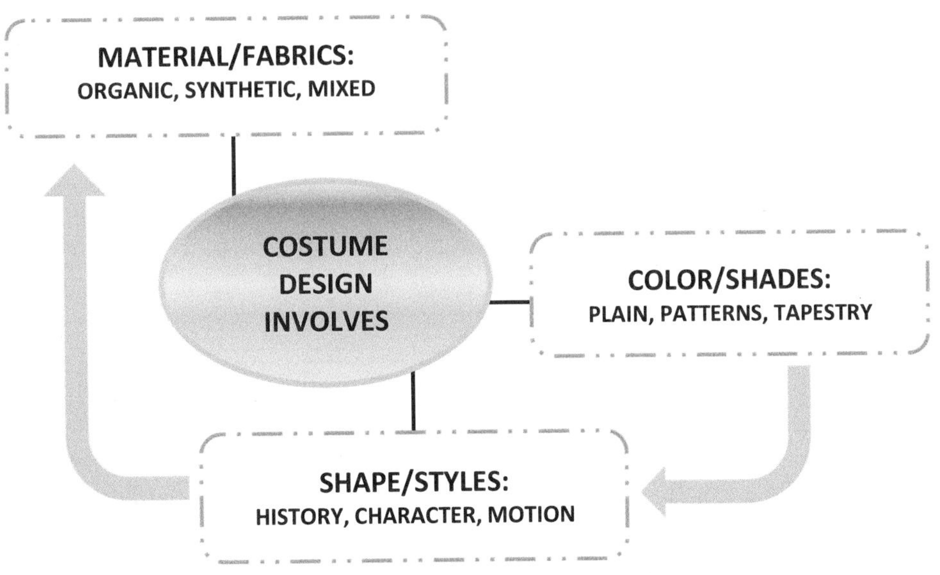

Figure 2

The technical elements of costume design addressed separately are:

◆ **MATERIAL/FABRICS:** Clothing and costumes are constructed from *fabric*, which is made of a basic filament and raw material—*fiber*. Fibers might have: a) *Organic origin*: Made from natural resources like plant or animal-based materials such as cotton, wool, silk, linen, and fur; b) *Synthetic origin*: Made artificially from chemical materials and petroleum products such as polyester, nylon, spandex, acrylic, and latex; c) *Semi-synthetic origin*: Made from a natural source but require processing to transform that natural source into a fiber that can be used for clothing such as rayon (aka viscose), modal, lyocell, and bamboo. There are also blended fibers, which are made from mixing two or more different materials together.[2]

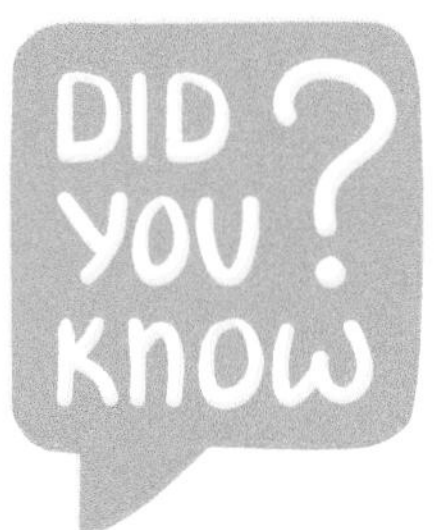

A microscope magnification can easily distinguish between fibers. Such a close look identifies the natural fibers as compared to human-made ones. Wool has an irregular, cylindrical, rough surface and scale-like structure, while silk has a smooth surface that is structureless, and in cross-section, it has a triangular-shaped transparent rod appearance. Cotton is flat with ribbon-like convolutions, while linen is smooth and bamboo-like with cross marking nodes. Finally, polyester has a uniform diameter and a smooth rod-like appearance.[3]

Fibers are made into fabric through weaving, knitting, and crocheting—see Figure 3. When worn by the dancers as costumes, various fibers and fabrics "behave" differently in terms of *weight*, *volume*, *flexibility*, and *mobility*. These qualities are called the *"hand" of the fabric*. A dance dress made of heavy cotton will "move" completely differently than the same dress made of lightweight silk. A fitted vest made of non-stretchy linen, instead of stretchy polyester, will affect the dancers' range of motion. In addition, fabrics absorb sweat differently. Some fabrics soak up sweat invisibly, while others develop visible wet spots where dancers prespire.[4]

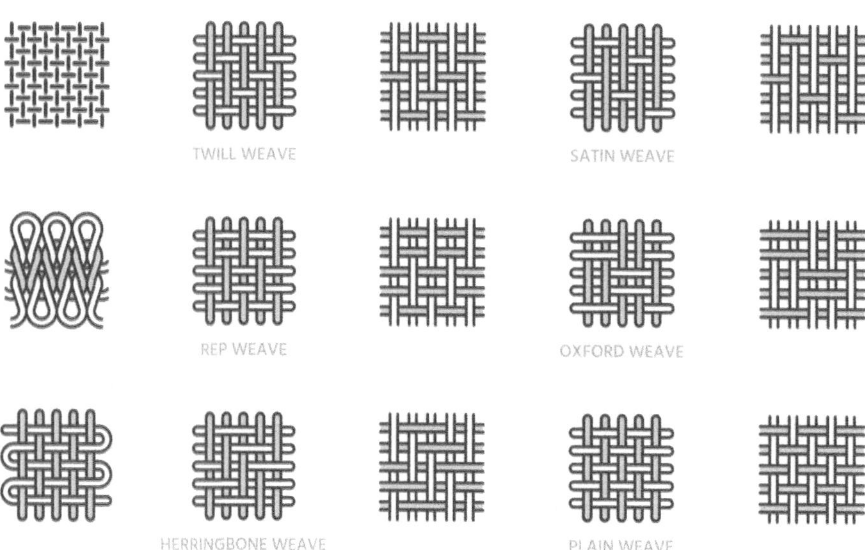

Figure 3 Textile swatches: weave types of different clothing materials, courtesy of iStock/Getty Images

◆ **COLOR/SHADES:** A color and its quality emerges as a property of an object or material to reflect, transmit, or absorb light, producing a specific visual effect. Colors can be warm or cool, bright or muted, and light or dark. The color of the fabric for costumes can be changed by dyeing, bleaching, or color removing.[5]

Colors have their own expressive language which speaks in bold or subtle messages. There are expectations and preferences for using certain colors for specific circumstances: a Flamenco dancer might be clad in a red dress to attract attention; a dancer portraying a snowflake—in a white tutu expressing snow and purity; or participants in a funeral dance scene—usually in black as a manifestation of mourning. There is a wide range in between. Costume and fashion designers develop a certain sensitivity to color nuances and have a deep understanding of using intricate shades, which they often express in figurative terminology:[6]

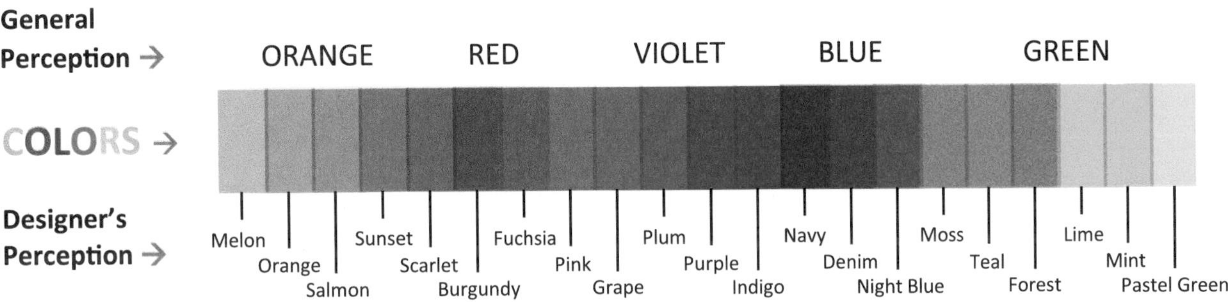

Figure 4

In costume design, colors can interact and can be mixed in a variety of ways. Colors of fabric for dance costuming can be categorized as a) *solid and plain colors*: these are not altered by mixing them with other colors. Plain colors can be primary colors such as red, yellow, and blue; secondary colors; as well as different hues, tints, and shades between black, gray and white; b) *patterns and motifs:* patterns are the repetition of an element, ornament, or theme to create a unique decoration on fabric through weaving. These patterns can be stripes, checks, plaid, patches, waves, diamonds, dots, and batik; c) *printing, dyeing and tapestry:* these can include embroidery of custom imagery, printed pictorial designs, air brush techniques, and specific dyeing with the goal to create a unique texture and give an exclusive look to the fabric.[7] A few samples of prints and patterns are:

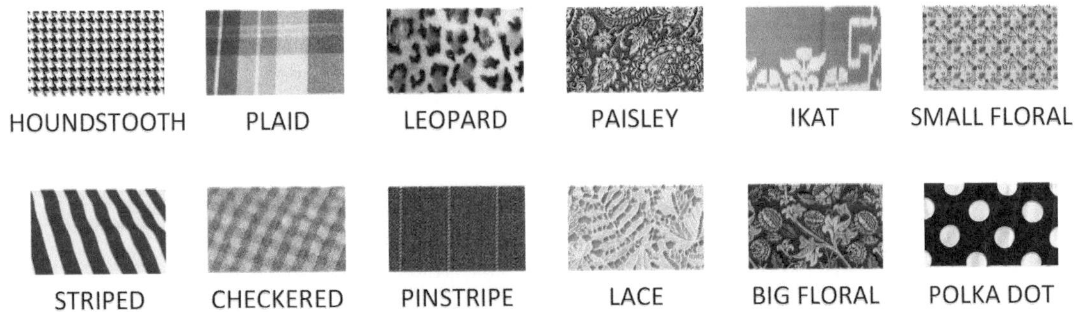

Figure 5 Samples of various fabric prints, patterns, and textures, from public domain images, sorted by Charles Scheland

◆ **SHAPE/STYLES:** Different types of fabric in a variety of colors are cut in patterns and then stitched together in different *shapes* and unique combinations forming a *style*. Style is the distinct conceptual arrangement and appearance of clothing that makes a visual and artistic statement. The latest style and trends in clothing are referred to as *fashion*.[8] There are multiple dimensions and references in regard to shape, style, and type of clothing and how they are related to stage costuming for dance.

➢ ***Historic reference:*** The anatomical structure of the average human body hasn't changed too much over the centuries. A naked body from the distant past and from today look similar; however, what covers it has changed and has defined clothing historically and culturally.

The initial purpose of clothing throughout the ages was to protect the body from the changing seasons and the elements. The first clothes were made from natural materials: animal skin and furs, grasses and leaves, and bones and shells. The history of clothing goes together with the history of textiles. Humans invented techniques such as weaving and spinning, and later the machines needed to make the fabrics used for clothing. Clothing also changed in functionality—from simply covering the body, to making *cultural, social, and fashion statements* that express personal preferences and taste.

Mainstream fashion and individual styles have also changed and evolved. In dance, all of these elements are taken into consideration alongside their historic and geophysical identity[9]—see Figure 6:

Figure 6 Images from left to right: Photography © Viktoria Ivanova and Sebastian Tornee, featured dancer Desi Jordanoff in a traditional outfit of Bulgaria, 2019; young Balinese dancer in traditional outfit; and Maasai lady in traditional outfit of Tanzania, 2019, courtesy of iStock/Getty Images

➢ ***Character reference:*** Clothing and garments in life and in dance express a lot about those wearing them. On stage, the dance costumes are the visual identity of the dancers who portray the artistic vision of the dance work. Dance costuming can communicate specific characteristics of an individual or a group and make an instant visual statement about context and circumstances. For example, the audience more accurately follows the storyline of *The Nutcracker* ballet when they first identify the stage costuming of the main characters: Clara, Fritz, Herr Drosselmeyer, the Nutcracker, the Mouse King, and the Sugar Plum Fairy. Building a stage costume for a character in narrative dance requires research, creativity, and clarity. There are seven elements that build a believable stage character and appropriate costume design: 1) time and place; 2) age and gender; 3) inner world and temperament; 4) socioeconomic status and occupation; 5) ethnic and religious affiliation; 6) circumstance and occasion; and 7) relationship to the other characters.

➢ ***Motion Reference and Movement Functionality:*** Non-literal and plotless dance works usually exclude historic and character references. In these cases, the goal of the dance costuming is to support abstract movement ideas and to fit the dancers well. For example, when we are about to buy a garment and we like the color and material, the key factor in our decision to buy it is a *right fit*.

MAKE IT FIT WELL!—is an efficient principle for successful collaboration between the choreographer and costume designer:

Functionality + Impression + Texture = FIT

Functionality is the assurance that the costuming is comfortable and allows the performers to execute the choreography effectively; *Impression* is the ideas and feelings that the costuming evokes to reach the desired artistic effect; and *Texture* is the physical and visual quality of the costuming that is expressed with the design elements affecting the dancers' movement and appearance.

◆ **REVEALING OR COVERING THE MOVING BODY** is another important aspect of costume design, determined by the amount and volume of fabric and the shape of the garment. Three guiding design strategies in alignment with the choreographic concept can help determine the degree that garments expose or conceal the dancer's body:

➢ ***Movement Extension*** is loose-fitting, extensive coverage of the body, in part or fully, with large volumes of fabric that emphasize the motion of the fabric. Such garments include full skirts, long dresses, scarves, capes, etc. The choreography utilizes the extra fabric by incorporating it with the movements of the dancers.

➢ ***Complementing Motion*** is close-fitting, balanced coverage of the body with overall garments or separates such as tops, bottoms, etc. The choreography utilizes a complementing balance between the motion of the dancers and the added visual and physical quality of the costuming.

➢ ***Second Skin*** is form-fitting, minimal coverage of the body with a moderate volume of fabric such as tights, leotards, unitards, trunks, bikinis, bras, etc. The choreography utilizes the exposed clear body shapes, the precision of movements, and the body's kinetic vulnerability.

Figure 7 Photography © Lois Greenfield, pictured from left to right: Nejla Yatkin, NY2Dance, 2011; Patrick Corbin, Corbindances 2006; Chad Levy, Amy Marshall Dance Company, 2011; Drew Jacoby, 2011; Joseph Gallerizo and Vanessa Lynn Campos, Dodge Dance Company, 2006.

◆ **ACCESSORIES AND PORTABLE PROPS** are stylistic and functional additions, and in some cases they are character enhancements to the dance costuming. They might include a variety of headpieces, as well as a range of jewelry, scarves, hats, gloves, eye glasses, etc. Portable props might include baskets, bags, canes, umbrellas, and other small portable objects. Accessories and portable props can be instrumental in shaping the features of the characters in their stage portrayal. For instance, carrying a cane would suggest someone of older age, a big spoon—a chef, a crown—royalty, reading eyeglasses—an intellectual, gloves—care and service, etc. To learn more about accessories and small props in relationship to the choreographer's concepts and dance dramaturgy, see Chapter 19.

◆ **DANCE FOOTWEAR** often determines the style of the choreography, and vice versa. "What kind of shoes do you want us to wear for your piece?"—The dancers always ask the choreographer during the very first rehearsal of a new work. And just as in *Cinderella's* shoe-fitting mystery, choreographers must consider fitting their creative vision to specific footwear and committing conceptually to it.

The choice of dance footwear should not be random. Dancing involves steps that are created on and executed by the feet. Therefore, the right footwear should support and fit the dance naturally. Multiple factors are at play, such as style, appearance, content, kinesthetic range, technique, ability, execution, and functionality.

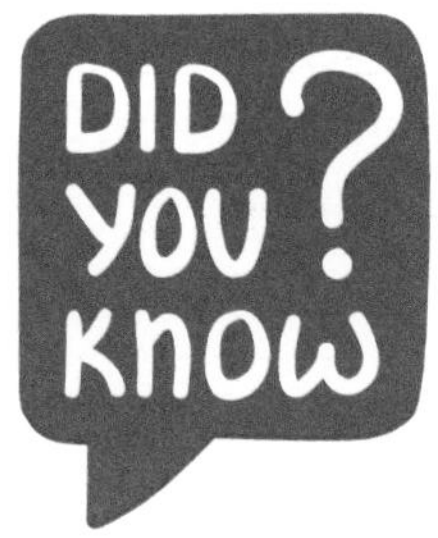

Shoes can tell a story! Dance genres are often determined by their footwear, or the absence of it. Early humans danced in bare feet, while later, ancient dancers used sandals, moccasins, and espadrilles. During the Renaissance and Baroque eras, dancers performed in fancy high-heeled shoes. In the Romantic era, ballerinas brought ballet slippers and pointe shoes on stage.

Spanish and Irish dancers introduced shoes to accommodate their percussive foot work. Modern dancers went back to performing barefoot, while contemporary dancers often use socks or grips to glide and turn while remaining grounded.

Figure 8 Images of shoes from upper left clockwise: Baroque shoes, tap shoes, sneakers, and pointe shoes, courtesy of iStock/Getty Images

The choice of dance footwear, or the absence of it, affects how the choreographer approaches the movement of the feet and the entire body. For example, choreographing for bare feet will instinctively generate grounded movement vocabulary, since the feet are in full and direct contact with the floor. Specialized dance footwear such as tap shoes will naturally allow elaborate rhythmic sequencing. Flat, non-heeled ballet slippers allow a dancer to jump higher and offer easy mobility across the dance floor.

Pointe shoes, on the other hand, offer a select and partial area of contact between the feet and the floor. Therefore, pointe shoe technique provides the opportunity for poses, shapes, and moves with extended suspensions, multiple turns, speedy steps, weightless-appearing moves, quick jumps, and complex, off-balance partnering work.[10]

The following is a brief summary of dance footwear's evolution and functionality:

Types of dance footwear through the ages						
RITUAL AND ANCIENT		MEDIEVAL, RENAISSANCE, AND BAROQUE		INDUSTRIAL, MODERN, AND CONTEMPORARY		
Bare feet	Bare feet	Bare feet	Bare feet	Bare feet	Bare feet	Bare feet
	Sandals	Sandals	Sandals	Sandals	Sandals	Sandals
		Court footwear	Court footwear	Court footwear	Court footwear	Court footwear
			Dance shoes	Dance shoes	Dance shoes	Dance shoes
				Ballet slippers	Ballet slippers	Ballet slippers
					Pointe shoes	Pointe shoes
						Sneakers

Footwear contact with the dance floor surface		
Direct and total	Fractional through shoe soles	Controlled through shoe soles

Footwear effect on footwork and overall body motion		
Grounded and sturdy	Contained and balanced	Lightweight and elevated

Figure 9

√ **COSTUME DESIGN** is a creative interaction between the subjectivity of the movement and the objectivity of the costuming. Providing the costume designer with content, context, and a description of the characters and the environment where the dance takes place serves as the beginning of the collaboration. Other important items for discussion are:

➢ **Artistic impression and visual/physical texture.** Dancers clad in casual, mass-manufactured garments will look like regular people on stage who happen to be dancing. A few alterations and modifications by a professional costume designer can turn manufactured clothing into effective stage costuming.

➢ **Functionality and mobility.** If the dancers perform choreography with extensive inversions and movements on the floor, then formal gowns or fitted, non-stretchy short skirts might impede their movements down to the floor and back up.

➢ **Presence of colors and color mixing—complementing, contrasting, and coordinating.** There are so many choices of colors. In most cases, the use of generic black costuming in dance is driven by a limited production budget, or by dancers who believe they will look more flattering. However, black costuming can be difficult to see on a black-box theater stage where the curtains, the dance floor, and the backdrop are black. Any color other than black might better complement the dance and other design and production elements.

?

When you begin choreographing, are dance shoes and costuming the first or last thing you consider, and why?

WORKING WITH THE DANCE COSTUME DESIGNER

– BASIC TERMINOLOGY AND COLLABORATIVE INTERACTION –

BASIC COSTUME CONSTRUCTION:	BASIC GARMENTS, OUTFITS AND STYLES:
Applique – a piece of fabric sewn atop another	**Leotard, Unitard, Corset** – form-fitting garments used in dance and classical ballet
Embellishment – special stitching, appliques, charms, or other decorations	**Collar, sleeves, cuffs, pockets, fly, waistband** – signature components of garments and clothing
Trim – any decorative item, ribbon, lace, or craft item that is sewn on	**Leggings, Tights, Pants, Skirt (circle, pencil, tutu)** – bottom garments that cover the lower extremities
Interfacing – fabric used between layers of fabric to provide stabilization and form	**Tank top, shirt, sweater, vest** – top garments that cover the torso
Lining – fabric used to finish the inside of a garment	**Dress, tunic, camisole, gown, cape, jumpsuit** – garments of different lengths that hang from the shoulders
Inseam – seam inside the leg of pants that runs from the crotch to the hem	**Knee-, Ankle-, Floor-Length** – ways to describe the leg coverage and the length of a dress or other bottoms
Hem – fabric that is turned up on the lower edge of a garment or sleeve to provide a finished edge	**Halter-, Strap-, Short-Sleeve, or Sleeveless** – ways to describe the shoulder attachment of a dress

Figure 10

HELPFUL TIPS & SUGGESTIONS

~ **Share your choreographic concepts, creative intentions, and dance content** with the costume designer. When possible, invite the designer to studio rehearsals during the early stages of the work-in-progress. Engage in a collaborative discussion about the total visual approach to the dance production.

~ **Provide references** and any visual samples such as drawings, photographs, or a magazine clipping of various designs you have encountered during your research to help the designers with the direction of their own research.

~ **Learn in advance the limitations** of the budget, technical logistics, and the timeframe for costume construction.

~ **Be flexible with the designer's modifications and suggestions for costume execution**, as some designers barely do cutting, stitching, and tailoring. Designers also assume a large responsibility for the realization of the designs, including construction, sourcing, and the final treatment and finishing.

~ **Review and agree on costume renderings and fabric swatches**, usually in the form of color sketches and sample fabrics in the proposed materials and colors.

~ **Consolidate an efficient costume plot** as the designer puts together a *piece list* and a *chart* of all the costumes needed before submitting it to the costume shop for budgeting and construction.

~ **Request mockup outfits and a rehearsal version of the costumes** to visualize the effect of the designs, test comfort and mobility, as well as to accommodate fitting and pattern drafting. The designs must also satisfy the movement range and practical needs of the dancers, including quick changes—if necessary.

[EN]LIGHTENING AFFAIRS
– THE BASICS OF LIGHTING DESIGN FOR DANCE –

The stars of a dance production are the choreography and the performers. However, a dance cannot be seen without the presence of light. A lighting designer is in charge of the location, direction, functions, design, and control of lighting. The lighting designer works with the choreographer to create an atmosphere that supports and enhances the concept and content of the dance work.

The lighting designer is also responsible for the dancers' safe stage entries and exits, as well as their performance in a visible environment, while maintaining the conceptual integrity and the desired visual effect of the dance work. A lighting designer will implement seven creative principles while designing specific moods and an overall atmosphere of lighting to accommodate the choreographer's vision.[12]

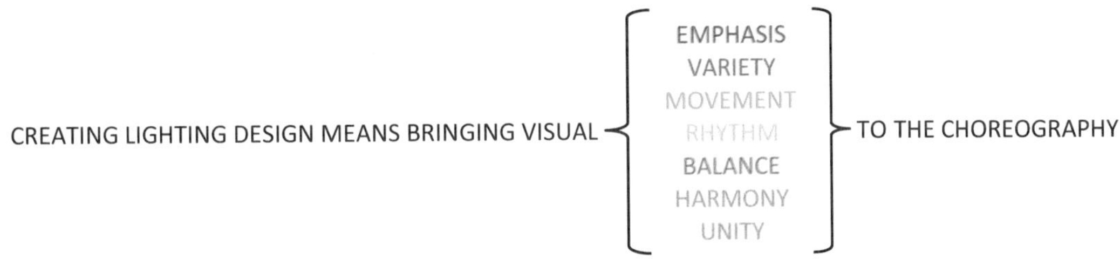

Figure 11

WHAT DO CHOREOGRAPHERS NEED TO KNOW ABOUT HOW LIGHTING DESIGNERS CREATE?

Before a choreographer engages in a passionate conversation with the lighting designer to provide an in-depth description of the dance work, the choreographer should learn how lighting designers think by stepping into their shoes. Similar to choreography, lighting design has its own creative foundation, tools, devices, and techniques, which can be summarized in the **three-dimensional thinking** diagram below that serves as the basis of any lighting design:

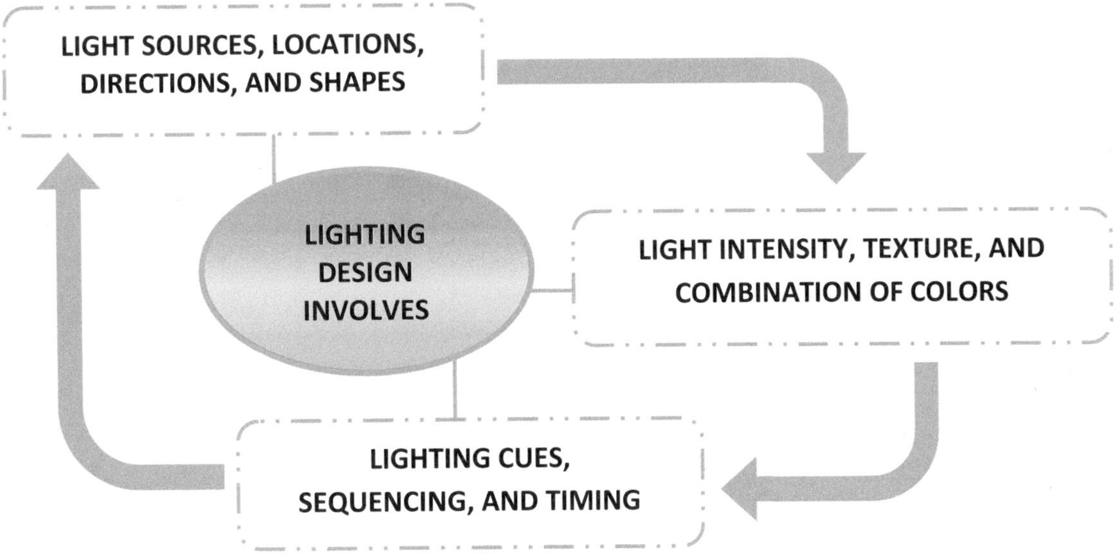

Figure 12

In the following pages, we examine the elements of lighting design separately:

◆ **LIGHT SOURCES, LOCATION, DIRECTION, AND SHAPES:** The lighting designer is in charge of the *lighting resources* and a variety of *lighting instruments,* as well as how they are positioned throughout the performance space. Light can come from the *lighting grid* above the stage, as well as from any position below, including the front, back, sides, and diagonals, or other positions. The direction of light is determined by the position, angle, and focus of the lighting instruments. Light can be shaped in certain forms and patterns. An intentional spotlight or moving light can bring a dramatic emphasis to a specific scene.[13]

➢ ***Location of lighting*** is where the lighting instruments are positioned. The stationary placement of the instruments is determined by the lighting designer and specified in a carefully pre-planned *lighting plot* that reveals where the lighting instruments will be located.

This chapter addresses lighting design for a *proscenium stage.* There is a distinction between lighting plots for theater, opera, and music concerts, and the lighting plots for dance. For productions with limited body motion, the lighting design focuses on the faces and the eyes to emphasize the work of the actors, singers, and musicians.

Dancers tend to move continuously and dimensionally on stage. The entire body should be lit not only from the front and top, but also from the sides. The lighting designer takes into consideration that all dancers should be fully visible at all times while moving throughout the stage space. Also, the type of lighting instruments chosen should provide an adequate amount of light and offer a variety of creative options.

In comparison to theater, opera, and music concerts, dance productions—especially in contemporary dance—frequently use an empty stage with a bare dance floor and limited props, sets, and elaborate constructions on stage. Outlined in the figure below are the locations and directions of light, the areas on stage, and the backdrop to be lit on a proscenium stage:

Light Locations & Directions

- Front and upper light
- Side, angle, and diagonal light
- Down light
- Back light
- Spotlights and specials
- Follow spot lights

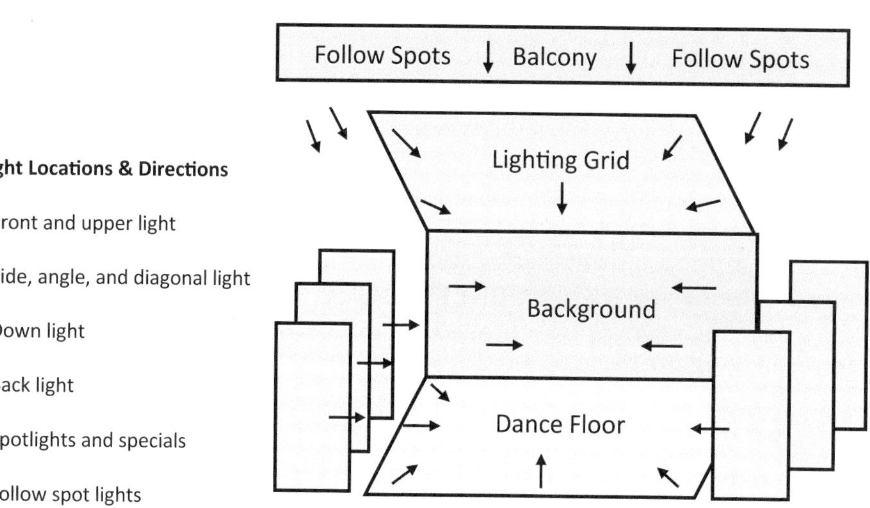

The areas to be lit are:

- The dance floor
- The background and cyclorama
- The stage space between the side curtains and the floor and the ceiling*

*This area is the most important visual field where the dancers' movements take place

Figure 13

➢ ***Direction of light*** is the path of light as it passes through space from the lighting instruments and arrives at a certain area, object, material, person, or group of people. Rays of light can also bounce off a surface, objects, or materials, causing *refraction*, which can change the direction of light.[14]

The light beam can travel from a variety of distances and angles through space without boundary, or it can be pointed and controlled with a specific *focus*. The focus is where the light instrument is pointed, which can be adjusted by the fixtures on the lighting instrument. *Selective focus* is when a certain area on the stage floor is lit, or a follow spot is focused on the performers' faces or on certain elements of the dance.[15]

The direction of light can be also determined by the source of light. For example, *motivated light* reveals the source of the light—a window, a lamp, or a candle carried across the stage. Revealing where the light is coming from creates a specific atmosphere on stage for the performers, as the lighting design "hides" behind it discreetly.

➢ ***Lighting shapes, patterns, and areas*** on stage are usually the lit areas where the most action occurs. A number of spotlights—specific light points or "specials"—can be required to cover the most important and dramatic elements of the dance. Frequent areas occupied by the dancers are upstage and downstage, the diagonals, and center stage.[16]

Lighting designers purposely attend dance rehearsal before technical rehearsals or study a video recording of the choreography, while taking notes about the movement placement, patterns, and pathways of the dancers. This is an important step when designing the lighting plot. Not only does the use of light affect the lighting plot, but so does the use of shadows. The three main concepts of lighting that a choreographer most frequently uses are:

— **Dance floor's** shapes, patterns, and zones are designed in certain forms to best reveal the most dramatic qualities of the dance. A series of general options is usually in use and available to the choreographer and the designer to choose what best suits each section of the dance. The dance floor lighting plan options may include some of the following:

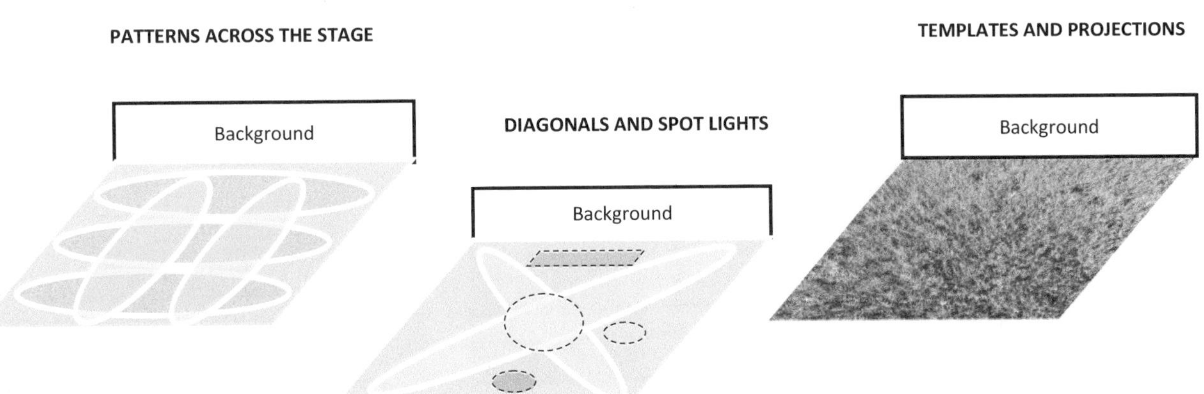

Figure 14

— **Backdrop and scrim** (cyclorama) lighting usually serves as the background for the dance. The cyclorama upstage could be left passively neutral, dim, or unlit. Alternatively, the cyclorama could be actively used to complement or contrast with the moving bodies in front of it. The back cyclorama could be lit partially or fully with single or multiple colors, with a variety of templates, or with a projection, such as a photo image of a sunset. Photos or live video projections need to be used selectively so they do not compete with the dance action in front of the backdrop.[17] Possible options to bring some dimensionality to the flat surface upstage are:

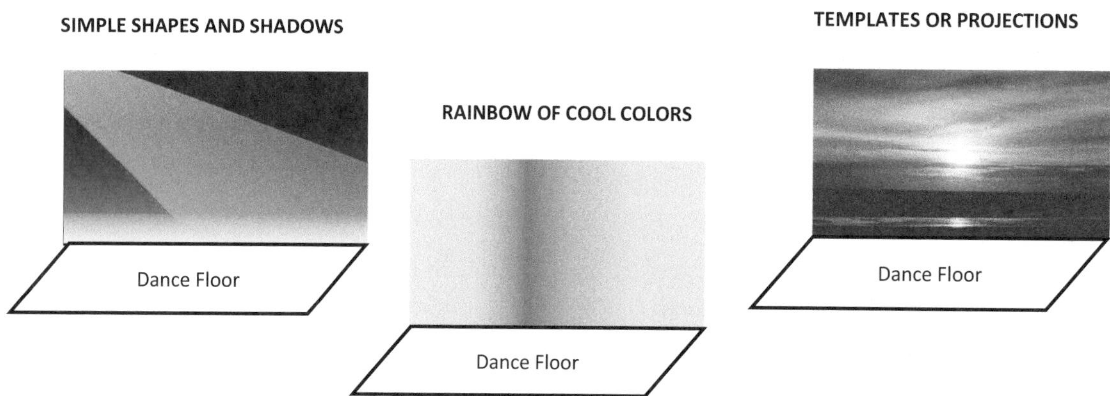

Figure 15

— **Side lighting** comes from different angles and diagonals from the side wings, with crossing trajectories above the dance floor, in front of the backdrop, and between the side curtains. Side lighting is most essential for lighting the dancers while in motion on stage. Even if the dance floor or the backdrop is not lit, the side lighting from the left and/or right side shins and booms can evenly light the dancers and provide enough visibility, as well as certain dramatic looks by sculpting the body with light.[18]

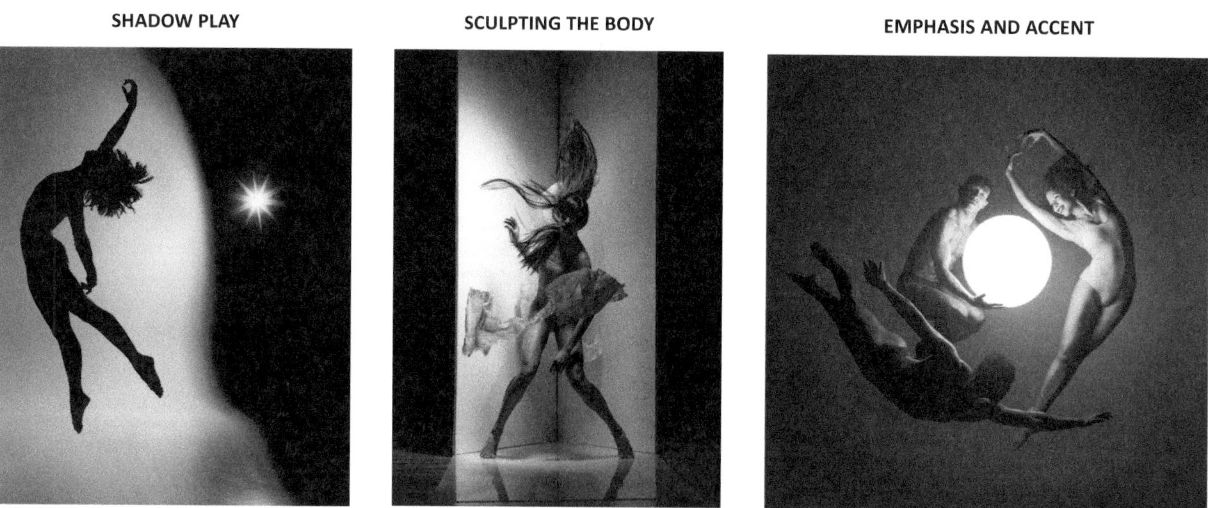

Figure 16 Photography © Lois Greenfield, image left—pictured Sumayah McRae, 2002; image center—pictured LaKendra Dennard, 2013; image right—pictured Michael Fielder, Andrew Pacho, Kara Sandberg, 2002

◆ **LIGHT INTENSITY, TEXTURE, AND THE COMBINATION OF COLORS:** Light intensity can range from total darkness to painfully bright. The timing of intensity serves as an additional artistic tool. The consistent brightness of the sunlight is different than brightness of a selected spotlight, which can be controlled with a fade-in and fade-out achieved with the instruments. The variation in brightness and colors creates certain moods. Traditionally, blue = evening, and bright yellow = sunny day, with endless nuanced combinations in between. The combinations of light intensity and color mix produce *light textures*.[19]

➢ ***Intensity*** is the amount of light distributed by the instruments. The lighting designer determines and assigns the percentage (%) of light intensity and light color temperature that each of the instruments will distribute. For example, use of excessive light (brighter) or less light (darker, dimmer) are artistic decisions made according to the amount of light necessary for both the dramatic effect of a particular scene and for safety.[20]

➢ ***Color selection*** for lighting design requires an in-depth knowledge of how a given color originating from a light source will appear on stage. The primary colors in lighting design are considered to be red, blue, and green, which can be mixed in endless combinations to create different nuances.[21]

➢ ***Combination of colors*** occurs when primary colors are mixed to produce secondary colors. In general, cool color + warm color = neutral color. In dance, a frequently used color is *magenta*, a color in between pink and purple, or red and purple which is composed equally of 50% red and 50% blue.[22]

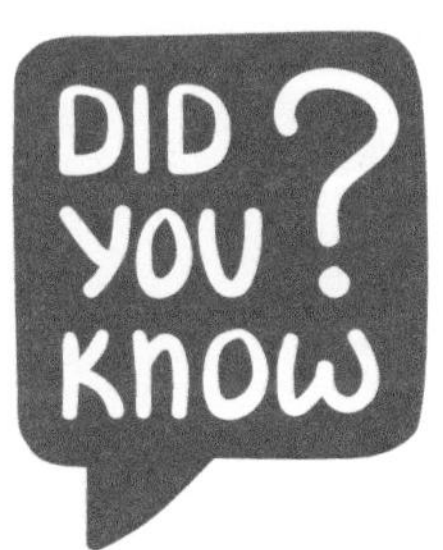

Pale lavender is frequently used as a neutral. Violet placed next to lavender will appear warmer and as light blue, while violet and blue mixed together will produce lavender. Two or more lights of different colors can create a new secondary color mix. Additive mixing of primary colors produces secondary colors—see the diagram right.

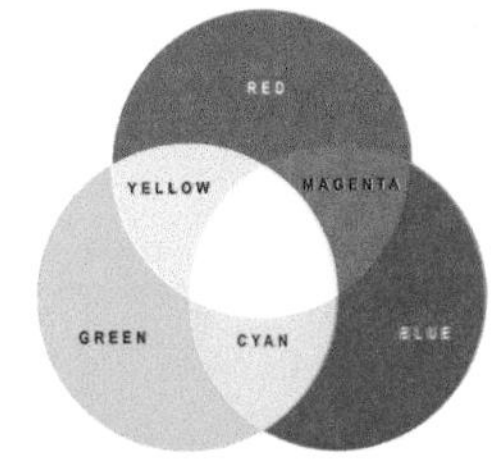

Figure 17 Image © Ferlixwangg, *The Three Primary Colors*, 2017, edited by Charles Scheland, 2021

The color of costumes is permanent, while the color of the lights can be altered. When the lights are pointed at the colored costumes, the color of the light can change the color of the costumes. As the color of the light interacts with the color of the costume, the color of the lights and the color of the costumes will mix and will create a new color. For instance:

Figure 18 Image © OpenClipArt, Lady Flamenco Dancer, 2018, and Theater Spotlight, 2018, edited by Charles Scheland, 2021

◆ **LIGHTING CUES, SEQUENCING, AND TIMING** is the collaborative designing process between the lighting designer and the choreographer. It follows the technical phase when the amount of lighting resources and instruments are positioned and focused, and the color palettes are determined and installed. Lighting cues are created and their sequencing is planned with precise timing of execution.[23]

➢ ***Lighting cue*** is the corresponding *lighting look* of a specific section of a dance piece that aims to visually support its content and increase the overall dramatic effect. There might be a single or multiple lighting cues, which change from one to another during the dance. Each cue has a different effect on the dance.

The cue sequence provides an overall variety, emphasis, and balance in the way a dance looks. For example, a brighter cue might be followed by a dimmer and more intimate cue that brightens gradually. It is impossible and unnecessary to write a lighting cue that covers every single movement of the dance. Too many or too few cues might have an obscure effect on the dance.

A wonderful example of a single *lighting look* or a *cue* that utilizes multiple lighting design tools and devices working together to create a stunning use of light is the painting titled "Calling of Saint Matthew" by the Italian visual artist Caravaggio, pictured right. The painting demonstrates the play of light and shadows, direction and intensity, refraction, and texture, as well as the use of specific colors. The artwork is an example of a perfect balance between darkness and brightness, emphasizing key visual elements by leading the eyes to what is important in the scene.[24]

Figure 19 *The Calling of Saint Matthew*, painting by Caravaggio, Contarelli Chapel, Church of San Luigi dei Francesi, Rome, Italy, 1599–1600, courtesy of Wikimedia Commons

➢ ***Cue Placement, Sequence of Cues, and Cue Calling*** are the progression and order of managing the stage action in relation to technical aspects of the production. The production team handles the lighting, music, and sets in coordination with the choreographer and the lighting designer, who determine the performance's technical demands.[25]

Since dance is related to music, changes in the dance sections and scenes are guided by changes in the music or are cued in coordination with the action on stage. Therefore, it seems organic that the sequencing of the lighting cues can respond to the changes in the dance and music. Each lighting cue has a number and timing to be called by the technical team for execution. For example: "Cue #127 is a fade-in; Cue #128 is a magenta wash; Cue #129 is a fade-to-black...," etc.

➢ ***Timing of cues*** relates to the length and speed of change of each cue, and it is crucial to the dramatic impact of the cues. The timing, execution, and transitions between cues should be carefully coordinated with the choreography to create a *rhythm of the lighting design* that is in sync with the dance.[26] The timing of cue calling might sound like: "Stand by Cue #12 (Called about 15 seconds in advance), and Cue #12—Go! (Called about 3 seconds before execution, in coordination with the timing of the dancers entering the stage)." The call and execution of each cue can be determined and recorded based on the dancers' blocking, the music score, or specific dramatic elements of the stage action.

Preprograming the lighting cues and creating a *cue sheet* with the sequence and timing of calling the cues has to be planned and practiced. This process will give the stage manager and the technical team the information needed to properly call the cues and run the entire performance—it is a "behind-the-curtain choreographic sequence" in its own right.

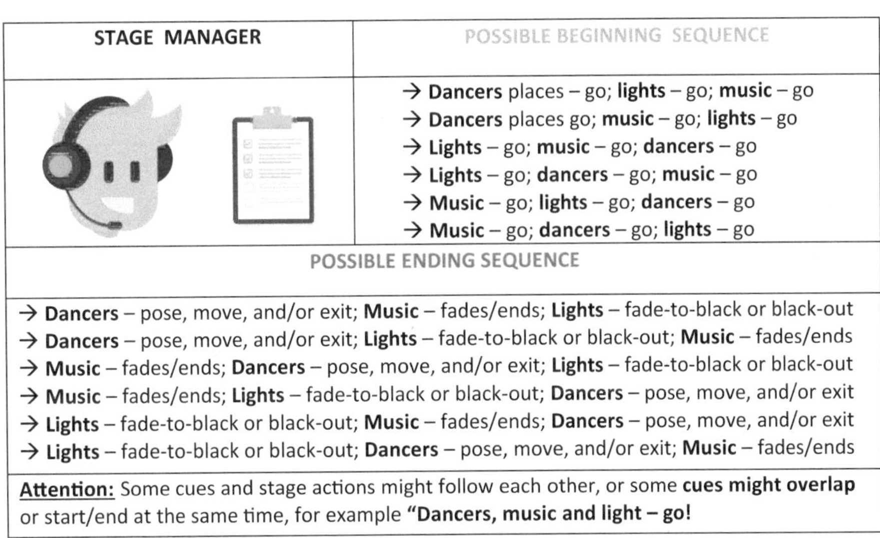

STAGE MANAGER	POSSIBLE BEGINNING SEQUENCE
	→ **Dancers** places – go; **lights** – go; **music** – go → **Dancers** places go; **music** – go; **lights** – go → **Lights** – go; **music** – go; **dancers** – go → **Lights** – go; **dancers** – go; **music** – go → **Music** – go; **lights** – go; **dancers** – go → **Music** – go; **dancers** – go; **lights** – go
POSSIBLE ENDING SEQUENCE	
→ **Dancers** – pose, move, and/or exit; **Music** – fades/ends; **Lights** – fade-to-black or black-out → **Dancers** – pose, move, and/or exit; **Lights** – fade-to-black or black-out; **Music** – fades/ends → **Music** – fades/ends; **Dancers** – pose, move, and/or exit; **Lights** – fade-to-black or black-out → **Music** – fades/ends; **Lights** – fade-to-black or black-out; **Dancers** – pose, move, and/or exit → **Lights** – fade-to-black or black-out; **Music** – fades/ends; **Dancers** – pose, move, and/or exit → **Lights** – fade-to-black or black-out; **Dancers** – pose, move, and/or exit; **Music** – fades/ends	
Attention: Some cues and stage actions might follow each other, or some **cues might overlap** or start/end at the same time, for example **"Dancers, music and light – go!**	

Figure 20

√ LIGHTING DESIGN is a creative interaction between artists working in two different types of media. *Enlighten Each Other!* is a great principle of a respectful, creative contribution and successful collaboration between the choreographer and lighting designer. For example, the choreographer might consider saying "The mood of the dance is sunset on the beach." Or "The dancers appear to be sleepwalking in the moonlight." Descriptive imagery is more helpful for the lighting designer than specific instructions from the choreographer such as "I need an isolated spotlight here," or "Can you put blue light over there?" Figurative descriptions are also more inspiring than technical instructions.

?

How much and what type of information do you share about your vision with the lighting designer?

WORKING WITH THE LIGHTING DESIGNER

– BASIC TERMINOLOGY AND COLLABORATIVE INTERACTION –

BASIC DESIGNING TOOLS:	BASICS OPERATIONS AND COMMANDS:
Scrim, Cyclorama – the backdrop on stage, which serves as the designer's canvas to support the actions in front of it	**Cue** – the lighting look of the scene and its sequence assigned by the designer and identified by a number – for example, "Cue #21, please, and stand by Cue #22!"
Specials, Spotlights, Isolated Areas – lighting instruments directed at and focused on specific stage areas	**Cue Speed** – the timing and duration of a cue execution programed by the designer and identified in seconds – for example: "Cue count transition of 7 seconds, please!"
Downstage, Diagonals, Upstage, Back Lights – instruments positioned in different locations around the stage	**Fade-in, Fade-out, Blackout** – the appearance and disappearance of light at the beginning and ending of a scene, identified in seconds, for example: "A 10-second fade-out, please!"
Side Lights, Shins, Booms – instruments positioned in each wing with the purpose to dimensionally light the moving bodies	**Light Intensity** – the presence of more light (brighter), or less light (darker), identified as a percentage – for example, "Decrease light down to 45%, please!"
Follow Spot Lights – freely mounted instruments following the action of the performers	**Magenta** – a color that is variously defined as purplish-red, reddish-purple, purplish, or mauvish-crimson, which is used periodically by designers
Templates, Gobos, Patterns – Stencils inserted into the instruments to manipulate the shape of the light	**Wash** – an even "fill" of light and color across the stage
Projections – still, moving, passive, or digitally interactive images projected on any of the stage surfaces	**"Going Dark!"** – a popular oral warning when designers briefly turn off all the lights on stage in order to write a new cue, or to make necessary technical adjustments

Figure 21

HELPFUL TIPS & SUGGESTIONS

~ **Prepare for conversation** with the designer including concept of the dance, description of moods, atmosphere, and approximate number of cues.

~ **Invite the lighting designer to dance studio rehearsals** prior to tech time for an initial introduction to the dance work and a discussion about the expectations in the lighting design.

~ **Provide information** about the colors of the costumes as you consider the colors for the lighting.

~ **Learn in advance about the technical limitations and time constraints** of the tech rehearsals.

~ **Use wisely the tech time for lighting design** and focus on working with the designer rather than with the performers.

~ **Anticipated time needed for the designer to experiment, build, modify, and demonstrate** the cues that you have discussed. Use: "Here is what we need. Please let me know when you are ready." Be prepared to wait patiently.

~ **The lighting design medium is different than choreography**—Make an effort to use the lighting design terminology and to consider the lighting designer's competency and collaborative input.

[INTER]ACTIVE PERFORMANCE SPACE

– SCENIC DESIGN FOR DANCE –

Dance always takes place in a specific environment—spontaneous or planned, existing or made, in nature or in architecture. Concert dance commonly uses theater and concert stages. In most circumstances, these stages are a configuration of a physical space with a designed area for performers and a calculated distance between the audience members and the stage action.

Typically, the stages used for dance are *proscenium*, *thrust*, and *arena*, as well as open/extended stage, outdoor improvised stage, and site-specific settings. For more information and features of site-specific work, please refer to *Being [Site] Specific* in Chapter 12. In enclosed traditional theater spaces, the *audience is the 4th wall*, and the three other walls are available to be shaped by the scenic design surrounding the performers.

Choreographers and dancers gravitate toward large open spaces so the dance may take place without being restricted by obstacles. A variety of traditional and proven décor practices create an architectural and visual setting for classical ballet and contemporary dance, such as design backgrounds and painted backdrops, drapes, curtains, flats, and platforms. Larger structures might be added such as a gate, arch, house, tower, road, bridge, and tunnel. Smaller objects refurbishing the space could be room furniture such as tables, chairs, and beds, as well as cycloramas, scrims, screens, banners, and panels. In contrast, interactive options could be outdoor and indoor site-specific locations, digital arts installations, projection mapping, or the incorporation of robots and flying drones. For more about advance planning of accessories, props, and sets, refer to Chapter 18.

As the choreographer and the scenic designer or the location facilitator prepare to collaborate, a few guiding questions can be considered: a) Where does the dance take place and what is the feel of the surroundings? b) What is the visual definition of the environment? c) How can this setting be recreated, constructed, or found to best integrate with the dance? There are a few main categories to define scenic surroundings and to strategically complement the overall concept of the choreography and the production:

◆ **SUPPORTIVE STATIONARY SETTING** is a setting found in nature or built to create a visual and architectural environment for the choreography to take place. The stationary set accommodates either the narrative of the dance work, or it is designed to visually enhance the choreographic concept. Stationary sets are usually conceived by professional set designers and built by a specialized team at a scenery shop. During the production, the technical and stage crew are in charge of placement of the sets and the changes of each scene.

Figure 22 Photograph © Ross Brown, pictured Gillian Murphy and Qi Huan in *Giselle*, a Royal New Zealand Ballet production by Ethan Stiefel and Johan Kobborg, costumes by Natalia Stewart, courtesy of the Royal New Zealand Ballet, 2012

◆ **INTERACTIVE SITE-SPECIFIC SETTING** is a specific site, a natural environment, or physical surroundings that serves as the stage where the dancing unfolds. The choreographic ideas are integrated into the given circumstances of the performance location. The choreographer also considers the advantages of the environment by incorporating its signature features, as well as its restrictions. In some instances, a vertical performance may seamlessly weave together dynamic physicality, intricate choreography, and climbing technology by turning the dance floor on its side and exploring unorthodox ways to use gravity and the natural landscape as part of the scenery.

Figure 23 Photography © Basil Tsimoyianis, BANDALOOP on Tianmen Mountain, Choreography by Amelia Rudolph and Melecio Estrella in collaboration with the performers, pictured Courtney Moreno, Becca Dean, Jessica Swanson, Tianmen Mountain, People's Republic of China, courtesy of BANDALOOP, 2016

◆ **KINESTHETICALLY INTEGRATIVE SETTING** is a flexible, nonstationary scenic environment that is maneuvered and manipulated by the performers or the technical crew under the direction of the choreographer. Objects, scenery, installations, and projections are in motion via manual, physical, or digital input—for example, via digital motion capture technology. The interaction between bodies and sets moving simultaneously is integrated organically with the concepts, content, and specific needs of the production.

Figure 24 Photography © Łukasz Łukasiewicz, PHOTON, *SYNTHESIA*, Aleksandra Słyż, performed by Anna Kamińska and Patryk Durski, Grand Hall of the Imperial Castle Poznań, Poland, 2018

√ SCENIC DESIGN is a creative interaction between the choreographer and the scenic designer regarding the environment where the dance takes place. Important elements are:

— **Perception of scale and dimension,** which is the consideration of how the scenic design relates to the content, visual balance, and architectural impact of the performance space arrangement in relation to the choreography. How do size and scope relate?

— **Dynamic engagement**, which is the use of the performance space and scenic design and its maneuverability in connection with the choreography and the relationship between the performers in their surroundings. How compliant is the setting?

ARTISTIC UNITY is the coordinated collaborative effort between the choreographer and the costume, lighting, and scenic designers to integrate all of the production elements with the choreography. How does everything fit together? Costumes, lighting, and scenic design all add to the overall appearance of the performance. Bringing together the entire production team and sharing artistic involvement is essential for reaching a desired outcome.

RESEARCH AND EXPLORATORY ASSIGNMENTS:

➡ **Costume Design:** Research the development of costume design in concert dance, especially in the last few centuries. One of the most prominent ballerinas of the Paris Opera Ballet in the mid-18th century, Marie-Anne Cuppi de Camargo, was known for adopting and wearing fashionable attire on stage. This *artful approach* in dance costuming led to the involvement of prominent fashion designers in working with choreographers and dancers, many of whom included Ballet Russes' Gabrielle "Coco" Chanel, all the way to the contemporary masters such as Yves Saint Laurent, Jean Paul Gautier, Christian Lacroix, Christian Dior, Isaac Mizrahi, Donna Karan, and many others. Groundbreaking dance shoemakers such as Salvatore Capezio and Gaynor Minden also contributed to the development of the best possible footwear for performers. In what ways did their inventions contribute to the development of dance costuming?

➡ **Lighting Design:** Research early revolutionary scenic and lighting designers, from Norman Bel Geddes and Robert Edmond Jones, to the first generation of professionals specializing in lighting design, such as Abe Feder, Jean Rosenthal, and Peggy Clark. The mid- and late 20th century lighting design was led by the accomplished Thomas Skelton, Jules Fisher, Peter Mumford, Mark Stanley, and Jennifer Tipton. The new generation includes Lucy Carter, Michael Hulls, Guy Hoare, Natasha Katz, and Brandon Stirling Baker, among others. How could their innovative ideas be useful in your work?

➡ **Scenic, Stage, and Set Design:** Research early prominent stage and scenic designers such as Adolphe Appia, Edward Gordon Craig, and Josef Svoboda, as well as the Ballet Russes' stage designers Léon Bakst, Natalia Goncharova, Alexander Benois, and Pablo Picasso. Important to also look at are the contemporary masters such as Santo Loquasto, John Macfarlane, Julian Crouch, and Bob Crowley, and the conceptual architectural sets of John Pawson and Frank Gehry. What aspects of their work are beneficial to you?

Figure 25 Photography © Lois Greenfield, pictured Jason Jordan, Ha-Chi Yu, 2001

★ **CREATIVE ASSEMBLING, PLANNING, AND COMMUNICATING:**

The choreographer strives to establish a productive work environment with the collaborators, to lead transparent communication, and to accommodate interactive conversations. A dance performance is a coordinated production team effort, where all collaborators are informed, updated, and invited to participate with creative ideas, artistic suggestions, and innovative solutions.

➥ Questions to prepare for a conversation with the costume designer

— What and who are the dancers representing in the choreography?

— How do the costumes contribute to the dancers' portrayal of movement ideas?

— How do the costumes visually enrich the content of the choreography?

— How do the fabric, colors, and style of the costumes add to the performers' appearance?

— Are the costumes functional? Is it easy to get them on and off—before, during, or after the dance?

— Are the costumes physically helpful to the dancers in performing the choreography?

— How many dancers are in the cast, and how does the choice(s) of dance footwear (or the lack of it) support the choreographer's movement language for the particular dance work?

➥ Questions to prepare for a conversation with the lighting designer

— Where does the dance take place in terms of the lighting environment?

— How does the lighting design help the audience to focus and understand the dance?

— Which areas on stage should be lit more than others, and where does intensity grow and decrease?

— Which dance scenes should be emphasized by the lighting design? When and why?

— Which performers should the lights follow, and when?

— Should the lighting design be noticeable and active, or discreet?

— How will the piece created in the dance studio, under "simple and plain" light, look different once on stage with "enhanced" light created by a designer?

➥ Questions to prepare for a conversation with the scenic designer

— Where does the dance take place and how does the scenic design support it?

— How minimal or massive does the stage design need be to assist the choreographer's vision—ranging from an almost empty stage to a full-scale theatrical set?

— How stationary or mobile will the stage set be, and how passive or integrated will the set need to be terms of its involvement in the choreography?

BIBLIOGRAPHY AND REFERENCES

[1] Liberman, Anne. *A Basic Course in Dance Costume Design*, Live lecture series, ICONS Choreographic Institute, Cohort 2017–18, Washington DC, USA, April 2018.
[2] Editors. *Natural vs. Synthetic Fibers: What's the Difference?* Masterclass.com, online article: www.masterclass.com/articles/natural-vs-synthetic-fibers, accessed May 2021.
[3] Editors. *Microscopic Appearance of Fibers*, Textile School, online article: www.textileschool.com/330/microscopic-appearance-of-fibres/, accessed May 2021.
[4] Liberman 2018. *A Basic Course in Dance Costume Design*.
[5] Liberman 2018. *A Basic Course in Dance Costume Design*.
[6] Liberman 2018. *A Basic Course in Dance Costume Design*.
[7] Picken, Mary Brooks. *Dictionary of Costumes and Fashion, Historic and Modern*, Dover Publications, Inc. 1957 and 1985, pp. 107, 111, 244.
[8] Picken 1985. *Dictionary of Costumes and Fashion, Historic and Modern*, p. 126.
[9] Hecht, Thomas. *Dance Costume*, LoveToKnow, Corp., online article: https://fashion-history.lovetoknow.com/clothing-types-styles/dance-costume, accessed May 2021.
[10] Steel, Valery. Editor. *Fashion and Dance*, Yale University Press & Fashion Institute of Technology in New York, pp. 143–167.
[11] Liberman 2018. A Basic Course in Dance Costume Design.
[12] Chan, Enoch. *A Basic Course in Lighting Design for Dance*, Live lecture series, ICONS Choreographic Institute, Cohort 2017–18, Washington DC, USA, May 2018.
[13] Wolf, Craig R. and Parker, Oren W. *Scene Design and Stage Lighting*, Harcourt Brace Jovanovich College Publishers, 1990, pp. 122–130.
[14] Chan 2018. *A Basic Course in Lighting Design for Dance*.
[15] Wolf and Parker 1990. *Scene Design and Stage Lighting*, pp. 467–468, 517.
[16-18] Chan 2018. *A Basic Course in Lighting Design for Dance*.
[19] Wolf and Parker 1990. *Scene Design and Stage Lighting*, pp. 37–41, 372.
[20] Wolf and Parker 1990. *Scene Design and Stage Lighting*, pp. 414–438.
[21] Wolf and Parker 1990. *Scene Design and Stage Lighting*, pp. 219–233.
[22] Wolf and Parker 1990. *Scene Design and Stage Lighting*, pp. 383–386.
[23-27] Chan 2018. *A Basic Course in Lighting Design for Dance*.

VISUAL REFERENCES

Figure 1: *Fantasy conceptual illustration for a fairy tale about the Naked King and his clothes*, Credit:Ann_Mei, courtesy of iStock/Getty Images

Figure 2: Diagram © Vladimir Angelov

Figure 3: Fabric sample flat line icons set. Weave types, different clothing materials, textile swatch, animal print, cotton, velvet vector illustrations. Outline pictogram for tailor store. Credit: Nadiinko, courtesy of iStock/Getty Images

Figure 4: Diagram © Vladimir Angelov, edited by Charles Scheland, 2021, and Elizabeth Gray, 2023

Figure 5: Samples of various fabric prints, patterns, and textures, by using public domain sample images, sorted and designed by Charles Scheland, list of samples:

Fabric Length, gift of Mr. A. G. W. and Mrs. Margaret M. Dunningham, collection of Auckland War Memorial Museum, 2017 (CC BY 4.0); *Flower Pattern*, Bergen Public Library, 2014, public domain; Kaushik Gopal, *Pinstripe*, 2007 (CC BY 2.0); RAJIVVASUDEV, *Fabric Stripe*, 2021 (CC BY 4.0); Peteski1, *Seersucker*, 2009 (CC BY-SA 3.0);

Peloponnesian Folklore Foundation, *Folded Red Sari*, 1970 (CC BY 4.0); MadrasFabricPreppy, *Madras Plaid*, 2019 (CC BY 4.0); G.cielec, *Pepitka*, 2014 (CC BY 4.0); William Morris, *Morris Way Fabric*, 1883, public domain; Riiksmuseum, Bruikleen uit de Koninklijke Verzamelingen, circa 1900 (CC0 1.0); Kürschner, *Lammjacke mit Leoparddruck*, 2009, public domain; Whiteghost.ink, *Polka Dot Printed Fabric*, 2014 (CC BY 4.0)

Figure 6: Images from left to right: Photography © Viktoria Ivanova and Sebastian Tornee, featured dancer Desi Jordanoff in a traditional outfit of Bulgaria, 2019; young Balinese dancer in traditional outfit and Maasai lady in traditional outfit of Tanzania, 2019, courtesy of iStock/Getty Images

Figure 7: Photography © Lois Greenfield, pictured from left to right: Nejla Yatkin, NY2Dance, 2011; Patrick Corbin, Corbindances 2006; Chad Levy, Amy Marshall Dance Company, 2011; Drew Jacoby, 2011; Joseph Gallerizo and Vanessa Lynn Campos, Dodge Dance Company, 2006.

Figure 8: Images from upper left clockwise: *Pair of antique women pretty shoes decorated with bows*, credit: serge-75; *A pair of black, leather tap dancing shoes*, credit: alenkadr; *Blue sport shoes on white background*, credit: talevr; *Pointe shoes isolated over white background*, credit: miss_j. All images courtesy of iStock/Getty Images

Figures 9, 10, 11, 12, 13, 14, and 15: Diagrams © Vladimir Angelov

Figure 16: Photography © Lois Greenfield, image left—pictured Sumayah McRae, 2002; image center—pictured LaKendra Dennard, 2013; image right—pictured Michael Fielder, Andrew Pacho, Kara Sandberg, 2002

Figure 17: Images © Ferlixwangg, *The Three Primary Colors*, 2017 (CC BY-SA 4.0), edited by Charles Scheland, 2021

Figure 18: Image © OpenClipArt, *Lady Flamenco Dancer*, 2018, *Theater Spotlight*, 2018, public domain, edited by Charles Scheland, 2021

Figure 19: *The Calling of Saint Matthew*, painting by Caravaggio, Contarelli Chapel, Church of San Luigi dee Francesi, Rome, 1599–1600, courtesy of Wikimedia Commons, public domain

Figure 20: Diagram © Vladimir Angelov, clip art of boy with headset and clipboard by iStock/Getty Images

Figure 21: Diagram © Vladimir Angelov

Figure 22: Photograph © Ross Brown, pictured Gillian Murphy and Qi Huan in *Giselle*, a Royal New Zealand Ballet production by Ethan Stiefel and Johan Kobborg, costumes by Natalia Stewart, courtesy of the Royal New Zealand Ballet, 2012

Figure 23: Photography © Basil Tsimoyianis, BANDALOOP on Tianmen Mountain, Choreography by Amelia Rudolph and Melecio Estrella in collaboration with the performers, pictured Courtney Moreno, Becca Dean, Jessica Swanson, Tianmen Mountain, People's Republic of China, courtesy of BANDALOOP, 2016

Figure 24: Photography © Łukasz Łukasiewicz, PHOTON, *SYNTHESIA*, Aleksandra Słyż, performed by Anna Kamińska and Patryk Durski, Grand Hall of the Imperial Castle Poznań, Poland, 2018

Figure 25: Photography © Lois Greenfield, pictured Jason Jordan, Ha-Chi Yu, 2001

Happiness is a state of activity.

Aristotle (384 BC–322 BC)

CHAPTER 25

A CAREER IN CHOREOGRAPHY

– DANCING DECISIONS MOVING FORWARD –

A career in choreography is similar to rock climbing—it requires infinite endurance, robust fitness, and ongoing risk management. And even when we finally get to place a flag on top of the mountain, we might wonder what it takes to keep it there.

As we enter the field of creating and crafting dance professionally, let's examine a few intriguing complexities in developing a sustainable career in choreography. We begin with mapping the field.

A dancer's first encounter with choreography might happen while enacting or performing someone else's choreography and offering a few innocent suggestions. Further interest and engagement might continue: a) by urge—when artistic individuals deeply desire to express and explore their own movement ideas; b) by chance—when an opportunity is given to dance artists to experiment choreographically; or c) by necessity—when a dance must be created, but there is no immediately available choreographer.

The career transition from performance to choreography might occur in diverse scenarios and multiple phases. Some dance artists begin choreographing very early while still in dance training. Others enjoy a substantial performance career before making the switch. There are also those who become increasingly involved in choreography while in the midst of a performance career, thereby developing two careers simultaneously. The latter leads to a smooth transition from one career path to another.

Various degrees of involvement and commitment are also at play. Generally speaking, the majority of aspiring choreographers begin creating dances early in life. They feel convinced right from the beginning that this is the most organic means of self-expression. Accumulating work at a younger age and over a longer period builds confidence and adds more meaning to their involvement. Intrinsic motivation and devotion are critical elements in the DNA of an emerging choreographer—see Chapter 9.

Many young choreographers create only occasionally by "testing the water" while maintaining a cautious distance. For them, partial involvement might produce partial rewards. Some choreographers prefer to *wait* for opportunities instead of *pursuing* them. A feeling of doubt may lead to a hesitancy to commit. The stakes seem too high. Choreography as a working field often appears highly unstructured, wildly chaotic, and very competitive. Managing the uncertainty is not for everyone.

Finally, many dance artists working as performers and educators—*outreach and teaching artists and practitioners*—also engage in choreography on a supplementary basis. Dance education and dance choreography are linked as practices but distinct as professions.

PROFICIENCY AND GROWTH
– MAINTAINING BALANCE WITH ALL BALLS IN THE AIR –

Choreographing on a basic level is a simple skill of putting movements together. Choreographing at an advanced level requires the development of multiple proficiencies simultaneously. Cultivating various creative abilities has been described in all of the previous chapters of this book, and it is humorously summarized in the image below.

Invention of Movement Material

Construction and Dramaturgy

Costumes, Lights, and Scenic Design

Improvisation and Experimentation

Concept and Context

Music, Sound, and Noise

Naming and Branding

Figure 1 Photography © Lois Greenfield, pictured Paul Zivkovich, 2014

➢ **Artistic growth** is an ongoing measurement of skills and craft proficiency—their efficiency and flawless execution. Artistic growth also helps determine the path of an artistic mission and a purpose for the choreographer: to be a groundbreaking visionary, an artful messenger, or a captivating acrobat. The choreographer Maurice Béjart dedicated a ballet to the choreographer Vaslav Nijinsky, naming him a "Clown of God," a character perhaps similar to the dancer pictured in the humourous image above.

➢ **Artistic maturity** is the choreographer's artistic confidence to take risks and experiment while seamlessly navigating through a *range of probabilities*. Evidence of mature proficiency is the choreographer's artful playfulness in response to any given topic or random idea and the ability to maneuver multiple options by *foreseeing various outcomes*. The ultimate proof of artistic maturity and proficiency is the ability to *craft convincing choreographic statements that organically connect* with an educated dance audience.

➢ **Developing healthy working habits** and learning how to foster creative skills are essential in preventing passion from becoming an obsession, because obsession is effective only in moderation. Although according to Oscar Wilde, we should pursue *everything in moderation, including moderation*. Like professional performers, with time and experience, choreographers develop self-awareness about their strengths and weaknesses. They also choose a strategy to deal with their weaknesses—to ignore and hide them, address and fix them, or turn them into strengths.

WORKING DRAFTS ARE HEALTHY CREATIVE HABITS

– BEING "IN" AND "OUT" OF THE ZONE –

Going back and forth, in and out, is healthy! When choreographers create in the studio, they are usually "in the zone," meaning they are in the creative mode, driven by their intuitive responses to artistic stimuli. As they sit and watch a run of their dance work, they take themselves "out of the zone" to evaluate the choreography's progress, making modifications and even significant changes.

Those shifts of being "in" and "out" of the zone are organic, healthy working habits of the creative process. Many choreographers generate movement material in the early stages of creation, experimentation, and improvisation by putting it together to serve as a *first draft*. Miscalculations are part of that process. Obsessing about perfection might be counterproductive—see Chapter 10.

Choreographers regularly work on improvements up to the moment before the dance goes on stage. Often, in one day and between multiple staging rehearsals, new information and more options become available. Some "edits" might be needed. Many choreographers work through *numerous drafts* to *finalize* their work.

Choreographers should never assume that their *first draft* is their *best option*. An enduring developmental process helps flesh out the movement material, clarify intent, and guide the performers; appropriate movement modifications will ensure the successful execution of the new choreography. With changes and rotation in the cast of performers—mostly when the dance has already been completed—the choreographer might consider further adapting the movement material to fit the performers' skills and strengths. Their first time might not be their best time.

The developmental principle of *drafts* is applicable when working with collaborators such as musicians, composers, and designers of lighting, costumes, and sets. A curving *In-and-Out* is a dynamic process of healthy and creative choreographic practices—summarized in Figure 2:

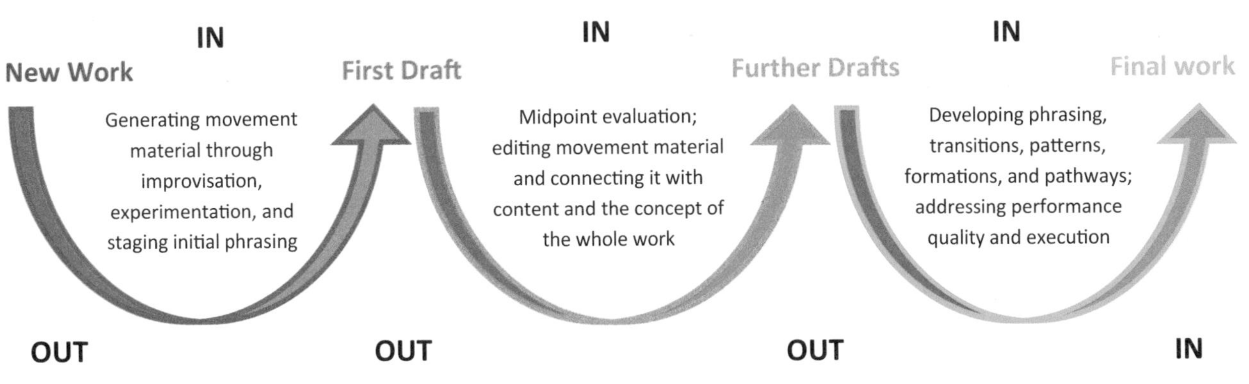

Figure 2

HOW GOOD IS YOUR BEST?

– DEALING WITH DOUBT AND THE PRESSURE TO ACCOMPLISH –

"I am doing my best!" the young choreographer exclaims defensively to an unenthusiastic audience after the opening night of his new work. The sentence is correct! As artists, we always try to do our best. It is also true that "my best" is very fluid, and it evolves.

Let's think about our first choreography, which was our "best" at the time of its creation. Decades later, and after dozens of works and gained choreographic experience, we might look back at our first choreography and wonder: "Oh...Was that my best?" Yes, back then it was. A "best" from the past will be different from a "best" of today. At the same time, a "personal best" might be further from the "Art Form's Best" and the "Current Field's Best"—see Figure 3.

"I will create a terrible dance today!" is something that a choreographer most likely would never say or intend. By default, we strive to create work that everybody will appreciate. When we see a dance that we do not like, it is not because of the choreographer's wish. Perhaps the execution was not as strong as the intention.

As creators, we may not always have a realistic evaluation of our creations. We may automatically assume that if we invest a lot of time and energy to create a dance, then that dance will be successful. We must realize that working in the arts is similar to working in science—not every experiment promises to be successful. In fact, a series of experiments may turn out to be unsuccessful in achieving a particular goal; however, these experiments can provide a powerful learning opportunity. We can ask ourselves how this process might help us acquire new knowledge, gain more experience, and bring us closer to achieving our goals.

"I'm getting more NO-s and Maybe-s, than YES-es!" choreographers may say early in their careers when seeking to expand working engagements. This is often the case when emerging artists feel their work has been ignored, misunderstood, and unappreciated.[1] Staying positive and hopeful in the early career stages is always challenging. It takes years, patience, effort, and endurance to become established in the field. Each creative voice has its independent strength and uniqueness. Yet it is often measured with the lens of the art form and the field's current urgencies. Choosing from the extremes of being uninformed and being too competitive has proven unproductive.[2] Good news! Each choreographer is in charge of how they use lenses and a magnifying glass.

Are you wearing the correct prescription lenses and using the right magnifying glass?

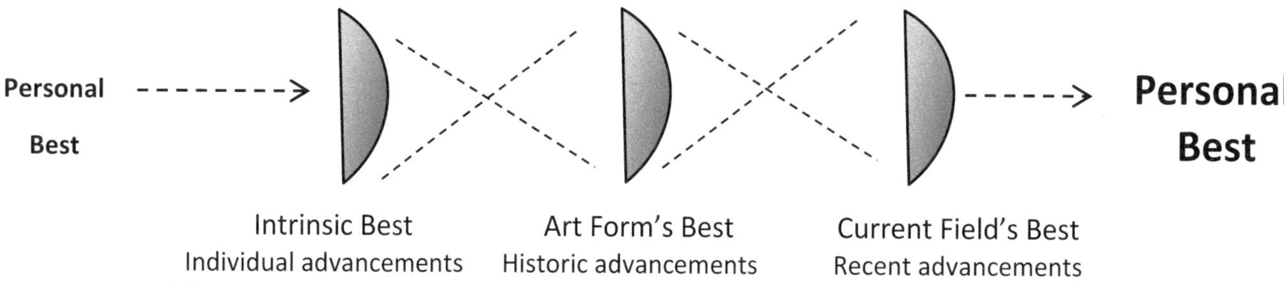

Figure 3

CAREER DEVELOPMENT PHASES
– BUCKLE UP FOR AN ENDURING CREATIVE JOURNEY –

A career in choreography is a long-term commitment involving ongoing progress through multiple career development phases. It is similar to running a marathon rather than a sprint—endurance is a must! Finding, retaining, and utilizing a support system and nurturing environment are essential, especially in the early phases of the choreographer's career. Career phases in choreography can be categorized according to the development and level of creative skills, frequency of exposure, scale of work, and caliber of presenting venues.[3] The seven phases of career development are:

PRE-PROFESSIONAL CHOREOGRAPHERS	a) ***Student Choreographer*** – has begun to learn the fundamentals of dance making and practice basic skills of choreography
	b) ***Budding Choreographer*** – has created short chamber dances and presented them in a safe learning environment and student venues
	c) ***Emerging Choreographer*** – has created longer solos, chamber dances, and group works and presents them in a variety of public venues
PROFESSIONAL CHOREOGRAPHERS	d) ***Early-Career Choreographer*** – has created long-format works and has presented in regional and national venues
	e) ***Mid-Career Choreographer*** – has created large-scale works and regularly presents them in major national and international dance venues
	f) ***Established Choreographer*** – has created large-scale, full-length professional productions and a substantial body of work, and regularly presents them in prestigious national and international venues
	g) ***Prominent Choreographer*** – has created a substantial body of work, award-winning and critically acclaimed works that are presented in high-ranking and prestigious performance venues

Figure 4

There are no rigid borders between the career development phases. Yet milestones and career-changing events are often linked to professional recognition, major publicity coverage, and engagements in special projects that enable choreographers to jump from one career phase into the next. However, a real "overnight success" is never the result of a little "work overnight."

With gained experience and an established presence in the field, the employment status also changes. During the stages of Early-Career and Mid-Career, choreographers might increasingly generate enough funding to transition from choreographing "part-time" to "full-time." The age of the choreographer is rarely a defining factor in their career development phase. Artistic advancement and gradual career development are realistic to achieve. A single accomplishment or a random success, however, does not guarantee a sustainable career.

?

Considering the chart above, which career phase you are in now?

CHOREOGRAPHIC SPECIALTY VS. CHOREOGRAPHIC VERSATILITY

As young dancers, many choreographers might have been educated in and exposed to various traditional dance techniques such as ballet, modern dance, jazz, etc. Others might have focused only on specific training such as ethnic dance or gymnastics, for example. While each dance genre has its own unique movement vocabulary, aesthetic, and philosophy, choreographic craftsmanship is generally applicable across movement forms.

Career choreographers might be asked to create works in various dance genres and mediums such as opera, dramatic plays, Broadway, TV, fashion shows, sporting events, etc. Some of these forms might not be familiar to the choreographer. At some point, choreographers might face a dilemma: Are they willing to take on projects related only to their artistic interest and specialty? Or are they willing to dive in and create in multiple disciplines?

Multi-genre and multi-disciplinary work is always exciting. It provides opportunities to expand versatility and: a) understand how different styles of dance, mediums, and art forms work; b) expand knowledge and artistically contribute to an unfamiliar project; and c) collaborate with different types of artists and organizations.

CHOREOGRAPHING BY DESIRE OR BY DEMAND

— BEING MISSION-DRIVEN OR CAREER-DRIVEN —

The field of choreography offers a wide variety of employment opportunities. Sometimes, however, the specifics of certain commissions might challenge the choreographer's artistic integrity and creative work—either productively or unproductively. Often, a particular project might not align with, or even contradict, the choreographer's artistic mission and career goals.[4] A simple sentence can help reveal the reasons to take on a new dance:

I ***NEED*** TO MAKE THIS DANCE! **OR**

I ***HAVE*** TO MAKE THIS DANCE! **OR**

I ***WANT*** TO MAKE THIS DANCE!

Figure 5

The last reason best fits the project! Yet there might be an occasion when there is a combination of all three, as long as the last line is the leading purpose. It is also essential to determine if the project is furthering a mission or a career. A career should be based on a mission and not the opposite. In summary: Create when it feels right! Mission, integrity, and being truthful are more important than a single project! Building a career based on mission means staying on course rather than continually changing course.

WHICH CAREER PATH IN CHOREOGRAPHY FITS BEST?

When it comes to developing a long-term career, choreographers intuitively consider numerous factors such as their own personality, temperament, needs, work habits, and satisfaction with their artistic freedom and growth. Creativity should also provide financial rewards. A starting point in a choreographic career is often rooted in and linked to the past. Many dancemakers have developed performing careers before they begin to choreograph. Their initial community of educators, colleagues, peers, mentors, and supervisors will become the beginning of a future network, bringing and fostering opportunities. People know other people. Sharing information has become the norm. Suddenly someone somewhere will need a choreographer for a project, and the seed for a choreographic career has been planted.

An initial career path might turn out to be temporary or permanent, as time will tell. There is no perfect career path promising only success and prosperity. To be realistic—all types of employment have advantages and challenges. The three primary career paths in choreography, which sometimes overlap and cross over, are:

→ INDEPENDENT/ FREELANCE CHOREOGRAPHER ←	
↓ **Description: Project by project choreographic employment** ↓	
ADVANTAGES:	**CHALLENGES:**
- Flexibility to choose best-fitting projects - Non-binding short-term commitments - Full control of employment arrangements and schedule	- Ambiguity in work schedule and creative goals - Inconsistency in engagements, revenue, and income discrepancy in long-term strategic planning
→ INSTITUTIONAL /RESIDENT CHOREOGRAPHER ←	
↓ **Description: Institutional umbrella choreographic employment** ↓	
ADVANTAGES:	**CHALLENGES:**
- Dependable income and schedule, employment security - Reliable advance programming and artistic management - Available institutional structure and support system	- Compliance with assigned projects - Demand for creative accommodations - Conformity with the institutional culture
→ DIRECTOR/HOUSE CHOREOGRAPHER ←	
↓ **Description: Dance company leadership choreographic employment** ↓	
ADVANTAGES:	**CHALLENGES:**
- Establishing individual artistic vision as an institutional vision - Retaining full institutional support for own artistic projects - Utilizing governing power as artistic power	- Balancing creativity with administrative management - Prioritizing institutional integrity over artistic integrity - Accommodating institutional complexities

Figure 6

DOES A CHOREOGRAPHER NEED BUSINESS AND MANAGEMENT SKILLS?

Yes! To gain full control of their careers, choreographers should cultivate fundamental business development skills to help them navigate through the complex landscape of professional opportunities. As in business development practices, all career choreographers should strive to build and develop a successful dance portfolio, artistic capacity, and assets.[5] Cultivating business development skills can be achieved by linking processes and combining efforts in three areas—figuratively expressed in the pyramid below:

STRIVING FOR QUALITY
when fostering new works, fresh ideas, and unique vision

ACKNOWLEDGING ACHIEVEMENTS
that foster further interest, support, and funding

BUILDING ANTICIPATION
that fosters excitement, enthusiasm, and engagement

Figure 7

Independent/Freelance Choreographers enjoy a fair amount of creative flexibility to choose the projects they want. Business-wise, the needed skills are to hustle, self-promote, inquire, network, engage, and manage all creative opportunities and administrative transactions, as well as negotiate contracts. While planting the seeds and preparing the groundwork for upcoming new projects, it is essential to nurture existing projects to ensure a promising career.

Institutional/Resident Choreographers can also act as *Independent/Freelance Choreographers* by acquiring outside projects while retaining employment positions with affiliated dance or educational institutions. Gaining the institution's trust is possible with good communication, coordination, and planning. Business-wise, the delicate balance here is addressing authorship and ownership. The artistic commodity of working and contributing to an institution should align with the choreographer's mission and integrity.

Directors/House Choreographers can also work occasionally as *Independent and Institutional Choreographers* by retaining their dance company leadership. In some instances, the *Director/House Choreographers* are also the *dance company's founders*, and their work might dominate the dance company's repertoire. For more about *Founding Director*, see *Institutional Naming and Branding* in Chapter 23. Leading a dance company does not necessarily mean loss of artistic liberties. However, there are substantial organizational management responsibilities. Business-wise, being a *Director/House Choreographer* is the most complex career choice. Since the dance company serves as an "artistic family," nurturing the choreographer's unique voice provides creative consistency. Yet administrative and logistics management is expected too.

HOW ABOUT CULTIVATING MULTITASKING SKILLS TO BETTER HANDLE LOGISTICS?

A composer needs a score sheet; a visual artist—a canvas, paints, and brushes, and an author—a blank page to write on. Choreographers express themselves through the bodies and minds of others—dance making is a collaborative process and experience. Having effective social skills and the ability to multitask are crucial—see Chapter 9. However, managing personalities and logistics is not always easy.

Turning a choreographer's initial idea into a completed production involves working with dancers, collaborators, designers, production crew, press, advertisement and administrative teams, and others. These interactions can be grouped into three essential clusters—managing and handling the participating *people*, the creative *process*, and the *production* logistics. The three Ps!

Interactions could include a range of *people* involved in the project, from friends to professionals.[6] Group creativity might unfold in multiple directions during the creative *process*, which could be collaborative, coordinated, or regulated. Finally, the technical logistics of each project determine the organization and management of the dance *production*, depending on whether it is self-produced, commissioned, or presented in other formats.

ENGAGEMENT	PROJECTS, GOALS, AND MANAGEMENT
& SUPERVISION	← ......LESS FORMAL -- MORE FORMAL....... →
People	...Family, Friends, Followers, Volunteers, Like-minders, Supporters, Professionals...
Process	...Experimental, Inventive, Collaborative, Integrative, Educational, Coordinated, Regulated...
Production	...Self-initiated, Self-produced, Co-presented, Commissioned, Funded, Hired, Ordered...

Figure 8

Unanticipated challenges might arise when misunderstanding and lack of coordination occur in *just one* of the three crucial PPP clusters. It happens frequently to various degrees. Choreographers' artistic skills might often conflict with their management skills. And yet just as dance involves kinesthetic balance, choreography involves a balance between creativity and practicality, as well as the development of management skills.

Engagement is the first step to establish a management process for completing the project. A choreographer could be compared to a military general who inspires and motivates his army to battle and win.

Becoming a leader and manager requires seven skills: 1) conceptualizing, 2) planning, 3) communicating, 4) decision-making, 5) delegating, 6) implementing, and 7) problem-solving.

In addition, *supervision* is an ongoing management process that involves dynamic strategizing, mid-point evaluation, and continual problem-solving. Supervision requires skills such as:

a) *multitasking* to simultaneously manage several pending tasks,

b) *situational awareness* to implement an ongoing assessment of surrounding conditions,

c) *prioritizing* the workflow challenges according to their importance and resolving each challenge separately.

WHO DECIDES HOW SUCCESSFUL AND WORTHY YOU ARE?

Luckily, no single person makes such a decision. As a matter of fact, you, the choreographer, are in charge of your worth and success. The following is a popular example that illustrates the concept of self-worth. Imagine that you are holding a $100 bill. Is it *worth* $100? Yes!

- If you crumple the bill, is it still worth $100? Yes.
- If you stomp on it, is it still worth $100? Yes.
- If you fold it into a tiny roll, is it still worth $100? Yes.
- If you hurl it at the wall, is it still worth $100? Yes.
- If you bury it in mud, is it still worth $100? Yes.
- If you submerge it in water for a while, is it still worth $100? Yes.
- If you throw it in the garbage, is it still worth $100? Yes.

The $100 bill never loses its value! No matter how mistreated it is, it's still worth just as much...and *SO ARE YOU*! Often you might feel worthless or mistreated. You might think, "Everyone is against me," and "No one cares about me." Aside from what has happened, what you have done, or what has been done to you, you're still just as valuable. You might *never* feel that *your work* is well recognized, and yet—you're precious, and neither you nor anyone else can take away your worth. However, if *you* as a person are always valuable and worthy, is the same true of the value and worth of *your art*?

WHAT IS THE COST, PRICE, VALUE, AND WORTH OF ART?

The point of art is to capture and aesthetically express the precious fabric of humanity. At the root of this grand idea, there is a practicing artist who is creating the work. The work might be evaluated and assigned a value and a monetary worth. Most artists, if not all, will be happy if their work helps them make a living.

Certain resources and conditions are necessary for an artist to create the work. An initial investment of time, effort, and materials is crucial for the art to take shape. These assets could be elaborate and expensive, or affordable and straightforward. These working resources could be provided either by the artists themselves or by other individuals and institutions. All of these initial factors put together will determine the cost for the work to emerge, materialize, and ultimately be produced.

As the work of art is completed, it takes on its own life of proving itself in various contexts. The field at large will analyze and dispute the quality of the work by identifying its strengths and weaknesses. Likability and popularity of the work might play a role. These aspects will determine the price of the work. The work will also face rigorous evaluation by an army of professional experts who will scrutinize its content, craftsmanship, and significance. All of these factors together will determine the value and worth of the work.

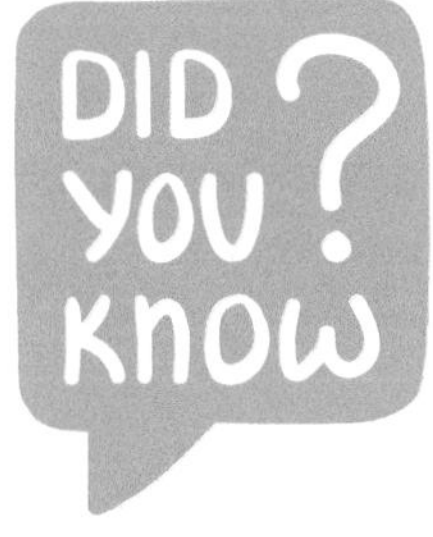

Pablo Picasso's *Nude, Green Leaves and Bust*, a 64-inch x 51-inch oil on canvas painting was created in a single day in 1932. The work depicts Picasso's lover, Marie-Therese Walter.[7] We will use this example to implement basic financial terms such as *cost*, *price*, *value*, and *worth* to help us understand the fundamentals of economics, also applicable in art. The dollar amounts are adjusted to today's standards. The fascinating fact here is the monetary range between the *initial cost* and the *final worth* of that single painting. The question is: How did the dollar amount grow from a few thousand dollars to many millions of dollars?

Current average PRODUCTION *COST* – $1,600
Based on the materials and the labor to produce

Current average MARKET *PRICE* – $16,000
Based on similar items in mass production sales

Current Value **and ESTIMATED** *WORTH* * – $106.5 million [8]
Based on the *significance* of the art work

Figure 9 Pablo Picasso, *Nude, Green Leaves and Bust*, 1932

**Value* and *Worth* are synonymous and often used interchangeably during a casual conversation. Yet there are some intricate differences. *Value* is mostly used as a *qualitative range* of importance and desirability—a level of excellence, meaningfulness, etc. *Worth* is mainly used as a *quantitative range* and a figurative estimate—a degree of craftsmanship invested and a monetary appraisal based on market demands and popularity, etc.

WHAT MAKES A PIECE OF CHOREOGRAPHY LIKABLE, SIGNIFICANT, AND VALUABLE?

"I like the piece you have choreographed!" is a common phrase, and yet choreographers work very hard to hear these words from the audience. But why is it so difficult to like something? Let's switch roles for a moment. Choreographers themselves are often members of the audience, and they see dances choreographed by someone else. Choreographers could be excellent adjudicators of their colleagues' work based on their professional involvement and competency in the art form. How can we explain the *likability* of choreography? What makes us like a dance?

There is a three-layer approach to evaluating the work that determines the stages and degrees of likability, and ultimately the value of the work:

✓ **Excited Anticipation:** We might form an initial impression of a dance work based on the preliminary information about it. Guiding details could be the venue, the title, the content, the music choices, and the dancers casted in the key roles. If the choreographer has an established name and existing repertory that has gained popularity, we might build certain *expectations* about what we *will see* or what we *want to see.*

In addition, press news about the new dance production or "word of mouth" can also provide information and build anticipation. This provided context might "set-up" expectations affecting *how we see* the work before actually seeing it.

✓ **Initial Reaction:** As we see the performance and after it is over, we could candidly ask a dance colleague or the nearby audience members: "What do you think, and how do you like this dance?"

We might expect responses expressing various *degrees of likability*. Short answers could range from "Not too bad" to "Good" and "Brilliant," while other replies might be: "Let's give it a chance"; "I am open to seeing more of it"; and "I cannot wait to see the next one." Finally, we can also expect a neutral phrase of uncertainty—"Not sure what to think about it."

An instant evaluation emerges in our minds once we have seen a dance work—an "internal inventory." Our thoughts, feelings, and impressions might *zig-zag*—see Figure 10, from "yes" to "no" in response to the sample survey below. The sub-questions in the parentheses could help us analyze and elaborate on what exactly is "likable" about the work.

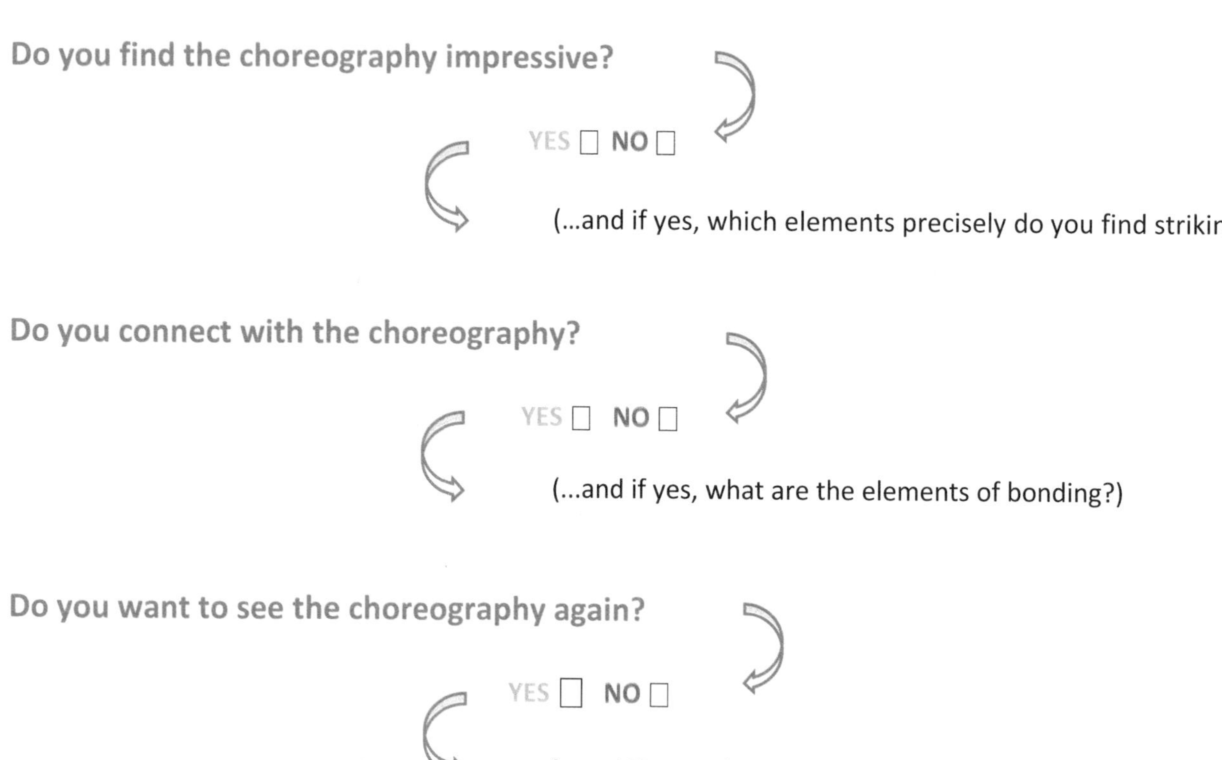

Figure 10

✓ **Identifying value and worth:** This sample survey suggests some initial criteria to evaluate likability based on how the work has been viewed and perceived. Yet further layers form the work's value and worth. At the same time, we do not assign value to the work—the work already *has* a value that we can *identify*.

We might think a dance piece is "good," but is this dance also "profound"? Since the choreographer and the viewers experience the work differently, the same dance might carry various degrees of importance and meaning to each person—see *Does Movement Have (To Have) Meaning* in Chapter 14. Leading factors for *identifying* value and worth are content, form, and craftsmanship. All three of these factors of a *creative-process-driven practice* will merge into the potential value and worth of the work, as shown in Figure 11:

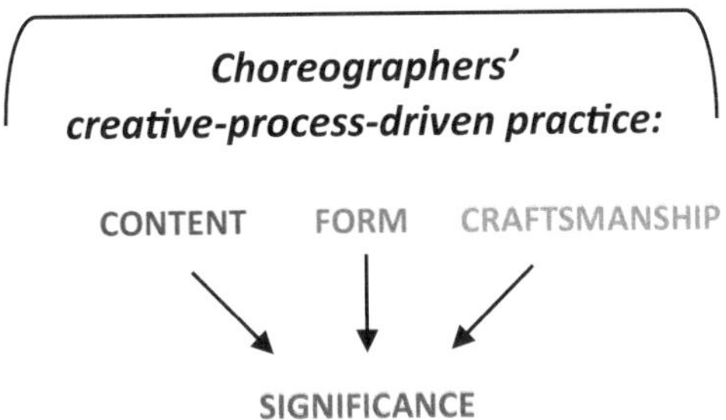

Figure 11

The next question is how significant is the work? *Significance* is also the work's *importance*, which determines its *value* and *worth*:

Figure 12

At first glance, however, significance might not provide an immediate measurement of value. A deductive approach can help us determine what significance includes. Let's break down *significance* regarding a choreographic work as an *outcome*:

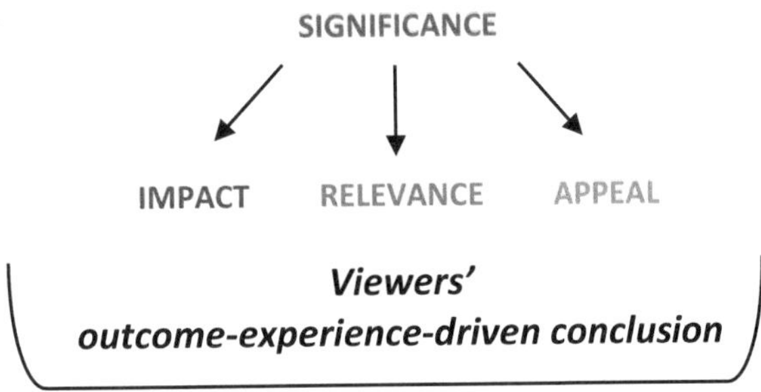

Figure 13

The *outcome-experience-driven conclusion* is the viewers' appreciation of the work. The work's impact is determined by the immediate impression it makes on the viewers and its commanding effect in the professional field, as well as its degree of relevance and appeal. In a reverse engineering approach, we can summarize in a few points the meaning of impact, relevance, and appeal, and how they function:

IMPACT: How to identify it and implement it?

➢ **One of Us!—Impact on the general audience.** Art often leads ordinary people to see life and the world in new ways. Audiences have a broad range of backgrounds, tastes, and cultural perceptions. A dance has a significant impact in that *broad field* when viewers can relate to the dance, and the dance *communicates* back to the viewers. The choreographer is "one of us (the audience)," and the work has a transformative impact—emotionally and intellectually—on the way ordinary people perceive art and life.

➢ **One of Many!—Impact on the professional field.** Colleagues, experts, and dance professionals have competence in the field and can identify a new trend. When a work stands out—one out of many others—by making an impact on that *specialized field*, it is proof that the artist-choreographer has significant influence within the field.

➢ **One of a Kind!—Impact on the art form.** Making great art and advancing the art form is any artist's ultimate goal. Accomplished artists are often placed in the context of the art form as a whole, and their work might be compared to present and past works of historic excellence. When a work stands out in that art-form's context, it impacts a limited field of historic heritage works. This factor proves the work has influence and would be seen as a remarkable contribution to the art form.

RELEVANCE: How to identify it and implement it?

➢ **The time is now!—Urgency of the present.** Bringing awareness to humanity's current struggles through dance demonstrates attentiveness and willingness to resolve them. Addressing the present is seeing, reflecting, and connecting with the world of today. Dance has the power to communicate current urgencies and tendencies. Contemporary interpretations of old classics could also be relevant to the present times.

➢ **Seeing the invisible!—Discovery and Re-discovering:** It is an enlightening experience when dance brings forth new ideas that have not been seen lately or known before. Often, ideas of substance are still present but somehow ignored, hidden, or forgotten; they are here but have become invisible. Rediscovering is also a form of discovery. Bringing forward and reconnecting to life's essentials, which are often overlooked on our daily horizon, carries great relevance.

➢ **Enduring the Test of Time!—Elasticity and Survivability:** Great ideas live a long time. And what makes ideas great is that they address humanity's actual state and the core of the human spirit. Timeless themes such as life and death, good and evil, love and prejudice, courage and heroism, survival and perseverance are always relevant. While a human life span is limited, great works of art live on—they are larger than life. Think big!

APPEAL: How to identify it and implement it?

➢ **United in our differences!—Uniqueness and Universality:** Dance is an art of sharing—it is by the people, for the people. Uniqueness, on the other hand, is often expressed through unusual qualities that might seem strange to the viewer. Common values and ideas that are relatable and unite people are enormously appealing.

➢ **Say little, yet mean a lot!—Simplicity and Complexity:** Since the beginning of humanity, expressing something meaningful in a simple way has always proven very appealing. In today's fast-paced world, content of great importance in condensed form is fascinating.

➢ **New and unique concepts are attractive!—Craftsmanship and Innovation:** We are drawn to the unique, and we are fascinated when ideas are executed skillfully and effectively. Striving for uniqueness is embedded in human nature, and we easily worship excellence. People's exceptional abilities are exciting and broadly appealing because they nurture hope and prove that people can be extraordinary.

WHAT MAKES US PAUSE AND WHAT KEEPS US GOING

Self-imposed limitations are the main hindrance to the creative and career-building processes. Will we believe that things cannot be done because of someone's judgment or when we are told that they are not significant? A new and big idea might seem odd to others because it is big and new. But if you need to *fight*, make sure you do not *fight alone.*

A support system might not be readily available, but it can be built. For institutional and resident choreographers, existing infrastructures are in place to build upon. Independent and company director choreographers might invest additional efforts to develop an inspiring environment to attract like-minders and collaborators: a) Convince and persuade others why *your idea* and *your mission* are essential, and why your choreographic work is impactful, relevant, and appealing. b) Clarify the difference between what *you can* do, and what *you should* do. c) Seek collaborators and partners, not just funders.

Measurement of success is criteria individually established by each choreographer.[9] We might always have an unsettling feeling about what we *wish* to achieve and what we *have achieved*. Can we handle the ups and downs? Let's remember that failure and success are part of the process.

How do we measure success in the first place? Is success determined by money, awards, recognition, and getting what we *want* and *need*? Or is it about fulfilling an *artistic vision* and *accomplishing a mission* that we deeply believe in, whatever others may think?

Here is some advice from the field: Allow for your mission to build your career, and not the opposite. Then you will share your art as work that inspires and not as work that sells. It is natural to strive towards building a *successful career* where financial stability and art-making exist harmoniously. It might not be easy, but it is possible. What does it take?

Figure 14 Photography © Lois Greenfield, pictured Alexandra Karigan-Farrior, courtesy of Amy Marshall Dance Company, 2010

BUILDING A CAREER IN CHOREOGRAPHY

– WISHFUL THINKING AND/OR FEASIBLE STEPS –

There is no instruction manual for building a career in choreography. Although we can guess what will work, we know what won't work. Waiting to be "discovered," or for someone to step in and do the work for us, or for opportunities to arrive at our doorstep—all these strategies are rarely effective. Waiting wastes precious time.

Instead, make a plan. Your plan can stretch three-dimensionally—write down what you would like to accomplish personally, artistically, and professionally.[10]

When we say *make a plan*, let's not confuse it with *make a wish*, which is not the same. Instead, *setting a goal* is much more helpful, and goals can be short-term or long-term. But what brings the real magic and turns dreams into reality in dance and in life is taking one small *step*, followed by another, and another...

Once the grand plan is outlined, you are ready to go. Transform your *wishes* into *goals*, and then break down your *goals* into feasible *steps*.[11] For example:

- "I want to get more exposure at major venues." (This is a *wish*.)
- "I am determined to present my work at a major venue." (This is a *goal*.)
- "I am about to meet the programming director of a major venue." (This is a *step*.)

The bigger the wish and the clearer the goals, the more and the smaller the planned steps need to be to make that wish a reality.

After all, the choreographer's work is to develop a plan for dance, create movements, and invent steps for the dancers to learn. The same applies to building a career. The choreographer creates a long-term strategy, clarifies upcoming goals, and breaks down these goals into feasible steps. Choreographing dance and life involve the same set of skills.

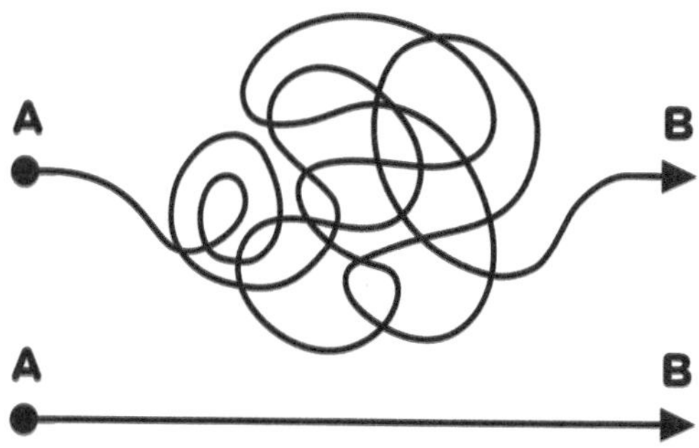

?

Can you identify your wishes, goals, and plans, and which of them are short-term and long-term?

INVENTING AND SELF-REINVENTING
– KEEPING THE CONSISTENCY OF NEWNESS –

Here is a short story: A famous sushi chef in Japan was asked by a customer how he made his sushi consistently delicious. The chef answered, "I make it *different* to taste the *same*." The customer was confused: "Aren't you using the same recipe? How do you always reach high quality?" The chef smiled: "Exactly! I do have a recipe. However, my customers wake up in a different mood every morning. Therefore, I have to *change* my recipe a bit every day so my sushi tastes *the same*. My success is not just my recipe, but the improvements and adjustments I make on a daily basis." Being truthful to a vision does not mean being repetitive. Every day is a new day bringing new excitement and challenges. The Greek philosopher Heraclitus said: "No man ever steps in the same river twice." Prepare yourself for ongoing artistic explorations by finding a balance between:

Retaining Your Unique Voice ← and → Reinventing Yourself Constantly

A process of reinventing begins with three simple questions:

➢ What in your work represents who you are?

➢ What is always consistent in your work?

➢ What is always changing in your work?

The last question is about inviting and welcoming new ideas and integrating them into your unique work. Expanding knowledge and integrating it into your artistic practice should become a self-sustaining creative habit.

"Choreography +..."

is an open framework of integrating choreography with other arts and disciplines. Never stand still. Choreographers should strive to be informed about the latest developments, investigations, and innovations in the arts, humanities, and sciences.[12] Interaction with other fields allows a fruitful cross-, inter-, multi-, and trans-disciplinary approach. Examples include:

◆ **Choreography + Movement Experimentation** involves the most fundamental aspect of artistic research concerning the choreographer's craft. The profession itself is about the art of movement and its emergence, invention, and development.

◆ **Choreography + Music** involves gathering resources on classical and contemporary composers, new trends and innovations in music, and sonic discoveries, as well as collaborations with musicians, composers, and sound artists.

◆ **Choreography + Literature and Theater** involves gathering resources on the latest publications in literary arts and in musical productions, drama, opera, and other performing arts that could potentially incorporate dance.

◆ **Choreography + Visual Arts and Design** involves gathering resources from the past and the latest in visual arts, fashion design, scenic design, and architecture.

◆ **Choreography + Science and Digital Technology** involves gathering resources on advancements in the sciences and digital technology, such as engineering, robotics, cyber innovations, Artificial Intelligence, Augmented Reality, Immersive Arts, and other new technologies.

◆ **Choreography + Environment and Social Change** involves gathering resources on the current status of the Earth's environment, how the socio-economic circumstances affect our perceptions, and how we interact with each other as a global society.

◆ **Choreography + the Human Condition** involves gathering resources on the essential concepts of existence such as survival and mortality, conflict and resolution, growth and progress, and economy and politics, and how all of these factors affect people across geographical borders, language barriers, and cultural backgrounds.

In conclusion, let's remember Albert Einstein's words: *"Life is like riding a bicycle. To keep your balance, you must keep moving."* Choreographing is not easy, but it is possible.

HELPFUL TIPS & SUGGESTIONS

~ Convert stumbling blocks into stepping stones
~ Manage work habits and prevent passion from becoming an obsession
~ Transform your wishes into goals; then transform your goals into feasible steps
~ Remember that disappointment and success are part of the process
~ Share your art as work that inspires, rather than work that sells
~ Choreography is not a career choice—it is a life choice
~ Have no regrets

... and a few parting words...

Who will be the one creating and sharing dance?

Who will be the one courageously moving the art form forward?

Let it be *YOU, THE CHOREOGRAPHER* reading this book!

assignments & exercises

"Choose a job you love, and you will not work for the rest of your life," is an old Arabic adage. When we enjoy what we do, work doesn't feel like a duty, but a pleasure. Waking up each morning with excitement and a positive mindset prepares us for a day of success and perhaps some challenges that we are happy to resolve.

Matching the right career path with personal abilities is mastery on its own. In many cases, we intuitively choose to work on something pleasant rather than something that feels unnatural and challenging. How do we sync our desires and abilities with our employment? It often takes trial-and-error to figure out what we gravitate towards, what we're good at, and what is the best way to help ourselves and others. All careers have their unique pathways and hybrid versions, and all have their advantages and challenges.

This assignment and exercise in the form of a questionnaire will help you navigate distinct career paths, as a specific choreographic career might match a certain mindset and temperament. What career path would be the best fit for you?

★ **Independent Choreographer: Developing and Sustaining an Artistic Presence**

In terms of employment consistency, a few guiding questions are:

- ➡ What is the extent and capacity of your network, and who might be able to offer you work?
- ➡ Do you regularly attend dance festivals, networking gatherings, and conferences to establish new contacts and seek further employment opportunities?
- ➡ Do you have the ability to hustle, self-promote, inquire, network, engage, and manage all of your creative possibilities and administrative transactions?

In terms of establishing an artistic presence and persistence, a few guiding questions are:

- ➡ Do you develop and regularly update your choreographic portfolio of existing and new work, and do you build a collection of media coverage and press reviews?
- ➡ How would you position yourself in terms of artistic vision/style, and how does your artistic vision/style align with upcoming artistic proposals to potential employers?
- ➡ Do you possess the endurance to self-manage and promote your own artistic work, even when it might be misunderstood or ignored?

★ **Institutional Choreographer: Offering a Fresh Perspective to an Existing Legacy**

⚲ In terms of employment commitment, a few guiding questions are:

➡ How well do you know the institution, and do you currently have an employment and artistic history with it?

➡ To what extent does your artistic engagement have an impact on the institution's infrastructure?

➡ Do you believe that your artistic personality fits with the institutional culture, infrastructure, and current artistic management?

⚲ In terms of artistic contribution, a few guiding questions are:

➡ Does your work offer a fresh perspective within the framework of the institution?

➡ To what extent do your abilities and artistic vision contribute to the institution's artistic vision?

➡ Are you aware of the expectations and the artistic compliance necessary for you to maintain your affiliation with this particular institution?

★ **Artistic Director: Supporting an Artistic Community**

⚲ After inheriting the leadership of a dance company, will you be able to maintain the institution's legacy and further develop it? For example:

➡ Do you embrace other choreographers' work and different repertories that fit the company's vision?

➡ Will you be able to accommodate the institutional integrity and complexities and prioritize them over your individual artistic interest?

➡ Will you be able to balance individual creative work with the rest of the administrative requirements such as personnel management, artistic programming, institutional development, fundraising, promotion, outreach programs, and long-term strategic planning?

★ **Founding Director: Building an Artistic Community**

⚲ Do you possess the commitment, excitement, and ability to build a start-up dance company and execute the *business development strategies* needed to establish and fund dance projects? For example:

➡ Can you identify individuals who will support, join, and build a Board of Directors to establish the new organization's basic institutional infrastructures?

➡ Can you identify a *Close Circle* of about 25–100 people who might include family members, friends, and artist collaborators who are willing to help logistically, organizationally, and financially by donating and contributing to your start-up?

➡ How about an *Extended Circle* and *Large Circle* involving 1,000 people and engaging with private and corporate funding, institutional partnerships, foundations, potential presenters, and promoters?

√ Based on your artistic and business proposal for establishing a new dance company, you will receive support and donations, which could be organizational, financial, and logistical. These contributions will plant the "seeds" of a new enterprise. If you could offer a small token of appreciation to your supporters, what would it be?

BIBLIOGRAPHY AND REFERENCES

[1] Moore, Rachel. *The Artist's Compass, the Complete Guide to Building a Life and Living in the Performing Arts*, Touchstone, 2016, pp. 98–99.
[2] Moore 2016. *The Artist's Compass*, pp. 2–3, 22–23.
[3] Content Editors. *Metrics for Professional Development and Careers in Choreography*, International Consortium for Advancement in Choreography, Dance ICONS, Inc—The Global Network for Choreographers, www.danceicons.org, accessed May 2019.
[4] Moore 2016. *The Artist's Compass*, pp. 24–25.
[5] Kaiser, Michael. *Capacity Building in the Arts*, by Day Eight, Inc., a live professional development seminar, Washington DC, May 2018.
[6] Moore 2016. *The Artist's Compass*, pp. 80–81.
[7] Content Editors. *Pablo Picasso, Paintings, Quotes, & Biography*, Online articles and data: www.pablopicasso.org, accessed May 2019.
[8] Pablo Picasso, *Paintings, Quotes, & Biography*, and as reported on May 5, 2010, by the British art auction house Christies, www.christies.com/.
[9] Simonet, Andrew. *Making Your Life as an Artist*, Artist U, 2014, pp. 85–87.
[10] Simonet 2014. *Making Your Life as an Artist*, pp. 95–97.
[11] Simonet 2014. *Making Your Life as an Artist*, pp. 97–110.
[12] Moore 2016. *The Artist's Compass*, p. 174.

VISUAL REFERENCES

Figure 1: Photography © Lois Greenfield, pictured Paul Zivkovich, 2014, clipart: *White ball isolated on white background*, credit: mirexon, courtesy of Adobe Stock

Figures 2, 3, 4,5,6, 7, and 8: Diagrams © Vladimir Angelov

Figure 9: Painting by Pablo Picasso, *Nude, Green Leaves and Bust*, 1932, sourced by Wikimedia, fair use, text and diagram © Vladimir Angelov

Figures 10, 11, 12, and 13: Diagrams © Vladimir Angelov

Figure 14: Photography © Lois Greenfield, pictured Alexandra Karigan-Farrior, courtesy of Amy Marshall Dance Company, 2010

Page numbers followed by *f* indicate figures.

BOOK CREATVE TEAM
– BRIEF BIOGRAPHIES –

Vladimir Angelov (Author) graduated from the National School for Dance Arts in Sofia, Bulgaria. He studied philosophy at the University of Sofia and completed his master's degree in dance and choreography at American University in Washington, DC. Mr. Angelov served as choreographer at the Washington National Opera at the Kennedy Center in Washington, DC, under the artistic direction of Placido Domingo, and he also has choreographed for diverse musical, theater, film, and television productions.

Mr. Angelov has created original contemporary ballets for companies such as Arizona Ballet, Atlanta Ballet, Indianapolis Ballet, Richmond Ballet, San Francisco Ballet, Washington Ballet in the United States, as well as Alberta Ballet in Canada, National Ballet of Finland, Ballet, National Ballet of Mexico, Ballet Manila in the Philippines, Tokyo City Ballet in Japan, Mariinsky Ballet in St. Petersburg, Russia, among others.

Mr. Angelov has been a regular guest lecturer at the George Washington University and the American University in Washington, DC, and has taught at numerous universities and seminars at dance companies in Austria, Brazil, Bulgaria, China, Finland, France, Germany, Japan, Mexico, and Russia. He is the Founding and Executive Director of the International Consortium for Advancement in Choreography - Dance ICONS, Inc., the International Choreographers' Organization and Networking Services—a global association for choreographers based in Washington, DC.

Camilla Acquista (Editor) graduated *summa cum laude* from the University of Maryland, College Park, where she earned her Bachelor of Arts in Psychology. For the next decade, she served as a personnel management specialist at the National Institutes of Health in Bethesda, MD, where she received accolades for her outstanding technical writing, editing, and project-management skills. A member of the Phi Beta Kappa Society, Ms. Acquista is a lifelong learner with an avid interest in the science of language. She studied Spanish, French, and Italian at the undergraduate level and today continues her coursework in Italian through the Italian Cultural Society fo Washington, DC. Ms. Acquista has served as Executive Editor and Programming Associate to Dance ICONS, Inc., since 2016.

Charles Scheland (Research Associate) is a New York City-based performance artist, educator, and researcher. He is a *summa cum laude* graduate of the Ailey/Fordham University BFA in Dance program, receiving departmental honors in majors of both dance and economics. As a professional dancer, he has danced for Carolyn Dorfman Dance, RIOULT Dance NY, and Michael Mao Dance, among others. Mr. Scheland is on the faculty of the Ailey School, Steps on Broadway, and the School of the Jacob's Pillow, teaching ballet and Horton technique. He also enjoys engaging in various types of dance research and choreographing chamber contemporary dance works. Mr. Scheland has been part of Dance ICONS, Inc., in various capacities since the inception of the organization.

Lois Greenfield (Featured Photographer) has created signature images for many major ballet and contemporary dance companies, from Alvin Ailey American Dance Theater to American Ballet Theater. Many of these photos have appeared in her three groundbreaking books: *Breaking Bounds* (1992), *Airborne* (1998), and *Lois Greenfield: Moving Still* (2015). Since her first exhibit at the International Center of Photography, her work has been shown in 52 museums and galleries around the world. Ms. Greenfield's unique approach to photographing the human form in motion has radically redefined the genre and influenced a generation of photographers.

Koranjali Alfonseca (Graphic Designer) graduated from the Corcoran School of the Arts and Design at The George Washington University in Washington, DC, USA. For the past two decades, Ms. Alfonseca has designed a wide range of projects for numerous clients in the corporate industry and the arts field. Passionate about dance and choreography, Ms. Alfonseca has been designing for Dance ICONS, Inc., since its inception and has created various promotional materials for the organization, including its signature logo. She currently works and lives in Florence, Italy, and enjoys spending time with her baby daughter, Dhani.

Liz Gray (Graphic Designer) is an artist, freelance graphic designer and consultant with 20 years of extensive work experience. Ms. Gray graduated with a BA in fine arts from the George Washington University, a master's degree in city and metropolitan planning from the University of Utah, and currently runs Liz Gray Design, LLC. For over a decade, she has collaborated with Vladimir Angelov on various dance-related projects. Aside from her love of art and design, Liz is a mom, owner of two cute pups, garden enthusiast, and nature lover.

Pilar Wyman (Indexer) studied Mathematics and Philosophy at St. John's College and UC Berkeley and has been writing indexes for books and other publications for over 32 years. Her areas of specialty include the arts, clinical medicine, and technology. Currently Ms. Wyman runs Wyman Indexing, as Chief Indexer and Consultant. In her youth, she studied ballet, modern dance, Sevillana, and salsa. She continues to practice yoga, as well as to support arts of movement.

PHOTO CREDITS: Vladimir Angelov, Photography © Krassi Genov, Camilla Acquista, Photography from personal archive, Charles Scheland, Photography © Michael Andre, Lois Greenfield, Photography © Kris LeBoeuf, Koranjali Alfonseca, Photography from personal archive, Liz Gray, Photography © Stacy Harvey, Pilar Wyman, Photography from personal archive.